FUND RAISING
in the
UNITED STATES

Its Role in America's Philanthropy

FUND RAISING
in the
UNITED STATES

Its Role in America's Philanthropy

---

by SCOTT M. CUTLIP

Foreword by MERLE CURTI

RUTGERS UNIVERSITY PRESS

New Brunswick   *New Jersey*

ACKNOWLEDGMENT

The author is grateful for permission to quote from the following:
BEFORE WE SLEEP, by Hank Bloomgarden, published by G. P. Putnam's
Sons; THE GENTLE LEGIONS, by Richard Carter, copyright © 1959 by the
Curtis Publishing Co., 1961 by Richard Carter, and reprinted by permis-
sion of Doubleday and Company, Inc.; VOLUNTARY HEALTH AND WELFARE
AGENCIES IN THE UNITED STATES, Robert H. Hamlin, ed., published by
Schoolmasters' Press; MEMORIES OF A HAPPY LIFE, by William Lawrence,
published by Houghton Mifflin Company; AMERICAN EPOCH, published by
Alfred A. Knopf, Inc.; MASS PERSUASION, by Robert K. Merton, published
by the Bureau of Applied Social Research; THE COOPERATIVE MOVEMENT
IN SOCIAL WORK, by William J. Norton, published by The Macmillan
Company and reprinted by permission of the Children's Fund of Michi-
gan; MAIN CURRENTS IN AMERICAN THOUGHT, by Vernon L. Parrington,
published by Harcourt, Brace & World, Inc.; COMMUNITY CHEST: A CASE
STUDY IN PHILANTHROPY, published by the University of Toronto Press;
DESIGN FOR GIVING, by Harold J. Seymour, published by Harper & Row,
Inc.; NATIONAL TUBERCULOSIS ASSOCIATION, 1904–1954, by Richard H.
Shryock, published by the National Tuberculosis Association; THE BAR-
GAIN HUCKSTERS, by Ralph Lee Smith, published by Thomas Y. Crowell
Company; CORPORATION CONTRIBUTORS TO ORGANIZED COMMUNITY WELFARE
SERVICES, by Pierce Williams and Frederick E. Croxton, published by the
National Bureau of Economic Research.
Specific citations appear in the notes to this volume.

To My Son
GEORGE CARPER CUTLIP

Preface

This book represents the convergence of two of my professional interests—the history of public relations practice in the United States and the impact of that practice on our society. Tracing the evolution of American fund raising reveals that public relations has been a substantial force in the rise of philanthropic giving to its present unprecedented heights. Assessment of the impact of organized public relations-oriented fund raising on our society finds that the results, over-all, have been highly beneficial for our welfare, health, recreational, and educational institutions. This is not to say that there are not dangers and adverse effects from today's highly organized fund-raising drives. There are, but the balance is clearly in favor of the public good.

This work started out as a monograph on the role of public relations in philanthropy, to be one in a series for the University of Wisconsin History of Philanthropy Project, with which I am proud to have been associated. As more and more information was found, my interest in the project mounted and the outline broadened. The present volume is the consequence of these developments. The original limits of my project were expanded once it became apparent that this significant story of fund raising had never been fully and factually set down in one volume. This I have tried to do. The focus of this history is on what has been termed *mass, operational, periodic,* and *secular* fund raising and its relation to our social history. Religious fund raising, which accounts for more than half of American giving, is treated only in a minor way.

The evolution of fund raising in the United States from the individual "begging missions" of the nation's early centuries into today's multibillion-dollar height is a typically American story. This evolution has had a profound effect on American philanthropy, on the institutions it supports, and on the increasingly broad segment of the public involved in the getting and giving of funds. The public relations expert and the professional fund raiser have played key roles in this evolution. The growth of American philanthropy in the twentieth century has been nothing short of spectacular.

The public relations and fund-raising professionals, versed in the ways of mobilizing effort and exerting pressure, are, in part, a reflection of this spectacular growth and, in part, contributing agents. Using an accumulating expertise and exploiting the growing power of the mass media, they have done much to educate the American people in the habit of giving. In the process they have lifted America's philanthropic gifts to more than ten billion dollars annually. Consequently, their related activities deserve more scholarly scrutiny than they have had.

In the more than four years that I have been working on this book, I have accumulated debts of large number and great magnitude, which cannot be fully repaid by mere acknowledgment here. The greatest debt I owe in this endeavor is to my dear friend and colleague, Merle Curti. Professor Curti enthusiastically approved the idea when I suggested it to him and gave me helpful counsel all the way. Most importantly, when I would grow weary of the tedium involved in such a project, he would renew my spirits with flattering encouragement. Professor Irvin G. Wyllie, associated with Professor Curti in the direction of the History of Philanthropy Project, was most helpful throughout. He gave me wise counsel, suggested good research leads, and always found ways to finance my research needs. I am equally indebted to Mrs. Mildred Lloyd, who served as secretary of the project in its five-year life, for typing and retyping most of this manuscript. She was as efficient as she was patient with my messy copy. Also of great help to me in this project was Dwight Teeter, who served as research assistant. His conscientious checking of all the footnotes is a task only scholars can fully appreciate.

I am profoundly grateful to the University of Wisconsin Research Committee, to the Dean of the Graduate School, and to the Ford Foundation, which financed the University of Wisconsin History of Philanthropy Project, for the time and travel money necessary to carry out my investigations for this book. Both agencies were helpful; without their financial support this book never would have been written. Two other persons especially helpful to me have been pioneer fund raisers David M. Church and Robert F.

Duncan. Both gentlemen provided much useful information but their greatest service was in the careful and critical reading of the completed manuscript except for the Epilogue. They saved me from many errors of fact and suggested needed additions.

Many, many others have been of help and encouragement to me in this long, tedious task. To all of these I am deeply grateful: The staff of the State Historical Society of Wisconsin—Librarian Benton Wilcox, Miss Ruth Davis, and their many cooperative associates; University of Wisconsin Librarian Louis Kaplan and his helpful staff; Donald T. Clark, former librarian of the Baker Library, Harvard University, and the Baker staff who did so much to facilitate my use of the John Price Jones Papers; President Charles W. Anger, Vice-President Theodore S. Ruggles, and Miss Dorothy Roche, librarian, of the John Price Jones Corp. who cleared the way for me to use the Jones Papers, both at the Baker Library and in the large library of the firm, all of whom lent much assistance to this endeavor; Dr. Arnaud Marts and Austin V. McClain of Marts & Lundy, who not only gave generously of their time but also turned over to the State Historical Society of Wisconsin valuable records for its philanthropy collection that were of immediate use to me; Mrs. Virginia Pierce Macpherson, daughter of Lyman L. Pierce, who graciously trusted me with her father's scrapbooks and papers; pioneer fund raisers Carlton G. Ketchum, Herman F. Reinhardt, Cornelius Smith, and Lowell Brammer likewise opened up their firms' records to me and gave me valuable information in interviews; T. J. Ross granted me access to the Matter Sent Out files of the Ivy Lee-T. J. Ross partnership; George Hammond, Gerry Swinehart, and Miss Elsie Simon, all of whom did much to build the Carl Byoir firm, provided much of the hitherto unrecorded information on the beginnings of what is now the March of Dimes; Ralph Blanchard, Henry Weber, and Miss Fay Webb, librarian, of the United Community Funds and Councils of America were all of great help to me in pulling together the community chest story; and Clyde E. Buckingham, director of research for the American National Red Cross, was of assistance to me above and beyond the call of his job. Both the Three Cs and the Red Cross have large libraries that are of inestimable value to scholars in this field.

Still others who assisted me in this project and whose debt I freely acknowledge include: Allen W. Ostar of the Joint Office of Institutional Research, a former student and friend; Edward M.

(Ted) Littlejohn, public relations executive with Standard Oil Co. (N.J.); K. P. Wood of American Telephone & Telegraph Co.; Irving Rimer of the American Cancer Society; Eldredge Hiller and Marie Medeo of the American Association of Fund Raising Counsel staff; John H. Watson III of the National Industrial Conference Board; Walter Barlow of Opinion Research Corporation; Allen H. Center, a collaborator of mine on another book; Harold N. Weiner of the National Public Relations Council of Health and Welfare Services; Mrs. Sallie Bright of New York's Community Service Society; veteran fund raiser Harold J. Seymour; Miss Dorothy Ducas, formerly of the National Foundation for Infantile Paralysis; William H. Baldwin, an early fund raiser and long a distinguished public relations counselor; and Professor Ralph O. Nafziger, a tolerant boss and wise counselor. I am certain there were others whose names have been inadvertently left out; I trust these persons will not think me ungrateful because of this oversight.

Finally, like most authors who finally get books written, I keep my warmest praise for my helpmate in all things—my wife Erna. She has helped with the fact checking, with the typing, and in countless other ways—and always with her cheerful spirit.

With these expressions of gratitude must go the customary absolution from any responsibility for the errors of fact or erroneous interpretation of facts herein recorded. These must be mine alone. The opinions and interpretations in the book are mine.

Scott M. Cutlip

Madison, Wisconsin
November, 1964

Foreword

Thanks to the interest of the Russell Sage Foundation, a pioneer in exploring in a scholarly way some of the problems associated with American philanthropy, and to the concern of the Ford Foundation for a deeper understanding of the nature, extent, and effects of voluntary giving for public purposes, a conference on the history of American philanthropy was held at Princeton early in 1956. The report which followed included a bibliography of available secondary materials and outlined needed researches. It called attention to the relevancy of several factors to the whole subject: the cultural differences between the United States and other countries, shifts in motives for giving and changes in beneficiaries, and the impact of philanthropy on American institutions and values. The report indicated the need for investigations of the history of institutions dispensing and receiving philanthropy. It called attention to the further need for studies of philanthropic habits in the several regions of the United States and in "typical" and "atypical" cities. The report also listed fourteen broad topics in the history of American philanthropy which needed study: relief and social welfare, religion, education, health services, the arts, charitable bequests, law, the economy, contributions to peoples beyond the national borders, and fund raising. As a result of the conference and of a Ford Foundation grant, researches conducted at the University of Wisconsin have contributed to our knowledge of philanthropy in seven or eight of these categories.

Except for the more or less incidental treatment of fund raising in the invaluable studies of F. Emerson Andrews and in two or three monographic treatments of particular agencies (such as Professor Richard Shryock's history of the National Tuberculosis Association), the bibliography in the Princeton Conference report indicated that no one of the fourteen areas had been as much neglected as the history of fund raising. In the year after the appearance of the Conference report the University of Toronto Press published a notable study, planned and undertaken in 1954, of the Community Chest in Indianapolis. This case study provides objective information, admirably organized, with important generalizations about fund raising in a city which is probably characteristic, in the problems of fund raising of many other places in the United States. *Community Chest, A Case Study in Philanthropy* was a pioneer undertaking which may come to be looked on as a classic in the field. Except for a brief over-all introductory essay, *Community Chest* was not concerned, however, with the history of philanthropy or fund raising in the larger sense.

The present book by Professor Scott M. Cutlip of the University of Wisconsin is, therefore, the first detailed and scholarly investigation of the history of fund raising in the United States. Because of his previous writings and work in the field of public relations and his acquaintance with key fund raisers, Professor Cutlip brought to the investigation invaluable assets. Apart from these he also has the equipment of the historian and the political scientist. His research, historical in nature, has been intensive and extensive. He has told an important and hitherto largely unknown story vividly and in the context of the development of philanthropy and of American social history itself.

Professor Cutlip's book speaks for itself. But I should like to call attention to a few of the contributions he makes which a prospective reader will not anticipate from scanning the impressive tables and from taking note of his use of manuscript as well as published sources and of oral interviews.

Although this study indicates the influence of a few British precedents in the development of certain techniques which the Americans carried much further, the history of fund raising in the United States is distinctively American. It is American in its functional relationships to our changing social structure, notably in the shift of philanthropy from a social elite to a mass base, from the predominantly religious to the predominantly secular auspices of appeals for funds, from the amateur volunteer to the professional fund raiser, from the expansion of the original agencies of press, pulpit, bazaar, and benefit to such agencies as the YMCA, *ad hoc* committees for social services in the two world wars, the Community Chest, United Givers, United College Appeal, and the great fund-raising firms which represent both a new business and a new profession. The revolution in fund-raising devices in the past decades has also been characterized by the effective use of almost never-ending slogans and gimmicks and, more important, the new mass media.

Professor Cutlip also reveals to us the fund-raising roles of outstanding Americans, including Benjamin Franklin and Bishop William Lawrence, who have been chiefly known for other things. He introduces us to a score of men and women whose names are little known to the general public but who have played creative parts in the history of the movement he relates and evaluates. These men and women, moreover, become for us not only "real" but unforgettable persons.

In these pages one also finds much new information and many valuable insights which broaden and deepen our understanding of just how money was raised and services recruited for emergency relief, education, health, and welfare. The study also enhances the meaning over time of such values as are connoted by the words "democracy, compassion, social conscience, civic responsibility" and, one must add, the proneness to yield to the pressure of mobilized opinion and to skillful organization.

But what stands out perhaps most of all is the way in which fund raising in our time reflects our business culture. The American flair for organization, the fetish of efficiency, the onslaught in the name of these against chaos, waste, conflict, and deception in organized giving, the uses of publicity techniques, and the introduction of scientific methods into fund raising—all these take on full and significant meaning. So does the increasing role of corporate giving in relation to tax exemption and to the effort to create a favorable image.

But this is not all. Professor Cutlip's story reflects and illuminates other changes in American culture, related to the dominance of business values and methods, but broader and more far-ranging. The great changes in the history of fund raising reflect shifts in roles—of the one-time passivity of the recipient and activity of the donor to a reversal of that relationship. It indicates the narrowing of the choices open to individuals in giving as in other aspects of life. The story before us also reflects the growing anonymity of personal relationships, for thanks to modern fund-raising methods and to the nature of our society the giver is relatively remote from the recipient. If America is creating a new industrial civilization, the shift from giving for the relief of the most desperate to giving for planned, long-range enrichment of our whole life may be both a reflection of and a contribution to the emerging civilization. These examples, which could be easily extended, suggest that the theme which Professor Cutlip develops for the first time in historical perspective is much broader than it might offhand seem to be.

For all these and for other reasons as well, it is a pleasure to write this foreword and to commend this book both to the specialist and to the general reader.

MERLE CURTI

Contents

FUND RAISING
in the
UNITED STATES

Its Role in America's Philanthropy

1

Fund Raising before 1900

Generally speaking, organized philanthropy supported by systematic fund raising is a twentieth-century development in the United States. Philanthropy, in America's first three centuries, was carried along on a small scale, largely financed by the wealthy few in response to personal begging appeals. In those years a small amount of excess wealth in the young nation went, for the most part, to the churches, to the pitifully poor, and to found schools and colleges. There were few organized drives, in the modern sense, before 1900. World War I and the decade that followed provided the seedbed for the growth of today's fund raising and today's people's philanthropy.

Nevertheless, America's modern high-pressure, fund-raising drive has its roots deep in the nation's history. As the skills and techniques of fund raising have advanced apace with America's ability to give, so has her philanthropy progressed, from the "begging mission" and lottery of the colonial period to the highly organized, concentrative $10 billion a year enterprise of our times. The public relations practitioner and the professional fund raiser have played vital roles in this advance. The modern fund-raising campaign, carefully organized, shrewdly promoted, and aimed at broad segments of the citizenry, has made American philanthropy a people's philanthropy. These methods, regrettably, are abused by charity bandits and sometimes are used for dubious or fraudulent purposes but, in total sum, popular philanthropy in the United States is a great democratic strength.

The first systematic effort to raise money on this continent was for a college. Harvard College, of course! In 1641 the Massachusetts Bay Colony sent three clergymen to England to solicit money for the college so that it could, among other endeavors, "educate the heathen Indian." That there was as much interest in getting desperately needed capital for the colony as in providing education for the Indians is seen in Governor Winthrop's statement of the objects of this mission in which he emphasized the need to explain the New England depression, "to satisfy our creditors," and "to make use of any opportunity God should offer for the good of the country." In historian Samuel Eliot Morison's opinion this last meant, in plain words, to raise money. Morison recounts:

> The Weld-Peter begging mission, which one may call, in modern terms, the first concerted "drive" to obtain income and endowment for the College, began early. On June 2, 1641, the General Court entreated their respective churches to release Hugh Peter of Salem, Thomas Weld of Roxbury, and William Hibbens of Boston "to go to England upon some weighty occasion for the good of the country." [1]

This was seventeenth-century circumlocution for seeking money. The Reverend Mr. Hibbens returned before the year was out, bearing some £500 for the college and the colony. Fund raisers Weld and Peter sent back an urgent request for "literature" to set forth the best "selling points of New England." In response to this request came *New England's First Fruits*, written in Massachusetts but printed in England in 1643. This surely was the first of millions of fund-raising brochures. Morison describes it as a "promotion pamphlet." This trio eventually fell out, and one of them denounced the whole expedition as a "cheat." Hugh Peter wound up on the scaffold and Thomas Weld became a rector in England. Such were the diverse rewards of early fund raisers!

In colonial days, as now, according to Beverly McAnear, "The greatest problem faced by the college administrators was that of getting the money necessary to keep the college open, for students' fees paid only a small part of the cost. In their search for requisite funds, promoters of the new colleges found that tapping the provincial treasury yielded only a trickle of cash. Harvard, Yale, and William and Mary all had been given both grants and annual subventions by their respective provincial governments or by the King. Among the newer colleges, only Dartmouth, King's and Philadelphia were voted money from the public treasuries, and King's alone was treated generously. None ever received an annual public subsidy, despite repeated applications." [2]

In this colonial period of 1745–1775 appeals to the general public by means of subscription lists and lotteries brought the infant colleges some funds. Occasional bequests brought in a bit more. Receipts from these sources usually went to meet recurring deficits. McAnear says that with the exception of King's, all the existing colleges were operating on deficit budgets after 1770. Understandably, the raising of funds for colleges was becoming increasingly difficult.

It is not surprising that these hard-pressed colleges turned to the dubious device of the lottery, with "Fair Harvard" leading the way. Tickets for the first Harvard lottery were to be drawn June 1, 1775, but before that date certain events took place that upset these plans, as cryptically reported in the Corporation's records: "N.B. The Managers of the aforesaid Lottery afterw'd gave it up, the war breaking out." A second lottery was held twelve years later and produced a few hundred pounds. A more ambitious one was launched in the 1790's to build Stoughton Hall. After only part of the money had been raised, however, this lottery was suspended amidst squabbles and lawsuits. A fourth and final lottery in 1806 yielded enough money to put up Holworthy Hall and pay off the balance of building Stoughton. Surely Harvard has never had a more costly and wasteful fund-raising method. Not only did sponsoring lotteries tarnish the good name of the college, but it received only 2.3 per cent of the money the public gambled for "the chance of enriching themselves." [3]

In 1745 Harvard, William and Mary, and Yale were the only colleges in the American colonies. In the next thirty years before the Revolution seven more had been founded: Dartmouth, Rhode Island (Brown), King's (Columbia), Queen's (Rutgers), New Jersey (Princeton), Philadelphia (Pennsylvania), and Newark (Delaware). Starting and maintaining these colleges took capital, in colonies where capital was scarce. As McAnear records, "The colleges were . . . saved by the development of widespread popular interest in higher education, interest intense enough to impel thousands of individuals, both in America and in the British Isles, to make cash gifts aggregating a very considerable amount." [4] This did not happen spontaneously in the seventeenth century any more than it does today. "The collection of funds from private individuals was systematized, and methods of organized effort and personal solicitation directed by persons closely connected with the colleges were developed." [5]

Among the pioneer fund raisers was a dynamic young evangelist who came from England to the colonies to preach and plead for alms. He was George Whitefield (1714–1770) who played a prominent role in the Great Awakening, the religious revival that swept across the American colonies in the 1730's and the 1740's. Bremner thinks that "Among the most important results of the Great Awakening were the fostering of humane attitudes and the popularization of philanthropy at all levels of society, but especially among the poorer classes." The young English evangelist in 1739 began "the most famous preaching tour in American history," exhorting not only against sin but crying out against the misery of the poor. In his seven visits to the colonies Whitefield "took up collections for poor debtors, raised money for the victims of disaster, and secured books and financial assistance for hard-pressed colonial colleges. Harvard, Dartmouth, Princeton, and the University of Pennsylvania all benefited from his assistance. If no single institution can be regarded as his monument, the reason is partly that he helped so many." [6]

In fund raising, as in so many lines of endeavor, Benjamin Franklin put his keen wit, capacious mind, and great tact to work for several philanthropic causes. Ben Franklin was a creative and highly successful fund raiser because he shrewdly planned his appeal and carefully catalogued his prospective donors. He would prepare a list of special prospects for each cause and then personally call upon each one. When the Reverend Gilbert Tennent came to Franklin to ask his help in raising a fund to build a Presbyterian church in Philadelphia Franklin declined to participate, but he did give Tennent this advice:

> In the first place I advise you to apply to all those whom you know will give something; next, to those whom you are uncertain whether they will give anything or not, and show them the list of those who have given; and lastly, do not neglect those whom you are sure will give nothing, for in some of them you may be mistaken. [7]

Franklin reports that Mr. Tennent took his advice "for he asked everybody, and he obtained a much larger sum than he expected." The great political leader-journalist-diplomat had a long record of fund-raising and philanthropic endeavors. He believed in a collective, voluntary approach to meet community problems. As early as 1727 Franklin helped organize the Junto, a club initially organized for the mutual improvement of its members, an organization active today. Junto's first fruit was a library set up in 1731. Bremner observes: "The voluntary method, as Franklin's success with it suggested, and as later events were to prove, was precisely suited to the inclinations of his countrymen." Franklin played a leading role in the founding and financing of the Pennsylvania Hospital and the Academy, which was to grow into the University of Pennsylvania. Franklin's advanced views on a citizen's responsibility to his community were shared by another of the Founding Fathers, Thomas Jefferson. The latter once said: "The duty of every man is to devote a certain portion of his income for charitable purposes and . . . his further duty is to see it applied as to do the most good." Franklin once confessed: "I do not remember any of my . . . maneuvers . . . wherein, after thinking of it, I more easily excused myself for having made some use of cunning."

By and large, fund raising in the nineteenth century was a matter of personal solicitation, often by paid solicitors, of passing the church plate, of staging church suppers or bazaars, and of writing "begging letters." The first feeble attempt to stage a federated fund drive was undertaken in Philadelphia in 1829 by Mathew Carey. A contemporary of Stephen Girard and Benjamin Rush, pioneer philanthropists, Carey was interested in the social questions of the day: immigration, tariff, wages for women, banking, health. It was probably an admixture of his economic and humanitarian interests that led him to make this first attempt at organized, federated fund raising although the campaign aroused no great enthusiasm, and never "got off the ground." In May, 1829, Carey sought the interest of ninety-seven "citizens of the first respectability" to sign an appeal for funds entitled "Address to the Liberal and Humane." In part, his appeal read:

In order to remove the inequality that prevails in the contributions, we most ardently invoke the general patronage of our citizens, for the following plan, whereby an immense mass of public good may be effected at a trivial individual expense . . .
An agent of courteous manners will be employed to call at every house in the city, which wears the appearance of being inhabited by

citizens in circumstances to contribute a single subscription of two or three dollars a year for the great and humane objects above specified. He will be provided with a book with as many divisions as there are societies for which patronage is sought. *To avoid offense, all appearance of importunity will be prohibited. He will merely present his book and wait the decision of the parties; and whether that decision be compliance or rejection, he will be directed to withdraw politely.* Although individuals may, if they choose, subscribe to more than one society, yet it is to be distinctly understood that *no more than one subscription is expected from any one person. And we go so far as to say that those who are already subscribers to any of those institutions, will be considered as exempt from a compliance with this call, although their names will be thankfully received,* if they judge proper to increase the number of institutions they patronize.[8]

Carey subsequently reported: "This experiment was tried for twenty days and a half. The last four days there were but twelve dollars received and on the last day there was but a single dollar collected, which was not sufficient to pay the collector." It was, as Carey said, "surely time to abandon the plan as hopeless." A total of 137 subscribers giving a total of $276.50 was the net result of America's first federated fund-raising effort. Little wonder that the idea was not soon tried again; and what a contrast to the forceful "over-the-top" climaxes to multimillion-dollar federated drives that were to come in less than a century! One feature of Carey's imaginative, if futile, effort does bear favorable comparison with fund raising today: its cost was 9 per cent, a figure Carey thought high. Whatever the result, the fact remains that here, in 1829, we find in embryo the elements of modern fund raising: the paid solicitor, the advance promotion, the classified prospect list, and the federated drive. Latter-day fund raisers have taken these basic elements and mixed with them precision, pressure, and public relations to create a significant vocation and to raise the billions United States philanthropy needs.

Carey's campaign was not the only fund-raising effort to fail in those years. Two separate campaigns to create monuments to the patriotism of the men of the Revolution failed. Bremner reports that "The Bunker Hill Monument Association of Boston ran out of money and into debt three years after laying the cornerstone of the monument in 1825." Similarly, the Washington National Monument Society, founded in 1833, sought to raise funds through popular subscription to build what has become a proud national symbol. The Society set its goal at $1 million. By 1847 the campaign had brought in only $70,000, but the Society proceeded to lay the cornerstone. A few years more and the Society had raised enough money to push the shaft to 153 feet in height. There it remained until 1883, when Congress appropriated funds to complete the Washington Monument. Of the total cost some $300,000 was donated by the public, in response to subscription appeals.

Yet, at the time these drives were faltering, young and none-too-affluent America was already beginning to respond to calls for help from overseas. In the 1820's Samuel Gridley Howe started a campaign to raise money for the cause of the Greeks in their war for independence. Volunteer committees staged charity balls, fairs, auctions, debating contests, and stage benefits as a means of raising funds. Bremner says that "The committees employed nearly all the devices of modern charity drives to levy contributions for Greek relief from merchants, shippers, laborers, and school children." Typical was the fair staged by the ladies of Baltimore in that city's Masonic Hall "that the women and children of 'the land of story and song' may be preserved from the horrors of starvation." "The splendid saloon of the Masonic Hall, was elegantly fitted up for the occasion, and on the tables with which it was lined, were to be found every variety of articles, prepared by the fairy fingers of the fair." [9] The ladies' show, incidentally, raised $1,600, no mean sum in those days.

Thus began the almost unbroken flow of American dollars and foodstuffs to the less fortunate peoples around the world. United States foreign relief is a much older story than many people realize. But the gifts were flowing both ways across the Atlantic, as indeed they had since the days of the "Weld-Peter begging mission." The year 1829 brought the death of the British chemist James Smithson, who left an estate of a half million dollars "to the United States of America to found at Washington, under the name of the Smithsonian Institution, an establishment for the increase and diffusion of knowledge among men." Congress finally accepted the gift in 1846.

To raise sizable amounts of money for a public cause, fund seekers placed their main reliance on personal solicitation, or "begging," as it was apt to be called by those approached for money. In the 1830's a dedicated teacher, Miss Mary Lyon, was deter-

mined to launch a college for women where she could put her own
educational ideas into effect. She set out to raise, by personal appeals to persons of means, the $30,000 she estimated she needed.
She traveled hundreds of miles, visited at least ninety communities,
and obtained 1,800 subscriptions totaling $27,000. The gifts ranged
in amount from six cents up.

The drive for money to found Mt. Holyoke was launched September 6, 1834, when "a few gentlemen met in Miss Lyon's private
parlor, in Ipswich, to devise ways and means for founding a permanent female seminary." The first free-will offerings in Ipswich
netted $267. Next, Miss Lyon herself "went from house to house,
to solicit subscriptions. She talked now with the lady of the house,
now with the husband. . . . She held before them the object dear
to her heart—the bringing of a liberal education within the means
of the daughters of the common people." Mary Lyon carried the
story of the liberality of the ladies of Ipswich "from town to town"
and "she wrote letters to former pupils of the Ipswich School,
soliciting their aid." Such was her dedicated perseverence that in
less than two months the sum of $30,000 was very nearly raised.[10]

Mary Lyon's heroic, singlehanded fund drive, lacking the elaborate organization and intensive public relations that would characterize college drives a century later, was typical of educational
fund raising in the nineteenth century. Dr. Arnaud Marts, veteran
fund raiser and former college president, writes:

> Colleges were using the "financial agent," frequently the president
> himself, who was sent to the eastern cities to preach in the churches
> and gather funds for the colleges of the west and south. Presbyterian
> financial agents went to New York and Pittsburgh; Congregationalists
> to New England; Methodists to New York and Philadelphia. . . .
> This personal search for gifts was the major technique used all
> through the Nineteenth Century for founding and maintaining our
> colleges. Indeed, it was the accepted technique for college fund-rais-
> ing in America right up to the close of World War I.[11]

The Irish Famine of the late 1840's produced another spate of
locally organized fund-raising efforts in the United States. Church
collections, bazaars and benefits, collections of foodstuffs, and direct newspaper appeals for cash were used by Irish relief committees in all parts of the country. Merle Curti describes this as "in a

sense, the first truly national campaign to relieve suffering in another land without respect to political and nationalistic considerations." He adds that the Irish relief campaign carried the Greek campaign devices of "the big meeting, the benefit, the church collection" much further.

This effort was powered by vast amounts of emotion-laded publicity, featuring graphic accounts of starvation in Ireland. *Niles' Weekly Register* observed, "Our desk has on it a pile of paragraphs that we have clipped from exchange papers evidencing a general sympathy in behalf of starving Ireland and Scotland." Even the Choctaw Indians were moved to respond to these heart-rending tales of woe. *Niles' Register* records that a "meeting for the relief of the starving poor of Ireland was held at the Choctaw Agency on the 23rd." A total of $710 was raised among the Indians assembled in meeting. The *Register* footnoted, "The 'poor Indian' sending his mite to the poor Irish!" [12]

But it was the Civil War (1861–1865) that produced an early model of the twentiety-century American high-pressure organized fund drive. Its initiator was the fabled financier Jay Cooke. Parrington calls Cooke the first modern American, "the first to understand the psychology of mass salesmanship." Cooke was largely responsible for the financing of the Union cause through the sale of government bonds to the public on a hitherto unprecedented scale. He pulled out all the emotional stops to "sell patriotism" to the North with thorough organization and effective publicity. His theme was that the soldier at the front must be supported at the rear. Parrington describes the Cooke-directed sales appeal:

It was every loyal American's war, and patriotism demanded that idle dollars—in greenbacks—should be lent to the boys in blue, and a grateful government would return them, both principal and interest, in gold. To induce slacker dollars to become fighting dollars he placed his agents in every neighborhood, in newspaper offices, in banks, in pulpits—patriotic forerunners of the "one-minute men" of later drives. They also served their country, he pointed out, who sold government bonds on commission. He subsidized the press with a lavish hand, not only the metropolitan dailies but the obscurest country weeklies. He employed an army of hack writers to prepare syndicate matter and he scattered paying copy broadcast.[13]

These "modern methods" brought widespread sale of government bonds—and profit to Jay Cooke & Company. Moreover, Cooke's methods provided a pattern for the sale of Liberty Bonds and other fund raising during World War I.

Also, during the Civil War there were fund-raising fairs in northern cities to raise money for bandages for the U.S. Sanitary Commission, forerunner of the American Red Cross.

With the exception of Jay Cooke's spectacular sale of government bonds through exploitation of patriotic appeals, most organized fund-raising efforts in America's nineteenth century were small-scale affairs designed to aid the church, the college, the relief of paupers at home, or the starving abroad. Indeed, welfare work was focused mostly on the destitute. For example, the New York Association for Improving the Condition of the Poor was organized in 1843, and from the very start proved a needed, useful organization. The need for welfare agencies and the demands for funds to finance them were greatly increased immediately after the Civil War. The close of that great national conflict unleashed political and economic forces that were to build the United States into a powerful industrial nation spanning the continent by the end of the century. The simple, hand-to-mouth old ways of helping the needy of colonial America could no longer meet the new needs of a booming industrial, urbanized nation with vast social problems.

Ironically enough, it was the same Jay Cooke who, through his financial manipulations, was indirectly responsible for perhaps the first volunteer door-to-door campaign to raise funds for charity. This is known in social welfare history as the "Germantown Experiment." In the winter of 1873 many of Philadelphia's factories and shops were closed by the depression and panic resulting from the failure of Cooke's banking firm and the consequent fall in security prices. "Continual were the calls at the back doors of the well-to-do for food, money, and help." Samuel Emlin, leading citizen in Germantown, a Philadelphia suburb, used the Germantown *Chronicle* to invite a gathering of all citizens of the borough "to provide for the poor of Germantown during the coming winter." A Unitarian minister, the Reverend Charles Gordon Ames, came to the meeting with a plan in his pocket, which was adopted: to divide Germantown into eight divisions and then appoint a visiting committee of citizens for each division. He also advocated a central office and a paid superintendent. Another public meeting was called, was well attended, and resulted in the formation of the Germantown Relief Society, one of the first societies for organizing charity in the United States. The Germantown experiment placed great emphasis on volunteer services, including solicitation for funds and goods.[14] Another early attempt at cooperative fund raising was that organized under religious auspices for the support of ten hospitals in New York City. On Hospital Sunday, December 28, 1879, funds were collected in the affiliated churches in an appeal directed by a committee of members. A little over $25,000 was obtained.[15]

The roots of America's developments in charity, welfare work, and fund raising extend back to the soil of the mother country, England. The YMCA movement, which was to have a profound impact on the nature of fund raising and philanthropy in America, was transplanted to North America from Great Britain in 1851, when the first associations were established in Montreal and in Boston. The Young Men's Christian Association found a favorable climate for development on the new continent. Its rapid growth in the United States was one of the early fruits of the waves of religious revival that rolled across the nation from 1849 to 1900.

In 1868 the first effort to improve philanthropic administration was also born in England, when the Charity Organization Society was founded in London. Finally launched April 22, 1869, to deal with the age-old problems of pauperism and poverty in London's East End, it was also "to be a center of harmonious cooperation between them and to check the overlapping of relief." [16] Thus, the problem of duplication of fund-raising efforts and welfare expenditures emerged early as a central problem of philanthropy— one that still remains to be solved. The Germantown Relief Society had created the first organized charity movement in the United States, but it was self-impelled to meet the immediate crisis of the hardships resulting from the Panic of 1873. The broader British approach was adopted in Buffalo, N.Y., in 1877. Watson thinks that "The influence of the London society was both marked and direct." Soon similar societies were organized in most of the larger cities of the United States.

Another central idea of modern philanthropy, that of the financial federation agencies, can also be credited to England. Although Mathew Carey in his unsuccessful Philadelphia campaign of 1829 had introduced the federated idea, the more comprehensive plan was developed in Liverpool in 1873. A few civic leaders made a study of the contributions to thirty-eight leading Liverpool charities. The study revealed that these charitites were being supported by 6,000 persons although an estimated 20,000 citizens in Liverpool were capable of giving money; that only 50 per cent of the contributors were giving to more than one agency, and only 16 per cent to more than two. After analyzing the study, a plan was recommended by which a group of charitable agencies were to make their appeals through one office and on one central pledge sheet. This list of endorsed agencies was circulated to givers, but no steps were taken toward effecting central accounting, central budgeting, or standardization—fundamentals of the present-day Community Chests in the United States.[17]

The financial federation idea was carried to America within the decade and first developed in Denver, Colo., by two clergymen —Father William J. O'Ryan, a Roman Catholic, and Dean M. Martyn Hart, an Episcopalian—both of whom had recently come to the United States from England where, presumably, they had got the idea of federating all charity appeals into one combined drive. What is now generally conceded to be the first earnest effort to centralize and correlate the financing of community charities was made in Denver in 1877. In the closing months of that year four religious leaders—two Protestant clergymen, a Catholic priest, and a Jewish rabbi—joined forces to organize and promote the Associated Charities of Denver. This effort, like other early federations, bore only a faint family resemblance to the twentieth century Community Chest and the United Fund. Both Liverpool and Denver experiments did give impetus to the long-continuing search for a central charity fund, and both certainly were products of the same philosophy and of the same discontent with the chaos which had accompanied charitable activities.

The four Denver clerics sponsoring the idea of one charity fund called a mass meeting and launched their project before a crowded house. Twenty-three agencies were brought into the federation, raising $20,000 in their first combined drive. Denver's first full-fledged Community Chest campaign in 1922 included forty-five organizations and raised $649,000. For the first decade the Associated Charities generated great enthusiasm among those concerned with the problems of the less fortunate.

The first annual meeting, held in November, 1889, packed the

Tabor Opera House from "floor to ceiling." The press reported that "the stage was occupied by representatives of every organization in the city."

Notwithstanding this show of support, the combined effort in Denver did not realize all the money needed for the support of its affiliated societies. Consequently a basic feature of a federated appeal, the immunity principle of only one drive a year, was ignored. This led to a rapid dissipation of the initial enthusiasm that had surrounded this new fund-raising idea which always appears attractively efficient and economical. William J. Norton observed:

> This first Denver attempt savored much more of the charity organization movement, then attracting wide attention, than of the later federation idea. . . .
>
> In structure, it was a chameleon, changing rather rapidly, four constitutions having been adopted by 1892 . . .
>
> By 1892 the flush of enthusiasm with which it had been launched was gone. . . . Several organizations had dropped out, and but fifteen benevolent societies remained cooperating with the Charity Organization Society as it was now named.[18]

By 1898, reflections of disappointment and unrest were showing in the Society's annual reports. Increased pressures, generated by a growing city and its multiplying needs, were being exerted on all agencies. The federated financing drive was not equal to these demands. In its twenty-first year the Society's collections dropped to $13,000. Up to this point the alliance had put its faith in volunteer fund raisers. The next year the president of the Denver Society wrote:

> A few of our institutions have received support that is entirely inadequate to their needs. Their friends, in order to maintain them, felt impelled to seek aid from outside sources. In their extremity they were persuaded to engage professional solicitors who retained the larger amount of the sums collected, giving the remainder to the institutions. This caused much unfavorable comment and met the disapproval of the Charity Organization Society.[19]

Thus just before the turn of the century the paid solicitor for charitable funds appears, one on whom great reliance was to be placed by philanthropic and eleemosynary agencies for the next two decades, in many cases with great regret. In the early years of American philanthropy the solicitor was almost always hired by only one organization, often on a percentage basis, which frequently led to abuse and fraud, or at the least to high administrative costs. The commission-paid solicitor disappeared from the philanthropic scene after World War I, with the emergence of the modern professional fund raiser and the Community Chest. But the stories of cheating by the first paid charity solicitors may well account for the donor's persistent resentment at giving part of his dollars to any paid fund raiser and the public's mistaken notions about today's ethical fund raiser who works for a fixed fee, not on a percentage basis.

The only other nineteenth-century attempts to forge federated fund-raising organizations were those originated by Jewish welfare groups "to simplify the method of collection and to save the contributors unnecessary annoyance." In 1895 leaders of the Jewish community in Boston decided to bring all their charitable institutions under one management and by June 1 of that year accomplished the reorganization. A year later Jews in Cincinnati established a federation of nine charities under the title United Jewish Charities. Both Boston and Cincinnati lay claim to having originated the idea of a Jewish welfare federation. A historian of Jewish philanthropy gives the honor to Cincinnati with this assertion: "We find that in 1895, in Boston, some form of a Federation was established, but the first true Federation was established in Cincinnati in 1896." [20] In 1900 Jews in Chicago followed suit, and in 1904 Philadelphia, Detroit, and Cleveland joined in the list of cities having Jewish welfare federations. These efforts, unlike their forerunners, met with success.

Bogen explains the impetus for the Jewish welfare federation in the nineties: "When Jewish philanthropy came face to face with the problem of mass immigration in the eighties, it became apparent that the isolated, uncorrelated agencies for relief, the different groups connected with the synagogue, were unable to cope with the situation. A more efficient organization became a necessity and the idea of cooperation arose." [21] Writing in the 1915 *American Jewish Year Book*, Dr. Joseph Jacobs asserted: "Thus far the history of federation in American Jewish Charity has been uniformly one of success. The advantages that have been claimed throughout have been in the first place a distinct increase in the amount collected." Bogen affirms this, saying "In every case, Federation has produced an increase, both in subscriptions and in numbers of contributors."

Bogen lists these advantages of the federation plan: (1) Increase the amount collected because "persons are often of the erroneous impression that they are contributing largely to charity when sending their gifts in driblets, and are frequently surprised at the comparative smallness when the different items are added up." (2) Elimination of indiscriminate, unauthorized solicitation. Federation tends to prevent the increase of unnecessary institutions. (3) Federation eliminates duplication and overlapping of the activities of the constituent societies. He thought that "the whole plane of Jewish philanthropy is raised by this more dignified method for collecting and distributing the means by which charity lives." [22] Certainly the federation was a step toward the desired goal of raising the greatest amount of money with the least possible expense and effort.

The "more dignified method for collecting" provided an early model of today's highly organized, specialized fund-raising machine. The Jewish Welfare Federation technique as it was developed in its early years followed this pattern: (1) A thorough canvass of the Jewish community would be made, and then a card catalogue compiled of all potential givers. (2) A circular letter setting forth the appeal for funds and a subscription blank would be mailed to those catalogued as potential donors. (3) This was followed by a personal solicitor from membership committees formed for this purpose. Each committee member would be given a certain district or, in some cases, committee members would select the names of persons they knew or could most easily contact. The Chicago Jewish Welfare Federation was the first to introduce the contemporary standard technique of setting up team rivalries to spur solicitations, but in that early period "these whirlwind campaigns" were spasmodic. The trends toward more systematic fund raising for the public welfare, sound though they were, were not widely recognized nor quickly copied.

For example, Jews in New York City, center of the nation's largest Jewish community, did not firmly establish a Jewish welfare federation until 1917. Denver's federated appeal to the public met with dwindling success after the initial enthusiasm generated by a new idea faded away, and it did not beget an imitator until the Jewish federation in Cincinnati in 1896, nearly twenty years later. In a speech at the Chicago World's Fair in 1893, Francis G. Peabody, the Harvard professor who played an influential role in developing the philosophy of modern social work, praised the Liverpool system and made a strong plea for adopting a similar plan in the United States. Arthur J. Todd, an advocate of federation, writing in 1931, noted Professor Peabody's speech and observed: "There is a bit of historical irony in the fact that such a plea should come from Boston and Cambridge which have consistently held aloof from answering the plea." As a matter of fact, no community took up the Liverpool-Denver idea until Elmira, N.Y., in 1910 started a plan which eventually gave it third place in the list of U.S. cities adopting a public financial federation plan to raise funds for charity.

As the nineteenth century moved toward its close those interested in providing relief for the poor, education for youth, and food for the hungry continued to rely on benefits and bazaars or on meetings called to meet some crisis in the United States or abroad. In 1876 Fisk University for Negroes in Nashville, Tenn., opened its new Jubilee Hall, built in large part with funds raised by the concert tours of its glee club, the Fisk Jubilee Singers. Three years later Booker T. Washington opened his Tuskegee Institute for Negroes with funds he obtained through personal solicitation.

Two years after the end of the Civil War, Samuel Gridley Howe once again undertook a campaign to provide relief for some 12,000 Cretans in Greece, refugees from "Turkish barbarism." He stimulated the organization of relief committees in Boston and New York and prodded the press to plead for American benevolence toward these starving, homeless people in the Mediterranean area. A few weeks after the campaign had started, Boston and its neighbors raised $37,000.[23] A few months later a successful fair in Boston's Music Hall brought in some $30,000 worth of food and clothing. The Irish Famine of 1879–1880 brought forth another series of now standard devices for raising funds for charity. Of this drive Curti writes:

> To an extent greater than in earlier campaigns, benefits, theatricals and auctions augmented the relief funds. Concerts, entertainments, billiards, boxing and bicycle tournaments were held in New York.

At the Stock Exchange public auctions of donated poultry, Irish greyhounds, and other items swelled the treasury. Approximately a thousand dollars came in from a sale of paintings donated by American artists. Mayo's Olympic Theater contributed ten per cent of gross receipts for each evening's performance over a considerable period.[24]

The most picturesque movement originated in Boston. Captain Bennett Forbes, who had conceived the idea of a relief ship for Ireland in 1847, proposed a similar effort on a larger scale. Theatrical and musical performances were held and Julia Ward Howe gave a reading. A large fair also proved successful. Within nine days the relief fund stood at $67,000. Before the movement closed its books $81,000 had been collected.

More than one struggling institution of higher education in America was kept afloat in the nineteenth century by the resourceful fund-raising efforts of a promoter-president. The primary task of the college president, then as now, was to find funds to keep the institution going and growing. Typical was the Reverend E. P. Tenney of Colorado College, described by a former student as a "promoter of no mean rank." James Drummond Ellsworth, pioneer public relations practitioner who served the Bell Telephone System from 1907 until 1930, recalls President Tenney in these words:

> Every now and then the College [Colorado] treasurer would report that the young, struggling institution was out of funds. Thereupon, "Prexy" Tenney would jump the next train for the effete East where by hook or crook he would procure enough money to keep going for another few months. As far as anyone knew he never came back empty handed and the College never closed down. . . . The enterprising president brought back from the East not only money for the College, but he also brought back students to fill the forms. . . .
>
> One of the president's fund-raising schemes was to get students to take up land by pre-emption claims in the upper Cheyenne Canyon, and a caravan started with a party of young women students riding donkeys and with the boys driving the pack animals. The enterprise collapsed because the Boston girls could not cook and did not like camp life. So like the Duke of York and twice ten thousand men, they marched up the hill and then down again. But President Tenney built a useful institution of learning on desert ground, nursed it through infancy and by its means gave a broader life to many an ambitious youth.[25]

The location of Smith College in Northampton was assured when the citizens of that small Massachusetts town met Sophia Smith's condition, set down in her will, that the college be located there "provided the citizens of Northampton within two years . . . shall raise and pay over . . . to the said Board of Trustees . . . the sum of $25,000." This was accomplished by public subscriptions and the college started in 1871—one of the earliest examples of the use of the matching gift as a stimulus to public giving. The college itself staged its first campaign for funds among its alumnae, in 1888–1891, to raise $23,500 toward erection of a $30,000 gymnasium.[26]

It was in this period that the American Association of the Red Cross was founded, destined from the start to play an influential role in American philanthropy. It came into being in 1881 as the result of the fierce, unyielding dedication and determination of Clara Barton. This strong-willed, resourceful woman had become convinced of the urgent need for an American Red Cross because of her experiences in the American Civil War and in the Franco-Prussian War. She had the acumen to realize that something more than a European war-assistance program was needed to build enthusiasm for the Red Cross idea in America, and in her appeals for support she placed emphasis on the need for a peacetime organization to assist victims of natural disasters in the United States. On May 21, 1881, a small group met in Clara Barton's house in Washington, D.C., to organize "the greatest venture of voluntary service in the world." From the start Clara Barton recognized the value of publicity and knew how to get it. In her little band of organizers were three able newspapermen of the time—Walter P. Phillips, George Kennan, and Colonel Richard J. Hinton.[27]

Even before the infant Red Cross had received its charter from the District of Columbia in October, 1881, Clara Barton had sent it on its first mission of mercy. In September of that year fires ravaged the forests of Michigan, causing great destruction, making hundreds homeless, and creating needs local authorities could not cope with. When the disaster struck, Clara Barton took the simple step of wiring the Associated Press and a few leading newspapers that the Red Cross would accept and distribute contributions. This powerful yet succinct message to the AP brought a national flood of gifts: "Everything is needed; everything is welcome."

"In such ways, based on constantly growing integrity, the Red Cross was to raise and distribute an estimated more than two million dollars worth of relief and rehabilitation supplies—about 90 per cent of the value in goods and only 10 per cent in cash—in the regime of Clara Barton [1881–1904]." Then, as today, the Red Cross efforts to aid those struck by disaster were frequently and sharply criticized. In 1889 when the Red Cross raised funds and food for the victims of the famous Johnstown, Pa., flood it was denounced by the New York *World* because "The Red Cross has introduced pauperism by giving out provisions and clothing to the more shiftless class" who desired only "to eat the bread of charity."

The poor and the homeless continued to be the objects of most charitable enterprises. Benefits, bazaars, charity socials, and appeals through the press were the old reliables of nineteenth-century fund raising. One of the giants in the field of social welfare emerged in this century in the person of Charles Loring Brace who founded the Children's Aid Society of New York in 1853. He soon came to realize that "one of the trials of a young Charity is raising money." Brace was among the first of our social welfare pioneers to rebel against the then common cheap exploitation of human emotions. Tugs at the heartstrings were then, are now, and perhaps always will be an almost surefire method of getting people to open their purse strings. Yet unrestrained exploitation of raw human emotions can create more problems than the money thus raised can ever solve. Nevertheless, tearful appeals, such as stories and photographs of pathetically crippled children, continue to be used in much of twentieth-century fund raising, and they remain a topic of fierce debate among social workers and fund raisers, particularly those involved in the national health fund drives. Another author, writing in 1958, was echoing Brace when he said: "Emotionally conducted campaigns whose purpose it is to call forth emotional reactions are no way to do the job objectivity demands be done." Writing in 1880, Brace recalled:

I was determined to put this [raising money] on as sound and rational a basis as possible. It seemed to me, that, if the facts were well known in regard to the great suffering and poverty among the children of New York, and the principles of our operation were well understood, we could more safely depend on this enlightened public opinion and sympathy than on any sudden "sensation" or gush of feeling. Our Board fully concurred in these views, and we resolutely eschewed all "raffles" and pathetic exhibitions of abandoned children, and "pedestrian" or other exhibitions offered us for the benefit of humanity, and never even enjoyed the perfectly legitimate benefit of a "fair." . . . The solid ground for us was evidently the most rational one.[28]

Brace was among the first of the fund raisers to realize that only an informed public support will prove to be a long-term support and that, conversely, emotional support though easily aroused can, and usually does, quickly vanish. Brace relied in the main on press and pulpit to build informed support for his work. "I was able to make use of the pulpits . . . and sometimes was accustomed to spend every night of the week and the Sunday in delivering sermons . . . throughout the Eastern United States." The "next great implement" Brace used in raising funds for the Children's Aid Society was the press. "I made it a point, from the beginning, to keep our movements, and the evils we sought to cure, continually before the public in the columns of the daily journals." Thus Brace anticipated and antedated the influential role of today's specialized public relations practitioner in promoting public philanthropy and, consequently, "was, in fact, often daily editor, in addition to my other avocations." [29]

One writer divides the history of financing social welfare services in the United States into four periods: (1) From colonial days to World War I; (2) from World War I to the great economic Depression of the 1930's; (3) from the Depression to World War II; and (4) from World War II to the present. He describes the first period as follows:

The first, and longest of these periods was characterized by a very laggard acceptance of community responsibility for anything remotely resembling adequate provisions for destitute and handicapped people. . . . As the country expanded, the number of organizations increased and some achieved a modicum of financial security through legacies and endowments. For the most part, however, until World War I, they were supported by the contributions of a very small minority and were chronically confronted by urgent needs they were unable to meet.[30]

While it is true that World War I brought intensive, hard-hitting campaigns that raised millions and established philanthropy on the broad, democratic basis that characterizes it today, the pattern was set well before World War I, as described in the following chapter. In the years 1875–1900, America doubled its population, jammed its people, including large waves of immigrants, into larger and larger cities, enthroned the machine and developed mass production of goods, and spanned the nation with rail and wire communications. It was a turbulent, frenzied period of development which made us into an interdependent society of specialists working along one massive national assembly line. These spectacular developments brought with them increasing social and welfare problems that could be met only through the collective efforts of the whole community.

The increasing needs of the poor, the handicapped, and the victims of technological change, resulting from America's headlong jump into the twentieth century as a major industrial nation of urban dwellers, could no longer be financed by nineteenth-century methods. There was increasing disenchantment with the benefit or bazaar as a means of raising funds on the part of both the money givers and the money raisers. The latter increasingly realized that in using such benefits a large part of the funds raised were consumed by the enterprise that produced them, and the net income seldom matched the toil and effort. Charity socials and entertainments became so common as to cause grumbling and irritation among the well-to-do who supported such enterprises and were gradually being replaced by subscription and solicitor methods of raising funds. But these, it was soon seen, were not adequate for the job at hand either.

In the closing decades of the nineteenth century and the first decades of the twentieth there came into the consciousness of American life a new emphasis upon social problems and new faith in the progressive spirit that was to reshape America. This increasingly sensitive social conscience was reflected in the rise of great numbers and varieties of social agencies, associations, and institutions. Some of these were started to alleviate suffering as it existed, some to bring greater opportunities to the under-privileged, some to spread education and recreation, some to fight disease. Such organizations multiplied at a rapid rate in the period described as "the watershed of American history." Not only was there an increasing attempt to meet the new problems through voluntary efforts; there was a growing demand for government intervention. Arthur S. Link asserts:

> The adoption of the Populist platform [in 1892] marked the end of an era when practically all Americans put their trust in the English Liberal ideal of a free, competitive economy, operating automatically in the general interest without decisive and planned intervention by government. The adoption of this platform heralded the coming triumph of a new progressive faith—a faith in the ability of men working together to overcome economic adversity and rectify social injustice by legislative action.[31]

In the America of small towns, small farms, small shops, the individual was glorified and each person was more or less on his own. Generations of Americans lived and died with little awareness of the need for social organizations to ease the blows of misfortune and soften the impact of the Industrial Revolution. Yet the very processes that exalted the philosophy of the rugged individual were building forces that ultimately brought today's highly complex, urbanized, and industrialized society, with its resultant maladjustments. As people crowded into ever larger cities they were thrown into intimate contact with one another, facilitating the spread of disease as well as ideas. As the cities grew, fed by waves of immigration from Europe and emigration from the farm, the existing health, social, and religious institutions were put to new stresses and strains.

Creation of the urban complex by the forces of industry and commerce had two by-products that are pertinent here: (1) the accumulation of vast new stores of wealth which were to release energies and capacities for attack on the problems of poverty, ignorance, and disease; (2) the growth of scientific knowledge of man and his environment, and increased faith in the solubility of man's perennial problems of pestilence and poverty. These profound changes built up slowly over the latter part of the nineteenth and early part of the twentieth century and were recognized by the general public at an even slower pace.

As America headed for a new century and a new day, this process of change in social direction was speeded up. "A strident and increasingly influential group of muckrakers, democratically inclined legislators, advanced social thinkers, and outright do-good-

ers was whipping up rebellion by emphasizing the disparity between American reality and the American dream. . . . The spiritual and financial parsimony of conventional charity was increasingly discredited by the words and deeds of workers such as Jane
Addams and Lillian D. Wald." [32] This was, indeed, in the words of
Richard Shryock, the period when "humanitarianism was rampant."

Norton observes:

> The private social service which looms so large today laid most of
> its foundation stones in those thirty years between the close of the
> Civil War and the Spanish-American War. Wealth developed at an
> enormous rate and people were free from their own affairs and could
> pay attention to philanthropy. Beginning with the last decade of the
> century two movements that had been brewing in the previous years
> began to accelerate. Public health conceptions suddenly became popu-
> lar and the effort to socialize the leisure-time activities of people found
> an instrument in the social settlement.[33]

As the new varieties and types of organizations concerned with
man's welfare continued to proliferate in the 1890's and early
1900's, it was inevitable that accompanying the growing demands
for philanthropic money there would be pleas for more cooperation and less confusion among these agencies. The American flair
for systematic organization and for efficiency was soon brought
to bear in this area of life. Already urban centers had begun to
develop councils of social agencies, welfare federations, alliances
of charities, and community funds. But most strident of all was
the increasing call for more money—money to be donated by the
growing body of affluent Americans or to be raised through taxation. Government was soon to cease being a narrow, negative
police instrument and to become, in the words of Felix Frank-
furter, "an affirmative mechanism for society."

The early federations relied upon letter appeals, upon personal
calls on prospective donors by the society's directors, or the paid
secretary, and, in many instances, upon paid solicitors. William J.
Norton, a pioneer in the federation fund-raising movement, recalls: "Although this combination of methods, in addition to the
publicity programs that were carried on, produced more money
than had been raised by the separate agencies previously, the in-

crease did not satisfy the pressure of the agencies for funds. Consequently the campaign method of raising money became . . . universal. It produced larger sums than any known means of fundraising."

The "campaign method" of money raising was to change profoundly the nature of social welfare, health, and educational institutions in the United States by making philanthropy a broad public enterprise, not just a hobby of the very rich. This campaign method had its genesis in the Young Men's Christian Association, just before America turned the calendar to a new and quite different twentieth century. The innovators were Charles Sumner Ward and Lyman L. Pierce, two young imaginative and ambitious Y.M.C.A. secretaries. Their pioneering played an influential role in developing a people's philanthropy in the United States.

NOTES

1. Samuel Eliot Morison, *The Founding of Harvard College* (Cambridge, Mass.: Harvard University Press, 1935), p. 303.

2. Beverly McAnear, "College Founding in the American Colonies, 1745–1775," *Mississippi Valley Historical Review*, Vol. XLII (June, 1955), pp. 24–44.

3. "Lotteries at Harvard," in *Harvard's Open Shelf*, Vol. 1 (October, 1948)—a fund-raising newsletter issued during the Lamont Library Campaign.

4. Beverly McAnear, "The Raising of Funds by the Colonial Colleges," *Mississippi Valley Historical Review*, Vol. XXXVIII (March, 1952), pp. 591–612.

5. *Ibid.*

6. Robert H. Bremner, *American Philanthropy* (Chicago: University of Chicago Press, 1960), pp. 21–23.

7. Quoted by Arnaud C. Marts in *Philanthropy's Role in Civilization* (New York: Harper & Row, 1953), p. 97.

8. From Mathew Carey's *Miscellaneous Essays* (1829), as reprinted in *Social Service Review*, Vol. 29 (1955), pp. 302–305.

9. *Niles' Weekly Register*, April 21, 1827, p. 130.

10. Edward Hitchcock, *The Power of Christian Benevolence: Life and Labors of Mary Lyon* (Northampton: Hopkins, Bridgman and Co., 1852; 7th ed.), pp. 200–204.

11. Arnaud C. Marts, *Man's Concern for His Fellow Man* (Geneva, N.Y.: W. F. Humphrey Press, Inc., 1961), p. 23.

12. *Niles' Weekly Register*, May 1, 1847, p. 139.

13. Vernon L. Parrington, *Main Currents in American Thought* (New York: Harcourt, Brace & World, Inc.), Vol. III, *The Beginnings of Critical Realism in America*, p. 36.

14. Frank D. Watson, *The Charity Organization Movement in the United States* (New York: Macmillan, 1922), p. 176.

15. John R. Seeley, Buford H. Junker, *et al.*, *Community Chest: A Case Study in Philanthropy* (Toronto: University of Toronto Press, 1957), p. 17.

16. C. Howard Hopkins, *History of the Y.M.C.A. in North America*, (New York: Association Press, 1951), p. 7.

17. Memorandum, "Study of Financing of Social Work," prepared by

Arthur J. Todd for Welfare Council of New York City, April, 1931, found in files of Council of Community Chests and United Funds, New York City.

18. William J. Norton, *The Cooperative Movement in Social Work* (New York: Macmillan, 1927), pp. 53–54.

19. *Ibid.*, pp. 55–56.

20. Boris D. Bogen, *Jewish Philanthropy* (New York: Macmillan, 1917), p. 44.

21. *Ibid.*, p. 364.

22. *Ibid.*, p. 48.

23. Laura E. Richards, ed., *Letters and Journals of Samuel Gridley Howe* (Boston: Dana Estes & Co., 1909), Vol. II, pp. 537 ff.

24. Merle Curti, *American Philanthropy Abroad* (New Brunswick, N.J.: Rutgers University Press, 1963), p. 91.

25. In unpublished manuscript, "Unforgotten Men," in Mass Communications History Center collection, State Historical Society of Wisconsin, pp. 16–18.

26. For this story, see L. Clark Seelye, *The Early History of Smith College, 1871–1910* (Cambridge, Mass.: Houghton Mifflin, 1923).

27. Charles W. Hurd, *The Compact Story of the American Red Cross* (New York: Hawthorn, 1959), p. 63. For fuller account based on series of Red Cross-produced monographs, see Foster Rhea Dulles, *The American Red Cross, a History* (New York: Harper & Row, 1950). For story of Clara Barton's life, see Ishbel Ross's *Angel of the Battlefield* (New York: Harper & Row, 1956).

28. Charles Loring Brace, *The Dangerous Classes of New York* (New York: Wynkoop and Hallenbeck, 3rd ed., 1880), pp. 280–283.

29. *Ibid.*, p. 282.

30. Wayne McMillin, "Financing Social Welfare Services," *Social Work Yearbook*, 1957, pp. 260–267. Quote is from p. 260.

31. Arthur S. Link, *American Epoch* (New York: Alfred A. Knopf, 1955), p. 11.

32. Richard Carter, *The Gentle Legions* (Garden City: Doubleday, 1961), pp. 32–33.

33. William J. Norton, *op. cit.*, p. 9.

2

From Wholesale to Retail
Philanthropy: 1900–1907

The Stage Is Set for Change

When Americans cheered the dawn of the New Year on January 1, 1901, they were knowingly celebrating the arrival of the New Century. Unknowingly they were ushering in a wholly New Era. The early years of the twentieth century in the United States were laden with significant changes, breath-taking in their swiftness, far-reaching in their impact. The momentous events of the period were to have their influence on American philanthropy and on the means of providing the money for its enterprises. The Republicans in 1900 had re-elected William McKinley as President of the United States and at the same time the conservative party leaders believed they had safely "shelved" the politically rambunctious Theodore Roosevelt in the Vice-Presidency. That same year the American National Red Cross finally obtained its charter of incorporation from Congress and in then faraway Germany Kaiser Wilhelm made an ominous speech declaring that Germany would no longer suffer "political impotence and economic submissiveness."

The dramatic changes of this era were signaled and symbolized more by the assassination of President William McKinley at Buffalo, N.Y., September 6, 1901, than by the turn of the calendar. With him the old order expired. Theodore Roosevelt's succession to the Presidency marked, in the words of one historian, "not only a change of Presidents but also the beginning of a new epoch for a people standing on the threshold of the most momentous century in modern history." [1] McKinley's death ended what William Allen

White had called "the alliance between government and business for the benefit of business."

The United States, then a nation of some 76 million people, had shed its nineteenth-century isolationism and moved into position as a world power in the wake of the Spanish-American War. The modern corporation that was to provide the economic engine to pull the nation ahead was created in 1901 when J. P. Morgan formed the United States Steel Company. With this move, control of the nation's industrial sinews passed from the steelmakers to the financiers of Wall Street.

The modern corporation, damned in its early years for its abuse of both its workers and its customers, would come to be looked upon as a major source of philanthropy in the second half of this century. In its early years the corporation permitted men, in the view of sociologist E. A. Ross, "to commit with clear conscience crimes which they would have abhorred as individuals."

In the same year, 1901, Henry Ford was building the motorcar that was to reshape life in the United States and make him a colossus of American industry. In January, 1901, the Texas oil boom began at Beaumont—a boom that was to provide the gasoline for the twentieth century's motorcars, trucks, trains, planes, and ships. In July of that same year the first turbine-driven steamship crossed the Atlantic and in December electric streetcars started rattling up and down New York City's Broadway. Also in 1901 the U.S. Navy decided that it could give up carrier pigeons because of the invention of Marconi's wireless. A year later the New York Central cut the running time of its trains between New York and Chicago to twenty hours, and Henry Ford drove a racing car at the unheard-of speed of a mile a minute. In another year, 1903, the first Pacific cable was opened and the Wright Brothers made their historic flight at Kitty Hawk. Their discovery of powered flight was to remake the world, as Henry Ford's automobile remade America.

Meanwhile, improved techniques of printing, the increased literacy of a people achieving more education, and heightened interest in public affairs combined both to reflect and stimulate the growth of mass media. The mass circulation daily newspaper and the growing numbers of popularly priced, widely read magazines were coming to be important factors in accelerating these profound changes and in generating a militant public opinion. The Associated Press, now the world's largest newsgathering organization, dates, in the modern sense, from 1900 though it can trace its history back to 1848. Until 1945 the AP, a nonprofit membership cooperative, could withhold its service from any publication competing with a newspaper published by an AP member. This monopolistic power forced E. W. Scripps to start the United Press in 1907 and William Randolph Hearst the International News Service in 1909 to compete with the greatly improved wire report the AP was providing its members. The advent of the national news wire brought a quick exchange of news and opinion across the nation, facilitating the agitation for change now abroad in the land.

The popular, widely circulated magazine was, likewise, a twentieth-century development. Before 1880 there were only a few important general magazines, *Harper's, Scribner's, Century, Atlantic Monthly,* and the *North American Review.* In the nineteenth century these magazines had small circulations and were sedate and literary in content. By 1890 the list of nationally circulated magazines had been increased by the *Ladies' Home Journal, Munsey's,* and *Cosmopolitan.* S. S. McClure, who was to play a key role in the wave of reform in the early 1900's, started *McClure's* in 1893 and stimulated the move from high-priced, quality circulation periodicals to popularly priced magazines with large subscription lists. Frank Munsey once estimated that the ten-cent magazine, between 1893 and 1899, increased the magazine buying public from 250,000 persons to 750,000. It was in 1900, significantly, that the first magazine—the *Ladies' Home Journal*—reached a million circulation. Political and social reformers now had a national forum, and they used it.

This was "the era of the muckrakers" who sped the process of change in the Age of Reform. These journalists—Lincoln Steffens, Ida M. Tarbell, Frank Norris, Upton Sinclair, Ray Stannard Baker, George Creel, and others—shouted the doctrine that the dominant trends in the United States were running counter to the American traditions of morality, liberty, and equality of opportunity. The movement got its direction and impetus from S. S. McClure whose failures in later years have too long obscured his important contribution to what has been well described as "a condition of excitement and irritation" in the land.[2] The simultaneous publication of three articles by Steffens, Miss Tarbell, and Baker in the January, 1903, issue of *McClure's* set muckraking on its way.

What was perhaps the first of the muckraking articles, one entitled "The Great Conflict," was published in *Arena* in August, 1901. The author, Professor Frank Parsons, decried the prevailing disparity of wealth in an era when Andrew Carnegie had a net income of $23 million in the same year that an average working man in the United States earned around $500. And Carnegie had no income taxes to pay! Even in 1910 the Pittsburgh Associated Charities found that if a steelworker worked twelve hours a day every day in the year he could not provide a family of five with the bare necessities. The lot of the steel worker, the farmhand, the coal miner, and the common laborer of industry was indeed cruel and harsh in this period. The muckrakers, political reformers, and social workers would eventually alter all this in what *Fortune* magazine well termed "The Permanent Revolution." Frederick Lewis Allen told the story movingly in *The Big Change*.

The plight of the coal miner was brought to the nation's attention by John Spargo in his *Bitter Cry the Children*. This was a time when children were put to work in the mines at the age of ten as "breakers" for as little as 35 cents a day and then, some thirty years later, were returned to this menial task as spent, crippled old men at the same rate of pay. In the same period Ida M. Tarbell was exposing the ruthless machinations of John D. Rockefeller in making his Standard Oil Trust a powerful monopoly and Lincoln Steffens was laying bare the graft and corruption in city and state governments. The horrors and stench of the slums as portrayed in Jacob A. Riis's *How the Other Half Lives* was reverberating in press and pulpit. In 1906 Upton Sinclair unmasked the terrible working conditions in the Chicago meat-packing houses. Sinclair's exposures were a vital force in bringing the nation's first Pure Food and Drug Act. Ray Stannard Baker and Frank Norris were reporting on the machinations of the nation's railroads. Revulsion, revolt, and reform were inevitable.

Others were promoting reform more by deeds than by words. In Chicago the great social work pioneer, Jane Addams, was demonstrating in her historic Hull House, founded in 1889, that human beings could live in dignity if given the opportunity. And in New York Lillian Wald was proving with her Henry Street Settlement House that "the health and happiness of even a depressed community could be improved if home nursing and other health services were made available in a spirit of democratic neighborliness." In the political arena Wisconsin's Robert M. LaFollette and New Jersey's Woodrow Wilson were pressing for political reform and demonstrating its efficacy at the state level. Political leaders were quick to capitalize on the unrest set loose by agrarian agitators and the muckrakers. Foremost in this group was Theodore Roosevelt who, by his own testimony, "collected and reflected the doctrines of the day." Frederick Lewis Allen thought Roosevelt's great contribution to American history was "to advertise and dramatize to the whole country a point of view on business, government, and the public interest that was refreshingly new, exciting, and contagious." [3]

As the historian Arthur S. Link sums it up: "Americans in the early 1900's launched a virtual crusade on all levels of government to revitalize democracy, bring the economic machinery under their control, and find an answer to the twin evils of privilege and poverty. The years before the first World War were, finally, a period when Christian moralism subdued the crass materialism of the Gilded Age, and morality and righteousness became the keynotes of politics." [4] Contagious, indeed, was the spirit of change and reform. It quickly spilled over into the fields of philanthropy and public welfare.

Big-scale Philanthropy Emerges

With Andrew Carnegie and John D. Rockefeller leading the way, the march of large-scale philanthropy and benevolent foundations across the national landscape began. Carnegie, who had already amassed a fortune in steelmaking of more than $30 million, published his historic essay, "Wealth," in the *North American Review* in 1889, stating his philosophy: that millionaires should, instead of leaving their fortunes to their families, administer their wealth as a public trust during life. Although Carnegie preached and practiced giving on a grand scale he did not believe that philanthropy should shoulder the whole burden of welfare. Rockefeller's philanthropy, on the other hand, was more from the old-fashioned religious principle of stewardship, which he had developed as a faithful churchgoer and church contributor early in life. In the same year that Carnegie's famous essay appeared John D. Rockefeller gave $600,-

ooo to help found the new University of Chicago, the first of millions the oil baron was to give that university. These two men plunged into a wholesale philanthropy that dwarfed earlier giving in the United States, in an effort to drain off their vast accumulations of wealth.

To take away the growing burden of hearing, investigating, weighing appeals for his millions, Rockefeller, in 1891, hired as his adviser the Reverend Frederick T. Gates, a young Baptist clergyman and fund raiser who played a most influential role in shaping Rockefeller's benefactions. Under Gates's guidance Rockefeller soon found himself—to use Gates's language—"laying aside retail giving almost wholly, and entering safely and pleasurably into the field of wholesale philanthropy." Rockefeller followed his gift of 1889 to the University of Chicago with gifts of a million dollars in 1900 and another million in 1901. In the latter year the Rockefeller Institute for Medical Research was launched on a small scale, but eventually received more than $60 million from Rockefeller.

With Gates's counsel, John D. Sr., in 1902, established the General Education Board which he endowed with more than $130 million to advance higher education and scientific research in the United States. In the same year Carnegie set up the Carnegie Institution in Washington, D.C. The steelmaker founded the Carnegie Institute of Technology in 1900, endowed the Carnegie Foundation for the Advancement of Teaching in 1905, and in 1911 made his largest gift to establish the Carnegie Corporation. The last-named foundation, like the General Education Board, has played an important and influential role in the advancement of American higher education and the extension of knowledge. The Rockefeller Foundation was chartered by the state of New York in 1913 after the U.S. Congress had refused to do so. These foundations, endowed with millions, made earlier American philanthropies seem trifling indeed. The Rockefeller Foundation, over the next fifty years, would give away $763 million, carrying out Rockefeller's instructions to "promote the well-being of mankind throughout the world."

At the time Rockefeller and Carnegie began their philanthropic gifts and foundations there were some 14,000 millionaires in the young, raw, resource-rich United States and other wealthy persons began to follow suit. The Milbank Memorial Fund was set up in 1905. Two years later Mrs. Russell Sage endowed the Russell Sage Foundation as a memorial to her late husband, a foundation which has played an important role in speeding and shaping the advance of social work in the United States. Fundamental changes in American philanthropy were under way, for even more significant than the growing list of large gifts to public projects was the fact that their donors were imaginatively breaking new ground in philanthropy. "Most earlier charitable trusts had been established for some narrowly defined purpose. . . . The major trusts founded by Carnegie and Rockefeller, however, were limited only to the advancement of knowledge and human welfare. Relieving the needy was not their objective. They would attack misery at its source through the weapon of research." [5]

The foundation was Rockefeller's answer to his insistence that "this business of benevolence" be more efficiently organized. Bremner thinks "Rockefeller's and Carnegie's chief contribution to philanthropy was to found institutions capable of distributing private wealth with greater intelligence and vision than the donors themselves could hope to possess." [6]

These large-scale philanthropies of a few rich men came at a time when popular revolt and resentment against the abuses of "the robber barons" was at its height. The trends in political reform through affirmative government and in putting surplus fortunes to work for the public good were not unrelated. Just as today's large business corporations give to earn public good will, similarly did the rich man of that day seek public esteem. But one oft-told myth should be laid to rest: The frequently made assertion that Rockefeller undertook his large-scale philanthropies at the urging of Ivy L. Lee, pioneer public relations practitioner, in order to change the public's image of Rockefeller from that of ogre to kindly old philanthropist has no basis in fact.

Lee was never employed directly by or for John D. Rockefeller, Sr. In fact, the father disapproved when John D. Rockefeller, Jr., borrowed Lee from the Pennsylvania Railroad for assistance in 1914 after the disgraceful Ludlow Massacre in the Colorado Fuel & Iron Company strike. But the father's long-standing policy of not interfering with his son's affairs stayed his protest. Lee's work for the younger Rockefeller in that bloody strike led to his retention as public relations counsel for the Rockefeller interests, a position of influence that he held until his death in 1934. In his work for John D. Jr., Lee did, in fact, carry out missions for Rockefeller Sr. and handled many news announcements involving him, including the announcement of his death. A trusted counselor to John D. Jr. for twenty years, Ivy Lee undoubtedly influenced his philanthropic decisions in some degree over those two decades although the extent of this influence is shrouded in their confidential relationship. Lee's role was probably a minor one.

Interestingly enough, the only time John D. Rockefeller, Sr., was moved to admit the need for public relations counsel in his relationships with the public was when his motives for philanthropy were damned in the "tainted money" controversy. He took this step reluctantly and only at the strong insistence of the Reverend Mr. Gates. In 1895 the Reverend Washington Gladden, a Congregational minister, had published an article, "Tainted Money," in which he denounced the benefactions of the rich "robber barons" and "pirates of industry" as a transparent means of buying public favor and heavenly salvation. In the article Gladden mentioned no names but the public thought most of his arrows were aimed at John D. Rockefeller, Sr. In 1905 Gladden renewed the charge and named Rockefeller when the minister violently opposed acceptance of a gift of $100,000 from Rockefeller to the Congregational Board of Foreign Missions. This became known as the "tainted money" controversy.

John D. Sr.'s tough business mind had long been inured to harsh public criticism of his ruthless business tactics. He never made an effort to reply to public attacks. Once, when questioned by a reporter about Ida Tarbell's attacks on Standard Oil, John D. Sr. replied, "Not a word, not a word about that misguided woman." But the criticism of Gladden and others cast a dark shadow across his philanthropies and cut deeply into Rockefeller's Baptist quick. In the midst of the 1905 dispute Gates wrote Rockefeller, plainly pointing out to him the error of his policy of secrecy. "While replying frigidly to Gates, Rockefeller gave way. He asked Gates to see [John D.] Archbold; and it turned out that he had sent Gates's letter to the head of Standard, and had frankly yielded the whole question." [7] This led to employment of Joseph Ignatius Constantine Clarke, colorful Irish newsman, as "publicity agent" for the Standard Oil Company in 1906, at a salary of $5,000 a year, later raised to $6,000.

Clarke worked to refurbish the Standard Oil Company's reputation more than to explain and publicize Rockefeller's philanthropies. "My contact was naturally with the Directors, [Henry H.] Rogers and Archbold particularly." [8] One of Clarke's first moves was to promote "an authenticated history of the Standard Oil," that is, one favorable to Rockefeller, to counter Ida Tarbell's *The History of the Standard Oil Company*, published in two volumes in 1904 and which, by now, was deeply impressed on the public's mind. "The Reverend Dr. Bacon was engaged," but "he passed away before he had taken the Company far on the road." However, Chancellor James R. Day of Syracuse University, a "booming flagellant of sinners . . . worshiped for his sense of justice," came to Standard's rescue with "a good clear story" but "the press pooh-poohed it." [9] Clarke was obviously referring to the book defending Standard Oil written by Chancellor Day—*The Raid on Prosperity*—published in 1908 by D. Appleton.

In his preface Day does seem to protest too much: "My convictions have not come to me out of the exigencies of a college presidency or by the contaminating influence of millionaires!" Yet that same year, 1908, Day's Syracuse University dedicated one of the first modern football stadiums in the nation—the gift of Standard Oil President John D. Archbold. Starting with an initial gift of $165 in 1886, Archbold had given Syracuse, through June, 1913, a total of $1,737,038.57, most of which consisted of gifts for current expenses, and the costs of erecting Sims Hall, and the stadium and gymnasium, both of which bear Archbold's name. [10]

Naturally such coincidences gave credence to the muckraker charge that the millionaires were seeking to buy good reputations with their philanthropies. Yet Raymond B. Fosdick, an executive in the Rockefeller Foundation for many years, vehemently denies this allegation as it pertains to John D. Rockefeller, Sr. "Critics have frequently charged that Mr. Rockefeller's benefactions were set up as a shield against public censure. . . . But this contention is not borne out by the Facts. The famous Ledger which he kept in his teens when he secured his first job as a clerk in Cleveland, a job which paid him six dollars a month, shows that he gave away 6 per cent of his total wage to the Sunday school and various missions related to his church interests. The obligation to give was an inseparable part of his religious conviction." [11]

Even such spectacular multimillion-dollar gifts were not sufficient to meet the increasingly evident welfare, health, and recreational needs of the twentieth century or to blunt the growing chorus of criticism aimed at rich businessmen. The early 1900's brought a boom in national voluntary organizations to bring relief to the pressing areas of community and social problems in America's new urban life. In Richard Shryock's opinion, "The custom stemmed from the combination, in this country, of a free society and of a *laissez-faire* tradition of government." With these multiplying organizations came public projects that had to be financed. As Bremner points out: "The continuing vitality of the voluntary principle and a broadening sense of responsibility for improving the social environment led to the formation of a host of new national organizations maintained by dues, donations, and subscriptions." [12] Demands on the public to give, and devices to raise funds, grew rapidly in the years from 1900 to World War I.

These years saw the start of the Boy Scouts, Girl Scouts, Campfire Girls, National Tuberculosis Association, American Cancer Society, the National Association for Advancement of Colored People, National Urban League, the Lighthouse, the National Child Labor Committee, and scores of other leagues, associations, and committees. In response to these organizations' need for money, modern techniques were developed; the public fund drive, the beginnings of the Community Chest, and the employment of fundraising and public relations experts to present their urgent pleas to the public.

With the increasing demands for publicly donated money came equally strong-voiced demands for system and efficiency in its solicitation. Organization leaders joined with the donors, particularly the bluntly critical businessmen, to echo Rockefeller in urging that "this business of benevolence" be more efficiently organized, particularly the raising of money. The American genius for system and efficiency was first applied to fund raising by two YMCA workers and an Episcopal bishop.

Ward and Pierce Launch the Big Fund Drive

The whirlwind, intensive campaign to raise large sums of money in a short period of time by bombarding the public with surefire appeals and by recruiting scores of volunteers to solicit many times their number had its origins in the Young Men's Christian Association. Developed initially to raise money for YMCA buildings, the successful techniques were soon utilized in the annual appeals of other gift-supported agencies to build hospitals, churches, colleges, civic centers, YMCAs, YWCAs, Boys Clubs, and to finance national health and welfare associations. The systematic solicitation of the public for gifts quickly proved its efficacy after the first experiment in Washington, D.C., in 1905. In the preceding fifty-five years the YMCA in the United States had accumulated a total capital investment of $35 million in buildings and endowment. In the decade 1905–1915 this amount was increased by another $60 million for capital funds through the newly fashioned YMCA campaign method of raising money.

The YMCA also was the first organization systematically to promote gifts from business firms and thus influenced the pattern of corporate giving which plays an important role in contemporary philanthropy. Business support of the Y began with the railroad YMCAs which undertook religious work among the laborers. This program started with the Union Pacific Railroad in 1868 when it was pushing its way westward from Omaha. In the early years of the railroad Ys, the railroads supplied about 60 per cent of the operating budgets, their employees the other 40 per cent. By 1912, however, this ratio had been exactly reversed. In the matter of the YMCA's promotion of business giving, Williams and Croxton state: "The intensive money-raising techniques developed and first applied by the YMCA professional and lay leaders early in 1904 [*sic*] unquestionably was the most important single factor in getting corporate contributions for the local Y programs." [13]

The builders of the model of today's fund drive were two YMCA officials, Charles Sumner Ward and Lyman L. Pierce. These two imaginative, resourceful fund-raising pioneers trained many of today's professional fund raisers, passionate disciples who insist one, not the other, is the father of the fund drive. Professionals still refer to "The Ward Plan" and to "The Pierce Plan." Naturally the early 1905 model campaign constructed by these two men, working together in the nation's capital, has been expanded and strengthened immeasurably over the years by other fund raisers and public relations practitioners.

Also, it is a bit of an oversimplification to say that the first modern fund drive dates from 1905. There are records in the YMCA archives of occasional "whirlwind" campaigns as early as 1884. The Seattle YMCA raised $12,000 in forty-eight hours in 1888. Howard Hopkins, author of a history of the YMCA in North America, records that "novel methods involving large numbers of solicitors and a short period of time were first tried out in raising the current expense budget of the Association at Burlington, Iowa, in 1891." [14]

Charles Sumner Ward, widely acknowledged as the prime originator of the short-term, intensive fund-raising drive, was a quiet, gentle, methodical New England Yankee with the traditional New Englander's reserve. He certainly was not the high-pressure, drum-beating ballyhoo artist some might picture as the man "who is responsible for the impressive fact that America now gives in millions rather than in thousands." Ward was born in Danville, Vt., on November 3, 1858, the son of Thomas and Ruth Weeks Ward. He received his preparatory schooling in the St. Johnsbury, Vt., Academy and was graduated from Dartmouth College in 1881, where he earned membership in Phi Beta Kappa. His Alma Mater called him back to the campus in 1912 to award him a master's degree in recognition of his service to his fellow man through the YMCA.

Soft-spoken, rather short in stature, Ward had gentle blue eyes and most of his life wore a closely cropped mustache. In the mid-twenties a New York *Evening Post* story described him as "a medium sized man, so mild of manner that one would never suspect him of the power to sway hitherto reluctant pocketbooks." Ward was a deeply religious man and an active worker in the Congregational Church all his adult life. A partner in his commercial fund-raising firm once described Ward this way: "A Vermont Yankee by birth, quiet spoken, shrewd in thought, Ward had an exceptionally large share of the New Englander's traditional concern over improving the lot of others." [15] Ward died in a Flushing, N.Y., hospital July 28, 1929.

Imbued with this "New Englander's concern" for helping others, it was natural that Ward would be attracted to the YMCA movement which was spreading across America at the time Ward was an undergraduate at Dartmouth. The Y was meeting with an especially enthusiastic reception on college campuses as a result of the work of its student department, organized in 1877, the year Ward entered Dartmouth. Soon after his graduation, Ward decided to make his career in YMCA work. After a brief training period, he became general secretary of an association in Lexington, Ky. One year later he moved to the same position in the larger New Britain, Conn., YMCA, where he organized and directed a successful effort to raise funds for a new building. Hopkins records that "Scattered

Associations utilized the short-term method of raising building funds at this time." In 1890 Ward was appointed to the general secretary's job in the Grand Rapids, Mich., YMCA, serving there for the next seven years, pondering and perfecting his ideas about the unpleasant task of raising the money to keep the Y's doors open.

In his early months at Grand Rapids Ward became increasingly irritated with the fact that he seemed to spend most of his time seeing people, or trying to see people, to beg for funds for the new YMCA. He was frustrated because fund raising and administrative detail left little time to give to the Y's program. Out of this irritation was born Ward's methodical plan for getting the fund-raising chore done all at once, and done quickly. He asked his directors to agree to close down their desks a part of each day for a short period of time and give wholehearted support to an intensive, organized effort to raise the Y's budget at the beginning of the year. In return Ward promised these men that they would not be called upon for begging chores the remainder of the year. The directors agreed and the plan was tried in 1892, with excellent results, and the year's budget was raised in a few days. Ward repeated the first-of-the-year short-term fund drive at Grand Rapids for the next five years.

From this simple experience Ward realized that the answer to getting funds donated to public causes "lay in organized and keen work concentrated into a small period of time." Ward learned another lesson at Grand Rapids he used with profit in later years. "You can get busy men to give a lot of time for only a limited period." He later explained the origins of his plan candidly, "To get the agony over with quickly was the main idea which prompted this movement."

Ward's skill in raising money was attracting the attention of the YMCA officials. In 1897 he was sent, on a loan basis, to rescue the Minneapolis, Minn., association which had recently lost its building. Ward quickly organized a drive to raise the money needed to redeem the building. Reports conflict as to the amount. Hopkins says Ward raised $25,000.[16] Press accounts say $75,000. In any case the sum was a wee drop in the bucket in the more than a billion dollars Ward was to have a hand in raising from the public before his career ended.

In 1899 Ward was promoted to the position of international field secretary and joined the YMCA's headquarters staff in Chicago.

For the next several years Ward gave his attention chiefly to aiding local associations out of their financial difficulties. "Those were the days of what was known as 'begging.' Philanthropic organizations had no definite system of collecting funds. One would start out to build a new building and it would be years in raising the funds. In Dayton, O., for instance, it took six years to get the money for a new building, and the secretary of the YMCA there died of over-work and worry brought on by the effort." [17]

Ward's early collaborator and later competitor in fund raising was Lyman L. Pierce, who was born May 14, 1868, in Stockton, N.Y., the son of Christopher and Salina Todd Pierce. He received his preparatory schooling in the Chamberlain Institute, Randolph, N.Y., and his college degree from the University of Minnesota. Like Ward, Pierce became interested in the YMCA as a college student and he, too, decided to make this his lifework. He, too, eventually became a professional fund raiser. He died July 20, 1940.

Upon his graduation from Minnesota in 1892, Pierce was sent to Denver and then to Omaha for training as a YMCA secretary. At Omaha he worked as membership secretary under Frank W. Ober, who was later to serve as editor of the Y's *Association Men*. Ober, like Ward, had hit upon the idea of having a short, intensive fund drive to raise the Y's annual budget. Ober and Pierce also put on a big membership drive when they enlisted a hundred of the leading men in Omaha to solicit one new member a month until the total membership should reach 1,500. These hundred men were divided into twenty teams. Printed matter was prepared and regular report meetings held. The drive was quite successful and news of the new method spread quickly through the Y movement.

His training completed, Pierce was sent to Cedar Rapids, Iowa, as the Y secretary in 1893. Naturally enough, Pierce soon used Ober's ideas to raise money for the Cedar Rapids association's annual budget. He moved rapidly in the burgeoning YMCA movement and in 1895 was made secretary for the state of Ohio. In 1897 he was appointed general secretary of the Trenton, N.J., Y and during his tenure there he tripled the membership from 400 to 1,200. Transferred to Washington, D.C., in 1901, he assumed the position of general secretary of the Washington YMCA on January 1. It was in the national capital that Pierce and Ward were to first join forces in fund raising.

Like Ward, Pierce was deeply religious and strongly motivated by his Christian beliefs. This early "YMCA School" of fund raisers, who were later to develop fund raising as a profitable private business, were impelled by a missionary zeal, regarded their work as "Christian stewardship," and said so on many occasions. At a welcome dinner in Cedar Rapids, Pierce responded: "I am not here to make any promises. I came to Cedar Rapids in the name of the Master, and in the name of the Master I shall do the best I can." Ward would sometimes describe fund raisers as "engineers of movements in service of other men."

Both men inspired great loyalty among their followers. Arnaud Marts describes Lyman Pierce as "a man of superior ideals and spiritual capacities." Herman F. Reinhardt sweepingly says of Charles Ward: "A Christian gentleman and genius whose remarkable understanding of human relations and inspired leadership resulted in a plan which revolutionized voluntary giving in America." On one occasion Ward is said to have asserted: "I would leave this work immediately if I thought I were merely raising money. It is raising men that appeals to me." [18] Yet a former partner who was in Ward's original fund-raising firm, founded after World War I, ruefully remarks: "Sadly, Mr. Ward came to value money very much." John Price Jones, who became well known when he turned the art of fund raising into a profitable business after World War I, frequently, in private, would derogatorily refer to the Ward-Pierce "YMCA School" of fund raisers as "the Christers."

With his characteristic energy and drive, Lyman Pierce soon set about to build a home for the Washington, D.C., YMCA. He got his board of directors to agree to raise $300,000 for a new building—quite a sum of money in 1902. The campaign was launched with a YMCA "Jubilee Banquet" at which it was announced that John D. Rockefeller had subscribed $50,000. This gift plus the conventional campaign of personal solicitation by Y board members and Pierce brought the total to some $270,000 in the next two years. Though the sum was large, the effort was spread out, the publicity quiet, and by early 1905 contributions had petered out. Raising the final $80,000, the sum needed to finish the building and furnish it, brought much more drama and publicity—and a change in American philanthropy. Pierce, of course, knew of Ward's work so he asked the international headquarters to send Ward to Washington to help him promote the final, intensive effort to raise the $80,000.

Ward came, and the April 5, 1905, Washington *Post* reported matter-of-factly that "Mr. C. S. Ward, one of the international field secretaries of the Young Men's Christian Association, is here giving valuable assistance in the Y.M.C.A. canvass." The collaboration of Ward and Pierce produced the modern fund-raising campaign techniques: careful organization, picked volunteers spurred on by team competition, prestige leaders, powerful publicity, a large gift to be matched by the public's donations, careful records, report meetings, and a definite time limit.

After thorough planning, Ward and Pierce launched the appeal with a pre-drive dinner, now a standard fixture in fund drives. They sent invitations to prominent Washington businessmen for a dinner the night of April 4, "To meet the Honorable Leslie M. Shaw [Secretary of the Treasury], Mr. Fletcher S. Brockman, Mr. Charles S. Ward of Chicago, and to confer about the organization of a Citizens Committee to Meet the Conditional Offer of $25,000 toward the completion of the building fund of the Y.M.C.A." They promised "no solicitations" at the dinner. As part of the pre-campaign effort the two young men had obtained from Woodward & Lothrop, a large department store, a gift of $25,000 on condition that the remaining $55,000 would be subscribed by the campaign deadline of May 1. Christian Dreshman noted later: "One of Ward's most effective devices for keeping public interest focused on a campaign was to announce in advance one large subscription—usually one-tenth to one-third of the goal—which was conditional on the whole amount being raised." [19] Also at the pre-campaign dinner Judge Thomas H. Arnold was persuaded to take the chairmanship of the Citizens Committee, thus adding his personal prestige to the appeal.

The campaign headquarters of this 27-day campaign to raise $80,000—a piddling sum by current standards but quite considerable in those days—was described by the Washington *Post* of April 4 in these words:

> . . . it was easily to be seen yesterday by a visit to the headquarters that no energy was lacking. The work of officials and clerks reminded the visitor of the stirring times at national headquarters during the recent political campaign. Exposed to the view of the passersby over the doorway appeared a huge sign in red and white, suitably inscribed, to show that this was the headquarters of the committees and the

work to be done. . . . Mr. Lyman L. Pierce, the secretary of the local association, was actively in charge throughout the day and until a late hour in the evening . . . other officials, together with members of the committee arranging tonight's dinner, paid frequent visits to the headquarters. [The headquarters were located in the old National Metropolitan Bank building on 15th Street.]

The campaign goals and the work of the campaigners were well publicized in the Washington newspapers for the next twenty-six days. For the first time in a Y fund campaign a full-time publicity man was used,[20] and he provided reams of copy which the newspapers used generously. This confirmed another of Ward's observations—that you could get the newspapers to support a philanthropic drive if it did not last too long. He recognized that fund campaigns extending over many months tend to become stale news, something a newsman shuns. This was the beginning of the elaborate, high-pressure publicity customarily used in the present-day fund drive. As Ward explained later: "The job of these publicity men was to make sure that the newspapers were supplied with the day to day material necessary to keep a campaign on the front page. Headlines, front-page editorials, and cartoons aroused the city's team spirit."

Ward and Pierce also used paid advertising in this campaign, the paid space being donated by Washington business firms. Woodward & Lothrop, continuing its earlier support of the Y building fund, provided one such advertisement with this explanation: "For today we are more interested in the results of the YMCA Building Fund canvass than in any feature of our own business." Typical was the full-page spread carried in the Washington *Times* Sunday, April 23, with the news-style headline: "The Y.M.C.A.'s Fight Against Time to Raise $50,000." These are early examples of public relations advertising, a standard part of present corporate public relations programs.

The two energetic fund raisers were quick to exploit the dramatic advantages of the time limit set for the campaign. Pressure on the campaign workers to complete their subscriptions by the May 1 "deadline" was dramatized by the "campaign clock." Thus, another standard fund-raising device of the future first appeared in the Washington Y campaign. The campaign clock, or campaign thermometer, or some such publicly displayed device to show the progress of the fund-raising effort became the hallmark of Ward's campaigns. Here, again, we find the authorship of a fund-raising idea blurred by counterclaims. Miner C. Williams, one of Ward's first assistants in the Y building campaigns, credits this idea to J. C. Pentland, physical director of the Omaha Association and thinks Lyman Pierce got the idea from Pentland.[21] Williams later claimed that many of the innovations attributed to Ward had originated with him, according to men who worked with both of them in the Y campaigns. Ward was generally acknowledged as the man who had developed the campaign clock, but in an interview in Pittsburgh, Pa., in 1914, where .he and Pierce were again collaborating in a fund-raising enterprise, Ward shared credit for the idea with Pierce. According to an interview reported in a Pittsburgh newspaper:

> Charles Sumner Ward, director general of the University of Pittsburgh's campaign for $3,000,000 which opens Thursday, this morning credited a Pittsburgher with having aided him in formulating the "campaign clock" idea, which in the last 9 years has won for Y.M.C.A.'s, hospitals, and colleges $23,000,000 in 85 campaigns.
>
> "They give me credit for originating the idea, but there is a man in Pittsburgh who had as much to do with it as I had," said Mr. Ward. "He didn't stay in the work, and I did. That's the only difference. He's over here in the Central Y.M.C.A. His name is Lyman Pierce.
>
> "Years ago Pierce and I got together to raise money for a Y.M.C.A. Together we hit upon the 'clock plan,' he contributing some of the features, and I others. Since that time I have been developing the idea and enlarging it by experience." [22]

However, in a pamphlet, *The Intensive Financial Campaign,* published by the Y's Association Press in 1916 Ward gives the credit to Pentland in these words: "The campaign clock invented by physical director J. C. Pentland of Omaha has proven the best device for informing the public of the progress of the campaign."

The Washington *Post,* on the morning of May 2, carried the happy news that the campaign to obtain the needed $80,000 by raising $55,000 to match Woodward & Lothrop's conditional gift was successful. The headlines read: "VICTORY IN LAST HOUR. Every Dollar of YMCA Fund is Subscribed. $15,687 Raised in Last 15 Hours." The paper reported that the goal was reached at ten o'clock, a fact announced at a conference at the Willard Hotel. The jubilation was echoed outside the hotel by loud honking of horns on the new cars. "Secretary Pierce was one of the happiest men in town last night." The Association issued a statement of thanks asserting that the Washington, D.C., campaign was unprecedented in the history of American philanthropy because it "was unparalleled in number of subscribers [over 3,000] and in the amount of money contributed, $350,000."

News of the effectiveness of this short-term high-pressure campaign soon spread among organizations needing public donations. It has been well said that "victory begets a thousand fathers, but defeat is an orphan." Many are the claims for authorship of the public fund drive idea. Ward's followers call it the "Ward Plan." Pierce's advocates say most of the effective ideas were his. Yet Miner C. Williams claims that he "largely made it the perfect instrument which it became," admitting that he built his campaigns on the work of Levi B. Mumma "who developed systematic procedures for the handling of the infinite details of the campaign." [23] The campaign idea obviously is the work of many minds over many years.

The Washington Y campaign created a new pattern in philanthropy and launched Pierce and Ward on their successful careers. In the next seven months of 1905 Ward helped organize and direct three 30-day YMCA campaigns that netted $180,000 in Duluth, Minn.; $225,000 in St. Paul, Minn.; $90,000 in Dallas, Texas. He also organized a 15-day campaign in Lincoln, Neb., that brought in $30,000. "Details were to be improved as Ward continued; in these initial drives broad plans and basic methods became fixed; in addition to the factors noted [team play, competition, mass psychology, and publicity], Ward insisted upon a carefully prepared list of prospects, a strong organization of workers with teams and captains, a dinner meeting at which the campaign was launched, and daily report meetings with effective publicity. With these devices he obtained some twenty-seven million dollars for the Y.M.C.A.s in the next decade." [24]

At the beginning of 1906 he was on the road again, starting in Denver, Colo., where the Denver *Post* of January 15, 1906, headlined: GREAT TASK OF RAISING TWO HUNDRED THOUSAND FOR YMCA BEGUN and the news story noted, several paragraphs down, "C. S. Ward of Chicago, member of the international committee, is in command of the campaign. He will direct the work of the committees and will advise with the local officers." Thus the pattern was repeated from one city to the next, one Y to the next. As the Ward "whirl-wind" blew across the country it not only raised funds for Ys, it made philanthropy a public task for all hands. But there were those who had doubts about the long-term value of these "whirlwind campaigns." For example, the Richmond *News Leader,* in the wake of a Ward drive there, editorialized in its February 1, 1907, issue:

> . . . a considerable number of our people shrank from and a few actually opposed the methods introduced here for securing the $200,000 for the new Young Men's Christian Association building. There was much hurrah and bustle and an aspect of intrusion and demonstration, contrary to all our traditions, precedents, and customs. Now that it is all over, the *News Leader* does not mind confessing that the scheme was not entirely to our taste; that we had grave doubts of the result. . . .
>
> Results tell. Nobody can argue against facts. The facts are that in fifteen days we have obtained the $200,000, although probably not one hundred men in the city believed fifteen days ago that it would be possible; and our chamber of commerce has been begging more than a year trying to obtain $30,000 from business men for a business enterprise.

Although there were some, like the editorialist of the *News Leader,* who found Ward's methodical ways of generating pressure on a community to give up its dollars not entirely to their taste, his spectacular results carried the systematically organized fund-raising campaign forward to higher goals and broader causes. The public fund drive was under way.

In working night and day to finance the new Washington, D.C., building and to expand the Y's program, Pierce had impaired his health. "Although Mr. Pierce has every appearance of being in robust health, he has never been a strong man physically. Within a year from the time when he arrived in Washington, Jan. 1, 1901, he was stricken with typhoid and lay ill for fully nine months." Pierce felt compelled to take a rest, and so resigned the Washington secretaryship in late December as of the end of 1905. At a farewell banquet in his honor January 31, 1906, Pierce could proudly say: "Financially, I believe we have made a new record. Three years ago we had the old building with a mortgage of $45,000. We had the lot on New York Avenue and a current expense debt of $18,000. Today we have the acknowledged finest and best equipped building extant.

Our boys' building holds the same place. Our assets are close to $550,000." Once he had his old vitality back, the restless missionary sought new worlds to conquer. He found them as national secretary in Australia and New Zealand. Pierce carried the gospel of the Y and the campaign method of raising funds to finance its buildings down under in 1906.

Pierce pushed and perfected the short-time campaign with great success in Australia. But this American high-pressure system brought criticism as well as results. For example, the Sydney (N.S.W.) *Bulletin* of August 1, 1907, commented: "The smart Yankee 'organizing' secretary of the Victorian Y.M.C.A. is growing monotonous with his glorious schemes for collecting cash. A report of his recent catchpenny proceedings at Bendigo and elsewhere disgusted a number of Melbourne capitalists who have given handsome subscriptions privately towards a building fund that has no end. The Y.M.C.A. is regarded by many people—especially merchants and employers of 'genteel' labor—as a very good cause provided it keeps the members from sinful manipulating of the ledgers, etc. . . . But it isn't good enough to justify the eternal importunities of a begging secretary, who presumably draws commission on his 'order' in addition to a fat salary. American methods for raising Australian money for highly moral purposes are not more deserving than Ada Ward's devices for raising a controversy." [25]

Nor did Pierce and his methods escape harsh criticism in New Zealand. The September 16, 1907, issue of the Christchurch *Truth* under a headline of SLICK UP TO DATE "CHRISTIANITY" declared: "A pushful American arrived here on Saturday to shove off a movement which he calculates and reckons will extract 15,000 pounds from the pockets of Christchurch people. It has been done in the magic name of 'Christianity' in Wellington and Dunedin, and this city will now be told to go and do likewise. The sum mentioned is a very large one . . . we hope Christchurch will pause before it allows any bustling stranger to bluff it into subsidising what is really a very questionable object." [26]

Despite the criticism, the "big begging" brought results. Pierce-directed campaigns in four New Zealand cities brought in £51,000 in fifty-one working days of campaigning. In Christchurch, where the *Truth* continued its attacks, Pierce raised £15,380 in twelve days, £380 over the announced goal. He scored comparable successes in several Australian cities. The YMCA firmly planted, and his campaign method of fund raising taught to Y leaders, Pierce, accompanied by his wife and a niece, Miss Louise Pierce, left Melbourne on November 30, 1907, for the United States. They took the long way home through Asia and Europe and Pierce spread the Y message as he traveled. He gave several lectures in India and in England.

While Pierce was in New Zealand, he was described in the September, 1907, issue of the *Spectator* thus: "Mr. Pierce is not at all the type one usually associates with movements for the uplifting higher of the Good Young Man. He is not the lean and hungry kind. He does not look as if the sins of the Bad Young Man were weighing him into an early grave. On the contrary, he is a splendid example of the motto, 'Laugh and grow fat.' He can laugh for sure and he's grown about as much adipose as a man can safely carry . . . he is of course a total abstainer."

Another Pioneer, Another Pattern

At the very time Ward and Pierce were attracting the notice of those confronted with the eternal problem of getting money for religious and philanthropic causes with their successful Washington campaign, another pioneer fund raiser was setting out to raise a really big sum, $2.5 million by an entirely different approach. He was Bishop William Lawrence, who also was to play a major role in the pattern of American philanthropy. A descendant of distinguished New England pioneers, Lawrence was born May 30, 1850, in a house on Pemberton Square, Boston, and lived until just a month before Pearl Harbor, dying November 6, 1941. Before he reached the twilight of his career the bishop became one of the big money raisers in America, though it always remained as a sideline to his church work. It was his "invigorating avocation."

He was the son of Amos Adams Lawrence and Sarah Appleton Lawrence. One great-grandfather, Samuel Lawrence, had fought for American independence on the green at Lexington and Concord. The future bishop's father and maternal grandfather undoubtedly did much to imbue him with a zeal for serving philanthropic causes. Of these philanthropist ancestors Bremner writes:

> Amos Lawrence, having disengaged himself from business, rode out on fine days to distribute tracts of the American Temperance Society and the Sunday School Union; on bad days busied himself

in selecting clothes, books, and other useful articles from storerooms in his house, bundled them into packages and sent them off to needy students, professors, and clergymen. . . .

It was a halcyon day for philanthropists when a man could say, as the very rich and very generous William Appleton did in 1853, "I part with money in various ways of charity but much like to do it in my own way and not be dictated to or even asked but in a general way to give with others." [27]

Grandfather William Appleton's views were to be reflected in Lawrence's approach to fund raising. The family, and New England influence, would repel him from the high-powered drives developed by Ward, Pierce, and John Price Jones. As the bishop later said: "I dislike the word 'campaign' in this connection almost as much as I abhor 'appeal.' 'Campaign' suggests force or pressure, methods whereby people are dragooned to give. 'Appeal' suggests a call upon the sympathies and emotions of people, melting them to give. Both methods are weak and liable to bring reaction; but as no other words have been invented to meet our ideas, we must use them." [28]

As befits the son of a New England first family, Lawrence studied at Groton, then entered Harvard College. His matriculation marked the beginning of a long and intimate association that was to prove mutually profitable to the institution and the man. He was graduated in 1871 and then entered the Episcopal Theological School, also in Cambridge. He received his S.T.B. degree in 1875. The year before his graduation from theological school he married Miss Julia Cunningham in a ceremony performed by the Reverend Phillips Brooks. His first charge was in Lawrence, Mass., where he spent eight happy years.

In 1884 the young priest returned to his beloved Cambridge to serve St. John's Memorial Chapel. Nine years later he was elevated to the bishopric and that same year was given an honorary degree, Doctor of Sacred Theology, by his Alma Mater. The next year, 1894, Bishop Lawrence was made an overseer by Harvard and in June, 1899, he was elected vice-president of the alumni association. In these positions and in his almost daily association with President Eliot and faculty members at Harvard the young bishop became increasingly aware of Harvard's need for broader support. In 1904 he became president of the Harvard Alumni Association and in his presidential address that June he called on the Harvard alumni to give $2.5 million to increase the salaries of the professors in Liberal Arts. As usually happens to a person who volunteers an idea, Lawrence was drafted by President Eliot to organize a campaign to raise this tremendous sum to strengthen the Harvard faculty. As Lawrence recalls in his memoirs:

> This was . . . long before campaigns for great sums were thought of or the word "drive" invented. There had, of course, been money-raising campaigns by the Y.M.C.A. and other organizations, but this industry, which has thriven since, was in its infancy.
>
> My experience had been limited to the Hasty Pudding Club and the raising of one or two sums of one hundred thousand dollars. We therefore had to feel our way. As the core of a committee of ten well-known alumni, three of us formed the working staff and later experience has shown me that three is enough: Frank Higginson, Robert Bacon, and myself. Our only central office was under my hat. Our publicity consisted in a few syndicated articles on Harvard at a total cost of five hundred dollars, and such editorials and news as we could get into the papers. It fell to me to supply the material for these and frame the circular letter to the alumni and friends of Harvard (only ten thousand at that time), who were our only constituency.
>
> We were agreed as to certain principles. The friends of the University were to be given an opportunity to strengthen the College by the increase of the salaries of the teachers in Liberal Arts; for we could not cover all teachers in the University. There was to be no crowding or jamming for subscriptions. It were better not to complete the full amount. As a matter of fact, the total gift fell short only about one hundred thousand dollars. We could doubtless have gotten the whole by pressure, but it was worth the amount to close with the good will and confidence of the alumni.[29]

Thus began the large-scale alumni fund drive which, in the present era, constitutes a substantial part of the public's support of American colleges, universities, and preparatory schools. And how different Lawrence's philosophy, that there be "no crowding or jamming," from that of Ward and Pierce, who exulted in their dramatic, last-minute push to meet a goal deadline by a fixed date and hour. But Lawrence, Ward, and Pierce did agree on one thing—the need for a few large, spectacular gifts before the drive opens. Bishop Lawrence wrote: "It also became clear to us that in raising of such a great sum—for it was great in those days—we must first have some large gifts with which to stimulate the imagination of all and to give a thrust to later action." [30]

The Harvard campaign of 1904–1905 which netted some $2.4 million also broke new ground in that the money was not obtained from donors to erect "monuments" to their memory. As the bishop noted: "The popular sentiment at that time was that people would give buildings which they could see, and would not give to the support of teachers." Alumni giving had been put on a retail basis and another pattern of American fund raising had been set in this formative period of the young twentieth century.

A Penny Seal to Raise Millions

While Bishop Lawrence was quietly but persuasively soliciting Harvard alumni and Ward and Pierce were perfecting their methods of raising money, another standard fund-raising device of today's people's philanthropy—the seal sale—was being developed. Only this time the idea was born abroad and imported to America. The National Tuberculosis Association's Christmas Seal—"the brightly colored stamp that has become so cherished a part of the Christmas tradition for so many Americans"—had by 1961 raised more than $500 million since the first American seals were put on sale in 1907. The sale of seals is now a much-used (and expensive) means of raising money but no organization has been able to match the success of the T.B. seal sale. "The mere mention of Christmas seals is enough to make fund raisers for other voluntary health agencies sob with envy," says Richard Carter.

The National Tuberculosis Association had its origins in the social ferment and scientific discoveries of the late 1890's and early 1900's. As urban America's health and social welfare problems grew in number and scope, organization of a voluntary association was usually the first step taken to meet newly recognized problems. Richard Shryock, who has written a definitive history of this association, says that "there is no way of knowing who first suggested the formation of the national tuberculosis association." The first society to fight T.B. was organized in Pennsylvania in 1892. With the advance of bacteriology and medicine, physicians insisted that T.B. was their problem too. In the end, both groups joined in organizing the National Tuberculosis Association in June, 1904, in Atlantic City, N.J. "Although it aspired to national status, the Association was at the start a small, private group, largely representative of the states on the northeastern seaboard." [31]

The only capital the new group had at the beginning was the ability and prestige of its members. In short, it needed funds to educate the public against the dangers of the disease and to provide care for sufferers. The national campaign for public donations for a health association was still in the future. A year before the National Tuberculosis Association was formed, a Danish postal official, Einar Holboell, had conceived the idea of selling Christmas stamps as a means of raising funds to care for Danish children who had contracted the disease. The idea took hold in Denmark. After the government approved the idea, more than four million of these stamps were sold in Danish post offices in 1904. Shryock says that the "idea spread rapidly in Europe, being adopted in Sweden in 1904, in Norway in 1906, and in other countries on the Continent soon after."

This novel and effective idea for raising funds to fight tuberculosis was carried to America by the stamp itself. Jacob A. Riis, a Danish immigrant whose crusading journalism did much to spur social reform, had lost six brothers to tuberculosis, so when he saw the Holboell-designed stamps on a letter from his native country it struck home. He investigated the stamp's origin and sale, and then took the idea to the public by writing an article for *Outlook* magazine. "What I want to know is why we cannot here borrow a leaf from Santa Claus's Danish year-book, and do as they have done. Why should we not have a Christmas stamp, printed by a Tuberculosis Committee, and sold by the government, for the purpose of rousing up and educating the people on this most important matter." [32] Thus was set in motion a chain of circumstances that was to make the Christmas seal an American tradition, and a lucrative device for raising millions with penny contributions. The history of the campaign against tuberculosis—or consumption, as it was called in those days—is tightly linked with the history of the Christmas seal sale.

Riis's article was read by Miss Emily Bissell, who was on *Outlook*'s editorial board. Miss Bissell has been well described as "an exuberantly energetic and imaginative young woman who earned her living as a writer and editor and was an inveterate volunteer." Her cousin, Dr. Joseph P. Wales, a physician, was at this time engaged in an experiment to prove that fresh air was the proper treatment for tuberculosis, a notion strongly decried at the time. He and two other doctors were treating eight charity patients in an open-air shack, rented from Alfred Du Pont for $1 a year, along the Brandy-wine River, in Delaware. Continued care of these patients called for money and "anti-tuberculosis dollars were hard to come by in those days."

Dr. Wales appealed for help to his energetic cousin. She suddenly recalled the Riis article and exclaimed, "That's our answer." That night Miss Bissell, at the time secretary of the Delaware Red Cross, sat down and sketched a rough design—a half wreath of holly centered with a red cross, and crowning the words "Merry Christmas." Her fellow officers in the Delaware Red Cross, when shown the design the next day, were not enthusiastic about the idea. Even so, they agreed to go along if the national Red Cross headquarters in Washington would approve. The Red Cross did, and thus made fund-raising history.

With Red Cross approval, Miss Bissell moved swiftly. A Wilmington, Del., artist agreed to refine her design. A printer agreed to do the $40 job on credit and printed 50,000 seals, in bright red on white paper. Then she worked furiously to promote the sale of the stamps, talking to newspapers, women's clubs, schoolteachers, shopkeepers, and labor leaders. Before the first stamps were off the press, much of Wilmington had heard about them. On Monday, December 9, 1907, a Red Cross volunteer, dressed in her uniform, took her place at a table in the corridor of the Wilmington post office to distribute pay envelopes bearing this legend:

25 CHRISTMAS STAMPS
ONE PENNY APIECE

ISSUED BY THE DELAWARE RED CROSS TO
STAMP OUT THE WHITE PLAGUE

PUT THIS STAMP, WITH MESSAGE BRIGHT
ON EVERY CHRISTMAS LETTER:
HELP THE TUBERCULOSIS FIGHT,
AND MAKE THE NEW YEAR BETTER

THESE STAMPS DO NOT CARRY ANY KIND OF MAIL, BUT
ANY KIND OF MAIL WILL CARRY THEM

Richard Carter recounts:

As social service chairman of the local Federation of Women's Clubs Emily had no trouble getting volunteers from the New Century Club to stuff the stamps into envelopes. The Du Pont advertising department prepared muslin banners that were carried on Wilmington streetcars for two weeks, proclaiming the new campaign. Red Cross ladies volunteered to appear in full, uniformed panoply and sell stamps in the lobby of the Wilmington post office. School children were recruited to help. Emily was the first customer. A queue developed behind her.

The printer hurried to crank out 50,000 more stamps. The doctors at Brandywine had hoped for $300 and would get far more.[33]

Fired with the enthusiasm born of seeing urgently needed dollars coming in, Miss Bissell decided to spread the word and try to get more money. On December 13 she went to nearby Philadelphia to call on the editor of the *North American,* a crusading newspaper interested in new social movements. A call on the paper's Sunday editor was unavailing. He told her he just could not see linking Christmans with "the curse." Rebuffed, she next turned to Leigh Mitchell Hodges, the conductor of a column, "The Optimist," which she read regularly. He quickly caught Miss Bissell's enthusiasm for the idea, seeing "a flaming banner to head the fight against a dread foe." He grabbed a sheet of the stamps from Miss Bissell and rushed downstairs to see E. A. Van Valkenburg, editor in chief. The editor, too, was quickly sold on the idea. "Drop what you're doing and give this your whole time. Take all the space you need. Ask her to send us fifty thousand stamps by tomorrow." Hodges gave his total attention to booming the sale of the seals with publicity in the *North American.* "All the make-it-known methods of a modern newspaper were set going—'scarehead' stories on Page One; endorsements from civic, religious, and political leaders; the Postmaster General's approval of Christmas Stamp sales in post office lobbies. Pictures of the stamp peppered its pages." [34]

The immediate result of this frenzied effort on the part of Emily Bissell, Leigh Hodges, and a few other dedicated volunteers was to sell 400,000 of the new Christmas stamps in eighteen days and clear about $3,000. One third of this goal was raised in Philadelphia by the Hodges-*North American* publicity campaign. The National Association's total 1906 budget was $15,000—far too little for the task it had undertaken nationally. A surefire way of getting money from the public to fight disease had taken "root, of all places, in the most conservative little state in the Union."

Miss Bissell's success was bound to beget repetition and, ultimately, imitation. She persuaded Miss Mabel T. Boardman and others in the American National Red Cross to undertake a nationwide Christmas seal campaign in December, 1908. Miss Boardman and her associates had been psychologically softened for Miss Bissell's determined appeal. They had heard, at the 1907 Conference of the International Red Cross in London, much discussion of tuberculosis as a "continuing disaster." The 1908 nationwide Christmas stamp sale was carefully planned and heavily promoted. Howard Pyle designed the 1908 seal and the American Bank Note Company and the U.S. Bureau of Engraving and Printing collaborated on its production. Sales were handled through Red Cross state branches in thirty-three states, through women's clubs, and certain of the local tuberculosis societies. These agents were given 80 per cent of the proceeds, the other 20 per cent being sent back to the Red Cross for preparing and promoting the seals. The national return reached $135,000 in 1908 and $200,000 in 1909, yet the Red Cross officials still thought this response would prove a temporary one.

A painless way of raising money would not long go unnoticed by the increasing number of nonprofit organizations springing up in that period. Shryock records: "The very success of the sales . . . threatened competition from other good causes in search of income. The Kentucky Tuberculosis Society, for example, reported that the Federation of Women's Clubs there would probably issue their own stamps; and that, in such case, the society would have to support the clubs' sale rather than that of the Red Cross. Tuberculosis units were also thinking of trying out sales for themselves. The Michigan society . . . experimented with 'Easter stickers' in 1910 and sold about 25,000 of them in the Detroit area." [35] The controversy was finally settled in 1910 by an agreement between the National Tuberculosis Association and the American National Red Cross to conduct the seal fund-raising sale in partnership.

Thus began the annual Christmas seal sale of stamps to "fight T.B." that today annually brings in some $26 million from the mailing of 40 million letters carrying some 12 billion seals to prospective givers. About one out of three letters brings results. The device of the seal to get money, and of high-powered publicity to sell it, had been harnessed together in a new pattern of public fund raising. Nor was the value of the seal promotion as an educational device overlooked.

Priscilla Leonard, writing in *Outlook,* also emphasized this aspect: "The Christmas Stamp is inspiring and educational, quite apart from its money-raising side. The vast majority of Delawareans . . . believed consumption to be incurable, non-contagious, and hereditary. They had never thought about either curing or preventing it. It was a scourge of God, to be deplored and let alone. The Christmas Stamp waked up every town, every post office, every club, every school." [36]

Dues and Donations Not Enough

The increasing number of voluntary societies formed in this period to promote better health and a better society, soon, one by one, came up against the hard rock of finance. The growing needs of these voluntary associations called for a more reliable means of financial support than the dues of a few dedicated members. For example, in 1904 the American National Red Cross had a total membership of 123 and $1,702 in cash assets. William J. Norton, a pioneer in the community chest movement, recalls that "when the twentieth century opened America suddenly awoke to the fact that it had a great body of social work fairly well organized as individual institutions but poorly organized as the basis of a community program. . . . The existence of these individual agencies then, together with the knowledge that more and more of them were being created constantly, gave rise to a three-cornered protest coming in part from social work itself, in part from the active supporters of social work, and in part from the general public." [37] It was increasingly recognized that fund raising must be an important and integral part of these missionary movements.

This awareness was first reflected in the annual meeting of social workers in 1906, when the Thirty-third Annual Conference of Charities and Correction at Philadelphia included a session on "Charitable Finance." Frank Tucker, vice-president of the New York Provident Loan Society, opened the session on money raising:

For years we have discussed policies for the use of public funds, raised by taxation, in the care of the dependent, delinquent, and defective. . . .
For the first time we are now to take up and discuss the problems of finance which grow out of the work of these organizations which appeal directly to the public for support, where the contributor gives

voluntarily, sometimes through conviction, sometimes through impulse, sometimes thoughtfully, often carelessly. . . .

We must first realize that a charitable or social activity is, in effect, a self-perpetuating trusteeship. . . . The function of trusteeship thus set up must do two things to justify its existence—it must raise money by convincing the public of its responsibilities for needs and conditions and it must expend the money so raised in such a manner as to warrant the public in believing that the investment is sound and productive of social profit.[38]

Typical methods of financing local charity and welfare societies in these years were described at the conference by Walter S. Ufford, general secretary of the Baltimore Federated Charities. He used as an example the Baltimore Association for Improvement of the Condition of the Poor which pitched its appeals on "sentiment" and "the primitive instinct for self-preservation." This group relied largely on the strength of a printed appeal to bring in its annual budget. Ufford continued:

In December, the annual report of the Year's work, which ended September 30, is sent with a treasurer's envelope and subscription slip enclosed. This goes to all who have contributed to the Association for the past five years. As these reports are delivered by hand within the business and residential section, we are able to verify mailing lists and to eliminate from them those who have died or moved from the city. This appeal is sufficient . . . to bring a response from one-third of the contributors the previous year. Then, in mid-winter, when living conditions are the hardest for the poor and givers have brought home to their own experience the need of warmth and shelter and proper food, the Association sends out a mimeographed letter with return envelope and donation slip to all who have not responded to the annual report. . . . On the first of April the Association had failed to receive . . . about 10 per cent of last year's contributions. For these the Association has been accustomed to use a collector.

The Charity Organization Society of Baltimore, unlike its colleague, the Poor Association, has found it necessary to use a collector throughout the year. This collector works upon a salary, not upon a commission. The salary basis is less open to criticism, as it does not meet with the objection that a certain proportion of the amount received is to be subtracted from every contribution. The method of the Baltimore Charity Organization Society is briefly as follows: At the beginning of each month, notices in the form of a mimeographed letter signed by the chairman of the Finance Committee and containing a return envelope addressed to the Treasurer, are sent to all who have contributed to the Society in the corresponding month of the previous year. After waiting a few days the Society's collector (a woman who has been employed several years) visits all those who have not responded. . . . It is our experience that about one-third of the contributors respond to monthly notices and that two-thirds wish to be seen.[39]

Such were the methods of raising money for the poor and the ill in the early 1900's. Society's needs would inexorably bring more effective ways. There was increasing realization of the value of the educational campaign which must pave the way for large-scale money raising, as Miss Bissell and others associated with the initial Christmas stamp effort soon recognized. Mina C. Ginger, financial secretary of the Newark Bureau of Associated Charities, pointed out to her colleagues at Philadelphia that "the collection of funds for the society should represent educational work, each contribution secured should indicate an understanding of the work and approval of it by the contributor." The educational value of their money-raising campaigns is the main argument used by contemporary national health associations in resisting their inclusion in either local united funds or in one national drive to cover all the health groups.

The mounting pressure to give to more and more causes brought a growing demand for a federation of charity appeals for money at the local level. Contributors began to insist on some order in the local philanthropies and to ask for guarantees that their money was not being wasted by duplicate agencies. In 1900 Cleveland, Ohio, businessmen, through their Chamber of Commerce, established the Committee on Benevolent Associations, which sought to guarantee to its businessmen-donors that their contributions would be properly used, a move that was to pave the way for the nation's first community chest in Cleveland in 1913.

Other chambers of commerce were quick to follow suit. In San Francisco in 1902 a committee representing both contributors and charitable agencies set up a Charities Endorsement Committee. Three commercial organizations in Seattle combined in a charities endorsement committee that same year. The New York City Charity Organization Society, in 1905, set up the Bureau of Advice and Information to provide a service that had been given informally up to that time. Mr. Ufford, among others, was aware of an increasing insistence from businessmen, usually the large local donors, for a consolidated appeal and for checks and controls on expenditure of their gifts. He told the Philadelphia conference of social workers:

> When one considers the multiplicity of appeals received by the average business man and thinks of the efforts that are being made by so many charities to secure adequate financial support in a given locality, one cannot fail to ask himself if much time, thought, and effort is not wasted that might be conserved. Do we not need a financial clearing house to assume responsibility for the support of our local charities? Let there be in every city and town a representative body or committee to review annually the charitable needs of the community. Let this committee receive and act upon all separate budgets of existing charitable agencies. Let it issue an annual appeal showing the amount of money needed by each charitable society, that this appeal be sent to every household and to all business firms in the community. . . . Let the committee's campaign be an educational one and so aggressively carried on that it shall be considered as much of a disgrace as tax dodging on the part of the residents . . . not to contribute to the support of . . . charitable work.[40]

Thus did this Baltimore charity leader perceive the needs that would be met, in time, by the community chest.

It is possible that businessmen of the early 1900's, not yet schooled in the ways of public relations and but dimly aware of their social responsibilities, resented the growing pressure to give money more than they worried about duplication and waste in the local charities. This was still the period of Darwin's "survival of the fittest" in a hotly competitive, buccaneering business world. Charity workers had long recognized the need for a central clearinghouse on recipients of aid. Charity givers would inevitably come to insist on a clearinghouse for their contributions.

The eight years from 1900 to 1908 were indeed meaningful, eventful years of the "Big Change," in the nation, in fund raising, and in American philanthropy. They brought the multimillion-dollar foundation and its wholesale philanthropy, the Ward-Pierce short-term YMCA fund-raising campaign method, the appeal of educational institutions for alumni support, the penny seal that would raise millions, and an ever-growing number of nonprofit agencies to require financing through public giving.

NOTES

1. For account of this sharp turn in our political history, see Eric Goldman's *Rendezvous with Destiny* (New York: Vintage Books, 1959, 4th ed.), Chap. 8.

2. For excellent biography of S. S. McClure, see Peter Lyon, *Success Story: The Life and Times of S. S. McClure* (New York: Scribner, 1963).

3. Frederick Lewis Allen, *The Big Change* (New York: Harper & Row, 1952), p. 97.

4. Arthur S. Link, *American Epoch* (New York: Knopf, 1955), p. 17.

5. Robert H. Bremner, *American Philanthropy* (Chicago: University of Chicago Press, 1960), p. 117.

6. *Ibid.*, pp. 120–121.

7. Allan Nevins, *John D. Rockefeller: The Heroic Age of American Enterprise* (New York: Charles Scribner's Sons, 1940), Vol. II, p. 350.

8. Joseph I. C. Clarke, *My Life and Memories* (New York: Dodd, Mead, 1925), p. 346.

9. *Ibid.*, pp. 354–355.

10. W. Freeman Galpin, *The Growing Years*, Vol. II, *A History of Syracuse University* (published by that university), p. 432.

11. Raymond B. Fosdick, *The Story of the Rockefeller Foundation* (New York: Harper & Row, 1952), p. 4.

12. Robert H. Bremner, *op. cit.*, p. 123.

13. Pierce Williams and Frederick E. Croxton, *Corporation Contributions to Organized Community Welfare Services* (New York: National Bureau of Economic Research, 1930), p. 52.

14. C. Howard Hopkins, *History of the Y.M.C.A. in North America* (New York: Association Press, 1951), p. 596.

15. Typewritten memorandum by Christian Dreshman in company files of Ward, Dreshman, & Reinhardt, New York City.

16. C. Howard Hopkins, *op. cit.*, pp. 597–598.

17. "Sought, Seen, Heard," New York *Evening Post*, April 23, 1925, p. 8.

18. Christian Dreshman, *op. cit.*, Memorandum.

19. *Ibid.*

20. C. Howard Hopkins, *op. cit.*, p. 597.

21. *Ibid.* Hopkins' account of the origins of the YMCA campaign method are based almost wholly on a typed manuscript by Miner C.

Williams, "The Growth of a Great Idea," which is in the Bowne Library, Springfield, Mass.

22. A newspaper clipping, unidentified by date or newspaper, in Lyman Pierce Scrapbook. In Philanthropy Collection, State Historical Society of Wisconsin, Madison.

23. Miner C. Williams' unpublished mss. as quoted by Hopkins.

24. C. Howard Hopkins, *op. cit.*, p. 598.

25. News clipping in Lyman Pierce Scrapbook.

26. *Ibid.*

27. Robert H. Bremner, *op. cit.*, p. 46.

28. William Lawrence, "An Invigorating Avocation," *Atlantic*, Vol. 132 (September, 1923), p. 318.

29. William Lawrence, *Memories of a Happy Life* (Boston: Houghton Mifflin, 1926), pp. 215–216.

30. *Ibid.*, p. 216.

31. Richard H. Shryock, *National Tuberculosis Association, 1904–1954* (New York: National Tuberculosis Assn., 1957), p. 78.

32. Jacob A. Riis, "The Christmas Stamp," *Outlook*, Vol. 86 (July 6, 1907), p. 513.

33. Richard Carter, *The Gentle Legions* (Garden City: Doubleday, 1961), p. 77.

34. Leigh Mitchell Hodges, *The People Against Tuberculosis* (New York: National Tuberculosis Assn., 1942), pp. 14–15.

35. Richard H. Shryock, *op. cit.*, p. 129.

36. Priscilla Leonard, "The Christmas Stamp in America," *Outlook*, Vol. 90, p. 266.

37. William J. Norton, *The Cooperative Movement in Social Work* (New York: Macmillan, 1927), pp. 10–12.

38. *Proceedings, Conference of Charities and Corrections, 1906*, pp. 196–197.

39. *Ibid.*, pp. 214–216.

40. *Ibid.*, pp. 221–222.

3

The Whirlwind Campaign Reaps Millions: 1908–1917

Federation Fund Raising Takes Root

At present our philanthropic activities rely chiefly upon "personal equation" methods of raising funds. Mrs. Earnest lunches with Mrs. Gushing and describes a visit to the day nursery that is suffering dreadfully for want of money; Miss Prominent invites a selected list to a parlor meeting where the needs of some worthy hospital or church club are touchingly presented; a wealthy treasurer, annoyed by a deficit, asks a business associate or his vis-à-vis at dinner to help him out. . . .

After appeals in person begin to affect one's invitations to dinner and to other social functions . . . the paid collector is tried . . . possessed of gluelike persistence that is sure to win some contribution if once granted a hearing.[1]

Thus did William H. Allen describe the methods of philanthropic fund raising in 1912. Allen, director of the Bureau of Municipal Research and National Training School for Public Service, New York City, 1911–1912, made an analysis of 6,000 letters appealing for charity addressed to Mrs. Mary Harriman, wife of the railroad magnate E. H. Harriman. Allen found both the getting and the giving of charity dollars in 1912 in a rather chaotic state. "Nowhere have givers adequate means of learning what is most needed in their communities" and "even the simpler forms of philanthropy are not comprehensively organized." [2] In his book reporting this study of fund seeking, Mrs. Harriman's plan for a central clearinghouse for "givers and appealers" is presented:

The logical home for a national center is the Mecca of appealers—
New York City. . . . At the outset several branches of its work would
be self-supporting; while other branches, such as advice to appealers,
givers and will-makers, might also in time become self-supporting.

Each patron would pay for the systematic analysis and handling of
letters sent by him. Service would be paid by the job, by commission or fee, or by the year.[3]

Allen specifically recommended in his findings that "there is a
need for a local clearing house in each state and each large city
. . . which shall welcome appeals from individuals and from organized agencies, study them and make educational use of them among
givers, appealers, newspaper writers and students of social forces."
He saw that reliance on the haphazard "personal equation" methods
of philanthropy would not serve the requirements of an urbanized,
industrialized America. The first thoughtful, definitive answer to
these problems on a community basis would come in Cleveland,
Ohio, the year after Allen's study was published.

On the afternoon of March 1, 1913, a group of businessmen, civic
leaders, and welfare workers met in the Cleveland Chamber of Commerce building that once fronted on Cleveland's public square. Before that historic meeting was over these civic leaders and social
welfare workers had created what is generally accepted as the prototype of today's community chest. On this day, a pale March sun,
softly cutting the gray over Lake Erie, witnessed the organization of
a fund-raising plan that was to play a central role in the public
philanthropy that finances America's community welfare, social, and
recreational needs. Today more than 2,500 community chests, or
variations thereof, raise millions of dollars and enlist thousands of
volunteer workers. As of January 1, 1961, it was estimated that more
than $4 billion had been raised by community chests in the United
States and Canada. Cleveland's federated fund was conceived as "a
new way out of perplexing problems of philanthropy" at the community level.

After considerable discussion, the new financial federation was
called the Cleveland Federation for Charity and Philanthropy. The
word "philanthropy" was added because for the first time such
agencies as the YMCA and YWCA, that were not charity agencies,
were included. After a clever bit of arithmetic the federation was
announced as embracing fifty-seven agencies.

The reporter who covered the organizational meeting says: "I remember what a discussion we had as to how many agencies we should figure there were in this federation. You can figure it in various ways you know by dividing an agency and its branches. Mr. [Whiting] Williams decided that we would use the number 57 that is well known now through Mr. Heinz and his pickles. We worked out subdivisions which produced 57 agencies." [4] Cleveland's move was not, of course, the first community effort to federate local money-seeking groups. But due largely to the public relations skill of Whiting Williams, the Federation's first paid executive, the Cleveland experiment became the most widely publicized one, and hence the most widely copied federation model.

Prior to this decade of 1908–1917 the city of Denver and the Jewish philanthropic agencies in several major cities were the main experimenters with federated fund raising. In Denver's case the effort had not been successful; by contrast the Jewish federated fund drives had brought in a steady increase in funds. For the Jews the federation plan had, in Bogen's opinion, met the test of securing "the greatest amount of money with the least possible expense and effort." As of 1909 there were 1,191 separate and distinct Jewish organizations engaged in philanthropic work, not counting mutual benefit societies, burial societies, trade unions, Zionists, and the like. Much of this growth had been stimulated by the success of the Jews' federated fund raising.

In 1908 the churches, charities, and missions of Elmira, N.Y., agreed to combine their efforts to care for the poor of that upstate city. To accomplish their goal these agencies set up the Social Service League. The next year the Women's Federation of Elmira and the League merged to form a broader Elmira Federation for Social Service. Five other social agencies dependent upon donations merged with the Federation to organize the Allied Charities in 1910, a loose federation embracing seven groups. This is said to be the first federation to put into effect the principle of immunity from solicitation by member agencies in separate fund drives.

At the start the Federation was little more than a joint campaign for a single year's funds. It is impossible to compare Elmira's first common fund appeal with previous years because reliable figures are not available for 1909. Elmira's first one-fund drive, a whirlwind-type of campaign, brought in only $14,156 of an announced $17,000 goal. "The budget was clearly excessive, however, for only $11,435 was appropriated to the organizations, $2,500 of the balance remaining being temporarily invested. There was no campaign the second year, and the amount collected fell off 17 per cent—from $14,156 to $11,786. Securities were sold to supplement these collections. In the third year the drop was still greater, and in April, 1914, with nearly six months of the year remaining, the 'Allied Fund' was almost empty. Another campaign was undertaken, and a professional manager employed." [5] This professional fund raiser was used during the remainder of 1914. From then on Elmira's united fund raising showed a steady climb, thus demonstrating the need for an intensive campaign if requirements of growing social services were to be met.

In the same period welfare agencies in Cedar Rapids, Iowa, had made a joint effort to collect, not raise, contributions. In 1912 San Antonio, Texas, made what Norton describes as "an abortive effort at federation." The wreck of the San Antonio movement was attributed to an effort by its Chamber of Commerce sponsors "to effect . . . standardization on the agencies." A chamber official reported at the time that "every effort to bring the organizations under one general head and clearly defined jurisdiction met with determined opposition." Others attribute the failure to public hostility toward San Antonio's Chamber of Commerce's effort to standardize giving.[6] It was evident that a federation of social agencies, to succeed, must be more than a common fund-raising effort. The special committee set up by the American Association for Organizing Charity in 1915 said in its report of 1917 that all federation attempts that have been abandoned were in the group "that attempted little or no work beyond the collection of funds."

Increasing sentiment for coordinating the work of agencies was manifested in that period. In a development contemporary with that of federated fund raising, the central council of social agencies emerged. In 1909 Milwaukee pioneered with the first Council of Social Agencies, set up to promote better planning among both public and private agencies. The Milwaukee group employed a half-time secretary to promote the desired coordination. Pittsburgh, Pa., set up a similar council later that year. The next decade saw councils organized in St. Louis, Little Rock, Ark., Cincinnati, Cleveland, Chicago, Detroit, Bethlehem, Pa., and many other cities. They were evidence of a growing concern on the part of both contributors and social agency workers for some centralized planning born of increasing conflict and collision among the multiplying efforts to improve community facilities. Conditions were ripe indeed for the community chest movement when it appeared in Cleveland in 1913.

The Cleveland Federation had its beginning in the Committee on Benevolent Associations set up in 1900 by the Chamber of Commerce, and was an outgrowth of its long struggle with the problem of endorsement of public appeals for funds. This Committee, which William J. Norton termed "painstaking, thoroughgoing," had over the years built up a set of sanctions and standards which came to be widely copied in the latter-day community chests. The Committee requirements for endorsement of an agency included: organizations should be incorporated; reports should be published; accounts should be audited by accountants; administrative committee of agency should meet at least quarterly; funds should be collected according to methods approved by the endorsement committee; proposals for new agencies should be reviewed and endorsed by experts in the field; new organizations, to be approved, should fill an unmet need in the community.[7] In this and other ways, the Cleveland Chamber of Commerce Committee worked hard at the task of bringing system and value to that city's philanthropies.

In 1904, the same Committee on Benevolent Associations, under the chairmanship of Martin A. Marks, earlier active in what is now the Cleveland Jewish Community Federation, was assigned a special staff secretary, Howard Strong. With the help of James F. Jackson, superintendent of the Associated Charities, and other social executives, the Committee studied the earlier but unsuccessful attempts at federation in Denver, Colo., and Liverpool, England. It also initiated studies of the various agencies, their problems and remedial practices. The Committee prodded these agencies to have annual audits made.

In 1907 the Committee made its first study of the financial support being given Cleveland's social agencies and found that "the present system is not only inadequate and unsatisfactory, from the standpoint of the organizations, but that it has become most unjust to a liberal public and tends through the innumerable appeals which constantly come to them to antagonize a large number of generous contributors."[8] The study grew out of the fact that reliable charity organizations had for many years been having difficulty raising needed budgets while "other societies doing a less important work have been laying up a surplus of receipts . . . and some wholly worthless institutions have collected from the public money which has been expended in maintaining an inefficient and needless work." [9] The Committee's study covered fifty-eight organizations endorsed by it, and three unendorsed agencies, practically all the legitimate money-seeking organizations in Cleveland. The report disclosed that these sixty-one agencies were spending something like $70,000 a year to obtain their donations and expressed the belief that a federated drive could accomplish the same purpose for some $12,000 to $15,000.

The Cleveland Committee again made studies and issued reports in 1910 and 1912 on the city's public philanthropy. These studies reflected mounting pressure for an economical, efficient method of raising charity gifts and a responsible agency to ensure wise expenditures of donated funds. In 1909 it was found that seventy-three institutions were attacking the problem of social betterment in Cleveland. The seventy-three agencies had by this time accumulated endowments worth $4 million. They were taking the full time of several hundred people and were calling for the expenditure of $1.5 million annually—a sum equal to $3 for every person in Cleveland. These agencies, in 1909, raised $650,000 of the $1.5 million, through public gifts, a sum contributed by only 5,386 individuals—less than 1 per cent of Cleveland's population. Of this number the six major donors were giving 42 per cent of all the money contributed. The 1910 study also showed that between 1907 and 1909 the amount given to charity in Cleveland had increased 22 per cent, but that the number of donors had decreased 11 per cent. Clearly the need for popular philanthropy had come to Cleveland.

Martin Marks was the moving force in bringing federation to Cleveland. He brought the Committee experience and values shaped by his work in the Jewish Charity Federation in that city. Almost from the start Mr. Marks asked repeatedly: "If the Jews can federate their charitable appeals why cannot the community as a whole?" In 1911, for example, the Jewish federated charity drive in Cleveland raised $91,500 from a Jewish population of 50,000—quite an impressive fund-raising feat. Marks's conviction of the value of federation was the motivating force behind the Committee's three careful studies of public giving in Cleveland.

Pressure was coming from the big donors too, particularly the few who were carrying more and more of the load. In its 1912 investigation the Chamber of Commerce Committee again learned, as they had in the 1910 study, that six givers were still contributing 42 per cent of the total raised for the seventy-three organizations soliciting gifts, the remaining 58 per cent coming from only 6,000 donors. One of the six major donors was John D. Rockefeller, Sr., who still maintained his residence in Cleveland. Retired from active management of Standard Oil, Rockefeller was giving more time and thought to philanthropy and it may be assumed that he expressed his convictions that the "business of benevolence" be more efficiently organized, meaning organized on business lines. Rockefeller was strongly sold on the federation idea and gave an increased contribution to the Federation in its first year to demonstrate his approval of the new plan.

Elwood Street, Cleveland newspaperman who was to become publicist for the Federation in 1913, says that the well-to-do of Cleveland at that time were finding appeals for contributions to social agencies "vexatious and numerous." Rockefeller made his start in business and his first millions in Cleveland, and from the 1880's on, until about the time of federation, he played an influential role in that city's church and civic life. He was long the pillar of the Euclid Avenue Baptist Church and returned to Cleveland every summer until his beloved Forest Hills home on a hill overlooking Lake Erie burned in 1918. His ideas on philanthropy were undoubtedly listened to!

Whiting Williams clearly reveals the impetus for the federation movement in an article published in the *Saturday Evening Post* in December, 1913. In "The Forlorn Philanthropist," Williams wrote: "The prime effort of the plan is to unfetter the philanthropist—to lessen the present pressure on him and free him, at least partially, from the present flood of solicitations."

The 1912 report reviewed the twelve years' work of the Committee and recommended the formation of the Cleveland Federation for Charity and Philanthropy. Williams recalls that the name represented the Catholic preference for "charity" and the Protestant for "philanthropy." He adds, "Together the two brought highly gratifying teamwork." The Committee suggested a board of thirty trustees and that organizations "with legitimate appeals for funds to the citizens of Cleveland without restriction to religious, denominational, or other special affiliation" be eligible for membership. "The painstaking kneading of the public mind at last produced results" and a meeting was called for January 7, 1913, to discuss the Committee's recommendation for a federation. The initiative in calling the meeting and in pushing the federation idea was taken by Cleveland's mayor, Newton D. Baker, who would, a few years later, as President Wilson's Secretary of War, take the leadership in establishing the first national federated fund drive.

Baker had strong support from the Chamber of Commerce, from Marks and his associates, who saw the need for raising more money at less cost, and from the large donors who wanted fewer "vexatious" appeals directed at them. The sense of the January 7 meeting was to recommend adoption of a federated fund-raising plan and to appoint a committee to work out the details. Meanwhile Whiting Williams, who was already deeply involved in the emerging federation, wrote in the February 1, 1913, issue of *Survey* that this "action is the result of five years' search for the cause of the constantly increasing difficulty of securing funds for maintaining and developing the work of the various charitable institutions of the city." Federation was conceived as a "new way out of perplexing problems of philanthropy." The plan was presented and adopted at the March 1 meeting described earlier.

One of the first moves of the newly organized Federation was to hire a full-time executive. The Committee chose Whiting Williams, then assistant to the president of Oberlin College, located just thirty-five miles from Cleveland. Williams had been serving Oberlin as a fund raiser and public relations man and, in the words of an associate, was "a pretty good propagandist." One of Williams' first acts was to hire Elwood Street as publicity secretary, the first known instance of a community charitable federation's hiring a full-time publicity man. Street had covered the March 1 organizational meeting as a reporter for the Cleveland *Leader*. He had worked his way through Western Reserve University by free-lance newspaper writing and photography, getting his A.B. degree in 1912. When Williams gave Street his job with the new Federation he launched the young reporter on a fruitful lifetime career in the community chest-social welfare field. Four years later, in 1917, Street himself would organize and head the Louisville, Ky., Federation of Social Agencies, that city's forerunner to its Community Chest. Williams and Street, both skilled writers with a flair for public relations, moved quickly to publicize the Cleveland Federation both locally and nationally.

Norton says: "Cleveland founded its federation on a wealth of evidence, planted it in extremely fertile soil, and promptly announced it to the world. Its federation succeeded from the start; it was advertised from the start; it prompted a dozen other cities to do the same thing; and it deserves to be known as the originator of the modern movement." [10]

Articles explaining and praising the new federation plan, written by Williams, were published in the February 1, 1913, issue of *Survey*, in the October, 1913, issue of *Review of Reviews*, and in the December 20, 1913, issue of *Saturday Evening Post*. In the *Review of Reviews* article, Williams reported: "The almost daily inquiries—received by wire as well as by post—from the leading municipalities of the entire country would indicate that the problem which Cleveland is thus attacking is one of nationwide proportions." [11] And of course it was. Chambers of Commerce in other cities—the chamber movement was now beginning to spread rapidly—were encouraged to make similar studies of local philanthropy.

Typical of the national publicity spreading word of the new plan was an article, "Putting the 'Cleave' in 'Cleaveland,' " in the July 5, 1913, issue of *Survey*. The article carried no by-line but presumably came from either Williams or Street. The article praised the Cleveland Federation as a plan for "benevolence by cooperation in place of benevolence by competition" and listed these advantages of the new one-drive method: the federation plan undoubtedly tends to make a person's gift larger than the aggregate of his gifts to separate organizations; federation makes it possible to keep a much closer record of the charity-giving habits of each donor; the economy of the new plan permits one firm to write one check to give $1,000 to thirty organizations and not have to write thirty checks and thirty letters; formerly commissions of from 15 to 50 per cent were paid to financial solicitors. The commissions of solicitors and the time of other administrative officers given to collection of funds were found by the Committee to cost an average of $1,000 per institution. This is at least four times as much as the cost will be under federation; now for the first time it was possible to give Cleveland a thorough-going course in social education. [12] Headlined UNIQUE ATTEMPT TO SOLVE PHILANTHROPY'S BIG PROBLEM, a full page in the *New York Times* of December 6, 1913, hailed the new approach. "Cleveland has organized a Federation which will make a concerted appeal for all charities and a gift to it will make the donor immune from separate gifts to institutions." Time has proved the latter assertion poor prophecy.

Williams and Street are among the early fund raisers who realized the need to build broad public support before attempting to achieve broad public giving. As Williams explained: "More givers and more effective givers are sure to be the result of the Federation's dependence on information and the live interest of the whole city rather than upon a fifty-fold pressure upon a few." Though they were quick to seize the national spotlight, these two skilled publicists did not neglect their first job of selling the Federation to the Clevelanders to achieve "live interest of the whole city." One of their first projects was a "house to house canvass for funds and friendships." They organized the week of June 2–9 as "goodwill week" and sent 300 social workers affiliated with the constituent agencies out on door-to-door calls "to inform the public of the nature, aims, and methods of the Federation and to stimulate interest in it. The three hundred visitors were specifically instructed not to urge anyone to contribute. Goodwill was sought more than money." [13] Nevertheless, contributions were asked for.

As the word spread of the Cleveland plan so did its adoption: in 1914 to Dayton, Ohio, New Orleans, Richmond, Ind., South Bend, Ind., Salt Lake City, and Birmingham, Ala.; in 1915 to Cincinnati, Ohio, Dallas, Texas, Oshkosh, Wis., Erie, Pa., and Baltimore, Md.; in 1916 to St. Joseph, Mo.; in 1917 to Buffalo, N.Y., Grand Rapids, Mich., Mt. Vernon, N.Y., and Milwaukee, Wis. By 1917 federations started in New Orleans, Salt Lake City, and Birmingham, Ala., had failed. With the exception of Cincinnati, the impetus for federation of social agencies came from businessmen through their chambers of commerce. Norton says that the federation movement in Ohio's Queen City "was the first to arise exclusively from agencies rather than the contributors." The Cincinnati Federation had its beginnings when a social workers' club called a meeting in 1911 to discuss coordination of the work of Cincinnati welfare agencies.

Driven by the desire to bring efficiency and economy to the growing list of voluntary welfare agencies, the businessman played a dominant role in the growth of community chests. The 1917 American Association for Organizing Charity Report recorded the fact that in ten of the first nineteen cities to organize federations the local commercial organization was the most influential in bringing federation into being. In this period the U.S. Chamber of Commerce was offering an outline of the necessary steps to organize a local community chest. This businessman's approach to the growing demands for popular philanthropy had, in the words of Lillian Brandt, "a flavor of the collective bargaining of the industrial world." Nationally the federation movement aroused much interest and discussion in the formative years. By 1920 there would be 50 community chest organizations in the United States; by 1930 there would be 233.

Reasons for the federation plan's growth were clear and compelling. These included: insistence by donors, mostly businessmen, on efficiency and economy and on fewer solicitations—the multiple drives for funds, "competitive finance," struck businessmen as wasteful and they keenly desired protection from repeated applications; social workers' desire for more effective coordination of the work of the multiplying agencies and to have a common forum for the exchange of ideas and information; need for more effective education of the public still not too generally sympathetic with the young social agencies. In some cities the financial considerations were by far the most important in setting up a federation. In others the motivation was a blend of financial, social, and educational motives.

Those interested in raising money for philanthropic causes, as well as the growing body of social workers who spent the funds, became increasingly interested in the federation idea now generating much heated discussion, pro and con. On May 11, 1915, the executive committee of the American Association for Organizing Charity appointed a special committee to study federations. The Committee was composed of: W. Frank Persons, chairman, director of general work, New York Charity Organization Society; William H. Baldwin, railroad executive and member of the board for Washington (D.C.) Associated Charities; Fred R. Johnson, secretary Boston Associated Charities; and Eugene T. Lies, general superintendent Chicago United Charities; none from a city which had tried the federation plan. At the time this committee was appointed at least forty-eight cities had considered the federation. The Committee began its work that December when the Russell Sage Foundation provided the services of Fred S. Hall to collect the data which provided the basis for its deliberations.[14] The Committee's conclusion at the end of its study in 1917 was that "it has not yet been demonstrated whether the federation plan means a net social advance or the reverse, and our recommendation is against the adoption of the plan *at present* in other cities." The 385-page report provides a wealth of data on public philanthropy for community agencies during that period.

The Committee's general conclusions were:

1. Measured by total contributions, financial success appears to have been usual in initial federation years except where there has been inadequate preparation and organization. Financial success is much less surely shown when later years are taken into account . . . the gains achieved have been based almost uniformly upon methods of financial work [granting of immunity from solicitation, use of whirlwind campaigns, and the encouragement of undesignated giving] which in our judgment do not tend to build up as stable a constituency as most organizations in non-federated cities now have.
2. On the educational side there has been an undoubted gain in certain cities, due to their federations' publicity efforts, and some gain in all cities to the extent that joint appealing makes the breadth and variety of social work better realized. But even in the federation cities that have done the best educational work we recognize a tendency, which seems to us inevitable, toward a loss of interest resulting from the lessened contact between givers and the objects of their gifts.
3. On the social side the gains of federations that have attempted social work have been considerable, and usually so far they seem not to have been offset by losses. . . .

   In many cities in which no federations exist progress has been steady and important, both in educational lines and in organized co-operative social work.[15]

The costs of fund raising and the results of the more intensified campaign for gifts are shown in Tables 1 through 4.[16]

Fund raising for the new federations accelerated the spread of the "whirlwind" money-raising campaign, as the Ward-Pierce technique was coming to be called. The AAOC Committee found that except in Cleveland, New Orleans, and Richmond, Ind., federations were relying chiefly on "campaigns of the whirlwind sort":

Usually the campaigns have been undertaken by means of teams of 100 or more persons, salaried and volunteer, furnished by the constituencies of the affiliated organizations, and in some cases by the commercial organizations. Gatherings of campaigners are arranged for, before and during the campaign, in the course of which instruction is given as to the methods of work and the aims of the various or-

TABLE I. CONTRIBUTIONS—PRE-FEDERATION AND INITIAL FEDERATION YEARS

Federated city	The year before the federation was formed		The federation's first year—"total contributions under the federation"		Per cent of increase over the preceding year	
	Contributions alone	Contributions and profits on entertainments, etc.	Year	Amount	Contributions alone	Contributions and profits on entertainments, etc.
Complete data						
Cincinnati	$118,015	$35,205	1916	$152,290	29.0	80.9
Erie	20,348	8,657	1915–16	63,700	213.0	16.3
Oshkosh	...	...	1915–16	10,067	...	...
Richmond	...	3,774	1914–15	7,035	...	86.4
Incomplete data						
Baltimore	164,820		1915–16	228,026	38.3	
Cleveland	281,584		1912–13	369,886	31.4	

TABLE 2. CONTRIBUTIONS—SUCCESSIVE FEDERATION YEARS

Federated City	The federation's first year	"Total contributions under the federation" with the per cent of increase (+) or decrease (−) over the first year in *italics*					
		First year	Second year	Third year	Fourth year	Fifth year	Sixth year
Baltimore	1915–16	$245,423	...	...	...	...	...
Cincinnati	1916	152,290	...	...	...	...	...
Cleveland	1912–13	429,180	$477,183 *+11.2*	$480,183 *+11.9*	$543,656 *+26.7*	...	...
Dallas	1915–16	39,992	...	...	...	...	...
Dayton	1914–15	30,784	34,878 *+13.3*	38,049 *+23.6*	...	...	...
Denver	1913–14	32,756	29,336 *−10.4*	41,986 *+28.2*	...	...	...
Elmira	1910–11	11,435	12,322 *+7.8*	14,026 *+22.7*	15,040 *+31.5*	$18,847 *+64.8*	$16,831 *+47.2*
Erie	1915–16	63,700	...	...	...	...	...
New Orleans	1914	49,695	...	...	...	...	...
Oshkosh	1915–16	10,067	...	...	...	...	...
Richmond	1914–15	7,035	7,707 *+9.6*	...	...	...	...
Salt Lake City	1914–15	19,212	...	...	...	...	...
South Bend	1914–15	22,401	22,437 *+0.2*	...	...	...	...

ganizations, so that the solicitors may be able to campaign intelligently. . . .

In most federations whirlwind campaigns have been supplemented by personal and letter solicitation. Directors and others closely connected with the federations have sometimes assisted in this. In Erie a solicitor has been employed, and in Cincinnati a collector of pledges.[17]

The AAOC found in its study that professional fund raisers were used in Elmira, N.Y., in 1914, in Baltimore in 1915 and 1917, Erie and Denver in 1915, and in St. Joseph, Mo., Milwaukee, and Dallas

TABLE 3. THE FEDERATIONS' COST

Federated city	Years	Contributions received by the federation	Cost of the federation office, campaigns, etc.	
			Amounts	Per cent of the contributions
Baltimore	1915–16	$156,891	$18,566	11.8
Cincinnati	1916	110,453	12,494	. . .
Cleveland	1912–13	152,473	17,789	11.7
	1913–14	291,487	29,201	10.2
	1914–15	309,280	32,731	10.5
	1915–16	411,559	32,660	7.9
Dallas	1915–16	29,021	5,481	18.9
Dayton	1914–15	29,854	1,858	6.2
	1915–16	34,030	3,489	10.3
	1916	24,829	2,870	11.6
Denver	1913–14	32,756	4,381	13.4
	1914–15	29,336	3,682	12.5
	1915–16	41,986	12,718	30.3
Elmira	1910–11	14,156	235	1.7
	1911–12	11,786	161	1.4
	Jan. 1, '14– Jan. 1, '17	56,052	6,245	11.1
Erie	1915–16	60,676	10,580	17.4
N. Orleans	1914	43,488	3,652	8.4
Oshkosh	1915–16	10,067	100	1.0
S. L. City	1914–15	19,212	1,377	7.2
South Bend	1914–15	22,401	639	2.9
	1915–16	22,437	1,342	6.0

TABLE 4. ESTIMATED COST OF COLLECTION—FEDERATED CITIES

Federated city	Years	Estimated cost of the federation's financial work	
		Amount	Per cent that it was of the federation's contributions as shown in Table 3.
Denver	3	. . .	14.5
Dallas	1	$ 3,421	13.8
Erie	1	6,241	10.3
Cleveland	4	198,234	10.3
Baltimore	1	15,000	9.6
New Orleans	1	3,652	8.4
Elmira	4½	6,641	8.1
Cincinnati	1	9,470	7.8
Dayton	3	6,717	7.6
Salt Lake City	1	1,377	7.2
South Bend	2	1,981	4.4
Oshkosh	1	100	1.0

in 1916. Cleveland's Whiting Williams did not accept the short, hard-hitting campaign idea. He believed in a quiet campaign, largely by circular letter and based upon the record of previous contributions, carefully tabulated. But "he admitted that the cost of the initial whirlwind campaign was less than the cost of circularizing, and that perhaps there was some initial advantage in the publicity of the campaign method, preceded by newspaper, church, street-car, window and other propaganda, as well as by meetings. The Erie initial campaign cost 7% of the $65,000 raised." [18]

Despite the hedging of AAOC's prestigious and painstaking committee, the united fund-raising campaign had too many strengths to be deterred and these early experiences in federated fund drives would provide a useful pattern for the greatly accelerated war fund drives that would come with America's entry into World War I. Whiting Williams propagandized far and wide that federation was bringing Cleveland "1. More Dollars; 2. More Effective Dollars; 3. More Givers; 4. Happier Givers; 5. A Better Cleveland." [19] Welfare workers could not resist the successful formula of the community chest plan which also sped the advent of planned publicity and public relations programs in the social welfare field. The Federation could afford a full-time publicity director whereas the individual philanthropic agencies could not. From the start federations appeared to be more sensitive to public opinion than had been the constituent agencies up to that time. Norton recalls:

> At the outset the modern federation [circa 1913] was compelled to recognize not only the value of educational publicity for social work, but the necessity for it as well, if the cooperative movement was to survive. The federation picked up the task of securing funds and popular support for social work at a point where the separate agency method of administration left off. This point was low in comparison to what ought exist.[20]

As mentioned earlier, it was fortunate that pattern-setting Cleveland employed a man as its first director who possessed "an acute sense of publicity values, a conviction in the efficacy of education that amounted almost to devotion, and a peculiar sensitiveness to trends of public opinion." [21] The Cincinnati and Baltimore Federations soon followed Cleveland's example in employing an experienced newspaper man as publicity director. The AAOC Committee found that "in Cleveland it is reported that the amount of newspaper space obtained has averaged nearly a page a week since the organization of the Federation." These publicists not only used newspaper space; they organized speakers' bureaus and promoted engagements for speakers; they embarked on systematic use of posters; started periodicals; issued yearbooks that were the forerunners of the annual report to contributors and community; and promoted the federated plan through articles in the national press. One of the first organizations to use the new medium of motion pictures was the Federation of Jewish Charities in Brooklyn, N.Y., in its 1916 fund drive. Bogen, writing in 1917, was dubious: "This, naturally, carries publicity to an extreme and may, unless judiciously presented, do harm, injuring the very elements whom the Charities are to serve." [22]

One of the pioneers in the community chest movement, Cincinnati's C. M. Bookman, observed in 1924:

> The Community Chest plan has made possible scientific methods of molding public opinion. The centralization and unification of social work has provided funds with which to carry on constructive educa-

tional programs; money with which to bring to the attention of the entire community the social ills of that community. A student of Community Chest cities will find that there has grown up in those cities the feeling on the part of the citizens that no one can be a true citizen and measure up to the real responsibilities of citizenship if he fails to identify himself with such a movement.[23]

Yet something as new, as flamboyant, and as tainted with overtones of "press agentry" as was publicity work would naturally draw the fire of many conservative businessmen and publicity-shy social workers. The new emphasis on public relations was not universally accepted. One social worker told the AAOC Committee that Cleveland's publicity was weak because "one is lost in the midst of detail and gets from it only a confused impression." A Cincinnati worker told the Committee that "the 'sob' appeal has been somewhat overworked and not enough emphasis has been given to constructive and rescue work."

There was understandable concern about the publicist's exploitation of the fear motive, an issue still with us. Yet Norton thinks no other single contribution could have been made to federation practice at that moment that would have done more toward assuring success. He adds: "In spite of a general acceptance of the necessity for public education, the cooperative movement found that the development of an effective methodology was beset with unusual difficulties. Social workers had been both too poverty stricken and too deeply absorbed with other matters to make progress enough in this [publicity] direction." The federation idea had brought the need for the intensive fund-raising campaign which in turn had necessitated intensive publicity, both important aspects of the unfolding philanthropic story. The publicity patterns, too, would be pushed and improved in the wartime drives to come. The next development in the federated plan of fund getting occurs when it has become a "war chest." Meanwhile, Charles Sumner Ward was at work perfecting the techniques of the short-term intensive campaign for money.

The "Whirlwind" Begins

Word of Ward's ability to organize and direct campaigns to raise large sums for new YMCAs quickly radiated throughout the Y and to other organizations dependent upon public largess. From 1905 on, the intensive campaign became "the well-nigh universal method of raising permanent funds" for the Y. In the 1905–1915 decade Ward and those using his tightly organized methods succeeded in raising some $60 million in capital funds for the Association. Writing in 1916, Ward said: "It is not claimed that the intensive method is the fundamental reason for this unprecedented growth [of the Y]. That reason lies in the record the Association has made for itself in its work for young men, and the practical appreciation by business men and others able to contribute money." [24] These concentrated campaigns involved large numbers of people who were schooled in the organized, intensive approach to the omnipresent task of getting money for public causes. In that decade Ward estimated, not less than 50,000 active businessmen had served on committees to solicit funds, that some 1.5 million persons had made contributions to Y drives. Little wonder that "the use of this plan of campaign speedily led to its adoption by other organizations. Some Association men have gone out to lead in various philanthropic endeavors, and many millions of dollars have thus been secured for hospitals, universities, and colleges." [25] Here, too, Ward led the way.

In 1907—just two years after the highly publicized Washington campaign—Ward was lent by the International Committee of the Young Men's Christian Association to organize and direct an appeal for funds for a new building for the Young Women's Christian Association of Pittsburgh, Pa. Ward's methods again proved successful and soon there were demands for his aid from YWCAs in other cities. In 1911 Ward took on his first hospital fund campaign, in Salem, Ohio. Ward was a strong believer in a saturation publicity drive to build a favorable opinion climate for the competing teams of solicitors. He usually hired a local newspaperman for the publicity task, an innovation in those days. For the Salem City Hospital campaign Ward hired a free-lance writer and former newspaperman, Frederick Courtenay Barber. Barber would, in time, organize the first commercial fund-raising firm and cut a colorful swath through the field of fund raising before his death on Jaunuary 1, 1937. Barber worked on and off for Ward for two years before starting his own business.

A flamboyant showman, Barber provided a sharp contrast to the rather solemn, dedicated, religious personalities of Ward, Pierce, and others of the Y school of fund raisers. For one thing Barber was a "hard drinker," the Y fund raisers were teetotalers. A former associate, Cornelius M. Smith, says of Barber: "Fred Barber was not only colorful but brilliant. He had great ability and energy with a magnetic and charming personality. His early campaigns for colleges, hospitals and character-building institutions were highly successful. It was unfortunate that his increasing success made it increasingly difficult to work with him." [26] Coupling his flair for showmanship with the lessons Ward had taught him, Barber set up Frederick Courtenay Barber and Associates in 1913. Almost from the start, Barber specialized in hospital campaigns and operated on a percentage fee basis, something the YMCA school of fund raisers would come to frown upon. Of Barber, Arnaud C. Marts, one of the giants in the commercial fund-raising field which came in the wake of World War I, once said:

> Mr. Barber was a spectacular personality who organized community campaigns with all the fanfare and spectacle of a circus. He put on a great show and charged substantial fees, and I suspect in many cases operated on a percentage basis. A friend of mine who participated in a hospital campaign which Barber ran in Memphis, Tennessee, in the years before the first World War, has told me of the parade which Barber organized as a part of his campaign publicity. At the head of the parade, in a beautiful phaeton, with high stepping horses, rode Barber himself, in a frock coat and a high silk hat. The contrast between the Barber type of circus and the Lyman Pierce and Charles Ward type of behind the scenes campaign is very striking. [27]

In Marts's opinion, Barber gave fund raising a "bad name" in its early years. Barber obviously did not fit into the staid, stable pattern of conventional fund raisers and went his way without leaving much of an imprint on the profession, which puts more emphasis on system and solicitation than on parades and hoopla. Two other publicists hired by Ward for other campaigns will appear later as leading professional fund raisers. One, F. Herbert Wells, became one of Ward's early partners when the pioneer campaigner set up his fund-raising business. The other, Carlton Ketchum, went on to establish his own firm which today is one of the largest of these commercial concerns. Ketchum was also tutored by Barber, but it was Ward's thoroughgoing methods that he used to build his thriving business after World War I.

Ward's success as a field secretary specializing in capital fund raising was recognized by the top officers of the Y when the International Committee called him to the New York headquarters to establish a Finance Bureau in 1910. In this post Ward proceeded to train a staff to direct fund appeals because, by now, he could not possibly meet the requests for his campaign leadership coming in from all parts of the country. In 1912 Ward was asked to carry his methods across the Atlantic, just as Pierce had exported the campaign plan to New Zealand and Australia a few years earlier.

The central YMCA in London invited Ward to come to England to organize a drive to raise a needed £100,000 to free the Association's palatial building in Tottenham Court Road from debt. The YMCA had been first organized in London, and Ward deemed it a great honor to be asked to lead this campaign. One London paper described him as "a quiet man with absolutely nothing of the sensational about him; yet at once he impresses all who meet him with his great force of character and his abounding resourcefulness. All his methods are those of a man who inspires confidence. . . . He is, in fact, simply a man in dead earnest."

Ward approached the London drive in his systematic way, stimulating publicity, organizing a committee, recruiting teams of solicitors, and, of course, erecting the big clock—this one on the Y building in Tottenham Court Road with "£100,000 in 12 Days for the Y.M.C.A. Building" across its face. A special dispatch to the Chicago *Daily News* of January 19, 1912, reported: "Charles Sumner Ward, who was in charge of the enterprise, was found at Guildhall today in the midst of the clatter and confusion of a roomful of stenographers, typists, and callers. The famous organizer looked a little tired, and just a little graver than he looked at the start of the fight."[28] Ward told the *Daily News* reporter "this is the most difficult campaign of my life." Conservative Britons did not readily respond to Ward's methods of publicity and pressure. Some London newspapers referred to Ward as the "Yankee Wizard." In the end he raised the amount needed to save the Y's home building. But in Ward's opinion "the biggest thing accomplished has been the advertising of the YMCA throughout the United Kingdom and the Continent. Scotland and Wales have requested me to help them in association work." The Dreshman Memo, quoted earlier, records that Ward did go to Edinburgh and there helped organize a Y campaign before his return home.

Having perfected his campaign methods in terms of thousands, Ward now decided the time was right to go after millions. In November, 1913, he guided the launching of a campaign to raise $4 million—an unprecedented sum to expect from public gifts—for the YMCA and the YWCA in Greater New York. New York was considered then, and still remains, the toughest city in the United States in which to carry out a successful fund-raising drive. Yet dramatically seeking to raise this tremendous sum in a short span of two weeks in metropolitan New York brought Ward new laurels. The New York *Globe* commented editorially: "The campaign to raise $4,000,000 . . . starts under the most auspicious circumstances. If thoroughly organized effort counts for anything the money no doubt will be collected within the time limit." [29] Ward put George W. Perkins "at the head of this whirlwind assault" on New York's pocketbook.

Ward used all of his tested techniques in this campaign. He erected the large campaign clock advertising the goal of $4 million at the corner of Wall and Broad streets on November 11. He had obtained in advance the large pace-setting gift to announce as the campaign opened—a check for $350,000 from John D. Rockefeller, later increased to half a million when other givers demonstrated faith in the Y's appeal. Ward amassed an array of prestigious backers and large contributors including: Mrs. Willard Straight, $300,000; Cleveland H. Dodge, $275,000; Miss Grace Dodge, $250,000; Mrs. Finlay J. Shepard, $200,000; Henry Clay Frick, $100,000, and Mrs. William D. Sloane, $50,000.

On November 26 the New York newspapers carried headlines reading, "YWCA-YMCA Fund Falls $126,498 Short; 24 Hours Added in Which to Make Total $4,000,000." And, sure enough, with the "crowding and jamming" eschewed by Bishop Lawrence, Ward pushed the drive over the stretched time limit and the November 27 issue of the New York *Tribune* carried this headline: "SHOWER OF GOLD RINGS MONEY CLOCK: YMCA Campaigners Pass $4,000,000 Goal With $62,501 to Spare." The drive brought in $4,095,000 from 17,400 donors. A two-week drive to raise $4 million in 1913 was bound to dramatize the Ward method and make fund-raising history with its consequent impact on American public philanthropy. Little wonder that the *Literary Digest* of December 13, 1913, would tag him "the whirlwind collector." His publicity associate, Frederick Courtenay Barber, wrote: "He sows the soil of necessity with the seed of genius, waters it from the springs of energy, warms it with the sunshine of good humor, and reaps bumper crops that would make the eyes of Wall Street bulge." [30] Yet Barber insisted that "Mr. Ward is the most unassuming of men."

Ward's spectacular success in the Greater New York YMCA campaign brought him to the attention of Chancellor Samuel Black McCormick of the University of Pittsburgh, then in process of transition from the old Western University of Pennsylvania. The newly organized University of Pittsburgh urgently needed $3 million to develop its new campus in Schenley Park, Pittsburgh. McCormick invited Ward to Pittsburgh to confer with Pitt's Alumni Fund Committee. Ward agreed to accept the challenge and began, in January, mapping plans for a whirlwind campaign to run for ten days in May, 1914, in his first attempt at college fund raising. Ward brought in Frederick Courtenay Barber to handle the publicity and asked Chancellor McCormick to provide two assistants from the university. Two Pitt students, brothers Carlton and George Ketchum, were the men chosen by the chancellor to assist Ward and Barber. Both had had some newspaper experience.

Carlton Ketchum recalls Ward as an "austere and reserved man, very far indeed from any of the campaign types which we all recognize." Ketchum thinks, in retrospect, that Ward's "effectiveness was that of the originator of a sane and practical method, and the firmness to insist on its thorough application . . . it was this, rather than any personal magnetism, that accounted for his success." Just how successful the Pitt campaign was is a debated matter. The president's report concerning this campaign states that in the allotted ten days "nearly $2,000,000 was raised" and that "the Committee will double its efforts until the remaining amount is raised." The records in the University of Pittsburgh Library give nothing to indicate that the remaining million was ever raised. Carlton Ketchum thinks $2.1 million was raised. Ward was retained and paid a fee by the Alumni Fund Committee, presumably out of the funds raised. [31] Out of this campaign experience with Ward, Ketchum recalls:

> The methods of the campaign would now be considered simple, if not naïve, but at that time caused a great deal of excitement and amazement because most of the people who served in the campaign or were affected by it had never seen such an operation or anything like it. As I recall it, a number of potential contributors were rather outraged at

the idea, but more of them accepted it and gave. In that early day, of course, with the income tax a negligible factor, individual giving was the big thing, and corporate support of any such project a minor factor.[32]

Ward was not only raising money for YMCAs and other philanthropic causes; he was teaching persons of means the often painful lesson of their obligation to support charitable causes and conditioning the public to the high-pressure fund drive which today is commonplace in our society. Ward's systematic organization of solicitation that brought the strongest possible pressure on those catalogued as able to give was bound to outrage many. But the system brought in the cash to meet campaign goals! Ward was also instructing men in the art of raising funds.

It was subsequent to the Pitt campaign that Frederick Courtenay Barber started his own fund-raising firm. He had been highly impressed by the energy and ability of the Ketchum brothers and hired both of them. They joined the Barber firm when Carlton was graduated from Pitt in June, 1916. George did not complete the work for his degree, but was soon using the lessons Mr. Ward had taught him to raise funds for the Rose Polytechnic Institute in Terre Haute, Ind.

Carlton's first assignment with Barber was to serve as publicity man in a campaign for a Salvation Army building in Great Falls, Mont., but he soon moved back to college fund raising. In the months preceding World War I, Carlton was engaged "in one of the very first organized campaigns for a woman's college—Elmira College." After the campaign in Elmira, Carlton worked on a public relations program for Lafayette College to pave the way for a fund-raising drive and then as director of a fund-raising effort for a woman's suffrage campaign in Illinois.

Carlton, as had his brother George a few months earlier, offered his resignation to Barber in the fall of 1917 to go into military service. When he told Barber of his intention to leave the firm and enlist in the army, Barber gave him "a good round denunciation." Ketchum and Barber were never friends again. Carlton Ketchum thinks that Barber "was a man of great inherent ability, but with absolutely no self-control and very few principles."[33]

Nearly four decades later, Ketchum looked back at the Elmira $3 million "Cyclone Campaign" as rather primitive compared to today's highly polished techniques for raising money for colleges. The Ward method of those days was designed for a community, not a widespread area. Ketchum reflects:

> One of the characteristics of the early college capital fund campaigns was that their planning customarily ignored annual alumni funds if such existed. Campaigners and colleges learned the hard way that this did not pay. . . . The early college fund campaigns, being patterned on those for the YMCA and like institutions, were short-term. Since most of them were chiefly local, appealing to the college's community, this was possible, but as they broadened out, it took a few years experience to demonstrate that a lot more time needed to be allowed for them. Preliminary public relations prior to the commencement of the official campaign period were seldom involved in the years before 1925. Report meeting methods were largely those of the straight community-type campaign.[34]

In the University of Pittsburgh campaign of 1914 we find the fragile thread of fate weaving together in common effort the labors of four men who stand in the forefront of American fund-raising history: Ward, of course; Carlton Ketchum (George was to make his mark in the world of advertising); Lyman L. Pierce, at this time the general secretary of the Pittsburgh YMCA, who served as leader of the volunteer workers in the Pitt campaign; and Arnaud C. Marts, who was serving as YMCA Boys' Secretary under Lyman Pierce and inevitably was drafted for service in the Pitt campaign.

William A. Littell describes how Marts and Ketchum, later to head two of the nation's largest fund-raising firms, first met. In June, 1911, young Carlton Ketchum arrived in Pittsburgh with $1.35 in his pocket. Immediately "he launched a whirlwind one-man campaign in which before sundown he (1) landed a summer replacement stenographer's job at Armstrong Cork, (2) hocked his watch to cover food until the first payday; (3) talked his way into the already-full Boys' Branch of the YMCA on the North Side. In the last he was aided and abetted by the sympathetic secretary named Marts."[35] All the Y's rooms were filled when young Ketchum applied but Marts agreed, at Ketchum's insistence, to put a bed in the hallway for him. Oddly enough, the paths of Ketchum and Marts did not cross again for thirty years, when they met to help organize the American Association of Fund-Raising Counsel.

Arnaud Marts, who would later join with another YMCA worker,

George Lundy, to organize the Marts & Lundy fund-raising firm, was a Phi Beta Kappa graduate of Oberlin College in 1910. He went to work as Boys' Secretary of the Pittsburgh YMCA under the tutelage of Lyman L. Pierce. This first work experience proved immensely valuable to young Marts. He still vividly recalls Pierce's qualities of "imagination, courage, faith, and zeal" which deeply impressed the young Y recruit. Marts attests with gratitude his "large debt" to Lyman Pierce. "When I graduated from college I was green and timid and didn't have any idea of my future. The chance contact with Lyman Pierce was the turning point in my life." [36]

But Marts did not get into fund raising until he had taken a slight detour. The ability of the handsome young Y official impressed officers of the Standard Life Insurance Company, headquartered in Pittsburgh, and they brought him into the firm as a vice-president, a position he held from 1914 to 1919. But during World War I Marts was drafted by Pierce to work in the first nationwide drive for the YMCA War Fund, and this led him to his fruitful fund-raising career. With fascination, he had closely observed the Ward-directed campaign to raise the $2 million for Pitt. He recalls that "Mr. Ward would come around to the Y.M.C.A. office at night to counsel with Mr. Pierce" though "Lyman had no official role in the campaign." Both the experienced Pierce and young Marts participated in the informal conferences.

Upon his return to the United States in 1908, after his campaigns in New Zealand and Australia, Pierce left Y work to accept a position as one of the general secretaries of the new Layman's Missionary Movement then gaining momentum in America. This movement was organized within the Southern Presbyterian Church and spread to other Protestant churches. In Pierce's words, the movement "was controlled and dominated by one purpose, *viz.*, to arouse the men of the Christian church to do a man's part in evangelization of the world." The movement was interdenominational. A Burlington, Iowa, newspaper of March 1, 1909, announcing Pierce's forthcoming visit to arouse interest in "the approaching Iowa conference of the Layman's Missionary Movement," glowingly described him as "one of the ablest speakers on the American platform and his experience with the great uprising for men in missionary work throughout the east insures a meeting of more than ordinary interest." In this work Pierce did not seek to raise funds directly. Advance publicity for these meetings to arouse "Christian men to undertake the evangelization of the non-Christian world" comfortably assured those urged to attend that no collections would be taken. Rather "the movement strives to build support for the mission boards of the churches." In this post Pierce developed the "every member canvass," widely used today in Protestant churches.

After a year's hard travel and much speechmaking, Pierce began to weary of the missionary movement and accepted an invitation to become general secretary of the Central YMCA of Pittsburgh in April, 1909. He held the position until January, 1915, when this task, too, had begun to pall and lose its interest for the active, restless missionary and fund raiser. The January 5, 1915, Pittsburgh *Sun* reported: "Lyman L. Pierce, general secretary of the local Young Men's Christian Association, has resigned to enter business, probably in Pittsburgh. His resignation, which is to take effect Jan. 20, was accepted with regret by the board of directors at a special meeting held yesterday." Lyman Pierce had once more used his ability to direct YMCA drives to build four buildings as well as raise the budget. His accomplishments in Pittsburgh were hailed in an editorial in the January 7, 1915, Pittsburgh *Press:*

> During the six years Mr. Pierce has occupied this position, the work of the association . . . has gone forward with a hopefulness and an energy unequalled in its previous career. It has been a period of uninterrupted growth and greatly extended usefulness. The number of branches in the city has increased to thirteen, all comfortably housed and some of them with buildings of a size and value which ten years ago would have seemed outside the range of possibility. . . . The annual contributions from the public have risen to $55,000 as compared with $18,000 six years ago.

In a few months Lyman Pierce returned to fund raising, after a rest to recoup a health and energy never equal to his supercharged drive. In the fall of 1915 he undertook his first non-Y assignment to raise funds for a Fremont, Ohio, hospital. With all the trappings of the Ward-Pierce method, a campaign was launched to raise $100,-000 in public gifts to match the $100,000 bequest for a Sandusky County Memorial Hospital. The bequest provided the spur to equal the big gift or lose it. The "clock" was used too. The Fremont *Daily Messenger* announced at the start that "the hands of the big clock at Front and State streets will be watched with interest. Near the end of the campaign it is predicted that the streets will be jammed four square with those anxious to see the big hand go around."

When Pierce got to Fremont in early October the *Messenger* under the headline PIERCE A REGULAR GINGERY GINGERJAR said: "Less than a month ago, Fremont people talked of a memorial hospital only in a vague sort of way. Now hospital is the sole topic of conversation among the vast majority of citizens. . . . Who is responsible?" Lyman Pierce, of course, was the answer. The paper then said of him: "One does not need to be around Mr. Pierce very long to realize that he is a big man in his line. Of medium stature and build, the possessor of keen, penetrating eyes and of a generally distinguished appearance, the master solicitor impresses one right off the reel as a man thoroughly fitted for his work."

And he was—he brought in over $99,000. The fervor these Ward-Pierce campaigns aroused is reflected in this news story in the October 21, 1915, *Daily News:* "Amid tears of joy and cries of exultation, the final announcements of success in the week's campaign . . . were made to 250 workers and crowds of spectators at the Armory Thursday noon. Men and women stood upon the chairs and cheered until the old building shook from wall to wall. Such a demonstration was never before witnessed in the old town." [37]

After this fling at commercial fund raising Pierce again returned to YMCA work, this time as general secretary of the San Francisco Y, a position he assumed November 1, 1915. Mr. and Mrs. Pierce, with their high school age daughters, Martha and Virginia, rented a home on Bellevue Avenue in the Golden Gate city, and once more he plunged into a building program for the Y. As the *Christian Advocate* of April 20, 1916, reported: "He has very quickly mastered the situation in San Francisco and every department of the work of the institution has felt the impulse of his inspiration and wise direction." And it was from San Francisco that Lyman Pierce answered the call of his nation at war to lend his talents across the country.

Though no records are available, it is probable that Pierce worked on a percentage basis for his fee in the Fremont hospital campaign, the standard practice in that time though today regarded as highly unethical by the members of the American Association of Fund-Raising Counsel. Carlton Ketchum explained:

Prior to World War I, professional campaign service was usually provided on the basis of a fee of 5% of the amount subscribed. Most, if not all, firms also charged the travel and living expense of their staff members and such supervision as there was to the campaign budget. Campaigns were costing 12 and 15% and even more. Naturally this whole scheme put a premium on padding up the reported totals on the part of the campaign firm and keeping subscriptions out of the campaign time so far as the client was concerned, and many abuses developed. It was a wholly indefensible scheme of things and was bound to fall of its own weight.[38]

Ketchum was working for the Barber firm in that period, which would confirm the assertion that Barber worked on a percentage basis. In his Y fund-raising campaigns prior to 1919 Ward charged no fees. *Munsey's* magazine reported: "Mr. Ward receives no compensation from the association branches he serves in this way. His salary is paid by the International Committee and is moderate. There is no percentage arrangement."

After more than a decade's experience Ward's campaign method had become routine and standardized. He put his emphasis on systematic organization and on pressure created through saturation publicity. "The press, pulpit, and the active propaganda form an educational force by which practically every individual in a community may be reached," he often told his campaign assistants. Ward, in outlining the campaign method in 1916, said that "the essential features of the campaign are suggested by the following words: CONCENTRATION, ORGANIZATION, SACRIFICE, EDUCATION, CUMULATIVE EFFECT, and CIVIC IMPULSE." He found that "this concentration greatly facilitates the publicity necessary for success." The Ward plan followed these steps:

1. A careful examination of the Y's affairs should reveal that the local association is in suitable condition to go before the public with an appeal for a new building.
2. The board of directors must weigh the plan carefully, note the sacrifice involved, and then commit themselves unreservedly to it.
3. An approximate date for the campaign should be set some months ahead so that detailed preparations can proceed with reference to that date.
4. In an advance publicity campaign the public, through the press, should be kept informed of the crowded condition of the old quarters and the immediate need of a new building.
5. One large subscription should be secured conditioned upon raising

the entire amount within the allotted time. The value of this large subscription in holding the canvass to the time specified and in bringing it to a climax on the last day is beyond estimate.

6. All the directors should be prepared to make their subscription as soon as the campaign opens as an example to others.
7. A list should be prepared on cards . . . of all prospective subscribers. Do not put estimates on cards.
8. When the list is complete, one half go to the Business Men's Committee, one half to the Young Men's Committee.[39]

One of Ward's associates in YMCA fund raising once neatly capsuled the Ward method in these words: "A large number of men willing to give definite time to personal solicitation for a limited number of days working under assignment is the factor that brings success."

The Bishop's "Church Pension Fund"

Bishop William Lawrence's talent and time were used far beyond the confines of his diocese. In 1893 he was elected a trustee of Wellesley College and for two decades played an influential role in shaping the policies of that famous woman's college. Bishop Lawrence was serving his second term as president of the Wellesley board when, on a bitter winter morning of March 17, 1914, disaster struck the college. Fire consumed all but the brick walls of the massive five-story building that housed the whole college in those days. Some months before the fire, a quiet drive to raise $1 million for an endowment had been started; $430,000 had been pledged in this endowment campaign when the fire struck. Insurance on the destroyed building brought in $593,500. Assessment of Wellesley's building needs made clear that $1.8 million would be needed to complete the endowment and build a new hall. Once more Bishop Lawrence answered the call to lead a drive for funds. His diary of March 30 recorded: "Presided at Trustee Meeting. Wish I were out of it, but can't shirk now they are in trouble; a big job."

One of the busy bishop's first moves was to visit the Rockefeller General Education Board and Mr. John D. Rockefeller, Jr. The latter advised putting the drive's goal at an even $2 million. Rockefeller wired Lawrence two days later that he would give $750,000 of this amount, with the understanding that the campaign was to end with the year. Lawrence recalls in his memoirs: "The alumnae organized and with fine leadership worked through the spring and autumn. I did little but obey orders when told to see individuals here or there. It was a very heavy bit of work. The national character of the College had distributed its alumnae throughout the whole country and many of them were teachers or were otherwise self-supporting. The quiet growth of forty years had not brought Wellesley to the attention of the business men of New York or even of Boston." [40] This deficiency the bishop promptly attended to. Lawrence even made an unfruitful trip to the Midwest and, called on, among others, James J. Hill, the brusque buccaneer of railroading. Lawrence recalls that Hill "began by frankly telling us that he would not give anything and he kept his word." Others did give, and on January 1, 1915, Lawrence could proudly announce that the $2 million goal had been reached—quite a marked advance in fund raising from that carried on by Mary Lyon for Mt. Holyoke only eighty years before, in nineteenth-century New England.

By the bishop's own testimony, the "stiff experience" and the "dogged perseverance and optimism of the campaigners" of the Wellesley campaign did much to prepare him for the larger battle ahead—the Church Pension Fund Campaign.

Early in the new century Bishop Lawrence became impressed with the need to provide for a decent retirement for ministers, not to cast them out to charity or require them to work beyond their useful years. "Without any conception of the size of the task that I was undertaking," Lawrence offered a resolution calling for study of a pension system for ministers at the 1910 General Convention of the Episcopal Church. The resolution passed and, as was to be expected, Bishop Lawrence wound up as committee chairman. He "soon found, that if work was to be done, I was expected to do it." The result of his study and committee report was action at the 1913 convention directing that "the Church should work towards the adoption of one pension system covering the whole Church." In 1915, after approval by the Diocesan Convention, the system was adopted and a charter obtained from the state of New York. Now came the task of raising the $5,064,000 required to start the Church Pension Fund. Once more Bishop Lawrence was drafted to lead the fund-raising army into battle. He later recorded:

The fourteen months from January 1, 1916, to March 1, 1917, were given to raising the sum: they were months of intense education in an intricate subject, exhilarating enthusiasm, fine loyalty and glad sacrifice. These were the months just before the War: before the country had accustomed itself to large figures by the Liberty Loans; before modern campaign methods had been developed or modern propaganda invented: it was the largest sum ever undertaken to be raised at one time for any religious purpose.[41]

Bishop Lawrence took leave of his diocesan responsibilities to undertake the "heavy load laid upon him." For two winters New York and the eastern part of the country was to be his home. The bishop once said of fund raising, "I hate the job at a distance but once I get started, trout fishing is not in it for excitement." Fired by the dread thought of "thousands of Clergy, their widows and orphans, thrown upon charity for generations yet to come," Bishop Lawrence plunged into this task of raising nearly $6 million in a nationwide campaign—a fund drive unprecedented in amount and in scope. "Every morning I had to lash myself to go downtown." Campaign headquarters were opened in the Bankers' Trust building. His right-hand man in the campaign was Monell Sayre who had served him ably in conceiving and creating the Pension Fund. Another key assistant was Guy Emerson, later to emerge as a leading fund raiser and financier in his own right. As Emerson was tutored by the bishop in the art of money getting, so did Emerson, in turn, tutor John Price Jones, Robert F. Duncan, and other professional fund raisers. Emerson, holder of both a bachelor's and a law degree from Harvard, was associate editor of the *Economic World* when the bishop tapped him to serve as manager of the Church Pension Fund. Emerson's journalistic experience was fully utilized in publicizing the needs of the retirement fund. George W. Burleigh managed the details and directed the clerical staff.

Bishop Lawrence was keenly aware of the reluctance of donors then, as now, to have their dollars go into overhead costs or fundraiser fees rather than to the purpose of the drive. His first task was to raise the $125,000 he estimated the year's drive would take in costs, and this he did. As he explained in his *Atlantic* article: "the raising before the campaign opens of a sum large enough to defray all the expenses of the campaign is a great asset . . . many people have a suspicion that campaigns are carried on wastefully sometimes, that professionals get a 'rake-off' of ten, twenty, or even fifty per cent; and they are a bit shy at having their expenses deducted from their gift."

This matter taken care of, the bishop then plunged into the task of perfecting his organization. "The connections were made between the office, the Bishops, the Diocesan Committees, and through them with the parishes, for we had in hand work in which every member of the Church was to take part." Bishop Lawrence rightly records: "Up to this time, before the War, there had been no campaign like it. Young Men's Christian Associations and other organizations had, of course, carried many drives for smaller amounts. There were no professional campaign firms, and but little skilled publicity. There were no precedents for the organization of our work, which covered the Church throughout the country and in the mission fields. . . . We had to blaze paths in many directions." [42]

And blaze paths he did, though he says "the first few weeks were like wandering through a bog under the mountain before one catches his breath above the trees." Like Ward and Pierce, Bishop Lawrence realized that a fund drive must be built upon a platform of public opinion conditioned by persuasive publicity. He thought publicity "was the great problem" because "there were no precedents." He tried two young men whose names he graciously did not record and found they would not do. Lawrence says he was "driven wild by their inabilities." In frustration he caught a train to Philadelphia to consult his friend Edward W. Bok, shrewd and successful magazine editor for the Curtis Publishing Company. Bok gave this public relations advice: " 'Go on as you are: only visualize your individuals; depict, describe your pathetic cases. Money for Belgium stopped flowing last summer; then I happened to see in the paper that Belgian babies wanted milk. We plastered the city with "Belgian babies want milk," and the flow began again. People give when their sympathies are touched.' " [43]

Elated by this guidance from a distinguished editor, Lawrence returned to New York and invited Ivy Lee to his office for a conference. By this time Lee had once more opened an office as an independent public relations counselor, though John D. Rockefeller, Jr., was still his principal client. Lee rejected Bok's advice, saying, "The sympathies of the American people are bruised and raw with the cry of Belgium; you cannot depict an old parson or his widow and orphan today in such a way to move people to give. Moreover, in the long run emotional appeals lose their force. The American people, intelligent, just, and generous to a cause that appeals to them, want facts and figures." [44] And a campaign of publicity based on facts more than on emotion is what these two shrewd students of public behavior agreed upon in conferences over the next week.

As one would expect of one so expert in promoting large philanthropic gifts, Lawrence possessed a shrewd sense of publicity and paid much attention to the press. He recorded in his memoirs on March 4, 1917: "At about 11 o'clock, as I was dozing, the thought suddenly struck me—this is the fourth of March, in an hour the President will quietly take his oath of office: for tomorrow is the ceremonial and the message. Monday's papers will lack news: here is a chance for a voice from Massachusetts to press and support the President towards leadership and action." And, as the bishop knew it would be, his telegram to President Wilson was featured Monday morning on the front pages "of every Boston paper" and many others, too. He wisely saw—long before many publicists realized it —that it is the content of publicity and not the quantity that counts in building public opinion. "Tons of paper and printer's ink are wasted every day . . . publicity should be so simple and clear that he who runneth may read." [45] The bishop wrote this in 1923 but many professional public relations practitioners still need to learn the lesson.

The first job, then, was organization and publicity. The facts of the Church Pension Fund campaign were announced on March 1, a Monday morning—always a time of little spot news and thus of maximum opportunity for publicists. "A majority of the daily papers throughout the country featured the statement that each bishop in his own diocese, North, South, East, and West, had said on Sunday morning that the average salary of a clergyman of the Episcopal Church was only $1,200 in probably the richest Church in the land. Simultaneous publicity was then in its infancy; by the courtesy of the New York papers we saturated the city with a few more facts, and attached to them the words, 'Church Pension Fund.' " Bishop Lawrence had learned that "if you expect a broad and popular support even the best cause must be linked up with some big cause, a problem touching the whole people." Lawrence and his associates realized that the pension system for the clergy of the Protestant Episcopal Church was a comparatively small cause in the public's eye, so they placed great stress on the provision for all elderly citizens, truly "a problem touching the whole people." For example, the bishop quickly won the support of Adolph Ochs, publisher of the powerful *New York Times* with the question, "Mr. Ochs, what are you going to do with the old people?"

As the publicity poured out, organization down through the church hierarchy was attended to, and soon "thousands of rivulets of assessments began to pour into the Church Pension Fund." By March 9 they had accumulated more than a million dollars in pledges and announced this news through a publicity release from the library of J. P. Morgan. Lawrence knew that a fund raiser must get a large initial gift or gifts to provide "thrust" to a money-raising campaign. On May 8, from Philadelphia, Lawrence announced through the Associated Press that the campaign had passed the $2 million mark.

Unlike the leaders of the "Y School" of fund raisers, Bishop Lawrence did not believe in making public the names of large donors, "but those who had large gifts in mind had a right to know who else were making them. Hence I carried with me on one or two sheets of paper, typewritten, a list: at the head was a list of the six donors to pay the expenses, amounting to $125,000. In this list my sister Sallie's name stood for $25,000 and mine for the same amount, that those who saw it might know that I was in the cause." [46] He had long followed Major Henry Higginson's advice: that leaders in a campaign must begin by "cutting into their own hides deeper than they expect any person whom they approach to cut into his." The cleric fund raiser explained the philosophy of not publicizing names of donors this way: ". . . in the long run those who give do not care about the public knowing it. If they give largely, their mail will be heavy with appeals; if in small figures, they would rather not be published." However, he always held that "a confidential list of large givers may rightfully be shown to those who consider giving largely." [47]

Once again the bishop's ability to organize carefully, publicize shrewdly, and persuasively lead a fund-raising campaign was demonstrated. In fact it became clear, as the drive deadline neared, that the Church Pension Fund would go over the announced goal of $5,064,000. And this posed a publicity problem. "Now that over five millions were in sight, were we under moral obligations to publish the fact?" He was under pressure from advisers in other parts of the country, especially the South, not to publish the fact that more than $5 million had been pledged because "the campaign was just beginning to move" at many points and publication of news of the goal having been reached would halt the flow of dollars. Bishop Lawrence agreed with these fears yet felt obliged to report the news. He finally solved his dilemma by giving "stuff to press for issue Monday night, putting in press general condition," and giving a more detailed report at a dinner Monday night, February 4, 1917, at the Waldorf-Astoria. The publicity of passing the $5 million mark nearly a month before the goal's deadline spurred gifts, rather than slowing or stopping them.[48]

On March 1—the campaign's deadline—Lawrence announced that pledges and cash had passed the $6 million mark, well beyond the original goal. The flood of contributions continued and by September, 1917, the total reached $8,750,000—making philanthropic history. By January 1, 1926, when Lawrence was writing his memoirs, this Pension Fund had grown to $20 million. Bishop Lawrence and his aides had successfully presented a nationwide church campaign for a rather narrow cause, viewed from the public standpoint, and raised nearly $9 million. Ward and Pierce had a new target to shoot at!

Bishop Lawrence had established himself, on the eve of World War I, as America's champion fund raiser. The wise bishop fully realized that "there are a thousand good causes but only a few of them may bring big money." Ability to organize and publicize a campaign for a cause usually made the difference. The importance of an effective public relations program in popular philanthropy was coming to be recognized—the lack of it would most likely bring frustration and failure. This lesson is to be seen in the early histories of the American Red Cross and the American Cancer Society, two of today's giants in the people's philanthropy of the United States.

Floundering Giants

Both the American National Red Cross and the American Cancer Society floundered about rather helplessly in the years prior to World War I for the basic reason that neither had learned the art of fund raising. The United States entry in World War I in April, 1917, was an event that would completely transform the Red Cross and make it the "Greatest Mother of Them All."

The American National Red Cross was on the verge of extinction in 1904. Active membership stood at 123 and its bank account at $1,702. The May 6, 1904, issue of the New York *Tribune*, termed

it "a discredited and decaying institution." The crisis inside the
Red Cross over the dictatorial rule of Clara Barton, its founder, was
eased on May 14, 1904, when she resigned her lifetime presidency.
Within less than six months, January, 1905, the Red Cross was incorporated under a new charter, passed by Congress and signed by
President Theodore Roosevelt, who had helped ease Miss Barton
out in favor of Miss Mabel T. Boardman. The new American National Red Cross was a feeble infant indeed. In its first year under
the new charter it spent only $2,902, most of which came from re-
sources of $10,000 which had been turned over to the new organi-
zation by Clara Barton. The enrolled membership in 1905 was 3,337
persons. Although it had been in existence a quarter of a century,
the American Red Cross had, in the words of the Madison Avenue
advertising man, "little public visibility." The dramatic and disas-
trous San Francisco earthquake changed this situation quite abruptly.

On April 18, 1906, when "hell itself seemed to explode in San
Francisco," President Theodore Roosevelt responded quickly and
named the Red Cross as "the best fitted organization to take over
relief work in the stricken city." Roosevelt acted without consult-
ing the Central Committee and placed a great burden on an organization which barely existed. Hurd says that "the Red Cross contributed mightily to the relief work in San Francisco, and it can be
added with equal honesty that the experience and reputation gained
by the new Red Cross in that work saved it from a questionable
fate. After San Francisco, the Red Cross was in business for keeps." [49]
Again the Red Cross followed the Barton plan of appealing for supplies and funds only at a time of disaster. More than $3 million was
contributed through the Red Cross for relief of victims of the San
Francisco earthquake.

Save for the appeals for supplies and money in time of disaster,
the Red Cross in those years tried to maintain itself on the dues
collected from members, a shaky support indeed. Publicity received
in the San Francisco relief work had caused Red Cross membership
to spurt to 9,262 members by the end of that year. But by 1907 this
figure had dropped to less than 6,000. Miss Boardman and her associates realized that the Red Cross must undertake a campaign to
inform the public and to recruit members. The *Red Cross Bulletin*
said frankly: "Publicity, in point of fact, is the great present need.
Relatively few people know what the Red Cross is." [50] The Red
Cross made a two-pronged attack on this problem of dwindling

financial support: it prepared documents almost legalistic in scope intended for the major societies whose support it must have; and in January, 1908, Miss Boardman persuaded the Executive Committee to hire Edward R. Johnstone, New York press agent, to solicit members. He was given the title of national registrar and a $6,000 salary, plus a commission on new members brought in.

Johnstone, a high-pressure press agent typical of the early 1900's, argued that "the only way to get big results is to make big expenditures." He convinced Miss Boardman that a goal of a million members was entirely possible. In this he was not wrong, only premature. Johnstone was to get a commission of 2½ percent on the first $50,000 net secured through his efforts at the end of the year; 5 per cent if the net passed $100,000. The breezy Johnstone was assisted by Dr. Louis Klopsch, editor of the *Christian Herald*. His efforts failed to achieve the spectacular results that he had promised and he was fired after a few months. The year 1908 closed with an enrollment of nearly 12,000 members. The Central Committee reported: "While the propaganda resulted in the accession of several thousand new members, the net result of the efforts did not justify the hopes that had been entertained of a large increase in membership. The cost of this work was paid from the fund created by the donors and without any inroads upon the resources of the Association." [51] Here we see the ever-present sensitivity of fund seekers to the common donor complaint of using gift moneys for fund raising.

The Red Cross not only felt disappointment when Johnstone failed to achieve his bright promises but was a bit taken aback by his aggressive publicity program. It should be said, in fairness, that Johnstone did double the Red Cross membership, and his publicity was a decade ahead of its time. One Red Cross historian, G. R. Gaeddert, has noted: "the experiment of 1908 must be regarded as the parent of the annual roll call so successfully used by Henry P. Davison." A writer in *New Outlook* pointed out that in the year 1908, when the American Red Cross netted $8,000 in annual dues, the Japanese Red Cross received over $1 million from its 1.5 million members. In spite of the increase in interest brought by the ARC's work at San Francisco and Johnstone's publicity campaign, the Red Cross was still financially feeble.

But in 1908, it will be recalled, the Red Cross hit upon its first fund-raising jackpot when Emily P. Bissell introduced the idea of the Tuberculosis Christmas seal. The T.B. Seal Sale evolved into a plan for Red Cross volunteers to sell the seals, at one dollar for a sheet of 100. The receipts from the 1908 sale brought in only $165,-899 but by 1916 the seal sale receipts for the Red Cross topped the $1 million mark. Charles Hurd estimates that "in the decade that the Red Cross developed, promoted, and sold the seals . . . sales aggregated $5,652,500, from which the Red Cross took a total of $489,800 and made a profit of $285,000.[52] The T.B. Seal Sale figures for this decade are as follows: 1908–$135,000; 1909–$250,-000; 1910–$300,000; 1911–$320,000; 1912–$402,256.09; 1913–$449,504.95; 1914–$555,854.13; 1915–$760,000; 1916–$1,040,810.02. The income from these sales encouraged the Red Cross to hire its first full-time administrator, Ernest P. Bicknell, a man with both newspaper and social work experience and one of the heroes of the rescue work in the San Francisco earthquake. When Johnstone was discharged, his place was taken by Bicknell, a believer in a more conservative, long-term public relations program. He was given the title national director, and the decade from 1908 to our entry into the World War in 1917 are known in Red Cross circles as "the Bicknell years."

It was a loose-knit, somewhat chaotic and feeble organization that Bicknell took over. "Problems of organization confronted us on all sides. . . . Inherited from a previous regime there existed at this time a partly developed system of State Branches and local groups called sub-divisions. This system was found not practicable as set up."[53] To correct this, Bicknell devised three classes of organization: chapters—the designation given local bodies which were made directly responsible to national headquarters; state boards—set up solely to collect and disburse relief funds when disasters occurred; and institutional members—the charity organization societies of the country, carefully chosen for "the high character of their work." Bicknell claims that "this happy arrangement met universal favor." He terms the period 1908–1913 "the organization era" of the Red Cross.

In addition to the small revenue from membership dues and the somewhat larger income from T.B. Seal Sales, the Red Cross obtained several large endowment gifts during this period. On December 1, 1908, the Red Cross endowment fund was worth $34,-634.25, and by the same day in 1913 the fund stood at $923,489.47. This was largely the result of Miss Boardman's untiring solicitation among her well-to-do friends. In her fund raising Miss Boardman had the support of President William Howard Taft, who was honorary president of the Red Cross.

James A. Scrymser offered $100,000 toward construction of a national headquarters building as "a monument to the loyal women of the Civil War," and suggested that the Red Cross raise $400,000 for this purpose and that Congress match it with a $400,000 appropriation. In this way the "Marble Palace" was built a stone's throw from the White House. In addition to Scrymser, the contributors were: Mrs. Russell Sage, $150,000; Mrs. E. H. Harriman, $50,000; and the Rockefeller Foundation, $100,000. The building was occupied on the eve of World War I. Under Bicknell's leadership Red Cross membership climbed slowly, but it did climb. By 1915 there were 22,000 members in 145 chapters scattered across the United States.

Interest and membership in the Red Cross had been accelerated by the Ohio River Valley flood of 1913 and the outbreak of war in Europe in 1914. The Ohio flood brought the first large-scale disaster operation under the reorganized Red Cross and was marked by extensive use of a staff of social workers borrowed from institutional members. In September, 1914, the *Red Cross*, a ship chartered by the ARC, sailed for Europe one month after the outbreak of war, carrying doctors, nurses, and medical supplies. (These hospital units were withdrawn from Europe in October, 1915.)

Both these events provided news pegs which the Red Cross publicists fully exploited. After the unhappy experience with Johnstone, the ARC was slow to set up a public relations department. A Division of Information was formed in 1914 and Austin Cunningham, Washington correspondent of the San Antonio *Express*, was hired as its director. To capitalize on the accelerating interest in the Red Cross that followed the start of war, a Membership Bureau was started in April, 1915, under Lewis E. Stein. Membership promotion began to take more and more of the publicity effort and ultimately the publicity function was virtually taken over by the Membership Bureau. From 22,449 members in 105 chapters in December, 1915, the membership increased to over 286,000 by December, 1916.[54] This growth was supported by an active public relations program. From 1908 to 1914 thirty-two articles appeared in national magazines publicizing the work of the Red Cross. The daily press had heavily publicized the role of the Red Cross in the San Francisco and Ohio Valley disasters.

This sharp spurt in Red Cross membership came from the Midas touch of Charles Sumner Ward, whose prowess in raising funds was by now widely known among philanthropic and social leaders. Ward was invited to Washington to confer with Red Cross officials on ways and means of increasing support for the Red Cross now that the dark war clouds of Europe were drifting toward our shores. Ward outlined a membership campaign and recommended that the Red Cross hire Harvey J. Hill to direct it; Hill, a young, energetic YMCA secretary was already widely known among fund raisers for his limitless energy and hot temper. Ward had met Hill in 1913 when Hill was general secretary of the Hazleton, Pa., YMCA and quickly spotted him as a "go-getter." It was Hill who finally persuaded Ward to leave the Y and set up his own commercial firm in 1919. Arnaud Marts says that Hill, as one of the founders, was "the dynamic and audacious member of the group."

In May, 1916, the Red Cross announced that it had hired Hill "who has done constructive work for the Young Men's Christian Association, and is therefore especially fitted to serve the Red Cross as membership builder." Granted a leave from the YMCA, Hill set to work, using tested techniques to build a membership base upon which a wartime structure might be safely constructed.

The growing membership required a more extensive change and at the end of 1916 the Executive Committee created "a special organization for handling all chapter and membership matters, making it an administrative department, directly under the supervision of the chairman." Hill's first effort was to promote establishment of Red Cross chapters in every county in the United States as groundwork for the all-out drive in 1917, destined to be a fateful year for all Americans and to transform the American Red Cross into a fundraising giant.

Another American fund-raising giant had its beginnings in this prewar era. In 1913, in the United States alone, more than 75,000 persons were dying each year of cancer and the number of victims was increasing at a rapid rate, mainly because of "medical fatalism and public ignorance." In 1900 cancer had ranked seventh in the causes of death, but by 1913 it had advanced to fourth, coming after circulatory diseases, tuberculosis, and Bright's disease. Public attitudes toward cancer in that period were an amalgam of "fear, fatalism, and ignorance." A few doctors and laymen decided something had to be done. This was a time "when discontent with the *status quo* was as acute in medicine as in social work." [55] Conviction among medical leaders crystallized at the May, 1912, convention of the American Gynecology Society when a motion was passed directing "the three men who have been doing the most work in regard to the propaganda of cancer, Drs. LeRoy Brown, Howard C. Taylor, and Frederick J. Taussig be appointed a committee . . . to draw up a plan of action."

In March, 1913, this committee met with Dr. Clement Cleveland, outstanding New York gynecologist, and asked him to appoint a committee to aid in establishing a national cancer society. These efforts were speeded by talks heard and publicized in the 1913 convention of the AGS. There doctors, and indirectly the public, were told that "the cancer death rate is increasing" and there was an imperative need "for educating the public at large in the absolute necessity of operative treatment at the earliest indications of cancerous growths. At the same meeting Dr. H. C. Taylor said, "There is beyond question a perfectly legitimate use, even for a medical man, of the publicity man and the press agent. He is constantly used in the political world and there is no reason why we should not also use him to accomplish medical ends." [56] Again, recognition was given to the importance of publicity.

In response to these urgings a meeting was held late in the afternoon of May 22, 1913, at the Harvard Club in New York City. Out of this meeting came the American Society for the Control of Cancer "to disseminate knowledge concerning the symptoms, treatment, and prevention of cancer, to investigate conditions under which cancer is found, and to compile statistics in regard thereto." [57] "Our society was founded for lay education," Dr. Taylor wrote. Dr. Livingston Farrand, then executive secretary of the National Association for the Study and Prevention of Tuberculosis, advised the cancer battlers that they faced the same task as that encountered by the Tuberculosis Association. "You have not only the ignorance of the laity to contend with, but curiously the ignorance of the medical profession as well. I speak frankly from my knowledge with regard to tuberculosis." Education of both the public and the medical profession then became the prime objective of the Cancer Society in these formative years. But this would take money. Both education and fund raising were public relations tasks.

The sparkplug of the Cancer Society in its early years was Mrs. Robert G. Mead, energetic daughter of Dr. Cleveland, chairman of the organizational meeting. Elsie Mead soon became, in fact as well as in title, "chairman of ways and means." "Her persistent enthusiasm kept the society afloat. It also kept the physicians mopping their brows. They might have been content with their new responsibilities, helping insurance companies prepare educational leaflets, issuing more leaflets of their own . . . but Elsie was forever bursting with additional projects . . ."[58]

The Cancer Society's program in those early years was modest and no great sums of money were needed. Even so, the small amounts required came with some difficulty, and the Society was still remote from becoming the national large-scale money raiser it is today. Mrs. Mead "almost singlehandedly developed the financial foundations of the Society." In 1915 officers of the impoverished Society decided that it must have a "guarantee fund" of $15,000 in the bank in case membership fees did not bring in enough for the limited educational program it had undertaken. Mrs. Mead, between November 8 and December 8, 1915, obtained pledges of $1,000 each from fifteen of her friends and for this the board gave her a "unanimous and hearty vote of thanks." The membership fee was put at $5. In 1913 there were 174 members, in 1915 this number had grown to 394, and by 1916 the total was past the 700 mark.[59]

The membership and interest in the Society were gaining momentum until public attention was diverted to participation in World War I. One writer commented in 1916, "the war effort claims everyone's attention and, in consequence, the work of the Society is handicapped but nevertheless continues." The report of the treasurer for the year ending December 31, 1915, showed a total expenditure of $6,997—a far cry from the American Cancer Society that today raises more than $30 million in an annual fund drive, pressures government to spend hundreds of millions on cancer research, and educates the populace on the "Seven Danger Signals of Cancer." Application of the skills and the power of public relations and fund raising would make the difference—as it does for all organizations—in the American Cancer Society, as it would come to be named, during World War II, not World War I. Here, too, was a slumbering philanthropic giant, waiting for the Midas touch of promoter and fund raiser. This would prove to be Albert Lasker, father of American advertising, who changed many of the nation's mores and made millions doing it.

NOTES

1. William H. Allen, *Modern Philanthropy. A Study of Efficient Appealing and Giving* (New York: Dodd, Mead, 1912), pp. 311–312.

2. *Ibid.*, Preface, p. vii.

3. *Ibid.*, pp. 280–281.

4. From manuscript of talk by Elwood Street given in 1949, supplied to the author by Mr. Street.

5. *Financial Federations*, Report of Special Committee of American Association for Organizing Charity, p. 141.

6. *Ibid.*, pp. 229–230.

7. "Chronological History of United Fund-Raising," mimeographed outline in files of United Community Funds and Councils of America, New York City.

8. William J. Norton, *The Cooperative Movement in Social Work*, p. 71.

9. *Ibid.*, p. 70.

10. *Ibid.*, pp. 68–69.

11. Charles Whiting Williams, "Cleveland's Federated Givers," *Review of Reviews*, V. 48 (October, 1913), p. 472.

12. Anon., "Putting the 'Cleave' in 'Cleaveland,'" *Survey*, Vol. 30 (July 5, 1913), p. 448.

13. *Ibid.*, p. 447.

14. Report of Special Committee of AAOC, *op. cit.*, p. 9.

15. *Ibid.*, pp. 63–64.

16. *Ibid.*, pp. 248–253.

17. *Ibid.*, p. 87.

18. William C. White in Memo addressed to "The Central Council of Social Agencies," dated May 20, 1916, giving report of his investigation of federated fund raising.

19. *Ibid.*

20. Norton, *op. cit.*, p. 279.

21. *Ibid.*

22. Bogen, *Jewish Philanthropy* (New York: Macmillan, 1917), p. 56.

23. C. M. Bookman, "The Community Chest Movement," paper read at National Conference on Social Work, Toronto, Ont., June, 1924, p. 5.

24. Charles S. Ward, *The Intensive Financial Campaign* (New York: YMCA), p. 3.

25. *Ibid.*

26. Letter from Cornelius Smith, Aug. 9, 1961.

27. In Proceedings of Marts & Lundy, Inc., Fourth Annual Staff Conference, Aug. 2–4, 1948, p. 55.

28. Chicago *Daily News,* dispatch from London dated Jan. 19 appearing in issue of that date; no byline.

29. Nov. 11, 1913.

30. In article, "Ward's Handpicked Millions," *Munsey's,* Vol. 51 (March, 1914), p. 322.

31. Information contained in letter from Judith Campbell, University of Pittsburgh, after a search of the university files. Letter to author, dated Aug. 2, 1961.

32. Carlton G. Ketchum in Memorandum dated March 1, 1960, addressed to David S. Ketchum, "Material for Article on the History and Trends of Fund Raising Campaigns for Colleges and Universities." In that firm's files.

33. Letter from Carlton Ketchum, Sept. 6, 1961.

34. *Ibid.*

35. William A. Littell, "Washington Calling . . ." *Philanthropy,* Summer, 1955, p. 94.

36. Interview with Dr. Marts in New York City, March, 1960.

37. Clipping in Lyman Pierce Scrapbook, State Historical Society of Wisconsin.

38. Ketchum Memorandum, *op. cit.*

39. Ward, *op. cit.,* pp. 9–10.

40. William Lawrence, *Memories of a Happy Life,* p. 344.

41. Lawrence, *The Story of the Pension Fund,* a pamphlet, p. 13.

42. Lawrence, *Memories of a Happy Life,* pp. 365–366.

43. *Ibid.,* p. 368.

44. *Ibid.*

45. Lawrence, "An Invigorating Avocation," *Atlantic,* Vol. 132 (September, 1923), p. 322.

46. Lawrence, *Memories of a Happy Life,* p. 375.

47. Lawrence, "An Invigorating Avocation," *Atlantic.*

48. Lawrence, *Memories of a Happy Life,* p. 377.

49. Charles W. Hurd, *The Compact Story of the American Red Cross* (New York: Hawthorn, 1959), p. 119.

50. American National Red Cross *Bulletin,* Vol. II, No. 4, p. 56.

51. American National Red Cross *Bulletin,* October, 1908, preface.

52. Hurd, *op. cit.,* p. 126.

53. Ernest P. Bicknell, *Pioneering with the Red Cross* (New York: Macmillan, 1935), p. 95.

54. Red Cross Annual Report for 1916, p. 6.

55. Richard Carter, *The Gentle Legions*, p. 143. © 1961 by Richard Carter. © 1959 by The Curtis Publishing Company. Reprinted by permission of Doubleday & Co., Inc.

56. *Transactions American Gynecological Society*, Vol. 38 (1913), p. 454.

57. *The American Society for the Control of Cancer*, published by the ASCC.

58. Carter, *op. cit.*, pp. 144–145.

59. Minutes of Executive Committee ASCC as quoted by Donald F. Shaughnessy in "History of the American Cancer Society," unpublished Ph.D. thesis, Columbia University, p. 34.

4

World War I and the Big Drive

The Red Cross Raises $114 Million in Eight Days

In the pre-dawn of April 1, 1917, in the White House, just hours before he was to ask Congress **to** declare war on Germany and the Central Powers, a tortured, troubled Woodrow Wilson told Frank Cobb, editor of the New York *World*, "this war will overturn the world we have known." It certainly did. When America shelved Wilson's crusade for domestic reform and set out under his leadership to "make the world safe for democracy," the nation set in motion forces that were drastically to change its way of life. Many were the consequences that would flow from the pervasive, powerful dynamism of our participation in World War I. Among them was the big nationwide fund drive that would bring the people's philanthropy we know today.

It was a confused, unprepared nation that President Wilson led into World War I. Arthur Link the historian holds

> . . . the American people entered the First World War, not knowing what the struggle was about or the objectives for which their new friends and enemies were fighting. . . .
>
> For Wilson's failure to educate the people to a realization of their vital stake in the outcome of the war, the American people paid a fearful price in divisions and doubts and organized efforts to sell the war to them. . . .
>
> In a stumbling manner . . . the American democracy organized for war. The industrial and military mobilization thus hastily accomplished produced the food, materiél, ships, and manpower that tipped the balance and broke the deadlock on the western front in 1918.[1]

Truly, this young industrial giant did not know its strength until forced to flex its muscles in a European war.

America's lack of readiness and ultimate all-out response to fighting a world war is fully exemplified in the story of the American National Red Cross. When Congress declared war on the Central Powers April 6, 1917, the Red Cross was far from ready to cope with the task that would be assigned to it. Yet by the end of the war it had become the world's largest relief agency. During its twenty months' operation under the War Council, the Red Cross made a phenomenal growth in every phase of its operations, originated new services, developed old ones more fully. From an organization forced to beg for money and for members, it grew into an agency closely identified with the national government, and one of world renown. In the process Americans were taught to give in the hundreds of millions in a national drive, not in thousands at the community level. And the art of fund raising became a polished art indeed.

When war came to America the Red Cross had a membership of 486,194 in 372 chapters scattered across the nation, $200,000 in working funds, and was loosely organized under the active direction of Eliot Wadsworth who carried the title of vice-chairman of the Central Committee. Former President William Howard Taft, then a none-too-active chairman, in August, 1916, persuaded Wadsworth, wealthy Bostonian and Harvard graduate, to accept the post without pay. Though only forty years old, Wadsworth had both executive and direct relief experience. In 1915 he had served in Europe with the Rockefeller Foundation European War Relief Commission. Miss Mabel Boardman was in the process of being eased out of power in the Red Cross just as she had maneuvered to shelve Clara Barton thirteen years before. Miss Boardman was completely bypassed with the creation of the American Red Cross War Council. In response to her protests, Chairman Taft admonished her: "You seem to be drifting into a bitter cleavage that does not make for the usefulness of the association." The Red Cross was gaining strength under Wadsworth when the war broke, but it was still not strong enough to carry the burdens that President Wilson would soon place upon it.

In April, 1917, the European war relief picture was chaotic and confused. In December, 1916, Wadsworth wrote to a friend that he had to deal with more than 130 societies, church organizations, relief societies and the like in distributing relief abroad.[2] The result was that foreign war relief, which obviously could have been better managed by a few well-organized, coordinated groups, was being distributed by more than a hundred. The Red Cross itself still had not learned that only by establishing an active chapter in every county in the Union would it be able to harness and use the interest and support of the civic-minded American people. A drastic overhaul of the Red Cross organization and its fund-raising methods was needed to equip it for participation in war. This was not long in coming.

A little more than a month after the United States entered the war, President Wilson created the Red Cross War Council and entrusted to it "the duty of responding to the extraordinary demands which the present war will make upon the services of the Red Cross both in the field and in civilian relief." He added, "The best way in which to impart the greatest efficiency and energy to the relief work which this war will entail will be to concentrate it in the hands of a single experienced organization which has been recognized by law and by international convention as the public instrumentality for such purposes." [3] The recommendation for the War Council had grown out of a meeting on April 21 of top Red Cross officials and nationally known civic leaders whom President Wilson had invited to advise him.

The meeting was promoted by Eliot Wadsworth and presided over by Cleveland H. Dodge, the temporary chairman. The President was represented in this meeting by U.S. Secretary of War Newton D. Baker, former Cleveland mayor. Speaking from his Cleveland experience, Baker strongly urged that the Red Cross was the agency which had both national and international recognition, and that it would be better to combine all relief efforts and do whatever had to be done through one organization. Baker outlined a long list of services that could and should be provided the armed forces.

The War Council displaced the existing leadership. "Former President Taft, still officially Chairman of the Central Committee, withdrew even more from direct participation in the society's affairs; Miss Boardman found herself largely ignored, and other members of the Central Committee were called upon to ratify decisions already made rather than to determine policy. Only Wadsworth, who was prepared to co-operate with the new leadership in every way, remained actively on the scene as a representative of pre-war days." [4] This is revealed in the fact that the Red Cross Executive Committee confirmed President Wilson's War Council order two days after it was published.

The War Council brought the leadership and methods of big business to the Red Cross. Wilson appointed Henry F. Davison, a partner in the firm of J. P. Morgan, as chairman. At first President Wilson was quite reluctant to appoint Davison or anyone else from Wall Street but was finally persuaded to do so by Cleveland H. Dodge, who worked through Wilson's confidant, Colonel Edward House. Wilson and Dodge had been warm friends since their student days at Princeton and Dodge was one Wall Streeter trusted by Wilson. Davison, then fifty years of age, was known to his friends as Harry, the name his parents had given him. He had later changed his name to Henry Pomeroy Davison. A member of the Morgan firm since 1909, he was described as "a man with keen insight, ability and courage and one whose judgment was highly respected." [5] Certainly he was a man of action. He took over the day the order was published and gave each member of the War Council staff a definite assignment. For himself he kept the publicity responsibility, thus giving public relations top priority.

To direct the tremendous task of raising the money needed to finance the activities assigned the Red Cross by Wilson, Davison summoned the champion money-raiser, Charles Sumner Ward, who served for the duration of the war on loan from the International Committee of the YMCA. Ward was given the title of secretary of the War Finance Committee. Ward then made Harvey J. Hill, already on the Red Cross membership bureau staff, his associate secretary. Early in June, Davison added another future fund raiser to the staff when he made Robert F. Duncan recorder of the War Council. Duncan, then twenty-seven, was secretary of the Harvard Endowment Fund Committee of which Davison's partner at the J. P. Morgan Company, Thomas W. Lamont, was chairman. A minor official in the War Council, Duncan would later make his mark with John Price Jones and Kersting, Brown & Company.

In a few weeks Davison persuaded Ivy L. Lee, the public relations counselor to John D. Rockefeller, Jr., and other industrialists, to become his personal assistant in charge of public relations.

Apropos of the coming of Davison, Lee, and Ward to the management of the Red Cross is this comment of Alfred McClung Lee:

With war fever obliterating such peace-time pursuits as muckraking, corporation heads, hitherto anathematized, were called to places of power. Millionaires, supposed to be the only ones to know how to think and act in millions and billions, were given charge of Government's "big business." And it "was not uncommon for the 'dollar a year' patriot to have his $10,000-a-year press agent." [6]

In his history of the Red Cross, Dulles describes Davison "as a man of great energy and vision who could command the services of any businessman in the United States upon whom he might call to do any particular job—someone who could make the Red Cross a '50 million dollar proposition instead of a 5 million dollar one.'" [7] The War Council, headed by Davison, represented a practical solution to the problem presented by the fact that the Red Cross, like all other agencies, was unprepared for war when it came. Davison brought to the Red Cross not only his administrative acumen but also the confidence of the rich men of business whose support the Red Cross must have if it was to raise big sums of money. As Dodge pointed out, "The great trouble is that the business men of this country today have not much confidence in the Red Cross due largely to the fact that until comparatively recently the organization of the Red Cross was not effective." [8]

The period from May 10, 1917, when it was first organized, to August 31, 1917, when the Council issued its first comprehensive organization chart, was "the formative period of study, program planning, selection of personnel and organization of machinery—including the $100,000,000 campaign to finance the organization. During this period the national officers defined the organization's functions and, to a large measure, its scope and authority in a war crisis." [9] Thus did the third generation of Red Cross leaders take over. Two important influences were introduced into the administration and policies of the Red Cross that would shape the organization from then on—the thinking and methods of Big Business and of Big Government. President Wilson placed it within the structure of the federal government by making it the nation's official relief agency in time of war or disaster, as well as an auxiliary of the armed forces. Davison brought the thinking and tight, clean administrative methods of Wall Street to the new "Marble Palace" that housed the Red Cross in Washington.

One of the first tasks of the War Council was to determine how much money would be needed and how to go about getting it. On the eve of the April 21 meeting called by President Wilson at Wadsworth's suggestion, Henry Morgenthau, Wadsworth, Dodge, and a few others dined together to discuss this problem. They agreed that the money should be raised in a great nationwide popular subscription but disagreed on how much could be raised. Morgenthau records, "The impression of all those present with the exception of myself, was that about five, or at the most ten, millions could be raised for this purpose." [10] Morgenthau scoffed at this and insisted that at least $50 million could be raised. "The next day, when the committee was in session, I made the proposition and was astonished that none of those present at first grasped the idea that the American people could be induced to subscribe fifty million dollars. I then spoke a second time and told the committee that the America Jews alone (of whom there were only three million) were then engaged in raising a fund of ten million dollars for their co-religionists abroad." [11] American philanthropists and businessmen had not been taught to think of philanthropy in terms of millions raised from the general public.

When Davison heard Morgenthau's figure he scoffed too—not because he thought the sum too much to raise, but too little. Morgenthau reports Davison as saying, "Mr. Morgenthau's proposal is absurd—absurdly inadequate. At least one hundred million dollars will be required and that is the amount we must determine to raise." Associates of Charles Sumner Ward insist that it was he who persuaded the War Council to undertake a drive for $100 million, not $50 million.

Dreshman, Ward's one-time partner, records, "Ward said he thought 100 million could be raised" and that "the council, incredulous at first, finally accepted this figure." [12] Dreshman's memo was based on his long association and conversations with Ward, so here again we find victory being claimed by many. There are other versions of how the unheard-of amount of $100 million was set as the goal. According to Dulles, Eliot Wadsworth told the story that one day Davison came into Wadsworth's office and said flatly, "We will make it $100,000,000." The goal was probably a joint decision. Thus America's first great nationwide fund drive was launched.

Chairman Davison confidently sounded the keynote for the first drive when he assumed the chairmanship of the War Council: "The Red Cross has given me a new conception of America and the

American spirit. It is with the zeal of a convert that I invite the American people to come in with me under President Wilson and make it the nationwide organization that is demanded by these times. . . . Our job in the American Red Cross is to bind up the wounds of a bleeding world." [13] The International Committee of the YMCA gallantly responded to Davison's requests for Ward's services to direct the big drive. He had little more than a month to get the nationwide campaign organized.

Ward swung into action, with Harvey Hill as his right-hand man. Next he sent an urgent plea to his old partner, Lyman Pierce, to ask him to take charge of the campaign in the states west of the Mississippi. A letter from President Wilson dated May 19, 1917, drafted Pierce to serve as executive secretary of the western section of the Red Cross War Finance Committee. Wilson wrote Pierce: "The enterprise which you will present to the leaders of the business and professional life in the West is at this time one of the most important contributions to the country's welfare which any patriotic citizen can make." [14] Pierce was serving as general secretary of the San Francisco YMCA when the call came. His services, too, were lent to the government for this cause.

The prestige and popularity of the nation's leader in war, President Wilson, was put behind the big drive when he proclaimed the week of June 18–25 as National Red Cross Week, one of the first intensive uses of the "week" idea in publicity. President Wilson's proclamations were copied by governors and mayors of cities, thus presaging another standard device of today's fund raising. The drive was opened with observance of Red Cross Sunday, June 17, in the nation's churches, where parishioners heard religious admonitions of their duty to aid the suffering and the homeless in time of war. Pulpit, press, and people responded in the fervor of war-born emotions and before the eight-day drive was done a total of $114,023,-640.23 had been collected, an oversubscription of 14 per cent. History had been made as the American people saw what large sums could be attained through the intensive fund-raising campaign hitherto used only at the community level for charity or a civic or church building. "The humanitarian impulses of the Amercan people had blossomed forth as a counterpoise to the brutality of war." This drive came right on the heels of the first Liberty Bond drive.

Although given great impetus by the feverish war spirit gripping the country by this time, the great outpouring of dollars was in no sense spontaneous. It was a systematic Ward campaign, however hurriedly organized. A quota was set for each city, town, and hamlet to give it a goal to reach, and a representative local committee put in charge. A proportion of the "war-drive" contributions collected within a community or county was retained by the local chapter or organization. City was matched against city in the fund-raising competition—an old technique of Ward's. The War Council utilized the services of community leaders and nationally known persons in carrying the appeal to every citizen. Dulles records: "Campaign material assiduously compiled at national headquarters was made available to countless volunteer speakers. They addressed gatherings in churches and schools, appeared on the platforms at luncheons of Rotary, Kiwanis, the Lions and other social or fraternal organizations, and interrupted theater performances, moving picture shows and popular entertainments . . . every existing agency of communication was utilized to promote the Red Cross cause." [15]

This unprecedented generosity blossomed in a fertile public opinion plowed by the shattering events of a great war, planted by intensive large-scale publicity programs, and then systematically harvested by Ward's organizational techniques for raising money. Ammunition for the first big Red Cross fund drive was provided in the form of advertising copy contributed by public-spirited advertisers, streetcar signs, banners across Main Street, lantern slides, sermons, lectures, speeches, and publicity in the nation's newspapers and magazines. All media vied to promote the cause of the Red Cross and thus prove their patriotism. President Wilson lent his prestige and idealism to the plea for funds with frequent statements. At every turn the American people were pressed to contribute. The *North American Review* told Philadelphians to aid "the hand uplifted over Hate," while the San Francisco *Chronicle* told its readers "there is no worthier cause than this" and that they "should give and give freely to the Red Cross fund." The Kansas City *Star* thundered, "Kansas City must have no slackers."

Ward realized the need to decentralize the national headquarters machinery of the Red Cross if he was to get the campaign organized in time for the kickoff on Monday, June 18. The country was mapped into four divisions, each with a director in charge, and under these were 114 field agents and an office force that grew to more than 300 members. The Red Cross still did not have its chapter in every county and "was not ready to deliver the message, awaken the interest, and get results." The size of Ward's task in getting this tremendous nationwide net organized in less than six weeks is seen in the fact that, finally, there were 3,929 campaign committees to cover the United States. For the campaign and collection expenses for this first wartime drive, the Red Cross spent $278,114.27 at the national level and it was estimated that the local committees or chapters spent another $500,000 for this purpose. It was claimed that "costs were less than seven-tenths of one cent for each dollar collected." [16]

Typical of the way the drive was carried out was the way Lyman Pierce, with his characteristic energy and drive, went at the job in the West. First he organized his home city of San Francisco. San Franciscans were told:

> San Francisco will raise $1,000,000 for the Red Cross National Fund for hospital work abroad, the care of dependents at home and general relief and rehabilitation work in devastated districts of Europe to be carried on by the Red Cross War Council. This sum must be pledged in full during National Red Cross Week from June 18 to June 25. . . .
> Campaign teams will be organized with from five to ten members. These teams will scour the districts for donations to be reported twice daily. Progress will be announced by public bulletins in Red Cross Centers from day to day. . . . Contributions will be acknowledged in the form of a pledge and may be made in four monthly payments. Liberty Bonds will be accepted as contributions. [17]

San Francisco organized, Pierce left the city on May 30 for a swing around the states west of the Mississippi, to set community goals and organize committees to reach them "in full" by June 25. Associated with Pierce in organizing the West in this first Red Cross drive were H. L. Corbett of Portland, Ore., John B. Miller, of Los Angeles, and Lawrence C. Phipps, Sr., of Denver.

Prodded by patriotism and the pressure generated by local committees determined to meet city quotas, rich and poor gave in the nation's first great outpouring of charity dollars. The rich men led the way to the collection box. The Rockefeller Foundation gave $5 million. George F. Baker, New York banker, started the New York City drive with $1 million. The drive brought the first major gifts in corporate philanthropy. The General Electric Company declared an extra dividend of $1 million and turned this over to the Red Cross. Anaconda Copper accepted the challenge and contributed a dividend of $1.5 million. Bethlehem Steel gave $600,000. Henry Ford, always with an eye alert to profitable publicity, gave 5,000 Model T cars to the Red Cross for its use.

The large gifts from wealthy philanthropists and from the corporations provided dramatic examples, but the contributions of middle-class America giving on a hitherto undreamed-of scale provided the bulk of the $114 million. Many factory workers, for example, gave a day's pay. The total collected represented more than one dollar for every man, woman, and child in the United States. This, *The Independent* held, was "further evidence that the public considered the Red Cross the agent of the whole American people, assigned to the relief of the suffering brought by war and disaster." [18]

Yet the *Literary Digest* noted some curious contrasts in the first 1917 drive when some towns reported as high as 95 per cent of the adult population giving to the Red Cross, while in Cincinnati only about 1½ per cent were moved to contribute.[19] Even so, this 1½ per cent gave "more than a million dollars." Cincinnati, oddly enough, a pioneer in federated giving, had long been noted for its generosity to local charities. All in all the June, 1917, drive demonstrated deep public support for the Red Cross, widened the horizons of public philanthropy, and raised the sights of the growing army of professional fund raisers. Little wonder that the *Outlook* called the results "generous and gratifying."

The publicity forces for this historic fund drive were augmented when the Red Cross Executive Committee, on May 12, 1917, hired Thomas R. Shipp & Company as "publicity agents" at the rate of $250 a week. The exact date when this arrangement was terminated cannot be established, but it apparently lasted six weeks, as there is a statement of July 1, 1917, that Mr. Shipp was leaving his position as "director of publicity" since the goal of $100 million had been reached.[20] Apparently Shipp was released when Ivy Lee came to the ARC on a full-time basis.

The Red Cross Booms Its Membership

The contagion of the war's fervent patriotism brought a boom in Red Cross membership. Some of the new members came in spontaneously but most were brought in by Harvey J. Hill's systematic solicitation. Hill had been recruited the year before to build up Red Cross membership and was hopefully headed toward a goal of a million members by December, 1917. The war quickly changed all this. Within a few days after America's entry into the war, national headquarters began receiving applications for membership averaging 3,000 to 4,000 a day. Some joined "for humanity's sake," others to support a son off to the army, but most joined as an act of patriotism. Ridgewood, N.J., with a total population of 7,000 enlisted 2,000 Red Cross members in two weeks; Bridgeport, Conn., enrolled 20,000 in ten days. Even the total inmate population of Michigan's Jackson Prison enrolled as Red Cross recruits.[21] Although the impetus of war was responsible for stimulating the mushroom growth of chapters and membership, most of the credit was due the leadership of Hill. He worked closely with Edgar H. Wells, formerly general secretary of the Harvard Alumni Association, and Charles J. O'Connor, director and assistant director of chapters, respectively. Assisting them in promotion were the division directors and state boards.

Hill was in and out of the Red Cross over the next two years. He was first hired March 27, 1916, as director for chapter membership extension. A letter dated November 1, 1917, shows Hill as "voluntarily relinquishing his salary since September 30" but on January 1, 1918, he is back on the payroll as "director of personnel." He was paid an "honorarium" of $2,000 for his services from January through April, 1918. It was not an unusual practice of the Red Cross in this era to pay honoraria instead of salaries. Initially, Hill did not envision a national membership campaign but proceeded on the old YMCA basis of organizing chapters in communities, and then pitting city against city to meet membership quotas.

One Red Cross historian reports:

It was a competitive game between cities. The idea was to organize the larger cities first. Each city was organized into committees and prepared for the campaign, which lasted only a week. Members enrolled after the specified time elapsed were not to be counted in the report, according to Hill. Arrangements were made also for the Red Cross director to address the various business and professional groups in the city. All gatherings were patriotic. Ministers were asked to preach. . . . Gatherings were told by Mr. Hill "Time should not be needed to decide whether one was back of the President. . . . Delay in enrolling may cast a suspicion that one is not an American." [22]

There was no hesitancy to exploit the war in any drive for funds even remotely related to it. By September, membership had mushroomed to 6 million belonging to some 3,000 chapters. But this was not enough to meet the needs of the Red Cross, in the eyes of Mr. Davison. He ordered a general membership campaign. "We shall call the roll of the nation," he declared and thus gave the Annual Red Cross Roll Call its name and created a fixed event on the nation's fund-raising calendar.

The pattern-setting national membership drive was carefully planned, largely the work of Davison, Ward, Lee, and Hill. The theme of the first Roll Call was to be "A Red Cross Christmas," thus capitalizing on the dual themes of Christmas and war. "The War Council of the American Red Cross has conceived that a great national purpose will be served by having membership in the Red Cross almost as universal as citizenship," the nation was told. Setting the Roll Call's goal at 15 million members because "we want the strength and support that will grow from this army of members," the War Council "set Christmas time to attain this goal, because we believe that the Red Cross and Christmas spring from the same spirit, and we wish to bring together these two great symbols of mercy, sacrifice and cheer. . . . We hope that from this Christmas campaign of 1917 will grow a permanent custom which will increase the significance of both Christmas and the Red Cross." [23] And such a custom did grow to increase the strength of the Red Cross, if not of Christmas.

The national Roll Call committee was headed by Theodore N. Vail, public relations-minded president of American Telephone & Telegraph Company. Other members of the National Christmas Membership Committee included the experienced fund raiser Bishop William Lawrence, editor Henry Watterson of Kentucky, baseball's Ban Johnson, publisher Frank N. Doubleday, and Mrs. William G. McAdoo, daughter of President Wilson. The national body was paralleled by a similar committee in each of the newly organized thirteen divisions of the Red Cross.

A campaign plan for the Roll Call was carefully prepared and published in booklet form as a guide to all participants in this drive for members. It was entitled "Red Cross Christmas Membership Campaign" and was 32 pages in length. Such plans for systematic solicitation became standard for the Red Cross in subsequent roll calls and have since been widely copied by the national associations seeking members and donations.[24] Dates for the Roll Call were December 17–25. The plan called for this calendar:

Monday, Dec. 17–Publication of Governors' proclamations arranged by division offices. Public statement by the chapter chairman and by the commanding officer of any army or navy post in the district.

Tuesday, Dec. 18–Civil Employees' Day. Proclamation by the mayor. Raising the Red Cross flag on the municipal building with flag to be displayed throughout the campaign.

Wednesday, Dec. 19–Women's Day, on which special tribute should be paid to the work which women are doing in the Red Cross. Meetings of local women's organizations. Peak of house-to-house canvass.

Thursday, Dec. 20–School Day, on which every teacher will speak on the significance of the Red Cross and upon the significance of the Christmas ceremony.

Friday, Dec. 21–Employees' Day, on which special tribute should be paid to the support which the laboring man is giving the Red Cross. Concentrate on certain large factories with speeches and solicitations.

Saturday, Dec. 22–Boy Scouts' Day, on which the Boy Scouts will be organized to canvass for membership.

Sunday, Dec. 23–Church Day, on which Christmas sermons on the Red Cross will be preached in every church.

Monday, Dec. 24–Red Cross Christmas Ceremony Day. At 7:30 on Christmans Eve, candles will be placed behind Red Cross Service Flags in every home. Workers will carol through the streets and church bells will chime.

Using the systematic campaign procedures developed in the YMCA, and making its appeal to patriotism through every citizens' organization, including schools and churches, the Red Cross War Council Roll Call was sure to triumph. And triumph it did—a total of 18.6 million Americans were enrolled, thus surpassing the goal by 3.6 million members. Dues collected were divided between the local chapter and the national headquarters. This principle had been established by Eliot Wadsworth late in 1916, because, as Red Cross membership and number of chapters grew, local autonomy and fund sharing had become thorny problems. Division of membership dues for 1917 between chapters and headquarters were set as follows: [25]

Class of membership	Amount of dues	Amount to National	Amount retained by the chapter	Amount applied by National to Magazine
Annual	$ 1.00	$ .50	$ .50	None
Subscribing	$ 2.00	$ 1.50	$ .50	$1.00
Contributing	$ 5.00	$ 3.00	$2.00	$1.00
Sustaining	$ 10.00	$ 7.00	$3.00	$1.00
Life	$ 25.00	$ 25.00	None	None
Patron	$100.00	$100.00	None	None

The revenues from Red Cross memberships were not small sums. The American Red Cross, as a whole, received approximately $42 million from membership dues during the twenty months the War Council was in command. "Of this total, about $3,700,000 from junior members was placed in school funds, approximately $18,500,000 was retained by chapters, $949,838.29 went into the Endowment Fund, and $18,930,056.17 came to the national organization for general uses." [26] The Red Cross established the Junior Red Cross membership for children in August, 1917. On September 15 President Wilson invited the nation's school children to sign up with the Red Cross because "Our Junior Red Cross will bring to you opportunities of service to your community and to other communities all over the world." By the war's end the Red Cross had a total membership of more than 20 million persons. Another rich money lode had been uncovered.

Publicity Paves the Way

This unprecedented outpouring of money was, in considerable measure, the end result of a shrewdly directed, large-scale publicity program that set new patterns for American publicists. After its unhappy experience with the promoter-press agent, Edward R. Johnstone, the Red Cross had pursued a halfhearted, haphazard public relations course until 1914, when Austin Cunningham was hired to head the Division of Information. Cunningham followed the limited publicity patterns prevailing prior to American entry into World War I, seeking to accomplish the objectives of his office "through press releases, magazine articles, monthly 'clips,' and monthly advance sheets to 2,500 newspapers. The news releases were used to solicit funds for the European and Mexican War Relief, and to announce important Red Cross changes." [27]

Cunningham put most of his effort into the *Red Cross Magazine*. He had built a circulation of 300,000 for this magazine by November, 1916, when its publication was transferred to Doubleday, Page & Company. Cunningham was stricken with tuberculosis in February, 1917, and left the Red Cross to recuperate. With his departure the Division of Information ceased to exist, and, with America's entry into the war and the designation of the Red Cross as the nation's relief agency, there was an urgent need for a bold, imaginative public relations program.

Such a program was gradually constructed by Ivy L. Lee, one of the first persons drafted by Davison. For the first few months Lee served on an informal, unofficial basis, commuting between New York and Washington. This explains why the War Council, when announcing its initial staff appointments, provided for only an official photographer and a recorder. However, Lee was quite active in the background. He helped Davison shape his May 10 announcement of acceptance as War Council chairman and at the same time got him to agree to a policy of full disclosure of all information pertaining to the Red Cross. As Lee explained later:

> The first thing I impressed upon him [Davison] was that we were going to handle many millions of the people's money, that we were largely a group of Republicans working under a Democratic administration, and that if the slightest breath of scandal attached to any of our actions, we might be subjected to a Congressional investigation at the first opportunity. Let us prepare for an investigation now, I said, and then there won't be any. Accordingly we prepared a system of records and checks against these records which covered every dollar. . . . And we took the people into our confidence from the start . . . and we came through clean.[28]

This policy of full disclosure was confirmed by Davison in a statement issued to the public under his name. In a press release dated August 4, 1917, marked for release Sunday, August 5, Davison declared:

> It is the earnest desire of the Red Cross that the American people, to whom the Red Cross belongs, should know all about its acts and its affairs. The people have given a wonderful exhibition of generosity and bigheartedness and at their bidding the American Red Cross has undertaken the most stupendous effort in the history of mankind to relieve suffering and distress.
>
> The accounts of the Red Cross are regularly audited by the War Department and an annual report is made to Congress. But it is the purpose of the War Council to take the people, day by day, as fully as possible into its confidence. Information as to Red Cross matters will accordingly be made public in great detail.[29]

And they were—under the deft hand of the man who probably wrote Davison's statement, Ivy Lee.

Lee consulted with Davison and other members of the War Council on questions of basic policy which arose in great number in the early, chaotic days of the Council when it was without patterns and precedents. Lee was helpful in shaping the plans for the first big fund drive, contributing the services of his staff in New York City to handle the publicity for the Atlantic Division. But the unofficial, part-time role of Lee did not suit Davison, and he pressed Lee to accept a full-time appointment without salary. Lee did so, and on July 11, 1917, the War Council appointed him "assistant to the Chairman of the War Council" "to give the utmost publicity . . . to the activities of the Red Cross." Lee was given authority, under Davison's direction, over "matters relating to publicity, publications, and The Red Cross Magazine." [30] Lee indicated that the choice of title was his, and that he eschewed the title of publicity director or press agent because "the public is suspicious." Lee correctly insisted that public relations must function at the policy level. In this Davison concurred. Lee became the right-hand man of Davison, living with him in Washington, eating with him, and traveling with him. A year later Davison told Lee, "I have come to feel a strong affection" for you.

Lee's publicity program for the Red Cross soon included:

The Red Cross Magazine. The editorial content was prepared under Lee's direction, picking up where Cunningham had left off.

Moving pictures, including their production and distribution, to show the work being done by the Red Cross;

News, to disseminate all information about the Red Cross' needs, services, and aims through all news channels;

The Red Cross Bulletin, an internal house organ to provide information to the various departments of the Red Cross, branches, chapters, and others interested;

An Information Bureau at national headquarters for the reception of visitors and the answering of routine queries;

Speakers' Bureau to arrange for lectures on the Red Cross in cooperation with lecture bureaus, clergymen, school teachers, etc.;

Advertising Section to present the Red Cross story through newspaper and magazine advertising, posters, and other forms of advertising that may be found possible.[31]

A general reorganization of the Red Cross Department of Publicity along these lines was effected September 1, 1917, after Lee had had sufficient time to observe, plan, and experiment with publicity patterns. Under this reorganization the publicity function was strengthened in subordinate units and a publicity director was named on the permanent staff in each of the fourteen divisions, to work in direct contact with the national headquarters. A year later the Department of Publicity consisted of a headquarters group, three main bureaus, and two coordinating divisions. Joseph Johnson was made director of the new department and there served as Lee's chief of staff.

The Red Cross Annual Report issued in June, 1918, described the Publicity Department as "the main channel of communication and understanding between those at headquarters . . . and the great body of Red Cross workers and the public." In something of an understatement, the Report continued: "By presenting to the public the need of an extra-military agency in the winning of the war, the Publicity Department aided in increasing membership and in raising funds." The Red Cross publicity machine, radiating from the "Marble Palace" to local chapters in the nation's more than 3,000 counties, was greatly augmented by the donated services of Lee's New York staff. Two volumes of clippings in Lee's "Matter Sent Out" archives attest to this contribution to the Atlantic Division and to Red Cross drives in New York City.

Lee himself was not really satisfied with the publicity organization until near the end of the war. On August 27, 1918, he wrote

Davison: "Our organization has been very weak, due to lack of personnel and for the past several weeks we have been trying to strengthen that organization. I now feel that we have an ample number of people to cover the whole field and that our staff includes as able a group of persons as it would be possible to get together in the world." [32]

To pave the way for the calls for members, for money, and for volunteer workers, Lee and the expanded Publicity Department bombarded the public from all sides with the Red Cross story. In outlining his program, Lee wrote:

> . . . we shall give to the newspapers some kind of story practically every morning and every afternoon; that these stories will be conceived with reference to relating our story as a whole over a given period; that we shall have speakers going all over the country giving our story by word of mouth, by lantern slides and pamphlets which will be placed in the seats of the people who attend the speeches; that we shall have our story told by the motion picture houses all over the country; that we shall have our story carried by preachers, labor leaders, Chautauqua speakers and others to their own particular constituencies. [33]

Lee also frequently used the staged event in attracting public attention. In August he urged Mr. Davison to make a trip to Europe to inspect the Red Cross work there

> so that you can come back . . . give out a big interview on your arrival in this country, and then make a quick tour of division headquarters, addressing large meetings at all the thirteen cities in quick succession. . . . All this program should culminate before December 15 when our Christmas membership drive will start with a great display of posters and specially prepared publicity material to the complement of a greater array of speeches by Four-Minute Men and orators of other kinds and our own soliciting organization. We would have a great hip-hip-hurrah time and have the population of the United States enrolled as Red Cross members. [34]

The Four-Minute Men were some 75,000 civic leaders enrolled by President Wilson's Committee on Public Information to speed war messages to the people in churches, in theaters, in civic groups, in fact to any assemblage of people they might find. Between drives

Davison, Lee, and others went on speaking tours to report on the work of the Red Cross.

While Ivy Lee was building and perfecting the Red Cross publicity program to saturation point, his old critic was doing the same thing on an even larger scale for President Wilson's Committee on Public Information, set up to propagate the story of America's war aims and to censor United States news media. George Creel, crusading journalist who had bitterly criticized Ivy Lee for his role in the Colorado Fuel & Iron Company strike, created a propaganda campaign unequaled in modern times. The work of the Red Cross Publicity Department and Creel's committee dovetailed and one agency's output reinforced that of the other. There is no evidence, however, that these old foes ever consulted each other in carrying forward their common effort. The two propaganda machines flooded every channel of communication with patriotic demands that people serve, people give, people believe in the struggle to make the world safe for democracy. In the process, Lee and Creel gave American public relations its greatest thrust forward by their wartime demonstrations of its worth.[35]

After the Publicity Department was functioning smoothly, Lee began to weary of his nonremunerative Red Cross chores. On June 11, 1918, he wrote Dr. Stockton Axson, secretary of the American Red Cross, "I have come to the conclusion that my duties at home compel me to relinquish my Red Cross work . . . there are certain mathematical equations I am compelled to face."[36] Apparently in response to Lee's continuing effort to resign, Davison wrote him on August 31, 1918: "This job as you know demands absolute concentration and continuity and a man better have nothing to do with it if he cannot devote all his time and strength to it. Your service to the Red Cross is incalculable and I should be distressed if it were not to continue."[37] His large ego caressed, Lee stayed to the end. He kept careful account of what his service to the Red Cross cost him. On December 12, 1918, he wrote Mr. Davison:

> The books of my New York office show that I have made an actual outlay in connection with my Red Cross work of approximately $11,000; this covering the expenses of some 30,000 miles of travel in this country and Europe, expense of living in Washington, and extra expenses of my department which I have assumed personally. In addition to this my New York office has rendered a very considerable

service to the Red Cross. . . . On any fair pro rata basis the actual cost to me on the part of my New York office would amount to $6,000 or $7,000, making a total expenditure . . . amounting to approximately $18,000.[38]

However much he may have grumbled about his sacrifice, Ivy Lee was astute enough to know he was putting money in the bank in terms of contacts and reputation that would pay off many times in the postwar years. Also, Lee unquestionably learned much from the public relations-minded Davison. Lee once told his Red Cross staff: "Mr. Davison has said time and time again that the publicity was the most important part of the Red Cross and that the Red Cross could not exist except for the interest stirred up in it by its Publicity Department."

Yet Lee himself thought the Red Cross intensive publicity program represented only a wartime need. In bidding farewell to the Publicity Department staff December 3, 1918, Lee said that "the time has come when we ought to consider, every one of us, the steady demobilization of the Publicity Department . . . there is no necessity to devote either the time or the money to a continued and active stimulation of the work of the Red Cross; that we ought to let the interest grow out of our work, instead of having a great organization that would merely stimulate that activity."[39] In this talk Lee showed lack of perception of the profound change in the Red Cross and proved himself a poor prophet as well. But his prodigious, professional public relations campaign for the Red Cross in wartime does him great credit. It brought in the money. His publicity patterns would be copied in future fund-raising efforts.

The Red Cross Does It Again

Less than a year after its spectacular, precedent-shattering $114 million drive the American Red Cross went back to the American people to ask for another $100 million. The public was told: "Although the demands upon our people are so great and so continuous, the War Council approaches the people for another $100,000,000 with no feeling of apology, but in the knowledge that this is the time for sacrifice, that continued giving is the spirit of the day, that nothing matters but the winning of the war." President Wilson endorsed the proposed fund drive and proclaimed May 20–27, 1918, as National Red Cross Week. Again, the one-week drive was to be preceded by observance of Red Cross Sunday in the nation's churches, May 19. Once more Charles S. Ward, as secretary of the Red Cross War Finance Committee, took charge. His lieutenants were Hill and Pierce and the campaign was backed up by the greatly strengthened publicity machine created by Ivy Lee.

For this drive there was ample time for more thorough planning, and with the experience of the first drive to serve as a guide there was much less confusion and wasted motion. A conference was held in Washington on January 16, and complete, detailed plans for the drive were laid down in a manual prepared by Ward and his associates and placed in the hands of all campaign workers well ahead of time. Ward described the manual as "a compendium of the best experience in campaigns available." Red Cross officials were admonished that "careful observance of these instructions is an obligation upon each chapter and is requisite to the proper conduct and promotion of the campaign and the collection of funds."

Ward directed that each community open a campaign headquarters no later than April 15 and proceed with thorough preparations. Again the drive was decentralized; this was easier now, with a Red Cross chapter in every county and in most large cities. A quota was assigned to each chapter on the basis of population, bank clearings, and other economic indices, and then local committees were organized to pit the community against its assigned quota. Competition among cities was again exploited. As before, the donations would be shared between the local chapter and the National War Fund.

Ward's campaign manual called for intensive publicity "to bring home to our people in the most vivid way the story of the help we are furnishing" our Allies. This time Red Cross publicists and solicitors could point to accomplishments, not just explain what the relief agency planned to do. All the ideas Ward, Hill, Pierce, and Lee could muster were utilized to emblazon the Red Cross symbol and its appeal for funds across the land. Few people, it is certain, escaped hearing the call to give. On the Sunday before the drive opened all those going to church heard the humanitarian appeal from the pulpit. On Monday, to open this second drive, some 2,000 parades were held simultaneously in cities and towns across the country. The biggest one was held in New York City where President Wilson led 70,000 men and women marchers down Fifth Avenue on a very hot day as thousands of citizens cheered the passing parade of troops, ambulance units, Red Cross nurses, and volunteer workers. Messages exhorting the people to give freely, from President Wilson, Chairman Davison, General Pershing and other wartime leaders, filled the nation's newspapers. Motion-picture, Broadway, and opera stars were again recruited to act, sing, or plead for funds for the Red Cross. John McCormack, the famous tenor, made a nationwide tour to promote Red Cross rallies.

Ward introduced a variant of his campaign clock idea in the New York City drive, in which he was quite active. It was arranged that at 3 P.M. each day every church bell would toll and every factory whistle would blow for one-half minute. Then a period of silence would follow for five seconds, at the end of which time every bell would toll, or whistle blow, once for each million dollars raised.[40] Similar programs were planned for other cities. This campaign produced perhaps the most famous of all Red Cross campaign posters, the portrait of a handsome, matronly Red Cross nurse holding war orphans in her arms as the "Greatest Mother in the World," drawn by Foringer. Motion pictures, now developing rapidly under the impetus of the war, were used more intensively this time. One, *The Spirit of the Red Cross*, written by James Montgomery Flagg, "was a romance in which the leading characters, an American soldier and a Red Cross nurse, vividly portrayed the trials and tribulations of the soldier on the battlefield." Flagg also designed many of the Red Cross World War I posters.

To provide thrust for this drive, Ivy Lee exploited the drama of the staged event by arranging for War Council Chairman Davison to return from Europe with a dramatic, firsthand report on the war and the work of the Red Cross in relieving its suffering and hardship, on the eve of the campaign. Davison returned on May 16, 1918, from an inspection trip of almost three months in Europe. Lee's release announcing Davison's return said, in part, "Mr. Davison hastened back to America at this time to be able to assist in conducting the war fund drive." A dinner was staged in New York City the evening of May 18 to provide a public platform for Davison's report on Red Cross accomplishments and needs in Europe. A long printed galley release on his talk had been sent out the day before from Red Cross headquarters marked for release after his talk. In such ways Ivy Lee used every publicity technique to arouse public opinion.

This was not difficult in a nation at war, caught up in a sense of

adventure and high purpose, fighting "a war to end all wars." All
the forces of opinion making—the press, the politicians, and the
pulpit—vied in their efforts to demonstrate patriotic support of the
Red Cross appeal. As Dulles observes: "The psychosis of war affected the drive even more than the campaign a year earlier, and
there was sometimes a hysterical note in the newspapers' repeated
demands that there must be no failure in backing the war effort and
no 'slackers' in the Red Cross drive." [41] Typical was this two-col-
umn headline in the May 9, 1918, Los Angeles *Times:* SMOKE OUT
'SLACKERS!' IS RED CROSS SLOGAN. In the middle of the campaign it
was reported that the Germans had bombed a Red Cross hospital
in France. American voices rose in indignation, and the Red Cross
campaigners moved to exploit this emotion-producing event. Said
the Washington *Evening Star:* "There had been no doubt about
raising the hundred-million Red Cross war fund from the start. But
this atrocity makes assurance doubly sure." The *Star,* in another
article, direfully predicted that "If this fund is not forthcoming our
men's wounds may have to be bound in hay or old newspapers." [42]

Ward and his associates worked tirelessly, traveling from city to
city, organizing committees to press the solicitation capitalizing on
this emotional support of the Red Cross. Ward had long since learned
that publicity alone does not collect gift dollars; that this is done
by ringing doorbells and knocking at office doors. He covered the
major cities of the East as he had done in the previous drive. Pierce
served as "secretary of the West-of-the-Mississippi share of the
campaign." Hill spent most of his time keeping track of the campaign at headquarters and the flow of materials and instructions
moving out to the field. Typical of the far-from-objective reporting to come from the meetings held by Ward, Pierce, and their
associates is this lead from a story in the Los Angeles *Times* for
May 9: "For the starving noncombatant victims of Prussian fright-
fulness in France as well as for the soldiers, gas-tortured and bullet-
torn by Teuton war methods, Los Angeles will be asked to give
$750,000 through the Red Cross from May 20 to 27. At the organ-
ization of the Second Red Cross War Fund Drive in Alexandria
yesterday this point was emphasized. . . . Nativity, creed or color
can raise no issue. There can be no slackers!' "

The contagion of war psychosis, the combined assault of all
public opinion media on the populace, Ivy Lee's saturation publicity
campaign, and Ward's systematic solicitation methods again paid

off. At the end of the one-week campaign for the Second Red Cross
War Fund Henry Davison jubilantly announced that some 43 million
adults and school children had given or pledged a total of $181.06 mil-
lion—almost double the goal set at the drive's start. Again, the gifts
came from the rich, the middle class, and the factory worker alike.
This time the Rockefeller Foundation began the drive with a gift
of $3 million. As a matter of record, by February 28, 1919, collec-
tions from the May, 1918, drive totaled only $169,575,598.84. Even
so this represented an oversubscription of nearly 70 per cent.[43]
The press concluded that this substantial oversubscription marked
a renewed endorsement of the work of the Red Cross. It did that
and it also attested to the power of perfected publicity and fund-
raising techniques. Collected contributions in the First and Second
War Drives are shown in Table 5.[44]

The Second Red Cross War Fund battle won, the public relations
and solicitation machinery was re-geared for the second annual
Christmas Roll Call, to bring in new members and more money. It
was predicted that this would be "the biggest single publicity campaign ever accomplished in the United States." [45] Preparation of
the publicity started in the late summer of 1918. "The aim and underlying purpose of this campaign is to recruit under the banner of
the Red Cross every loyal American no matter where he or she may
live," read the carefully prepared "Red Cross Christmas Roll Call
Plan Book." Again President Wilson led the Red Cross army into
battle. "I summon you to the comradeship," he exhorted the people.
The roll call was held December 16–23, again preceded by "Red
Cross Sunday, on which Christmas sermons on the Red Cross will
be preached in churches."

This drive did not meet the set goal of 20 million members for
two reasons: first, with the signing of the Armistice in November,
by Christmas time the war fever was fast subsiding and, second, the
influenza epidemic that swept the country prevented public meetings, struck down solicitors, and generally played havoc with the
well-laid plans of Messrs. Ward, Hill, Pierce, and their associates.
Nonetheless, a total of 18,602,759 members in a population of 105
million people had been enrolled, no mean accomplishment by all
previous standards of fund-raising and membership solicitation.

The Red Cross hit its peak membership in September, 1918,
as the war neared its climax, when it carried a total of 20,832,000

TABLE 5. COLLECTED CONTRIBUTIONS, FIRST AND SECOND WAR DRIVES COMBINED,
WITH COMPARISONS BY STATES
February 28, 1919

State	Collections	Per cent to total	Per capita	Per cent to wealth
Maine	$ 1,564,480.08	.6	$ 2.00	.15
Massachusetts	14,114,590.99	5.2	3.682	.22
Rhode Island	2,090,235.69	.8	3.279	.22
Vermont	503,222.10	.2	1.374	.10
New Hampshire	875,986.16	.3	1.962	.13
Connecticut	6,968,947.95	2.6	5.418	.30
New Jersey	9,775,739.48	3.6	3.173	.17
New York	69,331,242.69	25.4	6.511	.28
Delaware	3,273,524.41	1.2	15.089	1.06
Pennsylvania	27,283,990.90	10.0	3.101	.18
District of Columbia	1,471,045.04	.5	3.927	.13
Maryland	2,828,412.77	1.0	2.043	.13
Virginia	2,431,848.98	.9	1.088	.11
West Virginia	1,975,827.30	.7	1.373	.09
Florida	1,070,628.27	.4	1.140	.10
Georgia	1,632,179.60	.6	0.556	.07
North Carolina	1,442,430.18	.5	0.585	.08
South Carolina	1,421,146.56	.5	0.856	.11
Tennessee	2,473,516.85	.9	1.066	.13
Indiana	4,768,788.58	1.7	1.671	.09
Kentucky	2,627,823.14	1.0	1.091	.12
Ohio	17,737,755.61	6.5	3.363	.20
Illinois	15,116,986.97	5.5	2.393	.10
Iowa	4,190,483.36	1.5	1.884	.05
Michigan	6,557,562.93	2.4	2.093	.12
Nebraska	3,206,772.98	1.2	2.473	.08
Wisconsin	3,812,260.87	1.4	1.493	.08
Alabama	1,674,570.22	.6	0.699	.08
Louisiana	2,575,966.94	.9	1.367	.12
Mississippi	1,107,837.74	.4	0.554	.08
Montana	1,126,650.89	.4	2.316	.10
Minnesota	5,314,540.13	1.9	2.266	.10
North Dakota	767,235.52	.3	0.969	.04
South Dakota	565,908.51	.2	0.769	.04
Arkansas	1,591,943.01	.6	0.888	.09
Kansas	4,669,858.65	1.7	2.492	.10
Missouri	9,123,044.48	3.3	2.646	.16
Oklahoma	3,072,958.29	1.1	1.292	.07
Texas	5,256,699.55	1.9	1.142	.08

TABLE 5. (Continued)

State	Collections	Per cent to total	Per capita	Per cent to wealth
Colorado	3,281,983.86	1.2	3.235	.14
New Mexico	353,814.66	.1	0.810	.07
Utah	1,161,275.60	.4	2.560	.15
Wyoming	640,141.11	.2	3.362	.18
Idaho	984,112.14	.4	2.131	.16
Oregon	1,972,278.76	.7	2.220	.10
Washington	3,964,843.37	1.5	2.388	.12
Arizona	674,978.60	.3	2.481	.13
California	10,274,068.10	3.8	3.294	.12
Nevada	198,610.17	.1	1.731	.04
Alaska	161,220.43	.1		
Insular and foreign places	2,177,797.81	.8		
Total	$273,239,768.98	100.00	$ 2.373	.14

members on its rolls. This figure was not to be matched again until midway in World War II. The costs of the two membership roll call campaigns were put at $1,450,000 in round figures.[46] The Red Cross Roll Call was thus embedded in the fabric of our national life.

All told, in less than two years the people of the United States had contributed over $400 million to the Red Cross in gifts and membership dues, of which some $263 million was retained by national headquarters and $137 million by the 3,709 chapters. Of the $263 million kept by national headquarters, $110,422,134 was spent for relief abroad. In France alone the Red Cross spent some $57 million on medical care and relief work. At the end of the War Council's work in February, 1919, the Red Cross had nearly $100 million available to meet disaster and war relief needs.[47] A summary of War Council revenues and expenses follows in Table 6.[48]

The United Fund and Corporate Philanthropy

Although it raised some $400 million and spent $273 million in wartime services and ministrations, the greatly expanded American Red Cross had no monopoly on either the getting or the spending of philanthropic dollars during the war. To the contrary, many

TABLE 6. NATIONAL HEADQUARTERS FINANCIAL OPERATIONS
Twenty Months Ending February 28, 1919

Relief Fund balances, June 30, 1917	$ 3,134,904.33
Revenues from July 1, 1917, to February 28, 1919	
First war drive collections—national headquarters proportion	$ 92,947,388.54
Second war drive collections—national headquarters proportion	136,851,629.73
Membership dues—national headquarters proportion [1]	18,930,056.17
Donations of surplus funds from chapters	1,419,460.07
Interest	3,157,268.95
Other revenues	6,696,785.88
Total revenues	$260,002,589.34
Total available for appropriation and expenditure	$263,137,493.67
Appropriations from July 1, 1917, to February 28, 1919	
War relief in France	$ 57,207,003.95
War relief elsewhere overseas	63,840,655.04
War relief in United States	28,977,985.24
Disaster relief	938,420.87
Collections, enrolments, and publications	4,660,191.71
Operation of relief bureaus	2,727,055.90
Operation of bureaus for handling relief supplies; also transportation in United States of relief supplies	5,530,345.72
Operation of administrative bureaus at national and divisional headquarters	4,359,758.03
Other activities	853,694.87
Total appropriations [2]	$169,095,111.33
Balance in relief funds available for appropriations, February 28, 1919	$ 94,042,382.34

[1] Excludes $949,838.29 dues from life and patron members, all of which go to the Endowment Fund.

[2] Of this sum $152,380,671.07 had been spent or advanced to Feb. 28, 1919.

existing associations saw the war as an opportunity to gain national recognition and to build organizational strength, and many new ones sprang up to meet particularized needs. There was much jostling and crowding in the race to raise money and much waste and overlapping in the spending of it. By the time America entered the European war it was estimated that there were some 14,855 war relief organizations of one sort or another. The Council of National Defense, agency to coordinate civilian activities during wartime, managed to get this number consolidated into 159 in the months after April, 1917.[49]

Most of these agencies were centered in New York City. Typical ones included the Serbian Aid Fund, the French Heroes Fund, American Friends of Musicians in France, Free Milk for France Fund, Aid for National Allied Relief Commission, American Chocolate Fund for the American Expeditionary Forces, the Fatherless Children of France Organization, the Italian War Relief Fund of America, etc. In 1918 the State Councils section of the Council of National Defense made an investigation of all the agencies seeking public gifts to provide aid to the peoples of devastated Europe, to the fighting men, and to our own soldiers and sailors. Arthur Fleming, chief of the section, said after the investigation: "In my opinion the great work of war relief could be conducted much more effectively if the number of organizations in it were reduced to a very few, less than ten I should say. I believe it would be still better if the whole thing were turned over to the Red Cross. In the list of active war relief organizations there are numerous meritorious ones . . . but only in the case of the Red Cross do the methods in use provide for a complete official auditing of accounts, and surely every one who gives a dollar to war relief is entitled to this surety." He added that "flotation of Government loans, as well as subscriptions to worthy and legitimate purposes, would be endangered unless some method of regulation and control were adopted."[50]

Crowding hard on the heels of the Red Cross, in terms of vast sums raised and spent in World War I came the YMCA. The war brought to the Y, as it did to the Red Cross, its greatest period of expansion. After America's entry into the war, the American YMCA enlisted some 26,000 workers and spent a total of more than $152 million on war-related programs, mostly on recreational and religious programs for U.S. troops. The day the United States declared war on the German Empire, John R. Mott, general secretary of the International YMCA, acting on his own authority, wired President Wilson an offer of "the full service of the Association Movement." A week later the International Committee validated Mott's action and organized the National War Work Council, with Mott as its general secretary. William S. Sloane, New York furniture man, was named chairman of the 144-man Council, which included fund raisers Ward and Pierce. This step taken, the YMCA plunged into a war program and a fund-raising campaign to finance it.

Ward, Pierce, and Hill never officially took leave of their YMCA positions during the war. Their services were lent by the Y, without charge, to the Red Cross, to other welfare agencies, and to the federal government. These experienced fund raisers were racing up and down the land, shuttling back and forth from one campaign to another. They were always busy counseling and cajoling those involved in the fund-raising campaigns for the Y, the Red Cross, the Salvation Army, and other agencies.

This trio also served Herbert Hoover, director of the U.S. Food Administration, who had the task of building public support for food conservation and belt tightening. Early in the war Hoover called upon Ward for counsel and guidance on organizing a campaign of food conservation. On Ward's recommendation, Harvey J. Hill was again drafted to direct the work of the Household Enrollment Campaign, and a comprehensive organization was set up. This resulted in 13 million families signing pledges to conserve food needed by our troops and Allies. On September 24, 1917, Hoover sent the YMCA Board of Directors a wire requesting Pierce's services to organize the food conservation drive in the western states. Hoover added in his wire: "I have expressed to Pierce the hope that from time to time as occasion may arise he will find it possible in spite of other duties to give counsel and in some instances supervision to administration matters." [51] These three men also were quite active in the several Liberty Bond drives and gave themselves to the war effort without stint.

The YMCA had, of course, abandoned its capital fund building campaigns for the duration of the war, but soon put its techniques to use to raise a war fund. Led by the veteran trio of fund raisers, Ward, Pierce, and Hill, the Y's War Work Council planned a drive in September, 1917, for $35 million. This campaign followed the standard pattern, working through committees of local YMCAs with each community given a quota to meet. George W. Perkins, steel magnate, served as chairman of the War Work Finance Committee and lent his powerful backing to the cause. The one-week campaign was set for November 11–19, the goal was determined as the amount needed to carry the Y's war program to July 1, 1918— a budget nine times the total previous annual budget of all the Ys in the United States. Only $30 million was raised in this 1917 drive.

Although the Red Cross and the YMCA represented the main channels of American philanthropy to U.S. troops and to the victims of World War I, there were others in the field. In 1917–1918 Ward consulted on, or had a hand in, these wartime fund-raising efforts in addition to those of the Red Cross and the Y: National Catholic War Work Council, $30 million; War Camp Community Service, 1918, $15 million; Knights of Columbus of New York War Fund, 1918, $4.8 million; Jewish Welfare Board, 1918, $3.5 million; and the Salvation Army, $3.5 million. Four of these agencies sent personnel into the military camps and into the field with U.S. troops—the Red Cross, the YMCA, the Knights of Columbus, and the Salvation Army. These agencies provided morale-building and recreational facilities for American soldiers and sailors. The YMCA operated canteens for the troops in France, a program that was to bring bitter criticism to the Y. The War Camp Community Service was created to try to maintain "wholesome conditions" around military installations; it did not serve the troops directly, as did the others. The American Library Association embarked on a program to provide books for service men.

In a gross understatement one historian says that "the results in terms of teamwork were far from perfect." Inevitably there was overlapping and competition in the services to troops and to civilian populations, and ultimately this conflict showed up in the competition for donated dollars at home. Most serious was the duplication of effort to provide recreation for the troops at home and abroad. As Raymond B. Fosdick, appointed by Secretary of War Newton D. Baker to investigate the problem, pointed out: "A commanding officer interested in recreation and amusement for his troops might invite the YMCA, the Knights of Columbus, and the Salvation Army so as not to discriminate. The result was that in some places all three organizations would be found working side by side and at other points not one of them would be represented." [52] The same duplications and conflicts developed on the domestic fund-raising front.

Ultimately the same forces that produced federated fund raising in Cleveland and other cities a few years earlier began to manifest themselves on a national basis. Norton suggests: "Conservation was one of the slogans of that period, and it took a little less than a year from the time the United States declared war for both givers and campaign workers to realize that there was no conservation in these successive tremendous money-raising campaigns." [53] At the local level the community war chest was conceived as a means of financial

federation. At the national level Secretary of War Baker took the
lead, just as he had in Cleveland five years earlier. But a national
federated fund-raising effort did not come overnight or without a
great deal of struggle. Doubts and disagreements voiced years before at the community level were heard in the national forum, often
vehemently.

Early in June the YMCA revealed plans for another national drive
to raise $75 million or $100 million to finance its steadily expanding
war program.[54] A day later the amount was fixed at $100 million.
When finally formulated, the 1918 YMCA drive was to be a federated fund-raising effort of sorts, because the Y had agreed to include
the War Camp Community Service and the American Library Association in its appeal. This raised the total goal, first to $112 mil-
lion, then to $135 million. A few weeks later the Knights of Colum-
bus announced that they would launch a drive in January, 1919, to
raise another $50 million for their War Council. The Treasury De-
partment announced that it would set off the Fourth Liberty Loan
campaign on September 4. The Red Cross Roll Call for 1918 would
come the week before Christmas. With these announcements, the
pressure to federate the appeals—particularly those involved in similar morale-building services to the troops—came to a climax.

The summer months of 1918 were filled with parleying and maneuvering, as representatives of the federal government and the large
donors brought pressure to force the agencies providing auxiliary
services to the troops into one federated fund-raising appeal. The
officials of these agencies—YMCA, YWCA, Knights of Columbus,
the Jewish Welfare Board, and the Salvation Army—resisted the
pressure in varying degrees, for much the same reasons that the
major health associations today resist the common-sense demand
for one national health-fund drive. Also being heard with increasing
frequency was the question, "Why don't the army and navy provide
for the recreational and religious needs of our soldiers and sailors
and eliminate all this duplication of effort?"

The welfare worker's reply to this question, as it often is today,
was expressed in the words of John R. Mott: "The American people
want to have a chance to identify themselves with practical aid to
the troops." [55] The American people were being given plenty of
opportunities to identify themselves with the fighting of the war,
as they were bombarded by an unending fusillade of demands: to
donate, to buy, to save, to conserve. It was becoming ever plainer

that scores of organizations had seized upon the war as an opportunity to raise gift moneys and thereby grow. Many were mulcting a patriotic and often gullible public; and there was much wasted energy and expense in raising and spending philanthropic dollars. Public resistance was beginning to mount as the war effort moved into its second year.

The pressure for federation came from Secretary of War Baker, long a confirmed believer in federated fund raising, and through him from Raymond B. Fosdick, who handled most of the negotiations. In this effort they had the powerful support of President Wilson, who said this matter was engaging his thought "not a little." Shortly after the declaration of war Baker had appointed Fosdick, experienced Rockefeller Foundation official, as chairman of a War Department Commission on Training Camp Activities. Three months later Secretary of the Navy Josephus Daniels set up an identical commission for the navy and made Fosdick chairman. By early August the press was carrying news reports headlined "Propose Coalition in War Fund Drives" and asserting that "the suggestion to combine the drives of all the agencies working for the American soldiers and sailors was made by government officials." Most of the pressure to federate was being applied behind the scenes, and the resistance to federation was mostly just foot dragging, although the issue of religion often flared in public. The Knights of Columbus, meeting in New York for what was billed its "Victory Convention," agreed, on August 6, to the plan for a united fund drive. On August 15, the YMCA and the YWCA agreed to participate. The smaller agencies had no choice but to follow suit.

Complaints against the multiplying demands in terms of money and time for these independent high-pressure drives, including a growing number of dubious ones, brought other actions. Most significant was the organization of the National Investigation Bureau of War Charities as of October 1, 1918, "to investigate and endorse war relief organizations appealing to the public for funds." This was the forerunner of the National Information Bureau which, over the years, has exerted a strong influence in bringing order and honesty to public philanthropy. Like the community chest, the NIB has its roots in Cleveland, Ohio.

The generator of the idea for a national agency to check the legitimacy of public appeals for money was Paul L. Feiss, who, at the time, was serving as chairman of the Distribution Committee of the Cleveland War Chest. Feiss, when confronted with scores of requests for funds from wartime relief organizations, and with no reliable way of checking the organizations' reliability and effectiveness, decided something should be done to solve this problem. His first move was to take the train to New York to consult Henry P. Davison, chairman of the Red Cross War Council. Feiss relates that he urged the Red Cross to take on the task of evaluating the merit of the still multiplying wartime appeals. Davison declined, explaining that the Red Cross was a solicitor of funds and any effort to pass on the merit of other appeals would be misunderstood and maligned.[56]

Davison called Feiss's attention to the work of the Contributors Information Bureau sponsored by the New York Charity Organization Societies. This bureau, directed by Barry C. Smith, had been trying to help in appraisal of war relief agencies, in addition to its job of reporting to donors on the validity of appeals made by New York City charity organizations. Feiss appealed to Mr. Smith and his superiors to take on this task for the nation at large, but the group declined. He then asked if he might hire Mr. Smith to head such a national bureau if one could be organized. Apparently this idea was acceptable to Mr. Smith and his superiors. Late in the summer of 1918 a meeting of "representatives of the influential states" met at Cleveland, to discuss this "drive" problem. Out of this meeting came the NIB, first named National Investigation Bureau of War Charities. A draft news release states that the Bureau was organized by the War Chest Associations of Cleveland, Syracuse, Indianapolis, Columbus, Detroit, Rochester, Philadelphia, and Toledo. "Early in the picture were also wealthy individual donors of that era." [57] The Contributors Information Bureau continued its work of reporting in New York City and did not change its name. It confined its checking and reporting to organizations local to New York City.

The Council of National Defense quickly endorsed the plan of the NIB to pass on the merit and legitimacy of fund-raising appeals. The idea was enthusiastically approved by Secretary of War Baker. The former Cleveland mayor and Feiss were friends and it is possible that Feiss took the lead in this matter at Baker's urging. Mr. Feiss later became president of the Cleveland Chamber of Commerce. When World War II started, Feiss was drafted again to serve as president of the National Information Bureau for the war years. The newly formed NIB opened offices at 1 Madison Avenue in

New York City, October 1, 1918, with Barry C. Smith as the director. The reporting work he had started at the COS of New York was to be expanded. The opening announcement said that the first list of approved war charities would be issued January 1, 1919. At the outset the NIB's Executive Committee, which thus represented a substantial part of the giving public, determined upon the following minimum requirements for endorsement.

1. An active Board of Directors (both American and foreign for foreign organizations) of at least five unpaid responsible people holding meetings at least quarterly.
2. A necessary purpose with no unnecessary duplication of the work of another efficiently managed organization. To be determined after investigation by the Bureau.
3. Reasonable efficiency in conduct of work, management of institutions, etc. and reasonable adequacy of equipment for such work, both material and personal. To be determined after investigation by the Bureau.
4. No solicitors on commission or other commission methods of raising money. No street soliciting or selling of buttons, tags, etc. except during drives.
5. Non-use of "remit or return" method of raising money.
6. No entertainments the expenses of which exceed 30 per cent of the gross proceeds.
7. Complete audited accounts, both American and foreign, prepared by a Certified Public Accountant or the foreign equivalent, showing receipts and disbursements classified and itemized in detail for a six or twelve month period. . . .
8. Itemized and classified budget estimate for succeeding or current six or twelve-month period.[58]

Thus began an effort to bring honesty and order to the chaotic field of public philanthropy that continues to the present time, an effort still far from successful. Today, as then, the charity bandit exploits America's generous giving by operating just inside legal limits. The NIB has never possessed legal status. Arthur Fleming of the Council of National Defense lamented, "There is no practicable way for the Federal Government to control the situation."[59] But Senator Henry F. Ashurst of Arizona moved to answer the growing clamor, mainly from donors, that something be done. In late September he introduced a bill in Congress calling for control of all war charities by the Department of Justice, and for complete financial statements to be submitted monthly under oath from all agencies seeking public gifts for war work. The Department of Justice would have been empowered to suspend the activity of any war charity after a public hearing if it found reason to do so.[60] The proposed legislation died with the end of the war in 1918 leaving this difficult national problem unsolved, one for which there is still no adequate federal legislation.

More pressure for consolidation and federation of wartime fund-raising appeals came from the Council of National Defense report, issued in September, which asserted: "A great deal of money given for noble purposes is now being wasted. . . . Our investigation found the benevolent energies of the country were being dissipated by the solicitations of the many societies formed for this purpose." [61] The *Literary Digest* of September 21 under the headline, "High Cost of War Charity," commenting on the large number of agencies devoted to relief, said, in part, "the relief benefited the agencies of at least 50 per cent of the takings" in many cases. The time was ripe for action and Fosdick called a meeting of the World War I agencies concerned for September 4 in New York City—the day the Fourth Liberty Loan campaign was launched. Fosdick went to the meeting reinforced by an increasingly noisy public opinion and armed with a letter from President Wilson which declared: "It is my judgment, therefore, that we shall secure the best results in the matter of the support of these agencies, if these seven socieities will unite their forthcoming appeals for funds." [62] A United War Work fund campaign was the inevitable outcome of this meeting. It is hard to resist a President in wartime.

To demonstrate a newly found unity and to allay the religious feelings that had been aroused in all the backstage maneuvering and public discussion, John R. Mott of the YMCA was elected as director general on the nomination by John G. Agar of the Knights of Columbus. Mortimer L. Schiff of the Jewish Welfare Board seconded Mott's nomination to emphasize the nonsectarian character of the new fund group. Mott voiced his confidence that "the friction and misunderstandings that have occurred between members of the three principal welfare organizations can not be repeated under the new system."

Members of the United War Fund Committee working out the federated fund campaign were: George W. Perkins and Mott, representing the YMCA; Mrs. Henry P. Davison, representing the YWCA; Agar and James J. Phelan, representing the Knights of Columbus; Schiff; Myron T. Herrick, the War Camp Community Service; Frank A. Vanderlip, the American Library Association; George Gordon Battle, the Salvation Army; and Cleveland H. Dodge, treasurer ex officio. Fosdick was made chairman of this Committee of Eleven. It was agreed that he would supervise the expenditures of the money raised so that the donor would get the most for his dollar.

The agreement reached at this meeting provided for: a joint campaign; a joint pledge card; that all funds collected would be divided on a pro rata basis; that specified gifts were not to be solicited by anyone working in the drive; that all funds would be sent to national headquarters and there reallocated on the agreed basis; that expenses would be shared on a pro rata basis. A goal of $170.5 million was agreed to and dates for the campaign were set at November 11 to 19—the dates of the Y campaign already scheduled. These planners could not know what a historic date November 11 would prove to be. The committee decided on this budget: [63]

Agency	Amount	Per cent of total
War Work Council of YMCA	$100,000,000	58.65
YWCA	15,000,000	8.8
National Catholic War Council	30,000,000	17.6
War Camp Community Service	15,000,000	8.8
American Library Association	3,500,000	2.
Salvation Army	3,500,000	2.
Jewish Welfare Board	3,500,000	2.

The United War Fund campaign plan was quickly and heartily endorsed by President Wilson, who said all seven of these organizations were to be recognized as "instrumentalities through which men in the ranks are to be assisted in many essential matters of recreation and morale" and added, "they have given new evidence of their patriotic cooperation by uniting their appeals for funds." Secretaries Baker and Daniels quickly echoed the President's endorsement of the union of these "morale-making institutions."

But among those dissenting was Lyman L. Pierce, who said: "The joint drive is a condition brought about by the President's letter, which we must observe. We have been opposed to all mergers and war chest plans so far as the YMCA is concerned, because we believe our work should not be presented with any other. The only thing we can do now is to get in and make the drive a success. . . . The difficulties we will find along the lines of sectarianism will have to be overcome as best they can. We must make the drive a success in spite of any such difficulties."

The religious issue hovered in the background to complicate even further the difficult task of building a sense of unity among these competing agencies serving U.S. soldiers and sailors. As one Methodist minister in Texas put it: "There is naturally much rivalry between different organizations and denominations, and this rivalry is not altogether wiped out by our patriotism." [64]

The agreement signed, Director General Mott, aided by lieutenants Ward, Pierce, and Hill, set about the task of perfecting campaign plans for the nation's first united fund-raising drive. Bruce Barton was recruited to direct the publicity. They did not have much time. The goal was set at $170.5 million—more than the total cost of America's Revolutionary War. The full artillery of the new publicity and promotion weapons were wheeled into position.

In the well-known writer and publicist Bruce Barton the Committee had a tireless and imaginative publicity chairman. After the war Barton made his mark as an advertising man. Under his direction a large press book was prepared to provide editorial and advertising material to a press which was eager to demonstrate its patriotic support of these war-fund drives. For this book Barton wrote seven short editorials that were widely used; these pithy, powerful pleas were carried under captions such as "Never a Night Before Away from Home," "Somebody's Dollars Will Do It—I Wonder If They'll Be Yours," and "What Do You Think Is My Share?" The press book provided the print media with cartoons, with full-page and smaller size advertisements, and feature articles, such as "When the Engine Stalls on Dead Man's Curve." In addition to the press book mailed to daily, weekly, and college newspapers, to magazines and trade journals, and to farm papers, Barton's Publicity Committee disseminated large numbers of publicity releases. For this drive seven posters, not one, were designed but each carried the common theme, "Give to the United War Work Fund."

Barton sensed the publicity potential in the recently developed employee publication—or house organ, as it was then commonly known—and on September 28, 1918, he sent a form letter to each house organ editor asking not only for editorial support but for publication of a full-page advertisement on the date of publication nearest November 11. Barton's correspondence files show that most house organ editors were eager to cooperate with such requests. A form "thank you" letter was sent to the editors, similar to the one Barton wrote to G. H. Abercrombie of the Fuller Brush Company:

"The pleasant thing about this job has been that it has brought me into contact with so many people in different parts of the country who in their own way are doing so much for the common cause.

"It seems to me that there is a larger idealism in the nation today than ever before." [65]

Certainly there was a willingness on the part of editors to support these drives. Barton's war-drive records show the following known contributions of free advertising space to this united fund drive: [66]

	Insertions	Circulation	Value of space
General Magazines	164	38,286,353	$109,377.18
Farm Papers	105	10,903,049	29,920.19
Trade Papers	372	3,036,746	20,867.20
House Organs	86	1,791,350	4,345.00
Newspapers	29	198,013	1,008.50
College Newspapers	42	130,250	1,549.12
Totals	798	54,345,761	$167,062.19

While Barton and his volunteer aides were firing their publicity barrage, the emerging professionals in fund raising were at work on the organizational phase of the task. The tested techniques of the Ward system were followed right down the line. The local outposts of all these organizations were alerted and asked to collaborate by consolidating their campaigns at the community level to raise the assigned quota. But these carefully prepared campaign plans were thrown into panicky disarray when the premature news of an armistice raced across America November 7 on the wires of the United Press.

A cable signed by Roy W. Howard and William Philip Simms was received in the UP New York office at 11:56 in the morning and quickly relayed to the nation, setting off joyous celebrations of the war's end all across the land. The nervous tension built up by seventeen months of war was broken and bedlam broke loose.

"Sirens, whistles, bells rose in a resounding clamor." When it turned out to be a false report, the emotional letdown took all the drive out of Ward's campaign "drivers." "Mott stepped into this breach with a powerful appeal based on Mazzini's prophecy that 'the morrow of victory is more perilous than the eve' covered the nation with telegrams instructing speakers and solicitors to focus their appeal upon the potentialities of the peace and the dangers of demobilization." Mott wired the campaigners: "We need not be solicitous for our soldiers and sailors when they are drilling and fighting and confronting the great adventure of life and death, but rather when this great incitement is withdrawn and discipline relaxed and hours of leisure multiplied and temptations are increased . . . our organizations are more needed than ever to prevent the period of demobilization becoming a period of demoralization." [67]

The false story proved a blessing in disguise because between November 7 and November 11, when the official Armistice was signed, Mott and his associates were able to get their organizations regrouped and the emphasis in appeal shifted to the demobilization needs of American soldiers and sailors. The United War Fund drive was launched on schedule with the lighting of campfires in Washington and many other cities in pre-campaign ceremonies the night of November 10. But the starting event was lost in the excitement of a delirious nation crazily celebrating the victorious climax of the great crusade to "make the world safe for democracy."

The methodical Ward-directed campaign organization stubbornly, systematically plowed ahead with its solicitation. The main appeal was on the need to provide for the idle hours of U.S. soldiers and sailors. Campaign workers up and down the land exhorted: "Leisure has been the foe of every army that ever marched to war." More basic was the appeal directed at the sense of guilt of those who had stayed behind in the comfort of home instead of fighting "over there." Typical of this appeal: "When the boys return from the battlefields of France with the crown of victory upon their foreheads, the supreme test of loyalty of those who remained at home will be the extent of their personal sacrifices." Thus the United War Fund drive was presented as one last chance for those who had not fought in battle to expunge their sense of guilt.

Not only was the campaign thrown off the track by the coming of peace, but that fall the influenza epidemic of 1918 broke out and swept the country. Flu felled many of the campaign workers and forced cancellation of many campaign report luncheons and rallies. As the campaign neared its scheduled climax it became apparent that the goal would not be met on time. On November 15 President Wilson, in a message to Mott, had issued another strong appeal for citizens to give. The campaign deadline was first extended to November 20 "because the people of the nation have turned slowly from celebration of the war's end to the tasks which still remain in caring for the army overseas." By November 16, when the decision extending the deadline to November 20 was made by the Committee of Eleven, $108,847,408 had been raised." On November 21 the deadline was again extended, to November 25.

At a luncheon meeting of leaders in the New York City drive, which had a goal of $35 million, the drive chairman, John D. Rockefeller, Jr., said that he had a group of unnamed "guarantors" who would make up one-half of the $3 million deficit if "our city teams cover the rest." As of November 21, the New York goal was $3,247,378 short of fulfillment. But the deficit was made up in four days, the campaigners raising another $2.9 million and the Rockefellers, Sr. and Jr., contributing another $370,000. When the drive was over it was revealed that the Rockefellers had been the "guarantors."

In the last great surge born of increased pressure from headquarters, the nation's first United Fund Drive went far over the top—on November 25, it was announced that a total of $203,179,038 had been pledged or collected for the seven service agencies. This was the largest sum ever provided through voluntary offerings in the history of mankind. Mott said: "No great campaign was ever preceded by such a brief preparation. Even the scant two months left for this purpose were cut into for three weeks by the Fourth Liberty Loan, and, near the threshold of the campaign itself, by a general Congressional election.

"More serious still was nationwide spread of the deadly influenza epidemic, which had a death toll of twice as many lives as America has laid down in the war." [68] Mott hailed the tremendous sum raised through public philanthropy as a testimonial to the nation's cooperative spirit and religious unity. The successful climax of this campaign brought the total dollars raised by Ward-directed campaigns in World War I to more than $690 million.

Just as many of their latter-day counterparts in the national health-fund drives fail to realize the tremendous demands one drive after another puts on the civic workers in each community, so did Mott, Ward, Pierce, and the others involved in these national drives fail to sense the magnitude of the burden they were placing on those few people who take care of the public's business at the local level. "The authority of the federal government together with the general sense of harassment felt by local business and civic leaders as the result of the chaos of appeals which poured in from all quarters for the support of varied types of war welfare work tended to promote a uniting of the various war appeals into joint campaigns." [69] Those heading the drives for these national organizations apparently did not sense that the demands of each drive were so heavy that the people obliged to raise the money, in the separate cities, would be forced to pool their efforts to save themselves time, effort, and the embarrassment of repeatedly soliciting their friends or business associates for donations. Norton recalls: "The evil of this every-organization-for-itself basis, which had been only mildly apparent while local movements had the field to themselves, was thrust forcibly home by the medley of the new giant war activities. It came as an added burden to a people already distraught." [70]

These war-born forces, when coupled with the conflicts and needs that had given birth to federated fund raising a few years earlier, made the "war chest" inevitable. And the community war chest would in turn bring the community chest in the years of peace to follow. Syracuse and Rome, N.Y., were among the first to adopt the plan, and Syracuse proudly claims first place in war chest fund raising. The movement made sense and began to sweep the country. Columbus, Detroit, Cleveland, Rochester, N.Y., and Indianapolis soon followed suit. The war chests represented a givers' and workers' revolt against the incessant demands from the Wards, the Pierces, the Hills, and their lieutenants to give, to solicit, to work, to meet assigned quotas. Most of the war chests represented only united campaigns for funds, lacking the key principle of central budgeting and allocation to agency on basis of its need.

The organizers of war chests made one promise they could not keep, a promise the sponsors of a united fund drive have never been able to keep: the promise of a year's immunity from solicitation for funds or campaign work. For example, in Utica's first war chest campaign the mayor proclaimed "the citizens of Utica may not be asked for any war relief contributions during the year" with the exception of the Red Cross membership roll call in December. [71]

Utica, incidentally, demonstrated the power of a whirlwind war chest campaign—that upstate New York city of 85,000 people raised $1,078,000 in one week's campaign, well over the $700,000 quota. The director of the campaign explained, "The crux of the whole matter is organization. The city was organized so that the men directing the campaign would reach straight down to every individual citizen in town." The more than a million dollars was raised at a cost of $7,000, the sponsors claimed. Charles Sumner Ward had taught his lesson to the country: "The crux of the whole matter is organization." In perfecting and pushing his systematic campaign methods Ward and his associates had taught hosts of men and women the art of raising money. The warborn campaigns taught the American people to give as no people had ever given to public causes before.

Corporate philanthropy, today a major force in our society, also came to America during World War I. The modern corporation has slowly, often grudgingly, come to accept the social responsibility that its power and place in our society impose upon it. Part of this responsibility is discharged through gifts to public causes. Until World War I the gifts that did flow from the growing accumulations of wealth produced by the business machine were those of a few millionaires, led by the Rockefellers and Carnegie. The pressure to give and the participation of big businessmen in the fund drives of World War I led to the first major acts of corporate giving, some of which have already been mentioned. However, the legal advisers of many corporations held that corporations could not safely make gifts to the Red Cross, the YMCA, and other agencies without express consent of the stockholders. To get around this difficulty Ward and his associates, for the 1917 Red Cross drive, promoted the Dividend Plan whereby many corporations were induced to send out with dividend checks a form that would permit the stockholder to sign the dividend over to the Red Cross. A letter encouraged him to do so.

The idea was not too successful and was abandoned in the 1918 Red Cross drive because most stockholders had preferred to hold on to their dividend rather than sign it over to the Red Cross. Also, those corporations that had given directly to the Red Cross from company coffers had not been challenged in court and this emboldened many timid corporate officials. Corporation gifts made directly to the Red Cross were greatly increased in its second big drive. Detailed records on such gifts are not available on these major campaigns but all the evidence indicates substantial corporate giving to the several war charity drives of 1917–1918. The National Bureau of Economic Research, reviewing Red Cross files of contributors of $1,000 or more, discovered a total of 1,204 names of corporations spread over 210 communities in 27 different states. Contributions of $5,000 or more from named corporations in New York City totaled nearly $9 million in the Bureau's list.[72]

Corporations had even earlier started contributing to the YMCA, starting with the railways contributing to the associations organized to benefit their transient workers. In the nineteenth century the railroads supplied 60 per cent of the operating budgets of the railroad Ys. By 1917 more than 100 industrial YMCAs were maintained by the joint support of employers and employees in all types of industrial communities. In the November, 1917, Ward-directed national YMCA campaign, Judge Elbert H. Gary announced that U.S. Steel and its subsidiaries would give $500,000, and the press reported Standard Oil Company of New Jersey giving $250,000. Andrews estimates: "Data chiefly from contemporary newspaper accounts indicate that corporation contributions in various cities ranged from some 45 per cent of the total given [in Chicago] to 15 per cent in Louisville. It is quite possible that corporations contributed as much as $20 million to the second Y.M.C.A. drive."[73] Dr. Mott reported, at the end of the mammoth United War Work drive that " 'Never before have foundations, corporations, companies, banks, industries, and the rural population of America participated so generally and so generously in a great popular subscription.' "[74]

The extent that corporation giving grew under the hammering pressure of the campaigners set off on the trail by Ward and his peers is shown in Table 7, compiled in the National Bureau of Economic Research Study:

TABLE 7.[75] SUMMARY OF ALL CONTRIBUTIONS AND OF CORPORATION
CONTRIBUTIONS TO SECOND RED CROSS WAR FUND, MAY, 1918,
IN 26 SELECTED CITIES

City	Total amount contributed	Amount of corporation contributions	Per cent of total amount from corporations	Number of corporation contributions	Remarks
Baltimore	$1,391,102	$ 428,830	30.8	368	
Buffalo	?	357,523	?	450	
Chicago	6,250,000	2,450,086	39.2	435	
Cincinnati	2,541,782	572,535	22.5	219	
Denver	750,000	159,740	21.3	88	
Flint	343,000	150,000	43.7	2	
Grand Rapids	287,000	22,300	7.8	23	
Houston	450,000	126,450	28.1	145	
Louisville	540,000	85,220	15.8	221	
Lowell	244,201	55,944	22.9	61	
Milwaukee	1,109,203	261,500	23.6	118	{Contributions of $500 and over
Newark	1,188,348	335,700	28.2	285	
New Orleans	1,119,000	199,341	17.8	406	
Norfolk	261,000	48,695	18.7	133	
Omaha	300,000	87,375	29.1	56	
Providence	722,562	213,250	29.5	74	{Contributions of $1,000 and over
Reading	292,000	41,075	14.1	37	
Richmond	465,545	106,395	22.9	152	
Saginaw	370,000	29,785	8.1	34	
Scranton	520,000	57,700	11.1	19	
Wilkes Barre	350,000	30,600	8.7	15	
St. Paul	850,915	16,500	1.9	5	
San Francisco	?	230,490	?	483	
New York City	?	10,043,600	?	487	{Contributions of $1,000 and over
Boston	?	815,490	?	174	{Contributions of $1,000 and over
Lancaster	200,000	29,760	14.9	31	

NOTES

1. Arthur S. Link, *American Epoch*, p. 197.
2. Letter to A. A. Sprague, Dec. 2, 1916, No. 121.01 in ARC Archives.
3. Wadsworth to all Red Cross Chapters, May 10, 1917, No. 116, War Council. ARC Archives.
4. Foster R. Dulles, *The American Red Cross, a History* (New York: Harper, 1950), p. 140.
5. G. R. Gaeddert, *The History of the American National Red Cross*, Vol. IV, p. 84, in ARC Archives.
6. Alfred McClung Lee, *The Daily Newspaper in America* (New York: Macmillan, 1937), p. 453.
7. Dulles, *op. cit.*, p. 142.
8. Dodge to Colonel House, April 26, 1917, Colonel E. M. House Papers, Yale University Library, quoted from Gaeddert, *op. cit.*, p. 79.
9. Gaeddert, *op. cit.*, p. 89.
10. Henry Morgenthau, *All in a Life-time* (Garden City, N.Y.: Doubleday), p. 249.
11. *Ibid.*, p. 250.
12. Memo of Christian Dreshman, undated, in files of Ward, Dreshman, & Reinhardt, New York City.
13. Quoted in Charles Hurd, *The Compact History of the American Red Cross*, p. 145.
14. Woodrow Wilson's letter to Pierce in the Lyman Pierce Scrapbook.
15. Dulles, *op. cit.*, p. 149.
16. American Red Cross, *The Work of the American Red Cross during the War*, p. 19.
17. San Francisco *Examiner*, May 30, 1917.
18. G. Smith, "Your Servant—the Red Cross," *The Independent*, Vol. XCI, p. 479.
19. *Literary Digest*, in "War Speed of the Red Cross," July 28, 1917, p. 35.
20. Letter, Clyde E. Buckingham, dated Aug. 15, 1961.
21. *New York Times*, April 14, 1917, p. 3; May 30, 1917, p. 2.
22. Gaeddert, *op. cit.*, pp. 128–129.
23. Roll Call manual, Red Cross Archives 494.1, ARC 1103.
24. *Ibid.*, p. 32.

25. Wadsworth Letter to All Chapters, Secretaries, Dec. 1, 1916, No. 187.1 ARC.

26. American Red Cross, *The Work of the American Red Cross during the War*, p. 15.

27. Gaeddert, *op. cit.*, Vol. IV, p. 69.

28. Clipping from *Success* magazine, circa 1924, found in Ivy Lee Papers, Princeton University Library.

29. Press Release in MSO Books, American Red Cross Vol. I in archives of T. J. Ross Associates.

30. Minutes of Red Cross War Council for July 11, 1917, in ARC Archives, Vol. I, p. 59.

31. ARC "Organization of National Headquarters," ARC Archives No. 107, Aug. 27, 1917.

32. Lee Letter to Davison, in ARC Archives, dated Aug. 27, 1918. No. 301.

33. *Ibid.*

34. *Ibid.*

35. For account of Creel Committee, see George Creel, *How We Advertised America;* Mock and Larson, *Words That Won the War;* and Creel's autobiography, *Rebel at Large.*

36. Letter in ARC Archives dated June 11, 1918, No. 301, Ivy Lee.

37. Davison to Lee under date of Aug. 31, 1918, in Lee Papers.

38. Lee to Davison in ARC Archives, letter dated Dec. 12, 1918, No. 301, Ivy Lee.

39. Closing Remarks by Mr. Ivy Lee, Dec. 3, 1918, in ARC Archives, No. 140.11, Publicity.

40. *New York Times,* May 10, 1918, p. 11.

41. Dulles, *op. cit.*, p. 150.

42. Issue of May 24, 1918, p. 5: same issue, p. 6 in Sec. II.

43. *The Work of the American Red Cross during the War*, p. 19.

44. *Ibid.*, pp. 18–19.

45. ARC *Bulletin,* Sept. 30, 1918, p. 8.

46. *The Work of the American Red Cross during the War*, p. 9.

47. *Ibid.*

48. *Ibid.*, p. 5.

49. *New York Times,* Sunday, Sept. 8, 1917, Sec. IV, p. 6.

50. *Ibid.*

51. Copy of Postal Telegraph wire in Lyman Pierce Scrapbook.

52. Raymond B. Fosdick to Secretary of War, June 1, 1919, in National Archives.

53. W. J. Norton, *The Cooperative Movement in Social Work*, p. 113.

54. *New York Times,* June 3, 1918, p. 11.

55. *Ibid.*, Sunday, Sept. 8, Sec. IV, p. 6.

56. In conversations with Dudley Paul Reed, long-time executive director of the NIB, as recalled by Mr. Reed in "Notes on Early NIB History," ditto copy in NIB files.

57. In NIB files and quoted in "Notes on Early NIB History."

58. *National Information Bureau Report 1918–1919*, the NIB, p. 2. This was the NIB's first annual report.

59. *New York Times*, Sept. 8, 1918, *loc. cit.*

60. *Survey*, Vol. XLI (Oct. 12, 1918), p. 47.

61. *Literary Digest*, Vol. LVIII (Sept. 21, 1918), p. 4.

62. *New York Times*, Sept. 5, 1918, p. 15.

63. "Millions for Morale," *Survey*, Vol. 41 (Nov. 9, 1918), pp. 155–156. Table on p. 156.

64. Undated clippings from *Christian Science Monitor* in Lyman Pierce Scrapbook.

65. Bruce Barton Personal Papers, General Correspondence Box. No. 1. Mass Communications History Center, State Historical Society of Wisconsin.

66. *Ibid.* No explanation accompanies the tabulation to show on what data these figures were based.

67. J. R. Mott, *Addresses and Papers, of John R. Mott*, Vol. IV, *The Y.M.C.A.*, p. 797.

68. *New York Times*, Nov. 26, 1918, p. 7.

69. Arthur J. Todd, "Study of Financing of Social Work," confidential memorandum in United Fund-Community Chests and Councils Library, p 5.

70. Norton, *op. cit.*, p. 114.

71. *New York Times*, April 7, 1918, Sec. IV, p. 1.

72. Williams and Croxton, *Corporation Contributions to Organized Community Welfare Services*, p. 69.

73. F. Emerson Andrews, *Corporation Giving*, p. 29.

74. Williams and Croxton, *op. cit.*, p. 74.

75. *Ibid.*, p. 69.

5

Fund Raising Becomes a Business

Ward Starts His Own Firm—and Several Others

In the hindsight of history it appears obvious that the nation's newly discovered philanthropic potential—so dramatically uncovered in World War I—would be exploited to meet the dammed up needs of colleges, hospitals, preparatory schools, libraries, and the mushrooming social agencies. The YMCA campaign techniques which had been so spectacularly successful in raising more than a half billion dollars in national fund drives were bound to be utilized by organizations desperately needing big sums of gift money. Yet Ward, "the master campaigner," was a bit slow to see the potentialities of fund raising as a business. A conservative, methodical man, Ward was reluctant to cut himself loose from the $8,000 salary he was then receiving from the YMCA and gamble on a new enterprise. "I have no ambition to be the richest campaigner in the cemetery," he would tell his associates. The impetus that moved Ward from the Y to commercial fund raising was generated by Harvey J. Hill, "a scrappy, temperamental little dynamo." Hill had the aggressive attitude many short men take as a defensive posture; he was a gambler, a driver, a battler. Associates remember him as hot-tempered and profane, qualities not usually found in Y workers.

In the waning days of the United War Fund campaign and in the cleanup period after it was over, Ward, Hill, and their co-workers had many talks about the future of fund raising now that the war was ended. In the 40th floor office suite in the Metropolitan Tower—the United War Fund headquarters in New York City—they would often discuss the needs and potentials of a fund-raising firm serving colleges, hospitals, and other institutions on a fee basis. "Frequently Hill talked about his ideas for such a fund-raising firm, and dictated memos about it far into the night." [1] He kept pushing the cautious Ward until the latter finally accepted his idea. From the firm that Ward would soon organize came five of today's largest fund-raising organizations and scores of trained fund raisers—a development that would bring profound changes to American philanthropy.

After thirty-five years with the YMCA, an organization he had done so much to build in the United States, Ward resigned early in 1919 to plan for his new fund-raising organization. After his resignation, the International Committee of the Y established a Financial Service Bureau and made Ward's long-time assistant, Miner C. Williams, senior secretary. This bureau was created to provide the local YMCA associations, which were seeking help now that the war was over, with the services of campaign directors to guide building and membership campaigns. Williams provided the leadership for 938 campaigns over the next eleven years; campaigns that raised $103,665,238.[2] This was a remarkable record for that period. Williams welcomed the chance to take over the fund-raising campaigns; he had long resented the acclaim given to Ward, and always nursed the hurt that his contributions to the Y campaign method were not sufficiently recognized. Dr. Arnaud Marts, who knew the pioneers well, once explained this matter of dispute this way:

> . . . we don't know who created the automobile; we don't know who created the idea of mass merchandising. Neither are we quite sure who created the concept of the modern campaign. It seems clear . . . that the campaign was definitely developed by secretaries of the Young Men's Christian Associations about 1901–1902 . . . certainly Lyman Pierce, Charles Ward, and possibly Miner Williams. Each of these three men has told me his account of the circumstances under which the financial campaign was first used, and I can readily understand how each might think that it was he who actually invented the system. Knowing the three men, as I did, and their respective abilities, my own guess would be that Lyman Pierce actually had the creative idea, and that Charles Ward and Miner Williams made the application of it in a wider sphere of activity.[3]

Marts's interpretation is probably as close to the truth as a historian can come concerning what is still a matter of spirited debate inside the fund-raiser family, but of little consequence otherwise.

On May 1, 1919, the austere master campaigner Charles S. Ward and the peppery, aggressive Harvey J. Hill opened their pioneering fund-raising firm, Ward & Hill Associated. The new firm took offices in the Metropolitan Tower, 1 Madison Avenue, scene of their latest triumph, the United War Fund campaign. Here, too, Frederick Courtenay Barber had his offices. Once Hill had induced Ward to take the plunge, he began pressing Ward to bring the able and dynamic Lyman Pierce into the firm. This led to more discussion. Those who know the situation say that Ward was afraid that Hill and Pierce would gang up on him and run the firm their way, not his. "Being a cagey Yankee, Ward insisted that F. Herbert Wells be brought in at the same time. He thought this would preserve the balance of power because Wells had worked for him in the years past." [4] Out of these discussions and maneuverings came a new firm in September, 1919: Ward, Hill, Pierce, & Wells.

In September, 1919, Lyman Pierce severed his long association with the YMCA to become a partner in "the firm of Ward & Hill, counsellors in financial organizations and publicity," as the release read. In his letter of resignation Pierce said that he was not in good health and could not "continue at present with the strenuousness of the work" of general secretary. At a farewell dinner he expressed the hope that he would ultimately come back to the Y as "a general secretary of one of the city associations." But he never did—he completed his life as a professional and influenced fund raising as a business as he had earlier shaped the campaign method. Pierce joined the firm with the understanding that he would keep his home in Burlingame, outside San Francisco, and his office in San Francisco's Flood Building.[5] Pierce had, understandably, fallen in love with the Golden Gate and had no desire to move back to New York City.

The firm was a very loose partnership with Ward directing the work as "managing partner." In the beginning the central office was a headquarters, to receive visitors and to promote new fund-raising business, and did not provide research support and campaign direction as it, and similar firms, would do in the future. There was no lack of business. Ward's fame, and to a lesser extent Hill's and Pierce's, was widely acclaimed in philanthropic circles. F. Herbert Wells, after his work with Ward, had worked with Barber and for himself in hospital fund campaigns and thus brought many useful contacts from the hospital field. Wells's son, Louis, later founded the Wells Organization, a fund-raising firm specializing in church campaigns. This organization is now defunct.[6]

With peace came the great race for the lode of philanthropic gold that had been uncovered during wartime. Experienced prospectors, to lead money-hungry institutions to the gold, were in demand. Hill, more than Ward, had foreseen this situation. Hospitals, colleges, libraries, science institutes, art centers, religious and recreational agencies, community funds had laid plans calling for the raising of millions through public appeal. The great church denominations—influenced by Bishop William Lawrence's spectacular success on the eve of the war—began to think in terms of nationwide drives for rehabilitation abroad and for buildings at home. Community chests developed in city after city and soon turned to professional fund raisers for help. Ward and his associates knew the art of promotion, and the new firm had all the business it could handle.

To meet the requests for their services, the senior partners proceeded to recruit a staff of campaign directors. The first man hired was Christian H. Dreshman, who would eventually succeed Ward as senior partner. Dreshman, who died in 1955, had met Ward twelve years before, when Dreshman was serving as acting general secretary of the Pittsburgh, Pa., YMCA and Ward came there in 1907 to direct its building fund campaign. The veteran campaigner was quite impressed with young Dreshman's work, and when he set up his firm he persuaded Dreshman to leave the Y and cast his lot with the fund-raising business. Dreshman, "not particularly simpatico with Hill and Pierce," was brought into the firm by Ward to maintain his balance of power. Dreshman, later, was one of the three fund raisers who took the lead in organizing the American Association of Fund-Raising Counsel in the thirties.

Another early recruit to this burgeoning business was Arnaud C. Marts, who had worked under Lyman Pierce in the Y at Pittsburgh and had helped in Ward's University of Pittsburgh campaign. In 1914 Marts left Y work to go into the insurance business, but after the declaration of war he responded to a call from YMCA Secretary General John R. Mott to return as a fund raiser in the Y's 1917 $35 million nationwide appeal. Harry Blair, who had also served as a Y secretary at Columbus, Ohio, before going into the investment business in Philadelphia, like Marts, was recalled to duty by Mott. The two ex-secretaries, Blair and Marts, were sent to take over the YMCA campaign for Indiana which was floundering because the state Y secretary, an elderly man, was hostile to the wartime program.[7] Marts served as a lieutenant to Blair in this campaign. He also worked closely with Will H. Hays, then chairman of Indiana's State Defense Council, later to be national chairman of the Republican party and the first czar of the movie industry. The association with Hays was to prove fruitful for both men. From the YMCA fund-raising campaign Blair and Marts were drafted for the drive to raise $15 million for the War Camp Community Service. This led them to work in the United War Fund Campaign of 1918 and it was at headquarters there that Marts became participant in the discussions of Ward and Hill over the potential of fund raising as a lifetime work. Marts became convinced of the soundness of the idea and joined the new firm. Will Hays hired Harry Blair to direct the campaign to raise funds for the Theodore Roosevelt Memorial Association. The fledgling Ward firm sent Marts off to Memphis, Tenn., to direct a campaign to raise $35 million for the Southern Methodist Church.

As the Ward firm's business increased, other men were hired. These included George Lundy, Bayard M. Hedrick, and George Tamblyn. Lundy, later to become Marts's partner, was secretary of the Canton, Ohio, YMCA when war broke out. He took leave of his secretary's duties to work in the several wartime campaigns directed by Ward. He, too, became fascinated with the art of raising money and decided to join the new enterprise. George Tamblyn had worked with Hill in the Red Cross membership campaign, directing membership recruitment and roll call promotions for the Atlantic Division. Tamblyn would later found the firm of Tamblyn & Brown. Bayard Hedrick, another YMCA-trained man, would later split away with Marts & Lundy and then help organize still another firm, Pierce, Hedrick, & Sherwood.

Another recruit to fund raising was Olaf Gates, a "Ward man," who had also earlier served an apprenticeship in the YMCA. Gates was not known to the other partners and top campaign directors of the firm, and left no imprint on the fund-raising business after his some eight years in it. In January, 1921, in response to its growing volume of business, the firm opened three branch offices: San Francisco, in the Flood Building, with Lyman Pierce in charge; Chicago, in the Wrigley Building, with Gates in charge; and Nashville, Tenn., with Marts in charge. At the same time Dreshman, Marts, and Gates were made junior partners.

Given the growing demand for those skilled in the art of money raising and the ability of these able, ambitious men, it was inevitable that there would be friction and fragmentation in the young enterprise. Once the organizational work had been completed, a struggle for control developed between the Ward group (Ward, Wells, Dreshman, and Gates) and the Hill group (Hill, Pierce, Marts, Lundy). Clearly, Ward was in the position to call the shots and Hill could not remain happy in a firm dominated by the man he had pushed into the business in the first place. Hill had established strong connections with the Catholic Church in directing the National Catholic War Work $30 million fund drive during the war. In 1920 he directed the first Catholic Charities Campaign for the Archdiocese of New York and raised $2.7 million in this fund-raising "first." Though a Congregationalist, Hill subsequently directed several Catholic fund-raising efforts before his death on January 29, 1932, at his White Plains, N.Y., home.

At the end of 1921 Hill decided to pull out of the firm and set up his own organization, on a floor below in the Metropolitan Tower. Hill never prospered on his own. Business did not come to him in great volume and able men who had worked with him in the war fund-raising efforts obviously did not wish to associate themselves with his new firm. In the mid-twenties Hill was forced to swallow his pride and ask Ward for fund-raising assignments, which the pioneer campaigner gave him. At least this is the recollection of Arnaud Marts.[8] Marts sold out his proprietary interest in the Ward firm at the time Hill resigned, but agreed to continue as a campaign director.

Though he may have resigned from the San Francisco Y for reasons of health, Lyman Pierce was soon harnessing his restless energy to giant fund-raising campaigns managed by the new firm. He helped Arnaud Marts organize the $35 million "Centenary Movement" campaign for the Methodist Episcopal Church. The campaign plan for this drive records that "Messrs. Lyman L. Pierce and Arnaud C. Marts have been taken into the council by the Director-General as Advisory Directors with the purpose of bringing into the campaign their experience in nation-wide campaigns."[9] Once this campaign had been launched, Marts was put in full charge, and Pierce was off to Wisconsin to direct the first united-fund-raising effort on behalf of colleges. Nine Wisconsin denominational colleges—Beloit, Campion, Carroll, Lawrence, Marquette, Milton, Milwaukee-Downer, Northland, and Ripon—made collegiate fund-raising history when they sought to raise $5 million in one joint campaign, a fund drive that was not very successful. From this campaign he went, early in 1920, to the Interchurch World Movement campaign headed by John D. Rockefeller, Jr. Thus the busy, energetic Pierce was always on the move, sprinting from one campaign to the next, and often guiding two or more at once.

Meantime Ward, as the managing partner, was, in the bitter words of one, "just sitting in the office." While Marts, Pierce, and the others were out driving hard to raise new campaign quotas they became irritated because they did not seem to get any help from the home office. There was a growing feeling that the "master campaigner" was becoming more interested in making money than in raising it. The always restless Pierce was swamped for demands for his skilled service so, in 1922, he decided to establish himself as an independent operator. The separation was amicable, on the surface at least, and he maintained a friendly relationship with the firm until he joined with Bayard Hedrick in 1927 to establish the firm of Pierce & Hedrick, today known as Pierce, Hedrick, & Sherwood. Pierce opened an office in San Francisco, which he directed until his death on July 20, 1940, and Hedrick one in New York City.

When Pierce quit the Ward firm, the two remaining junior partners were brought into full partnership and the firm became known as Ward, Wells, Dreshman, & Gates. In February, 1928, the first three partners bought out Gates's share because he "proved of no value to the firm," and his name was removed from the office door. Today the Ward-founded firm is known as Ward, Dreshman, & Reinhardt, headed by Herman F. Reinhardt, who entered the firm from the YMCA in 1928, the year before Ward's death. Reinhardt, a native of Taylor, Pa., started his Y career as a secretary in Scranton, Pa., in 1910, was brought to the headquarters staff in New York in 1912, met Ward, and was immediately attracted to him. Reinhardt deeply reveres Ward's memory.

In 1926 Marts, Lundy, & Hedrick decided to quit the Ward firm and organize one of their own. Marts recalls, "My two major friends in the firm had been Harvey Hill and Lyman Pierce." The three campaigners incorporated under the name of Hedrick, Marts, & Lundy with offices at 527 Fifth Avenue, New York City. The firm operated only one year on this basis when "because of differences in viewpoint" Marts and Lundy bought out Hedrick's interest. It was inevitable, in a young, untried enterprise, that there would be strong clashes of viewpoint. Their differences centered more on such questions as "fees, contract forms, staff members and their remuneration, and the matter of dealing with prospective new clients" than with the campaign method. The Ward-Pierce-Y method was being followed without much innovation these first postwar years. The Ward firm operated on a fixed fee basis from the start, eschewed the percentage of funds raised method of pay, and thus fixed a basic policy for ethical firms to follow. "Most of these decisions were made at midnight discussions in the midst of the pressure of campaigns, which each of us were directing while we were also forming the new firm. Harvey Hill and Lyman Pierce were the leaders in the determination of most of these matters." [10]

Dr. Marts explains the founding of Marts & Lundy, one of the largest firms in the field, in these words:

> In 1925 he [George Lundy] and I began to discuss the matter of starting a new firm in order that we might develop a service which we felt the changing conditions in fund-raising needed. As I look back on our reasons for wanting to break away, I think they were almost wholly connected with a desire to do a creative job and to work out client relationships which we thought were fitting and necessary. . . . The urge that drove us into Marts & Lundy was the creative urge that stimulates people to try their own wings. . . .
>
> Another member of the original firm, Mr. Bayard Hedrick, joined us in our creative aspirations, and in the summer of 1926 we received a charter from the State of New York for the firm of Hedrick, Marts & Lundy. Mr. Hedrick was a very able campaign director and a good business man. . . .
>
> I think one of the basic reasons Mr. Lundy and I were willing to make the effort both in time, energy, and loss of personal income to build up this Firm was a desire on our part to help give dignity and effectiveness to the whole program of Financing Philanthropy. . . .
>
> We felt, and still feel even more deeply, that the voluntary endeavors of free men in our Republic to create and maintain churches, colleges, hospitals, YMCA's and the like, is American democracy at its very best. [11]

You see reflected here a deep sense of religious motivation which plainly shows in the work and thoughts of many of these early YMCA-trained, commercial fund raisers. Yet this motivation did not make them immune to the quest for power and profit. When the new Hedrick, Marts, & Lundy firm had been formed, the three partners did not know each other very well. Marts recalls, "Lundy and I were soon rather surprised to discover that Hedrick had conceived his role in our firm to be that of general manager just as Charles Ward had taken that role for himself in the parent firm. This was rather a shock to Lundy and me especially when we discovered that Hedrick did not intend to go out into the field and direct campaigns as we were doing. At the end of the first year . . . it was agreed that he should withdraw. We then dropped his name from our firm." [12]

Another firm that quickly spun off from the pioneering Ward organization was that of Tamblyn & Brown, founded in 1920. George Tamblyn had worked for Harvey Hill in the Red Cross membership campaigns and was recruited for the new firm by Hill. Tamblyn's first campaign was one to raise money to rebuild the devastated churches of France and for this drive he sought a publicity director. By chance he met John Crosby Brown and offered him the job, though Brown said: "I have never done any publicity. I have never done anything but graduate from Yale and serve in the Army." Brown at first feigned indifference, though he had been seeking a job as a reporter without luck for several weeks, but when Tamblyn offered him $50 a week, big pay in those days, he accepted with alacrity. "I did take it and stayed with Mr. Tamblyn for eighteen months doing publicity for him. He was first working with Mr. Ward and then independently free-lancing. At the end of the eighteen months he saved three thousand dollars and I saved one thousand dollars and we started the firm of Tamblyn & Brown" [13]— a firm still in business.

This team brought more emphasis to the publicity aspects of fund raising than the Ward firm was giving. Tamblyn undertook to handle the organization and Brown the publicity. Brown recalls: "I made up my mind that I would build up the best publicity staff in the country and really tell the story of our universities and colleges and hospitals in a truthful and dignified way . . . to attract understanding and support. . . . Our basic policy was organization and publicity. There are two oars on a boat and you both have got to pull the same way and you have got to pull in harmony." [14] But Tamblyn & Brown had difficulty in pulling on the oars the same way "in harmony."

A later president of Tamblyn & Brown explained that, in view of their different backgrounds, "it was natural for them to think of organization and publicity as being separate, and perhaps it was difficult for them to gain a concept of 'public relations' as an exercise which would, in fund raising, embrace both organization and publicity. . . . Many memoranda passed between the two partners in the early days in an effort to define their respective roles. . . . In that Mr. Tamblyn was the senior partner it might be said that the major emphasis . . . in the early days was on organization services, but that this emphasis shifted when Mr. Brown became president of the corporation in the early 1930's." [15]

When the Ward firm started, fund raising appeared to be a spotty, seasonal enterprise with no assurance of continuous employment for those hiring themselves out as campaigners. Ward and his associates hired campaign directors only for a specific campaign and charged a fee roughly double the director's agreed-upon fee or salary. George Tamblyn disagreed with this policy, so Tamblyn and Brown started on a shoestring to build up a permanent staff. They thought that the prospect of steady, regular employment in a profession would appeal more to people of ability. "We started on that basis and Mr. Ward, every time he saw George Tamblyn, would say, 'I see you are still in business but I know it won't be very long. You can't swing a permanent staff in that field.' " Tamblyn & Brown has operated on a permanent staff basis from its inception.[16] Other firms have long since followed suit.

Another Ward recruit to the field of fund raising, who would later head his own firm, was Howard T. Beaver, who joined the Ward firm as western manager on September 1, 1924. Beaver served in this capacity until December 31, 1935, and then, in 1936, opened his own fund-raising firm in Chicago. Beaver, as most of the other Ward recruits, had formerly worked with the YMCA. He was graduated from William Jewell College in 1913 where, as an undergraduate, he had become deeply involved in the Y association. "The Y amounted to something in colleges in my time," Beaver proudly said. In his junior year, while serving as vice-president of the college YMCA, Beaver helped run a fund-raising drive for the William Jewell YMCA, so that it could engage a professional secretary. "We got no help from national headquarters."

When he left the campus Beaver went to work for the YMCA promoting college Ys in midwestern colleges and universities. In 1917 he was sent abroad by the Y, going to Persia with the Mesopotamian Expeditionary Force. In 1919, on the Persian Gulf, he contracted tropical malaria and was returned home. In Baghdad,

Beaver had become acquainted with Y worker Wayne A. Saarcka, a former associate of Harvey Hill's. After he had recuperated from his malarial attacks, Beaver entered the University of Wisconsin graduate school to study economics. At Wisconsin Beaver was active in the Luther Memorial Church, which borders the campus. Saarcka had been recruited by Hill as a campaign director for the Ward firm, and when Saarcka came to Madison to direct a fund-raising effort for the Luther Memorial Church he and Beaver renewed their wartime friendship. The outcome was that Saarcka talked Beaver into abandoning his graduate work and taking a job with the Ward firm a year later. Saarcka left the Ward firm in the depression. In his tutoring of Howard Beaver, Ward trained another champion fund raiser.[17]

Howard T. Beaver died September 14, 1962, just two weeks after he had presided over his staff's annual conference. Shortly thereafter, his thriving firm Howard T. Beaver Associates was merged with that of the American City Bureau in the first merger of two major fund-raising firms. The merger, agreed to September 29, 1962, climaxed negotiations that dated back to 1959, when the late Bart Brammer of American City Bureau approached Beaver, who declined the proposal at that time. In August, 1962, Beaver reopened the negotiations with Lowell H. Brammer, now chairman of the board of American City Bureau. The merger became operative January 1, 1963. The new firm, American City Bureau/Beaver Associates, is under a single management with headquarters in Chicago and regional offices in New York, Atlanta, Houston, and Sacramento, and employs more than a hundred professional fund raisers.

Two other men whom Ward had introduced to the systematic techniques of money raising were the brothers Carlton and George Ketchum. Unlike the other fund raisers who sharpened their methods in money raising during the war, the Ketchums served as officers in the U.S. army. Carlton was discharged early in 1919 and went to work for the University of Pittsburgh as publicist and fund raiser. George arrived home early in August, and on September 1, 1919, opened the office of Ketchum Publicity—"an organization consisting of George, a stenographer full time and such part of my time as could be had on evenings and Saturdays," Carlton recalls. Norman MacLeod, now executive vice-president of the Ketchum firm, joined in 1920, and Carlton quit his university job to work full time in the firm in the summer of 1921. The firm was incorporated in 1923 as Ketchum, Inc. At the same time an advertising firm was organized as a separate agency, Ketchum, MacLeod & Grove. For the first year and a half Carlton was the whole staff of the advertising firm. As both firms grew, separate staffs were built and the functions separated, and ultimately the two firms became distinct entities. George moved over to head the advertising agency, Carlton back to head Ketchum, Inc., which grew into one of the nation's largest fund-raising firms, though it had been initially organized as a public relations enterprise. But there was more demand for help on fund raising than there was for public relations counsel.

Carlton Ketchum recalls: "We set out to be a public relations firm but when we were only a year old we directed a campaign for the Industrial Home for Crippled Children in Pittsburgh, then one for the Y.W.C.A. in Wilkinsburg, Pa., a Pittsburgh suburb, and Ketchum was launched on a campaign career, not a public relations business." [18] These were the first of some 2,400 fund-raising drives the Ketchum firm would direct over the next forty years and marked the beginning of a steady growth that would, by 1960, carry it to the top of the heap in volume of business. Similarly, Ketchum, MacLeod & Grove is one of the nation's largest non-New York based advertising agencies. The Ketchums, unlike the other Ward protégés, had had no YMCA experience but they had picked up a lot of pointers from Ward and from Frederick Courtenay Barber. All in all, one way or another, Ward had stimulated organized fund raising as a lifework for those in his firm, and the leaders in the firms of Pierce, Hedrick, & Sherwood, Marts & Lundy, Tamblyn & Brown, Ketchum, Inc., and Howard T. Beaver Associates. These would spearhead the Y school of commercial fund raisers.

Ward might claim credit too, at least indirectly, for another fund-raising firm that started in 1919. This was the firm Will, Folsom, & Smith, Inc., started by five former Barber staff members. The initiative was taken by Cornelius M. Smith, a former newspaperman who had come to fund raising via the publicity route. Smith's first interest in fund raising had been whetted in 1907 when, as a reporter for the Baltimore *Sun,* he was assigned to the paper's campaign to raise funds for a new tuberculosis hospital in a Baltimore suburb. Smith left newspaper work in 1915 to work for Barber as a publicity director on hospital campaigns but remained only two years.

In 1919 Smith, Charles D. Folsom, a lawyer, and Dr. Allen Sinclair

Will formed a partnership, Will, Folsom, & Smith, "To conduct fund-raising and public relations programs exclusively for hospitals," a policy to which the firm still adheres. Folsom had worked for Barber, and before that had been a member of the New York law firm Williams, Folsom, & Strouse. Dr. Will was on the *New York Times* staff at this time and really never became active in fund raising. Smith explains: "It is true that Dr. Will was not long an active participant in our firm. . . . Our plan was that Dr. Will would develop a department to conduct the public relations programs which we believed were urgently needed in the hospital field. This sound objective turned out to be premature by many years." [19] Dr. Will retired from active participation when he left the *Times* to become head of the department of journalism at Rutgers University in 1923, but his name was continued in the firm by common consent. Will died on March 10, 1934.

In addition to Smith and Folsom, three of the new staff members in their firm had served apprenticeships with Barber: Mrs. Maude L. Johnstone, Barber's sister; Erna Fyfe; Helen McCauley. All three had left Barber because they found him increasingly difficult to work for. "Mrs. Johnstone and Miss Fyfe continued well into the mid-twenties to direct highly successful campaigns for us. Clients, however, became increasingly reluctant to accept guidance from women directors, regardless of their ability, and so there was no longer a place for them. Miss McCauley served for years as one of our campaign office managers." [20]

Mr. Smith recalls that in these pioneering days "almost anyone of good appearance with a flair for selling, organizing, and publicizing could conduct successful campaigns to raise moderate sums for popular causes. . . . After a few years the novelty wore off and more carefully planned procedures had to be developed." And the man who was to perfect these planned procedures and carry fund raising to new levels of exactness and results was to come from the world of journalism, not from the YMCA school. He was John Price Jones.

John Price Jones Moves in

A bright new star appeared in the World War I fund-raising constellation and started moving across that firmament in the immediate postwar years bringing new light and brilliance to the field.

From the time he undertook fund raising as a lifework in 1919 until he sold his firm in 1955, John Price Jones had directed money appeals netting a total of $836,380,351, of which $746,625,351 was given to philanthropy. Jones came from the world of journalism to bring a new approach and new intensity to the art of getting people to give money. He developed a lucrative fund-raising business quite independent of the influence and ideas of the Ward-Pierce-Y school.

In the early years of commercial fund raising there was little exchange of ideas and information in a field marked by competitive hostility. Jones's fetish for research, for careful record keeping, and for thorough planning made the methodical Charles S. Ward appear slovenly and haphazard by comparison. Jones brought to fund raising a deep appreciation for the value of research and planning, an increased emphasis on public relations, and in his penchant for paper work he codified the principles and procedures of fund raising. The London *Economist* has called him "the most famous of the expert fund-raisers."

John Price Jones was born August 12, 1877, at Latrobe, Pa., in the heart of the anthracite coal region, son of a mine foreman. His parents were David F. and Leah Price Jones. He would years later be characterized by one associate as "a hard-bitten Welshman." Jones was fired with ambition as a boy and meant to pull himself out of the coalfields. He saved his childhood earnings and managed admission to Phillips Exeter Academy. A neighborhood grocer, admiring the boy's spunk, lent him $150 to round out his preparatory school budget. The lender was astonished to receive an initial installment on the repayment during the first weeks of Jones's stay at Exeter. He had obtained a half dozen jobs, including waiter and campus agent for the tailor. Before he finished school he had repaid the storekeeper's loan. Jones finished Exeter in 1898 and entered Harvard that fall. He earned his way through Harvard by serving as correspondent for several daily newspapers.[21] He was graduated in 1902 and from then on Exeter and Harvard were to play influential roles in his life.

Upon leaving college he became private secretary to Congressman Samuel L. Powers, for whom he worked in Washington for two years "doing also a certain amount of newspaper work." Jones then took a reporter's job on the Washington *Post*, where he stayed until 1911. Realizing the need for the broadening experience of travel, Jones quit the *Post* and took off for Europe. He traveled steerage and returned to New York on December 13, 1912, with exactly one dime in his pocket. He quickly landed a job on the New York *Globe*. Next he "tried some publicity work, and then transferred to the New York *Press*. I worked on that paper until Mr. Frank A. Munsey bought it. As he considered me a too-high priced man, he fired me. I then went to the *Sun*, where I remained for almost four years, until Mr. *Munsey bought* that paper too. He and I did not meet on the *Sun,* for after a few months, I decided not to let the lightning strike twice in the same place, so I went into the advertising business." [22] Jones took a job in the H. K. McCann Company advertising agency, forerunner to today's McCann-Erickson. It was from the McCann agency that Jones was drafted to handle the publicity for the Liberty Loan drives in New York City, an assignment that was to launch him on his highly successful career as a fund raiser. Jones served in the Liberty Loan campaign post for two years, on loan from McCann.

Jones was put to work under the direction of Guy Emerson as "assistant director publicity Liberty Loan Campaigns, Second Federal Reserve District, 1917–1919." Emerson, it will be recalled, had been tutored in the art of fund raising by Bishop William Lawrence, in the Episcopal Church Pension Fund campaign on the eve of the war. From this point on Guy Emerson, Harvard '08, would work closely with Jones, Harvard '02, in pioneering fund raising, public relations, and philanthropy. Emerson put Jones in charge of the Press Bureau for the Second Liberty Loan drive. The former reporter quickly brought his urge for system, detail, and planned procedures to bear on the campaign, and in the Second Liberty Loan campaign a well-thought-out plan of publicity was coordinated with the vast soliciting effort.

After America entered the war, $13,856,484,000 was raised in five successive drives. Speakers, posters, pamphlets, and press bureau were skillfully coordinated and exploited in developing an emotional reaction that repeatedly sold the bonds. Jones induced leading screen and stage stars, such as Douglas Fairbanks, Mary Pickford, Charles Chaplin, and Lillian Russell to promote bond sales. One historian asserts, "Where the movies really helped to win the War was in the Liberty Bond drives when the Chaplin-Fairbanks-Pickford triumvirate loosed the purse strings of an adoring nation." He also persuaded New York's utility, Consolidated Edison, to imprint campaign appeals on gas and electric bills, milk companies to put slogans on bottle caps, and banks to insert patriotic appeals with their monthly statements.

For the Fourth Liberty Loan campaign Jones organized a "Features Bureau," an effort to crystallize and standardize the work of using special events as a means of stirring enthusiasm of both the workers and the public. During the Victory Loan drive after the Armistice, Jones took on, in addition to his press and features bureau work, direction of a speakers' bureau. A great believer in putting down on paper all lessons learned, after each campaign Jones would write up lessons that could be utilized in the next drive. "These studies demonstrated conclusively that a new era in fundraising was at hand." [23] Jones would soon put these lessons to work for his Alma Mater.

Thomas W. Lamont, Harvard '92 and partner of J. P. Morgan & Company, had accepted the plea of President A. Lawrence Lowell to lead a drive for a $10 million teachers' endowment fund for Harvard in 1916. Lamont hired a bright young Harvard graduate, Robert F. Duncan, '12, to serve as secretary of this endowment fund campaign, which was launched at a black-tie dinner in the Metropolitan Club in New York City, in November, 1916. Duncan, a native of Clinton, Mass., was recruited from the circulation department of the Springfield *Republican*. The Harvard drive stopped, of course, with America's entry into the war. Lamont quickly persuaded his partner, Henry P. Davison, to take young Duncan to Washington and give him a job in the Red Cross, where he became recorder for the Red Cross War Council. "It would have been a dull youth who didn't see this rope ladder out of the burning building," Duncan recalls. All that was required was a call over the Morgan intercom system. Duncan tells the next chapter of this story this way:

The day after the Armistice in November, 1918, I was back at Morgan's. Mr. Lamont wanted to get right at the job. Before the war, I had known that Guy Emerson '08 had had a part in the Episcopal Church Pension Fund through which Bishop William Lawrence '79, a member of the Harvard Endowment Fund Committee, had raised some $9,000,000 [*sic*] for the Episcopal Church. One of my first calls on returning to New York was on Guy. . . . He told me, "There's a man named John Price Jones '02 handling publicity for the Liberty Loans with whom you ought to talk. He'll be finishing up soon at the

Liberty Loans and he'd be a great help to Harvard." To make it short, I talked promptly to John Price Jones, saw quickly that Guy was right, talked to Mr. Lamont, brought the two together, and in a few weeks Mr. Jones was on the Harvard Endowment Fund payroll—my recollection is at $7,500 a year. Few people ever realized the far-reaching effects for Harvard and the fund-raising profession of Guy's suggestion.[24]

Jones and Duncan took command of the Harvard Endowment Fund campaign and began a collaboration that was to last more than thirty-one years. Jones was made general manager and Duncan continued as secretary. Offices were rented at 165 Broadway and the staff was completed by three wartime Red Cross workers: Edgar H. Wells, '97, Eliot Wadsworth, '98, and Miss Jeanette Sherman who had been Wadsworth's secretary in the "Marble Palace." John W. Prentiss, '98, a partner in Hornblower & Weeks, was fund treasurer and he did much of the personal solicitation of the big givers. "Much of what we now call 'Special Gifts Solicitation' was done by those two men [Lamont and Prentiss] at luncheon clubs and in personal calls within a couple of hundred yards of 23 Wall Street." [25]

When the campaign to raise $10 million for the Harvard Endowment Fund was launched, it not only made fund-raising history but changed the course of American higher education, for Harvard was dramatically telling the nation and sister colleges that the old methods of financing higher education in America were passé. Guy Emerson observed, shortly after the drive was over: "For years men who undertook campaigns of this kind were obliged to shoot almost entirely in the dark. They never could get an accurate estimate of their expenses in advance and they had only the most sketchy idea of the character of the campaign they were going to undertake, what it would involve in energy, what the essential talking points were. They knew in a general way that they were after money and the net result of their appeal usually was 'Please give us some money because we want it.' " [26]

Not so with the Jones-Duncan directed campaign. Efforts to obtain gifts were preceded by an intensive, intelligent publicity program documenting the service which the university, by the training of young people and the research work of its professors, had furnished the nation. The educational program made clear Harvard's pressing needs, as well as her opportunities for greater service, if the money were given to her. The way for the solicitor was paved with forceful publicity. What Jones had learned during the Liberty Loan drives about organization of fund drives—mostly from Guy Emerson—was utilized. Jones made it clear to his associates that he sought to develop enthusiasm for giving to Harvard by dignified means, "without rough and tumble methods." He wisely saw that the publicity must reflect the nature of the institution and that donors must be shown reasons for giving.

Thorough organization preceded the solicitation. Jones and his staff marked out the United States into divisions, subdivided into districts. Under the district chairman there was appointed a vice-chairman for each state within the district. Campaign committees were appointed in each major city. Divisions, districts, states, cities, and clubs were given quotas. The systematic solicitation provided for a visit to every Harvard alumnus. Stag smokers, luncheons, and dinners were staged in every city where there was an appreciable number of Harvard alumni. Rivalry—a stimulus always exploited by the shrewd fund raiser—was stimulated among the classes of Harvard and among the many Harvard clubs. Publicity, directed specifically to Harvard alumni and more generally to the public, stressed that there was a great need for educated men in all important walks of life and that Harvard was producing educated men of the highest culture.

"With a gradual crescendo, as the gifts began to pour in, everyone connected with the University was swept into the movement to push the fund over the top. Over the top it went. $14,200,000 had been raised by November, 1919—and the big movement of organized giving to American education was under way." [27]

Little did Harold J. Seymour, later a pioneer Jones employee, and Robert F. Duncan dream, as they wondered and fumbled in this 1919 Harvard campaign, that they would have a deep professional interest in a Program for Harvard College some forty years later, with its unprecedented goal of $82.5 million. In that campaign Duncan, then a consultant with the firm of Kersting, Brown & Company, Incorporated, was at first the campaign director and later the consultant, while Seymour was consultant to the same firm. Here we have dramatic demonstration of the growth of America's public philanthropy, from the shades of Messrs. Peter, Weld, and Hibben, who went to England in 1641 on behalf of Harvard and produced only £500 for the college and the colony.

With the publicizing of Harvard's great success it was inevitable that other institutions, hard pressed to meet expanded postwar demands, would plan fund drives with the aid of the new professional fund raisers. Smith College was among the first to seek Jones's help in organizing a fund appeal. Duncan recalls that Mrs. Harold C. Greene invited him to her Bronxville home to discuss Smith's needs and the possibilities of a fund drive. Mrs. Greene arranged for Duncan to meet Mrs. Hannah Dunlop Andrews, a Smith alumna, who asked if the "Harvard group" would take on the task of raising funds for Smith.

Duncan reported this to Jones, who mused, "Maybe there's a business in this." On this cue Jones and Duncan went to see Mr. Lamont to discuss the feasibility of starting a small corporation to specialize in directing fund campaigns. The Morgan partner lent encouragement to the idea. Next the pair talked with Guy Emerson, who also gave the idea his hearty approval, which was all the young enterprisers needed. The one person who discouraged the proposal was Eliot Wadsworth, who proved himself a bad prophet in saying, "this business won't last." [28] Wadsworth may well have said this to Jones and Duncan "but when he was offered John Price Jones stock he bought it and collected good dividends for many years thereafter, holding it when it was in demand from the staff." [29]

The John Price Jones firm was incorporated under the laws of the state of New York November 23, 1919, "to give counsel and service in organization and publicity to business houses, institutions of public, semi-public and private character, and to individuals." It was created, Jones's announcement said, "to meet a demand for highly specialized knowledge in these fields." The corporation was formed with these directors: Jones, Duncan, Emerson, George A. Brakeley, H. K. McCann, Parke F. Hanley, Bayard F. Pope, Edward Harding, and Harold W. Thirlkeld. Emerson, his mentor, was at this time vice-president of the National Bank of Commerce. In turn the directors elected Jones president, Brakeley vice-president and general manager, Hanley vice-president, Thirlkeld vice-president, and Duncan secretary and treasurer. Jones rented 5,200 square feet of office space at 150 Nassau Street, at Printing House Square, in the old New York *Sun* offices. The building was owned by the American Tract Society. This area at one time was the center of New York's newspaper industry. It was a matter of great pride to Jones to put his desk in the exact spot where his desk as business editor of the *Sun* had stood. "Jones was always quite sentimental about the old *Sun*," one associate recalls. When the furniture had been bought and the firm was ready to open there "was still a little money in the bank," Duncan recalls.

Jones's first task was to recruit a staff. Two key workers on his Harvard campaign staff were brought to the new offices on Nassau Street: Harold J. Seymour, Harvard '16, moved over to the Jones payroll immediately; Chester E. Tucker, Harvard '19, joined the Jones staff December 15, 1919. Miss Jeanette Sherman, Wadsworth's secretary in the Red Cross, joined the Jones organization as a secretary in December, 1920, serving until 1953 when she retired. Both Seymour and Tucker would attain vice-presidencies in the Jones firm before moving on to other pioneering tasks in fund raising. Tucker also was president for a time.

Like Duncan, Tucker had worked on a Springfield, Mass., newspaper, as Fort Devens correspondent for the *Daily News*, whence he joined the Harvard Endowment Fund Committee staff. Seymour had read proof for the Harvard *Crimson* when in college and was a competent writer with a talent for publicity. Two decades later he would direct the National War Fund drives of World War II. Tucker later became vice-president in charge of development for the University of Pennsylvania, long a Jones client. These three men were Jones's anchor men for a quarter of a century and contributed greatly to his success. In the opinion of those familiar with the situation, Jones never gave this trio due recognition for their contributions to the art of fund raising, nor did he offer them any substantial part of the business. Consequently, all eventually left him.

To take charge of the public relations services in the new firm Jones tapped a former newspaper associate on the New York *Sun*, George A. Brakeley, a Princeton graduate. Starting as reporter, Brakeley successively was assistant night city editor, assistant city editor, assistant editor, and Sunday editor on the *Sun*. From there Jones had drafted him for publicity work in the 1918 and 1919 Liberty and Victory loan campaigns. After the war Brakeley had taken the job of managing editor of the *Red Cross Magazine*, a job he quit to join Jones. He would ultimately return to his Alma Mater as treasurer in charge of fund raising and development. Hanley had managed the Features Bureau in the Liberty Loan publicity department under Jones's tutelage.

Hanley's right-hand man in the Features Bureau—today it would be called special events—H. W. Thirlkeld, was also brought into the new firm. A nonjournalistic recruit to the staff was Frederic W. Allen who had directed the War Savings Stamp campaign in the state of New York. The heavy journalism orientation of this eager young staff naturally resulted in heavy emphasis on the role of publicity in fund raising. Jones's staff thus offered a sharp contrast to the Y-secretary orientation of the other young fund-raising firms splintering off from the pioneer Ward firm.

Heavily influenced by his experience as a reporter, business editor, advertising writer, and Liberty Loan publicist, Jones conceived of his new enterprise as both a public relations and a fund-raising business and envisioned extensive possibilities in both fields. Down through the years he sought to put equal stress on these two fields in obtaining business and in serving clients; but it was in fund raising that he became best known and it was from fund raising that his principal income came. Postwar America was ready for the commercial fund-raising expert; it was not as receptive to the need for the public relations expert.

The Ketchum brothers were learning this in Pittsburgh. Unlike Jones, they pulled back on public relations and concentrated on fund-raising campaign management. The dramatic demonstrations of power staged by George Creel in his direction of the Committee on Public Information and by Ivy Lee and Charles Sumner Ward in the giant Red Cross fund drives had awakened great interest in the art of influencing public opinion through barrages of publicity. Yet the public relations counseling business grew slowly in the 1920's in sharp contrast to the tremendous boom in public relations practice that followed World War II. Jones sought to ride both horses all the way, never too successfully in public relations as separate from fund raising.

Early in 1920, for example, Jones issued a pamphlet: "We take pleasure in announcing the organization of a special bureau devoted to publicity for social affairs. In this bureau are competent writers and skilled organizers ready for the instant service of corporation clients. This bureau is prepared to give service as follows: Publicity Advance, Announcements, News Stories, Special Articles, Executive direction in organizing features [special events], meetings, dinners, bazaars, balls, entertainments. Mail service in sending out invitations, announcements, appeals." In another promotion pamphlet issued in Jones's ceaseless quest for new business, he promoted

"A Summary of Services That Will Crystallize an Idea, Advance a Cause, Sell a Product." The pamphlet promoted these services: public relations, publicity, fund raising, direct mail advertising, and a letter shop. Early in the business Jones created a direct-mail organization for his fund-raising campaigns and then sold this as a service to keep the large mail-room staff busy. Jones hated to see employees idling away company time.

Under the heading "How the Corporation Can Serve" the 1920 pamphlet read: "Does your enterprise need publicity or organization or both? Do you want to secure funds in behalf of a college, school, or some other public enterprise? Do you need advice in campaign organization? Do you need a new and different point of view in your advertising? Do you wish to know the attitude towards your concern or your product? Do you want to win increased confidence from your employees? . . ." Here one sees Jones envisioning the money-making possibilities of today's separate and lucrative fields of fund raising, public relations, public opinion research, advertising, and employee relations services. Of the many services he offered in an effort to keep a growing staff profitably occupied, it was in fund raising that Jones was to make his mark.

In the post-World War I era of public relations the Jones firm was competing against the well-known Ivy Lee, Pendleton Dudley, Harry Bruno, William H. Baldwin, Edward L. Bernays, and other public relations pioneers—and without spectacular success. In a printed "Survey of the Margarin Industry and Its Public Relations"— obviously a presentation designed to land this PR account—found in Jones's papers, 1920–1922, Jones claims, "The John Price Jones Corporation which in point of personnel and in number of accounts is the largest public relations corporation in America." This was obviously a severe stretching of the essential truth though it may have been literally true. Duncan never shared Jones's enthusiasm for building up the public relations side of the business or his penchant for detailed paper work. Duncan insisted then, as he does today, that these were two separate fields. The test of time validated his position. Today fund raising and public relations, in terms of business organization, are distinctly separate professions, though the two functions are inextricably intertwined in the art of raising money. Duncan took the same position in regard to the conduct of a fund appeal. The peppery Duncan held that "organization is the heart of the business. . . . Although publicity is essential, organization bears the ultimate responsibility of producing the funds."

It is Duncan's view that Jones's fame as a money raiser led to business in the one field and blocked off the other: "We became so labeled in the philanthropic field that our PR business didn't develop." This became a perennial topic at the annual staff conference Jones initiated as part of his systematic training of his staff— an idea pioneered by the American City Bureau and one all the other large fund raisers ultimately adopted. At the 1935 staff conference Bayard F. Pope, Jr., asked an obvious question that eternally bothered the Jones executives, "Why, if we are equipped to conduct a public relations account, don't we have a few public relations clients?" Pope answered the question with these reasons:

1. Because most of our staff are engaged in fund-raising and seldom think of the commercial side of our service.
2. Because few members of the staff realize how much commercial experience we really have had and because they try to sell commercial jobs on the basis of our fund-raising experience.
3. Because we are regarded by the public as a fund-raising organization and because the public fails to see the similarity between the two types of work.[30]

In a plans book dated March 1, 1921, Jones set forth this as the purpose of his firm:

The purpose of the Corporation is to originate and promote an idea, to develop an intangible thought into a concrete reality which the public can hear or see or read about and understand and through understanding be moved to a definite course of action or be restrained from action. In the development of this work, the Corporation is much like the selling or promotion department of a big corporation. We originate ideas for our clients, ideas that help in the development of a smoothly running organization, that help in putting that organization in a better light before the public or help that organization sell more goods, or help in the spreading of a humanitarian, religious, economic, or educational idea that works for the general good of all. The Corporation, furthermore, serves a client in need of publicity or organization advice in much the same way that a lawyer gives legal counsel. To carry on this work with the utmost effectiveness requires the application of new methods within the Corporation and the generation of new ideas for general distribution in behalf of its clients.[31]

To carry out these objectives Jones, in his reorganization plan of 1921, set up six departments: Executive, New Business, Planning, Organization (the fund-raising operation), Production, and Controller. With the new organization plan went a manual of standard practices which Jones laid down for all hands. A great memo writer and rule maker, Jones kept a taut rein on his staff and required them to submit daily reports. One former staff member recalls: "The daily report was a nightmare to the staff but a great boon to the business. It established a system of control which made it apparent from day to day where a job was going. He also required you to report on 'Work to Be Done' so you had to plan ahead."

Though he spelled out the plans, the function, and the objectives of the new firm in minute detail in 1919 Jones was to admit a decade later: "At the start of our business we were pretty vague about our task. We were hazy about publicity. We have learned a lot in ten years, and most of what we have learned you will find in Standard Practice." [32] Jones and his associates did learn because when he sold control of the firm to Charles W. Anger, in June, 1955, the Jones firm had directed campaigns raising $836,380,351 broken down as follows: [33]

Categories

Higher Education	$237,206,696
Secondary Education	15,357,571
Education for Handicapped	872,390
Health Organizations, Hospitals, Homes	88,793,225
Organized Social Work	41,995,931
Civic Projects	36,627,156
War Relief and National Defense	128,469,539
Emergency Relief	78,913,640
Membership Drives	4,316,299
Political Committees	8,856,163
Religious	12,160,877
John Price Jones of Canada	70,893,145
Total Amount Raised in Fund-Raising Campaigns	$746,625,351
Total Raised in Business Reorganization Work	89,755,000
	$836,380,351

In accomplishing these business goals Jones made himself quite wealthy and firmly established his name in the history of American philanthropy and public relations. What manner of man was John Price Jones?

Jones often remarked that anybody by the name of Jones who could make a success of anything was entitled to double credit. He thought this would be especially true of one named John Jones. He knew the importance of establishing himself as a distinct personality and thus began using his full name, John Price Jones, in 1917. There are two versions of his decision. He once told his staff: "During the Liberty Loan campaign somebody asked me what my middle name was. I said Price. They were getting out a letterhead and put my name on it as John Price Jones, and within a week after the appearance of the letterhead everybody called me by my full name. They said it was easier than saying John P. Jones." [34] On other occasions he said it was suggested to him by his friend the poet Vachel Lindsay, a man Jones deeply admired. "Vachel Lindsay told me John Price Jones had a swing to it," he would often explain. Jones and Lindsay, a lonely, troubled man who later took his own life, found solace in each other's companionship. Jones was later active in organizing the Vachel Lindsay Association.

Whatever its origin, the name John Price Jones gave its owner a distinctive brand that suited his ego and his business objectives. He was a man small in build, large in ego though often described as self-effacing, tireless in determination, and great in ability. The success of his fund-raising firm provided the big drive for Jones's life. While still a cub reporter on the Washington *Post*, Jones married Miss Frieda B. Suppes at Johnstown, Pa., December 5, 1905. They never had any children. Jones had few hobbies and few close friends. His work was pretty much his whole life save for an annual vacation on a dude ranch near Cody, Wyo., where he liked to ride. In the early years of the firm Jones lived in a New York City apartment but later bought a farm at Pineville, Pa., in Bucks County. In later years he commuted to work from there and puttered about the farm now and then.

Jones was a short, compactly built man with dark eyes and a ruddy face. He had been a gymnast at Harvard, excelling on the parallel bars. Until middle age he played handball, usually at his favorite haunt, the Harvard Club. Jones was a moderate drinker but a heavy cigar smoker and as he moved through his offices at 150 Nassau giving out directives he would leave a heavy odor of smoke in his wake, much to the annoyance of his staff. Much like Charles Ward, Jones was a rather shy man who did not mix easily in social gatherings. He once confessed that though he had been instrumental in raising nearly a billion dollars he had never personally asked anyone to contribute to any cause.

Whereas Ward was described as "austere" by his subordinates, Jones was said to be inarticulate. Yet he could write memos, plan books, and directives, and did so, endlessly. As an employer he was a paradox. He was considered a martinet, yet never had the heart to discharge those who proved to be incompetent. He was a determined man and brooked no opposition from his staff when he decided to set a new policy or adopt a new procedure. Yet he was receptive to ideas and generous in sharing ideas, but was jealous of ever sharing his power. Jones drove his staff hard but always drove himself harder.

Jones was a precise, punctual man and insisted on the same qualities in his staff. Office Bulletin No. 4, issued January 21, 1920—in the early months of the firm—carried this as its lead item: "LATENESS: A record kept of attendance this morning shows that of 83 employees of the John Price Jones Corporation, 32 arrived after 9:10. It has come to the attention of the Accounting Dept. that persons arriving at 9:15 or 9:20 have charged the half hour on the time cards from 9 to 9:30 to various clients. This is obviously unfair to our clients. All members of the staff should report promptly at 9 o'clock." [35]

Jones wasted hours of company and employee time in detailed, meticulous record keeping and in reports. Donald Hammond once recorded in a memo, "Some of us, I feel, do a vast amount of futile and unnecessary paper work." A mild understatement indeed. In the opinion of one long-time associate, "Jones had very little sense of humor. He was all business and damn well determined to put his ideas into practice." Another says, "He always drove volunteers hard. To Jones nothing was ever impossible." Another describes him as "a great checker upper."

Unlike the Pierce-Ward school of fund raisers, Jones took no interest in religion. His official biographies list no church affiliation. His great loyalties were to Exeter, Harvard, and the Republican Party. Jones was an archconservative politically. He did not encourage intimacy and very few people called him "Jack." Robert F. Duncan was one of the few who did. Once, in a Memo to the

Staff dated May 5, 1936, Jones tartly wrote: "Men in your type of business have one serious fault and that is speaking of important men by their first name." While a former Jones vice-president could well say he was "a slow man with a buck," he was a soft touch for loans from those in the fund-raising field and was often used as such. Another associate says that in this respect he was "not a good judge of character and not a shrewd employer of people." From those who worked with Jones comes a typical picture of a man who pretended to be tough; gruff on the surface to hide his shyness but softhearted underneath. Jones well knew the value of self-promotion.

Jones brought great advances to the art of fund raising as well as financial success for himself. He had a genius that enabled him to harness the newly discovered power of publicity to the efficient business methods he admired, and thus to create a wholly new approach to fund raising. He undergirded fund appeals, from the early twenties on, with thorough research on the institution to be served, its degree of support, and the case to be presented in the fund appeal. He insisted on standardizing the procedures of fund-raising, yet knew that each campaign must be tailored to the institution for which it was waged. He would tell his staff: "Standard Practice [the firm bible] doesn't tell you how to handle your job. It tells you how to handle the various parts of your job, but not the job complete. It is not desirable that it should. Every man must be free to work out his own plans, his own philosophy, his own psychology, his own pattern, his own fundamental principles." [36]

Because he accepted the fact that to obtain and keep able men he would have to hire them on a yearly basis, Jones saw to it that their slack time was put to good use in doing research and in planning new campaigns. Out of these slack season researches came new procedures and recodification of experience learned in previous campaigns. The Jones firm invested large sums in building a strong central library, an effort still not fully matched by the other fund-raising organizations. His flair for promotion and heavy emphasis on a planned publicity program to precede fund raising represent another contribution to this field. In every endeavor he insisted upon pinpoint targeting and "raised merry hell" about wasted motion. In a typical memorandum to his staff dated June, 1925, Jones reveals his philosophy in these words:

Facts first.

Then analysis.

With complete information, intelligently classified, a reasonable plan will reveal itself.

If there is time, make a preliminary test.

Beware of irrelevant stunts. Every shot should be carefully aimed at the target. . . .

Think it out first, then write. After that it probably won't need much talking over.

JOHN PRICE JONES [37]

As the voluminous records of the John Price Jones Corporation make abundantly clear, Jones preferred to think things out first, then write a memo or plan, and not spend much time talking things over. He was brisk, sometimes brusque, and always businesslike. Making fund raising a business was his business, his life, his hobby. It is an extra legacy of Jones's work that he kept such careful, complete records and then made these available to students of public relations and philanthropy by turning them over to his Alma Mater when he sold his business in 1955. The Jones records provide the most complete picture of the operations of a fund-raising organization openly available.

The new Jones firm prospered from the start and its young but experienced staff was soon involved in several fund-raising appeals. The methods and manner of the Harvard Endowment Fund campaign were quickly put to work for Smith College. Publicity again stressed the institution's services to the nation and its increased opportunity to serve if supported. Jones "carefully mapped out the length of the campaign, quotas, purpose and tone of publicity, the best channels for driving home the appeal. The basic theme of the Smith appeal was "the widened scope of women's activities today meant that Smith had greater potentialities of service than ever before as the largest institution of its kind." The campaign was obviously linked to the campaign for woman suffrage, now nearing a climax in America. This appeal, "Smith Must Go Forward," was widely publicized through the activities of the Press Bureau, a Speakers Bureau, a Features Bureau, advertising, pamphlets, and a national campaign bulletin to keep workers and donors informed.[38]

Jones had been deeply impressed by his exhilarating role in the stirring Libery Loan drives of World War I. Of this period he once wrote:

Now, for the first time, a well thought out program of publicity was coordinated with the raising of money. After America entered the struggle, $13,856,484,000 was raised through five Liberty Loans which were the immediate ancestors of the modern campaign since they undertook to educate people to giving. . . . Speakers, pamphlets, and a press bureau united in developing an emotional wave which repeatedly swept the entire country. The "feature" [special event] came into being as a means of focusing and concentrating the feelings thus aroused. The high degree of organization characteristic of American business was now applied to the problem of working out plans by which groups of men and women rapidly assembled, could be directed efficiently, co-ordinated in their activities, and kept happy in their work. . . . The first few years after the Armistice saw the lessons learned in the Liberty Loan campaigns applied to many other projects.[39]

In his written records Jones never took cognizance of the dramatic fund-raising efforts of Charles S. Ward and the Red Cross during the war. Harking back to his Liberty Loan experience when he had observed the value of using the friends and relatives of men in uniform, Jones and his associates pressed into service "all the friends and relatives of Smith women." The result of this effort was that the campaign goal of $4 million was passed on June 1, 1920, by a total of $21,893. Success begets success and in the next few years the Jones firm was retained to direct campaigns for Bryn Mawr, Mt. Holyoke, Barnard, Wellesley, and Simmons.

As the Harvard campaign was nearing its climax and he was working out the details of organizing his business, Jones was undertaking another campaign for his Wall Street sponsor, Thomas W. Lamont. The Brooklyn-born painter and sculptor, Frederick W. MacMonnies, was a close friend of Lamont's and had sold the Morgan banker the idea of erecting a colossal statue by MacMonnies on the battlefield near Paris, to commemorate French heroism in the Battle of the Marne in 1914. The sculptor and the banker estimated that $275,000 would be needed to finance the project, including a substantial commission for the artist.

Lamont called Jones, and out of this came the appeal for "America's Gift to France." The idea was presented to the American people this way: "since the rich and poor, the young and old of France had all contributed towards the gift of the Statue of Liberty in 1879, it was thought desirable by the sponsors that the gift should be through popular subscription with expenses of the campaign underwritten."[40] America had become quota conscious during the war and this drive was made "representative" by establishing quotas, first by states, next by cities. Each community had its America's Gift to France Committee, usually headed by the mayor. Anything over the cost of the monument was to go to French charity.

All the wartime techniques were pulled out of the Jones kit. Motion pictures of MacMonnies working on the statue and of President Wilson making the first donation were widely shown in movie theaters. Buttons, suggestive of those used by the Red Cross, went to all subscribers. Posters by Albert Sterner were tacked up in every city, town, and hamlet informing the people where they could make their contributions. Cartoons, photographs, news stories, Sunday features, and magazine articles supplemented thousands of leaflets distributed in the drive. Yet this fund appeal, small in comparison to the multimillion dollar drives of wartime, got short shrift from the *New York Times*. The *Times* carried the opening announcement under a small 10-point head on its editorial page January 26, 1920. This story quoted Lamont as saying that "no campaign drive will be made, but committees will be named in each State to have charge of the collection."

The drive was staged the week of March 20–27 and during this week the *Times* carried a tiny, one-paragraph story on page 21 of its Saturday, March 27, issue. This item announced that the prize-fighter, Georges Carpentier of France, would speak that afternoon from a platform in Times Square where a 10-foot container for gifts was located. Nonetheless, by July, 1920, the goal of $275,000 had been met and Jones's fame as a fund raiser thereby enhanced.[41] The direct-mail campaign was directed by Robert F. Duncan and was aimed, in the words of Harold J. Seymour, "largely at Francophiles and friends of Tom Lamont." Seymour continues: "The campaign was professionally notable for the prose style of one Harry Powers Story, who wrote the leaflet and perpetrated the following emetic in describing the point at which the statue was to be placed: 'God marked his finger in the sand, and smiled.' "[42] The statue, "not one of Mr. MacMonnies' greatest triumphs," was subsequently placed at Meaux, supposedly the farthest point of the German advance toward Paris. The statue was presented to the people of France on September 11, 1932, by U.S. Ambassador Walter Edge.

The first public relations accounts obtained and serviced by the Jones firm were those listed simply as "Coal Operators" and the National Budget Commission. On the night of October 31, 1919, nearly 400,000 soft coal miners had struck against the operators of the bituminous mines of the nation, from Illinois to Pennsylvania, despite a temporary injunction obtained by U.S. Attorney General A. Mitchell Palmer. The *New York Times* of November 1, 1920, reported that 394,600 miners had gone out on strike, though their leaders had been silenced by the court order. Coal operators, meeting in Cleveland, vowed to keep the mines running.

Thus began one of the bitterest struggles in American industrial history with federal troops and state guards being used, finally, to crush the miners' strikes. Jones's financial records show that the firm started billing the "Coal Operators"—as it was carried on the books—November 29, 1919. Unfortunately the casebooks on this early Jones account have been discarded. Firm records show only that the client's headquarters was in Washington, D.C., and that the firm did a survey, prepared a plan, and did publicity work. Jones's records also show some work for the Bituminous Coal Operators and the National Coal Association in 1921 and 1922. Harold J. Seymour, who worked on the "Coal Operators" account, today says: "I don't think it amounted to much more than the fact that Jones had need of clients even more than money in this commercial field. . . . I'm as sure as anything can be that John L. Lewis was never caused even one extra heartbeat, let alone any loss of sleep." [43] Later entries showed the West Virginia Coal and Coke Company as a public relations client. These would not be Jones's last services to employers engaged in a bitter labor battle. He aided the steel companies in the bloody 1937 Little Steel Strike when anti-unionism met an unlamented and violent end in the New Deal era.

The National Budget Committee represented an effort of big taxpayers to cut costs of government in this era of "normalcy." The stated goal was "to promote efficiency and economy of Government finances" by getting new budget laws adopted by Congress. This campaign was led by John T. Pratt, national chairman, and Henry L. Stimson, a director of the Committee. R. Fulton Cutting served as chairman of the New York Committee. Conservative businessmen then, as today, were convinced that the nation was headed for financial ruin because of its large debt and "many of the friends of Mr. Jones in Wall Street and State Street, Boston, were positive that the days of great fortunes were at an end." The National Budget Committee campaign was directed by George A. Brakeley. Seymour wrote a series of editorials for the Committee's house organ in the style of Mr. Dooley, but he doubts "if this had any lasting effect on the public passion for thrift and economy." The main effort was the promotion of a National Budget Club chain and a *Fortnightly* magazine. The Fortnightly Clubs were organized to "serve as forums for discussions of public finance." This account terminated in 1922.

A financial statement for January 3, 1920, when the firm was two months old, shows these Accounts Receivable: [44]

America's Gift to France	$4,555.90
Bryn Mawr	2,015.78
Coal Operators	4,777.46
Harvard Endowment Fund	5,004.01
Intercollegiate Treaty Referendum	1,149.25
National Budget Commission	4,958.30
Smith College Fund	7,284.53
Haarlem House	266.38

By November 20, 1920, at the end of the first year's operation, the John Price Jones Corporation had accumulated assets of $90,862.24, earned a net profit for the year of $33,973.80, and firmly established the name of John Price Jones at the head of the fund raisers' parade to the rich fields of public giving.[45] The firm's assets, in another twenty-five years, would be more than a half million and Jones would be an affluent citizen.

On the occasion of his eightieth birthday, in 1957, it would be glowingly said of John Price Jones: "This is the man who did the hard work—the work of building up a new profession—who trained and nurtured more men and more companies of men in this new profession than any other teacher . . . the man who has developed among business and civic leaders a greater sense of responsibility for giving, for leadership and for public service than they had had before." [46] Praise exaggerated and not quite accurate, to be sure, but nonetheless this determined little man with big ideas and big goals saw the potentials of a people's philanthropy and drove toward them systematically and relentlessly.

A third group of prospectors joined in the rush to the philanthropic gold fields that had been struck during World War I. These
were the trained campaigners of the American City Bureau, the
organization that had spearheaded the Chamber of Commerce movement which spread across America just before World War I. The
American City Bureau brought to the new commercial enterprise
of fund raising a wealth of campaign experience but little background in philanthropy. This firm dates back to 1911. That year
Harold and Edgar Buttenheim, two young and ambitious brothers
who were working on McGraw-Hill trade publications, bought
an anemic *American City* magazine from the Civic Press for $2,000.
Harold, the older of the two, was on the editorial staff of *Iron Age*
and Edgar was an advertising salesman for the same publication.

Harold S. Buttenheim's career in trade journalism started in 1898
when, shortly after his graduation from Jersey City High School,
he went to work as an errand boy for the *Street Railway Journal*.
Harold Buttenheim recalls: "If my memory serves me correctly,
the combined advertising and subscription revenue was less than
$200 per month," [47] when they bought the magazine. Edgar
Buttenheim took over the business side and Harold assumed the
editorship of the magazine designed primarily for municipal officials; "they divided the task between them on this functional basis
and during the subsequent 35 years neither has wished that he had
the other's job." At first the Buttenheims held on to their jobs on
Iron Age until their new magazine looked as if it would be successful. First Harold resigned to devote full-time to the magazine, and
a few months later he was joined by Edgar. From then on the two
worked closely to build a successful magazine, promote municipal
reform, build the chamber of commerce movement, and finally
emerge as one of the giants in the fund-raising business. When
Harold Buttenheim retired in 1956 the magazine was averaging 300
pages an issue.

The Buttenheim brothers moved on to the municipal scene as
the era of reform was still in full flower in the wake of Lincoln
Steffens' muckraking exposés, *The Shame of the Cities*.[48] This was
the period of Woodrow Wilson's "New Freedom" reforms. Through
the editorial pages of their new magazine, they quickly joined in

support of better, cleaner municipal government. Editorially, Harold Buttenheim started hammering on the need for citizens to become involved in local government, on the need for "a group of organized citizens within every community which influence and check on elected officials."

Harold kept pounding at the need for "organized citizenship" and out of this came the establishment of the American City Bureau on April 22, 1913, to "promote the general welfare and prosperity of communities of any and all kinds, the health, safety, and comfort of the citizens thereof respectively and to raise money for civic and philanthropic purposes." The ACB, as it is known in fund-raising circles, was organized by the Buttenheims more to promote civic progress than to raise money. Initially they had no plans for going into fund raising. The brothers, though no longer active in the management of the ACB, still retain 51 per cent of the voting stock and thus retain control.

The initial field staff of the ACB included three men: Daniel A. Reed from upstate New York, later to serve many years in the House of Representatives; J. Harold Braddock, and Lowry W. Statler. Reed left the firm in 1918 when he was first elected to Congress. Three chamber of commerce campaigns were conducted in 1913.[49] The first one, in Olean, N.Y., brought in $15,750 in membership dues. The other two were in Syracuse, N.Y., and Reading, Pa. The ACB collected only $40,000 in its first year and charged its fees on a basis of a percentage of the intake, the common practice in those days. In organizing and directing these membership campaigns for chambers of commerce, the three campaign directors borrowed heavily and openly from the techniques developed for the YMCA by Ward and Pierce.

The Bureau was but one of many concerns engaged in organizing chambers of commerce and promoting the civic booster spirit which was fervently embraced by American businessmen in this period. This era saw the birth of the businessman's service club, utterly American. The first Rotary club was organized in Chicago in 1905 and in August, 1910, sixteen Rotary Clubs met there to organize the National Association of Rotary Clubs. Two years later this service club idea spread to Canada, England, and Ireland—and ultimately around the world. The first Kiwanis Club was organized in 1915 in Detroit and Lions International's first club was organized in 1917. The object of these clubs, in the expressions of their promoters, was to get the merchant to see beyond his store door and realize that he had a responsibility for improving the community, and, despite their many shortcomings, the clubs did teach the self-centered merchant and professional man to set aside part of his time for civic tasks. It was this civic booster spirit—later to be satirized by Sinclair Lewis in *Babbitt*—that the American City Bureau capitalized on and furthered in its promotion of community-minded chambers of commerce.

In 1920 the Bureau, under the leadership of Lucius Wilson, was affluent enough to start a promotional publication for the civic and chamber field, *Community Leadership*. Its announced purpose was "further stimulating civic activity by chambers of commerce." On this occasion *Survey* magazine said of the ACB: "With a field staff of 69 it has become one of the largest national influences for civic betterment." [50] And in the Buttenheims' eyes the most wholesome. The first issue of *Community Leadership* asserted this in reference to the start of the Bureau:

Six years ago a group of four men came together to form the American City Bureau. The Bureau at first was regarded as merely another addition to a number of concerns already engaged in "organizing" chambers of commerce. It soon became apparent, however, that the service it offered differed in a number of ways from the service obtainable elsewhere. The vital difference lay in the fundamental philosophy on which the service is based. These other concerns were asking men to join chambers of commerce because such organizations would "bring factories to town," fight railroads, boom real estate, and for other similar reasons—purely selfish. The American City Bureau made its appeal squarely to civic patriotism. Its representatives asked men to give their money and energy to make their communities better places in which to live and do business. . . . Ensuing events have shown that this confidence in the idealism of America's leading citizenship has been justified. The Bureau is today practically the only institution of its kind in the world. [51]

Word of the ACB's success in reorganizing and organizing chamber of commerce bodies with membership campaigns was intensively promoted through the parent magazine. In 1914 the field staff was increased to eight men and they staged campaigns for the trade bodies in Johnstown, Pa., Youngstown, Ohio, Bluefield, W.Va.; Petersburg, Va.; South Bend, Ind., Williamsport, Pa., and Glens

Falls, N.Y. By the war's end the ACB had "more than fifty" men on its field staff and the combined office and field staff of the campaign bureau and the magazine totaled more than a hundred. Another concern active in the promotion of chambers of commerce in these early years, the Town Development Company, was absorbed by the ACB in August, 1918.

The ACB claimed in its house publication, *Bureau News*, started in 1919, that "One hundred and twenty Chambers of Commerce in as many cities owe their present strength to the services of the American City Bureau. . . . During the past twelve months the Bureau has become an international institution. Six vigorous Chambers of Commerce have been developed in Canada under the Bureau's direction. More effectively to care for the needs of these two hundred organizations and of others which are continually being added to our clientele, three new offices are being opened—in Chicago, San Francisco, and Toronto.[52] To train secretaries for these new chambers now burgeoning across the land the ACB started a "Summer School of Community Leadership" in 1915 and continued this school until 1921, when it was crowded out by the now-vigorous Chamber of Commerce of the United States, and the National Association of Commercial Organization Secretaries (NACOS).

The purpose of these summer schools, according to Harold Buttenheim, was to train chamber of commerce secretaries and other community leaders to run a successful local organization and to suggest a wider variety of civic activities than most commercial organizations had previously undertaken. He recalls with pride that "in 1920 and 1921 we had attained sufficient prestige to be welcomed by the Board of Regents of the University of Wisconsin to the lecture halls and fraternity houses of that great educational institution." [53]

After World War I, as the chamber movement grew in numbers and in strength, the chamber of commerce professionals began to look askance at the American City Bureau and to resent its domination of the movement in which it had long played a major role. The national chamber of secretaries' newly organized trade group, in 1921, arranged with Northwestern University to run a competing summer course to be known as the National Institute for Commercial and Trade Organization Executives. That year competing schools were held. Buttenheim claimed: "Many a Chamber of Commerce secretary who would have preferred to attend the ACB school at

Madison, was induced by his board of directors or by his desire to stand well with the powers that be in the National Chamber or NACOS, to enroll at Evanston. So fine a reputation had the Bureau gained from its previous schools, however, that the actual enrollment in 1921 at Madison was greater than that at Evanston." [54]

Even so the Bureau dropped its summer school after the 1921 session and this symbolized its gradual shift from chamber of commerce organizing to community fund raising. Buttenheim's explanation of the withdrawal is this: "The Summer Schools of Community Leadership had been a serious drain on the Bureau's finances, which had been further hit by the nation-wide depression of 1920–21. So we did the sensible thing: we told the National Chamber and NACOS that if they would continue the Institute at Evanston as an annual event, we would consider that our pioneering effort had served its purpose and would pull out. . . . This proposition was accepted, and the National Institute has continued ever since." [55]

The fact was that the chamber movement had developed a trained body of secretaries who moved about the country much as the professional city manager, who emerged in the same period, was doing. These "professionals" resented, understandably, the dominant role ACB had won for itself because it was, after all, a commercial concern out to make a profit. Consequently, these new professionals maneuvered and pressured to gain control and direction of this movement for themselves. The chamber movement was now generating its own leadership as men came into large chambers as assistants, then moved out to become secretary of a small-town chamber of commerce, and from there started the climb up to the largest cities with such trade groups. ACB-designed membership campaign procedures were by now common knowledge among these secretaries.

The civic booster-chamber of commerce rah-rah movement had its heyday in the 1920's—the period when Calvin Coolidge blandly said that "the business of America is business." The best interests of the Buttenheim magazine, the *American City*, dictated that these new foci of community power, the chamber secretaries, not be alienated. Thus the ACB discreetly and gradually withdrew from the chamber of commerce organization business. The Bureau would learn, to its dismay, how completely independent the chamber movement had become when, in 1949, it launched and tried to sell a public relations counseling service to chambers of commerce. This effort, fathered by John Mack, an ACB vice-president for many years, never got "off the ground." Lowell Brammer, who today heads ACB, explains: "Jack Mack failed to realize that the Chamber of Commerce field had professionalized itself and did not need such aids and assistance. The bureau folded with his retirement. We were not equipped to compete in the general field of public relations." [56] Mack, incidentally, started his career with the old Town Development Company, leaving it to join the ACB four months before the latter firm bought out Town Development on August 1, 1918. The Bureau's influential role in building and shaping the chamber of commerce movement is an important chapter in American social history.

Harold S. Buttenheim—the editor of *American City* and guiding force of the Bureau—had never thought of fund raising as a possible work of profit for his business concerns until the decline of his civic betterment and municipal reform programs. He was a great believer in the power of "organized citizenship"—one of his favorite phrases. He was the motivating force behind the Tax Institue of Princeton, N.J., the Citizens Housing and Planning Council of New York City, and the National Association of Planning Officials.[57] Buttenheim retired from active participation in his two enterprises in 1956 just before he reached his eightieth birthday. (In 1906 Mr. Buttenheim married Margaret E. Stoddard, daughter of William O. Stoddard, Abraham Lincoln's private secretary and biographer. She died in 1924. They had no children.)

The farsighted Buttenheim brothers were willing to plow back profits from their chamber campaigns to build up their staff, train it, and develop useful information for city governmental and civic leaders. The ACB, almost from the start, emphasized the need for research to develop information useful to community leaders and to improve the ACB's campaign techniques. The Bureau, to train members of its staffs and the new secretaries for the chambers, spent large sums in educational programs and pamphlets. It initiated the staff conference that today is a standard fixture of the major firms in commercial fund raising. The Bureau held its first staff conference in 1915 at the old Hardware Club in New York City, according to Harold Buttenheim's best recollection.

This useful means of the staff's exchange of experiences and methods has been continued to this day on an annual or sometimes a semiannual basis. The proceedings of the staff conferences of the major fund raisers offer a rich source material on the specific campaigns directed by these various firms. The Bureau also was instrumental in its early years in organizing a special committee of educators, called "National Committee for Chamber of Commerce Cooperation with the Public Schools." Aided by a foundation grant, this committee prepared and distributed three pamphlets bearing the general title, *Know and Help Your Schools*—one of the early efforts to promote stronger support of public schools.

Although the Buttenheims had originally conceived of the American City Bureau as "a clearing house for information concerning every activity making toward municipal improvements and community advance," [58] it was inevitable that the Bureau's demonstrated prowess in organizing campaigns for chambers of commerce would be sought to raise money for civic philanthropy. As did most of the pioneers in commercial fund raising, the Bureau got its first experience in World War I when several members of the ACB staff were turned over to the War Camp Community Service to conduct that warborn agency's 1917 nationwide drive for $3,750,-000. In 1918 the Bureau was hired to direct the Baltimore War Chest Campaign and its success led to many repeat campaigns there. From 1919 to 1959 the ACB directed sixty-nine separate fund drives in that Maryland metropolis. Initially the Buttenheims did not exploit this early success in fund raising. The work of organizing and re-organizing defunct chambers of commerce went steadily ahead, war or no war. The campaign records in ACB's archives show this record of chamber of commerce campaigns for its first ten years:

Year	Number chamber campaigns
1913	3
1914	5
1915	13
1916	14
1917	14
1918	27
1919	66
1920	109
1921	97
1922	46

As these figures clearly show, once the war was over there was a tremendous spurt in the growth of the chamber movement. A hint of the reason for this is found in the foreword to the 1919 Lectures for the Summer School of Community Leadership: "There are numerous indications that America wishes to capitalize the spirit of cooperation and service which flamed forth everywhere during the war. It has been shown by the widespread organization of community bodies . . . for the purpose of bringing together community leaders and those who desire to work for the common welfare in civic and commercial activities. It was demonstrated by the unexpectedly large attendance at the 1919 session of the Summer School of Community Leadership. Every part of the Union and of Canada was represented . . . more than two hundred strong."

These figures also show that the ACB reached its peak in chamber campaigns in 1920. As indicated earlier, in the early twenties the ACB was being slowly crowded out of the chamber of commerce field by the newly organized National Association of Commercial Organization Secretaries and the Chamber of Commerce of the United States. As a consequence the Bureau came upon hard times. Harold Buttenheim recalls:

> In 1921–1922 the Bureau nearly went on the rocks financially, owing largely to the fact that a substantial part of the payments for our services in those days was represented by notes from Chambers of Commerce payable out of their second and third year collections following a campaign. When times were good, these notes were usually good, too, but the business recession of the early 1920's resulted in a substantial shrinkage of Chamber of Commerce collections—and in the shrinkage or repudiation of many of their notes.
>
> As one means of retrenchment to meet this situation, the size of the staff was drastically reduced, and the San Francisco and Canadian offices were closed. Then Chicago became the main office.[59]

This shrinkage of business and loss of accounts receivable brought internal wrangling as well as economic adversity, and led to the exit of Vice-President Lucius Wilson. He had originated the plan for the Summer School of Community Leadership and was bitter about its extinction. In fact the first session of ACB's summer school was held in 1915 in East Dorset, Vt., where Wilson had a summer home. In 1919 Wilson authored a booklet, *Community Leadership— The New Profession* which was widely distributed and somewhat influential in shaping the civic movements of that day. He also edited the publication, *Community Leadership,* started in January, 1920, and dropped in 1923 with the economy wave and his exit from the ACB. Starting as a biweekly and ending as a bimonthly, this publication served as a house organ and promotional piece for the Bureau, and also as a means of exchanging news and ideas among local commercial-civic organizations in the United States. In 1919 he also wrote another pamphlet, *Building Cities for Tomorrow,* which was widely distributed by the ACB over the next two years. Economy forced curtailment of such publications and business discretion dictated dropping the summer school, yet Wilson and the Buttenheims parted with bitterness. O. Ray Stone, who had a strong background in statistics and research, was named general manager to succeed Wilson and served in this capacity until he died in 1932.

Unlike the other giants in commercial fund raising, the ACB has never been identified with a "big name" personality, such as Charles S. Ward, Lyman Pierce, John Price Jones, Arnaud Marts. The man who was most influential in turning it from a civic-booster campaigner into a fund raising organization was James E. Almond. Stone hired Almond, a veteran newspaperman, in 1923. Almond sold his newspaper in Wabash, Ind., to take the job. Almond had first become acquainted with the Bureau in 1915 when, as a newspaper publisher in Riverside, Calif., then a small town, he served as a volunteer in a Bureau-directed campaign to organize a chamber of commerce in that city. Subsequently Almond attended two of the Bureau's summer schools, the one in 1918 held at Eagles Mere, Pa., and the one in 1920, held at the University of Wisconsin. When Stone died in 1932 Almond was promoted to the post of general manager and four years later was made president. Almond died March 13, 1960. He was a graduate of Hanover College, which gave him an honorary degree in 1950. As a newspaperman Almond served on the staff of the old Chicago *Record-Herald* and published papers in North Dakota, California, and Indiana. He was one of the organizers of the American Association of Fund-Raising Counsel in 1935.

Almond's first assignment out of Chicago was in nearby Racine, Wis., where he handled the publicity for Racine's Welfare Fund, the first of thousands of community chest campaigns this organization would direct in the next thirty years. The Racine campaign fell short of its goal of $91,906; only $85,819 was raised. The Racine campaign was directed by Earl J. Smith, a veteran chamber of commerce organizer.

Almond moved on from Racine, in late September, to direct the only community chest campaign he ever ran on an in-charge basis —the one for Spartanburg, S.C., that October. He raised only $69,-013 toward the goal of $90,000. Next he went to Denver, Colo., to promote an ACB-directed chamber of commerce campaign early in 1924. Out of these three experiences Almond perceived that ACB's long-term future lay with the fast-multiplying community chests and straight fund raising. Thus another commercial organization of skill and experience moved into the new field—and with profound consequences for America's public philanthropy.

Associates recall hearing Almond remark many times that "the only good thing that came out of the World War was the Community Chest," a campaign that he frequently described as "an annual harvest of goodwill." Certainly the community chest was a good thing for the Bureau—it saved its life. Pushed by Almond's enthusiasm, the ACB turned to fund raising on an intensive basis in 1923. Community Chest business kept the ACB going in the period between the two World Wars. The Bureau directed its first capital fund-raising drive in 1925 for Colorado College; its first hospital campaign two years later. Almond, Stone, and their associates became strong advocates for federation of appeals of local welfare agencies. In 1923, the year it entered the community chest field, the Bureau directed six such campaigns. By the end of 1958 the American City Bureau had managed 1,476 community chest drives.[60]

Though Almond directed only one of these campaigns, he sold scores of such drives to local welfare agencies and intensively promoted public support for the federated fund idea. Thus did the ACB, in the words of one of its officers, "fall into fund raising" after World War I. Its next major transition would come after World War II when it would move to the field of capital fund raising for colleges and universities. This transition came under the leadership of Almond and Bart Brammer, who succeeded Almond. When Bart Brammer died he was succeeded by his nephew, Lowell Brammer.

NOTES

1. Arnaud C. Marts, *Man's Concern for His Fellow Man* (Geneva, N.Y.: Humphrey), p. 31.

2. C. Howard Hopkins, *History of the Y.M.C.A. in North America* (New York: YMCA, 1951), p. 600.

3. A. C. Marts, "Historical Sketch of the Fund Raising Profession," in Proceedings, Fourth Annual Staff Conference of Marts & Lundy, Inc., 1948, p. 52.

4. Interview with Dr. Marts, Feb. 25, 1960.

5. Clipping in Lyman Pierce Scrapbook, from *Christian Advocate*, Sept. 18, 1919.

6. The Wells Organization folded July 31, 1960. It was heavily in debt when it went out of business, one of the few large firms to fail in this generally lucrative field.

7. Marts Interview, Feb. 25, 1960.

8. Letter from Marts dated Aug. 25, 1961. This was confirmed by Howard Beaver in an interview, Aug. 29, 1962.

9. Lyman L. Pierce, *How to Raise Money* (New York: Harper, 1932), p. 136.

10. Proceedings Marts & Lundy Fourth Annual Staff Conference, p. 55.

11. Arnaud C. Marts, "The Evolution of Marts & Lundy, Inc.," in Proceedings Seventh Annual Staff Conference, 1951, p. 3.

12. Letter—Dr. Marts, Aug. 25, 1961.

13. John Crosby Brown in Proceedings Marts & Lundy Fourth Annual Staff Conference, p. 66.

14. *Ibid.*

15. Letter from the late Alexander MacIntosh, then president of Tamblyn & Brown, Sept. 20, 1960.

16. Proceedings Marts & Lundy Fourth Annual Staff Conference, p. 66.

17. Interview with Howard A. Beaver, June 16, 1960.

18. William Adams Littell, "Washington Calling. . . ." *Philanthropy*, Summer, 1955, p. 94. Letter from Carlton Ketchum dated Sept. 6, 1961.

19. Letter from Cornelius M. Smith, Aug. 9, 1961.

20. *Ibid.*

21. A biographical sketch issued by John Price Jones, Inc., dated Nov. 19, 1959.

22. John Price Jones in *Twenty-fifth Anniversary Report of Class of '02*, Harvard University, 1927.

23. Wolcott Street, "John Price Jones Corporation History," p. 15, (unpublished mss.) in John Price Jones papers, Baker Library, Harvard Graduate School of Business. Street's mss. was clearly designed as a business promotion piece. Hereinafter this collection of Jones records and papers will be referred to as the John Price Jones Papers.

24. R. F. Duncan in mimeographed memo of reminiscences dated Sept. 30, 1959.

25. *Ibid.*

26. Wolcott Street history mss. in John Price Jones Papers.

27. *Ibid.*

28. Interview with Robert F. Duncan, March 29, 1960.

29. Letter from David M. Church, June 6, 1962.

30. In Proceedings John Price Jones Annual Staff Conference for 1935, in John Price Jones Papers.

31. Jones Plans Book in John Price Jones Papers.

32. Jones in Annual Staff Conference Proceedings for 1929.

33. Confidential Report dated June 15, 1955, in John Price Jones Papers.

34. Jones in Proceedings 1936 Staff Conference, John Price Jones Papers.

35. Office Bulletin in John Price Jones Papers.

36. Jones in Proceedings 1929 Staff Conference, John Price Jones Papers.

37. In John Price Jones Papers.

38. Wolcott Street mss., *op. cit.*, pp. 20–21.

39. John Price Jones in unpublished mss. in John Price Jones Papers.

40. Wolcott Street mss., *op. cit.*

41. *Ibid.*

42. Letter from Harold J. Seymour, Sept. 5, 1961.

43. *Ibid.*

44. John Price Jones Papers.

45. *Ibid.*

46. Taken from a testimonial scroll prepared by the Jones staff for his 80th birthday, Aug. 12, 1957.

47. Harold S. Buttenheim, "Then and Now," mss. of talk given at 1946 Staff Conference of American City Bureau. In ACB's files.

48. A series of articles first published in *McClure's* magazine; later collected and published in book form under this title by McClure, Phillips in 1905. Republished by Hill & Wang in 1957.

49. *Ibid.*

50. Bruno Lasker, "Community Leadership," *Survey*, Vol. 43 (Feb. 14, 1920), p. 588.

51. *Community Leadership*, Vol. 1 (Jan. 1, 1920), p. 4.

52. ACB *Bureau News*, Vol. 1, 1919.

53. Buttenheim, *op. cit.*

54. *Ibid.*

55. *Ibid.*

56. Interview with Lowell Brammer, June 9, 1960.

57. *New York Times*, Sunday, April 8, 1956, p. 76.

58. *American City*, Vol. 8 (Jan.–June, 1913), pp. 465–466.

59. Buttenheim, *op. cit.*

60. American City Bureau Campaign Record in ACB Files, Chicago Office.

6

The 1920's: Exit Charity, Enter Popular Philanthropy

America Accepts a New Level of Giving

Paradoxically it was the grim pursuit of victory in World War I, not the biblical impulses of brotherhood, that brought on the change in American philanthropy, the ways of financing it, and, consequently, to the nature of the benefiting institutions as well.

In the great postwar rush of public giving the word "charity" itself disappeared from common usage along with the fuzzy connotations it gave to the ancient religious injunction that we are "our brother's keeper." As one writer puts it: "What the scriptures had commanded to be done in secret would before long be celebrated in public and shouted from the rooftops by a different name: philanthropy." [1] And the shouting would in time become shrill and incessant as it sought billions of dollars for welfare needs. In this profound change from charity to public philanthropy the skilled fund raiser and his high-pressure methods played a key role. "Each year the springs of charity poured out a golden flood: $1.75 billion in 1921, $2 billion during 1924 and 1925, almost $2.5 billion in 1928." And in 1964 the flood of public giving topped the $10 billion crest line.

Accurate reports of America's giving over the years are not possible. Estimates of the growth of American philanthropy in these postwar years, based on "careful compilation of statistics by the John Price Jones Corp.," show that, from 1921 to 1927, "donations totalled roughly the following amounts: [2]

1921	$1,719,000,000
1922	1,787,760,000
1923	1,859,310,000
1924	2,000,320,000
1925	2,068,570,000
1926	2,192,680,000
1927	2,219,700,000

In the 1920's the fund raisers had larger fields to plow and harvest. William J. Norton, a participant in this profound change, reflected: "The giant campaigns and the numerous appeals placed in an enormous setting, stimulated by a vast emergency, opened wide the hearts and purses of the people who poured into the lap of philanthropy sums equal to the ransom of kings. Once acquired, this habit could never shrink to the minor proportions prevailing before the war." [3] War chests were quickly changed to community chests and the new band of professional fund raisers were soon mobilizing capital fund drives for colleges, cathedrals, and hospitals so that there was little loss in the momentum of giving, or little relief in the pressure on the newly tagged donor to give, and to give again.

Amid the clamor created by drive upon drive in the 1920's there were voices of pessimism crying out that "the community of the present will no longer support private charities on the scale and in the manner it has done in the past." The author of this statement, Cornelia J. Cannon, wrote: "For thirty years the philanthropists of America have indulged in a perfect orgy of charitable activity. . . . But something has happened in the last year or so. . . . The apparently solid support has shown signs of giving way. We confess to a harried feeling in the presence of the grim alternatives daily offered to us, of either surrendering our money or accepting a major responsibility for the downfall of philanthropic institutions . . . there is a revolt of the giving public." [4] Mrs. Cannon contended that it might well be possible "that this revolt of the giving public was not altogether selfish."

Before World War I giving in America was widely presumed to be both a prerogative and a responsibility of the wealthy and of the businessman. The emphasis was on needs for relief, not for health, recreation, and rehabilitation. All this the war changed dramatically, drastically. Before the war, Norton recalls:

It is true that the tag days growing up in the early years of the twentieth century had expanded this [giving] habit somewhat; but its application was sporadic and haphazard through this medium. It is true that the churches, particularly the Catholic Church, took up collections for parochial charities among their parishioners; but at this time little less than one-half of the American population acknowledged allegiance to any church; and the ways and means of gathering these collections was not very productive. The Christmas seal also had come into widespread vogue, and in a small way was reaching a larger constituency than previous methods had permitted.[5]

Although the word "charity" was rapidly disappearing from the public's lexicon, the fund raiser continued to exploit the sure appeals of poverty, pity, and emotion. Lillian Brandt asserted in her *How Much Shall I Give?* that "the fundamental, primitive, probably instinctive, desire to relieve physical suffering is still no doubt the most general and strongest of all motives." Elwood Street, while secretary of the Welfare League of Louisville, Ky., made a survey in 1921 of all donors contributing more than $5, as to why they gave, with these results: pity, 568 persons listed first; humanity, 483; religious obligations, 437; sympathy, 429; justice to those who have not had a fair chance, 402; duty, 389.[6] Of course, as Miss Brandt observed, "The relative weight which various considerations have in determining contributions to philanthropy in America at the present time can only be a matter of speculation . . . as we notice how the public responds to appeals today, this much at least seems clear: that this is not so much a matter of reason or of conscience as of habit, tradition, imitation, social pressure, and sentiment."[7] It was for this reason the new level and habit of giving stemming from the war period had profound social consequences.

Accurate figures on the amount, spread, and purposes of giving for the early 1920's are not available, but all the evidence points to the growth and spread of public giving in this era. Late in the 1920's the National Bureau of Economic Research undertook a study to assess the trends in philanthropy—and this means trends in fund raising. The study proposed to answer such questions as: "Are more dollars contributed for philanthropic purposes now than formerly, or is it merely true that a few large organizations have taken the place of many small organizations?" "Have per capita contributions, if measured in dollars of constant purchasing power, increased during the last quarter century?" The study was made by Willford Isbell King of the Bureau's staff and published in 1928. Because of the lack of adequate data on a national basis, on the part of either the recipient agencies or the givers, those in charge of the study decided that "the only feasible way of obtaining any light on the trend of philanthropy was to select a single community, as nearly typical as possible, and study it intensively." New Haven, Conn., was chosen as best meeting the criteria set up by the study committee. Trends in American giving, as measured by this detailed study of New Haven, for the 1900–1925 era were found to be as follows:

1. The number of dollars contributed to philanthropic organizations in New Haven has grown very greatly from 1900 to 1925, the amount at the close of the period being about 4½ times as great as the former. . . .
2. When contributions are reduced to terms of constant purchasing power, a decided growth in the total still appears.
3. When the contributions so deflated are converted to a per capita basis, we find that the amount contributed per person in New Haven has averaged about the same during the last five years as in the first five years of the twentieth century.
4. People today are contributing to philanthropic organizations about the same proportion of their total wealth that they did in pre-War times. . . .
5. Earnings and investments constitute a growing percentage of the total receipts of all philanthropic organizations in New Haven. In 1900 approximately one-fifth of the total receipts came from these sources, while in 1925 the fraction had risen to two-fifths.
6. . . . it appears that large gifts are much more important than small gifts in swelling the aggregate, two-thirds of the money contributed being received from persons giving $100 or more.
7. A study of the percentages of the total direct expenditures made by all organizations for philanthropic purposes shows that the fraction of the total used for relief of the poor, afflicted, and delinquent has remained about constant. . . . On the other hand, health work has been steadily absorbing an increasing percentage of the total expenditures. . . .
8. One of the most striking features brought out by the investigation is the marked strength of the cyclical movements in individual contributions. . . . The quarter century from 1900 to 1925 includes six distinct waves in contributions, the crests in 1902, 1909, and

1918 being the highest peaks. . . . The average wave length appears to be about 4 years. The correlation with the criteria usually taken to represent the business cycle is not at all close.[8]

As the ability and willingness to give had been vastly broadened and deepened by the developments in philanthropy in World War I, more and more hands were forcefully reaching out for the gifts. Those who would give found themselves besieged with pleas to give, the situation that plainly prevails today. Since the turn of the century the number of national organizations financed by public giving had been steadily growing, as an industrialized-urbanized society created new needs and new wealth to meet these needs. The growing demands upon the new philanthropist, big or little, can be visualized in the following list tracing the growth of national fund-seeking social, health, religious, and welfare agencies:

GROWTH OF NATIONAL FUND SEEKERS 1900–1922 [9]

Increase in Number of National Organizations

Prior to 1900

Young Men's Christian Association	1866
National Women's Christian Temperance Union	1874
International Sunshine Society	1879
Salvation Army	1880
American Red Cross	1882
Needlework Guild	1885
Young Women's Christian Association	1886
American Humane Association	1889
Council of Jewish Women	1893
National Children's Home Society	1897
National Florence Crittenton Mission	1898
National Consumers' League	1899

1900–1916

Society for the Friendless	1900
National Child Labor Committee	1904
National Tuberculosis Association	1904
Boys' Club Federation	1906
Playground and Recreation Association of America	1906
National Probation Association	1907
Federal Council of Churches of Christ in America	1908
National Association for the Advancement of Colored People	1909
National Committee for Mental Hygiene	1909
Boy Scouts of America	1910

GROWTH OF NATIONAL FUND SEEKERS 1900–1922 (*Continued*)

American Association for Organizing Family Social Work 1911
National Federation of Settlements 1911
Camp Fire Girls 1912
National Organization for Public Health Nursing 1912
American Rescue Workers 1913
American Society for the Control of Cancer 1913
American Social Hygiene Association 1914
Girl Scouts 1915
National Committee for the Prevention of Blindness 1915
National Congress of Mothers and Parent-Teacher Associations 1915

1917 and Since

National Association of Travelers' Aid Societies 1917
National Committee on Prisons and Prison Labor 1917
American Association for Community Organization 1918
Community Service, Incorporated 1919
National Catholic Welfare Council 1919
National League of Girls' Clubs 1919
Circle for Negro Relief 1919
Jewish Welfare Board 1920
Child Welfare League of America 1920
American Federation for the Blind 1921
Big Brother and Big Sister Federation 1921
National Alliance of Legal Aid Societies 1922
American Child Health Associations 1922

The proliferation of these welfare and recreational associations and their resultant impact on each community across the land can best be seen in the microcosm of one community—for example Sioux Falls, S.D.[10] In the early 1920's Sioux Falls, with a population of 25,000, was the largest city in the state, a main railroad junction and trading center for parts of three states. A fairly typical community, the city had no millionaires but many well-to-do citizens, an active chamber of commerce, and the normal quota of citizens who pay their civic rent by promoting community betterment. Prior to World War I no national fund-raising agency had made intensive contact with the citizens of Sioux Falls. The National Tuberculosis Association had organized a nursing service for the state; the local Humane Society paid a $10 membership fee to the American Humane Association; the National WCTU had established a local chapter, one that never had more than forty members; and the International Sunshine Society had associated with it one of the departments of the Sioux Falls History Club. Before the war the

YMCA had attempted to organize in Sioux Falls but failed, and though there were Boy Scout troops the Boy Scout organization was not successful in organizing a council. This calm of inertia and isolation prevailed as the war clouds broke across the country in 1917. Sioux Falls would never be the same once the feverish activity of warborn fund raising began to subside.

The fervor of war and the ensuing Liberty Loan campaigns and fund drives apparently awakened the Sioux Falls community consciousness to its social needs, and national organizations found the field more fertile. Beginning in 1917, national fund seekers began to take root in Sioux Falls thus:

1917: An American Red Cross Chapter was organized. The Salvation Army established a headquarters and organized family welfare and religious work.

1919: The YMCA successfully organized a Y in Sioux Falls and launched a drive for a $450,000 building.

1920: The American Association for Organizing Family Social Work, at the request of the Chamber of Commerce, made a survey of the community and established a family welfare society.

The National Association for the Advancement of Colored People organized a branch.

The Child Welfare League of America admitted the South Dakota Children's Home Society to membership.

The YWCA established a local unit and organized educational and recreational activities.

The National Council of Catholic Women appointed a Sioux Falls representative to organize a unit in this territory.

The National Congress of Mothers and Parent-Teacher Associations accepted one PTA as an affiliated member.

1922: The National Tuberculosis Association sent a representative to Sioux Falls to assist the State Association in uniting in one League four groups in this county which had previously been selling Christmas seals and undertaking separate activities.

The American Society for the Control of Cancer organized a committee of physicians to obtain publicity on the prevention of cancer.

The National Committee on Visiting Teachers financed a visiting teacher to work in Sioux Falls.

Thus in five years ten local units of national organizations had been formed and two other national affiliations had been established in this community. And thus were sown the seeds of the competition and conflict between the national agencies and the community welfare agencies for volunteer time and donated dollars that continues to this day. A social worker, writing on philanthropy in 1920, re-creates for us the mood of the period:

> As social agencies multiplied, and as they developed their appealing powers, the competition they plied for the attention of those who were known to be able to contribute became so intense that neither of these methods [chamber endorsement and bureaus of information] suffice. Neither one was any defence against incessant bombardment by appeals from more organizations than any one person could interest himself in. . . . Neither one helped him decide how to apportion his contribution among them, or which to refuse altogether. And so there arose, here and there . . . a veritable insurrection of givers, a revolt against the harassing competitive methods of the local charities which led to the development of "financial federations." [11]

Although the World War I fund drives and bond sales had set new patterns for giving to public causes, it was inevitable that there would be reaction to the high-pressure campaigns once the crisis had passed. The big money raiser of the war, the American Red Cross, was the first to suffer the consequences of this understandable emotional letdown.

The American Red Cross began 1919 with total resources of $127,000,000, of which the national treasury held $41,000,000 in money and $53,000,000 in supplies, and the chapters had $33,000,000. But the cost of the foreign program was so great that in 1919 a new fund drive was held.

The response to that drive was crushing. The subscribing members, who had exceeded 20,000,000 in 1918, dropped to under 9,000,000. And subscriptions in response to a modest appeal of only $25,000,000 compared with wartime gifts, yielded only $15,000,000 despite a campaign led by an appeal from President Wilson himself.[12]

Not only did the 1919 Red Cross fund drive fail dismally, there set in a wave of bitter criticism that was to haunt the Red Cross from that day to this. Hurd recounts:

> In the fund campaign of 1919 the first charges of waste and mismanagement were made. . . . Similar charges were leveled at every

other major organization, including the Y.M.C.A. whose overseas hostesses formed unofficially their own organization bitterly termed the "damned Y girls." . . . That the Red Cross had "charged the soldiers for supplies" flared into a burning issue. The moral behavior of nurses and social workers became a favorite morsel of alley gossip . . . the Red Cross suddenly found itself pilloried for "destroying American youth" by free distribution of cigarettes to soldiers.[13]

The most brutal attack launched against the Red Cross was that made by Hearst's New York *American*. That paper's assault virtually summarized all the important criticism that plagued the Red Cross from the close of the war through the 1920's. In a series of articles lasting from May 25 to July 26, 1921, the *American* leveled a bitter tirade of charges with such headlines as "GIFTS INTENDED FOR ARMY SOLD TO PROFITEERS." One article asserted that the Red Cross had not aided army veterans since the war. Another described the ARC as "a cold-blooded, highly professionalized charity trust." It proclaimed that speculators and Red Cross officials worked hand in hand and waste inside the organization was commonplace. The Hearst paper editorially demanded a Congressional investigation but none came.[14]

With the end of the war, control of the Red Cross reverted to the Central Committee and there ensued a difficult organizational shakedown period. Financial support of ARC programs during the 1920's and 1930's would come from three sources: (1) use of surplus funds left from World War I drives; (2) contributions to special drives following major disasters; (3) the annual "roll call" or membership drives. The 1921 by-laws set up these classes of memberships: Annual, $1; Contributing, $5; Sustaining, $10; Life, $50; Patrons, $100. In 1927 an additional class, "Supporting Membership," costing $25, was established. Memberships fell off drastically, and the downward slide that began in 1919 continued until the low of 3 million members was reached in 1926. "No public health programs, no appeals by presidents, no tricks of publicity availed against the 'normalcy' spirit of the times. The belief of the public (or its apathy) that the Red Cross had fulfilled a splendid function in wartime but should not return to prewar status held firm. The third, fourth, and fifth roll calls, spanning the years 1919 to 1922, were marked by the same publicity methods that characterized the fund drives of the war era. . . . Still membership decreased."[15] Thus the technique of tapping the increased flow of charity dollars did not produce automatic results.

The "old pro" of the public fund raisers, the YMCA, took its portion of postwar criticism and had comparable difficulties in sustaining its capital drive momentum after the war's interruption. A common charge against the Y was that "the overseas canteen service was operated at a profit and that the organization gave away free nothing but writing paper." Such a charge stung veteran Y fund raiser Lyman Pierce to retort: "the association has used every effort to run down the weak spots in the organization's work overseas, and sent home 200 of the 6,000 men who have gone overseas because they were not qualified. The universal verdict is that our overseas work is at least 80 per cent excellent. . . . If any man who has a criticism . . . will put it in writing I will have it investigated immediately." [16] The hangover of wartime criticisms, the depression of 1921–1922, and the loss of the skilled fund raisers Charles S. Ward and Lyman Pierce all served to make the Y's fundraising row more difficult to hoe. Also the YMCA found the emerging financial federated drive as developed by the community chests a new and vexatious problem. Hopkins records:

When the metropolitan secretaries met in 1918, Secretary L. Wilbur Messer of Chicago presented the results of a survey which led the organization to again go on record as believing it "unwise for the Young Men's Christian Association to unite in local financial federations." Despite the militant efforts of Messer and others, the next few years saw the gradual adherence of scattered Y.M.C.A.'s to chests. A few champions of the chest arose, notably Secretary Robert E. Lewis of Cleveland, but most viewed this development that was then "sweeping the country" as a menace to the Associations. Again in 1920 Messer polled the secretarial brotherhood, obtaining overwhelming majorities against affiliation. The primary post-War recession of 1921 brought failure to many federated drives and for a time clouded the issue, but the number of Y.M.C.A.'s related to chests steadily increased as the chest movement spread. [17]

The growing number of social needs met by a growing number of agencies financed by donations and manned by volunteers, coupled with the war-awakened community consciousness, sped the idea of financial federation and sharpened the wits of fund raisers. The war chests and bond committees that had been organized in

America's villages, towns, and cities across the land were eager for new challenges. "Substituting the word 'community' for the word 'war' in their names, they stopped selling bonds and sold the juice of human kindness instead. The idea was to pool all the needs of all those who had, in one way or another, been bested by their environment—the crippled, the sick, the hungry, the ragged. Pool them all and pay the bill in one grand swoop, as true brothers should. And the people in the villages and the towns and cities paid gladly." [18]

The stage was set for financial federation, the community chest, and the trained fund raiser.

The Community Chest Movement Spreads

One of the socially significant consequences flowing from the giant fund drives and war chests of World War I was the community chest—today a standard fixture in every community of any size. Unification of fund-raising campaigns for voluntary health, welfare, and recreation agencies now exist in one form or another in more than 2,000 American communities. The federated fund-raising idea, as developed and nurtured in America, has spread to Canada, Australia, Japan, and the Philippines. In 1957 it was estimated that "all united campaigns now secure gifts from 26 million individuals and companies through the efforts of 3 million chest solicitors and in turn supply these funds to 21,000 agencies." [19] By 1960, some forty years after the emergence of the Community Chest, more than 2,000 chests were raising annually some $450 million for health, recreational, and welfare needs—mostly on the community level. By 1950 these chests had raised more than $3 billion for community welfare. Moreover, they had spread the base of charitable giving until three out of every four families in chest-organized cities were listed as givers. Community chest professionals have brought community fund-raising campaigns to a high point of perfection and have provided the main thrust in the evolution from charity on the part of the rich to the poor to a truly public philanthropy.

The community chest, spawned as the war chest, spread rapidly in the 1920's. The rate of growth is shown in Table 8. C. M. Bookman, pioneer in the federated fund-raising movement, said in 1924, in a five-year look backward, "No movement in the long history of social work has so quickly caught the popular fancy. Through community

TABLE 8. THE COMMUNITY CHEST STORY AS SHOWN BY THE TOTAL RAISED
BY ALL RECORDED CAMPAIGNS, 1920–1961

(Figures supplied by United Community Funds and Councils of America, Inc.)

Year	Number of campaigns	Amount	Raised for specified year	
			Per cent of goal	Per cent of previous year *
1920	39	$ 19,651,334	95.0%	...
1921	61	22,781,834	93.0	111.6%
1922	96	28,568,453	87.7	124.9
1923	147	40,280,649	92.9	139.4
1924	203	50,351,190	95.5	123.3
1925	240	58,003,965	94.0	113.8
1926	285	63,677,235	94.7	108.3
1927	308	66,432,072	94.4	105.1
1928	314	68,664,042	96.2	104.4
1929	331	73,276,688	95.9	107.6
1930	353	75,972,555	95.5	103.4
1931	386	84,796,505	98.7	112.1
1932	397	101,377,537	96.8	122.0
1933	401	77,752,954	83.7	77.3
1934	399	70,609,078	83.2	91.1
1935	406	69,781,478	87.2	98.4
1936	429	77,367,634	91.8	110.8
1937	452	81,707,787	93.8	105.0
1938	475	83,898,234	93.3	101.7
1939	523	82,771,362	91.2	96.9
1940	561	86,297,068	95.3	103.6
1941	598	90,379,099	98.0	103.4
1942	632	104,575,890	99.6	113.9
1943	649	162,334,486	107.0	156.0
1944	703	210,415,187	100.9	118.6
1945	772	221,272,950	101.9	102.5
1946	798	197,048,839	89.8	87.9
1947	841	168,521,984	96.6	86.3
1948	1010	177,082,356	95.3	102.7
1949	1152	188,061,328	91.9	104.7
1950	1318	192,933,988	93.1	101.1
1951	1498	212,987,292	94.9	109.2
1952	1500	240,920,220	93.8	113.6
1953	1560	266,124,734	96.1	109.6
1954	1690	287,539,960	96.7	107.2
1955	1858	302,023,059	95.9	104.3
1956	1939	339,706,067	98.4	112.4
1957	1961	378,382,274	98.1	111.1
1958	2041	414,575,641	95.3	108.6
1959	2104	427,262,622	94.7	102.3
1960	2147	458,252,609	97.0	107.3
1961	2186	477,979,689	95.9	103.8

* Based on campaigns for which figures for both years are available. Includes "new" United Funds.

chest methods practically the entire populations of many cities have become interested in social work." [20] Elwood Street recalled in 1949, "The Community Chest movement is the most widespread of American social movements, the product of a classless mutually considerate society." [21] By war's end there were some twenty war chests operating. As the decade opened there were thirty-nine community chests in operation and from this base the movement grew rapidly.

The community chest movement in the twenties was given considerable impetus by the new professional fund-raising firms always on the competitive quest for business. The Charles Ward and the American City Bureau firms took the lead in promoting acceptance of the community chest idea and in managing campaigns. Then local federated drives were staggered and this made it feasible for the professionals to serve many chests during the course of the year.

Rochester, N.Y., a city of strong civic spirit and a generous philanthropy financed in large part by George Eastman, was the first city to convert its war chest into a community chest. The significant and successful conclusion of Rochester's first community chest drive was faintly heralded in a small filler item in the June 12, 1919, _New York Times:_ "Rochester has just completed a campaign of one week devoted to raising $1,250,000 for the community chest. The city 'went over the top' with $1,000 to spare last night. The community chest is designed to care for all the city charities and the rehabilitation of returned soldiers. George Eastman contributed $200,000."

The multiplying World War I drives for money and for volunteer time had brought on a givers' and workers' revolt. The logical answer to the endless demands for money and for work in campaigns seemed to be financial federation, an infant idea struggling for acceptance at the war's start. The war chest had been conceived on the principle of financial federation and little else. Syracuse and Rome, N.Y., took the lead. The idea quickly spread to Rochester, N.Y., Columbus, Ohio, and other cities and by 1918 there were some twenty war chests, largely the creations of givers and volunteer workers. Norton recalls:

. . . there was a good deal of justification for the revolt. The big agencies, long organized and well equipped for war work, made demands that were hard to meet, both in funds and in time. In addition to these an increasing horde of new enterprises started begging, some poorly conceived, others good enough in conception but badly led and organized. The old home charities had to keep on asking. And finally there were the demands of the government, exacting and insistent. The evil of this every-organization-for-itself basis, which had been only mildly apparent while local movements had the field to themselves, was thrust forcibly home by the medley of new giant war activities. It came as an added burden to a people already distraught.[22]

The appeal of the financial federation that can take the ever-growing requests for money and for volunteer time and bundle them into one easy package and one total annual effort is illusory but well nigh irresistible. The war chests and the community chests that followed them made a promise no chest or united fund-raising organization has ever been able to keep—to stop all other solicitation for funds for health and welfare purposes. On this Norton says: "Such a promise was impossible of delivery.

"Out of the experience . . . came a lesson to many parts of America, that federation, while offering membership to any responsible charitable, philanthropic or civic agency coming within its general scope, may yet not attempt the impossible task of trying to stop all solicitation for charitable work." [23] Yet the appeal of the united fund drive persists for understandable human and economic reasons. These have been listed by Thompson:

1. It conserves the energy of volunteer solicitors.
2. It protects the contributor by affording him the opportunity to give to a group of certified agencies whose budget requests have been screened.
3. It relieves major agency boards and staffs of major responsibility for raising their own funds, thereby enabling them to give full attention to the services for which they are founded.
4. Through an expanded campaign it spreads the base of giving with greater public participation at all levels.
5. It helps insure greater continuity of support for community services by providing a recognized and acceptable vehicle for winning that support.
6. It encourages cooperative planning for meeting health and social welfare needs.
7. It helps provide a more balanced spread of financial support of the various service agencies.

8. It helps build community *esprit de corps* and common interest among all races, creeds, and economic levels.
9. It reduces fund-raising costs to a minimum.[24]

However logical and attractive the reasons may be, federation is still stoutly opposed by most national health fund-raising organizations. In fact, the battle and bitterness between the advocates of federated versus nonfederated fund-raising drives has grown, not abated, over this 40-year span. The National Tuberculosis Association, the first agency to make a national drive for public gifts, in the early 1920's offered to cooperate with the new community chests on stipulated terms. Hints of the inevitable public battle were given by Philip Jacobs in 1923:

> The development during and since the war of the so-called community chest or financial federation presents a situation to thoughtful tuberculosis workers that requires careful consideration, particularly from the point of view of conservation of the Christmas seal. . . .
> The attitude of the outstanding leaders in the development of community chests, such as those in Cleveland, Detroit, Cincinnati and Rochester, as unfortunately as not being emulated by many other similar leaders of funds of this character in other cities . . . where the use of high-handed tactics by a small coterie of large givers has alienated the tuberculosis group from the other social agencies.[25]

Contrast Jacobs' mild warning with the 1961 battle cry of Basil O'Connor, long-time head of the March of Dimes, that efforts to create a National Commission on Voluntary and Health Agencies would destroy "one of the most cherished privileges of democracy by inflicting on volunteers a government by vigilante." [26] O'Connor has adroitly and determinedly campaigned against what he likes to term "the Super Fund" idea, to be related later.

The National Tuberculosis Association, which had terminated its arrangement with the American Red Cross in 1919, was now raising funds through its seal sale through state and local associations, or a local charity as an agent where it had no association. The Association at this time took no flat stand against the emerging community chest: "The National Tuberculosis Association is not opposed to community chests as such. It stands for the closest possible coordination of community health and social activities, official and non-official." The Association set down these three conditions for local cooperation with the chests:

1. Preservation of the seal idea. This may be done by distribution to chest contributors without cost or by allowing a limited seal sale by mail.
2. The local association must insist that a community federation give proper recognition to the claims of state and national associations. The entire tuberculosis movement has developed upon the idea that only by presenting a solid phalanx, with national, state, and local agencies can proper progress be made. . . .
3. A local tuberculosis agency has a right to demand, and should demand, as a condition for entering a community fund, that its integrity shall be guaranteed.[27]

The seeds of conflict that would ultimately take the tuberculosis associations out of the Community Chest can be seen in these stipulations.

Accurate determination and discernment of the costs involved in raising money for the proliferating health and welfare agencies was as difficult in the 1920's as it is today, yet the donor, as always, wanted to know what portion of his dollar went to the cause and what went to the fund raiser. The group making the National Bureau of Economic Research study, "Trends in Philanthropy," in New Haven threw up its hands in despair on this problem:

There is a strong popular desire to know what proportion of the money collected by philanthropic orgnizations is used to pay for the cost of collecting funds and for administrative purposes. . . .

To satisfy this demand is, however, not an easy matter. The financial offices of philanthropic organizations feel that the public expects them to do the impossible—raise money without expense—and hence they are reluctant to reveal the actual costs of money-raising. . . .

In view of the difficulties just described no effort was made to estimate the cost of money raising for more than a single year. Fairly complete estimates covering 1925 were compiled for certain organizations but these were so few in number that . . . it seems unwise to publish the results.[28]

There is no evidence, one way or another, concerning what pressures, if any, were brought to bear to bar publication of fund-raising costs in New Haven.

In 1924 the National Information Bureau, led by Allen T. Burns and pressed by the community chests, urged a study of the internal financial management of the voluntary health societies. The oldest and largest of these was the National Tuberculosis Association. Shryock records:

> In 1921 the amount of Seal income available for the work of the Association from the 1920 sale was about $153,000. The Association's total income was about $167,000 and its total expenses about $7,000 in excess of income. The upward trend in income continued, so that by 1928 the Seal return from the 1927 sale reached $270,000 and the total income was above $300,000. . . .
>
> During the interval 1920 to 1928, receipts from dues declined from $18,000 to $13,600 but this loss was minor under the circumstances. . . . Salaries were naturally a major item in the costs of most divisions.[29]

It was the National Tuberculosis Association that blocked efforts to publish a study of fund-raising costs promoted by Burns and financed by the Rockefeller Foundation. The study was proposed by a general committee set up by the National Information Bureau and financed by the Foundation when a number of voluntary health agencies agreed to cooperate, including the Tuberculosis Association. In fact, Philip Jacobs, its publicist and executive, became chairman of the general committee. Mark M. Jones of the Rockefeller Foundation was retained to direct the investigation. His first step was to probe the Association's finances and fund-raising costs. Shryock reports:

> Taking 1923 as a test year, he [Jones] reported that the Association costs were only .9 per cent of the total sales but represented 16.7 per cent of the amount retained as its share. State society costs averaged a ratio of about 10 per cent of the total sales but represented 42.5 per cent of the amount retained as its share. [State bodies acted largely as distributing agencies.] The local societies' costs averaged about 15 per cent of the total Seal sales and 21.3 per cent of the amount they retained.
>
> Jones reached these results by including under expenses certain items which the Association had not listed. Whenever a staff member did part-time or incidental Seal work, for example, Jones added a proportionate amount of his salary to campaign costs. On this basis, and

viewing the Seal picture as a whole, he concluded that the tuberculosis societies had spent $1,104,645 in raising about $4,262,000—a ratio of costs to returns of nearly 26 per cent. The latter figure was viewed as too high and as indicative of inefficient methods.[80]

As would be expected, the Association protested loudly. Then as now the professionals insisted that a fund-raising campaign is educational as well as remunerative and part of the costs are properly chargeable to education and public relations. Shryock tells us, "The reaction against the Jones survey, both in the Association Office and in the field, was such that the bureau never published it." Understandably, the National Information Bureau dropped its efforts to probe the financial management of other voluntary agencies who were competing with the community chests for funds at the local level.

It has been ever thus with efforts to probe the finances of the voluntary health and welfare agencies. Despite the fact that they beseech the public to give and thus incur the obligation of a public accounting of their finances, it remained, in the year 1964, difficult to discover accurate figures on the income and outgo of money they have raised. In 1945 another Rockefeller Foundation-financed study of voluntary health agencies, this one conducted under the auspices of the National Health Council, came to their reluctant conclusion:

> Methods of arriving at the cost of raising an agency's budget are highly variable. There are no standardized procedures and valid comparisons cannot be made. Moreover, fund-raising is often inextricably interwoven with the educational efforts of an agency. Under these circumstances some of the organizations hesitated to furnish estimates of what it cost them to raise money. . . . While all of the agencies employ conventional recording and accounting methods . . . there is need, if comparable figures are to be obtained, for national agencies to agree on uniform principles and procedures to be used in arriving at the cost of raising money.[81]

Fifteen years later the Rockefeller Foundation financed a third study of the management of these voluntary health and welfare agencies. This study was conducted under the auspices of an *ad hoc* committee and directed by Dr. Robert Hamlin of the Harvard School of Public Health. Again the investigators ran into a wall of confusion and complications in trying to arrive at fund raising costs. The Hamlin report urged: "*A system of uniform accounting and financial reporting is potentially the most important method for obtaining more objective information about voluntary agencies.* It has been discussed for years, but has not been developed because of the difficulty of the task and the fears of voluntary agencies." [32]

Thus does history repeat itself. Several of the bureaucrats of the social and health agencies financed by public giving resent or resist giving the public the full information that is the donor's due. A few of the lesser agencies make no public report. However, as of 1963 twenty-seven states had laws requiring more or less detailed financial reports from fund-seeking agencies.

Three Influential Organizations Emerge

In the post-World War I growth in public philanthropies, people with money to give found themselves besieged with more and more appeals. Consequently, they became irritated and bewildered in trying to sort the worthy cause from the unworthy one, the honest appeal from the fraudulent one. The multiplying number of health and welfare agencies competing for the public's dollars found the competition stiffer, particularly in the depression year of 1921. Leaders of the agencies saw the need to sharpen their public relations tools and to train the specialized personnel that modern fund raising requires. The community chests springing up across the nation needed guidance and cohesion to promote and protect the principle of financial federation. The outcome of these and kindred needs was the development of an agency and organizational bureaucracy. Three national organizations that were to exert much influence on the growth and direction of American philanthropy emerged at this time. They were: The Community Chests and Councils, now the United Community Funds and Councils of America; the National Information Bureau; and the National Publicity Council for Welfare. Their impact on philanthropy warrants a brief recounting of their beginnings.

The Three Cs

The community chest movement was propelled and shaped by a small band of pioneering paid professionals who, in 1918, organized an association that is today the powerful, articulate, and affluent United Community Funds and Councils of America, Inc., quartered in an imposing edifice near the East River in the heart of Manhattan.

William J. Norton, who had pioneered federated financing in Cincinnati and was now with Associated Charities in Detroit, and the man who succeeded him in Cincinnati, C. M. Bookman, took the initiative in calling a meeting of war chest officials in Chicago in February, 1918. Out of this meeting came the American Association for Community Organization "to encourage and stimulate collective community planning and the development of better standards of community organization for social work." [33] Elwood Street, the first publicity professional in this field and then volunteer secretary for the Louisville, Ky., war chest, participated in the meeting at Chicago. He gives the credit to Norton, who was the first president, and to Bookman.[34]

The original idea of the association called for some central headquarters where communities desiring to adapt the federated plan could obtain reliable information and guidance. Although the organization, over the years, developed and emphasized its function as "a center for information and guidance," it has increasingly become the public relations agency to lead the battle of the community chests against the multiplying fund appeals put forth by independent agencies. But there is no indication that this prime public relations role was foreseen by the organizers. In fact, one student of this subject wrote in 1937: "The association, in neither its original nor its developed form, has ever been primarily or essentially a propaganda, missionary or evangelistic agency." [35]

This statement does not square with reality. Certainly the founders of the community chest association knew the importance of public opinion. Bookman, in 1924, said: "The Community Chest plan has made possible scientific methods of moulding public opinion. The centralization and unification of social work has provided funds with which to carry on constructive educational programs, money with which to bring to the attention of the entire community the social ills of that community." [36] Norton had early recognized the necessity of "educational publicity for social work" if the "cooperative movement was to survive." Street had started as a publicist for federated financing and ardently preached the importance of "continual year-round interpretation to educate the public as to social needs and social services . . . to help in bigger and better campaigns next time." Thus the possibility of providing an articulate voice in the national forum to promote federated giving may well have been an agreed, if unstated, purpose of the new association. These founders were wise in the ways of public relations.

At first the Association's secretarial and information service was performed by volunteers, with Norton, Bookman, and the others taking turns. With the booming growth of community chests in the early twenties it became obvious that this task could not be handled on a makeshift, part-time basis. The National Information Bureau, the history of which will be described later, provided the first home for the American Association for Community Organization. Allen Tibbals Burns, one of the main forces in building the community chest movement, became full-time director of the National Information Bureau on July 1, 1922. Burns, born in Haverhill, Mass., and educated at the University of Chicago, was directing the "Study of Methods of Americanization" for the Carnegie Foundation when he was offered the NIB job. He had served on NIB's board of directors in that agency's formative years, and as president of the National Conference of Social Work two years before. The community chest movement boomed in the mid-twenties and subsequently, in January, 1926, Burns quit the NIB to become full-time executive director of the community chest organization, now showing more vigor than the NIB.

Allen T. Burns was the prime mover in promoting and guiding the growth of the community chest idea, and in his term of office he saw the local chests and welfare councils increase from a mere handful to 650, including the major cities of the United States. To his leadership goes much of the credit for the steady growth of the movement. A year after setting up new headquarters for the Association Burns persuaded the members to change the name to Association of Community Chests and Councils. The "Three Cs" organization—as it soon became widely known—financed an expanding array of informational and promotional services by assessing the member chests 1/10 of 1 per cent of the money they raised each year. In 1933 the Association incorporated and changed its name to Community Chests and Councils, Inc.

In 1923, with the election of a layman as president, the professional chest executives retreated to the wings and put the lay leadership out in front of the movement. As in most associations of this kind, the direction and cues continued to come from the professionals backstage. Burns retired from his post in 1943. He died in Fort Myers, Fla., March 9, 1953, at the age of seventy-seven. His wife, Florence Seder, also was widely known in the field of social welfare. Burns was succeeded by his assistant, Ralph Blanchard, who directed the community chest movement until his retirement in 1960. Blanchard had come to New York City from Buffalo, N.Y., to be Burns's assistant in 1928. The name was changed once more, in 1956, to its present United Community Funds and Councils of America, Inc., thus reflecting the emergence of the broader, more inclusive United Fund in the 1950's. The organization is today financed by a budget of more than $1 million and staffed by men and women "who have one thing in common, a strong belief in the principle of united local community planning and financing of voluntary health, welfare, and recreational services."

According to Ralph Blanchard, who in a real sense grew up with the community chest movement and profoundly influenced it, the national headquarters staff of the Three Cs housed in the Carnegie International Center, has four functions: (1) to provide service to local chests, councils, and funds; (2) to serve as a stand-by squad to rescue chests or funds when they flounder financially; (3) to organize and direct the national public relations program, e.g., getting the President of the United States to launch each fall's chest campaign; (4) to provide national leadership in the field of health and welfare.[37] To carry out these responsibilities the Three Cs today maintain a large staff organized in these divisions:

Executive—the executive director and his assistant directors. *Public Relations*—devoted to the effective promotion and interpretation of the federated way of planning and financing services. It conducts a national public relations program on behalf of the united community campaigns. *Campaigning*—this division is responsible for providing special services, including campaign materials and how-to-do-it kits which will help local chests operate more effectively. *Field Service*—campaign and labor staff men are on the road a great deal of the time, providing consultation field service upon request from chests, councils, and funds. All staff field trips are coordinated in this division. *Personnel*—this division has as its responsibilities: (a) setting professional standards for all chest, council, and fund staff positions; (b) raising salary levels to compare favorably with business and industry; (c) recruitment and training of high-caliber men and women for these jobs; (d) assisting local communities to find chest executives. *Research and Statistics; Library and Loan Service; Health and Welfare Planning;* and *Labor and Federations.*[38]

The newly organized national association quickly saw the need for qualified personnel to staff the community chests springing up across the land. In 1923 it sponsored, in cooperation with the Ohio State University Graduate School of Social Administration, a training course for federation secretaries. In 1931 a graduate course leading to a social work degree in community organization was initiated at OSU. In 1938 special training for the chest and council field was also introduced at Boston College. In 1924 the Association, in cooperation with the Welfare Federation of Cleveland, pioneered in setting up registration areas of social statistics through which common measures as to volume and rates of social service could be established and related to costs. In 1930 this undertaking was assumed by the Children's Bureau of the U.S. Department of Labor, but in 1945 this function of the Children's Bureau was cut and the service was resumed by the Three Cs.

Today, the once struggling American Association for Community Organization is a well-staffed, affluent organization of tremendous power, The United Community Funds and Councils, providing a persuasive voice for philanthropy and standing as a bastion of defense against the growing encroachments of the new and aggressively independent money seekers.

The National Information Bureau

The need for a reliable, objective check on the validity of the increasing appeals for money became apparent as the number of drives multiplied and the amount of chicanery in the charity field mounted. The seekers of the easy dollar are always quick to seize a new opportunity. This wartime need was met initially by the organization of the National Investigation Bureau of War Charities in the fall of 1918, as related earlier. The work of the NIB under the direction of Barry C. Smith met an obvious need and its sponsors decided to continue it on a permanent basis after the war's end. The name was changed to the National Information Bureau on August 1, 1919, the board of directors was expanded, and the NIB's scope was broadened to include study and endorsement of national organizations seeking public gifts to work to maintain sound standards in public philanthropy. The National Information Bureau was rooted in the proposition that "philanthropic operations entail a high degree of responsibility because of the element of public trusteeship." The NIB holds to that basic proposition today, some forty-five years later.

Thus began a continuing and still not wholly successful effort to provide objective methods to evaluate the merit of voluntary agencies and thus channel contributors' dollars only to agencies equipped to use them in the public interest. The National Information Bureau, early described as "an information service to protect charitable contributors and conserve charitable resources," has accomplished much in this effort. Yet some forty-two years after it was founded the Rockefeller Foundation's study of voluntary health and welfare agencies in the United States concluded that "The public, in the absence of objective methods to evaluate voluntary agencies, gives too little consideration to the quality of agency services, and to the priority of community health and welfare needs." [39]

Thus it was a long, complex, and difficult task the NIB undertook when it was reorganized August 1, 1919, "to study and endorse agencies of national scope engaged in social, civic, or philanthropic work and supported in whole or in part by voluntary contributions." In the reorganization the board was expanded to bring in leaders of organized social work to serve alongside representatives of the contributing public. Officers of the newly organized NIB were: Gustavus Pope, Detroit, president; Paul L. Feiss, Cleveland, vice-president and treasurer; Paul D. Cravath, New York, second vice-president; and Allen T. Burns, Carnegie Corporation, secretary. Among those on the initial board of directors was Samuel Insull whose utility empire crashed in a sensational scandal in the depression of the thirties. It proved ironic indeed to have Insull cooperating in an effort to prevent charitable frauds on the public!

The Bureau from the start has been supported by membership fees and voluntary contributions. At the outset two classes of dues-paying memberships were established: *Organizations:* Active—for community chests, federations, and similar organizations representing charitable contributors; Associate—for chambers of commerce, women's clubs, and similar organizations. *Personal*—Individual or Service, or Associate. In its first annual report the NIB reported (in an audited statement, to be sure) that it had an income of $37,-427.15 in the fiscal year of September, 1918, to September, 1919. Of this sum $32,041.58 had been spent. [40]

Early in its history the NIB started printing what are now known as its *Giver's Guides* although copies of the first one are not in NIB's files. In the files in New York City are copies of Bulletin No. 2, "Approved War Activities," dated February, 1919, a report on "Foreign Relief Conditions," April, 1919, and Bulletin No. 4, "Approved War Activities Abroad." These bulletins were published somewhat irregularly until 1940. This service was resumed in 1945–1946 when, under the leadership of D. Paul Reed, the annual publication of *Giver's Guide, National Philanthropies*, was instituted. The new National Information Bureau set down these requirements for its endorsement to the public as an agency deserving of public support:

1. An active and responsible governing body holding regular meetings or other satisfactory form of administrative control.
2. A necessary purpose with no avoidable duplication of the work of another efficiently managed organization.
3. Reasonable efficiency in conduct of work, management of institutions, etc. and reasonable adequacy of equipment for such work, both material and personal.
4. No solicitors on commission or other commission methods of raising money.
5. Non-use of the "remit or return" method of raising money by the sale of merchandise or tickets.
6. No entertainments for money raising purposes, the expenses of which exceed 30 per cent of the gross proceeds.
7. Ethical methods of publicity, promotion and solicitation of funds.
8. Agreement to consult and cooperate with the proper social agencies in local communities with reference to local programs and local budgets.
9. Complete annual audited accounts prepared by a Certified Public Accountant or trust company showing receipts and disbursements classified and itemized in detail. . . .
10. Itemized and classified annual budget estimate.[41]

These standards set down as a yardstick of the merit of national fund drives did not use the word "charity" at all and thus signified the historic transition that took place in the wake of World War I, the transition from charity to philanthropy. These standards also give us some insight into the fund-raising methods prevailing in public philanthropy in the years after the big drives of World War

I. The situation confronting the young National Information Bureau when it was initially organized was seen by its officers in these terms:

> Lack of proper coordination in war relief, resulting sometimes from ignorance, sometimes from personal or political jealousy, has at times flooded the country with duplicating appeals. Needless agencies have been launched. . . .
>
> A New York physician, for instance, organized a society to furnish medical supplies to American military hospitals. It seemed to him a wise and good purpose. . . . The fact that the United States authorities had arrranged to care fully for this need does not appear to have entered his head. . . .
>
> A committee organized to ship individual packets of cigarettes overseas was so much interested "in getting cigarettes to the boys" that it was "blinded" to the fact that a profit of 30 cents was made on each dollar contributed and that other tobacco funds were already well covering the field.
>
> One of the numerous funds raising money from a single profession for war victims of the same craft was especially anxious to be approved by the Bureau—in spite of duplication—because the sponsors hoped through the consequent advertising to secure applicants for relief.
>
> Their one difficulty, they explained, was in spending the money they had collected! . . .
>
> The classic example of imposition in war relief is the Army and Navy Bazaar held in New York in October, 1917, at which, the District Attorney reports, it cost over $71,000 to raise $645 for relief. . . .
>
> The public has been pretty thoroughly aroused to a healthy skepticism, and fraudulent enterprises on a large scale are not so easily floated as during the early part of the war. The vitality of many relatively small enterprises of a very suspicious, if not actually criminal character is, however, surprising. . . . The Bureau is frequently called upon to investigate organizations on the borderland between gross carelessness and downright fraud.[42]

In his first report Barry C. Smith, the first director of the NIB, reported that to date the Bureau had made 320 separate investigations and disseminated the results to members and made endorsed lists available to the public. He reported that "Ninety-four war relief agencies have been endorsed; 110 have been refused endorsement. In addition the Bureau has withdrawn its endorsement from one organization." In Smith's opinion this work of the NIB "has relieved war chests, chambers of commerce, and individual givers from the burden of original investigations and, by the same token, has relieved busy war relief executives from a needless duplication of inquiries into their administration." [43] Almost from the beginning Smith and the officers of the NIB saw its purpose as twofold: not only to evaluate the merit of agencies seeking public gifts but to seek to raise the standards of their administration and cooperation. "The Bureau will thus continue to conserve charitable resources by protecting the public and hopes to exercise a constructive influence on the methods adopted by social agencies."

The minutes of NIB board meetings in the early 1920's reveal and reflect a variety of efforts, mostly unavailing, to bring about better cooperation and higher standards of operation by the national agencies. Included was the project, mentioned earlier in this chapter, of making a series of depth studies of national agencies seeking charity dollars. There is indication in NIB files that the impetus for these studies came from the Rockefeller Foundation, which offered to finance them. The project started and stopped with the study of the National Tuberculosis Association, already discussed. In a mild understatement, Dudley Paul Reed says, "It is my impression that this type of depth analysis stopped in part due to the unwillingness of national agencies to cooperate." [44]

Taking another tack in pursuit of this objective of "exercising a constructive influence on the methods adopted by social agencies," the NIB called a Conference on National Social Agencies to meet in Washington, D.C., in April, 1921. The call described the conference "as an effort to effect better cooperation between the growing number of national organizations making annual appeals for public giving." This conference passed a resolution calling for a "study of the work of national agencies in several local communities . . . to determine the facts as to the interrelation of the work of national agencies in those communities." To carry out this resolution the National Information Bureau, in the fall of 1921, appointed Professor Porter R. Lee, Professor Walter W. Pettit and Miss Jane M. Hoey as the staff to make the study. Professor Lee was director and Professor Pettit was on the staff of the New York School of Social Work. Their investigations culminated in a 157-page report published a year or so later.

The study focused on the relationships of forty-six national fund-seeking organizations with their local chapters or affiliates in Atlanta, Ga., Bridgeport, Conn., Burlington County, N.J., Cleveland, Ohio, Grand Rapids, Mich., Memphis, Tenn., Minneapolis, Minn., Plainfield, N.J., Rochester, N.Y., St. Louis, Seattle, Sioux Falls, S.D., Springfield, Mass., and Wilson County, N.C.[45]

Chief among the conclusions of this study were "National organizations are recognized in local communities as necessary and useful," but "there is a widespread feeling in some local communities that the chief interest of national organizations in the local community is the raising of money for the national budget." [46] The investigators also found that "There is a feeling in some local communities that there are too many national organizations and that too many national headquarters are located in New York City." [47] Thus was highlighted an old problem in popular philanthropy—the necessity to establish a mutually satisfactory relationship between the ever-growing national headquarters of a philanthropic agency in faraway New York City and its local chapter in Sioux Falls. This report created much heated discussion in philanthropic circles and may be presumed to have had some impact on these agencies in improving their national-local relationships and in modifying their publicity practices. At least this report gives us a view of the beginnings of a general attitude toward the national organizations on the part of donors and volunteers in the local community in this seedbed period.

With growing support, the National Information Bureau found its work rapidly developing during its second year, 1919–20. To keep up with the increasing volume of inquiries, it began 404 new investigations, more than one a day during the year. Progress in these formative years is seen in this table: [48]

	Year 1918–19	Year 1919–20	Per cent increase
Inquiries received	1309	2472	89
Reports issued	1533	2772	80
New investigations begun	179	404	126

Barry Smith reported to the NIB board: "The period of fantastic memorials of the war is not yet over. The welfare of man and beast is still sought by new, inexperienced and often superfluous committees. Meanwhile the reaction from the generous giving of the war is hampering legitimate agencies, and has forced them to give more careful consideration than ever to economy and efficiency." [49] In March, 1920, the NIB published a *Giver's Guide* approving 82 agencies for general purposes and 41 war relief organizations. Later in the year 12 other organizations were approved, including four for war relief, and endorsement was withdrawn from three which failed to maintain the standards to which they had agreed. Although the NIB still has not solved the problem of channeling charity dollars only to those organizations that deserve them, it has almost from the start exerted a beneficial impact on fund-raising and fund-accounting practices. In his second annual report, Mr. Smith could claim:

> In order to secure endorsement exactly half of these 82 national agencies improved their methods. Of all the organizations approved since the formation of the Bureau in 1918, 80 have begun to have their books audited by a certified public accountant . . . 48 have bettered their financial methods in other ways, 34 have reorganized or modified their operations, 17 have bettered their cooperative relations, and 53 have adopted budgets. [50]

Not only did the public appeals multiply. So did efforts to profit by exploiting the nation's sense of debt to those who had fought and the sense of sorrow for the war-shattered nations of Europe and the Middle East. "Patriotic efforts don't seem to be appreciated any more," complained the promoter of a new Americanization agency to the National Information Bureau when it was making an investigation in 1919. This was one of twenty-nine such agencies attempting to work side by side on the same problem. "The promoter's patriotism during the war had taken the form of a soldier-magazine; his interest in Americanism dated from the time when the magazine ceased to pay." [51] Another of these Americanization societies was found devoted "entirely to Americanization by 'geometrical' taxation"; another was serving as a cloak for a lobbying campaign against certain liberal legislation; still another appealed for funds in the name of a treasurer whose connection with the organization was both involuntary and unconscious. One very ambitious Americanization agency was found by the NIB to be accomplishing nothing save paying its chief executive "a salary of five figures."

Backed by the reputable social agencies, the Bureau proceeded aggressively against the fraudulent and unsound charity appeals.

Late in 1919, for example, it succeeded in blocking altogether "an undesirable campaign for $50,000,000 for which national headquarters had already been opened, a quantity of monumental mahogany furniture installed, and an expensive campaign manager retained." [52] In another instance, as a result of the Bureau's investigation, a swindler, with a police record in two cities and two aliases, was sentenced to federal prison for use of the mails with intent to defraud. The NIB discovered early that much chicanery in charity can be accomplished without breaking the law. "Control by state law or municipal ordinance is difficult." The NIB has always used "judicious publicity" to expose charlatans as the most effective method of protecting the unwary giver.

The NIB did not confine its checking on the validity of public appeals to national and local agencies in the United States. As pointed out in its first report, "Since the larger part of the money actually spent for relief was disbursed in Europe, the Bureau found it necessary to study relief operations there." In February, 1919, it sent to France, Belgium, and Italy W. Frank Persons, who had for two years been director general of Civilian Relief for the American Red Cross. Persons devoted his probing exclusively to a survey of American war relief organizations at work.

A second field study was made in Austria, Germany, Poland, and Serbia in the winter of 1920. When Maxim Gorky appealed to Americans for food for starving Russians, in the summer of 1921, American knowledge of Russia had for three years been a matter of conjecture and contradiction. During the fall and winter of that year several organizations undertook to raise money and food to send to the Russians. The reports from these agencies as to the need in Russia were vague and sometimes contradictory. Therefore the directors of the National Information Bureau, on May 16, 1922, voted "the organization of a Commission on Russian Relief to study the situation in Russia after the harvest of 1922 was accounted for, so that some sort of forecast could be made of conditions during the coming winter." [53] Members of the Commission were: Allen Wardwell, New York City attorney and member of American Red Cross Commission to Russia, 1917; Graham R. Taylor, then executive secretary of the American Association of Social Workers; and Allen T. Burns, director of the National Information Bureau since July 1, 1922.

Apparently the NIB, in its effort to clarify the picture of the true needs in Russia and thus better advise those being asked to give, collided with Herbert Hoover's organization for relief work in Russia in this period. The minutes of the board of directors' meeting on February 9, 1923, read: "The Director presented briefly the negotiations conducted by the Bureau and the Commission on Russian Relief, with Mr. Hoover, regarding the prevention of duplication of appeals and controversy in the field of Russian Relief. It was indicated that after a great deal of work, the efforts had been unsuccessful in getting Mr. Hoover to make any public statement regarding the present famine need in Russia and that Mr. Hoover would not occupy any more of the field of Russian Relief than he was doing at the present time." [54]

The NIB Commission entered Russia by way of Riga on September 6, 1923, and the last member left that country on December 14. The Commission issued its report in February, 1923, recommending "continued aid from outside Russia until the emergency is over." The report concluded: "American aid has not hitherto been conditioned on approval of the Soviet's economic or political policies. It has been given, in fact, in the face of almost universal disapproval of Soviet policy, because of the wish to meet a demonstrated human need. In our judgment the facts we observed in Russia point inescapably to the conclusion that if widespread suffering and death from starvation this year are to be prevented, American help must be continued on a large scale." [55]

Barry C. Smith, who had pioneered the patterns of investigation and the philosophy of protecting the giver, first in the Contributors Information Bureau of New York City's Charity Organization Society, then in the National Investigation Bureau of War Charities, left the increasingly active NIB to take a better job with the Commonwealth Fund in 1921. Barry's son Geddes, whom he had brought to the NIB from the COS, remained on with the NIB as acting director until July, 1922, when he, too, joined the Commonwealth Fund staff. Allen T. Burns, who had helped organize the Bureau while serving as director of the Americanization Study for the Carnegie Corporation, was named to succeed Geddes Smith. He served in this post until he became director of the Community Chests and Councils of America January 15, 1926.

A full-time director to succeed Burns was not named until 1928, when Mrs. M. H. Harding was appointed. Mrs. Harding served until 1940, when Leonard C. Cushing was brought in as staff head. Mrs.

Harding continued on the NIB staff until 1945 and then retired. D. Paul Reed, present director of the NIB, came to this post in May, 1941, as acting director and subsequently the title was changed to executive director. Mr. Reed "has functioned in his present role of quasi-public conscience for two decades." A writer in 1961 observed: "Mr. Reed and his staff are justifiably proud of the National Information Bureau's performance. At the same time, they are honest in pointing out that they were unable to prevent contributions totaling an estimated $75,000,000 last year [1960] to agencies that didn't deserve the trust." [56] In 1964 as in 1919, "the messages that people are most eagerly waiting to hear are the types of messages that can most easily be distorted."

The National Publicity Council

The writing of persuasive messages to raise more and more charity dollars increasingly became a more difficult, more specialized task. This brought the professional publicist to the field of public giving. Improvement and extension of publicity techniques for the community chests and other charity organizations was spearheaded by the work of the indefatigable Evart G. and Mary Swain Routzahn of the Russell Sage Foundation.

The increased emphasis on publicity in the philanthropic field was reflected in the organization of the National Publicity Council and of a Health Education Section in the American Public Health Association in the early 1920's. In the birth and development of these two organizations the Routzahns played the key role. The importance of publicity in stimulating the public to give money to public health and welfare causes has been recognized almost from the start, but in line with the intensive and extensive fund-raising efforts in the postwar era, the emphasis became more pronounced, the techniques more professional, and the media more varied.

Evart G. Routzahn began his lifetime work of promoting support for health and welfare services with the newly organized National Tuberculosis Association in 1905. The Association's first traveling exhibit was placed under Routzahn's direction and sent to the major cities along the eastern seaboard in December of that year. The exhibit proved extremely popular and the Association officials decided to keep it on the road indefinitely. The Association received grants for this purpose from the Russell Sage Foundation in 1907, the first funds the Association had obtained, apart from donations and dues.[57] "During the era of exhibits, 1906–1912, the National Association experimented with other means of publicity. In 1908 . . . it established a Publicity Bureau which was probably the first of its kind." [58] The latter claim is not valid. In this six-year period Routzahn had charge of the Association's Southern Traveling Exhibit. He also directed the exhibit at the International Tuberculosis Congress in Washington, D.C.

In mid-1912 the Russell Sage Foundation decided to establish a Department of Surveys and Exhibits to serve as "a clearing house for advice and information on social surveys and exhibits, and for field assistance in organizing surveys and exhibits." The new department was headed by Shelby M. Harrison, formerly of Pittsburgh, Pa., a man experienced in the then rudimentay techniques of the social survey. Routzahn was brought in from the Tuberculosis Association as associate director to handle the exhibits and publicity phase of the new department's work. Routzahn started work at the Russell Sage Foundation September 1, 1912, and worked in this cause until he retired in 1934. One of the first persons to be hired in the surveys and exhibits unit was Miss Mary B. Swain, a former English teacher. She and Routzahn fell in love, courted, and then married in 1914 as they worked day and night to build understanding of publicity techniques. They worked tirelessly as a team until Mr. Routzahn's retirement; then Mrs. Routzahn carried on the work until she retired in 1945.[59]

Mrs. Sallie Bright, outstanding public relations leader in social work who followed in Mrs. Routzahn's footsteps, says of the Routzahns: "Mr. Routzahn was the spark that powered them to their accomplishments. Mrs. Routzahn didn't have his keen imagination but she effectively complemented him in many ways. He was primarily interested in the health field, she in social welfare. He was a great gadgeteer and exhibits were always his first love. As a former English teacher she was more interested in the written word. He was utterly uninhibited as a person; she was more sedate. They worked well together and accomplished much for our field." [60]

Mr. Routzahn provided the spark that kindled widespread interest in social work publicity when he read a paper, "Elements of a Social Publicity Program," at the National Conference of Social Work in New Orleans, April 17, 1920. Spontaneous response to his demand for a "new type of worker in the social welfare field . . . trained in the technique of expressing social information in ways that will attract attention and create interest on the part of people" resulted in formation of a Committee on Publicity Methods in Social Work. This organization, which has pioneered public relations thinking in the health and welfare fields, was set up by twenty-two health and welfare workers the year after Routzahn's urging at New Orleans. Evart G. and Mary Swain Routzahn were the principal organizers. A year later, in 1922, the Committee was reorganized as the National Publicity Council for Welfare Services; this title was changed to Social Work Publicity Council in 1939 and then to National Publicity Council for Health and Welfare Services in 1943. Finally, in January, 1961, the title was changed to National Public Relations Council of Health and Welfare Services.

From its inception, in 1922, until 1940 the Council was the vehicle of the Routzahns and used by them to transport new ideas, new techniques, and missionary zeal to the novices in health and welfare publicity work. And novices there were in numbers. The increasing demand for publicists, coupled with a high turnover of personnel in the field, intensified the need for help and training in the ways of expressing information "that will attract attention and create interest on the part of people."

Simultaneously, the Routzahns were kindling interest in public relations and publicity techniques among workers in public health. In 1921 and 1922 they conducted sessions on publicity and educational methods at the annual meeting of the American Public Health Association. Enthusiasm generated by these sessions led to creation of a Health Education section in APHA's national headquarters, a department in the Association's monthly journal, and a place on the APHA annual program. Routzahn was appointed editor of the journal's department on publicity methods. "Throughout the twenties Mr. and Mrs. Routzahn spent a great deal of time in helping develop these two agencies for the improvement of educational methods and publicity. In each case meetings, exhibits, and consultations at the annual conventions and interim bulletins were the chief methods. Many of the meetings were in the popular form of 'clinics,' at which examples of publicity were criticized by experts and discussed by the audience." [61]

The study of the interrelation of the work of national social agencies sponsored by the National Information Bureau—a study started in 1921 and completed in 1922—found publicity programs then being used to be rather primitive and based almost wholly on the emotional appeal. This report had criticism to offer at both the national and the local level. Of the national social agencies studied, the authors concluded: "The educational work of the national organizations, whether printed publicity, addresses, or something else, is not fundamental and it is relatively ineffective." [62] Yet the authors did say, "National agencies have undoubtedly rendered valuable service to local units in supplying them with information which would make good publicity material." Then the report strongly criticized social agency publicity at the local level in these words:

> From evidences in local communities of the lack of appreciation of the need for publicity and methods of securing it on the part of so many local workers, a further problem is presented to national agencies. It is one thing to put printed material into the hands of local executives. It is another thing to demonstrate to local workers how it can be used effectively. The training of personnel in the art of publicity has apparently not yet been worked out. Many of the local executives especially in the chest cities were willing to have the programs of local and national work presented once a year in newspaper articles with emotional appeals. This method does bring in funds for the agency but it is not adequate for the edification of the community in the fundamental principles upon which the programs of the social agencies are based. [63]

Use of the emotional rather than the educational approach to getting money for popular philanthropy continues, though perhaps not to the same extent as was practiced in the early 1920's. Then this study found, "To a considerable extent the appeals of community chests give the chief emphasis to work for the alleviation of human misery. . . . The outstanding slogan of chest publicity as we encountered it is 'Suppose Nobody Cared.' Publicity which is written around this idea does not, in the judgment of the executives of many social agencies, do justice to the work they are doing." [64] In sum, these scholars found that national publicity material was getting limited local attention because it was ill adapted to local needs, and that local publicity material exploited the emotional appeals because this was the easiest way to get money. It still is.

This twofold problem outlined in the NIB report had a wide hearing and was the focus of the efforts of the Routzahns in their untiring work to bring efficacy, responsibility, and competence to

the field of philanthropic publicity. In stimulating publicity awareness in the closely related fields of welfare and health, Routzahn
worked primarily with the Health Education section in the American Public Health Association and Mrs. Routzahn gave her time to
the National Publicity Council. In 1923 this husband-and-wife team
introduced a full course on publicity in the New York School of
Social Work, one of the first publicity courses to be offered at the
college level in the United States. This course became an established
part of the school's curriculum. In 1929 Mrs. Routzahn added a second course to offer "practice in writing and other forms of expression." During the twenties the emphasis in publicity teaching and
practice was on printed matter.[65] Even so, as the NIB report indicated, "it is usually not wholly satisfactory, even to the agency
which prepares it."

In 1923 Mrs. Routzahn got out the first mimeographed *News
Bulletin* for the National Publicity Council. This now common
means of exchanging ideas and news among social work publicists
was issued from six to eight times a year from Mrs. Routzahn's office
at the Russell Sage Foundation. The *News Bulletin* was changed
to a printed monthly magazine entitled *Channels* in 1938 after fifteen years as a mimeographed letter. The Russell Sage Foundation
contributed Mrs. Routzahn's services as executive secretary of the
Publicity Council. In 1931 the Foundation started supplementing
her services with a cash grant of $1,000 for an editorial assistant.

In 1929 the name of the Council was changed to Social Work
Publicity Council, directed by officers and an executive committee.
At this time publicity work for community chests and kindred
fund-seeking agencies had become sufficiently widespread to produce 1,000 members for the Council. In 1935 a constitution and
by-laws were adopted which provided for a board of directors as
the governing body. The same year the Russell Sage Foundation
increased its grant to $3,500 and a membership secretary was em-
ployed. To take advantage of the new Internal Revenue Act of 1935,
which encouraged gifts to philanthropic organizations, the Council
was incorporated under the membership laws of the state of New
York in 1937. By April, 1940, the Russell Sage Foundation found it
necessary to withdraw Mrs. Routzahn's services as the Council's
executive and she was succeeded by her protégé, Mrs. Sallie Bright,
who had joined the staff in 1936.

The Council changed its name and broadened its field of service in 1943, when it became the National Publicity Council for Health and Welfare Services. The change of name was occasioned by the fact that by this time half the Council's services were going to the organizations in the health field. By 1948 the Russell Sage Foundation had severed its last ties with the Council, cutting it loose to navigate on its own course in the seas of philanthropic public relations. The NPC has had some rough going but it has stayed afloat and today seems to be on a steady course. When the Council became wholly self-supporting in 1948, *Channels* became a bimonthly four-page newsletter, one of several economies effected. The publicity seeds planted by the Routzahns have borne much fruit since the early 1920's. The focus today, as four decades ago, is on ways and means of building public support to raise funds for these agencies.

NOTES

1. John Lear, "The Business of Giving," *Saturday Review*, Vol. 44 (Dec. 2, 1961), p. 63.
2. John Price Jones, *America Gives Away $2,219,700,000 in a Year*, pamphlet in Jones company files, dated 1928.
3. William J. Norton, *The Cooperative Movement in Social Work*, p. 121.
4. *Atlantic Monthly*, Vol. 128 (September, 1921), pp. 289–290.
5. William J. Norton, *op. cit.*, p. 127.
6. In "Why Do People Give?," *Survey*, Vol. 46 (Aug. 16, 1921), p. 611.
7. Lillian Brandt, *How Much Shall I Give* (New York: Frontier Press, 1921), p. 25.
8. W. J. King, *Trends in Philanthropy* (New York: NBER, 1928), pp. 75–76.
9. Found in National Information Bureau's *Report of a Study of the Interrelation of the Work of National Social Agencies in Fourteen American Communities*.
10. The account of the national organization impact on Sioux Falls is condensed from pp. 95–98 of the NIB study.
11. Brandt, *op. cit.*, p. 111.
12. Hurd, *The Compact History of the American Red Cross*, p. 182.
13. *Ibid.*, pp. 182–183.
14. See *American* for dates of May 25, May 31, June 1, June 29, July 1, July 5, July 19, July 20, and July 25, 1921, for the grim details.
15. Robert K. Murray, *A Study of American Public Opinion on the American National Red Cross*, p. 81.
16. *San Francisco Chronicle*, Dec. 29, 1918.
17. Hopkins, *History of the Y.M.C.A. in North America*, p. 601.
18. Lear, *op. cit.*, p. 63.
19. Guy Thompson, "Community Chests and United Funds," in *Social Work Yearbook*, 1957, pp. 175–179.
20. In address, "The Community Chest Movement," given at Toronto, Canada, June, 1924.
21. In address given at Pinewoods Institute, quoted from mss. he provided.
22. Norton, *op. cit.*, p. 114.

23. *Ibid.,* pp. 116–117.

24. In *Social Work Yearbook,* p. 175.

25. In *The Tuberculosis Worker,* p. 205.

26. Lear, *op. cit.,* p. 69.

27. Jacobs, *The Tuberculosis Worker,* paraphrased from p. 207.

28. King, *op. cit.,* pp. 18–19.

29. Richard H. Shryock, *National Tuberculosis Association, 1904–1954,* pp. 213–214.

30. *Ibid.,* p. 215.

31. Gunn and Platt, *Voluntary Health Agencies* (New York: Ronald), pp. 212–213.

32. *Voluntary Health and Welfare Agencies in the United States,* An Exploratory Study by an Ad Hoc Citizens Committee. Study Director Dr. Robert H. Hamlin (New York: Schoolmasters' Press, 1961), p. 20.

33. "Chronological History of Fund Raising," mimeograph in files of organization.

34. Letter from Elwood Street, May 11, 1960.

35. Arthur J. Todd in Confidential Memorandum, "Study of Financing of Social Work . . . ," for Welfare Council of New York City Research Bureau, April, 1931, p. 7.

36. In address, "The Community Chest Movement," at National Conference on Social Work, Toronto, Canada, June, 1924.

37. Interview in New York City, March 20, 1960.

38. Mary Dabney, "Profile: Community Chests and Councils of America," *Philanthropy,* Vol. 3 (Spring, 1955), pp. 42–48 ff.

39. *Voluntary Health and Welfare Agencies in the United States,* pp. 16–17.

40. *National Information Bureau Report, 1918–1919,* the NIB, p. 16.

41. *Ibid.,* p. 14.

42. *Ibid.,* pp. 9–10.

43. *Ibid.,* p. 10.

44. Dittoed, "Notes on Early NIB History," circa 1960.

45. National organizations cooperating in the study were: American Association for Community Organizations, American Association for Organizing Family Social Work, American Child Health Association, American Foundation for the Blind, American Humane Association, American Red Cross, American Rescue Workers, American Social Hygiene Association, American Society for the Control of Cancer, Big Brother and Big Sister Federation, Boys' Club Federation, Boy Scouts of America, Camp Fire Girls, Child Welfare League of America, Circle for Negro Relief, Community Service, Council of Jewish Women, Federal Council of Churches of Christ in America, Girl Scouts, YMCA, International Sunshine Society, Jewish Welfare Board, National Alliance of Legal

Aid Societies, National Association for the Advancement of Colored People, National Association of Travelers' Aid Societies, YWCA, National Catholic Welfare Council, National Child Labor Committee, National Children's Home and Welfare Association, National Committee for Mental Hygiene, National Committee for the Prevention of Blindness, National Committee on Prisons and Prison Labor, National Congress of Mothers and PTAs, National Consumers' League, National Federation of Settlements, National Florence Crittenton Mission, National League of Girls' Clubs, National Organization for Public Health Nursing, National Probation Association, National Tuberculosis Association, National Urban League, WCTU, Needlework Guild of America, Playground and Recreation Association of America, Salvation Army, and Society for the Friendless. Only one organization invited to participate declined—The Volunteers of America.

46. Report of a Study of the Interrelation of the Work of National Social Agencies in Fourteen American Communities, the NIB, circa 1922, p. 9.

47. *Ibid.*, p. 9.

48. *National Information Bureau Report, 1919–1920*, NIB, p. 5.

49. *Ibid.*, p. 3.

50. *Ibid.*, pp. 4–5.

51. *National Information Bureau Report, 1919–1920*, NIB, p. 3.

52. *Ibid.*, p. 5.

53. *The Russian Famines 1921–22, 1922–23*, Summary Report Commission on Russian Relief of the National Information Bureau, Inc., New York City, 1923, p. 3.

54. Minutes of NIB on file in its headquarters.

55. *Ibid.*, p. 40.

56. Lear, *op. cit.*, p. 64.

57. Shryock, *op. cit.*, p. 101.

58. *Ibid.*, p. 102.

59. Glenn, Brandt, and Andrews, *Russell Sage Foundation*, Vol. I, pp. 68 and 179.

60. Interview with Mrs. Bright, New York City, March 10, 1960.

61. Glenn, Brandt, Andrews, *op. cit.*, Vol. II, p. 363.

62. National Information Bureau, *Report of a Study of the Interrelation of Work of National Social Agencies in Fourteen American Communities*, NIB, circa 1922, p. 127.

63. *Ibid.*, p. 94.

64. *Ibid.*, p. 112.

65. Glenn, Brandt, Andrews, *op. cit.*, p. 367.

7

The 1920's (continued):
Cash for Colleges and Cathedrals

Capital for Colleges

The nation's educational, religious, and health institutions moved swiftly to capitalize on the new spirit of philanthropic giving in the United States. More donors gave more dollars, usually under the heavy pressure of the new expert fund raiser, to build colleges, hospitals, libraries, churches, and even two cathedrals in this rip-roaring postwar decade. The Republican-coined word "normalcy" was used to describe an era which included the flapper, the gangster, and Joe College in a decade that was anything but normal.

Growth of philanthropic support for the nation's institutions of higher education—most of it obtained in capital fund-raising drives —can be seen in the carefully kept records of the John Price Jones Corp. Jones, a great believer in statistics, kept such records when no one else did. When the Jones firm sought information on the total gifts and bequests for higher education, fifty representative institutions reported a total of $28,145,000 for the 1920–1921 fiscal year. Though a small sum by today's billion-dollar standards this was a great deal of money for colleges in 1921. Thirty years later, these same fifty institutions received $112,790,000 in gift moneys. Allowing for the depreciated dollar value, the 1949–1950 total was still an estimated $28.8 million greater in purchasing power than the 1920–1921 amounts. And forty years later, in 1960–1961, gifts and bequests reported by these fifty institutions was $345,953,000, an increase of 22 per cent over the 1959–1960 total and a sum twelve times greater than the sum reported in the first compilation. The $345,953,000 received during 1960–1961 raises the 41-year total of private giving to these colleges and universities to $3,838,301,000—with $2,239,049,000, or 58.3 per cent, having been raised since 1950–1951.[1] This 41-year statistical record carried forward by the Jones firm covers only an undetermined fraction of the total giving for American educational, health, and religious institutions. The gushing rivulets of the 1920's have become the mighty streams in mid-century America. In 1960 it was estimated that the nation's colleges received $608 million in gifts, grants, and bequests.

Prior to addressing the Association of Alumni Secretaries in 1923, Jones sent a questionnaire to 150 universities and colleges to provide facts for his talk. Of the 109 institutions that returned the questionnaire, 64 had conducted fund-raising drives since the close of World War I.

> The statistics sent in by the 64 colleges and universities . . . show that the total amount sought was $113,664,689. The amount sought in each case ranged from $1,189,000 for the University of Utah to $15,250,000 for Harvard. Of this amount $85,803,500 was needed for endowment . . . and the rest was to be used for buildings, war memorials, gymnasiums, and stadiums. . . .
>
> Of the total of $113,664,689 sought by these institutions, the university presidents and treasurers have reported that in all $90,246,-385.38 was paid in or pledged. It is interesting to note that of the total sought in each case only 36 colleges and universities reached their goal. . . . This total amount of gifts by no means represents the grand total of money pledged to American educational institutions in the last four years.[2]

Yet these figures give us an idea of the great spurt in capital giving to colleges in the 1920's, the decade in which Americans thought they had found perpetual prosperity. The figures also tell us that even in those lush days of fund raising not every drive was successful.

The 30-year trend of gifts and bequests to educational institutions in general followed the trend of economic conditions. It was gradual and upward after 1921. It reached a peak in 1925–1926 due to several unusually large gifts (George F. Baker's gift of $5 million to Harvard for its Graduate School of Business), and then fell back to a normal increase until it reached a new peak of $92,007,000 in 1929–1930. Then came the depression and a fairly rapid decline in capital fund raising. The low point of this 30-year span was reached in 1933, when only $23,174,000 was donated to colleges. From there on there was a fluctuating upward trend until the post-World War II years were reached—since then the upward movement has been rapid and steady. Where it will stop nobody knows. It is worth noting that the greater part of this philanthropy has been in contributions by the living, less than one-third in bequests, reflecting the sure hand of the fund raiser. Over the 30-year span gifts constituted 69.37 per cent of the total, bequests the remainder.

Of the fifty-one institutions on which the Jones organization kept records, five universities received nearly half—46.10 per cent to be exact—of the total philanthropy he reports: Harvard, Yale, Chicago, Northwestern, and Columbia. In these thirty years Harvard received a total of $229,875,000; Yale was second with gifts and bequests adding up to $213,647,000. Only Harvard and Yale held places in the first five throughout the three decades reported. Johns Hopkins was in the first five in the 1920 decade and in the last decade reported Cornell and Princeton moved up to displace Chicago and Columbia. These trends—as reflected in the gifts and bequests to the fifty-one colleges and universities—can be studied in Table 9 and Chart 1 (on pp. 246 and 247) showing the figures extended for a 31-year span, or from 1920–1921 through 1950–1951.[3]

Leading the professionals into these new areas of philanthropy was John Price Jones and his newly organized fund-raising and public relations firm. Jones's successful part in raising nearly $14 million for Harvard not only led him to establish a new firm; his success brought him the choicest clients in the college drive field. Soon Jones and his growing staff were at work for Wellesley, Mt. Holyoke, Johns Hopkins, the University of Pennsylvania, the University of Chicago, Ohio State University, and others. In its first six years, 1919 to 1925, the John Price Jones Corp. managed fourteen college and university campaigns to raise nearly $68 million for endowments and buildings. These campaigns were conducted at a cost of $1,576,-731.13 or a percentage cost of 2.34 per cent of the sums raised, according to Jones's records. As of January 1, 1926, the Jones firm could post these results in higher education:

Institution	Amount sought	Amount obtained	Percentage of goal
1. Harvard University	$15,250,000	$13,931,780.69	90.7
2. Northwestern University	5,050,000	9,599,243.27	190.0
3. Hampton and Tuskegee	5,000,000	9,269,840.49	185.4
4. University of Chicago	17,500,000	8,664,797.50	49.3
5. University of Pennsylvania	5,000,000	5,344,366.00	106.8
6. Johns Hopkins University and Hospital	10,890,000	4,505,395.45	42.0
7. Smith College	4,000,000	4,021,893.91	100.5
8. Wellesley College	2,700,000	2,740,779.10	101.5
9. Lehigh University	4,000,000	2,625,000.00	65.6
10. Bryn Mawr College	2,000,000	2,204,412.39	110.0
11. Pennsylvania State College	2,000,000	1,612,442.60	80.6
12. Ohio State University	1,000,000	1,040,000.00	104.0
13. Trinity College	1,500,000	1,030,000.00	68.6
14. Tufts College	750,000	700,000.00	93.3

Jones could report with satisfaction to his second annual staff conference June 29, 1925, that:

> . . . there have been developments of great interest . . . and other promising accounts have been added to our business. The Hampton-Tuskegee Campaign for $5,000,000 . . . has succeeded in raising over $4,500,000 with Mr. Eastman's additional gift of more than $2,000,000 available if the four and a half millions are increased to five millions by the end of the year—a goal which will be attained.
>
> At the University of Chicago subscriptions to about $7,500,000 have been raised towards a Development Fund of $17,500,000, which it is hoped to complete this year. Three million and a half have been subscribed at Johns Hopkins. The University of Pennsylvania has reached its first objective—the raising of $5,000,000, indeed has gone beyond it by $200,000. . . . All told the Corporation has been instrumental in raising, during this year, more than $20,000,000.[4]

For this effort in 1925 the Jones firm, after paying substantial salaries to Jones and other members of the organization, showed a net profit of $41,053.33, a healthy increase over the net profit of $16,148.37 earned the previous year.[5]

Typical of these Jones-directed harvests was that managed in 1924–1926 for Johns Hopkins University and Hospital under the direction of Harold J. Seymour, destined to become one of the major

TABLE 9. RECAPITULATION. THIRTY-ONE YEAR RECORD OF GIFTS AND BEQUESTS * TO
FIFTY-ONE COLLEGES AND UNIVERSITIES, 1920–1921 TO 1950–1951
(In Thousands of Dollars)

| | Thirty-one year totals and averages 1920–1921 to 1950–1951 | | Ten-year averages | | | 5-year averages | |
| | | | 1920–1921 to 1929–1930 | 1930–1931 to 1939–1940 | 1940–1941 to 1949–1950 | 1945–1946 to 1949–1950 | Record for 1950–1951 |
	Total	Average					
Gifts and Bequests							
28 Larger Colleges and Universities	$1,506,677	$48,602	$48,649	$37,271	$54,945	$70,662	$ 98,017
14 Smaller Colleges and Universities	107,795	3,477	3,478	2,896	3,716	5,129	6,896
9 Women's Colleges	89,669	2,892	3,005	1,927	3,549	5,554	4,846
51 Institutions	$1,704,141	$54,971	$55,132	$42,094	$62,210	$81,345	$109,759
Gifts							
28 Larger Colleges and Universities	$1,053,948	$33,998	$36,383	$23,940	$37,082	$52,224	$ 79,896
14 Smaller Colleges and Universities	76,738	2,475	2,880	1,642	2,617	3,875	5,348
9 Women's Colleges	63,502	2,048	2,050	1,352	2,648	4,442	2,991
51 Institutions	$1,194,188	$38,521	$41,313	$26,934	$42,347	$60,541	$ 88,235
Bequests to 47 Colleges and Universities							
25 Larger Colleges and Universities	$ 452,729	$14,604	$12,266	$13,331	$17,863	$18,438	$ 18,121
13 Smaller Colleges and Universities	31,057	1,002	598	1,254	1,099	1,255	1,548
9 Women's Colleges	26,167	844	955	576	901	1,111	1,855
47 Institutions	$ 509,953	$16,450	$13,819	$15,161	$19,863	$20,804	$ 21,524

* *An Index of Giving to Higher Education,* John Price Jones Corp., copyright 1952.

CHART I *

THIRTY-ONE YEAR RECORD OF GIFTS AND BEQUESTS
TO FIFTY- ONE COLLEGES AND UNIVERSITIES
(1920-21 TO 1950-51)

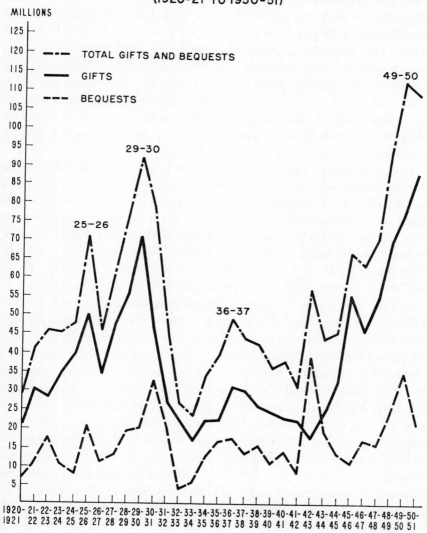

* *Ibid.*

figures in professional fund raising. The details of this campaign reveal the influential role fund raisers often play behind the scenes and reflect the campaign methods of the 1920's.

Quite early in their study of the Johns Hopkins situation, Seymour and Harold W. Weeks, who would handle the publicity campaign, found that the public thought that Johns Hopkins had left enough money to put both the University and the Hospital on easy street. This impression persisted although a financial crisis had almost wiped out the university in the 1880's. The University had made only one general appeal to the public in all its history, that in 1910. "Although the Hospital had been more fortunate in conserving its endowment, its officials left the public in the dark as to its finances. For more than 20 years it not even as much as published a financial statement as part of its annual report." [6]

The University and the Hospital had been established by the wealthy Baltimore merchant, Johns Hopkins, who had amassed a fortune of some $10 million by the 1870's. Reportedly Hopkins' decision to perpetuate his name by endowing a university and hospital grew out of a chance social conversation with philanthropist George Peabody at the home of Robert Garrett, Washington, D.C., shortly after the Civil War. Hopkins, like Peabody, was a bachelor. Hopkins' and Peabody's careers had many parallels.

In 1920 the Johns Hopkins Hospital and Medical School officers realized that they needed a great deal more money if these institutions were to measure up to the opportunities for research and meet the nation's growing health needs. After a survey, they laid out a scheme for expansion that required big sums of money. At this time the Hospital and the University were separate corporations but with interlocking boards of directors. Despite this there "has been . . . a certain feeling that they could not go together too closely, and it has taken time to sort of weld the two things together," Seymour told his Jones colleagues.[7] By the time Seymour entered the picture, the Medical School-Hospital had raised $8 million for its expansion but the University was in dire straits. The University "had very pressing needs of its own because its work had not received any help at all with the exception of an annual grant of $30,000 from the General Education Board. The problem was to erect an organization which would be centralized in that we could use the name of Johns Hopkins to include both things and yet wouldn't hurt anyone's feelings." [8]

The blunt fact was that Johns Hopkins University was in both financial and public relations trouble when the Jones organization was called in. Hopkins officials agreed to the Jones recommendation for a Half-Century Campaign, jointly sponsored, to raise money for the University and the Hospital. A campaign, Daniel Willard would explain later, "occasioned largely by the expansion program of the Medical School and Hospital, and by the losses of academic income due both to the termination of the $30,000 grant from the General Education Board and the construction of the Alumni Dormitory and the Chemistry Laboratory." The drive was scheduled to start April 1, 1924, and reach its climax on February 22, 1926, the fiftieth anniversary of the inauguration of Daniel Coit Gilman as the first president of Johns Hopkins University. Gilman was the first great apostle of university research.

Seymour's first task—as a mediating outsider—was to organize a Joint Committee of Trustees from which he could get support and authority to proceed with a fund-raising campaign. This Joint Committee was made officially responsible for erecting a campaign organization but "all they did was to get our plan, approve the plan and the budget, and then get a chairman and from that point on the Joint Committee of Trustees ceased to function." [9] Seymour admitted later that this was a mistake. But the Joint Committee could not agree on a campaign chairman and Seymour had to solve that problem too. He recounts:

> . . . they [the Joint Committee] began to lose a lot of time and to just chew the rag a whole lot . . . eventually it got to a point where we had to interfere because they were not getting anywhere. The first important thing that we did was to get a chairman . . . Daniel Willard [president of the Baltimore & Ohio R.R.]. . . . From that point on things moved pretty fast. Willard was wise in seeing that we didn't want a big executive committee.

Willard and Seymour, following the original Jones plan, first concentrated on assembling the Hopkins case and in building prospective donor lists. "The only way you can get names of potential donors is by digging down and scratching. I secured the names of people all over the country who have come there as patients." Seymour first assembled the total Johns Hopkins University and Hospital case for funds, then prepared the appeal for each institution.

"Then we are going to sub-divide this appeal into lesser stories for the school. . . . There will be a statement of the Medical School to give to Mr. [Henry] Ford. He made a personal visit to Hopkins, thinks highly of it. Then the next step is to get up a special statement on the different departments. . . . We have got a tremendous story . . . research is the surest road to practical discoveries." [10] The importance of research was a basic campaign theme.

The alumni are the first to be mobilized in a college money-raising campaign but at Hopkins Seymour "had absolutely nothing to go on." The lists were inaccurate, there was no addressograph mailing list and no alumni association to amount to anything. The alumni secretary was a faculty member who worked at the job part-time. Seymour arranged for the appointment of Dr. Charles K. Edmunds, later to become provost, as the director of the association and they brought in a man to edit the alumni magazine and compile accurate alumni mailing lists. Seymour found much disgruntlement among Hopkins alumni because "they haven't got enough members on the Board of Trustees."

Building a strong alumni organization was often the first step fund raisers took on a college campus. Seymour postponed any solicitation of the alumni until their relationships were in better order; "we are not going to begin until we are absolutely right, I don't care when it is." The state of Hopkins alumni relationships had been dramatically exposed just a few years before when the University tried on its own to raise $5 million among alumni and got only $150,000 in pledges on which, at the end of five years, $70,000 had been paid. Seymour was certainly right in proclaiming to his colleagues, "We have got to revive that dead horse."

The Hopkins alumni problem was aggravated by the fact that more of its alumni had been graduate students than undergraduates. For the graduate student there is less of an emotional tie to Alma Mater. In 1925 Johns Hopkins would announce discontinuance of the bachelor's degree and the abandonment of the first two years of ordinary college work, a fact that was to hamper the money getting. Typical was the fund-raising dinner for Hopkins alumni staged by Seymour in New York October 26, 1925, at the Town Hall Club. Seven hundred and ten Hopkins alumni in New York City were invited, 135 attended, and 67 of them made pledges totaling $20,820.

Recognizing the limited interest of alumni in the University, Seymour hit upon the idea of organizing them through the departments in which they "were most intimately concerned," giving each group an opportunity to contribute and solicit funds for its own particular department. Also a campaign for bequests was undertaken. "I believe we have contributed something new in giving material to lawyers in a form ready to be filed." He also solicited holders of life insurance policies to consider Hopkins.

One of Seymour's big tasks was to get both university and hospital to overhaul their public relations policies; neither had a publicity man. Here again the new professional fund raiser was an effective stimulus in prodding colleges and universities to put in publicity and public relations departments in the 1920's. "The most important piece of work in this direction has been organization of the Johns Hopkins Hospital Association. . . . Another important contribution . . . has been our attempt to change the general atmosphere at the . . . Hospital with regard to the handling of patients. A code for the hospital is being framed and hung in all important places throughout the hospital." [11] After a year on the Hopkins campaign, Seymour shared these conclusions with his colleagues:

1. Trustees should be put on the job, and kept on the job, from the very start of the campaign.
2. Great caution should be observed in selecting the committee which is actually to run the campaign. In the early stages such a committee should be only temporary.
3. A schedule should be laid down and rigorously followed for the achievements to be met each month.
4. Those parts of any general plan which are independent in character should be allowed to proceed by themselves.
5. In special gifts work, for large projects, it is better to concentrate upon one project at a time.

Because of the disorganized state of the University's alumni and public relations, the drive proceeded slowly at first. As of June, 1925, Seymour reported to the Jones staff: "We are out for $10,800,-000 for the 50th Anniversary. . . . There are less than 200 subscriptions on the books. . . . The 21 Trustees pledged a total of $195,000. There are four of these Trustees reputed to be millionaires. Mr. Willard will not take the battle ax and go after them. He himself is not a rich man. He has given only $5,000 . . . we had a list of prospects and there was a list committee that was supposed to go over the cards and evaluate them but they did not do it. So I did it." [12] Typically, here is the way he "did it":

> I went to the bankers and got the dope; went to a Jew if there were Jews on the list, and got the dope on them. There was a man on the list named Abraham Hutzler. The cards . . . showed that he had given small sums to the University. He was a millionaire. I went to the bank and asked if he could endow a chair. I went to another Jew in the clothing business who knew him well and asked how to go about approaching Hutzler. The merchant told me that Hutzler's son-in-law was a professor at the university. So I saw the professor. He suggested that President Goodnow and Mr. Kaiser of the Board of Trustees [would be the best ones to talk to his father-in-law]. They were not very keen . . . they had no claim on him. . . . Finally they agreed to see him and Goodnow nearly spoiled it by asking for $100,-000. Hutzler said he would think about it. I let the matter slide for six weeks. Then I got hold of Ames [Joseph S. Ames, provost] and Kaiser. . . . I told them they must see this man, he was 90 years old. I made the appointment and told them to ask for the endowment of a chair in political economy. . . . The first thing Hutzler said was, "I will give you $50,000," but Kaiser said that would not do, that they wanted to set an example for other people in Baltimore and that Johns Hopkins wanted Hutzler to give $250,000. Finally Hutzler agreed to give $200,000.[13]

At the June, 1925, Jones staff conference, in the discussion of the Hopkins campaign, it was brought out that Hopkins faculty members were not cooperating as the campaign directors thought they should. Vice-President Robert Duncan chimed in: "In Chicago [the University] we brought a message direct from the Board of Trustees that if they [faculty members] valued their jobs they must play ball." [14] Duncan, too, knew the ways of putting pressure on potential donors. He would tell his Jones colleagues this story at the 1930 Annual Conference:

> A few weeks ago in Chicago we had the task of organizing a group of special gifts workers to raise $1,250,000 for St. Luke's Hospital by June 30. For certain reasons there could be no newspaper publicity whatever. The entire activity had to be conducted quietly. Mr. Insull [Samuel Insull the notorious utilities manipulator], a great campaign leader, was Campaign Chairman, but out of the city most of the

time. . . . We started off bravely to form a Preferred Gifts Committee. . . . Shortly it became evident that . . . many of them did not qualify. Few of them would go out and ask for money for St. Luke's . . . time was flying.

. . . The class of men whom we did want who would do what Mr. Insull asked them to do were those financial men who handled the far-flung Insull security business. It required little insight to see that that was our best bet. . . . Knowing that a certain house did most of the Insull financing, we conferred with the head of that house and, almost overnight, a splendid, though small, group of workers sprang into being. The men referred to took about ten prospects, got a pledge from each, gave $3,000 himself and got his house to pledge $10,000 . . . the enlistment of a few effective . . . workers came at just the right moment and enabled us to push our total at a luncheon which Mr. Insull gave to $800,000. The present total is more than $1,000,000.[15]

The "enlistment of a few effective workers" and polite business blackmail was an effective fund-raising technique even then!

In a report dated December 29, 1926, Chairman Willard, now also president of the Hopkins Board of Trustees, gave this accounting of the active campaign directed by him and Seymour:

The results of the canvassing undertaken by the campaign organization, with the attending publicity, were estimated on Dec. 18, from 3,982 subscriptions as follows:

Recorded gifts to University	$4,375,403.19
Recorded gifts to Hospital	1,527,514.89
Reported subscriptions	1,112,550.00
Income from Unrestricted Funds	7,160.23
Income from Restricted Funds	391.01
Est. Total Half Century Fund	$7,023,019.32

The cost of the campaign, estimated to December 31, will be approximately $225,769.90 which is about 98½ per cent of the budget of $229,398.97 allowed by the Trustees. The University and the Hospital, under the original agreement, each will have spent about $113,800 on the campaign. Of the total expenditure, which represents about 3 per cent of the amount raised, the John Price Jones Corporation will have received about $94,600 for the services of Mr. Seymour and Mr. Weeks, and for consultation with Mr. Jones and other associates. The balance of the expenses were incurred for office help, rent, furniture . . . etc.[16]

The Hopkins campaign budget—a typical one—was as follows: [17]

Item	Budget	Expended
I. General Salaries	$ 53,934.00	$ 48,623.14
II. Rent	7,119.97	6,330.21
III. Office Furniture	1,000.00	1,226.76
IV. Office Supplies	3,350.00	4,291.50
V. Office Equipment	2,620.00	2,888.25
VI. Telephone, Telegraph	2,950.00	1,977.30
VII. Travel	8,500.00	7,584.80
VIII. Entertainment	6,000.00	2,537.66
IX. Printing and Engraving	24,200.00	39,008.40
X. Postage	8,500.00	7,584.80
XI. Mailing Service	3,950.00	4,291.91
XII. Photography	2,250.00	2,165.38
XIII. Motion Pictures	1,500.00	260.50
XIV. Campaign Library	550.00	226.65
XV. Publicity General Expense	2,500.00	1,366.33
XVI. Advances to Local Chairmen	2,000.00	none
XVII. Advertising	5,000.00	none
XVIII. Contingency Fund	6,000.00	934.69
XIX. Professional Services of John Price Jones Corp.	87,475.00	93,199.33
Totals	$229,398.97	$224,179.83

At this time Willard announced the close of the Half-Century Campaign on December 31, 1926, after which the University and the Hospital would "manage individually the conduct of their respective efforts to raise funds." The University continued its fund-raising activities "though in a less intensive way" and retained the Jones Corporation and Seymour on a part-time basis. Willard could have added that, as a result of the work of Seymour and Weeks, the financial straits of Johns Hopkins University had been greatly eased and the public relationships of both the University and the Hospital greatly improved. A great educational institution that had pioneered in offering graduate study under the leadership of President Gilman had its direction turned upward once more. Viewed in this light, the fees charged by the fund raiser were not high.

Thus the Johns Hopkins Half-Century Campaign to raise $10.8 million, though it fell short of its goal, was typical of the increasing number of such drives on behalf of colleges and universities in the 1920's, drives made necessary by World War I and the increased cost of living. John Price Jones said in 1923: "High costs made the endowments of colleges of less and less value. Those institutions had to have money. But it did another thing. It organized the alumni as they had never been organized before, and aside from getting money the next most important thing is the organization of the alumni. . . . These campaigns have brought the alumni closer to the college than ever before." [18]

Some three decades later, as he neared the end of his career, Jones would reflect: "To have participated in any degree in the immense development of philanthropy in the higher educational field since World War I has been a gratifying experience. During that period, professors' salaries have risen to a more equitable level—though not enough; great university building programs have been launched and carried to completion; large sums of money have been poured into fundamental research in university laboratories. It has been a stimulating venture to help channel some of the currents of this great philanthropic stream." [19]

And channel the philanthropic stream Jones did. From the time of the first Harvard campaign, to 1952, his organization had helped America's colleges raise more than $1 billion in gifts and bequests through the carefully organized, high-pressure methods he did so much to perfect and record. Jones often asserted: "The fund raiser is entitled to take pride and satisfaction in his work. He serves a social need far beyond that served by a mere press agent or publicity man." [20]

But there were those who did not view this boom in higher education with wide-eyed approval. In raising funds for colleges and universities in the 1920's Jones and his colleagues "sold" higher education in the process. Much of the fund appeal was on the value of a university education. The public relations efforts of colleges were strengthened and intensified in conjunction with these drives. This led the dour Dr. Henry S. Pritchett, head of the Carnegie Foundation, to complain: "Oftentimes the byproducts of giving to a good cause result in social toxins which do enough harm to more than counteract the benefit that may come from the original gift." [21]

The pleas of poverty emanating from the college campuses of the 1920's—pleas usually framed by the new professional fund raiser —were even more shrill than those we hear today across the land. In probably what was the first of the college federated fund-raising drives—now commonplace in the philanthropy of higher education —nine Wisconsin private colleges banded together to seek an endowment of $5 million under the guidance of pioneer fund-raiser Lyman L. Pierce. The sum raised was divided among institutions on a pro rata basis of student enrollment.

In a publicity release, akin to those we see today, Pierce told the people: "The life of many a small college is hanging by a tenuous financial thread. The situation is intensified because nearly all colleges this year are being overwhelmed with a two or three years' grist of students whose school-going days have been delayed by the war. This has called for a bigger faculty and more buildings. In some of the schools, salaries have not been revised generally since 1905." [22] The Minneapolis *Tribune* took cognizance of this pioneering move of private colleges to join in a common appeal: "What has appealed to the educators of the nation is that these institutions—some of them denominational and some non-denominational, some Protestant and some Catholic—have forgotten their rivalry, and are in battle, shoulder to shoulder to maintain college faculties and standards." [23] The college federated fund drive became commonplace in the years after World War II.

The Wisconsin Colleges Associated—as the temporary federation was called—fund drive was formally launched in September, 1919, with a 10-city statewide tour starring eight of the college presidents involved in the drive. The tour was arranged and guided by Pierce, who had the title "director general" of the campaign. The tour was widely publicized by Carl Getz, state publicity director for the campaign. Announcing the unprecedented statewide tour of these college presidents, Pierce said: "These presidents will attempt to inform the people of the state exactly what is the part played by a small college in the state's educational system. To illustrate: Of the 8,000 living alumni of these eight institutions more than one-fourth are in the professions. The ministry, education, and social service are largely dependent upon the college for new men and women." [24] This refrain is a common one used in today's spirited competition for gifts to higher education, particularly as between the private and the state-supported institutions.

The sum of $1,014,423 was collected in the allotted time, according to the Milwaukee *Sentinel* of November 25, 1919. In the summer of 1923, President Plantz of Lawrence College announced that the fund had reached $3.5 million, and that it was expected the goal of $5 million would be attained. These figures included pledges, but as of that date Marquette University had received about $40,000 as its share of the general cash returns.[25] In a footnote, Father Hamilton adds: "Evidently pledges were not redeemed, because by 1929 when the University closed the books on this episode a total of $57,928.85 had come in according to records in the Marquette Office of Accounting."

Even though not wholly successful, this first attempt at federated fund raising among colleges drew the interest of educators across the country. For example, at the time the Stoughton (Wis.) *Courier-Hub* quoted Louis Smith, president of Washington and Lee University, as saying: "Wisconsin sets the pace for . . . the rest of the states in the Union. Here the privately endowed colleges of the state, regardless of whether denominational or non-denominational, Catholic or Protestant, have joined hands to work out their common problems. . . . Again Wisconsin leads the way." With the completion of the Wisconsin college drive, Pierce, at this time a partner in the Ward firm, took an assignment to direct a campaign to finance the Inter-Church World Movement staged in the spring of 1920, a campaign with a fund goal of $336,777,572.

Early in 1922 Pierce had returned to college fund raising and proceeded to organize an intensive hard-hitting campaign to raise $3 million for Stanford University's endowment fund. He assumed active charge of the drive to raise the "First Million." Pierce enjoyed this campaign because it enabled him to be at home with his family in nearby Burlingame. The drive started with Stanford's students who were assigned a quota of $200,000 by Pierce. The Stanford President's Report of 1921–22 records that the students made pledges totaling $105,965 and noted that "The future growth of Stanford is assured when the student body of today has joined the alumni." During this same period Pierce was also directing a drive to raise $400,000 for the Greater Northern California Campaign to finance a "new effort to advertise and develop Northern California." In mid-1922 Pierce received a call from his Alma Mater, the University of Minnesota, and he was soon back amid old haunts, fund raising harder than usual. One writer observed: "Pierce just walks, talks, eats, and sleeps University of Minnesota."

In the fall of 1922 Pierce launched a drive to raise $2 million among Minnesota alumni and students to build a large football stadium and an auditorium. The stadium was to be dedicated to the soldier dead of World War I and the auditorium was to honor Minnesota's former president, Cyrus Northrop. Pierce assigned one-fourth of the quota—$500,000—to the current student body. He rightly predicted: "There won't be a University of Minnesota student or faculty member who will escape the corps of 1,100 students who will collect $500,000 of the $2,000,000 Cyrus Northrop memorial fund on the University campus Oct. 30 to Nov. 4." By now Pierce knew well the technique of getting large numbers of people to ask even larger numbers of people to give.

By June, 1923, a total of $1,593,660 had been raised for the stadium and the auditorium and of this sum $668,008 had been raised in 8,122 pledges from faculty and students. Of the total sum pledged by June, 1923, nearly half had been obtained in the three cities of Minneapolis, St. Paul, and Duluth. Altogether, some 15,000 pledges of gifts had been secured since the beginning of the drive in the previous October.

As is usually the case, there was some shrinkage in pledges by the time the collections were made. Reporting in the March, 1928, issue of Minnesota's *Alumni Weekly*, the president of the Greater University Corporation reported considerable difficulty in collecting from those who had made pledges as students. He reported over $400,000 was still due on student pledges. In contrast, 80 per cent of the faculty pledges and 90 per cent of the businessmen and alumni pledges had been paid by this date. The corporation president, Thomas Wallace, thought that the agricultural depression of 1925 was the principal factor in this defaulting on pledges. Wallace reported in this alumni publication that the Pierce-directed drive of 1922–23 had, by 1928, netted the following: total pledged by students, $667,807.78; total pledged by faculty, $100,000; total pledged by alumni and friends, $1 million. The stadium was completed in 1924 and the Northrop Auditorium in 1929. Total cost of the two structures came to more than $2 million, all privately subscribed. Thus Minnesota led the way for state universities in the systematic solicitation of gifts.

One of the most spectacular of the capital drives in the twenties was that which raised $8.1 million in five months for a spectacular building—the University of Pittsburgh's Cathedral of Learning. This effort was directed by Carlton and George Ketchum who had, more than ten years earlier, learned the rudiments of the intensive campaign on the Pitt campus from Charles Sumner Ward. The 1925 campaign was the first of fifteen fund drives the Ketchum firm would direct for Pitt over the next thirty-five years. George and

Carlton Ketchum shared direction of this first Cathedral of Learning campaign, but Carlton directed the three subsequent drives. The dramatic nature of the building and the term, Cathedral of Learning, provided the theme for the Ketchum whirlwind campaign conducted through a Citizens' Committee of nearly a hundred business and civic leaders of western Pennsylvania. In this drive the Ketchums tapped corporation treasuries as they had never been tapped before. The daring idea of a skyscraper university was conceived by Chancellor John G. Bowman, but the name for it was not his. He disliked the attention-getting phrase.

Chancellor Bowman, who became head of the University of Pittsburgh in 1921, soon found himself frustrated as the Pitt enrollment steadily mounted and the University ended each year with a deficit. Furthermore, land in the campus area was scarce and high-priced. Pitt's enrollment had increased nearly 100 per cent between 1916 and 1923. Out of wrestling with these problems came Chancellor Bowman's dream of a skyscraper of fifty-two stories to house the university. He later explained: " 'The usual appeals had been made and failed. Every word that could be used had been used, every argument exhausted. Cold arguments would only be a waste of time. Something was needed that people could *see*, that would arouse their imaginations, stir their feeling and pride in the university. It had to be as modern as the age . . .' " [26] Later he said that "the primary object of the building was to arouse the community to the importance of the university to Pittsburgh." [27] He retained the architect Charles Z. Klauder. The two men finally found their basic concept for the building while listening to Wagner's *Die Walküre*. The skyscraper would, like the opera, pile climax on top of climax.

The happy name for the building (at least from the fund raiser's point of view) was first coined by Charles D. Armstrong, president of the Armstrong Cork Co. and a trustee of the University. "It was first used by Mr. Armstrong in a meeting with three or four trustees and the Chancellor to look over the first drawings of Mr. Klauder for the building. Mr. Armstrong, moved to admiration by the bold conception, said, 'Why, it's a veritable Cathedral of Learning.' " [28] Dr. Bowman in turn repeated the term to Judge Elbert H. Gary, who gave it publicity. It was used by the U.S. Steel magnate, in an interview with reporters in Pittsburgh, January 29, 1925. After covering many topics of the day, Judge Gary endorsed the skyscraper plan of Chancellor Bowman in these words: "There has been adopted a plan which will provide an educational home for 12,000 or more students at one time. The capacity is very large. The form is monumental. . . . Here in this populous and prosperous city, this cathedral of learning will stand for ages as an example and an inspiration." [29] Ketchum recalls, "The interview with Judge Gary was front page news and almost everyone thought he had originated the name. Dr. Bowman . . . would have prevented its use if he could, but it took hold almost immediately." [30]

Judge Gary was among the first of the nation's corporate leaders strongly to endorse the then dubious idea that corporations were obligated to support institutions of higher education. This was the year of big fund drives for Gothic cathedrals in America. This same year Bishop William Manning was seeking public gifts to build the Cathedral of St. John the Divine on Morningside Heights, New York City, and Bishop James E. Freeman was asking the nation to finance completion of the Washington Cathedral on Mt. St. Alban in the nation's capital. Both of these cathedral fund drives were being conducted by professional fund raisers. At any rate Ketchum knew a happy fund-getting term when he heard it and exploited "Cathedral of Learning" to the hilt, in the campaign that spring.

The dramatic idea of a 52-story skyscraper university had not at first "aroused the community to the importance of the university to Pittsburgh" after Chancellor Bowman had publicly unveiled the architect's drawing. "Chancellor John G. Bowman of the University of Pittsburgh had spent 18 months and $80,000 trying to sell the idea of a tall building which had come by accident to be known as the Cathedral of Learning." [31] Little wonder that Chancellor Bowman would lament: "We have become unbalanced. We have grown industrially and materially but have lagged spiritually and intellectually. Football has superseded the classroom." (And nowhere was the primacy of football greater than at Pitt in the 1920's. Near the Cathedral of Learning a giant football stadium was built to seat 65,000 fans!)

Chancellor Bowman turned to alumnus Ketchum, whose firm was making a name for itself as a fund getter for local charities and eleemosynary institutions. This was Ketchum's big challenge and one that launched him into college fund raising and national operations. He organized a hitherto unorthodox campaign to reach the whole community, not just the social elite and the affluent. Ketchum had observed the lessons taught in the war drives. In three months nearly $10 million had been given or pledged to the university, $8.1 million for the Cathedral of Learning. "This money came from the wealthy; it came from the poor. Steel workers by the thousands, and bankers . . . almost 100,000 school children who 'earned' what they gave." [32] The great sums of money came from Pittsburgh's wealthy steel and coal fortunes and from the corporations. However, as is always true, building costs kept going up and by the time Pitt filed its building plans with city officials in September, 1926, the tall Gothic structure had been scaled down to forty-two stories.

Many fund-raising campaigns of that period were to build larger football stadiums. In 1923 when Lyman Pierce was whipping up support for Minnesota's Memorial Stadium, Dr. Arnaud Marts, still with the Ward firm, directed a campaign to raise $500,000 to build a stadium on the campus of his Alma Mater, Bucknell University—an institution he would later serve as president. Incidentally, it was during the Bucknell stadium drive that Marts met Louis Robey and Thomas F. Morgan, Jr., both of whom played major roles in the development of the Marts & Lundy firm.

The 1920's was the era of the raccoon coat, the Greek letter fraternity, the hip flask, and of course the big football game, glorified both in Hollywood and in the groves of academe. Most college presidents either acquiesced to or openly encouraged the overemphasis on big teams, big crowds, and big stadia to house them, for a more basic reason than to provide Joe College and his dad, Bill Alumnus, an excuse for a rah-rah weekend. They were deluded into thinking that football teams represented an effective money raiser and recruiter for the college or university.

Dr. Marts, looking back on these developments a decade after his all-out effort to build a stadium for Bucknell, reflected:

> A great many colleges, during the 1920 decade, were induced to go in for football in a big way in the expectation that a winning team would be of great help in attracting both gifts and students to their campuses. The pretensions of football have been considerably deflated in the past few years. . . .
>
> . . . I have heard many a college trustee say something like this: "What we need is a football team. I mean a team that can win games and make newspaper headlines. If we could turn out a first-class team, we'd have no trouble in getting all the students we could admit and in getting the friendship of men with money. . . ."

. . . let us examine the actual experience of colleges with football as a promotional technique during the 1920 decade. . . . I have taken the . . . Bulletin No. 23 of the Carnegie Foundation . . . and have selected from it just as fairly as could be done 16 colleges . . . mentioned as having spent much time and money in building up their football teams. I have selected 16 other colleges mentioned as having regarded football as an amateur sport and as not having spent money to get players. . . .

The aggregate property value of the "football" group in 1921 was $28,237,130. In 1930, this aggregate property value had increased to $61,295,639, a gain of $33,058,509; in percentage a gain of 117 per cent.

The aggregate value of the "non-football" group in 1921 was $27,-195,348. In 1930 this aggregate property value had increased to $61,-403,921, a gain of $34,208,573; in percentage a gain of 125 per cent.[33]

Dr. Marts concluded that as a means of building student enrollment football's net rating would be low and that as a means of building college endowment football's net effect "would seem to be minus." In this he was echoing the famed Carnegie Foundation study of college football which, in its Bulletin No. 26, asserted: The notion that winning athletic teams bring the college increased attendance, contributions for endowment and for academic purposes, or higher reputation among those whose good opinion is worth having, is erroneous.[34]

The quota system that had worked so effectively in local YMCA campaigns and now in community chest drives was soon incorporated into the drives for college capital. Of Tamblyn & Brown's early days, John Crosby Brown recalls:

One of the very first campaigns we had was for Colgate University. Mr. Tamblyn was a Colgate man. It was for a Million Dollars. It so happened that there were 3300 Colgate alumni at that time. An interesting and ingenious man named Hod Stokes Cohen conceived the idea that if you divided 3300 into One Million Dollars you got 333. He said: "Let's have an independent quota for alumni gifts of Three Hundred and Thirty-Three Dollars." We had a minimum payable over five years, which is the way we used to do it in those days. Tamblyn and Brown had nothing to do with that but we tried it out and it worked like a dream. Some people couldn't give that much; others would give a lot more. We got this series out, 333, nothing else, on a blank piece of paper, that we sent to all the alumni. We explained it and got people interested, and for many years we used that individual quota.[35]

The same independent quota approach was used by Tamblyn & Brown in a 1923 drive for Mt. Holyoke, founded by one of the first fund drives in America nearly a century before. "Mt. Holyoke had been going along for a year and a half and on a $3,000,000 campaign had raised only $800,000. Finally in desperation they wrote us in 1923 and we took them on. We brought it up to $2,600,000 mark in quite short order by an individual quota for Mt. Holyoke." [36]

The American City Bureau made its first attempt at capital fund raising on behalf of Colorado College, Colorado Springs, in 1925. In a campaign which opened that December the ACB set out for a goal of $365,000 and raised $417,000. From that drive until 1939 the ACB managed only one or two college capital fund-raising drives each year. Just prior to World War II the Bureau began to shift to the capital fund-raising field and by 1958 it had managed 178 college drives. In the early twenties the ACB was a prime promoter of the emerging community chest, entering the field in 1923, as "a strong advocate for the federation of appeals of local social welfare agencies" and urged that these federated drives be "professionally directed." By the end of 1958 American City Bureau had directed 1,476 community chest or united fund drives, according to its office records.

Ivy Lee, whose work with the Red Cross War Council had done much to set the new pattern of money drives, took his newly enlarged public relations firm into the fund-raising field in its early years. Princeton alumnus Lee's firm played a major role in the Princeton Endowment Campaign of 1919–20 for $14,325,000, launched in September, 1919, with the announcement that Henry Clay Frick had given Princeton 30 per cent of his residuary estate. Moses Taylor Pyne was the chairman of this campaign; Lee's office prepared the publicity. The news releases went out on Princeton letterheads. Lee, taking a leaf from Charles Sumner Ward's book, dramatically publicized the little gift as well as the large. On January 22, 1920, Lee's office issued a release carrying President John Grier Hibben's praise of a Negro janitor's small gift and another on February 8 reporting a gift of $5 by a high school teacher to be paid in five installments of $1 per year. A March 26, 1920, release reported that a total of $6,059,703.63 had been pledged in gifts of $350,000 to the janitor's $1.

Pyne and Lee turned the heavy pressure on Princeton's alumni, who were told that it had cost, based on 1912–1917 figures, an average of $641.60 annually to educate an undergraduate. A national alumni association was organized in 1921. Princeton officials realized the need to give the alumnus service as well as admonishments about his debt to Alma Mater, and consequently announced the Princeton Lectures on April 3, 1920, which were billed "a first step in a plan to make every one of the 11,000 alumni of Princeton students and continuously active participants in the work of the university." "It embodies the beginnings of an effort on the part of the university to take Princeton to her alumni, to do something for them and not merely to be asking them to do something for Princeton." [37]

Lee's files show that his firm prepared the Princeton Endowment Bulletin, designed to stimulate workers and donors; booklets, such as "The Princeton Campaign As Affected by Mr. Frick's Bequest," "Why Princeton Needs $14,325,000," etc.; placed an article by President Hibben, "Are Cheap Teachers Going to be Good for Your Children?," in the *American* magazine for September, 1919, staged dinners, wrote speeches, and counseled President Hibben and Chairman Pyne on strategy and tactics. By June 16, 1923, a total of $9,706,-480.14 had been raised in addition to the Frick bequest. The latter amounted to only $6 million after the 1921 plunge in stock values.

Ivy Lee and his associates also were active in other fund-raising drives the first six years of that decade. After the 1926 Presbyterian Pension Fund publicity service, Lee either voluntarily or involuntarily abandoned this type of account to those specializing in fund raising. In January, 1920, Lee's firm ran a campaign to raise $500,000 for the Dobbs School for Girls at Dobbs Ferry, N.Y., formerly the Misses Masters School. To promote this appeal, Lee's office initiated a campaign newsletter, "Do It for Dobbs." In 1923 his firm provided the publicity for the public appeal of the American Jewish Joint Distribution Committee raising money for relief of famine in Europe. This committee was headed by Felix M. Warburg, chairman, and Herbert H. Lehman, vice-chairman. A November 4, 1923, Ivy Lee release reported that the Committee "has spent $60,000,-000 for relief work in Europe, $12,000,000 of which was devoted to relief work in Russia." Lee's records show that this campaign was promoted by Lee's publicists through the year of 1923.

The Ivy Lee firm handled the publicity for the drive of the Woman's Roosevelt Memorial Association, a national organization headed by Mrs. John Henry Hammond. Mrs. Leonard Wood was made honorary president of this drive so her name could be exploited. The appeal for $250,000 to restore Theodore Roosevelt's birthplace at 28 East 20th Street, New York City, was opened January 4, 1920, the first anniversary of the former President's death. An Ivy Lee news release of April 19, 1920, reported: "Including $140,000 already subscribed, the Association has raised $175,000 since it was organized a few weeks after Colonel Roosevelt died." [38] This drive was a retread on an earlier effort that was short-lived. Soon after former President Roosevelt's death a memorial association was formed to raise $2 million to restore his home and provide other memorials. The honorary president, William Boyce Thompson, multimillionaire mining engineer, underwrote the costs of the campaign, according to Arnaud C. Marts, who worked on this drive for a brief period. Marts was brought in by his old friend Will Hays, then Republican party national chairman and a vice-president of the Memorial Association. Marts is of the opinion that Thompson expected a political job from Hays for his effort but did not get it. [39] Thompson had been a delegate to the 1916 GOP convention and again was a delegate in 1920.

In the Roosevelt fund drive, Lee repeated the big gift-small gift technique. An April 15, 1920, news release reads, in part: "Today's mail at national headquarters brought a $5,000 pledge from Mrs. Willard Straight; a crumpled two-dollar bill sent more than six weeks ago from a U.S. Signal Corps private stationed at Kokrines, Alaska; and a contribution from Mrs. F. Hein Siang of Nanchang, China, who is studying in America."

In 1921 the Lee firm handled the publicity campaign for a capital fund-raising drive of the Broad Street Hospital, New York City.

Not all the fund raising for colleges in the 1920's was done by the newly established commercial fund raisers. Bishop William Lawrence, pioneer college fund raiser extraordinary, managed quite a *coup* for his Alma Mater, Harvard, in the mid-twenties. From 1913 on Bishop Lawrence had been serving as a member of the Harvard Corporation, a position he found "responsible, interesting, and engrossing." Though the 1919–1920 Harvard Endowment Campaign had raised some $14 million by 1923, "the University was clearly suffering for lack of material construction: every room and bit of space was overcrowded; the chemical laboratories were in lamentable condition. The freshman dormitories were almost the only evidence of recent construction: and another hall was needed there." [40] In September, 1923, Dean Wallace B. Donham of the Harvard Graduate School of Business Administration successfully persuaded the busy bishop to be honorary chairman of a campaign to raise $5 million for this school at Harvard. The business school had been founded in 1908 and Donham had succeeded the first dean, Dr. Edwin F. Gay, in 1919. The bishop accepted Donham's challenge: "Loyalty to the business traditions of my family and a conviction that this was a real missionary enterprise for the welfare of the country made me consider his appeal."

Bishop Lawrence was much more than honorary chairman. He took charge and undertook direction of a $10 million fund-raising campaign. As before, his first step was the careful laying of plans. "It fell to me to have the general oversight, to advise, and to speak when and where I was told to, and present the facts to individuals here and there who might give large sums." Because the University's need for business, chemistry, and art buildings and endowments to support these courses had no direct relation to each other they were lumped under the common appeal of "An Opportunity for National Service." The bishop insisted that this was an honest appeal because Harvard was, "in fact, a national university." The appeal for the $10 million was to be directed to the public, particularly the rich, not to Harvard alumni as such because Alma Mater's sons had been put through the John Price Jones fund-raising wringer only three years before. The campaign appeal was directed to "citizens as citizens," and the "campaign methods and education were adjusted to the search for large gifts." [41]

After six months' careful planning and preliminary solicitation of major prospects, Bishop Lawrence publicly launched the drive for $10 million with a dinner at the Harvard Club in New York City, on March 31. The *New York Times* publicized it as a "campaign to raise $10,000,000 by public subscription to develop the public service of Harvard University for the benefit of the nation." The bishop delivered a stirring address to the gathering of prominent men, all potential donors, to be sure, and to the public over the still primitive medium of radio. He had arranged to have the program carried over Station WJZ. In his appeal, which carried the lengthy title "Three Unappreciated Factors Vital to America's Commonwealth and a Great University's Relation to Them," the bishop sweepingly generalized that these three factors were "essential to the character, safety, and prosperity of the country." [42] The bishop was not one to be modest in asserting the merits of causes for which he sought money.

As he had proved before, he knew where to get the large gifts. Early in January, 1924, he went to see George F. Baker, the "dean of the business of this country," to ask the financier to give the first million dollars for the Graduate School of Business. "Later he [Baker] kindly talked over the subject and took the matter under consideration. Weeks passed, three months, indeed." On April 21, 1924, the fund-raising bishop was en route to New York City when he was given a telegram at New Haven from Mr. Baker asking to see Bishop Lawrence that evening at six o'clock. Philanthropist and fund raiser met at the home of the latter's daughter at the appointed hour.

The teasing way in which Baker broke the news to the persuasive bishop is told by Lawrence in his memoirs:

> We sat down, passed a friendly word or two, and then he said, "Bishop, I have been thinking over the matter of the Business School. I have lost interest in your suggestion that I should give the first million. I am not going to give it or a half million either." He paused, and then told an anecdote, while I sat tight, for he evidently had something more to say. He went on, "If, however, by giving five million dollars I could have the privilege of building the whole School, I should like to do it. If it were one of several such schools or an old story, I should not care to do it, but my life has been given to business, and I should like to found the first Graduate School, and give a new start to better business standards. I want to do it alone. Do you think Harvard will let me?" [43]

Harvard would and did. And that is why a large portrait of Bishop William Lawrence hangs, unexplained, in the lobby of the George F. Baker Library, near a portrait of Mr. Baker. Financier Baker's gift was announced to the public in the lead story of the *New York Times* of June 2, 1924. Baker, then in his eighty-fourth year, was estimated to be worth $300 million at the time he made this gift to Harvard. He was generally considered one of the five wealthiest men in the nation. The gift to build the home for Harvard's business school brought Baker's philanthropic gifts to nearly $12 million. According to the *New York Times*, he had made these contributions in recent years: Red Cross drives in World War I, $2 million; Cornell University, $2 million; Metropolitan Museum of Art, $1 million; New York Hospital, $750,000; Columbia University (for Baker Field), $700,000; Museum of Natural History, $250,-000; Teachers College, $100,000; Morgan Hall, $100,000, and the $5 million to Harvard. In the press release announcing the Baker gift, Bishop Lawrence termed him "the dean of American business" and said, sweepingly again, "Mr. Baker's gift is unique in the annals of American education." [44] And indeed it was the largest single educational gift since the days of John D. Rockefeller, Sr., and Andrew Carnegie.

On June 20, 1924, during Harvard's commencement, Bishop Lawrence announced that a total of $9,289,595, including Mr. Baker's gift, had been raised in the "Opportunity for National Service" fund-raising drive. The shrewd, persuasive cleric had thus pushed the campaign near its goal when he again fell ill from the strain of his many religious and philanthropic endeavors. This was his last multimillion-dollar fund-raising effort. However, in the 1930's he undertook a $60,000 campaign to build a chapel in the Massachusetts General Hospital where he had spent much time as a patient. In this latter effort he was "like a war-horse who again scents the smoke of battle. At once he began preparing lists of possible donors, and especially arranging for the necessary printed material for the appeal. He always did this with the utmost care, writing and rewriting, and being most particular as to the printing and even the type and color of paper used." [45]

In the opinion of his biographer, Bishop Lawrence's secret in eliciting large sums for philanthropic causes was his faith in people. "Here is found the real keynote of Bishop Lawrence's success as a money raiser. To be sure, he spent untold hours in securing the right publicity, in the arranging of lists, in the writing of letters in his own hand. But fundamental was his faith in the sense of responsibility of the average man and woman. He felt this for himself." [46]

Another early fund raiser of the 1920's who eschewed the highly organized, high-pressure campaign method for the more traditional personal solicitation of wealthy persons was William H. Baldwin III, who was to make his mark in public relations, not fund raising. Baldwin, scion of a distinguished New England family, was graduated from Harvard in 1913. Through membership in the prestigious and powerful Harvard Club of New York he came to know John Price Jones. Baldwin had worked on the New York *Post* from 1914 until he became a naval censor in the war. Because of his newspaper experience, Jones hired him to manage the office at Cambridge in the 1919 Harvard Endowment Campaign that was to set the pattern for the capital fund drives of the twenties. Pleased with Baldwin's work on the Harvard campaign, Jones invited him to join his firm when it was being organized. Baldwin declined, saying, "Johnny, you and I will remain better friends if I don't come to work for you." [47] Baldwin had already learned what others, over the years, would come to know—that John Price Jones was not an easy person to work for. Instead, Baldwin took a public relations job as an assistant to Thomas E. Woodlock in the International Shipbuilding Corp.

In 1922 Baldwin was asked to organize and manage a fund-raising drive for Fisk University, Nashville, Tenn., that was to result in the first million-dollar endowment fund for a Negro college in the South. Baldwin's fund-raising and publicity experience made him a logical choice for this assignment. It was an invitation that Baldwin, because of his rich family heritage, could not turn aside. His grandfather, William H. Baldwin, Sr., had quit the life of a prosperous Boston merchant to devote his energies to building and spreading the YMCA movement in America. His father, who had died at the untimely age of forty-one, was a staunch friend of Booker T. Washington, and played a helpful role in getting Tuskegee Institute on its feet. His mother was Ruth Standish Bowles, daughter of the distinguished Sherman Bowles, founder and editor of the Springfield (Mass.) *Republican*. She helped found and nurture the National Urban League. Thus, when Paul D. Cravath, chairman of the Fisk board of trustees, put the pressure on Baldwin to take over the Fisk fund drive, the latter felt obliged to accept. Actually Baldwin's task was to raise only $500,000 for Fisk because the Rockefeller-financed General Education Board had agreed to match this sum if Fisk could raise a half-million dollars. To raise such a sum for a little-known Negro college in the South was no easy task in the 1920's, and Baldwin knew it.

He tackled the job with dedication born of his family heritage and with confidence born of his experience in the Harvard drive. As a condition of acceptance he demanded that he be made a member of the Fisk board and head of its executive committee. This not only gave him authority to cope with Fisk's administrators but it gave him more status in dealing with the major philanthropists of the day. (In 1963 Baldwin was still serving as a dedicated member of the Fisk board of trustees.) Baldwin soon decided that a national campaign for a single Negro university in the South would cost more than it would bring in. "I decided this would have to be a rifle shooting proposition." [48]

The money was raised chiefly by Baldwin's pinpointing a potential donor, figuring out how to approach him, and going after the money. For example, he planned to approach the Carnegie Board for a donation. A friend tipped Baldwin that his best chance of getting a sizable contribution was to work fast because Henry Pritchett was leaving as Carnegie president and his successor was not likely to be too sympathetic. After considerable difficulty Baldwin got to see Pritchett and his plea was effective. A telegram was subsequently sent to Pritchett and a gift of $250,000 was forthcoming. Half the goal had been reached. The timing was so close that Pritchett had already closed his last formal board meeting and only took up the Fisk matter as an addendum.[49] Other contributors to Baldwin's goal included Julius Rosenwald, Chicago merchant, and Samuel Mather, Cleveland industrialist.

One of Baldwin's adroit public relations moves was to outlast the two-year fund drive he managed. For many years Fisk University had used the Fisk Jubilee Singers as a publicity and fund-raising vehicle. This group had been a great money raiser for the University in the years before the turn of the century, but in the two decades prior to this fund drive Fisk officials had slipped into the demeaning practice of having these singers go, hat in hand, to perform in the parlors of the rich. These concerts for wealthy men would conclude with "passing the hat." [50]

This begging approach was repugnant to Baldwin, who was already campaigning to bring respect and equality for the Negro. Baldwin argued that if these singers were qualified—and they were —they should perform in public and be compensated accordingly. He insisted that the Fisk Jubilee Singers become a concert group and give public concerts. This they did, attracting favorable notices of music critics and winning respect for their race. They raised money for Fisk too.[51] In two years Baldwin raised the $500,000 and this gave Fisk its first million-dollar endowment.

As Baldwin was winding up the Fisk drive in 1924 he was approached by Carl W. Ackerman, former Hearst newspaperman and then public relations practitioner, to assist the latter with the fund-raising campaign for the National Episcopal Cathedral being built in Washington. Ackerman, later to become dean of Columbia University's School of Journalism, had been favorably impressed by Baldwin's work for Fisk. And this brings us to two major campaigns to raise money to build two giant, Gothic Episcopal cathedrals during the mid-years of the "Roaring Twenties."

. . . and Cathedrals Too

One of the largest and undoubtedly the most controversial of the many large fund drives put on in the bountiful twenties was that launched by Episcopal Bishop William T. Manning in 1925 to complete the Cathedral of St. John the Divine on Morningside Heights in New York City. This fund drive was planned and directed by Tamblyn & Brown. The intensive campaign brought in $10 million, $5 million short of the announced $15 million goal—an impressive sum nonetheless. The idea of this massive Cathedral was first conceived and voiced by Episcopal Bishop Horatio Potter some thirty-five years before. At Potter's urging, the Episcopal diocese of New York had bought the Cathedral's commanding site, at the time occupied by an orphan asylum, "standing isolate on a rocky hill."

Construction was commenced in 1892 and the Cathedral was designed so that it could be built in sections. The choir and chapels were completed and consecrated on April 19, 1911. Bishop William Lawrence tells us that Bishop Potter who first posed the plan for a great cathedral "where the great preachers of the country would be heard," had earlier "forbade the Reverend John Cotton Smith, Rector of the Church of the Ascension, New York, to invite the Reverend Doctor Adams, President of Union Theological Seminary, to preach in his church of a Sunday evening." [52]

That shrewd money getter, Bishop Lawrence of Boston, more than once advised fund raisers that "if you expect a broad and popular support, even the best cause must be linked up with some big cause or problem touching the whole people." When the controversial Right Reverend William Manning finally attained the bishopric of New York he had, in the words of his critic Elmer Davis, "the misfortune to inherit a Gothic cathedral half finished along with other problems of his diocese." [53] Many saw no reason for finishing the Cathedral at all. Bishop Manning and his fund raisers knew that to raise the huge sum of $15 million they must appeal to givers beyond the Episcopal parishes of New York City. Consequently, they set out to make the cathedral "A House of Prayer for All People"—at least for the purposes of the fund-raising campaign. Davis wrote at the time: "instead of trusting to the Christian stewardship of the faithful, he [Bishop Manning] is going out after Jews and Catholics and Baptists, Parthians and Medes and Elamites. He is trying, and it seems successfully, to make the building of the cathedral a sort of community crusade in which all of New York will participate." [54]

In the language of the professional fund raiser, "this campaign enlisted the cooperation and support of people of many faiths, races, and walks of life, and contributions came from the millionaires and from small children." [55] The slogan, "A House of Prayer for All the People," not only brought in money; it brought much internal wrangling and outside criticism. Many Episcopalians feared that Bishop Manning would pollute the purity of the faith in his determined effort to get dollars. Others, some of them old clerical foes, resented this diversion of money from church needs to an ornate building. Outsiders, at least a perceptive few, saw the slogan as a hypocritical fund-raising device and nothing more. The bishop's chief critic wrote: "If the merchandiser had been any but a Bishop, offering holy wares, this would have seemed perilously like misrepresentation of the quality of the goods." [56]

Bishop Manning was elected bishop of the New York diocese in January, 1921, after having been defeated two years earlier in his long-time ambition to advance from his post as rector of the famed and wealthy Trinity Church. Bishop Manning first gained public note in 1908 when he became rector of Trinity at the very time it was "feeling the claws of the muck rake." The New York *World* had been exposing the fact that much of Trinity's property in downtown New York was in a wretched slum condition and many of the church's properties were housing prostitutes. "In short, Trinity real estate had become a scandal." [57] Manning cleaned up the mess and employed a young public relations counselor, Pendleton Dudley, to see that he got credit for doing it.

Manning became bishop in the face of strong opposition. Opponents said it was the violent attacks of William Randolph Hearst that elevated Manning. The cleric had antagonized Hearst when Mayor John Hylan had included the publisher and the bishop on a committee to welcome home the soldiers from France. Manning thought it an outrage for Hylan to put Hearst, who had opposed America's participation in the war, on such a committee. He resigned and helped organize another welcoming ceremony in Madison Square Garden, an event that was something of a flop. Manning had also been involved, over the years, in a bitter doctrinal dispute over the Virgin Birth and in his effort to organize an American Catholic Church along Anglican lines. It was inevitable that the roiled religious waters would eddy in and out of the cathedral campaign.

Once the bishop felt that he had sufficiently consolidated his new position of power, he set about the task of bringing the monumental Cathedral to completion. By this time only the choir and crossing had been built. He shared his dream with Franklin D. Roosevelt. By late 1924, F.D.R. had partially recovered from the tragic, crippling attack of poliomyelitis that struck him down at Campobello the year Manning became a bishop. Roosevelt was receptive to any task that would provide diversion and would bring him back to public life. Certainly his political and public relations mentor, Louis M. Howe, was looking for ways to bring Roosevelt back into the public spotlight in his long-term campaign to put F.D.R. into the White House—a goal that Howe had set for himself in 1911 and had never given up, even in the black hours of Roosevelt's illness. Thus it was easy for the bishop to get Roosevelt to accept the chairmanship of the Committee for Completing the Cathedral.

Of necessity much of the hard work, the telephoning and the errand running, on the St. John's campaign fell to Howe. A historian who studied the Roosevelt-Howe relationship asserts: "He [F.D.R.] could seldom say no to the causes in which he believed, but he did little about them himself. The hard work was necessarily left to Howe. Louis was delighted, for heading fund-raising committees kept the boss's name in the papers and helped to build a public image for him, despite the Republican monopoly of politics. But before the twenties were done Louis would be swamped." [58] Howe saw mostly the public relations advantages in F.D.R.'s role in the Cathedral campaign.

F.D.R. had a deeper purpose in the view of Frank Freidel, a biographer, who says: [59] "Both he [F.D.R.] and his half-brother, James Roosevelt Roosevelt, took the keenest interest in this project. More than his deep pride in and devotion to the Episcopal Church motivated him, for he felt strongly that the Cathedral must be built above creed and faction." In these years Roosevelt also occupied himself with fund-raising efforts on behalf of his own Warm Springs Foundation, the American Legion, and the Richard E. Byrd polar expeditions.

Tamblyn & Brown was retained and this firm assigned Walter Dickinson to direct the intensive New York City-wide drive in Roosevelt's name. Dickinson, Bishop Manning, and F.D.R. fully agreed that it was absolutely necessary to do something dramatic in New York City which would attract the public's attention and "make the people of New York think they had a great spiritual asset in that Cathedral and make them feel it was their Cathedral." [60] Bishop Manning's basic theme—as phrased in a talk to the League for Political Education the day before the drive opened—was "The Cathedral will symbolize the brotherhood of man as already people of all races, colors and creeds visit it. The Cathedral as a spiritual influence will grow with time." [61] Elmer Davis put it more bluntly: "twentieth-century New York is not Gothic; twentieth-century New York is split up among a hundred religions and only about one per cent of its inhabitants belong to Dr. Manning's church. The other ninety-nine per cent had to be dragged in somehow." [62] Davis thought that "it would be an act of genius" to put the drive over. He did not reckon with the new professional fund raiser.

Dickinson, counseled by his partners Tamblyn and Brown, presented a plan for a big public rally in Madison Square Garden—a site more associated with big prizefights, six-day bicycle races, circuses, and dog shows than with the church. An interdenominational committee had been carefully selected to lend the appearance of broad public support of the fund drive. Bishop Manning carried the title of honorary chairman and F.D.R. was chairman. Other members were: Edmund L. Baylies, Frank L. Polk, James R. Roosevelt, Elihu Root, George W. Wickersham, Bertram H. Borden, Nicholas Murray Butler, Vernon M. Davis, and Dr. Edward Hall.

Dickinson put before this committee a plan for bringing 15,000 persons together in a public rally in the Garden on Sunday afternoon, January 18, 1925, to start the public drive. His presentation provoked much debate and many gloomy predictions that the rally would fail. Perhaps members of the committee were silently recalling Bishop Manning's role in the welcome for American soldiers home from Europe that had drawn only some 3,000 to 4,000 persons to the cavernous Garden a few years before. In any case, the committee voted 8 to 2 not to risk the rally in Madison Square Garden. But F.D.R., with his characteristic daring and sure sense of public opinion, waved aside the vote and said, "Sure, we can do it—and we will." Perhaps he was moved by the thrilling thought of standing before a great audience of some 15,000 persons once again.

By the time Tamblyn & Brown's publicists finished their campaign more than 15,000 persons had crowded into the Garden that Sunday afternoon and another estimated 5,000 had been turned away. To promote attendance Dickinson and his aides had borrowed a trick from the well-known evangelist Billy Sunday—some 13,000 tickets to the rally had been distributed to persons of various religions and no religion "who had joined in the project of building the Cathedral as a civic and national institution and as a center of the city's spiritual life." [63] All evening services were canceled in the city's Episcopal churches and the faithful admonished to attend the rally. The program was opened with music provided by the Police Band and hymns sung by the massed choirs, 2,000 voices in all, of the Episcopal churches of the diocese. The Reverend Adye Richard, acting dean of the cathedral, gave the invocation. Chairman Roosevelt opened the meeting, presented the campaign workers to Bishop Manning, and praised the bishop for his effort to complete the cathedral.

Bishop Manning spoke next, announcing that some $4.1 million of the needed $15 million had been raised in a year of private solicitation and that $11 million must be raised in the next month. He announced several large gifts of $100,000 or more from such well-known donors as J. P. Morgan, Vincent Astor, and Frank A. Munsey. He took special pains to praise a gift of $25,000 from Mortimer L. Schiff, noted Jewish financier, to emphasize the interdenominational nature of the fund drive. The bishop was followed by five-minute speeches in support of his drive by Mayor John Hylan, Elihu Root, distinguished statesman and Presbyterian layman, President Nicholas Murray Butler of Columbia University, Actor George Arliss, the Reverend S. Parkes Cadman, president of the Federal Council of Churches of Christ in America, Frank L. Polk, and George W. Wickersham. The press reported that the 15,000-odd persons "were brought to their feet" when a telegram from President Calvin Coolidge endorsing the campaign in carefully chosen ambiguous words was read. Taking a leaf from Bishop Lawrence's book, Bishop Manning assured the assembled audience, and those listening on the radio, that the costs of the campaign had been underwritten and therefore every dollar given would go to building the Cathedral.

The Monday edition of the *New York Times* spread the news of the rally as its lead story and gave virtually all of its second page to the campaign. It supported the drive with stories on forty-two days of the 65-day campaign. The daily press generally supported the bishop's fund-raising effort and none openly challenged his sincerity save Elmer Davis. And the only outlets he could find for his criticism of the drive were the *New Republic* and *Harper's*. Davis challenged the sincerity of the campaign slogan, when in fact only Episcopalians were allowed to take communion in the chapel and because, though non-Episcopal ministers were allowed to preach from the pulpit, "their unordained feet did not tread the holy ground of the sanctuary." He pointed out that the "House of Prayer for All the People" was owned and controlled by 1 per cent of the people!

This issue of whether the Cathedral was to be truly for "all the people" was dramatized in the dispute between Bishop Manning and John D. Rockefeller, Jr. Rockefeller, a Baptist, the campaign's biggest donor, accompanied his gift of $500,000 with the plea that the "large outside friendly interest should be represented on the Cathedral's Board of Trustees by a small number of laymen of sister churches." He made it clear that he was giving because the Cathedral was to be "for the use of all people" and because he was "deeply interested in every well conceived and wisely directed effort, by whomsoever initiated, looking toward the cooperation of all good men and women in opposing evil and furthering the application of Christ's spirit in human living." [64]

Bishop Manning accepted, with alacrity, Rockefeller's check for a half million because "the clause which you [Rockefeller] add to your gift makes no condition as to its acceptance and imposes no obligation" but turned down his request to bring non-Episcopalians into the Cathedral's board of trustees. Rockefeller made his gift on February 5 and this brought the sagging campaign back to the front pages. The dispute between the philanthropist and the cleric continued through the campaign though the bishop pleaded that Rockefeller's suggestion was "manifestly not one to be taken up during the heat and stress of a campaign."

Rockefeller's letters and statements were issued through his public relations counsel, Ivy L. Lee, while the bishop's statements were processed through the Tamblyn & Brown organization. Copies of Rockefeller's letters and the releases are to be found in the files of the Ivy L. Lee firm (now T. J. Ross and Associates). Lee unquestionably assisted in the writing of Rockefeller's letters and statements in this delicate area of public dispute. Dickinson says that he and Ivy Lee never met during their battle of press releases over this "outside trustee" issue.

Interestingly enough, Lee also represented the Copper & Brass Research Association in those years. Near the end of the Cathedral fund drive Lee, for the copper trade association, put out photographs and a release supporting the appeal for public gifts. Why? Down in the release describing the church, we find "Its walls are of massive masonry, *while the roofs and other important metal parts . . . are constructed of copper, a metal whose worthiness has been proved by its centuries of service on churches and cathedrals in England and on the continent.*" [65] Incidentally, cathedrals were a hobby of public relations counselor Lee.

From the time of the rally on, the Tamblyn & Brown campaign for the cathedral followed the standard Ward-Pierce pattern. Teams were organized in divisions and divisions were assigned quotas in pursuit of what Elmer Davis aptly characterized as "organized nagging." Two days after the rally it was announced that the Division of Businessmen would raise $2.5 million of the $15 million goal. This release described the Gothic structure as "a national shrine of religion and temple of beauty as magnificent and noble as any of the architectural feats of the Old World." On January 22, Franklin D. Roosevelt pleaded for public support in one of his first talks over the radio, the medium he was to use so skillfully in his later political career. Even laboring men and women were asked to support this Episcopalian cathedral and on January 23 a building trades employees committee was organized and assigned a quota. On March 1, two union leaders presented a gift of $1,000 to the bishop.

But as the deadline of February 1 neared and the campaign was far short of its announced goal, Bishop Manning announced, on January 26, that the drive would be extended and that $5 million had been raised, which meant that the days after the rally had brought in only $900,000. This low point of the drive was bolstered by a big play given the $100 gift of Alfred E. Smith, governor of New York and a Roman Catholic, an act for which he was criticized by Catholic priests. All sorts of benefit events were used to raise money. A track meet, starring Pavo Nurmi, was held in Madison Square Garden February 25 and a prizefight on March 12. The Sports Division of the campaign was responsible for building one bay in the nave of the cathedral. Collection booths were set up in restaurants and department stores as the appeals for dollar gifts were stepped up. Elsie Janis put on a stage benefit.

Not only did the money not come in as fast as Manning, Roosevelt, and Dickinson had thought it would, criticism of the drive from both within and without the church would not die. An old church foe of Bishop Manning's, the Reverend Leighton Parks, rector of St. Bartholomew's Episcopal Church, preached from his pulpit on Sunday, February 22, that "merely to allow anyone to enter a church, to receive a cordial welcome, and to listen to the service did not make a church 'a house of prayer for all people.' " Mr. Parks insisted that "the central act of worship is the Lord's Supper" and that only Episcopalians could take communion in the "House of Prayer for All People." Sunday, March 15, the Reverend Mr. Parks distributed printed copies of this sermon to his congregation and to the news media. He said his parish could not support the drive.

To counteract this criticism Bishop Manning and his fund-raising campaigners planned and staged an interdenominational service for Sunday, March 15, with the Reverend S. Parkes Cadman of the Federal Council of Churches of Christ as the guest minister. Cadman roundly rebuked those who questioned the bishop's sincerity. The *Times* headlined this story, "Cathedral Opened to Joint Services of Many Creeds." Elmer Davis saw these interdenominational joint services only as a fund-raising device. He wrote a year later: "There have been no interdenominational services lately, but it is a safe bet that there will be, if, as, and when required. For money is still needed for the cathedral and Jews and evangelical Protestants still have it." [66]

But the bishop would not take every gift offered. On February 8 he dramatically refused to accept a personal gift of $500 from an old church foe, The Reverend Wm. Norman Guthrie, rector of St. Mark's in the Bouwerie. A few years earlier the rector of St. Mark's had enlivened his services by the use of dancing girls; "artistically expressed religion," the rector termed it. Bishop Manning termed this "pagan" and cut St. Mark's off from Episcopal visitation and ministration. Rector Guthrie announced to his congregation that the bishop had refused his personal gift and said that differences in church policy should not be a barrier to giving. At least he gave the Cathedral some publicity.

The campaign ground on, pressuring the well-to-do and the not so well-to-do to give. On February 11 Elihu Root issued an appeal for more public support. The next day circulars were posted in all New York City police stations suggesting 25-cent gifts. On February 18 it was announced that the drive had reached the halfway mark with $7.5 million. This represented a total of 35,000 separate gifts according to the fund raisers' statistics. With half the money in hand or at least in sight, the bishop went ahead with his building plans. Work on the nave began with ground-breaking ceremonies held May 6.

That same day the *New York Times* reported that John D. Rockefeller, Jr., Elihu Root and Arthur Curtiss James were to be nominated for the Cathedral's board of trustees at the 142nd annual meeting of the Episcopal Diocese of New York the following week. The news report stirred hot debate inside the Episcopal Church and its some 60,000 communicants in New York City but no effort was made to change the Cathedral's charter at the annual diocesan meeting. Bishop Manning righteously assured the assembled churchmen that he deemed preservation of the Church's fundamental doctrine "more important than building 1,000 cathedrals." At the same time he made no offer to return Mr. Rockefeller's half million dollars.

Growing resentment of the diversion of Episcopalian funds to the massive, monumental Cathedral did break through the proceedings of the annual meeting. On May 12 the Reverend Frank Warfield Crowd, rector of St. James Church and a cathedral trustee, introduced a resolution that congratulated Bishop Manning on his success in raising $10 million for completion of the Cathedral of St. John the Divine but asking that the fund-raising efforts of the diocese be concentrated on meeting the benevolent needs for the next three years. The rector's resolution was successfully shelved by Bishop Manning's forces and on May 13 a substitute resolution was adopted that said, in essence:

That this convention congratulates the Bishop of the Diocese on the extraordinary response to his appeal for funds to complete the Cathedral of St. John the Divine, and rejoices with him that the building has actually commenced; we trust that the great work so auspiciously started, may go steadily forward.[67]

The bishop's professionally directed fund-raising campaign, slated to be a hard-hitting short-term one, came to a close for all practical purposes late in June, when Bishop Manning announced that $10 million had been subscribed to complete the Cathedral, that 300,000 had visited it in the past year, and that "this great undertaking will give strength to the whole cause of religion in our land." Thus was a gargantuan, twelfth-century Gothic cathedral erected on Morningside Heights with twentieth-century fund-raising methods.

When George Washington and the Frenchman L'Enfant were dreaming their dreams of our nation's capital their plans included a "church of national purpose" and they designated a site for it. The site was later given to the U.S. Patent Office. Seeing the opportunity or sensing the need, depending on one's view, the Protestant Episcopal Church took up Washington's idea near the turn of the century. In 1893 the Congress granted the Episcopal Church a charter to build "a house of prayer for all the people forever free and open." Thus the way was paved for the solicitation of members of all faiths to build Washington's Episcopal Cathedral. The church bought a commanding site on Mt. St. Alban, highest point in the city, and eventually acquired a wooded area of more than sixty acres.

In 1907, with President Theodore Roosevelt looking on, Bishop Henry Yates Satterlee laid the cornerstone for the apse of the grim, Gothic structure that would eventually be the Cathedral Church of St. Peter and St. Paul. One observer recorded: "The model of the Washington Cathedral shows that its architects have gone for their inspiration to England, above all to Canterbury and York. . . . The sympathies of the founders of the Cathedral are Anglican and to them, the English cathedrals of the Middle Ages are the truest architectural expression of their faith." [68] By 1925 the building was one-eighth completed. Since then the work of building the Cathedral, second in size in the United States only to St. John the Divine, has proceeded in short spurts and long stops. By 1962 the building was 62 per cent completed. In that year carvers were working on the south transept capped by the turreted Gloria in Excelsis tower. This tower, when completed in 1964 or thereabouts, will dominate the Washington skyline and house the "world's most awesome bell chorus—a ten-bell peal and a 53-bell carillon." By 1962 some $12 million had been spent and *Time* magazine estimated "$15 million more will be needed to finish it down to its final gargoyle and grotesque." [69]

Washington Episcopalians, inspired and encouraged by the success of Bishop Manning's fund drive for St. John the Divine, decided in 1925 to launch a similar campaign to get nationwide gifts to complete their "House of Prayer for All the People." By 1925 the apse had been finished and contained the Bethlehem Chapel where daily services were conducted. "Preparations have been made to interest the nation in concluding the construction of the entire structure within the next five years at a total cost of $12,000,000 of which approximately $5,000,000 has been raised. This sum has been contributed by more than 12,000 persons of all church affiliations and from all parts of the United States. Approximately $4,000,000 came from Washington [D.C.]." [70] The Right Reverend James E. Freeman, Bishop of Washington, had the determination to launch the giant fund-raising effort to complete the cathedral. He worked tirelessly and preached endlessly to accomplish his goal.

It was no accident that early in 1925 magazine articles and news stories started appearing in the nation's press to publicize Bishop Freeman's goal of building a "Westminster Abbey for America." The bishop had retained the publicist Carl Ackerman to promote support for his fund-raising campaign. For example in the *New York Times Magazine* of May 3, 1925, we find a handsomely illustrated article, "A Westminster Abbey for America," which said, "the cathedral stands in the minds of its founders as the Westminster Abbey of the New World." Provision of an appropriate burial place for the nation's great was one of the strong campaign appeals used from the beginning. Already the bodies of Admiral George Dewey and President Woodrow Wilson had been placed in cathedral crypts. Incidentally, when the Washington Cathedral fund raisers scored a publicity coup in arranging to have the remains of Admiral Dewey dug up and placed under its nave, "a freshman employee of Tamblyn & Brown was so impressed that he immediately got off an office memorandum suggesting that the firm keep its eye on ex-President William Howard Taft (then alive) for its client, the Cathedral of St. John the Divine." [71] No wonder *Time* was moved to comment that these professional fund raisers "have had to be patient, elusive and resourceful, with the corporate manners of an undertaker and the understanding of a Freud."

The *New York Times* supported the fund drive for the Washington Cathedral with the same enthusiasm that it was manifesting on behalf of Bishop Manning's project. On March 13, 1925, the distinguished Jewish leader, Dr. Felix Adler, in a New York speech raised the question whether persons who are not members of the Protestant Episcopal Church are being "rightly urged" to contribute to the building of the two cathedrals. The *Times* rapped Dr. Adler's knuckles: "Those who do not wish to contribute are not asked to explain and may with propriety keep quiet." In this same editorial, carried in the March 15 issue, the *Times* praised the National Cathedral as a shrine "where men of all creeds may come and utter their messages." Parenthetically, it is worth noting that Dr. Adler expressed great loathing for the now popular term "fund drive." To him the word "drive," he said, suggested the herd, the driver, and the driven. He said he preferred the term "appeal."

Ackerman hired William Baldwin to assist with the fund raising. The latter's major task was to work with Bishop Freeman in soliciting large individual donations. Apparently Baldwin was retained to open doors to prominent and affluent eastern families with whom Baldwin, because of family, social, and civic connections, had entree. As Baldwin, a Unitarian, puts it: "I became the Unitarian chaplain to the Bishop of Washington, accompanying him to 'put the bite' on wealthy dowagers and other prospects." [72] Bishop Freeman's principal aide in the fund drive was the Reverend Canon Anson Phelps Stokes, of Washington, D.C. Both clerics believed in the individual, personal solicitation for gifts rather than the public broadcast appeal. Baldwin tells this story about the Canon Stokes: "The Reverend Stokes was working to raise money for Yale University. One objective was a large donation from a wealthy dowager who regularly read and believed in the *New York Tribune*. The reverend, through a friend and fellow alumnus on the *Tribune* staff, got a carefully worded editorial run in the paper, expressly written to appeal to this prospective donor. The dowager saw the editorial and was moved to make a sizable contribution." [73]

When, early in 1926, Bishop Freeman decided to invade Bishop

Manning's money fields of Gotham he put his faith in the direct, personal confrontation of prospects in the manner of Bishop Lawrence. In January, 1926, Bishop Freeman preached sermons in the Episcopal churches of St. Bartholomew, St. Thomas, and famed Trinity. In each instance he made it clear that he would "not make any appeal in the service but through personal visits." Supporters of the National Cathedral campaign arranged a series of fund-raising dinners for the bishop. One such was that put on by Mr. and Mrs. Henry White on January 28. Ackerman saw to it that the bishop's remarks were appropriately publicized in the next day's *Times*. In these meetings Bishop Freeman was urging support of the Cathedral as "a shrine of all Protestantism." White, former ambassador to France, was serving as chairman of the New York Committee of the National Cathedral Foundation, the fiscal and fund-raising agency.

In his sermons and in his private meetings with prospects the bishop repeatedly exploited the theme of peace, then a matter of concern in the days after the world's first global war. "I do not think large gifts to museums of art would help to bring permanent peace to the world as would large gifts to either of the two Episcopal cathedrals." [74] Apparently Freeman avoided any possible conflict with Bishop Manning's fund drive by praising and endorsing the appeal for St. John the Divine in all his public appearances. Repeatedly Bishop Freeman asked: "Shall we let this age sweep on its way, throwing up monuments to its industrial, commercial, and educational program, not daring to emphasize the priority of God in two great cities?"

Canon Stokes played a somewhat different tune in his appeals for money. He linked the need of the Cathedral to the spectacular wave of crime that was spreading across the country in the wake of national prohibition. He asserted that "one great factor in the crime waves and the present spirit of lawlessness in America was the lack of a vital religion." Stokes described the building of a National Episcopal Cathedral as "a monument to Christianity and an attempt to improve Christian morals." "Why not a monument to Jesus Christ?" he thundered. [75] Both clerics freely used President Calvin Coolidge's endorsement of the Cathedral as "an adornment and an inspiration in the national capital." Freeman assured the gathering at the Whites' that "a current of deep religious feeling governs President Coolidge in his official as well as in his private life." Another oft-repeated theme in sermons and publicity was "The capital city of Washington belongs to the whole country and all citizens should support this shrine to Christianity in the nation's capital."

The Reverend Mr. Stokes did not hesitate to take a hand in the public dispute between Bishop Manning and John D. Rockefeller, Jr., then raging around the St. John the Divine campaign. On February 10, 1925, Stokes wrote a letter to the *Times* supporting Rockefeller and differing with the position of his fellow Episcopalian cleric. "There is an excellent precedent for Mr. Rockefeller's suggestion in connection with the Washington Cathedral . . . its charter does not limit board membership to Episcopalians. . . . There have been two or three non-Episcopalians on the Board of Trustees, including Daniel C. Gilman." Stokes concluded pointedly, "I hope that the Washington precedent may prove suggestive and perhaps of some help to Bishop Manning." [76]

Surely the letter did not please Bishop Manning but it may have curried favor with Rockefeller. The Washington campaigners, like Bishop Manning and his committee, hammered hard on the "house of prayer for all people" as a means of getting gifts from non-Episcopalians. There were even fewer Episcopalians in Washington than in New York City. "'Great preachers will here proclaim their messages. . . . It will be available for great public services'. . . there will be no subsidized or rented pews; it will be a people's church." [77]

To build a "people's church" takes publicity, promotion, campaign organization, and doorbell ringing. Ackerman and Baldwin worked together in 1925 to build the requisite public support and Ackerman carried on alone in 1926. They relied primarily on publicity. Baldwin quit the campaign in 1925 to become secretary of the Arbitration Society of America, forerunner to the American Arbitration Association. The following year Ackerman left public relations counseling to take a job with General Motors. Baldwin took over his business, but not the Cathedral campaign. Late in 1926 Bishop Freeman and his committee hired the fast-growing John Price Jones firm to take charge of the campaign, the goal of which was now up to $15 million. Jones managed the Cathedral drive until the depression struck in 1931. During his association with Bishop Freeman, Baldwin made two suggestions. One was to hang in the nave of the Cathedral the flag of each state from which a stated total of contributions was received. This was designed to exploit a tested appeal in fund raising—spur competitive rivalry among groups with pride of identity. This idea was adopted several years later, Baldwin says. The other suggestion, not adopted, was that the Cathedral acquire a wave length for radio broadcasting to establish "The Voice of Religion" from the nation's capital. "This would have had assets far beyond fund raising," in Baldwin's opinion.

Radio broadcasting, developing rapidly as a mass medium in the twenties, was ultimately used by the National Cathedral in its fund-raising efforts. The Jones firm arranged for and planned a nation-wide broadcast from the Cathedral on Good Friday, April 18, 1930. Staffman Jed Fiske told his colleagues: "A mass by Bishop Freeman was most impressive and probably caused thousands to inquire as to how this great church is being supported. It would be interesting to know, although impossible to estimate—how much money was raised by this broadcast." [78] No evidence was to be found in the Jones record as to the effectiveness of this Good Friday broadcast.

Jones and his staff, upon acquiring the Washington Cathedral account, made an extensive survey as to the Cathedral's "comprehensive needs, its general policy, future plans, past fund raising activities, and relations with the lay public. Twenty volumes of records . . . were digested." [79] Out of the survey came a campaign plan that focused on this appeal: "Washington Cathedral should function as a fortress for the preservation of religion and religious knowledge, a training ground for the dissemination of religion and religious knowledge and a headquarters for the extension of the bounds of religion and religious knowledge. Publicity must demonstrate the significance of a 'witness for Christ in the Nation's Capital.' " [80] The campaign analysis suggested a series of recurrent campaigns, at intervals of three to five years, to raise $30 million.

The immediate Jones objective was to raise $6.8 million through nationwide publicity. The plan called for a great organization spreading through every diocese where permission to canvass could be obtained. Under the nominal leadership of General John J. Pershing, chairman of the National Committee, and Senator George Wharton Pepper, chairman of the Executive Committee, the Jones firm began its publicity and appeals to wealthy prospects. In two years, from May, 1927, to May, 1929, Street reports that more than $4 million had been raised for the Cathedral. Pershing and Pepper provided a prestigious front for the Jones-directed campaign. Jones often said: "I have always sought to work quietly. My work is that of stage director, laying out the work for the other person and staying out of the spotlight. It has been our aim to get the work done and not fight for the credit." [81] Jones had ruefully learned a few years earlier not to claim all the credit in a fund drive. After the Johns Hopkins campaign the Jones firm put out a pamphlet taking credit for having "raised" the Johns Hopkins sums. This brought a blistering attack from Abraham Flexner. Thereafter Jones, in public utterances, was careful to claim only that he had "assisted" in raising the money.

Another massive religious fund-raising effort was the one-year drive directed by Will H. Hays, erstwhile Republican politician and now movie czar, and Arnaud C. Marts that raised more than $15 million for the Presbyterian Church Pension Fund in 1926–1927. Hays triumphantly announced to the church's General Assembly in San Francisco on May 28, 1927, that the campaign had "$15,045,000 in hand and more coming," stoutly declaring "a new standard of giving to Christian causes has been set." Editorially the *New York Times* termed the drive "a great practical achievement," adding "it has a spiritual corollary that is more significant." [82] This campaign, which ultimately reached into every Presbyterian church and home, was originally conceived in the older nineteenth-century pattern of quiet solicitation of multimillionaires, but ended in the new post-World War I pattern of high-pressure methods and widespread solicitation.

The Presbyterian Church's plan to raise $15 million to start a pension fund for its aged ministers, missionaries, and educators was first announced March 1, 1926, because "a sufficient number of churches have now voted to accept the plan to justify commencement of the drive." Hays and his former Cabinet colleague, Secretary of the Treasury Andrew Mellon, made the initial plans. They thought they could raise this tremendous sum by a quiet, systematic solicitation of some one hundred multimillionaires who were Presbyterians. Hays told the General Assembly, meeting in Baltimore, Md., May 29, "It may be desirable to raise the bulk of the $15,-000,000 from a limited group of individuals. We are planning to that end." [83]

The General Assembly voted approval of the Pension Fund campaign despite Hays's report that "it is being delayed through the failure of members and churches to subscribe to it. Only 3600 ministers of the required minimum of 4000 have signed." Hays also announced that all contributions would go to the Pension Fund because "all campaign expenses will be borne by Andrew W. Mellon, Richard B. Mellon, and William B. McKinley." Thus he took a leaf from the book of the first big pension fund campaigner, Bishop Lawrence. But still the drive did not catch fire.

At this point Hays called in an associate of earlier money-raising drives—Arnaud C. Marts, partner in the newly organized Hedrick, Marts & Lundy firm. Marts and Hays had worked together in Indiana in war drives. Again in 1922, when the Republican party had a $500,000 deficit, National Chairman Hays asked Marts to assist with a drive to clear this debt before the 1922 Congressional campaigns. Marts set up fund-raising drives in Rochester, Dayton, and Cleveland for the GOP. At this time Marts was still working with the Ward firm.[84]

Hays, a native of Sullivan, Ind., and a lawyer, served as chairman of the Republican National Committee from February, 1918, to June 7, 1921. In return for this service President Harding appointed him postmaster general to handle the new administration's patronage, a post Hays held for one year. He quit the Cabinet in March, 1922, to become the president of Motion Picture Producers and Distributors of America, the first "movie czar"—a post created after the movies had been threatened by Hollywood scandals. Hays held this post until 1945. He died in 1954.

Hays turned to Marts for aid when his 100-multimillionaire idea fizzled. Marts persuaded Hays to change his concept of the campaign, arguing that only by going into every state and into every church could such a staggering sum of money be obtained. Consequently, Hays announced on June 9, 1926, that a Layman's National Committee of One Hundred would conduct a fund-raising drive "in every state through the synods." The worship of business as well as of God in the 1920's is reflected in Hays's assertion: "The world's one essential industry is religion, and being an industry it must adopt industry's methods." Because the campaign was "considered purely a business affair," Hays said the ministers would not be asked to participate. But they were utilized before the campaign was over. Hays was chairman of the drive, Andrew W. Mellon treasurer, and Arnaud C. Marts director.

Before hiring Marts to take charge, Hays had retained the Ivy Lee firm to provide publicity for the campaign. Hays turned to Lee presumably because of the latter's work for Bishop Lawrence in the

1916–17 campaign for the Episcopal Church Pension Fund. According to John Park Lee, an employee of but no relation to Ivy Lee: "Mr. Lee agreed to do this job for the Presbyterian Church at cost to him. I presume he billed the Layman's Committee for a portion of my salary. . . . I was the only one who traveled in connection with this campaign, and did public relations for Marts & Lundy in connection with campaign dinners." [85] Marts does not recall that either Ivy Lee or John Park Lee played an important role in the drive.

Marts says: "The successful campaign has been over for 33 years and my fund-raising associates and I put it across as the result of two years of very strenuous activity from New York to San Francisco. We wrote the brochure; we prepared the spot news as it was produced by meetings and activities throughout the field, and the Ivy Lee representatives remained behind in the New York and Philadelphia office without much knowledge of the campaign procedures except in those two cities." [86] Both John Park Lee and Marts recall another publicity man on the Hays committee staff. Lee thinks he was an Ivy Lee employee but Marts says, "He was an ex-newspaper man who was sort of a political hanger-on and I think Mr. Hays paid his salary in our pension fund office because he did not know where else to put him. It was hard to find anything he could do." Apparently Hays found a place for patronage in his philanthropic organizations too! John Park Lee subsequently left the public relations firm and became secretary of the Presbyterian Church's Board of National Missions.

Reflecting today's expanded dimensions of American fund raising and money giving, John Park Lee, as executive secretary of the Presbyterian Church's Commission on Capital Needs, in 1964 was perfecting plans for a drive to raise $100 million. This drive, to provide money for replacing old buildings and building additional churches, was to start in May, 1965.

Marts himself knew the art of using emotion-laden publicity methods. In something of a slap at the Ivy Lee effort, he writes: "One of the most striking newspaper releases for stirring a lot of action and emotion happened in Steubenville, O. We had our campaign on in the Steubenville Presbytery and in the midst of it an old retired Presbyterian minister was found slumped against a wall in the city, too weak to talk. He was given emergency treatment and then it was found that he had not had anything to eat for some time.

This was the sort of local news that we developed in the process of the campaign that, of course, could never come out of the New York publicity mill." [87] At any rate there is a bound volume of 128 releases in the offices of the one-time Ivy Lee firm demonstrating that the Lee firm provided much of the publicity for the local campaigns in New York City—where $950,000 was raised—and in Philadelphia. Lee's office issued the opening announcement. Credit for success—or failure—in fund drives can be a touchy matter.

Marts and his associates planned that the yearlong campaign would start in New York where the big moneybags were stored and then move across the land to a climax at the church's General Assembly in San Francisco in May, 1927. In the words of Mr. Hays, it would prove to be a triumphant "march to the sea by 30,000 laymen starting on the Atlantic Coast last fall and winding up on the Pacific Coast today." By April, 1927, the canvass had reached Chicago and the western states and some $9.2 million had been pledged.

Despite Hays's earlier promise not to involve the ministers in pleas for their own welfare, Sunday, April 24, was designated Pension Day. The next day's newspapers reported: "Four thousand Presbyterian ministers in 3500 cities from Illinois to California preached on the pension plan to aid the Pension Fund campaign being conducted now in the Western States." This same month there was another story publicizing the fact that all contributions went to the Pension Fund because the campaign costs had been underwritten. The April 20 news release added the names of Captain Robert Dollar of San Francisco and George G. Barber of New York City as underwriters of campaign costs.

To bolster the campaign as it moved across Ohio, Hays announced in Columbus on February 12, 1927, that he had had "his worldly possessions appraised and would give one-tenth of his fortune to the Pension Fund." The *New York Times* account continued in deadpan fashion, "The exact amount of his gift was not disclosed." The usual quota and district system with campaign committees and subcommittees was followed in this "march to the sea" which brought the Presbyterian Church a $15 million Pension Fund, Will Hays a gold watch from the grateful clergy, and Marts & Lundy their first big success as a fund-raising firm. Hays wrote Marts in a letter dated June 10, 1927: "I cannot overstate what you have meant to the cause. The entire denomination is under real obligation to you for the ability and wisdom, the understanding, the Christian character and deep devotion with which you approached this task. And you brought with you the experience which is so necessary in proper accomplishment of such an undertaking." Thus a chance wartime contact in Indiana had led to a new fund-raising coup.

At least one American did not view all this drum beating for colleges, churches, and cathedrals with either wide-eyed enthusiasm or caustic criticism. Will Rogers looked on with wry amusement. In his gentle, genial way Rogers could bite deeply into pomposity and pretension, and his quick shafts of humor brought more than one issue into perspective. His kind of person is not found on the American scene today, and we are the poorer. The great humorist and entertainer sent Will Hays this letter during the campaign, written on the stationery of Hotel Jamestown, Jamestown, N.Y., with his own typewriter:

> Dear Willie Hays
> Say, I got your letter about raising 15 Millions for the Presbyterians. My Lord, since you went into the Movies you got the Churches talking in Millions, 15 Millions, say, all the Presbyterians I ever knew couldn't even SAY 15 MILLIONS. Who's going to count it if you do get it, You will have to get an Episcopalian to explain to you how much it is.
> 15 Million, What are you trying to make out of them? A Feature Church? They are nothing but an ordinary program church, along in the class with the Baptists, and Camelites, and Holy Rollers. Their Sales quota on the entire United States and Europe and Australia couldn't gross over two million.
> If you get 15 million for the Presbyterians you are going to have to organize a Jewish Branch, call it perhaps "The Presbyterian Sons of Israel." . . .
> I see by your advance publicity that "Andy" Mellon is mixed up with you. That Guy is mixed up in every business in the world and now he is in the Church business, Treasurer as usual. I will help you on one condition, that is you Presbyterians get your 15 Million you will help us Methodists get $483.27. That's this year's quota and we feel that we shot a little high on it. Do you know of any rich man we could advertise as our Treasurer? Is Hoover working at any religion? If neither one of us get what we are after it looks like we will have to go to saving Souls instead of money, and that's a mighty old fashioned thing to have to get back to. Enclose find check for $100. to compensate you for your ambition. You notice the check is made out to "Andy."

I don't want you to think I didn't trust you, I do. In fact I trust you just as much as I do him. It should have been made out to "Hays and Mellon Probable beneficiaries Presbyterians." Please don't allow Mellon to apply this on National Debt, I would just as soon it would reach the Foreign Missions as that.

You may raise this, Bill, anything is possible in politics. Look what Vare and Smith raised. When you do get it "save the heathen and the Movies first."

I am praying that justice won't be done in your case, William.

An Amateur Highbinder
Yours
WILL ROGERS [88]

NOTES

1. John Price Jones Co., *American Philanthropy for Higher Education* (copyright 1962, Inter-River Press), pp. 1–2.

2. "Methods and Costs for Raising Funds for Colleges and Universities," address by Jones given in Cleveland, Ohio, April 13, 1923, and reprinted as a pamphlet.

3. Above data is from "Three Decades of Philanthropy for Higher Education," John Price Jones Corp. multilithed report, copyright 1951. In corporation's files.

4. *Conference Proceedings*, Vol. 2, in John Price Jones Papers.

5. John Price Jones "Annual Report," John Price Jones Papers. AG-1.

6. "Publicity Problems at Johns Hopkins," Harold W. Weeks, in *Proceedings Semi-Annual Conference of the Staff, June 29–30, 1925*, John Price Jones Papers, BF-2. (Weeks died Oct. 12, 1962.)

7. "The Johns Hopkins Campaign," *Staff Conference Proceedings*, 1924, in John Price Jones Papers.

8. *Ibid.*

9. *Ibid.*

10. *Ibid.*

11. Seymour, "Strong and Weak Points at Johns Hopkins," in *Proceedings Semi-Annual Conference of the Staff, June 29 and 30, 1925*, John Price Jones Papers, BF-2.

12. *Ibid.*

13. *Ibid.*

14. *Ibid.*, p. 63.

15. *1930 Annual Conference Proceedings*, John Price Jones Papers, BF-5, pp. 5–7.

16. John Price Jones Papers, Johns Hopkins Campaign Book, v. C 42.

17. Monthly Budget Report, Jan. 1, 1927, *Johns Hopkins Campaign*, John Price Jones Papers.

18. In address to Association of Alumni Secretaries, April 13, 1923.

19. In "An Index of Giving to Higher Education," John Price Jones Corp. files, copyright 1952.

20. Unpublished mss. in John Price Jones Corp. files.

21. In "The Difficult Art of Giving," *Current Opinion*, Vol. 74 (April, 1923), p. 465.

22. Minneapolis *Tribune*, Oct. 12, 1919.

23. *Ibid.*

24. Eau Claire *Leader*, Sept. 21, 1919.

25. Raphael N. Hamilton, S.J., *The Story of Marquette University* (Milwaukee: Marquette Press, 1953), p. 197.

26. Sherman Gwinn, "John Bowman's Fifty Story Dream," *American*, Vol. 105 (May, 1928), p. 90.

27. *Ibid.*, p. 94.

28. Letter Dec. 28, 1961, from Carlton G. Ketchum.

29. *New York Times*, Jan. 30, 1925, p. 3.

30. Ketchum letter to author, Dec. 28, 1961.

31. Littell, "Washington Calling," *Philanthropy*, Summer, 1955, p. 94.

32. Gwinn, *op. cit.*, p. 92.

33. "College Football and College Endowment," *Oberlin Alumni Magazine*, April, 1934.

34. For elaboration of these allegations, see: Howard J. Savage *et al.*, Bulletin No. 23, *American College Athletics, 1929*, and *Current Developments in American College Sport*, Bulletin No. 26, 1931, both published by Carnegie Foundation for the Advancement of Teaching.

35. In talk to fourth annual staff conference of Marts & Lundy, Aug. 2, 1948, in *Marts & Lundy Staff Conference Proceedings*.

36. *Ibid.*

37. Printed lecture by Edward Grant Conklin of this date, based on stenographic notes and found in Lee's MSO Book for the Princeton Campaign.

38. In Ivy Lee MSO Book, 1920.

39. Interview with Dr. Marts, Feb. 25, 1960.

40. Lawrence, *Memories of a Happy Life*, p. 417.

41. *Ibid.*, p. 418.

42. *New York Times*, April 1, 1924, p. 23.

43. Lawrence, *op. cit.*, p. 420.

44. *New York Times*, June 2, 1924, p. 1.

45. Henry Knox Sherrill, *William Lawrence* (Cambridge, Mass.: Harvard Univ. Press, 1943), pp. 103–104.

46. *Ibid.*, pp. 101–102.

47. Interview with W. H. Baldwin, New York City, May 20, 1960.

48. *Ibid.*

49. *Ibid.*

50. G. Robert Tipton, in *Musical Gems from the Reader's Digest* (Pleasantville, N.Y.: The Reader's Digest Association), pp. 44–48.

51. Letter from Baldwin, Oct. 20, 1959.

52. Lawrence, *op. cit.*, pp. 248–249.

53. Davis, "Dr. Manning's Pious Anachronism," *New Republic*, Vol. 41 (Jan. 28, 1925), p. 256.

54. *Ibid.*

55. Memorandum on this campaign prepared for author by Tamblyn & Brown.

56. Elmer Davis, "Portrait of a Cleric," *Harper's*, Vol. 153 (June, 1926), p. 20.

57. *Ibid.*, p. 11. For one account of the Trinity scandal, see Charles Edward Russell, "The Tenements of Trinity Church . . ." reprinted from *Everybody's*, July, 1908, in Weinberg, *The Muckrakers*.

58. Alfred B. Rollins, Jr., *Roosevelt and Howe*, pp. 198–199.

59. Freidel, *Franklin D. Roosevelt*, Vol. 2, *The Ordeal*, p. 109.

60. John Crosby Brown in remarks made at Marts & Lundy Fourth Annual Staff Conference, Aug. 2, 1948, New York City. Found in conference report, p. 68.

61. Tamblyn & Brown Memorandum, "Cathedral of St. John the Divine."

62. Davis, "Portrait of a Cleric," p. 17.

63. *New York Times*, Jan. 19, 1925, p. 1.

64. *Ibid.*, Feb. 7, 1925, p. 4.

65. Pringle, Henry F., *Big Frogs* (New York: Macy-Marcus, 1928) p. 114. Italics are mine.

66. In "Portrait of a Cleric," p. 21.

67. *New York Times*, May 14, 1925, p. 3.

68. Elizabeth Robins Pennell, "Building an American Cathedral, *Harper's*, Vol. 148 (February, 1924), pp. 343, 346.

69. *Time*, May 4, 1962, p. 53.

70. Tom Everritt, "The National Cathedral at Washington," *Review of Reviews*, Vol. 72 (December, 1925), pp. 623–627.

71. "Touch System," *Time*, Vol. 45 (Jan. 15, 1945), p. 79.

72. Letter to author, Oct. 12, 1961.

73. In interview with Major John Forrest, April 4, 1961.

74. *New York Times*, Jan. 18, 1926, p. 24.

75. *Ibid.*, p. 24, same column.

76. *Ibid.*, Feb. 12, 1925, p. 18.

77. Everritt, *op. cit.*, pp. 625, 627.

78. John Price Jones Papers, 1930 Staff Conference, BF-5, "Radio and Fund Raising."

79. Street's history of the Jones firm, unpublished mss. in John Price Jones Papers, p. 60.

80. *Ibid.*, p. 61.

81. *Ibid.*, p. 67.

82. *New York Times*, May 29, 1927, p. 16. Editorial comment on p. 8, Sec. II.

83. *Ibid.*, May 30, 1926, p. 10.

84. Interview with Dr. Marts, Feb. 26, 1960.

85. Letter from John Park Lee to author, April 18, 1960.

86. Letter dated April 27, 1960, written by Marts in response to being shown letter from Lee to author.

87. *Ibid.*

88. Copy of letter kept by Dr. Arnaud C. Marts in his personal files.

8

Fund Raising in the Depression

Raising Money for Relief

The decade of 1919–1929, termed by John Price Jones "the golden age of fund-raising," came crashing down in economic ruin and social chaos as the Great Depression followed in the wake of the Stock Market crash of October, 1929. This bitter climax to the false prosperity of the 1920's brought an end to "the greatest era of voluntary giving any nation has ever witnessed." David Shannon succinctly summarizes the onset of the depression:

> After several months of depression America was indeed a place turned topsy-turvy. Even the surface appearance of the cities changes. Former bond salesmen were on the sidewalks trying to sell apples. Former clerks roamed the business districts in an attempt to make a living by shining shoes. Unemployed and homeless men welcomed arrests for vagrancy and the warmth and food to be had in jail. Over a hundred thousand American workers applied for jobs in the Soviet Union. Shanty towns appeared in an around the industrial cities, and the inhabitants of these housing developments born of desperation bitterly named them for the President of the United States.[1]

The searing, shattering years of the depression left no American institution untouched and unchanged, least of all fund raising for philanthropy.

The capital fund drives for colleges, churches, and hospitals faltered or limped to a close as one prospective donor after another went into bankruptcy. For example, the John Price Jones tabulations on capital gifts to forty-six colleges show that these institutions received $77,867,380 in gifts and bequests for the year ending June 30, 1930, but the same colleges and universities collected less than half this amount, $31,083,828, for the year ending June 30, 1935. The fund raisers shifted their talents to raising money for relief. The American Red Cross was caught in the vortex of the political battle between conservatives who stoutly held that relief was a matter for private philanthropy to solve—not the government, as liberals argued. Yet the ARC, much against its will and past traditions, "was soon acting as an unemployment relief agency." The community chests turned, temporarily, from general welfare and recreational programs to providing food, shelter, and clothing for the mounting millions of unemployed workers and their families. From the crash in October, 1929, until March, 1933, when President Franklin Delano Roosevelt took office, private philanthropic agencies and their fund raisers made a determined but futile effort to cope with the greatest suffering this nation has ever known in peacetime.

President Herbert Hoover steadfastly insisted that the relief of millions of distressed Americans was a local responsibility. On December 13, 1930, he declared that the transfer of this local obligation to the national government would sap that "spirit of responsibility of states, of municipalities, of industry and the community at large, [which] is the one safeguard against overwhelming centralization and degeneration of that independence and initiative which are the very foundations of democracy." A few weeks later, February 3, 1931, he again asserted that federal relief would destroy "character" and strike at "the roots of self-government." [2]

Consequently, in these early depression years, 1929–1933, private agencies had to try to carry the rapidly mounting load with money raised in emergency drives. This meant work for the fund raisers at least.

The question of private philanthropy versus governmental relief on a grand scale provoked one of the fundamental political struggles of our time.

In contrast to Hoover's insistence on local relief by private agencies, Franklin D. Roosevelt, as early as 1931 while governor of New York, had asserted, "One of these duties of the State is that of caring for those of its citizens who find themselves the victims of such adverse circumstances as to make them unable to obtain even the necessities for mere existence without the aid of others. . . . To these unfortunate citizens aid must be extended by Government, not as a matter of charity, but as a matter of social duty."

As President he implemented these views and created what his opponents derisively termed the "welfare state." Caught in the crossfire of the conflicting philosophies of Hoover and Roosevelt was the American National Red Cross.

The Red Coss had traditionally assumed, from the days of Clara Barton on, that economic distress was not a natural calamity calling for emergency relief. In the nation's brief depression of 1921 it had held the position that caring for the unemployed was a community and not a Red Cross problem. As the depression crisis mounted the Red Cross insisted that "the whole disaster relief structure" might collapse if the Red Cross allowed itself to become too deeply involved in aid for the unemployed. Yet as the depression's impact grew in severity, the Red Cross could not resist involvement. "The great drought of 1930, beginning in Arkansas, gradually developed until twenty-three states were affected; Arkansas, Kentucky, Oklahoma, Texas, and Louisiana were most severely affected. Since Red Cross chapters had, in many instances, become active in aiding sufferers from the drought, the organization was asked by President Hoover to "stand by" in case the drought should become a "serious calamity." [3]

In early August, as winds blew rising clouds of dust across the scorched fields of the West and the South, President Hoover called a meeting of the governors of the affected states. John Barton Payne represented the Red Cross at this conference held August 14. On the previous day Payne had announced that a disaster reserve fund of $5 million was being held in readiness for emergency use. The onset of winter only deepened the suffering of the families in the drought-stricken areas where disaster had been piled on top of depression so the Red Cross committed the $5 million fund on December 10, 1930. Early in January, 1931, Judge Payne was still insisting that "we might get through the winter with our present funds." But only a week later the Red Cross issued an appeal to the citizens of the United States for $10 million for drought relief. President Hoover, at Red Cross request, designated the ARC "as the nation's sole agency for relief in such a crisis," and on January 13 appealed to people to give to this emergency fund drive.

While the drive for funds was under way, a political storm broke in Congress when the Democrats proposed that an appropriation of $25 million be given the Red Cross " 'for the purpose of supplying food, medicine, medical aid, and other essentials to afford adequate relief in the present national emergency to persons otherwise unable to procure the same.' " [4] The Red Cross immediately responded, saying it would refuse such government moneys. "It was felt that to do so would involve the Red Cross in work duplicating that of other agencies, impose responsibilities that could not be adequately met, and completely destroy the voluntary character of Red Cross activity." This brought the issue of private relief versus government relief squarely into focus. The Red Cross, the community chests, and other privately directed although publicly supported philanthropic agencies—all dominated by conservative businessmen —had long held that philanthropy and relief of distress were private matters. Their leaders were determined to restrict government to the narrowest sphere possible.

In World War I, a J. P. Morgan banker, Henry P. Davison, as chairman of the Red Cross War Council, had said that the consequence of acceptance by the Red Cross of any government financial contribution "would be the discouragement and discontinuance of private support and its conversion ultimately from a great voluntary humane movement to a department of government supported by taxation." The astute banker knew that so long as the wealthy could keep the "taxation" for relief in their hands they could control the amount given and the ways in which it would be expended. Refusal of the money proposed in Congress made the Red Cross the subject of heated controversy and posed one of its most difficult public relations crises in a long history of such crises.

Public opinion divided sharply on this fundamental philanthropic and political issue. The Providence (R.I.) *News-Tribune* said that the Red Cross had either underestimated or misrepresented the needs of the drought sufferers "and the charge is openly made that it misrepresented them." On the other side of the fence, the Cleveland *Plain Dealer* voiced full confidence in the ability of the Red Cross to handle the drought relief problem. The *Outlook* expressed many citizens' views when it declared that it was ridiculous to refuse the $25 million from Congress and then appeal to the public to give $10 million. Meantime, the subsidy proposal was defeated in Congress.

The bitterest attack on the Red Cross in this depression period came in 1934, from John Spivak, one-time reporter for the *Daily Worker* and a frequent contributor to the *New Masses*. Spivak's attack, entitled "Shady Business in the Red Cross," was published in the November, 1934, issue of the *American Mercury*. In essence Spivak charged that the ARC placed the contributions of "working people and school children" in the hands of a clique of bankers for their advantage and attacked the disaster relief program as being a "salary relief for thousands of Red Cross employees." He concluded his vitriolic article by urging, "Certainly the Congress . . . should get to the root of the Red Cross financial dealings and its methods of distributing relief. With millions of our people starving, it is time 'The Great Mother's' skirts were cleared." [5]

Paul Kellogg, editor of *Survey*, came to the defense of the Red Cross and dismissed Spivak's charges as "cockeyed reporting." [6] Moreover, Kellogg argued the case for voluntary giving for private relief work as against direct government aid. Despite charges that it had ample reserve funds for such emergencies and amid the controversy over whether relief was a matter for private agencies or for the government, the Red Cross went ahead with its 1931 emergency fund-raising campaign. It started slowly and the first million dollars was not obtained for ten days. Judge Payne persuaded fifty-seven outstanding public figures, including former President Coolidge, General Pershing, Thomas W. Lamont, Owen D. Young, William Green, and John L. Lewis, to serve as sponsors. A nationwide broadcast urging contributions was made in their name. Hoover repeatedly pleaded for gifts to the Red Cross on the grounds that this was "the American way" of meeting an emergency.

Hoover himself gave $5,000 to the San Francisco Red Cross chapter to dramatize his support of the campaign. The usual benefits and bazaars were held. An unusual benefit was a competition for the best bootjacks—a contrivance used by Westerners to get boots off—held in Kansas City on April 4. This auctioning of glorified boot removers netted the Red Cross only $300, yet merited a story in the *New York Times*. At the very moment the Red Cross was putting on the publicity pressure to raise the $10 million drought relief fund, it was being attacked for "letting people starve." On April 2, 1931, Brant A. Scott, vice-president of the West Virginia Mine Workers Union, told a Senate Committee holding hearings in Charleston, W.Va., that the Red Cross had refused to aid hungry and destitute miners even though people in the coalfields were idle, hungry, and half naked. " 'The Red Cross has never helped the miners. I went to Charleston three times but they refused any aid outside the city. They said the money was not for the rural districts, but did not explain why.' " [7] Two days later Judge Payne replied by announcing that the Red Cross might send a representative to the West Virginia coalfields to investigate these reports of starvation and by asserting, " 'The Red Cross has been confining its activities to drought sufferers but that in communities partly agricultural and partly industrial no discrimination had been shown.' " [8]

Of this Red Cross drought relief campaign, Abraham Epstein, executive secretary of the American Association for Old Age Security, wrote critically:

> Never in the history of American philanthropy has a charitable appeal received so much publicity as the recent drive for $10,000,000 . . . by the Red Cross. Never before had there been such a concentration of energies. Night after night the greatest national and international stars played to the radio audience. . . . And never before was Big Business so genuinely eager to raise the quota, for it wanted to prove to Congress that its appropriations were unnecessary in a land where every heart flows dollars upon the slightest touch.
>
> Yet in spite of all these efforts the original period of the drive expired with only 70% of the money raised.[9]

Nonetheless, despite these twin handicaps of the deepening depression which cut people's ability to give and of the widening controversy over the relief role of the Red Cross, the ARC plodded relentlessly ahead with its emergency fund-raising effort and eventually raised more than $13 million for this purpose. The Red Cross had raised $10,589,780 by June 30, 1931. The next year, 1932, the ARC pleaded for more money to help persons who had suffered losses by the continuing drought in the West and by the plague of grasshoppers. A total of $2,267,000 was raised for this "Grasshopper and Drought Relief" fund, making a grand total of $13,366,722 given by the American people to the victims of the drought in response to repeated ARC appeals from January, 1931, to June, 1932. In summary, the Red Cross spent $11.1 million in assisting 614,504 families (approximately 2,765,000 persons) in 1,057 counties in this emergency effort. In addition the Red Cross distributed food and relief supplies valued at nearly $1 million to drought victims.[10]

As public pressure mounted, the Red Cross retreated a bit from its official position when on September 9, 1931, Judge Payne wrote local chapters that they could participate in unemployment relief

providing local funds were available or could be raised for that purpose. The 1931 annual report states that 2,276 ARC chapters were
engaged in some type of unemployment relief. In 1932 the Red Cross
took on, at President Hoover's request, distribution of 85 million
bushels of government-owned wheat and 844,000 bales of government-owned cotton to provide food and clothing for the needy and
distressed. Acceptance of these commodities, valued at $73 million,
was somehow viewed differently by Judge Payne than the offer
of money by Congressional appropriation. He said: " 'Commodity
distribution can be handled without creating the precedent resulting from the appropriation of government funds to the Red
Cross.' " [11]

"In the months that followed the Red Cross, working through
chapters and local charities both public and private, distributed ten
million barrels of flour to five million families as well as sixty-six
million ready made garments, thirty-eight million chapter made
garments and three million blankets." The Red Cross was removed
from the horns of the dilemma posed by its adherence to private
philanthropy and by the needs of millions of starving, homeless
people when Franklin D. Roosevelt became President. In May, 1933,
Harry Hopkins announced that "all public relief funds must be
administered by public agencies."

In the 1930's the Red Cross found it necessary to conduct three
more emergency fund-raising drives, one each in the years 1936,
1937, and 1938, due to "natural disasters." In 1936 to aid the victims of the spring floods that brought damage to seventeen states
and the District of Columbia, the Red Cross asked the public to give
$3 million. By June 30, 1936, the ARC had raised more than twice
that amount—$7,955,963—for flood relief. In 1937 the Ohio and
Mississippi valleys were again struck by devastating spring floods.
This time the Red Cross launched an emergency drive to raise $10
million and received two and one-half times that amount. By June
30, 1937, the American people had given, through the Red Cross,
$25,312,168 to the victims of the rampaging floods along the Ohio
and Mississippi rivers.

The next year, when New York and New England were struck
by both hurricanes and floods, the Red Cross again issued a special
appeal for funds and raised $930,748 in this 1938 campaign. Relief
in the amount of $1,682,000 was dispensed in the New York-New
England area, the balance coming from the ARC Disaster Revolv-

ing Fund. As the nation regained its health and the relief role was taken over by the federal and state governments, the Red Cross found fund raising easier. Or at least these emergency appeals would so indicate.[12]

The impact of the depression years on the Red Cross annual Roll Call fund-raising effort to support its ongoing program is a bit difficult to determine. From 1931 on, Red Cross records show only the amount remitted to national headquarters for support of the National Red Cross; thus no records are available showing the total amount of funds raised by the chapters. Records showing total memberships and contributions to the national headquarters would indicate that the ARC hit its low point in this decade in 1933 and then started its climb back. Given the depressed economic conditions of the early 1930's and the criticism brought on by the private-versus-government relief controversy, the Red Cross membership, and thus its income, held up well in those years. The full picture can be seen in Table 10.[13]

For the first year of the depression Hoover stoutly, stoically in-

TABLE 10. RESULTS OF ANNUAL RED CROSS ROLL CALLS, 1926–1939

Fiscal years	Amount raised	Number adult members
1926	$3,201,000	3,012,055
1927	3,351,000	3,087,789
1928	4,556,000	4,058,949
1929	4,721,000	4,127,946
1930	4,554,000 *	4,130,966
1931	2,018,000	4,075,649
1932	1,974,579	4,004,459
1933	1,782,922	3,701,866
1934	1,873,856	3,802,384
1935	1,889,584	3,837,941
1936	2,038,563	4,137,636
1937	2,413,964	4,904,316
1938	2,724,805	5,523,585
1939	2,781,325	5,668,680

* Last year totals for national and chapter fund campaigns were recorded by American National Red Cross headquarters. Totals for years 1931–1939 show only National ARC's share of receipts.

sisted that private social institutions could meet the situation in the "American way." But by October, 1930, he felt compelled to act. That month he sought the advice of Mrs. William Brown Meloney, an editor of the New York *Herald Tribune*, on appointment of an emergency committee. He asked her to suggest the names of a prominent man for chairman, an outstanding woman, and a public relations expert. Mrs. Meloney suggested Colonel Arthur Woods as chairman, Dr. Lillian Gilbreth, an industrial engineer, and Edward L. Bernays, widely known publicist. Bernays' main contribution was the naming of the committee—the President's Emergency Committee for Employment (PECE). To discourage "negative thinking," Bernays counseled against using the word "unemployment." Bernays participated only in the organizational phase of this committee. Woods chose as his two assistants Fred C. Croxton and Edward Eyre Hunt. Hoover publicly launched the committee on October 30 "to encourage local responsibility for unemployment relief," making it clear that the government's role would be minimal.[14]

As privation and starvation spread in the spring of 1931, the President's committee moved to spur a nationwide fund-raising drive at the local level. The move to launch a united appeal in the nation's 376 cities of 25,000 population or more was disclosed on June 13, in Minneapolis, at the annual convention of the Association of Community Chests and Councils. Fred C. Croxton, acting chairman of PECE, told the community chest officials: "Experience has taught us that primary dependence for meeting this need must be placed on local resources."

Croxton's announcement of the united fund-raising drive slated for the autumn created some confusion in philanthropic and governmental circles. Judge Payne quickly issued a statement from ARC's headquarters denying that the Red Cross would participate in this united campaign. "I have nothing whatever to do with such a campaign," he said. U.S. Secretary of Commerce Lamont quickly dissociated the government from the drive by saying, "I have never approved anything of this nature." [15] It subsequently came out that Allen T. Burns of the Three Cs had approached Payne but was turned down on the grounds that the American Red Cross did not participate "in such general movements." Then, as later, the ARC resisted being included in united fund drives.

The coordinated campaign for funds got under way almost immediately with the appointment, on June 16, of J. Herbert Case, chairman of the board of the Federal Reserve Bank of New York and president of the National Association of Community Chests and Councils, who accepted the "summons" of the President's Committee to lead a drive to raise $82 million in some 376 cities of 25,000 or over. In launching the drive, Mr. Case said that this was the first time that the community chests of the country had been summoned collectively for national service. But he made it clear, "There is to be no subordination of community interests and no pooling of funds for national disbursement." To provide a factual basis for the fund appeals the Three Cs immediately launched a survey of the 376 localities, 244 of which already had community chests. The survey questionnaire went to local welfare organizations in the other 132 municipalities. The dates for the drive were set for October 19 to November 25. The campaign committee included the community chests' pioneer publicist, Elwood Street. The drive's theme was "the principle of local responsibility for local needs." The Three Cs Welfare Relief Mobilization, as the campaign came to be titled, spurred organization of emergency committees in the non-chest cities and this in turn ultimately led to more community chests being organized.

On July 21 Burns reported to the President's Committee that "unless there was improvement in business soon the relief requirements probably would be twice as great the coming winter as in 1930–1931." He reported that much of the privately raised money for relief had been expended. Burns saw the handwriting on the wall: "Private philanthropy cannot possibly raise all the funds needed to meet the aggregate demands." On the eve of the campaign Burns announced that the Three Cs survey showed that immediate emergency relief needs of 314 cities—the number that responded to the questionnaire—excluding community chests and other local welfare programs for the coming year, amounted to $170,090,130, of which $142,670,130 would be required for direct aid to the needy. Burns explained that no estimate of amounts needed for relief in the nation as a whole had been prepared.

On October 18 President Hoover launched the fund drive with an appeal broadcast by radio to the nation from Fortress Monroe, Va. He told the nation, "Through these agencies Americans must meet the demands of national conscience that there be no hunger or cold among our people." The *New York Times* account said, "Mr. Hoover is depending on efforts of individual communities to preclude appropriation of relief funds by Congress." The drives proceeded intensively at the local level with supplemental supporting publicity sent out from the Three Cs headquarters, with the approval and support of PECE. The costs of the fact-finding survey and the campaign publicity were underwritten by the Rockefeller Foundation. The Three Cs sent its seasoned campaign staff across the country to assist both chest and non-chest cities with the plans and promotion for the local campaign.

Skilled campaign direction and careful planning were developing as field services in the chest movement. The standard campaign devices were used and a wide variety of benefits were staged. Football fans attending the Army-Navy and Rose Bowl games gave an estimated million dollars. By December 7 the National Association of Community Chests and Councils reported that 174 of the drives had been completed and $63,441,995 raised in these cities. Of these, 123 local committees had met or passed their goal. But more were lagging. Chest records show a total of $84,796,505 raised in 386 campaigns for 1931 and note that this sum represented 98.7 per cent of the campaign goal, though Case had earlier set the national goal at $82 million. The source of the discrepancy in these figures is not clear.

The next year, 1932, Burns, Blanchard, and their associates saw the need to broaden the appeal of the fall campaign in order to save the traditional welfare and recreational programs, such as Boy Scouts, Girl Scouts, and others. They had become alarmed at the number of long-established welfare programs being cut down by depression economizing. Burns and Blanchard were among the first to see that private giving could not cope with unemployment relief and to urge governmental action. "This irritated and angered many of our lay leaders," Blanchard recalls. "During the Depression the tremendous need for unemployment relief put terrific pressure on our local agencies and in some cities many worth-while programs were dropped. We had to head this off and thus the Mobilization for Human Needs was launched in 1932." [16]

To emphasize the need to hold the fort for the long-established programs, the National Association of Community Chests and Councils had for its convention theme that year, "Man Does Not Live by Bread Alone." The Mobilization became an annual chest campaign drive and continued until World War II and the advent of the National War Fund. The annual Mobilization was launched each year with a meeting of laymen and executives in Washington, D.C., key-noted by the President of the United States. Thus was born the now standard fund-raising fixture of a coordinated nationwide drive each fall for welfare needs. Until 1931 the timing of local drives had not been coordinated and had been spread across the calendar year (usually spring or fall)—a fact that suited the fund-raising firms very well.

Raising the desperately needed relief moneys at the local level gave the professional fund raiser the chance to keep his organization intact and at work. The firm's records show that the Jones Corporation did not suffer heavily in the depression. This organization directed relief appeals that brought in $63 million in the first three years. A competitor was driven to appeal to the emergency relief leaders to "divide the work" and not give it all to Jones. Jones, who was at the top of the fund-raising field in that period, did give employment in the emergency campaigns to a considerable number of men who had been laid off by other fund-raising firms. The magnitude of the burden of providing relief to the hapless victims of the depression can be seen in the nation's largest city where the money spent on unemployment relief rose from slightly more than $10 million in 1929 to sixteen times that sum by 1934. This is shown in Table 11. In raising the funds used by private agencies, John Price Jones and his staff played a large role. As Jones noted in a memorandum dated June 30, 1933, "the provision of food, clothing, and shelter to the destitute has been the chief task of American philanthropy during the past three years." [17]

In the fall of 1930 the Jones staff directed three emergency relief campaigns in New York City and one in Philadelphia where it had developed strong contacts through previous campaigns. In New York the Jones firm provided the direction and publicity for the drive of the Emergency Employment Committee which raised $8,518,137, or $518,137 more than the last announced goal; the appeal of the Woman's Fund Committee which had been for $400,000 brought in $590,184; and the drive of the Brooklyn Unemployment Emergency Committee which had a campaign goal of $500,000 and raised $554,231, or 110 per cent of the goal. The campaign in Philadelphia, sponsored by the Philadelphia Committee for Unemployment Relief, had a goal of $5 million, but obtained only $3,801,934, or 76.04 per cent. According to Jones's records, total cost of these four campaigns averaged only 1.43 per cent of the amount raised, "largely

TABLE 11. PRIVATE AND PUBLIC EXPENDITURES FOR UNEMPLOYMENT RELIEF, 1929–1934 [*]
Prepared by Research Bureau, Welfare Council of New York, May 16, 1935

Source	1929	1930	1931	1932	1933	1934
Private Agencies	$ 2,549,881	$ 5,289,771	$15,354,435	$18,821,275	$ 13,211,332	$ 6,016,099
Semiofficial (Mayor's Official Committee; Board Education Relief Fund)	—	361,451	2,135,606	3,689,018	2,643,250	1,850,406
Public	7,493,412	9,021,041	28,768,074	57,673,506	93,427,242	157,161,233
Totals	$10,043,293	$14,672,263	$46,258,115	$80,183,799	$109,281,824	$165,027,738

[*] *New York Times*, July 28, 1935, Sec. II, p. 2.

due to donated headquarters, space, equipment, executive and clerical assistance."

The main fund appeal of 1930 in New York was that headed by Seward Prosser of the Bankers Trust Company and sponsored by an Emergency Employment Committee of financiers and industrialists. When the drive sponsored by Prosser's committee and directed by Jones's firm opened October 15, the goal was set at $4 million— $150,000 a week to provide jobs for 10,000 men at the rate of $3 a day. It was quickly seen that this goal was too low to meet the city's need and that more could be raised, so it was first advanced to $6 million on November 5, and finally to $8 million in December. Most of the sum came from large gifts, including $1 million from the Rockefellers, $500,000 from Edward S. Harkness, and $250,000 from the Milbank Memorial Fund. This committee's work program provided relief to only a small fraction of New York's jobless. Jones probably got this assignment because he had had the Bankers Trust Company as a client in 1929.

Of this John Price Jones Corp.-managed campaign for the unemployed, Abraham Epstein wrote:

> The recent Prosser Committee drive for unemployment relief which for weeks was trumpeted on the front pages of every newspaper in New York, received almost a third of its $8,000,000 from a half dozen extraordinarily generous individuals. Contributions which in any way could be called voluntary came from less than 4,000 persons.[18]

Epstein wrote his article to assert "that private charity will be unable to cope with the [relief] problem" and to debunk "our pretentious claim to be almoners to a world which spends untold millions on self respecting social insurance." Epstein concluded, "Indeed, when we talk of caring for unemployment and drought by private philanthropy, we talk nonsense. Private philanthropy is confessedly unable to meet the present situation. . . . Under this system the burden of social ills falls almost entirely upon the few generous rich and the bulk of the poor wage earners. The bulk of the well-to-do escape entirely from paying their share."

These were the lessons learned in the 1930 drives as put in the rather formal language of one fund raiser:

1. Unemployment and starvation present a case. However, a solution, even if temporary, will strengthen such a case tremendously. Em-

ployment in the form of made work succeeded better than ordinary family relief.

2. The appeal must be emotional. Facts must be faced and conditions not minimized. Stress must be placed upon local need and need for local support, on the fact that outside aid will not be forthcoming.

3. Leadership is just as important as in any campaign. Two campaigns fell down in calibre of leadership and neither met its goal in time set. Two campaigns having sterling leadership increased their goals by 33.3 per cent and 14.3 per cent respectively.

4. A popular appeal needs publicity to focus public attention toward it. . . . The newspapers literally "ate up" all material supplied them and were constantly hungry for more. Radio time was donated and used many times a day.

5. Such an emotional appeal must be dramatized. Billboards, advertisements, leaflets, etc. with pictures having such captions as, "I don't want charity—all I want is a job," "Share your job with the jobless" . . . all aided materially.[19]

On the basis of its performance in 1930 in New York City drives, the Jones organization was retained by Harvey D. Gibson, chairman of the Emergency Unemployment Relief Committee, to direct the 1931 campaign that raised $18 million for relief in New York City. Gibson, it will be remembered, got his baptism in fund raising and welfare administration when he was called into the Red Cross War Council by Chairman Henry P. Davison to straighten out the ARC's tangled business affairs. Gibson and his committee did much to set the pattern for work relief by providing meaningful jobs. For example, he used unemployed white-collar workers to compile the first city directory New York City had had for a decade.

Of the $18 million raised in the Gibson-Jones 1931 fund appeal, it was estimated that more than $5 million came from some 7,500 "corporations and business firms." That same fall Jones men managed a campaign for the Philadelphia United Committee which raised $10,408,674. In 1932 Jones was retained to direct the Baltimore, Md., Relief Campaign, raising $1,676,213 there. Also in 1932 his firm handled the second campaign for the Emergency Unemployment Relief Committee in New York, one for the Salvation Army, and one for the Musicians' Emergency Aid which raised $238,415. The 1932 Gibson Committee—as it came to be widely known—fell far short of Gibson's ever-mounting goals, raising only $13.5 million. David Church recalls: "Those of us working on the campaign never knew what the goal was. Every time it seemed in sight Gibson would go out on his own and announce a new goal." Showing the relentless march of the depression, in 1932 corporations could give only $4.2 million to the Gibson appeal.

The Gibson Committee was disbanded in September, 1933, when governmental relief programs had taken on the task that was too large for private philanthropy. But once again private giving had provided experimentation in the field of social welfare. The Gibson Committee program was the first to establish work relief which placed the beneficiaries in the position of earning rather than receiving relief. This program was administered by William H. Matthews, described by associates in this effort as "a zealot and exceedingly courageous individual." Matthews frequently "laid down the law" to this campaign committee of bankers and industrialists. He would tell them "he was going to spend all the money he could wisely spend and they had better raise the money to meet the commitments he had made." [20]

Jones's firm directed drives for the Salvation Army in 1932 and 1933 and in these two "United Appeal" campaigns raised more than $1 million for that long-time friend of the poverty-stricken. The theme used in these appeals was "Help to Put Some One Back on His Feet." This campaign brought Jones some harsh criticism. A person signing himself only as L.B. wrote to James G. Blaine, chairman of the 1933 Salvation Army appeal:

> Dear Mr. Chairman
> The method of distributing relief in this City is to be blamed for your difficulties. The Gibson committee showed shameful preference. Relief was handed out to persons with automobiles smoking good cigars, while other suckers had to wait 14 days to get their pay. . . .
> Queens County, especially, is the victim of a rotten management under irresponsible persons led by the so-called John Price Jones Outfit, professional grafters. . . .
> P.S. In the Bronx and in Queens County twice the money could have been raised had it not been for these Price Jones grafters and their high powered salesmen. . . .[21]

The Jones firm's income held up in these depression years although its accumulated assets in securities and stocks took the beating all investments suffered. John Price Jones Corp. financial records show that in 1930 it earned a net profit from ordinary operations

of $151,845.18 but that a loss of $108,706.96 on sale of securities
and a provision for contingencies brought the net income down to
$19,533.88. As of 1930 the Jones firm held securities which cost
$468,144.35 but then had a market value of $305,533.75.[22] The next
year, 1931, the firm had a gross income of $647,685.83 and an op-
erating profit of $166,822.91. Again losses on securities brought this
down to $40,175.30.[23] In 1932 the firm earned a gross profit of
$72,176.16 and a net profit from all sources of $42,215.88. As of
January 30, 1932, the firm had accumulated assets of $436,059.92
in addition to providing Jones and his top officers with good salaries
in the depression years.[24] In 1933 the net profit before taxes had
dropped to $12,272.55 on a gross operating income of $441,282.74
reflecting the take-over of the federal government in financing relief. But in 1934 the firm had weathered the readjustment and earned
a profit of $46,642.28 and as of January 30, 1934, its assets were
valued at $525,919.98, according to the 1934 annual statement.[25]

Other fund raisers turned to depression-created tasks in order to
keep going. The impact of the depression on the work of these firms
can be seen in the tabulation of drives conducted by the American
City Bureau. In 1928 the ACB provided the direction for 35 community chest drives, 38 chamber of commerce membership drives, and
6 capital fund drives. In 1929 its accounts show 35 community chest
campaigns, 38 chamber drives, and 5 capital fund drives. In 1930,
after the depression had set in, the ACB managed 52 community
chest appeals, 23 chamber drives, and 8 capital fund drives. In 1931
its community chest accounts dropped to 36, its chamber campaigns
to 29, and its capital fund campaigns down to one church drive.
From 1933 on the American City Bureau's emphasis shifted to community chest campaigns and capital fund drives with the chamber
of commerce accounts dwindling to as low as 9 in 1933 and 10 in
1939.

The American City Bureau made an important contribution to the
work of fund raisers in the mid-thirties, with the "Unit Account
Plan for Community Chest Campaigns." This was a refinement of
the old quota system developed in the early days of fund raising
by Ward and Pierce, although American City Bureau described it
as "a revolutionary departure from traditional fund-raising practices and theories" and claimed "this plan established a procedure
through which there was achieved fair and universal support of
worthwhile causes." The basic idea was to make the giver a cam-

paigner. When the plan was formulated, the ACB explained to prospective customers: "If we agree . . . that our main objective is to secure unit consciousness of the responsibility for providing a given portion of the Community Chest fund we are attempting to raise; and if we agree, further, that the ideal unit is the business establishment or office in which the potential donor is employed, then we have automatically set up for ourselves the mechanics of our campaign. . . . We are going to appeal to all persons identified with one of these predetermined units to conduct their own campaign on behalf of the Community Chest." [26] Improvement and intensification of this unit plan carried the system of "voluntary taxation" for public welfare almost to the point of assessment on ability to pay, in the years that were to come. In 1946 ACB President James Almond could say that "practically every Community Chest of any importance in the country is using at least a limited application of our Unit Account formula which is easily the last word in fund-raising for these institutions." [27] It also brought the ACB more chest business!

Other Depression Fund Drives

There were other important and interesting developments in fund raising in the 1930's. The most spectacular and significant advance in the art of raising money from the public for philanthropy was the Roosevelt Birthday Balls and later the March of Dimes to fight polio. This story is significant enough to warrant a detailed accounting in a later chapter. The art of raising large sums by getting small dime and dollar contributions was beginning to attract the study of the professional fund raisers. At the 1933 staff conference of the John Price Jones firm, Bayard F. Pope, Jr., presented a paper "The Dime and Quarter in a Fund Raising Campaign." He concluded, "As a fund-raising device, it is felt that an effort to obtain small gifts is effective in a very limited number of types of campaigns—campaigns in which the general public is interested. This would have to be either a national or civic issue, such as 1. unemployment; 2. prohibition; 3. veterans." [28] He overlooked disease which would be the motivating force behind the lucrative nationwide dime and dollar campaigns to come. Pope did say that the dime-and-quarter campaign "can be effectively adapted to almost any type of campaign purely for its emotional appeal and publicity value." He wisely saw that seeking small gifts can "create an atmosphere of universality and obtain wide participation."

One drive failed totally in the thirties because the sponsors mistakenly assumed that publicity in itself could raise a substantial sum of money. This was the appeal for funds to create a memorial to America's beloved humorist, Will Rogers, who was killed along with his pilot, Wiley Post, in a plane crash near Point Barrow, Alaska, August 16, 1935. A few of his friends, including publicist Steve Hannagan, Texans Amon G. Carter and Jesse Jones, John W. Davis, and Will Hays, met in New York and decided to start a public fund drive that was to be "well planned spontaneity at its very best." Fund raiser Harold J. Seymour tells what happened:

> There was to be no dollar goal, no specific program on which to spend the money, no state or local quotas, and no attempt to set patterns of giving by a few pace-setting contributions. The campaign opened in September, with an announced conclusion for Thanksgiving Day. Steve Hannagan and all his associates never did a better publicity job; in newspapers, magazines, radio, and all the popular media of the day. Every bank and post office in the country was reported to have had signs at all windows for customers—"Contributions for the Will Rogers Memorial Received Here." There were state chairmen in 47 states, and 2,732 local chairmen. But on Dec. 14, 1935, after an extension of the campaign, and with 105,176 givers on the books, the total reported at national headquarters was $63,802.72. . . . Meanwhile, on the same date, despite all the free services, free space, free talent, and free radio time, the campaign expenses had been $59,716.92.[29]

Thus, despite a good cause—and an ace publicist—Steve Hannagan—the drive was a failure, amply demonstrating that a planned campaign and systematic solicitation are essentials to bring in money.

The depression caused even the staid Metropolitan Opera Company to turn to the public with an appeal for funds to keep "The Met" going. In January, 1933, its directors "with great reluctance came to the conclusion that the only salvation for the Metropolitan Opera lay in a public appeal," something unheard of in its annals. The opera company hired the John Price Jones firm and, after due consultation, it was decided to launch a public appeal for $300,000 which would enable it to plan for the 1933–1934 opera season. Because the Metropolitan Opera had always operated in an air of exclusiveness, wealth, and glamour, and in "a quiet and secretive manner," the press took keen interest in the drive and gave it wide publicity. For the Jones-directed campaign, a Committee for Saving the Metropolitan Opera was organized with opera star Lucrezia Bori as chairman. Cornelius Bliss, chairman of the opera's executive committee, and Harry W. Brown of the Jones firm directed the campaign from backstage. Jones's firm was hired for only the intensive period of the drive—from February 15 to March 29. Cornelius Bliss officially announced the appeal to the public for money to save the Metropolitan on February 26.

The campaign "was conducted much as any of our campaigns," Brown told his colleagues at John Price Jones. Three successful benefit operas were staged and an Opera Ball benefit was held, these events netting $25,200. The direct-mail appeal to known opera fans brought 1,533 contributions totaling $35,793. The Juilliard Foundation gave $50,000 and the Carnegie Foundation another $25,-000. During the campaign four operas were broadcast and the intermission periods used to appeal for money. Brown says: "Although there was evidence that radio had served as a precipitating agency in certain cases, only $8,734 could be credited to this source of appeal." [30] This is another bit of evidence to show that radio appeals, unless followed by solicitation, are not highly productive in fund raising. At the close of the Jones phase of the drive a total of $275,000 had been raised and "the balance was in sight." The Opera Ball was held on April 28 and officially closed the campaign.

A total of 5,827 gifts had brought the Met $320,256, or 106½ per cent of the announced goal. This was a public response because only 11 per cent of the subscribers came from the Metropolitan's season ticket holders. Brown reported that the cost of raising the money was only $4,656, or 1.45 per cent of the amount raised. Beyond the money raised, the opera broadcasts and the public fund appeal broadened the public's interest in the Metropolitan and brought it growing support in the years to come. "It broke down barriers of exclusiveness and secretiveness that had in the past prevented its acceptance by the general public as a civic or national institution." It is revealing that virtually every state was represented in the list of contributors.

In the latter half of this grim decade of depression and war there were multiple public fund drives for those caught in the vise of religious persecution and in the throes of civil war. With the advent of Hitler and his fiendish plan to exterminate the Jews of Germany, there came, naturally, increasing cries for help from across the Atlantic to Americans in general and Jews in particular. In 1934 a United Jewish Appeal raised $2,169,832, despite the unfavorable economic conditions. Another nationwide United Jewish Appeal was made in 1935 under the chairmanship of Felix M. Warburg. This drive was launched by a spectacular show, *The Night of Stars*, in Madison Square Garden starring Eddie Cantor, Al Jolson, and Irving Berlin. Twenty-one thousand persons attended and the show netted $45,000.[31] Of the large cities only Cleveland met its quota, but many of the 700-odd smaller communities where drives were staged did better. Even so the expectation of a return to the scale of pre-depression giving was not realized. Only $1.6 million was in hand by autumn.[32] In October, 1935, the executive committee of the United Jewish Appeal voted to discontinue the joint campaign which had been sponsored by the American Jewish Joint Distribution Committee and the American Palestine Campaign.

The people of impoverished Spain were caught up in a violent, bloody civil war in 1936 that served as prelude and testing ground for the war between totalitarianism and freedom that was to follow in 1939. The Spanish Civil War bred strong feelings in America, emotions that led to fund drives in support of both factions. The Loyalist, or democratic, forces raised a total of $1.6 million while the pro-Franco forces raised only $200,000 and this largely through the Catholic Church, which was supporting Franco. One Franco group, the American Committee for Spanish Relief, organized a spectacular pageant held at Madison Square Garden in May, 1937, that received lots of publicity but netted little cash. Fifteen thousand persons attended but of the $30,753 collected $25,793 went for expenses. The pageant created quite a stir when musician Lionel Hampden withdrew from the show at the last minute after discovering its partisan nature.

Merle Curti thinks that the poor showing of Franco groups in raising money here "can be attributed in part to the fact that the Nationalist agencies relied chiefly on the Church's established mechanisms for collecting money, agencies already burdened with commitments to Catholic charities. It also appears, however, that there was truth in the frequent complaints of the hierarchy and of the Catholic press that the laity was not responding in sufficient numbers or with 'proper generosity' to the Nationalist relief agencies."[33] Whatever the underlying reasons, the fact remains that the Loyalist forces raised eight times as much money by reliance on the modern fund-appeal techniques. This story of fund raising for aid abroad is told in Curti's *American Philanthropy Abroad.*

All along the fund-raising front the task grew tougher and the methods of the professional tighter, in those depression years. Year in, year out the fund-raising campaign depends quite heavily on the large, wealthy donor for the bulk of its funds and these were the persons hit hardest by the nation's economic collapse in 1929. John Price Jones told his fellow fund raisers in 1935 that these people of property and wealth "who must contribute at least 60 per cent of the money" were giving less because of "political uncertainty and economic pressure," and they were giving "more critically, thoughtfully, and with greater discrimination." The result, Jones said, "has been that fund-raising has become more difficult." [34]

This increased resistance by the larger giver "made it all the more necessary to present the strongest facts." Jones emphasized that it was necessary for the fund-raising director to prepare better and to pinpoint his appeal to the large donor because of this increased resistance and "the increasing competition of charitable agencies." All of this, Jones admitted, was causing fund-raising costs to go up. And radio was no new, cheap way to raise funds either. Jones concluded, "Fund raisers have found, too, that they cannot raise substantial sums over the radio." As the number of drives multiplied in the depression years, as charity drives were imposed on top of the regular drives of long standing, the fund raiser found it harder and harder to recruit workers. Jones said, "The fact simply must be faced that by and large people work on campaigns not so much because they love the various causes represented as because they respond to the influence of adequate leadership." John Price Jones was never misty-eyed in his approach to raising money.

Though as an ardent conservative Republican who yielded to no man in hating "that man in the White House," Jones took cognizance of the growing demand of citizens that many of the services long unevenly or inadequately supported by voluntary gifts be taken over by the government. More and more the solicitor of funds was hearing, "Why doesn't the government do this?" As Jones wrote in 1937, "The remarkable growth of the community-chest idea shows that public opinion favors consolidation of social welfare service, elimination of duplication both in service and appeals, and economy in administration." He added, "At this point the depression brought only social gain, for in places our private social welfare structure was topheavy." [35]

A Jones executive, A. C. Gumbrecht, took another look at the impact of the depression on fund raising in 1936 and came to these conclusions:

1. Obviously, the decrease in the amounts of large gifts means that a broader basis of support for any campaign is essential if it is to be successful.
2. Greater stress must accordingly be placed on long-term cultivation of interest through educational programs designed to develop interest in those prospects not previously interested, and to strengthen the interest of an institution's casual or older friends.
3. In any such long-term program, "participation" as a successful fund-raising fundamental becomes most important.
4. Greater care must be taken insofar as the larger givers are concerned to determine interests and attitudes so as to make the most effective appeal along the avenue of least resistance.
5. Insofar as possible the services of the institution should be interpreted in terms of their relationship to solution of the problems of the day. Existing economic conditions have broadened the humanitarian basis of philanthropic support.[36]

Legal Gate Opened for Corporate Philanthropy

One of the significant, far-reaching developments in American fund raising in the depression years was the governmental green light given to corporate contributions to philanthropy by the passage of the 1935 Revenue Code with its 5 per cent deductibility clause. By 1960—a quarter century later—American corporations were giving some $400 million to philanthropic causes each year, dollars given to obtain public good will and to create a favorable opinion climate for the corporation's operations. The big spurt in giving came in the prosperous years after World War II when American corporations accepted the public relations doctrine lock, stock, and barrel. Corporate gifts to public causes increased twelvefold from 1940 to 1958, from $38 million to $395 million.

In the postwar years, 1945–1960, corporation executives and their public relations counselors talked much of "serving the public interest" and "playing the role of good corporate citizen" and many supported their platitudes with philanthropy. The Rockefeller

Foundation financed the Hamlin study, published in 1961, which predicted that corporate giving would reach the annual mark of $750 million by 1975, but the same year Richard Eells, an authority on the subject, was predicting that corporate giving "will probably level off to something like a half billion dollars a year." In any event the corporate portion of public philanthropy is important and highly influential because of its absolute size and because of the strings attached to many corporate gifts. With its increasing largess, the corporation inevitably influences institutions it supports. Today the corporate gift committee is a prime target for the fund raiser.

Corporate philanthropy may be traced to the late nineteenth century when the railroads began to support the railroad YMCAs, created initially to provide housing and wholesome recreation for their transient workers. The first organization of men into a railroad YMCA was begun in Cleveland in 1872. By 1890 associations had been organized at eighty-two divisional and terminal points and in every case the railroads were contributing financial support. Andrews records, "A usual practice at this stage was for railroad corporations to pay about 60 per cent of the operating budgets . . . the employees making up the remainder." [37] By 1911 there were 230 railroad Ys but the ratio of support had been just about reversed. Railroad owners soon realized that the employee welfare services being proffered by the burgeoning YMCA movement were a good investment. Hopkins, who recorded the history of the Y movement, says, "The Y.M.C.A. thus completely allied itself with the employing class in a paternalistic service to workers," and consequently, in his opinion, "The American Y.M.C.A. had always a bad conscience about the industrial worker." [38]

One of the first to see the Y's value to railroads was Cornelius Vanderbilt, Jr., who first granted use of a clubroom in his new Grand Central Station and then, in 1888, provided a building at Madison Avenue and 45th Street costing $225,000 for New York Central employees. "When the status of the railroad associations was reviewed by Col. John J. McCook of the Santa Fe before the Jubilee Convention in 1901, they were well on their way to becoming a Y.M.C.A.-managed company welfare program." [39] A like result follows many corporate contributions to philanthropy today. Corporations and business firms generally became, as American philanthropy developed in the pre-World War I years, large contributors to YMCA capital fund drives and to local charity campaigns.

With America's entry into World War I and the resulting patriotic fervor, there came more intense pressure on the corporation to contribute to wartime causes. Yet, as recorded in an earlier chapter, corporation officials were genuinely troubled as to whether they had a right to give stockholders' profits to any cause, however noble. Most corporations, guided by their cautious legal advisers, held that they could not safely make a contribution to the American Red Cross or a like cause without express stockholder consent. It was to get around this difficulty that the Red Cross had suggested its Dividend Plan which did not prove highly effective. In the first war drive the Red Cross sent the following form to corporations who held they had no legal right to give stockholders' dividends to any cause. This issue was to be legally tested in 1951. The form letter and dividend order the Red Cross prepared for corporations to use in getting contributions follow:

FORM OF LETTER FROM CORPORATION TO ITS STOCKHOLDERS

Dear Sir:

The Board of Directors at a meeting held the   day of   , 1917, passed a resolution, copy of which is enclosed.

On May 11, 1917, President Wilson appointed a War Council of the Red Cross and it is under the direction of this War Council, and by proclamation of the President, that a nation wide campaign is to be conducted during the week of June 18 to June 25, for the purpose of raising a very large sum of money for the American Red Cross War Fund.

Your Board of Directors adopted the aforesaid resolution for the purpose of enabling every stockholder of this Company to share with it in a joint contribution to this cause. The destruction of property and the injury to business throughout the world on account of the War need not be here emphasized, as it has been vividly described in the press and from the platform. It is apparent that every interest in this country should exert itself to the utmost in the alleviation of suffering and in aiding in the rebuilding of the social and business structure upon the ruins caused by the War.

The plan described in the resolution was adopted in order to enable the stockholders and the corporation together to help to swell the Red Cross War Fund in a way devoid of any criticism. Many corporations in England and Canada have, during the War, contributed directly from their funds to the Red Cross and similar purposes. This plan permits of a joint effort through the medium of the corporation, which it is hoped will be welcomed by all.

Let me urge that every stockholder sign the enclosed dividend order and return it to the office of the Corporation, No.
Street,   , immediately.

Yours respectfully,

President

SPECIAL RED CROSS DIVIDEND ORDER FOR USE ONLY IN CONNECTION WITH DIVIDEND OF   Date.

TO BE SENT TO ALL STOCKHOLDERS FOR RECEIPT BY THEM ON JUNE 23RD, OR AS SOON THEREAFTER AS POSSIBLE.

To the Treasurer of   Corporation:
The undersigned stockholder of   Corporation hereby consents and directs that the extra Red Cross Dividend declared by the Corporation on the   day of   , 1917, payable to the undersigned as such stockholder, be turned over and paid to the American Red Cross War Fund

Name_____

Address _____

Note: Under arrangements made with the Red Cross it is understood that the Corporation shall be authorized to enroll every stockholder whose share of such extra dividend exceeds $1, and who signs a dividend order as above, as an annual member in the American Red Cross for the period of one year.[40]

Some 150 corporations declared such Red Cross dividends, collecting $17,948,969.[41] Most of the dividend gifts were set at 1 per cent of the par value of the stock; others at the sum of 15 to 50 cents per share. Many corporations gave directly. (As recorded earlier, despite doubts of legality, the General Electric Company gave $1 million to the first Red Cross drive in June, 1917, and that this was followed by gifts of $1.5 million from Anaconda Copper, $600,000 from Bethlehem Steel, and 5,000 Model T cars from Henry Ford.) No detailed records of this first Red Cross drive are available and thus it is not possible to say what portion of the total came from corporations. As the wartime pressure to give mounted and the number of drives increased, more corporations threw legal caution to the winds and gave money. In the November, 1917, YMCA drive, Chairman Elbert H. Gary announced that the United States Steel Corporation would give $500,000 and Standard Oil was reported in the press to have given $250,000.

Valid records on corporate contributions to the drives of World War I are not available but press reports indicate that they were substantial. Andrews thinks, for instance, that "it is quite possible that corporations contributed as much as $20 million to the second Y.M.C.A. drive." [42] Williams and Croxton assert: "To these national war service funds of 1917 and 1918 as well as to the local war chests, corporations contributed generously. Unlike the pre-war federations, however, the war service appeals had not only an appeal to the entire community, but they had a tested money-raising technique. This was the intensively organized campaign." [43] Thus, in the view of these pioneer students of corporate philanthropy, the Ward-Pierce short-term drive had much to do with the first sizable corporate gifts to public causes, clearly indicated in Table 7.

Thus the role of businessmen in promoting the community chest movement in the post-World War I years made these donors better able to control the welfare programs in their communities and, with authority, insist on "businesslike" administration of charity agencies. Corporations played a strong role in the expansion of community chests because, as Andrews notes, "chests were excellently suited to many of the conditions of corporate giving." In 1925—on the eve of the depression—22 per cent of the money raised by 129 community chests studied by Williams and Croxton came from corporations. These chests raised $58,801,872 in 1929 and $12,954,769 of it was given by incorporated business firms. There were some 322 chests in existence in the United States in 1929 and these chests raised a total of $70,320,427 that year according to the records of the National Association of Community Chests and Councils. Williams and Croxton could get accurate records on 13 chests for each year of the 1920–1929 decade. "Over the ten-year period the budgets of these 13 chests increased 14.9 per cent, the number of corporate contributions has grown from 2,652 to 5,127 or 93.3 per cent, and the amount contributed by corporations has increased 10.4 per cent from $2,535,819 to $2,799,192." [44]

Corporations also gave, in increasing numbers and increasing amounts, to YMCA, college, and hospital fund drives in the twenties, and to special causes too. Williams and Croxton were able to identify gifts totaling $1.5 million as corporation contributions out of the some $4.5 million Americans gave Japan in 1923 after that country's devastating earthquake. These gifts represented some 34 per cent of the amount raised in that nationwide campaign. Corporate officials and employees usually provided the direction and manpower for the annual community chest campaign and in other fund-raising drives as well. The growing number of corporate publicity men were often used in these drives. Yet the Williams and Croxton study clearly shows that in the prosperous year of 1929 corporate giving was at a low level. Nonetheless, the corporation was the mainstay of the community chest. This is shown in a general summary of corporation support received by community chests (Table 12).[45]

TABLE 12. SUMMARY OF ALL CONTRIBUTIONS AND OF CORPORATION CONTRIBUTIONS TO ALL COMMUNITY CHESTS STUDIED, 1920–1929

Year	No. of chests	Total amount contributed	Amount of non-corporation contributions	Amount of corporation contributions	Per cent of total amt. from corporations	Number of corporation contributions
1920	13	$10,654,941	$ 8,119,122	$ 2,535,819	23.8	2,652
1921	22	12,143,537	9,327,554	2,815,983	23.2	4,667
1922	29	15,796,696	12,662,562	3,134,134	19.8	6,759
1923	49	23,234,874	18,258,913	4,975,961	21.4	10,819
1924	73	35,390,361	27,679,153	7,711,208	21.8	17,219
1925	94	41,354,365	32,312,353	9,042,012	21.9	21,873
1926	109	48,343,599	37,586,260	10,757,339	22.3	26,335
1927	119	52,053,112	40,037,890	12,015,222	23.1	30,301
1928	124	54,556,718	42,290,868	12,265,850	22.5	31,978
1929	129	58,801,872	45,847,103	12,954,769	22.0	33,977

With the onset of the depression the pressure on the corporations to give to the needy intensified as their ability to give declined. How well they responded is not known. There are no reliable records on corporate giving from 1929, when Williams and Croxton completed their study, until the beginning of government statistics on corporate gifts in 1936. The National Association of Community

Chests and Councils did not keep as careful records then as the organization does today. As welfare and charitable agencies tried, albeit feebly, to cope with the staggering demands for food, shelter, and clothing, undoubtedly intense pressure was applied to the corporations which had provided about one-fifth of community chest budgets over the previous decade. Community chest collections rose from $73 million in 1929 to $101 million in 1932, but then as the depression deepened the contributions fell back to $78 million in 1933. Undoubtedly much of this decline was due to the continued downward spiral of business income. Then in December, 1934, another heavy blow was struck at all publicly supported institutions in general and at the struggling community chests in particular when the United States Supreme Court affirmed a government ruling that a corporate contribution to a community chest was not deductible as a business expense. This ruling came in the Old Mission Portland Cement case.

The legal right of corporations to give to philanthropic causes never had been perfectly clear. Certainly there was no federal authority expressly granting corporation directors the right to give away stockholders' money. Corporate officers had long been conscious of the legal dictum, "Charity has no business to sit at boards of directors *qua* charity," that had originated in England in 1883. Because corporations are chartered by states, it was there they sought legal permission when World War I brought heavy pressure on them to give to war drives. As early as 1917 Texas passed permissive legislation, with New York following in 1918, Illinois in 1919, Ohio in 1920. Most states now have such legislation, that is, legislation which does not prohibit a corporation's making gifts to charitable causes. But Andrews, writing in 1951, said: "The laws differ widely in their provisions, and a final question may remain in some states as to whether they apply to corporations chartered before the respective dates of enactment." [46]

Under federal tax law, corporate giving had developed on the theory that the corporation had a right to spend money on local charities because the benefits of these charities accrued to the corporation's employees and to the welfare of the business itself. The right had been based on Treasury rulings and court decisions, not on any laws passed by Congress. In fact Congress had rejected such a proposal in 1918. As Justice Harlan Fiske Stone wrote in the

opinion in this landmark case—*Old Mission Portland Cement Co.
v. Helvering, Commissioner of Internal Revenue:*

The privilege of deducting charitable donations from gross income,
conferred on individual taxpayers by Para. 214 (a) of Revenue Acts
of 1921, 1924, and 1926 has not been extended to corporations. A proposal to extend it to them was rejected by Congress pending the
passage of the Revenue Act of 1918. (*Congressional Record*, House,
Vol. 56, Part 10, 10426–10428.) Section 234 (a) of Revenue Acts of
1921, 1924, and 1926 authorizes corporations to deduct from gross
income "all the ordinary and necessary business expenses paid or incurred during the taxable year in carrying on any trade or business."
Article 562 of the Treasury Regulation 62, interpretative of the 1921
Act, declared that corporations were not entitled to deduct charitable
donations. But it recognized the right to deduct donations "made by a
corporation for purposes connected with the operation of its business
. . . when limited to charitable institutions, hospitals, or educational
institutions conducted for the benefit of its employees, and also donations which legitimately represent a consideration for a benefit flowing
directly to the corporation as an incident of its business." These provisions were retained without substantial change, in the regulations
promulgated under the 1924, 1926, and 1928 Acts.[47]

Corporate giving had developed under the limited authority of
Treasury rulings and liberal interpretation of them by Internal Revenue officials when suddenly Commissioner Guy T. Helvering low-
ered the boom by ruling that the Old Mission firm's contribution
to the San Francisco Community Chest was not "for the benefit of
the donor's employees." The company, at the urging of community
chest officials, appealed the ruling. The commissioner's ruling was
affirmed by the Board of Tax Appeals and the Court of Appeals for
the Ninth Circuit of United States courts,[48] and then appealed to
the United States Supreme Court. The high court upheld the lower
court by ruling that "It is a question of fact in each case whether
a donation is made to an institution conducted for the benefit of
the donor's employees or is a consideration for a benefit flowing
directly to the donor" and then asserting that determination of fact
is a matter for Internal Revenue officials, not the courts.

Commissioner Helvering had ruled in the Old Mission case that
gifts of petitioner were made in the belief that "they resulted in
good will toward the petitioner and increased its business." In so

ruling the commissioner muddled corporate giving policies and threw the community chest officials into despair. By the 1930's it was the general practice to pool charity contributions in a central chest and this decision ruled out corporations as general contributors. They could still, presumably, give to a hospital used by their employees but could no longer get a tax deduction for contributions to the organized philanthropies of the community. This new and stricter interpretation of the law was a severe blow to the community chest movement. Quickly there began an almost endless series of conferences, correspondence, and phone calls in and out of community chest headquarters in New York as Allen T. Burns took the lead in planning a campaign to get legal authority for corporate giving. Unless this could be obtained, Burns saw a bleak future for community chests. He asserted that "resentment has been growing over the discrimination against [corporations] in taxing their *pro bono publico* expenditure and it is becoming increasingly difficult to persuade them to make liberal contributions." [49]

Burns and his associates saw their chance to act when President Roosevelt, early in 1935, asked Congress for new tax laws. They persuaded Senator Walter F. George of Georgia and Representative John W. McCormack of Massachusetts to introduce a measure which would legalize corporate contributions and make them deductible up to 5 per cent of the corporation's net income. The bill was introduced on July 12. Two days earlier, Frederick R. Kellogg, president of the National Association of Community Chests and Councils, had pleaded with the House Ways and Means Committee: "Private philanthropy has had a progressively more difficult task to hold up its end of the national charitable responsibility during the depression. . . . Private charity cannot carry on without the help of the corporation to which it has become accustomed. When this help amounts to between $15,000,000 and $20,000,000 in 400 of our American cities, it is clear why Community Chests and Councils—the representative of private charities in these 400 cities —feels the necessity for doing its utmost to remove the barrier against continuing corporate generosity. The sum that the Treasury would lose in taxes is nothing compared with Treasury expense if private giving is not encouraged to resume in its old time terms." [50] Kellogg suffered a paralytic stroke the day after he testified and died a month later.

As the chest officials moved to mobilize public support for corporate giving they were dealt another heavy blow when President Roosevelt issued a withering blast at the proposed tax exemption for corporate gifts to charity. Roosevelt told his July 24 press conference that "Granting the exemption from profits thus contributed would mean the sanctioning of two unsound practices. First, the purchase of goodwill by corporations, and, second, the authority of corporate officials to exercise a right in bestowing gifts that belong properly to the individual stockholders in the corporation." [51] In effect, in the view of Walter Lippmann, "the President of the United States had declared that corporate contributions were immoral." [52] Yet the President conceded that "many arguments in favor of encouraging corporate gifts to charities were based on humanitarian purposes and particularly that Y.M.C.A.'s and similar organizations in small cities benefited by contributions from industry which in turn were thus saved the expense of providing recreational facilities for their own employees."

But the President went on to point out: "On the other side of the picture was the fact that corporate gifts to charity were made to obtain goodwill. He referred to an unnamed power company in a Southern state whose president he quoted as having told him [F.D.R.] that agents of the company were ordered to see that the company made the first contribution to all charity drives conducted in cities and towns in that state." [53] The President pointed out to the press that the George-McCormack bill allowed up to 5 per cent and that on this basis a person deriving an income of $5,000 in dividends could have $250 given to charity without having any say in the matter.

F.D.R.'s barbed shafts struck home. The National Association of Community Chests and Councils immediately issued a protest and again told the public that corporations were giving some $20 million to social agencies in 417 cities and asserted that "to discriminate against corporate gifts would be against the keystone of support for private social agencies." The *New York Times* supported the chests in an editorial on July 26 in which this powerful voice asserted: "Granting this exemption would doubtless stimulate the flow of funds so badly needed if private philanthropy is to be kept alive." The *Times* of July 27 reported a "mixed reaction" in Congress to Roosevelt's statement. Representative Robert Doughton, venerable chairman of the tax-writing House Ways and Means Committee, indicated no serious consideration was being given the 5 per cent proposal when he was queried by reporters after the President's press conference.

Allen T. Burns, Gerard C. Swope, president of General Electric and chairman of the Three Cs 1935 Mobilization for Human Needs drive, and Newton D. Baker, Wilsonian Democrat and long-time promoter of the chest movement, joined forces to stimulate pressure on Congress from business leaders and chest supporters in the 417 cities then served by community chests. Three days after F.D.R.'s blast the *Times* was predicting a floor fight in the House on the George-McCormack measure as "scores of Congress members continued to receive letters from individuals and charitable organizations urging the exemption." Burns persuaded Swope to appeal directly to the President. Swope was able to get a promise from Roosevelt that he would not veto the 1935 revenue bill if it did contain the 5 per cent clause. Beyond this F.D.R. would not go, Swope reported to Burns.[54] In 1947 the National Association of Community Chests and Councils gave their first Red Feather Award to Swope for his "outstanding service." On this occasion Swope recalled that "I was introduced to the Community Chests by Newton Baker." The industrialist served as chairman of the National Mobilization for Human Needs in 1935 and 1936, took the lead in organizing the National War Fund in 1943, and was the first chairman of the Three Cs National Health and Welfare Retirement Association.

Baker had, as mayor of Cleveland, promoted the first community chest and as Secretary of War had forced the first nationwide united fund campaign. Now in 1935 he once more played an influential role in American philanthropy. He worked on his conservative friends in Congress to gain support for the measure and got it written into the tax bill in the House. As honorary president of the National Association of Community Chests and Councils, he testified before the Senate Finance Committee on August 1 in support of the 5 per cent exemption. In this session he encountered opposition from two powerful Democratic senators, Alben Barkley of Kentucky and Tom Connally of Texas. At the same hearing Secretary of the Treasury Henry Morgenthau, Jr., refused to take a stand on any provision of the pending revenue bill, including the

5 per cent clause. In announcing Baker's appearance, Burns said Baker "was associated in the administration of the 1935 Mobilization for Human Needs." The Burns-Swope-Baker campaign succeeded. With justification, Ralph Blanchard claims the Three Cs were "100 per cent responsible for the 5 per cent deduction."

The House of Representatives amended the 1935 revenue bill to include the George-McCormack provision permitting corporations to deduct up to 5 per cent of net income for philanthropy before passing the measure on to the Senate. The Senate passed the bill on August 14 and from there it went to joint conference and was finally passed August 24, 1935. President Roosevelt, keeping his promise to Swope, signed the measure into law on August 30, 1935, a historic date in the chronicles of fund raising and philanthropy. The law became effective January 1, 1936. A later Treasury interpretation of the 5 per cent clause held that "Under the 1935 Act, corporations are permitted to deduct from gross income contributions or gifts made within the taxable year to or for use of a domestic corporation, trust, community chest, fund, or foundation exclusively operated for religious, charitable, scientific, literary, or educational purposes to an amount not in excess of 5 per cent of the corporation's net income." Thus began the modern and meaningful role of the corporate giver.

By and large business firms were slow to take advantage of this new legal right to give stockholders' money to charitable causes. One result of the law was to provide statistics on corporate giving in so far as such gifts are reported for purposes of tax exemption. The immediate effect was not dramatic, for reported contributions averaged only $30 million annually for the years 1936 through 1939. Corporate philanthropy did not loom large in American fund raising until World War II when, under wartime pressures and stimulated by heavy excess profits taxes, corporate officials moved into philanthropy on a much larger scale. As a matter of fact, only in one year since the 1935 revenue law was passed—1945—has corporate giving exceeded 1 per cent of corporate net profits—quite a long way from the 5 per cent ceiling. Corporate giving to philanthropy from 1936 through World War II is shown in Table 13.[55]

Corporate givers now had the green light from the federal government. They were to be reminded of this with increasing frequency by fund raisers.

TABLE 13

Year	Net corporate income before taxes (millions)	Tax exempt corporate expenditures for charitable, educational, etc., purposes (millions)	Expenditures as per cent of net income before taxes
1936	$ 7,356	$ 30	0.41
1937	7,387	33	0.45
1938	3,700	27	0.73
1939	6,766	31	0.46
1940	8,957	38	0.42
1941	16,391	58	0.35
1942	23,150	98	0.42
1943	27,978	159	0.57
1944	26,538	234	0.88
1945	21,405	266	1.24
1946	25,407	214	0.84
1947	31,663	241	0.76
1948	33,900	239	0.70

Backlash of Criticism

Elmer Davis, though the most articulate and biting, was not the only critic of the expertly led fund-raising campaign using the methods of "organized nagging." As the expert's methods were perfected and polished, the criticism mounted in corresponding ratio. Evidence of a deepening resentment of what John Price Jones called the "scientific method of raising funds" began to appear in the mid-twenties and has grown into the crescendo of criticism of the never-ending list of money appeals we hear so frequently today. Edward S. Martin, writing in *Harper's* "The Easy Chair," decried "an over-development of that great industry of raising money by drives and campaigns and organizations for purposes which the organizers and drivers believe to be good may come—if it runs to excess—to be open to the same objection which concerns the diffusion of the funds of the taxpayers. It may take away from the givers whom it reaches the ability to give their own funds to objects they think about and care about." [56] Martin proved himself a poor prophet by asserting that "When these great ebullitions of

money raising go out of style," the lack of choice in one's philanthropic gifts would be one of the reasons.

Martin wrote:

> The process of getting it [money]—the mechanism—is so perfectly
> understood, so systematized, organized, and lubricated that a new busi-
> ness has come into being: that of conducting financial campaigns to
> raise money. . . .
>
> No doubt most readers get in the mail suggestions to subscribe for
> this or that. . . . In larger centers of population such suggestions
> come daily by handfuls to anyone suspected of ability to give. . . .
> When one opens one of the appeals he finds some familiar and re-
> spected name at the bottom of it and usually a row of other highly
> respectable names set down elsewhere. Suppose the name is signed
> Henry Bolton, and suppose we have heard of Henry Bolton as a rich
> and generous philanthropist. We read the name and we see Henry
> Bolton in our mind's eye. We do see him; that is the magic of it;
> but it is getting to be, nowadays, that we also see something else—an
> office building somewhere; a large room full of girls operating type-
> writers and duplicating machines; somebody with a rubber stamp
> being "Henry Bolton." Of course that is the way it is done, the way
> it has to be done on the scale that obtains nowadays. . . . But how
> long can it be kept up? How long can the magic of the rubber stamp
> continue to bring in money? [57]

We now know that the magic of the rubber stamp still works
for causes both good and bad.

Actually the professional fund raiser took a dim view of mail
solicitation for funds; he preferred the direct confrontation of the
selected prospect. Charles Sumner Ward said, in 1926: "Mail order
appeals . . . are justified only in calling in contributions from those
who have subscribed regularly in the past. I make an exception in
the case of the tuberculosis Christmas Seal campaign and perhaps
one or two others. But in the main the postage stamp symbolizes
excessive cost in benevolence, ranging from 50 per cent for large
and worthy campaigns to 100 per cent for smaller ones. The man
who will respond to a mail-order appeal, excepting for a cause with
which he is intimately familiar, belongs to Easy Mark Lodge." [58]
Yet today Easy Mark Lodge still has a large membership.

There was also growing criticism of the "high cost of giving." Crissey wrote:

> From the viewpoint of the professional philanthropist, the high cost of giving is the little joker that takes the joy out of generosity and leaves the intending benefactor cold, suspicious, and irritated. With some exceptions, benevolence of all kinds is subjected to a heavy overhead and selling expense before it can distribute a dividend in the coin of actual charity or helpfulness.
>
> A man who has spent more than a quarter of a century investigating solicitors in this field, and the causes and institutions for which their appeals were made, assures me that not one-half the money given charity reaches the ultimate consumers. In his opinion about 60 per cent of this rich harvest from the soil of human generosity is absorbed by the thrifty gleaners.[59]

As we have indicated before, arriving at accurate costs for fund raising campaigns is tricky and difficult. For many of the mail type of charity campaigns Crissey's source could have been correct. For the large capital fund drives of the 1920's, as managed by those new gleaners, the costs of raising money were far less. This was seen in the Johns Hopkins campaign, for example. In 1952 a John Price Jones officer took a look at campaign costs from the 1920's on:

> In the 1920s, it would have cost a client about $35,000 to raise one million dollars, or about 3½ per cent of the amount raised. Today it would cost him from $75,000 up. That's quite an increase, but still this figure compares favorably with the costs of many current non-John Price Jones campaigns, most of which—on the same basis—would need budgets of at least $120,000.
>
> Putting it another way, this means that for every dollar spent on a Jones campaign, thirteen dollars come back in contributions. . . . Where does the money go? If the total cost of a campaign is, say $100,-000, then we might find our major costs breaking down like this: Professional fee, $30,000; general office salaries, $20,000; printing, $10,-000; rent and maintenance, $6,000; lettershop work, $4,000—or about 70 per cent of the total cost. Sub-technical men, too, are frequently hired to do organization or publicity work on some of the larger campaigns. The cost of their services ranges from 10 to 20 per cent of the total cost.
>
> . . . Looking at the cost figures over the past 25 years, we find that the company's fee as a percentage of total cost is less today than it

was in the twenties, having dropped from 46% to 30% of the total cost. In relation to the amount raised, the professional fee has gone up slightly from 1½% to 2⅓% of the amount raised. In the main increases in the company's professional fees have lagged well behind the general trend of prices.[60]

Crissey made another criticism in the mid-twenties that has reverberated down the years becoming ever more valid and shrill. "According to men who advise the rich regarding their philanthropic investments, a great many charities don't know when to die; they have outlived their usefulness owing to changed public conditions, but persist because they have called into being an organization of human beings who hate to give up their jobs." [61] This critics have said of the National Foundation's course, for example, after the Salk vaccine had been perfected.

As we have indicated, colleges and universities were the major users of the fund raiser's sharpened skills and those first to feel the hot breath of Alma Mater's solicitor were the alumni. This led to what Arnaud C. Marts has termed an "alumni revolt." In 1960, looking back across forty years of money raising, Marts recalled that the giving public, in three separate decades, had rebelled against fund raising.

> The first time was in the mid-1920s when hundreds of colleges took up the new campaign methods with a rush and all over the land began to pressure their alumni to "pay their debt to *alma mater*." Too little was said to the alumni about the greater and nobler service their alma mater could render mankind if she were supported more generously. And too much was said about the fact that alma mater had given them an education below cost and that they should now pay up. This worked well enough once, but when alma mater made a big point of the same debt a few years later in a second appeal to the same alumni, some cynicism and resentment resulted.[62]

Alumni were not the only ones to question these multiplying drives in the 1920's to "sell" higher education and raise capital funds thereby. Other voices were raised to protest the pressure of these fund drives and to question whether this broadened, enlarged support of higher education was a good thing or not. Dr. Henry S. Pritchett, a former president of the Massachusetts Institute of Technology and a long-time president of the Carnegie Foundation, in his report in 1923 decried this intensive promotion of higher education in these words:

> All giving, like all accomplishments intended for human betterment, cuts more than one way. Oftentimes the byproducts of giving to a good cause result in social toxins which do enough harm to more than counteract the benefits that may come from the original gift. . . .
> . . . One such byproduct is an overemphasis on going to college. As a result we have today an army of youth pressing into the colleges so great that the colleges cannot deal with them efficiently. . . .
> Another byproduct has been a tendency to transform the American college president into a soliciting agent. Scholarly men today hesitate to take the place of college president, and they may well do so, because today the typical board of trustees is not seeking a scholarly president; it is seeking a president who can get money.

Pritchett was not only unduly pessimistic about the ability of the nation's colleges to provide better education for more and more young people but proved himself a poor prophet in this same report when he expressed doubt "whether a science or even an art of public giving can be developed." History has recorded the results in both instances.

Letters to the editor do not accurately reflect public opinion but they do reveal the flotsam of discontent in the stream of public opinion. The hard-hitting drive Lyman Pierce staged for the University of Minnesota in 1922–23 brought a typical complaint to the editor of the Minneapolis *Star* signed A.L., St. Michael, Minn., and said:

> In the last few years we have had drives galore; liberty bond drives, charity drives, church fund drives, Rockefeller church going drives, poppy drives, and liberty drives. "Drive" is a good word and well describes the procedure. . . .
> In these drives there must be drivers, professional drivers. These drivers are in a class all their own. . . . Parasites, all, of course, these drivers are individuals that don't work and that won't work. . . . Why did this Y.M.C.A. driver light on this section of the country to conduct a stadium drive? Will someone explain that? And why a stadium drive? . . . Let light be shed on this stadium drive, ere we submit to being plucked or shorn.

Pierce, of course, had heard similar complaints years before in Australia. He would hear them again many times before his career as a professional fund raiser ended with his death on the eve of World War II, and so would others.

One of the fund raiser's prime assets was the compilation of lists of givers to charitable causes. A consequence of these lists was that the same donors were selected for pressure in campaign after campaign. In due time many rebelled. One was Mrs. Bayard James, New York City, who wrote John Price Jones on December 18, 1936, as follows:

> As a member of Mr. [Walter S.] Gifford's Committee I have seen the list of "prospects" prepared for the C.O.S. Campaign.
>
> I should like to ask why it is that my 1936 contribution of $7500. to the Citizens Family Welfare Committee which I specified was to be anonymous is listed under my name?
>
> I should also like to inquire how your firm obtained the fictitious figures which have been listed . . . in the case of myself, of my mother, Mrs. W. Bayard Cutting, and of my niece, the Marchesa Origo. . . .
>
> Meanwhile, will you kindly see that these three entries are removed from all existing and future lists prepared by your organization? [63]

Jones replied apologetically to Mrs. James in a letter dated December 22, 1936, saying that "the basic principle behind the preparation of our lists is to collect and post on prospect cards only gift information which is a matter of public record and on which there has been no restriction. . . . There is no question regarding our mistake here as your gift was clearly marked anonymous. . . ." [64]

Jones's response brought another letter from Mrs. James reflecting the rich donor's growing exasperation with the systematic pressuring stemming from the professional fund raiser. In a letter dated January 19, 1937, she wrote:

> . . . I hope that my having called these particular matters to your attention may result in greater care in the future on the part of your staff because I believe some of them (in their zeal for raising funds) are not always as scrupulous as you would wish them to be, either in their methods of obtaining information or in their respect for the wishes of contributors. I say this because of past experience. Each year, since the first EURC [Emergency United Relief Campaign] campaign, I have protested at my anonymous gifts having been listed and each time have been told that "Anonymity" applied only to press reports. . . .

The John Price Jones Corporation has contributed so much to the

welfare of New York during these difficult years by its effective
fund-raising methods that it has attained a position of unique importance in the community. Anything that lessened its continued usefulness would be deplored by all thoughtful people. Yet for some time
I have questioned whether the high-pressure methods used might not
eventually prove a boomerang which could defeat their purpose. I
myself have nearly reached the conclusion that henceforth I must
refuse to contribute to any "drive" conducted by or with the help
of the John Price Jones Corporation. . . .

To my mind the chief danger of the present system is that it
penalizes generosity. An individual makes a contribution, which is
perhaps out of all proportion to his income and which may have been
taken out of capital, is from that time on the victim of practically
every money seeking agency in the City. The (to me) dreadful publicity of your lists; the fact they are used by so many agencies and
by thousands of individuals; the method of grading prospects on varied
color lists, according to the amount of previous contributions, and
your instructions to workers to base their demands upon the amount
of such contributions, plus the insistence of a personal interview or
at least a telephone call, creates a situation which is practically intoler-
able for the person of a moderate or even a large income, provided
such person has a sense of civic responsibility. . . .

. . . since the first Emergency Unemployment Relief Committee
drive, the volume of appeals has steadily increased, until now it is well
nigh overwhelming. It takes over an hour a day merely to open the
mail and glance at—far less digest and consider them. To answer them
requires the greater part of a secretary's time; if one does not answer
the "follow-up" system comes into play and one is hounded by telephone calls, and by letters, the tone of which is often . . . objection-
able.

In addition to the mail appeals, there are now the members of your
competing teams with their "assignments" who telephone for appointments; the calls themselves are a nuisance and time consuming;
further, it is impossible to refuse to see at least some of the personal
acquaintances who request an interview . . . it seems to me that *most*
people are not only annoyed or offended by this method but that it is
distinctly inhibiting to generous impulses.

The most serious feature . . . of the present system is that a contribution once made becomes the criterion for future gifts to all campaigns for every kind of charitable and educational work. Not only
is one bombarded by appeals but one is met with grave disapprobation
if one refuses to give or even if one's contribution is less than the
expectations raised by your lists . . . the only alternatives are either

a change of the present method or else for individuals like myself to refuse to give to charity as generously as they would otherwise wish to do.[65]

But Mrs. James was not the only one becoming irritated under the steady bombardment of appeals for the needy during the depression. A memo in the Jones' papers from staffman Henry E. Abt to Vice-President Harold J. Seymour dated September 11, 1936, reflects the same complaints from business firms.

Reporting on an interview with J. D. Twiname, secretary to the president of the B. Altman & Company department store, Abt wrote Seymour as follows:

> Mr. Twiname and his assistants are bitterly resentful of our Corporation on the following grounds:
>
> 1. We have several times sent them letters referring to one or more of their contributions made . . . in other campaigns and, as he states it, virtually all demanding equivalent percentage contributions in then current campaigns.
> 2. They have a feeling that the Corporation is peddling . . . information concerning the amount of their contributions and, as a matter of fact they have adopted a policy hereafter to make all contributions anonymous if the John Price Jones Corporation is on the job.
> 3. In several recent instances . . . we seemed to have made some clumsy boners working with Messrs Burke [John S. Burke, president of B. Altman] and Twiname.[66]

John Price Jones made this defense of the repeated use made of lists of known givers: "There is a definite need, we believe, for a list of prospects; but the manner in which the list is to be compiled and the facts to be gathered are subjects for careful consideration. Because I believe this material is, in an emergency, a community asset, not merely the property of John Price Jones Corporation, I should be happy to have a committee of proper people decide upon the scope and limitations of such a list." [67] There is no evidence that anything ever came of this offer by Jones.

There was also growing criticism of the fees being collected by the expert fund raiser for direction of campaigns. One philanthropist who rebelled at the cost of professionally directed campaigns was Edward S. Harkness. Writing on behalf of Mr. Harkness, Malcolm P.

Aldrich wrote Stuart M. Crocker, chairman of the United Hospital Campaign Fund, under date of December 10, 1936:

> . . . Mr. Harkness wished me to let you know that he will contribute $20,000 to the campaign this year. . . .
>
> Also, he wished me to tell you that as he has never approved of the continued use by organizations of professional money raising concerns, due as you well know to the large amount of money necessary for their fees, he may decide not to contribute next year if the Fund finds it necessary to again employ such organizations.[68]

Both of these criticisms are reflected in this anonymous letter written to Mrs. August Belmont, who was serving in the 1933 Emergency Relief Committee drive in New York City:

> Everyone with intelligence is tired to death of the endless claims made on a good natured public by this so-called Emergency Relief, Adopt a Family, Block Aid, etc. etc. or what have you: Where have the thirty-nine millions, collected last year and this gone . . . ? Congratulations on having the press subsidized. . . . It wouldn't be a bad idea if that firm on Nassau St. [the Jones firm] and its employees who have made so much money out of the Depression adopted a few families. It is said they have made over a million dollars.[69]

Jones's financial records refute this wild assertion.

John Price Jones was extremely sensitive to such criticisms and took steps to meet and counter every specific complaint that came to his attention. As the depression increased the number of fund drives and cut down the number of donors, the pressure grew more intense and the criticisms louder. On April 5, 1934, Jones sent a memo to his staff, "Attitudes Toward the Corporation," and asked for "any comments you may have heard similar to these. We shall then get together and have a discussion."

ATTITUDES TOWARD THE CORPORATION

1. That the Corporation is too expensive.
2. That the Corporation is not geared to do small jobs at a price commensurate with the size of the job.
3. That we have a lot of stock surveys and plans.
4. That we have a tendency to overload jobs we secure with our staff.
5. That we are very good while the job is being done, but hard to get rid of when our services are no longer vitally needed.
6. That the Corporation has made money out of the Emergency and Blaine [Salvation Army] campaigns.

7. That the Corporation wields too much influence, is too much the power behind the throne on a campaign.
8. That we threaten the permanent jobs of the technical men employed by various institutions.
9. That the Corporation has had its lists maintained at the expense of its clients, specifically the Emergency Unemployment Relief Committee and the Blaine Committees.
10. That the Corporation does too much planning and paper work.
11. That the Corporation contributes few ideas and little originality to a job and that these are up to the permanent staff and volunteers heading the campaign.[70]

Thus we see that Jones insisted on the same searching self-analysis for his firm as he did for its clients. And in these periodic reports of complaints and criticisms we have a candid view of the resentments incurred. It may be safely presumed that similar complaints were being voiced with equal force against the other major fundraising firms of these years though we do not have their records to document this.

There were those who questioned whether support of such programs as Boy Scouts was a proper function of the community chest. In a letter to the *New York Times*, Henry Ware Allen of Wichita, Kan., wrote:

These are two observations that may be made relative to the Community Chest drives recently concluded the country over. It is a fact easily proved that 100 per cent contributions invariably involve coercion of a certain proportion of employees. To avoid this, subscriptions should always be solicited by an outsider and never by an officer or employee of a plant. The second mistake made in so many towns and cities is that of including in the Community Chest such institutions as Boy Scouts commendable though these may be. The majority of Boy Scouts come from families who would scorn to accept charity direct.[71]

And of the community chest drives, Abraham Epstein had this to say:

What is the real extent of America's generosity? . . .

In the cities in which money is raised through community chests or welfare federations the contributors never exceed 17% of the total population. The 360 American community chests, in spite of the energetic trumpeting, cajolery, and high pressure salesmanship that go with them, do not raise more than $80,000,000 a year—less than half the sum now spent through workmen's compensation laws alone.[72]

Much of this criticism flows from the basic fact that many people do not really enjoy giving to public causes and most do so only under pressure. As the pressure mounts so does their resentment. The criticism serves the healthy purpose of toning down some of the flagrant practices of the commerical fund raiser and is needed to keep the less ethical, more exuberant ones of them in line.

The Fund Raisers Organize

As the competition during the depression sharpened, criticism of the professional fund raiser mounted and the need to perfect campaign procedures grew, the pioneers in the business felt the need to unite in a professional association. Whether such an association is to be properly called a professional association or a trade association is open to debate. At any rate, nine of the major, long-established fund-raising firms organized the American Association of Fund-Raising Counsel, May 13, 1935, and twenty years later set up a central executive office.

Who took the initiative in bringing the association into being is, as of so many matters of historic import in this field, also a matter of debate. In an undated memorandum compiled by Christian H. Dreshman of the Ward, Dreshman, & Reinhardt firm, Dreshman takes the credit in these words:

> During the summer of 1934, following the Depression of the early thirties, Mr. Bayard Hedrick of Pierce and Hedrick, Inc., and C. H. Dreshman of Ward, Wells and Dreshman were meeting frequently at luncheon discussing various matters pertaining to the fundraising business . . . at one of our luncheons Mr. Dreshman suggested the advisibility of bringing together the leaders of the then top firms to explore the possibility of forming an organization to set common standards of practice and ethics as well as charges for service.[73]

Dreshman continues his account:

> Mr. Hedrick concurred in the suggestion and urged that Mr. Dreshman should take the initiative in bringing the leading firms together for discussion. Mr. Dreshman consulted with Dr. Arnaud C.

Marts, George Tamblyn, and Mr. Hedrick, all former associates with him in the firm of Ward, Wells, and Dreshman, as well as Cornelius Smith of Will, Folsom, and Smith, Inc., and James Almond of American City Bureau.

Carlton G. Ketchum has a different recollection of the Association's origins. He writes:

The founding of the American Association of Fund Raising Counsel has been somewhat clouded by conflicting recollections. My own is quite distinct that Cornelius M. Smith, founder and president of Will, Folsom and Smith, had the idea and proposed it at lunch one day at the Royal Restaurant, at Fifth Avenue and Forty-Third Street to Chris Dreshman and me. The three of us invited the representatives of the other known firms. . . . Whatever credit attaches to the establishment of the Association, and I believe there is a good deal because it has exerted a wide-spread and wholesome interest, belongs to Corny Smith.[74]

The first general meeting of which there is a record was held October 8, 1934, at the Advertising Club in New York City with ten firms represented. Cornelius Smith presided at this meeting and his minutes record that he was elected acting chairman. Plans to establish "professional standards" were tabled at the urging of John Price Jones, who thought the group should get better acquainted before tackling such a ticklish matter. On Jones's motion, "the group voted to hold monthly meetings at which papers would be read and discussions held." The following firms were represented in this first general meeting: American City Bureau, James Almond; John Price Jones Corp., Jones and David M. Church; Ketchum, Inc., George Ketchum; Marts & Lundy, Inc., Dr. Arnaud C. Marts; Mac-Art & Campbell, John Campbell; Pierce & Hedrick, Bayard Hedrick; Tamblyn & Brown, Ralph Hedges; Tamblyn & Tamblyn, George Tamblyn; Ward, Wells, & Dreshman, Chris Dreshman; Will, Folsom, & Smith, Inc., Cornelius Smith.

After these few exploratory meetings during which these long-time competitors in the field became better acquainted, a decision was made at the January, 1935, meeting to form a permanent organization. Harold J. Seymour, veteran Jones fund raiser, was named chairman of the committee to draft a constitution and by-laws. Joseph Nate of American City Bureau was elected as secretary and his first recorded minutes are from the May 13, 1935, meeting when the organization was formally voted. Nate's minutes record the nomination and election of the following charter members: American City Bureau; John Price Jones Corp.; Ketchum, Inc.; MacArt & Campbell; Marts & Lundy, Inc.; Pierce & Hedrick, Inc.; Leo Redding; Tamblyn & Brown, Inc.; Tamblyn & Tamblyn; Ward, Wells, & Dreshman; Will, Folsom, and Smith, Inc. Two of these firms, MacArt & Campbell and Leo Redding, never accepted the membership tendered them. Cornelius Smith was elected as the first president, a tribute that would appear to validate Ketchum's assertion that "Corny Smith" deserves the credit for starting the Association. Dreshman explained the need for such an association this way:

> Many firms had grown up since 1919, each going their own way, setting their own standards of ethics and procedures, as well as charges to the client for services. Some firms and individual operators were engaging in certain practices that were definitely harmful to the prestige of the comparatively new fund raising profession. There were considerable variations in charges, some operating on a percentage basis instead of the fee basis, while others were including in their compensation the overall cost of the campaign including printed matter, luncheons, publicity, etc.[75]

In short, the matter of charges, the pressure of competition, and the sting of growing criticism of the professional fund raiser stimulated the formation of this association to promote and protect what had become a lucrative business. Once organized, the Association provided a forum where the members and their staffs could meet and exchange ideas on improved ways of raising money for philanthropy. It took the group twenty years to take the next major step of establishing a central office and hiring a full-time executive. Over the intervening two decades the Association was a loose roundtable sort of discussion group that met "from time to time to talk shop and palaver about professional ethics." "The AAFRC lacks the power to enforce its stated code of ethics but the members all adhere to it, although, as one professional stated, 'some do it a damn sight better than others.' "[76] This may be true in regard to nonmembers but it does exert control over its membership. On one occasion an AAFRC member was suspended for six months until he corrected what was considered a violation of the code. Members have been given warnings on a few occasions. From 1945, when the Tamblyn & Tamblyn firm ceased operations, until 1949 when the AAFRC extended its membership to the major fund-raising firms, it existed with only eight member firms.

Decision of these charter members to establish a central office and hire a full-time director came in the wake of New York State's legislative investigation of fund-raising practices in 1953 and 1954. By concurrent resolution the legislature of the state of New York on March 31, 1953, set up a Joint Legislative Committee on Charitable and Philanthropic Agencies and Organizations. The Committee's probe, climaxed by a report submitted on February 15, 1954, was headed by Senator Bernard Tompkins and came to be known as the Tompkins Committee Investigation. Publicity attendant upon the airing of many fraudulent practices brought organized fund raising under public scrutiny and increased the protests against those who exploited America's charitable instincts for personal gain. One consequence of this probe was the passage of New York State's trail-blazing legislative act requiring registration and reporting by fund-raising organizations and professional fund raisers. Some twenty-five other states had followed suit by 1964. At the conclusion of its investigation the Tompkins Committee asserted that "the public is being mulcted of millions of dollars each year," and "these vast sums are being diverted away from worthy and necessary philanthropies." [77] The work of the Committee will be recounted later. In 1954 the AAFRC opened offices at 500 Fifth Avenue with a secretary and with Dr. Marts, then president, giving part time to the Association.

After a considerable search for the right man to head the new central office, the AAFRC officers chose David M. Church, veteran executive in the John Price Jones organization, then in a period of transition. Church opened the office across the street from the New York Public Library on a full-time basis in April, 1955. He served as executive director until his retirement on January 1, 1962. In his career with John Price Jones and in his seven years as the executive officer of the fund-raisers' association, Dave Church left a strong imprint on professional fund raising—on its practices, on its literature, and on its ethics. Church came to fund raising by a circuitous route; the Berkshire *Evening Eagle*, the University of Pennsylvania, the Marine Corps, press association work in New York, Washington, and London. "A long way round," thinks Church who says his first contact with public relations was after his graduation from the University of Pennsylvania when he became a clipping clerk in the Pennsylvania Railroad Publicity Department. By this time Ivy Lee had left the PRR and his brother, James W. Lee, was the railroad's publicity chief. Church remembers no contact with either Lee while on the clipping clerk's job.

In August, 1916, Church joined the United Press to work as a reporter under Roy Howard and Carl Groat. A year later he switched to Hearst's International News Service and then in 1918 quit INS to join the Marine Corps. After the war Church found it impossible to get a newspaper job, so he took temporarily a job as an information man for the government's War Risk Insurance Agency. But in 1920 he was rehired by the INS and served that press association until 1929, when he was hired by John Price Jones. Church had been exposed to the art of fund raising years earlier when he had served on the "high school team" in a fund drive for the Pittsfield YMCA directed by Charles Sumner Ward. At the time this work, Church said, "inspired no aspirations to follow in the footsteps of the fund-raiser." His work with the Jones firm was largely to promote the firm and Mr. Jones. "Jones enjoyed being promoted as an individual," Church recalls.[78] The John Price Jones papers reveal that much of the writing for which he is credited was largely Church's work.

Church joined the Jones organization in what he thought was an interlude between press association jobs. But he remained with the firm a quarter of a century. Jones was not a facile writer, yet sought to bring a scholarly atmosphere to fund raising through the publication of books and pamphlets. John Price Jones, Church recalls, was not as easy to write for as were his clients. "Mr. Jones," says Church, "was brilliantly fruitful in ideas but lacked the patience, or perhaps the facility, for putting his ideas on paper. Therefore, like today's television stars, he had his writers. The only publication bearing his name in which he did much of the writing was *The Technique to Win in Fund Raising*. If Jones was disinclined to do a great deal of actual writing, he was not loath to order re-writing and re-writing. It is to his credit that his ideas developed into some of the early literature of fund raising. *The Yearbook of Philanthropy*, published during the 1940's and 1950's, *The Technique to Win in Fund Raising*, *The American Giver*, and *At the Bar of Public Opinion*, were the product of John Price Jones's mind, if not of his pen. These books are still frequently quoted in current writing on fund raising and philanthropy."[79]

Decision to strengthen the Association and take positive public relations steps to protect the ethical fund raiser led to an expansion of the heretofore small, clubby group of eight professional firms, and as of 1964 the AAFRC had a total of 26 member firms on its rolls. This spread the expanded costs of the Association over a larger base. These are: Aderton-Trostle Associates, Harrisburg, Pa.; American City Bureau/Beaver Associates, Chicago; G. A. Brakeley & Co., New York and San Francisco; Burrill, Inc., Kansas City; Community Counseling Service, Inc., New York; Community Service Bureau, Dallas, Texas; Holland Estill & Associates, New York; Charles R. Feldstein & Co., Chicago; Thomas Richard Finn & Associates, Kansas City; Haney Associates, Inc., Newtonville, Mass.; Hogan Winters & Co., Rye, N.Y.; Hopkins-Manspeaker Associates, Englewood, Colo.; John Price Jones Company, Inc., New York; Kersting, Brown, & Co., Inc., New York; Ketchum, Inc., Pittsburgh; James V. Lavin Co., Boston; Marts & Lundy, Inc., New York; Harold L. Oram, Inc., New York; Pierce, Hedrick, & Sherwood, Inc., New York; Richard Pontz & Associates, Lancaster, Pa.; John F. Rich Co., Philadelphia; Tamblyn & Brown, Inc.; Ward, Dreshman, & Reinhardt, Inc., New York; Milton Hood Ward & Co., Inc., New York; Will, Folsom, & Smith, Inc., New York; G. A. Brakeley & Co., Ltd., Montreal, Canada.[80] Harold J. Seymour, one of the pioneers, was given the status of honorary member by the AAFRC in 1958 in recognition of his many contributions to the development of this field. Honorary membership was given Church at the time of his retirement in 1961.

The Association uses its growing strength to promote and publicize its Fair Practice Code. It seeks to encourage fair legislation regarding charitable contributions as public demand for some check on fraudulent fund raisers results in more and more legislation, such as that passed in New York in 1955. The AAFRC has prepared a model law for control of charitable solicitations which has been used by many legislative committees in drafting these registration-control laws.

FAIR PRACTICE CODE
American Association of Fund-Raising Counsel, Inc.

One—Member firms will serve only those charitable institutions or agencies whose purposes and methods they can approve. They will not knowingly be used by any organization to induce charitably-inclined persons to give their money to unworthy causes.

Two—Member firms do business only on the basis of a specified fee, determined prior to the beginning of the campaign. They will not serve clients on the unprofessional basis of a percentage or commission of the sums raised. They maintain this ethical standard also by not profiting, directly or indirectly, from disbursements for the accounts of clients.

Three—The executive head of a member organization must demonstrate at least a six-year record of continuous experience as a professional in the fund-raising field. This helps to protect the public from those who enter the profession without sufficient competence, experience, or devotion to ideals of public service.

Four—The Association looks with disfavor upon firms which use methods harmful to the public, such as making exaggerated claims of past achievements, guaranteeing results, and promising to raise unobtainable sums.

Five—No payment in cash or kind shall be made by a member to an officer, director, trustee, or adviser of a philanthropic agency or institution as compensation for using his influence for the engaging of a member for fund-raising counsel.

The Association's central office has taken over the task of compiling comprehensive statistics on American philanthropy, the gist of which is published annually in a report entitled *Giving, USA*. This fact book has appeared each year since 1956. The AAFRC and its officers were largely instrumental in establishing a course on fund raising at Teachers College, Columbia University, in 1960. In the years 1956 to 1958 the AAFRC's Committee on Personnel made a thorough study of the need for more systematic recruitment and training of personnel for this field because "there was agreement on the difficulty in finding competent staff personnel." Thus, out of the informal meetings over lunch in the early 1930's came the Association that today exerts considerable influence on the practices of fund raising and, beyond these, on American philanthropy.

NOTES

1. In a book of readings, *The Great Depression*, p. 1.
2. Hoover, *State Papers*, Vol. 1, pp. 470, 496.
3. Buckingham, *Red Cross Disaster Relief* (Washington: Public Affairs Press, 1956), p. 38.
4. F. R. Dulles, *The American Red Cross, a History*, p. 281.
5. Spivak, "Shady Business in the Red Cross," *American Mercury*, Vol. 33 (November, 1934), p. 287.
6. Kellogg, "ARC," *Survey*, Vol. LXX (December 1934), p. 383.
7. *New York Times*, April 3, 1931, p. 14.
8. *Ibid.*, April 5, 1931, p. 22.
9. "Do the Rich Give to Charity?" *American Mercury*, Vol. 23 (May, 1931), p. 25.
10. "Disaster Preparedness and Relief, Final Study Report," January, 1935, p. 14. *ARC Archives*. For this story, also see ARC, *Relief Work in the Drought of 1930–1931*, official report covering activities from August, 1930, to June 30, 1931, published in 1931.
11. Buckingham, *op. cit.*, p. 40.
12. Letter dated June 15, 1962, from Clyde E. Buckingham, Director, Office Research Information of the ARC.
13. Bernstein, *The Lean Years* (Boston: Houghton Mifflin, 1960), pp. 302–303.
14. *Ibid.*
15. *New York Times*, June 14, 1931, p. 26.
16. Interview, March 30, 1960.
17. John Price Jones Papers.
18. Epstein, p. 25.
19. Proceedings Twelfth Annual Staff Conference, pp. 85–89, John Price Jones Papers.
20. David M. Church Letter, Sept. 2, 1962. See Matthews' account of this program in his *Adventures in Giving* (Dodd, Mead, 1939).
21. "Criticisms of John Price Jones Corp.," in John Price Jones Papers. In fairness it should be noted that Jones never had any part in spending the relief funds he helped raise.
22. "John Price Jones Annual Reports," John Price Jones Papers, v. AG 11.
23. *Ibid.*, v. AG 12.

24. *Ibid.*, v. AG 13.

25. *Ibid.*, v. AG 14 and AG 15.

26. In outline of plan copyrighted in 1936 by the ACB. In ACB files.

27. In "Call to Order," talk given at ACB's 1946 Staff Conference. In ACB files.

28. In 1933 Staff Conference Proceedings, John Price Jones Papers, BF 10.

29. In multilithed memo, "Fund Raising's Two Mossiest Myths," published by the American Association of Fund Raising Counsel, September, 1958.

30. "John Price Jones Staff Papers for Staff Conference, 1933," John Price Jones Papers, BF 10.

31. *New Palestine*, Oct. 4, 1935.

32. *Ibid.*, May 31, July 12, 1935.

33. Merle Curti; *American Philanthropy Abroad*, pp. 399–400. Published in 1963 by the Rutgers University Press.

34. "Recent Trends in Fund Raising," staff paper prepared for American Association of Fund Raising Counsel, May 13, 1935. In John Price Jones Papers.

35. Jones, "Public Opinion, the Depression, and Fund-Raising," *Public Opinion Quarterly*, Vol. 1 (June, 1937), pp. 142–147.

36. In 1936 Staff Conference Proceedings, John Price Jones Papers, BF 13.

37. F. Emerson Andrews, *Corporation Giving* (New York: Russell Sage Foundation, 1950), p. 24.

38. Hopkins, *History of the Y.M.C.A. in North America*, p. 237.

39. *Ibid.*, p. 236.

40. Williams and Croxton, *Corporation Contributions to Organized Community Welfare Services* (New York: NBER, 1930). In Appendix, pp. 234–235.

41. *Red Cross Bulletin*, Vol. 2, Jan. 14, 1918.

42. Andrews, *Giving*, p. 29.

43. Williams and Croxton, *Corporation Contributions*, *op. cit.*, pp. 33–34. This study provides the best record on corporate giving up to the depression years.

44. *Ibid.*, p. 92.

45. *Ibid.*, p. 93.

46. Andrews, *op. cit.*, p. 235. See also Ray Garrett, "Corporate Donations to Charity," *Proceedings* of the Section of Corporation, Banking and Mercantile Law, published in the *Business Lawyer*, November, 1948.

47. *Old Mission Portland Cement Co.* v. *Helvering, Commissioner of Internal Revenue*, 293 U.S. 289 (1934); affirming 69 F. (2nd) 676 (1934).

48. For Court of Appeals decision see 69 F (Ind) 676.

49. Burns, "Tax Exemption of Corporation Gifts," *Survey*, Vol. 71 (September, 1935), p. 262.

50. *New York Times*, July 11, 1935, p. 6.

51. *Ibid.*, July 25, 1935, p. 27.

52. Column in Aug. 1, 1935, issue New York *Herald Tribune*.

53. *New York Times*, July 25, 1935, *loc. cit.*

54. This information was relayed to Burns's assistant, Ralph Blanchard, who told it to the writer on March 30, 1960. Blanchard told me he had confirmed this story with Swope shortly before the latter's death.

55. Beardsley Ruml and Theodore Geiger, *The Five Percent* (Washington: National Planning Assn., 1951), p. 8.

56. "Drives and Economy," *Harper's*, Vol. 150 (May, 1925), p. 766.

57. *Ibid.*, pp. 763–764.

58. Quoted by Forrest Crissey in "The High Cost of Giving," *Saturday Evening Post*, Vol. 199 (Dec. 11, 1926), p. 82.

59. *Ibid.*, p. 74.

60. Robert Bochat, "Campaign Costs," in *1952 Staff Conference Proceedings*, June 11, 1952. In John Price Jones Papers.

61. In Crissey, *op. cit.*, p. 82.

62. Marts, *Man's Concern for His Fellow Man*, p. 55.

63. In John Price Jones Papers.

64. *Ibid.*

65. *Ibid.*

66. *Ibid.*

67. Letter to Mrs. James dated Jan. 20, 1937, in John Price Jones Papers.

68. John Price Jones Papers.

69. Letter in John Price Jones Papers.

70. "Commendations and Criticisms of John Price Jones Corp.," John Price Jones Papers.

71. *New York Times*, Dec. 16, 1934, Sec. IV, p. 5.

72. Epstein, *op. cit.*, p. 23.

73. Undated Memorandum, "A Brief History of the Origin of the American Association of Fund-Raising Counsel," in files of AAFRC central office, circa 1955.

74. Letter from Ketchum to author, dated Sept. 6, 1961.

75. Undated Memorandum, *op. cit.*

76. Anon., "Fund Raising Agencies," *Tide*, Jan. 16, 1948, p. 13.

77. *Report of the Joint Legislative Committee on Charitable and Philanthropic Agencies and Organizations*, Albany: State of New York Leg-

islative Doc. No. 26, 1954, p. 37. Henceforth this will be referred to as the Tompkins Committee Report.

78. Interview with Mr. Church, Dec. 28, 1959.

79. *Ibid.*

80. American Association of Fund-Raising Counsel, Inc., *A Directory of Members, 1964.* New York: The Association, 1964.

9

F.D.R., Polio, and the March of Dimes

F.D.R. Discovers Warm Springs

In 1958 Americans contributed some $325 million to national voluntary health agencies—nearly 5 per cent of the total giving of individuals and corporations for that year. It is estimated that contributions to these national health agencies will reach $575 million by 1970.[1] In 1958, nearly $40 million of this sum was raised by the pioneering and powerful National Foundation for Infantile Paralysis through its March of Dimes. An idea born of desperation in late 1933 had evolved into a highly successful pattern to raise money and interest people in the conquest of diseases that afflict mankind. The now familiar national health fund drive had its origins more in the Roosevelt Birthday Balls and March of Dimes than in the older Christmas Seal sale. The essential difference was supplied by bold managerial leadership and the sure touch of the modern public relations man.

A rare combination of personalities and events converged at precisely the right moment in history to launch the successful crusade against crippling poliomyelitis. But more than prevention of polio was found in the process. Successful nationwide fund-raising patterns were developed that have been utilized by those battling cancer, heart disease, muscular dystrophy, and the host of other still unconquered diseases. High-pressure publicity and skilled organization methods are used to get millions of volunteers to solicit gifts from as many as 80 million Americans in a single drive. The health drives are truly a people's philanthropy. A blending of the talents and energies of shrewd, persuasive Carl Byoir, doughty, tough-minded Henry L. Doherty, supersalesman Keith Morgan, and last, but far from least, bold, thick-skinned Basil O'Connor in exploiting

351

the magic name of Franklin D. Roosevelt built a National Foundation for Infantile Paralysis that "stood beyond all challenge as the most successful voluntary health organization on earth." Because of its significance as the most successful money getter among the health drives and because it demonstrates the influential role of public relations in today's philanthropy, the story of a fund-raising idea that, between 1934 and 1960, inclusive, raised $618.5 million in pennies, dimes, and dollars deserves to be chronicled in detail.

On a hot August day in 1921 on Campobello Island, New Brunswick, a happy, healthy Franklin Delano Roosevelt was vacationing with his family. The thirty-nine-year-old former Assistant Secretary of the Navy had left a steaming, humid Washington, D.C., in July, not knowing that he carried with him the deadly virus of polio. F.D.R. had been shunted to the political sidelines by the defeat of the Democratic presidential ticket of James M. Cox and F.D.R. in the 1920 election, when the voters chose to evade the harsh realities of the war-racked world and, instead, fled to the never-never land of "normalcy." Roosevelt was stricken with infantile paralysis, as polio was called in those days; he escaped death by a narrow margin. He was never to walk again yet he was destined to lead his nation through some of its most perilous hours; to be the only man ever elected President of the United States for four terms. In the long, vexing struggle to regain his health and to make his political comeback Roosevelt had, in the words of Frances Perkins, "the intelligent support of Mrs. Roosevelt and Louis Howe, his faithful aide of Navy Department days." Louis McHenry Howe had, years earlier, made up his mind to guide F.D.R. to the Presidency of the United States, and he succeeded.[2] Most of all, F.D.R. had his own courage and determination to live a useful life and not retire to Hyde Park a hopeless cripple, as his mother encouraged him to do.

In mid-1924 philanthropist George Foster Peabody had acquired control of the Warm Springs, Ga., resort hotel then "in genteel ruin." He sensed the spa's possibilities as a recuperation center for the crippled victims of infantile paralysis. Peabody, described as "a man of great caution and persistence, in some ways philanthropic," instructed his manager: "I know a man named Roosevelt who just last month made quite a speech in Madison Square Garden. . . .

"He ought to be interested in this place. . . . Ask him to come down for a visit. He's a wealthy man. Terribly crippled I understand. We must be practical." [3]

Informed of the spa's therapeutic possibilities, F.D.R. decided, in late 1924, to visit Warm Springs, 75 miles southwest of Atlanta— the place where Roosevelt would die early in his fourth term as President of the United States. The resort was already renowned for its constant tepid flow of crystal-clear water heavy with mineral salts, and after his visit F.D.R. decided to try the Warm Springs treatment. He returned there in the spring of 1925 and spent several weeks exercising and swimming in the pools of the resort controlled by Peabody, who originally came from nearby Columbus, Ga. Roosevelt was so impressed with the improvement of other patients, as well as his own, that in 1926 he decided to conduct some experiments. Twenty-three patients were placed under observation for periods of five to seventeen weeks. All made improvement, some to remarkable degrees. F.D.R. called in orthopedic surgeons and each voiced approval of his idea to establish a hydrotherapeutic center at Warm Springs. In the blunt language of Basil (Doc) O'Connor, F.D.R.'s law partner who became the powerful and controversial head of the National Foundation:

I was drafted. George Foster Peabody had this old broken-down resort in Warm Springs, Georgia, and Roosevelt got the idea that the swimming was helping his paralyzed muscles. He bought the place to help other polio patients. We went down in 1924 and I thought he was crazy to want that big goddam four-story firetrap with the squirrels running in and out of the holes in the roof. I couldn't have been less interested in the project. But in 1928 he ups and becomes Governor of New York and nonchalantly says to me, "Take over Warm Springs, old fella, you're in." I tell you I had no desire to be "in." I was never a do-gooder and had no aspirations of that kind.[4]

And Doc O'Connor has been "in" from that day to this; in the thick of the battle to conquer polio and to resist those who would restrict in any way the national professionally directed volunteer money-raising campaign which he, more than any other campaigner, has perfected. Carter thinks O'Connor "is the toughest, most stylish, most uncompromising individual in the voluntary health field, knows it, and enjoys it. Persons impressed by his conspicuous self-esteem and impeccable tailoring sometimes write him off as a peacock, which is a grievous underestimation. The man has a quick, highly organized, and—most unusual—principled intellect." [5] Surely O'Connor is a shrewd, strong-willed individual who will, if he can, ride roughshod over all who differ with him.

O'Connor fought his way to the top the hard way. He was born to a poor family living on the wrong side of the tracks in Taunton, Mass., January 8, 1892. He often recalls an incident that left an indelible impression on him and fired him with the zeal to succeed and to make money. When O'Connor was a child his father was an $18-a-week tinsmith in the railroad yards. One day his father lost his job and the boy found the penniless man crying. Carter speculates: "Those who love O'Connor say that his social consciousness and his hatred of injustice date from that day. Those who dislike him maintain that his father's grief left the boy determined to become rich and invulnerable." [6]

O'Connor put himself through Dartmouth in three and a half years by earning money playing in a dance band. After getting his A.B. from Dartmouth in 1912 he went on to Harvard Law School and got his law degree three years later. After four years' employment in New York and Boston law firms he started his own firm in 1919 and practiced under his own name until 1924. In 1925 he formed a partnership with F.D.R., Roosevelt & O'Connor, which continued until F.D.R. assumed the Presidency in March, 1933. He was more than a law partner; he was an intimate friend and respected counselor.

More and more Roosevelt gave his heart and mind to Warm Springs. He became increasingly convinced of its possibilities as a center for research and cure of polio. Roosevelt set his mind on buying Warm Springs. O'Connor found that Peabody controlled the option to buy the property for $100,000 but that he wanted twice that much from Roosevelt. After lengthy negotiations with Charles Peabody, a nephew, Roosevelt on April 29, 1926, signed an agreement to buy the entire property—springs, hotel, cottages, and 1,200 acres of land for $195,000. For Peabody this was profit, not philanthropy. The deal was finally consummated on February 1, 1927. After his purchase of the "fire trap" at Warm Springs, Roosevelt proceeded to organize the nonprofit Warm Springs Foundation to develop the old spa as an orthopedic center. The certificate of incorporation, dated July 8, 1927, set down the Foundation's purpose "to stimulate and further the work being done anywhere in the field of infantile paralysis, including the advancement and diffusion of knowledge concerning such work and the coordination and correlation of the efforts of all those engaged therein." Members of the board of the new Foundation were Roosevelt, Henry Pope, James T. Whitehead, George Foster Peabody, Leroy W. Hubbard, Herbert N. Straus, and the ever-faithful Louis Howe.

Warm Springs had stimulated F.D.R.'s mind and broadened his outlook as well as strengthened his shrunken muscles. He became increasingly aware of the large number of people who were victims of polio and was stirred by the idea that something could be done for them. He put a great deal of his own money into the Foundation and persuaded his friends to do the same. According to Frances Perkins, his long-time friend and aide, F.D.R.'s "plan was to keep the place simple and cheap, to make it possible for people to help themselves, to give them something to do if they were able. . . . "He thought that, above everything else, there should be medical research into the causes of paralysis and into methods of preventing it or curing it in the early stages." [7]

When Roosevelt was elected Governor of New York in 1928 he realized he would not have the time to raise funds and guide the program at Warm Springs so he airily turned it over to his trusted friend and law partner, O'Connor, with the terse command: "You'll have to run Warm Springs now." O'Connor—a manager who insists on managing—moved to tighten up the Foundation's rather loose business operations and to give more direction to the medical treatment offered at Warm Springs.

Hard pressed for money to repair and rehabilitate the rundown resort, O'Connor turned to Keith Morgan, a million-dollar-a-year insurance salesman, as the money raiser. Morgan's interest in Warm Springs had been enlisted through his friendship with one of the first patients, Arthur Carpenter. Carpenter, at the time advertising manager of *Parents' Magazine*, first went to Warm Springs in the spring of 1928, and a few weeks later Keith Morgan went down to visit him. There Morgan met F.D.R. and was captivated by the man's personality and courage. After chatting for a while with Morgan, F.D.R. said: "Carpenter tells me you can sell anything. How about selling this place to a lot of wealthy people who've never heard of it?" And this Morgan was to spend much of his next thirty years doing because that summer O'Connor followed up F.D.R.'s suggestion and drafted Morgan "for the duration."

"Warm Springs grew, and its methods grew. Franklin Roosevelt, his friends say, grew there, too. His horizon had broadened at Warm

Springs in the 20s and early 30s. He talked to neighboring farmers and little business men. . . . He never stopped going to Warm Springs. In 1931 he built himself a simple six-room house there, white clapboard, green shutters, rambler roses climbing the proch columns, tall Georgia pines overhead. It became a second White House." [8] Of the part Warm Springs played in Roosevelt's outlook, Frances Perkins writes: "When Roosevelt took a little house in Warm Springs, he did not know that part of the country well and he immediately became interested in the people and the area in which they lived." [9]

By the time Roosevelt was elected President in 1932 the Warm Springs Foundation was nearly bankrupt. The bills were piling up. Just as O'Connor and Morgan had begun in 1929 to raise money to put Warm Springs on a sound financial base, the stock market crashed and the depression set in. O'Connor recalls how he and William (Willie) Woodin, then president of American Car and Foundry Co. and later F.D.R.'s first Secretary of the Treasury, "walked off shoe leather trying to raise money." O'Connor wrote begging letters by the score. One prospect replied in the bleak, hungry March of 1932: "Thanks for the compliment of asking me for $1,000. I haven't $1,000, Doc, and if I did I think there are many cases [at home] that could use a little money very nicely." In this era rich men were the mainstay of public philanthropy but in the severe depression few of them had money to give. Even Roosevelt's election to the Presidency did not make a great deal of difference at first. O'Connor had thought the soliciting of gifts would be easier now with the president of the Foundation in the White House. O'Connor pitched his renewed appeals on "helping the President" in the nation's dark hours. Most of the replies were still the same: "Sorry, Doc, but I just can't afford to give now." One banker thought it best to make his contribution "a small and personal one" in view of a coming Senate investigation.

Yet the bills piled up. Suppliers were demanding their money, and hundreds of polio victims were begging to come to Warm Springs. O'Connor recalls wryly that "Warm Springs could not pay for its pots and pans." He called a meeting of the trustees, who voted to authorize a public campaign. It became apparent that a new approach and a nationwide effort would have to be made if Warm Springs was to become a reality, not just F.D.R.'s personal dream. Whose idea it was has been lost in dimmed memories but Keith

Morgan decided to put the problem before Carl Byoir, a new star then shooting across the nation's public relations firmament. Out of Morgan's call on Byoir at the latter's office, 10 East 40th Street, would come the President's Birthday Balls, the March of Dimes, the National Foundation for Infantile Paralysis, and, finally, victory over the disease itself. It was perhaps fateful that Morgan turned to a public relations man, not a professional fund raiser.

Carl Byoir and Henry L. Doherty Enlist

Carl Byoir, though he already had a rather dazzling career behind him by 1933, was not yet the celebrated and controversial public relations counselor he was destined to become before he died on February 3, 1957, at the age of sixty-eight. Byoir was born in Des Moines, Iowa, the son of a none-too-successful hotelkeeper. A brilliant youngster, he started work as a reporter on the Des Moines *Register* at the age of fourteen and by the time he was seventeen he was city editor of the Waterloo (Iowa) *Times Tribune*. He entered the University of Iowa in 1906 with only $30, yet graduated four years later with all expenses paid and $6,500 in the bank.

Demonstrating the drive and imagination that were to carry him far, he earned this money by managing the university's annual yearbook and by selling the printing jobs on other college annuals for a Des Moines printing house. In his senior year Byoir prepared a written course on how to make annuals pay and sold this manual and printing contracts in one package. He then went on to Columbia University Law School. Here he paid his way by organizing the House of Childhood to sell Maria Montessori's kindergarten training methods in the United States. At the age of twenty-three he was in part responsible for the spread of the Montessori-method kindergartens in this country. He got his law degree in 1912 and with $9,000 he had saved he started *John Martin's Read Aloud* magazine for children. Then he sold out and went to work as an advertising salesman for Hearst magazines. He was circulation director for the Hearst magazines when America entered World War I.

Soon after George Creel had taken on the staggering, unprecedented task of selling America's war aims at home and abroad with propaganda through the Committee on Public Information he ran into a snag on pamphlet production. Creel's aide, Edgar Sisson, knew Byoir and in June, 1917, asked him to come to Washington to help. An accumulating number of patriotic pamphlets that Creel had persuaded historians and scholars to write—the Red, White, and Blue textbooks—were logjamming in the Government Printing Office. Byoir quickly broke the jam by shuttling these booklets to catalogue publishers in their slack seasons. He got the booklets flowing to the public and also saved CPI money. His success led to his appointment, when he was only twenty-eight years old, as associate chairman of the Committee.

In this role Byoir, among other things, organized the League of Oppressed Nations to sap the morale of the enemy with propaganda. This led, after the war, to his helping the new Republic of Czechoslovakia get established. Byoir handled the public relations for President Masaryk and the new nation. His work, during the war and after, led to his association with Emanuel Voska, head of the Masaryk ring of espionage agents working against the Central Powers in the United States during the war. Voska and Byoir went into the export-import business to capitalize on their "in" with the new republic and its leaders. For a while they made fabulous profits. Then the foreign exchange market collapsed and they lost everything. Byoir, spurred no doubt by the failures of his father, aspired to great wealth. He was crushed, but not for long.

Byoir was urged to go into bankruptcy and get a fresh start. This he refused to do. Determined to pay off his debts, he turned to the field of patent medicines. He worked his way into a firm making Nuxated Iron, a high-priced iron tonic of low cost and little value. From Nuxated Iron Byoir went on to peddle Seedol, a bowel tonic; Kelpamalt, a weight builder; Viaderma, rub-on reducing compound; and, finally, Blondex. To sell Blondex Byoir promoted and popularized the platinum blonde—a species of American woman now grown in number and in variety of hues. His debts paid off, plagued by a painful sinus condition, and probes being made by the Federal Trade Commission and the American Medical Association into such products, Byoir sought rest and recuperation.[10] First he tried Arizona and then, in 1928, he went to Cuba.

After a good rest and improvement in his sinus condition, the restless, energetic Byoir leased two Havana English-language newspapers, the *Post* and the *Evening Telegram*. He soon realized that to make these papers profitable, Cuba would have to lure more tourist dollars into Havana's cash registers. He began the promotion of American tourist travel to Cuba. After considerable effort he persuaded President Gerardo Machado, a Cuban dictator in the now all too familiar pattern, to set up a promotion office in New York for this purpose. In 1930 Byoir opened an office at 10 East 40th Street with the name "Havana Post" on the door. This was subsequently changed to Carl Byoir & Associates. He had for his base a retainer of $60,000 a year from Machado, but this account was lost in August, 1933, when the dictator was expelled from Cuba by his countrymen. Naturally, Byoir was eager to find new clients to maintain his growing staff in these depression years. Among the first in a long list of clients to be served by the Byoir firm was "Colonel" Henry Latham Doherty, another of the major characters in the March of Dimes drama. Doherty was made a colonel by a Florida governor in recognition of the hotel man's intensive efforts to promote Florida's tourist business during the depression. Byoir, in contrast, was a lieutenant colonel in the U.S. Army Reserve and thus was fully entitled to be called "Colonel," as he frequently was.[11]

Colonel Doherty was born and reared in the era of Horatio Alger, Jr. He probably read some of that celebrated author's novels which did so much to construct the American Dream of rags to riches. In any event Doherty's life could have been taken from the pages of the Alger stories. He was born in Columbus, Ohio, May 15, 1870, of poor parents. At the age of twelve he quit school and went to work as an office boy with the Columbus Gas Co. He had the ability and drive to advance steadily in supervisory positions until, at the age of twenty, he set out to make his fortune. A bold, buccaneering utility tycoon and financial manipulator, he gained his wealth, as did the other utility barons of the pre-New Deal era, by exploiting the nation's resources, by financial rigging, and through municipal franchises granting monopoly of service without adequate rate fixing.

In 1890 Doherty took a job with the Madison, Wis., utility and for the next fifteen years worked for or managed utility companies in twenty-five cities across the country. In 1905 he organized Henry L. Doherty & Co., a banking firm and owner of utilities, a stock firm of which he was sole owner. Five years later he put together the Cities Service Co., a holding company for 190 public utility and petroleum properties with assets estimated at more than $1 billion. When Doherty had reached his sixty-fifth birthday his fortune was variously estimated from $300 to $500 million and he was holder of 150 patents or inventions for utility and petroleum operations.

Doherty, a dapper, dynamic little man with neatly trimmed white chin whiskers, had long been a controversial public figure by the time Roosevelt came to power. In 1906, a year after founding his holding company, Doherty was involved in a dubious franchise election in Denver, Colo. In the ensuing investigation Doherty was held in contempt of court by the famous Judge Ben Lindsey for refusal to testify. "Mr. Doherty, to his rage and surprise, found himself in a cell. But not for long. The utterly lawless action of a notorious judge set him free, and he fled across the state line. . . .

"Some months later, Mr. Doherty's right hand man either lost his memorandum book or had it stolen from him. Pages from it, reproduced in Senator Patterson's paper, showed that he had paid $67,690 to candidates and leaders of both parties." [12] Early in the depression the Kansas City *Star* launched a campaign to get Doherty's company to lower its gas rates. Doherty tried to scare off the *Star* with a series of libel suits. "By July 6, 1932, he had four suits pending against the *Star* and its officials asking total damages of $54,000,000. Aiming at ousting the editors of the paper, he also tried to frighten the W. R. Nelson Estate trustees into canceling their agreement with the purchasers of the *Star* and, to have a mouthpiece, bought partial control of the *Star*'s local competitor, the *Journal-Post*." [13]

In 1933, the year Roosevelt was inaugurated, a Federal Trade Commission probe of Doherty's dealings revealed that he had realized a net profit of $17,748,032 in the 1929 sale of 200,000 shares of Cities Service stock, a profit made at the expense of Cities Service stockholders. He ultimately paid back to these stockholders $1,250,-000 to settle their suits out of court.[14] In 1931 he bought the Miami Biltmore Hotel and Country Club and, though this was in the depth of the depression, searched for a publicity team to promote tourist trade for the new property. This led to Doherty's connection with Carl Byoir and Byoir's right-hand man, Gerry Swinehart, one long skilled in developing tourist trade. Byoir had hired Swinehart away from the West Palm Beach Department of News and Advertising when the former started his firm in 1930. Doherty's hotels represented the Byoir firm's first United States account, landed because Byoir and Swinehart submitted the boldest plan with the highest price tag, as Doherty later confided to them.

Keith Morgan put his case to Byoir bluntly, explaining that he knew that Byoir represented Doherty and that Doherty ought to be interested in helping Warm Springs. "Why?" asked Byoir. "He has a public reputation as a pirate of finance. Aside from the annoyance, it must get in his way," Morgan replied. Byoir readily saw the possibilities of refurbishing the wily oil magnate's reputation. He told Morgan, "The colonel is at the Shoreham in Washington. I'll phone him, but you'll have to go down and talk to him yourself." In that Washington hotel Morgan found "the remarkable Doherty in a big bare top-floor suite, clad only in red woolen underwear which he claimed was the most sensible attire." In response to Morgan's plea for help Doherty bluntly asked, "Why should I?" "Because it might get an old pirate like you into heaven," Morgan answered. Doherty first glared, then laughed and said, "Who's the head of your organization? Byoir says you're a good outfit. I'll talk to the head man." And with that Doherty and Morgan were off to the White House to see President Roosevelt. The next move was to invite Carl Byoir and Doherty to Warm Springs for the traditional Thanksgiving celebration to discuss specific ways and means of raising money. Doherty liked what he saw and Byoir was enthusiastic.[15]

Doherty suggested that some sort of fund-raising celebration be planned and he volunteered to underwrite the publicity and administrative costs. "I'll put up a hundred and fifty thousand, maybe a little more, to finance a practical program for raising some really important money." (He ultimately put up $25,000 and got more than his money's worth of favorable publicity in return.) Those conferring agreed that the appeal must be nationwide and that it should be a quick drive. Doherty barked, "Give 'em one event that will stir them up, make them contribute, and then go home to bed." Byoir spoke up: "I like the idea of a party, of people dancing." This idea would later be cast into a memorable slogan, "Dance so that a child may walk," by Columnist Walter Winchell. "When could we hold it?" someone asked. "The President's birthday," Byoir responded. "What an idea!" he added as the possibilities paraded across his imaginative mind. Morgan telephoned for Roosevelt's permission. "If my birthday will be of any help, take it." He, too, saw the possibilities of getting big money for the project nearest his heart, even if it meant dealing with one of the "money-changers" he was then publicly excoriating.

Byoir later confided to his associates that "F.D.R. is scared about what the public reaction might be to this fund-raising effort because of the bonds outstanding against Warm Springs."[16] The subterranean charge that F.D.R. was using the money raised for Warm

Springs to pay off his personal debts, incurred in starting the Foundation, continued to circulate for years. This bothered him considerably. Harold L. Ickes recorded in his carefully kept diary for April 21, 1936:

> James Waldo Fawcett, of the *Star*, came to see me at my invitation a couple of days ago. He confirmed the fact that Farley is saying I am to be one of the principal Democratic speakers in the campaign. He told me that the story is going around that the President has received AAA benefit checks and that the money that was raised at the first President's birthday dance for the Warm Springs Foundation was used to lift a mortgage on the Warm Springs Foundation that was held by the President. I repeated these rumors to the President today when I had lunch with him at the White House. He said the Warm Springs Foundation actually hadn't paid the interest due him; that he had refused to accept the interest because it would have had to be paid out of the fund that was raised in his name in celebration of his birthday.[17]

These recurring rumors went back to 1928 and grew out of the efforts to persuade F.D.R. to run for Governor of New York on the Democratic ticket and thus improve Al Smith's chances of carrying the state. In declining the offer of the nomination made by Smith and others, F.D.R. gave as one reason his heavy financial obligation in Warm Springs. John J. Raskob, wealthy General Motors executive who had just been named chairman of the Democratic National Committee, put the pressure on Roosevelt. "Damn the Foundation. We'll take care of that!" he shouted over the telephone to F.D.R. That night he mailed Roosevelt a check for $250,000. A few days later Roosevelt returned the check, saying, "I can't take this check, John. You didn't promise to give me the money. All you did was promise to underwrite it and I am satisfied with that." Shortly after this the committee to raise money was formed under the chairmanship of Will Woodin. Raskob subscribed $50,000. His contributions ultimately totaled $113,000. A Roosevelt hater, John T. Flynn, complained in his *The Roosevelt Myth* that F.D.R.'s supporters "never mention the fact that it was a group of rich men interested in Al Smith who put up the money to pay the debts incurred by Roosevelt in the [Warm Springs] enterprise."[18] But as the historian Frank Freidel says, "It would be hard to establish any significant relationship between Raskob's gifts and Roosevelt's personal finances. Raskob gave an initial 25,000 dollars in October, 1928. Roosevelt did not receive the first installment on his note—approximately 14,000 dollars—until Jan. 31, 1930. . . . Raskob could be considered no more than an especially generous contributor. . . . Yet as late as the campaign of 1950, Republicans of New York cited these contributions as justification for some highly intricate transactions involving their own leaders." [19]

Mrs. Roosevelt documents, in *This I Remember*, that F.D.R. originally lent $201,677.83 to start Warm Springs and received in return from the Foundation a demand note. This was ultimately paid back by the Foundation, some of it after his death, with the receipts from the insurance policy carried by the Foundation on Roosevelt's life. The records show that Roosevelt personally contributed $53,-008.91 to the Warm Springs Foundation. This sum includes $3,000 given by his mother and $9,508.91 in book royalties from *The Public Papers and Addresses of Franklin D. Roosevelt*.[20] In the depression when the Foundation was still plagued by financial woes, "Keith Morgan, working with O'Connor's approval, had arranged to have Roosevelt's life insured by twenty-two of the nation's biggest insurance companies, in the amount of $560,000." [21] The insurance was properly publicized to dramatize to the nation that doctors had found F.D.R. in good health, an insurable risk. Like the loans to Warm Springs, it was the subject of much misinterpretation.

Thus it was understandable that those around Roosevelt were a bit apprehensive about the public's reaction to use of the Presidency in a fund-raising venture, however noble the cause, especially Marvin McIntyre, one of his press secretaries. McIntyre and Byoir had become friends in World War I when McIntyre was serving as F.D.R.'s press secretary in the Navy Department and Byoir was associate chairman of the Committee on Public Information. McIntyre is reputed to have told Byoir, "Carl, for God's sake keep this business away from the White House." [22] Whatever the fears of F.D.R. and his coterie, the decision was made to use a celebration of the President's birthday to raise money to fight infantile paralysis.

Doherty was made chairman of the National Committee for Celebration of the President's Birthday and contributed $25,000 to underwrite the costs of organizing and promoting the affair. Byoir and Keith Morgan presented their idea to the American people, Byoir directing the promotion and Morgan handling the housekeeping. O'Connor joyously looked forward to an end of Warm

Springs' hand-to-mouth, debt-ridden existence. F.D.R. watched from the White House with deep satisfaction but was careful to take no visible role in the staging of the fund-raising campaign. He did, year after year, go on the national radio hookup to address all of the Birthday Balls across the country. The drive was launched by a resourceful trio: the shrewd, not always scrupulous Doherty; the imaginative, energetic promoter Byoir; the intelligent, egotistical O'Connor. These three men, who had fought their way to success from poverty and were not accustomed to failure or halfway measures, began the crusade to conquer polio.

The President's Birthday Party

In baseball parlance Carl Byoir was very much a "take charge guy" —imaginative, tireless, and persuasive. Once the decision was made, in early December, to celebrate the President's birthday on January 30, 1934, Byoir became general director. Doherty, who was taking the public bows, persuaded the Waldorf-Astoria Hotel to provide free space for the committee headquarters. In mid-December Byoir moved out of his own firm to set up shop at the Waldorf and quickly assembled a staff. He recruited his close friend, the late J. Stephen (Steve) Flynn, to be executive secretary and serve as Byoir's alter ego in campaign direction. His able personal secretary, Mrs. Elsie Simon Sobotka, worked for these two men day and night, taking calls, making appointments, arranging trip schedules, and straightening out one minor mix-up after another.

Byoir used his own staff to provide the publicity. Most of the promotion came from the typewriters of Gerry Swinehart and Jane Buck, with frequent assistance from Carl Dickey, Howard Swain, and Alden Calkins. George Hammond, now president of the Byoir firm, recalls that he stayed at the firm and "kept the store." Byoir made no charge for his day-and-night services. In fact, he spent about $2,000 out of his own pocket in organizing the celebration. Keith Morgan served as committee treasurer and lent a helpful hand in many ways. Committee workers recall Morgan as "a great organizer."

January 30 was only six weeks away. Byoir had envisioned a birthday ball in every American community "to stamp out infantile paralysis." Most people's thoughts were centered on Christmas. How could so many events be organized in so many cities and towns in so little time, and in the absence of a functioning national organization? He and his public relations aides decided to get newspaper editors involved. Wires were sent to one newspaper in each city and town, asking the editor to nominate a chairman to organize a Birthday Ball in honor of President Roosevelt. Where the editor failed to respond, Byoir turned to the local Democratic party chairman or the Roosevelt-appointed postmaster. There was no time to observe nonpartisan niceties if a successful event was to be planned and promoted. Byoir's associates recall: "No question about it. Our approach in those days was 90 per cent political. It had to be. We had to work with our friends."

This association of the fund-raising effort with political partisanship would, in future years, haunt Warm Springs fund raising. Basil O'Connor recalled in 1955: "To this day in some parts of the country the National Foundation for Infantile Paralysis is suspected to be a part of the Democratic national committee. . . . The amazing thing is how well the money was spent. Little if any was stolen or used for politics." [23] Byoir's secretary, Miss Simon, recalls that "it was always a source of great pride to Mr. Byoir that he accomplished so much at so little cost." He held down expenses by recruiting volunteers and by persuading suppliers to provide free materials and services. Action and ideas started exploding around the Waldorf like Chinese firecrackers.

"Byoir swamped the nation's press and radio with publicity material. Democrats, especially postmasters and collectors of internal revenue, rallied to organize local balls. 'We couldn't wait to find out where the Republicans were,' explained a member of the national committee." [24] Byoir got Wiley Post—the one-eyed around-the-world flier—to fly him across the country to create publicity and to arouse the local committees. He persuaded Howard Chandler Christy to create a poster to publicize the event and as a cover for a fund-raising book published by the committee. Pictures of crippled children filled the nation's newspapers. Radio personalities tried to outdo one another in promoting the event over the nation's airwaves. Walter Winchell, gossip columnist and broadcaster with a large following in those days, presented a potent appeal that would be used repeatedly in Birthday Balls and March of Dimes to come. In his Sunday night broadcast a few weeks before the celebration, Winchell closed with these words: "And so until next Sunday night. . . . I remain Mrs. Winchell's bad little boy, Walter, who urges all of you to attend the various dances held in honor of the President on his birthday, January 30th. Because if you buy a ticket to dance, then some little child who can't even walk may be able to dance some day." The response to this appeal was swift and sure. Byoir's publicists quickly took it up and dinned the ears of the nation with the slogan, "Dance so that a child may walk." [25] George M. Cohan wrote a song for the occasion, and Edgar A. Guest a poem. Every available big name in American public life was mobilized. Every appeal was exploited.

The idea of celebrating the President's birthday to raise money for polio victims quickly stirred national enthusiasm. In those days F.D.R. was seen as the courageous leader who had overcome a great handicap and was now leading the nation out of its slough of despond. Byoir, the public relations man, knew that the timing was right. F.D.R. was now the nation's hero, not yet "That Man in the White House," to be revered and reviled with equal vehemence in his later years. Columnist Mark Sullivan wrote at the time: ". . . neither party is really functioning. What is going on for the present is a form of personal government by general consent." The Providence (R.I.) *News Tribune* editorialized: "Insofar as the people of this state shall respond, we shall be paying tribute to a man who overcame a great affliction to rise to the highest position." Forty thousand persons in Alabama sent F.D.R. a telegram 1,280 feet long, that took three days for transmission, to tell him, "Our gift, the remembrance of a grateful people, we send the Warm Springs Fund for Crippled Children. With it goes our earnest hope it may unfetter tiny feet and help them overhaul truant, youthful spirits which will not be repressed." [26]

An editorialist for the *New York Times* accurately reflected public opinion when he wrote: ". . . we have seen the fact that he [Roosevelt] has appeared to the country to be a spirited and gallant commander-in-chief in a time of national crisis. Not to give him loyal and almost unquestioning support has been all through regarded as something next door to treason." [27] Here was double-barreled appeal hard for people to resist. As Carter says, "The 1934 balls transcended their original purpose and became a national celebration of the fresh hope that Americans felt for their country, as well as an honor to Roosevelt and an occasion to 'Dance so that others may walk.' "

There is no sure count as to exactly how many events were held,

The common estimate in the press was that some 6,000 events were staged in 3,600 communities. Birthday Ball attendance ranged from 10,000 persons crowding a mammoth ball in Philadelphia to one attracting fifteen couples in a small Illinois town. Five thousand persons paid a minimum of $5 a ticket to participate in a gala ball in the Waldorf-Astoria, a dance graced by the presence of the President's eighty-year-old mother and Mayor Fiorella LaGuardia.

Byoir used his Palm Beach connections to stage a lucrative Birthday Ball in that winter capital of the social elite, a dance described by the *Times* as "the largest and most brilliant event held here in many seasons." *Newsweek* reported: "Elks, Moose, Owls, United Mine Workers, and ambassadors danced. . . . In Washington, Myron C. Taylor, board chairman of U.S. Steel, paid $1,000 to go to a party and Negroes in Grafton, W.Va., paid 50 cents for admission to Stozenfel's Hall." The *Times* reported the next day: "Hundreds of thousands of persons joined in these tributes in every State in the Union . . . in the icy reaches of Alaska and Admiral Byrd's camp in Little America, in Hawaii, the West Indies, and the Canal Zone, wherever the Stars and Stripes flies . . . a turnout of the whole people."

In New York City alone forty different fund-raising events were held on January 30 under the leadership of Frank W. Smith, New York Edison utility executive. The clergy paid tribute to F.D.R. at a dinner arranged by the insurance industry because of F.D.R.'s former connection with that field. Five hundred wine and liquor dealers, grateful for the repeal of prohibition, staged a benefit dinner at the Hotel Roosevelt. Centenarians in the Home of Old Israel had their party. Fashionable folk danced at Newport and staunch Republicans danced in Upshur County, W.Va. In Washington Will Rogers was master of ceremonies at a party at the Shoreham Hotel that raised $30,000. Mrs. F.D.R. made the rounds of the Washington parties to say thank you for the President. And the President spoke over the largest radio network in the nation's history—a decision he had made only the day before—to say a heartfelt thank you. "No man has ever had a finer birthday remembrance from his friends and fellows than you have given me tonight. This is the happiest birthday I have ever known." All kinds of people—rich man and poor, old and young, city man and farmer, conservative and radical—had joined hands in a heart-moving common cause.

The Baltimore *Sun* said: "It was a revolutionary event, not politically but socially revolutionary, indicative of the profound social change that has affected this country since the New Deal began." Through it all ran a strong note of faith and deep emotion cleverly exploited by the untiring public relations genius Carl Byoir. The next day the Associated Press made a nationwide survey through its bureaus and stringers and found that 737,067 persons had attended reported parties and that receipts of $839,568 were in hand. The AP predicted, optimistically, that a total of $1.5 million would be raised. It was truly, as the *Literary Digest* headlined, "The Nation's Great Tribute to the President."

When all the receipts had been collected and all the bills paid, the Doherty Committee had raised the more than million dollars Byoir predicted. On May 9, 1934, a presentation ceremony was held in the East Room of the White House. A proud Byoir presided. (He was still so little known then that the *New York Times* spelled his name Byers.) Mr. Doherty was unable to be present because of his illness. Byoir introduced Rear Admiral Cary T. Grayson who presented the yard-long, 18-inch wide parchment check for $1,003,-030.08 to Roosevelt as president of the Warm Springs Foundation. F.D.R. in turn handed the check to O'Connor and quipped, "I am going to appoint all of you a committee to watch Doc O'Connor." In accepting this gift Roosevelt "gave assurance that none of the money would be used to repay advances from those interested in the foundation." [28] And Roosevelt meant it. A gay President cheerily said aloud once more, "A million dollars, Doc." O'Connor quickly replied, "Less the money the Foundation owes you." F.D.R. started to protest and O'Connor hastily interjected, "That's only fair, Franklin." "Not a penny from this money, Doc, and let's not mention it again." O'Connor half muttered to himself, "Damned stubborn Dutchman," an affectionate epithet he often used when balked by his partner and friend.[29] A jubilant F.D.R. grinned and turning to Byoir said, "Carl, I'll bet you a good tie that you can't top this figure next year," thus making it clear that he hoped that this fundraising plan would be used again. Byoir took the bet and a new and powerful pattern of nationwide fund raising was put on a permanent basis.

The Warm Springs Foundation announced a week later that of the $1,003,030.08 raised by the Birthday Ball, benefits of $100,000 would be used "to stimulate and further the meritorious work being done in the field of infantile paralysis," $650,000 for "furtherance of the work at Warm Springs," and that the remaining $253,030.08 would go into the "Warm Springs building and contingency fund." Thus began a stepped-up program to stimulate polio research and to care for the victims of the disease, providing, in F.D.R.'s words, "for the care and cure of crippled children in every corner of this kindly land." There were no accurate figures available but it was estimated in May, 1934, that some 200,000 victims of infantile paralysis were then living in the United States. Roosevelt was sure that the fund raising would do more than raise urgently needed money for his pet philanthropy; he knew that it would arouse great interest in the disease itself. Mrs. Roosevelt said in an interview March 27, 1934, "My husband was quite right that it [the Birthday Ball] would stimulate interest and activity on behalf of crippled children." Among other things the pressure for access to the Warm Springs curative waters grew as the place became nationally known.

Foundation officials were hard pressed to find more funds to build new facilities, and to finance possible provisions for non-paying or part-paying patients. O'Connor and his associates gave consideration to a capital fund-raising drive for two new buildings, apart from the Birthday Balls. John Price Jones's records show that his firm was invited to submit a proposal in June, 1934, for getting money to build two new buildings. Nothing came of Jones's 38-page proposal. The firm recommended a campaign based on these appeals: inspiration of new hope for the crippled; Warm Springs— the means of achieving this new hope; the greatest remaining need —buildings. Doherty's right-hand man and chief executive of the Doherty oil utility empire, W. Alton Jones, was on the building committee. Jones, later to achieve public notice as an intimate friend of President Dwight D. Eisenhower, died in a plane crash in March 1962. Other members were John W. Harris, chairman; Winthrop Aldrich, treasurer; Douglas Gibbons, secretary; Clarence Woolley, vice-chairman; Rex Cole, Grantland Rice, Charles F. Neergaard, Vincent Cullen, and Albert L. Scott. Personal solicitation of large givers continued quietly but more birthday balls were planned. Modern public relations techniques and the national appeal for health needs had been welded into a sure technique for raising millions.

The 1935 Birthday Ball for the President represented another crowning achievement for the hard-driving Byoir and his able, energetic crew of public relations aides. The successful pattern of the first Birthday Ball was repeated with even more flourish. Byoir won his bet with the President by raising more than a million in gross receipts and the tie, with the initials F.D.R. woven into it, became a prized possession. The mass media were saturated with publicity urging support of the President and of the battle against polio. Byoir again took command as general director and did the work while his client, Henry L. Doherty, took the public bows. Byoir again drafted his friend Steve Flynn to serve as committee secretary and look after the details. Keith Morgan continued as treasurer. Added to the general staff this time were Emile E. Watson, director of state organization, and Avery C. Marks, Jr., radio director. All served without compensation, a fact Byoir took pains to make known repeatedly.

Byoir's firm again provided the publicity support. The nation was told by press, radio, poster, town assembly, newsreel, telegram, telephone, and letter that President Roosevelt "has given his 53rd birthday to the cause of Infantile Paralysis which means the present welfare and future safety of American children." This time, to spur broader local support, the Birthday Ball Committee announced that 70 per cent of the receipts would stay in the community where they were raised and 30 per cent would go to the newly organized Commission on Infantile Paralysis Research, also headed by Colonel Doherty. None of the money would go to Warm Springs Foundation this time. The decision to share the funds with the community and to start support of research was attributed to the President in the Birthday Ball releases.

Day and night, for two months, Byoir, Gerry Swinehart, Jane Buck, George Hammond, and others of his staff publicized the President's Birthday Ball. Newspaper publishers across the nation were again asked to foster affairs for their cities and towns and to encourage more community participation. Placards were placed in the nation's show windows, in the New York subways, and on motorbuses. Howard Chandler Christy again painted a campaign poster. Radio personalities were encouraged to repeat the appeal again and again, and they did. Newsreels reached movie audiences with publicity messages weeks before the celebration. Everywhere a person turned he was reminded that he should "dance so that a child may someday walk." Big-city hotels and country schools furnished ballrooms. Even country barns were dusted out and used for "hoedowns" to raise money to fight polio and honor the still popular President. Again Byoir publicity succeeded.

Many new approaches were tried in 1935. Taking the cue from the Birmingham *Post*'s idea of a telegraphic birthday greeting to the President, Byoir set up a Birthday Greeting Committee with Postal Telegraph's Clarence H. Mackay as chairman. Byoir wheedled both Western Union and Postal Telegraph to agree to contribute their facilities for birthday telegrams to the President. Thousands of persons went to telegraph offices across the nation, paid 25 cents to have their names added to the huge roll at the bottom of a gigantic birthday greeting. Western Union and Postal sent the names free and turned over a total of $11,343 to the Birthday Ball Committee.

By the time January 30 rolled around fund-raising events had been organized in 5,600 separate cities and towns. Chicago turned out the greatest number of ballgoers at a single celebration when an estimated 35,000 persons jammed the International Amphitheater of the Union Stockyards. The Kelly-Nash machine could promote birthday balls, too! But Detroit raised the most money, netting $31,-534.51 from several balls. New York's celebration was again marked by pageantry and the heterogeneity of the celebrants. *Time* reported: "Park Avenue rubbed elbows with Avenue A when 15,000 debutantes, ward heelers, American Legionaires, professional party-trotters, bearded Henry Latham Doherty, head of the national Ball Committee, and Mrs. Sara Delano Roosevelt mingled in the five ballrooms of the Waldorf-Astoria."

This was at a time when Doherty was spending thousands to battle the President's proposal to break up the notorious holding company scheme in the utilities which had profited Doherty much. The night of January 30 became a second New Year's Eve in New Deal Washington under the masterful touch of George Allen, confidant of Presidents Roosevelt, Truman, and Eisenhower. In the nation's capital a party was held in every major hotel and Mrs. Eleanor Roosevelt visited all of them to say a personal thank you for the President. F.D.R. again expressed his thanks over a nationwide radio network. In Little America Admiral Byrd blasted a greeting on the Jacob Ruppert's whistle. Five hundred Alaskans waded through snowdrifts for a dance at Ketchikan. Fun-loving Puerto Ricans made the occasion a saint's holiday and celebrated for a whole week. A ringside table at the Tampa, Fla., Colony Club cost $250. A triple wedding was solemnized during the party at Monroe, Wis. There was no end to the ideas dreamed up at the local level to gather a crowd and raise money to fight polio.

When all the celebrations had ended and the expenses had been paid, only something like $750,856, according to Keith Morgan, had been realized in the 1935 Roosevelt birthday parties. Total receipts were not announced until November 19, when Colonel Doherty notified President Roosevelt at a White House luncheon that a gross total of $1,071,000 had been raised. F.D.R. presented Byoir with the victory tie at this luncheon. Others present included Edsel Ford, who had given an indoor pool to Warm Springs in 1928, and Paul de Kruif, the science writer, who played a prominent role in the research side of the fight against polio. At the White House luncheon Doherty told F.D.R. that of the national committee's gross receipts of $326,062.39, a net sum of $241,000 would be turned over to the President's Birthday Ball Commission for Infantile Paralysis Research.[30] Two days later Byoir gave out a more detailed financial accounting in New York City. He said the national committee's expenses for telephone and telegraph, clerical services, travel, and printing totaled $65,056.19. He said 100 cities raised one-third of the more than a million dollars, $305,027.74, with Detroit and Chicago showing the way. As some of the repeat events took on more glitter the net return dropped. For example, the gross receipts from the gala pageant and dance at the Waldorf was $21,960 but when all the bills had been paid a net of only $7,695.91 was left.[31] Whether or not a million dollars was netted to fight polio, the cause of research to find the polio killer and crippler surely received a million dollars' worth of publicity. This was a frequent assertion of Byoir's. The great outpouring of dancers and diners to celebrate the President's birthday also indicated that his popularity was still high. The Republican New York *Herald Tribune* editorialized: "If any one had any doubts of the continued personal popularity of President Roosevelt, the enthusiastic nation-wide celebration of his 53rd birthday ought to end them."

Byoir, Doherty, Morgan, and O'Connor certainly had no doubts because they went ahead with plans for a third fund-raising celebration on January 30, 1936. Doherty made the official announcement on December 3 and again appointed Byoir as general director, Morgan as committee treasurer, and Steve Flynn as executive secretary. The same organization went at the task with the same basic plan, including a split of receipts with the local communities, exploiting the same publicity patterns of appeals to help crippled children and demonstrate support of the President. The biggest innovation in the 1936 Birthday Ball celebrations came from George Allen, who brought the magic of Hollywood to them. "This movie star thing grew like wildfire," one of Allen's associates recalls. Allen tells this story:

> I had been Washington chairman of the President's Birthday Balls from their beginning in 1934, working closely with Basil O'Connor . . . and Mrs. Roosevelt. They were more elaborate affairs in the capital after 1935, when I arranged with Woody Van Dyke, one of the top directors at Metro-Goldwyn-Mayer, to send movie stars to Washington to provide glamour for a city where other kinds of public personages were a dime a dozen and therefore not glamorous. That first time we got Jean Harlow and Robert Taylor. When I called Mrs. Roosevelt to suggest that she invite these two attractive people to tea, she declined but suggested instead that she have them to lunch and invite the press, too. That luncheon became an annual affair, as did Mrs. Roosevelt's evening rounds of the hotels where the balls were held. I customarily accompanied her on these rounds.[32]

Of all this, Mrs. Roosevelt says: "My husband's birthday was always a busy day for all of us. The movie stars took part generously in the celebrations held for the benefit of the victims of polio, and it was great fun to have them lunch with us. . . .

"In the evening I made the rounds of the hotels . . . and, usually, came back to the White House in time to hear my husband broadcast, in the company of many of the stars. I know how touched and deeply grateful for their cooperation Franklin was and how glad that his birthday could be made the occasion for helping the victims of polio." [33]

To promote the 1936 Birthday Ball celebration, in the year that Roosevelt was up for re-election, Byoir and his staff asked Howard Chandler Christy to paint his third official poster for the programs, billboards, and placards; got the advertising agencies and major advertisers to contribute ads and space to publish them; announced the balls over every radio station and through every major program; issued reams of copy for press and periodical; developed new sequences for the newsreels; and publicized harder if perhaps more routinely. Colonel Doherty repeatedly pleaded, through Byoir's publicity, that "only nation-wide generosity can remedy the plight of the nation's

300,000 infantile paralysis victims" and repeatedly reminded Americans that "from the scourge of 1935 . . . this dread disease added approximately 10,000 victims to its rolls." One of the reasons that it was relatively easy to dramatize the threat of polio was the fact that it was an epidemic disease and, unlike heart disease or cancer, periodically dominated the nation's front pages.

President Roosevelt continued his public support of the Birthday Ball fund-raising effort. On Saturday night, January 18, he told the National Committee for the President's Birthday Ball by telephone, and the nation by press release, that "My birthday has been chosen as the occasion for helping this noble work which evokes from me my most profound gratitude." He also used this occasion to refute the Warm Springs rumors by telling the nation, "Last year not one penny of the money given went into the work of the institution in Georgia." Roosevelt saw, rightly, that "this fight against infantile paralysis is constantly assuming a greater and greater national character." [34] Although F.D.R. publicly endorsed the Birthday Ball enterprise each year, activity was kept away from the White House and the presidential staff did not become involved.

For the third time admirers of Roosevelt, the rich and poor, philanthropists and fun-seekers, danced and dined to celebrate the President's birthday and to give money to fight polio. Some 20,000 dancers crowded Convention Hall in Philadelphia where Governor and Mrs. George Earle led the grand march. Another 5,000 persons dined, drank, and danced in three Miami hotels. James A. Farley was the honored guest at the party held in Colonel Doherty's Miami Biltmore. Once more some 3,500 of New York's social and economic elite and not-so-elite swarmed into the swank Waldorf-Astoria to celebrate and to watch another glittering pageant, this one entitled "Health, Wealth, and Happiness." And again the President's venerable mother was the honored guest. Just before the President spoke to the celebrants Doherty and Byoir made short speeches. Fifteen hundred people danced at fashionable Newport. The President's Birthday Ball on Staten Island ended in a pre-dawn riot. At 4 A.M. when the dance ended some 4,000 guests converged on a thronged cloakroom served by two hapless women. Pushing and shoving started, the clothes racks were upset, and a melee ensued. Police reported the riot was "adjusted" by 7 A.M. In the nation's capital some 18,000 persons purchased tickets at $2.50 each to dance or to watch dancing at six balls held in hotels. Again Mrs. Roosevelt, guided by Chairman George

Allen, and flanked by movie stars, made the official rounds. Again the President said thanks over a nationwide radio hookup. According to the *New York Times* account the next day, some 5 million persons had attended some 6,000 fund-raising events. As before, no accurate count was made.

One sharp difference in 1936 was the President's own private birthday party, which was somber and subdued because his faithful aide and wise public relations mentor, Louis Howe, lay fatally ill in the naval hospital in Bethesda, Md. The afternoon of his birthday F.D.R. and his two press secretaries, Steve Early and Marvin McIntyre, visited Howe for an hour. Until then Howe had been the planner and promoter of F.D.R.'s private birthday celebrations. Mrs. Roosevelt recalls: "In our pre-White House days Louis Howe, who was a versatile person, had always spent a great deal of time and thought on my husband's birthday parties; as long as he was able to direct them, they were always amusing. He wrote special songs and poems for them and assigned everyone some particular stunt." [35] His illness cast an air of gloom over the day's events and his death took from the President his valued and devoted counselor, who had spent twenty years making his dream of an F.D.R. presidency come true. [36]

One new promotional idea was introduced to give support to the 1936 balls—that of sponsored advertising. This was in the days before institutional advertising for public relations purposes had become as widespread as it did in World War II and thereafter. To promote the idea Byoir and his staff put out the *Bulletin* in newspaper format with promotional ads of varying sizes that enterprising advertising salesmen could sell to local merchants and other business firms. The 14-page promotional newspaper, distributed to local committees, advertisers, and advertising agencies, also carried news stories and news pictures that could be and were utilized in local publicity campaigns. The *Bulletin* was produced by the William H. Rankin Co., which also produced the annual *Birthday Magazine*, another money raiser. A review of the 1936 publicity effort indicated that some 10 million lines of advertising costing $1 million had been contributed by commercial advertisers to promote the sale of Birthday Ball tickets. Byoir asserted that this was the first fund-raising effort to receive the benefit of sponsored advertising, an invalid claim. But it was certainly the most intensive use of paid advertising for fund raising up to that time.

Yet, despite the million dollars' worth of advertising and the millions of dollars' worth of free publicity Byoir's staff obtained, the 1936 Birthday Ball was less successful than the first two. News reports, obviously stemming from the Doherty Committee, put the gross receipts at $1.5 million a few days after the party.[37] Doherty later said the gross receipts totaled $750,000. Carter puts the 1936 Birthday Ball proceeds at $573,000. In 1937 Keith Morgan said the 1936 receipts were $572,756. Again the receipts were shared, with 70 per cent staying in the community where it was raised and 30 per cent going to research. This fact made accurate accounting of amounts collected difficult.

The context in which the 1936 celebrations were held was sharply different from that in the dark days of 1934. The nation was slowly recovering from the depths of depression. Roosevelt had become "That man" to many taxpayers who were back on their feet and now worrying about the mounting national debt. This was an election year and F.D.R. was being bitterly assailed from the political right. There was more talk of his benefiting from the Birthday Ball receipts. A bitter political foe, the rabble-rousing Governor Eugene Talmadge of Georgia, called Warm Springs "a racket" in a letter that was given wide circulation. Many Republican newspapers now editorially questioned the suitability of making the President's birthday a fund-raising device.

Keith Morgan blamed the drop in receipts on "the falling off of the President's universal popularity, particularly among the class of people accustomed to giving large sums of money." And, as Carter recalls, "mendacious gossip that the Roosevelt family bled profits from the polio institution was conscientiously repeated in syndicated columns." Moreover, the bloom of novelty had worn off the Birthday Balls and many apolitical persons were simply growing tired of this appeal. Whatever the factors involved in the decline in receipts, there were many signs that a new approach would ultimately have to be taken. O'Connor, Morgan, and Byoir were becoming aware that there could be dangers in overidentifying Roosevelt with the polio drive. However, Basil O'Connor today asserts that, to his knowledge, there never was a time when he was involved in a discussion about moving the fund-raising campaign away from the F.D.R. figurehead. On the contrary, he points out, binding the National Foundation ever closer to the President seemed to be the technique that was followed.

In 1936 the officers of the Warm Springs Foundation began to think in terms of a long-range program. Endorsed by President Roosevelt, a national campaign opened in Georgia on December 26, 1936, for a permanent endowment of the Warm Springs Foundation. The goal was $2 million of which $42,611.30 was raised in a year's time. Harrison Jones, a vice-president of the Coca-Cola Co., was the chairman for the drive. As a matter of fact, the solicitations for large donations among persons of wealth continued through all the years of the Birthday Balls. In 1935 Georgia Hall, central administration building, was erected with $100,000 given by citizens of Georgia. The same year two dormitories were built with funds contributed by the Kress brothers, Samuel, Rush, and Claude.

Doubts about the declining popularity of President Roosevelt and the waning power of the President's Birthday Ball as a money raiser were convincingly dissipated by F.D.R.'s overwhelming re-election in November, 1936, when he carried every state except two. In the wake of this sweeping triumph at the polls, Colonels Doherty and Byoir and Warm Springs Foundation officials O'Connor and Morgan began to make plans for the 1937 Birthday Ball.

Carl Byoir again took charge of the fund-raising promotion as executive director. His firm sent out reams of publicity copy and placed scores of plugs with columnists and radio personalities. Again Howard Chandler Christy contributed an official poster and program cover. Once more the people were told: "The proceeds of all these entertainments—every cent of them—go to carry on the fight against infantile paralysis. Seventy per cent remains in the community which raises it, to support local hospitals that treat the disease and its after effects. The remaining thirty per cent goes to Warm Springs Foundation in Georgia where so much is being learned about the treatment for disabled victims—where, in a sense, are the headquarters of this whole organized attack on poliomyelitis. . . . A great deal of money is needed." [38]

As before, prominent persons representing all segments of society were used on the national committee: Colonel Doherty, Ambassador Joseph E. Davies, Charles G. Dawes, Edsel Ford, Walter S. Gifford, William Green, Patrick Cardinal Hayes, General John J. Pershing, William Randolph Hearst, and Bishop William T. Manning. There is no record of a committee meeting that would have brought together those ancient foes, Hearst and Manning! Loyal workers, many of them volunteers, put in fifteen and sixteen hours a day at committee headquarters, under the inspiring leadership of the tireless Carl Byoir. Again, the fund-raising events ranged widely, from checker tournaments to box suppers to the now standard gala pageant in the Waldorf-Astoria where Mrs. Sara Delano Roosevelt was the honored guest. This time the Byoir staff estimated that some 6,000 events drawing 5 million persons were held across the nation—and even on the foreign soil of Bermuda. In 1937 $1 million was raised in gross receipts.

In a statement issued September 14, 1937, Chairman Doherty said that a gross of $1,090,779 had been realized in the 1937 celebrations. Of this amount $325,000 had been sent the National Committee from 3,591 communities and another $15,000 was expected before the books were closed. Doherty reported that Western Union and Postal Telegraph had, between them, raised $80,106.19 from the birthday greeting messages sent to President Roosevelt. The colonel explained that he had given $50,000 to underwrite the expenses of the 1937 birthday party. This presumably is the same $50,000 he announced as a gift to the National Committee on January 30, when he wrote President Roosevelt that "I want to support your own leadership in raising both flood and paralysis relief funds." The 1937 polio fund raising came in the midst of the tragic floods in the Ohio and Mississippi River valleys. The Red Cross was appealing for flood relief money at the same time that Byoir was appealing for money to battle polio. The Doherty gift, duly publicized by Byoir, was apparently an effort to prod people to give to both causes and make them appear noncompetitive.

Although the Birthday Balls had once more grossed more than a million dollars, there continued a rumble of criticism, both within and without the Foundation. Dr. Michael Hoke, surgeon in chief at Warm Springs, was deeply pained by the emotional appeals Byoir and his aides used to promote the polio crusade. "He was angry that the medical methods used at his institution had been publicized, dismayed that patients had been interviewed on the radio, horrified that polio sufferers throughout the country had been misled to think that they could come to Warm Springs, where there was no room for them, and be cured, which was impossible." [39] Other physicians were unhappy about the high hopes raised by the Byoir-directed campaigns. Republican editors continued to carp at the idea of linking a political leader with a philanthropic appeal. And when the General Asembly of the Presbyterian Church met at Columbus, Ohio, in May, 1937, a resolution "objecting to the annual Birthday Balls given throughout the country in honor of President Roosevelt" was introduced but not passed. O'Connor and Morgan realized that another plan was needed.

At this point Carl Byoir resigned. His associates give two reasons: first, his break with Roosevelt over the President's effort to "pack" the Supreme Court early in 1937; second, what he considered Roosevelt's ingratitude to Doherty in refusing to name him a trustee of the about-to-be-formed National Foundation for Infantile Paralysis. Byoir had been an enthusiastic political supporter of Roosevelt from 1930 on. The public relations counselor had seen the consequences of the depression in 1932 when he tried, heroically but unsuccessfully, to promote a "Share the Job" campaign as the "War Against the Depression." This campaign had been sponsored by the American Legion, the American Federation of Labor, and the Association of National Advertisers. Byoir publicity was no match for the overpowering economic forces then gripping the nation, and Byoir admired Roosevelt's attack on the depression when he came to office.

In 1936 Byoir raised large sums for the Democratic National Committee with his Roosevelt nominators plan whereby a person could join in the nomination of Roosevelt by signing a nomination certificate and contributing a minimum of $1. As part of this fund-raising campaign Byoir staged Nominator Rallies acros the nation to coincide with Roosevelt's ringing acceptance speech in Franklin Field, June 27, 1936—the speech in which he introduced the stinging epithet "economic royalist." And certainly one of these was Doherty. In appreciation of Byoir's efforts, Roosevelt wrote him this letter under date of July 10, 1936:

Dear Carl:
I am just off to start my cruise but I do want to send you this line to tell you how much I appreciate all that you did in organizing the "Roosevelt Nominators." I know what a tremendous amount of hard work this entailed, and I hope much that you are going to get a little holiday yourself. My thanks to you and my very best wishes. I hope I shall see you soon.

Byoir ultimately became a Republican and, at different times, a vigorous supporter of Senator Robert A. Taft and Governor Thomas E. Dewey for the Presidency.

The original copy of the following letter, written for President Roosevelt's signature but never agreed to, was found in Carl Byoir's papers:

Nov. 10, 1937

Dear Mr. Doherty:

When you wrote me on October 12th that, despite your long siege of treatment, you had not reached at any time a state of recovery that would justify you in attacking a problem of the first magnitude, such as is represented in the attempt we are going to make through the new national foundation for infantile paralysis, I was, of course, keenly disappointed. I realized then that no one ought to urge you to take any risks that might retard your complete recovery, particularly in view of the great contribution you had already made in the fight against infantile paralysis through your four-year chairmanship of the National Committee for the Birthday Ball for the President, and the raising, through the cooperation of our fellow-citizens everywhere, a fighting fund that approximates $4,000,000. The very fact that the larger part of this fund remained in the communities where raised assured that the very task of administration by local committees would create an ever-widening interest in this fight.

Since it would obligate you to no active part in the work to be undertaken, and because it would keep alive your own interest in and association with all that we hope to do in the fight against infantile paralysis, I am wondering if you wouldn't agree, at least for this year, to accept the honorary chairmanship of the birthday celebrations.

Although your present health prevents you from actively participating in the larger plan I have outlined, I am indeed heartened to know of your confidence in an early and complete recovery, and I earnestly hope that the day will not be long delayed.

You will always have my personal appreciation for the service you have rendered.

Very sincerely yours,
FRANKLIN D. ROOSEVELT

Surely another factor in Byoir's decision to retire from Birthday Ball campaigning was the fact that the pattern had become routine and the task had lost its challenge. In the estimate of his associates, Byoir was primarily an idea man and an organizer; once a challenge had been met and solved Byoir tended to lose interest in it. He was not a detail man and needed the fresh stimulation of new tasks to keep going at his fast pace.

No one can surely ascribe the motives that move men but it seems apparent that both Doherty and Byoir had entered into the campaign to get money for Warm Springs with mixed motives. Doherty suffered painfully from arthritis in his latter years and was intensely interested in it and related diseases. He was equally aware of Roosevelt's animosity for the utility magnates who had bilked the nation's consumers and investors in the freewheeling days of "normalcy." Carl Byoir was an enthusiastic Roosevelt political supporter and was, of course, anxious to refurbish the rather tarnished reputation of his client Doherty.

Byoir also was pioneering in a new field, not as widely accepted then as now, and knew that the aura of association with the President of the United States would be a valuable asset. Neither of these men was anything but shrewd, but so was Franklin D. Roosevelt. He was quite willing to use the money and talents of Doherty and his public relations man, Byoir, but had no intention of being gulled by them. When Doherty did try to cash in on his work for Warm Springs with the President he was rebuffed. George Hammond, Byoir's longtime and devoted co-worker, stoutly insists that there was never a *quid pro quo* in Byoir's work for the President. But surely the astute Byoir knew the value of having an entree to the White House and resultant publicity as a leader in a noble cause. In those years, 1933–1937, both Doherty and Byoir needed favorable publicity to offset the questionable reputation each was getting.

Shortly before Keith Morgan made his first appeal to Doherty for support of Warm Springs, *Newsweek* had reported: "In the mad New Era days when bankers and bootblacks bought stocks at fancy prices, high-pressure salesmen scoured the country boosting Cities Service Co. common. Not even the campaigns of the National City Co. rivaled this one in intensity. The drive was directed by Henry L. Doherty Co. to raise money for Cities Service, parent organization of a $1,000,-000,000 oil and utility empire. Every known device was used." [40] This was in reference to the Federal Trade Commission's investigation of the near $18 million profit that Doherty had made in a 1929 stock juggle. In the mid-thirties, when this was exposed, Doherty had to pay up $1,250,000 to settle Cities Service stockholders' suits out of court. In those same years Doherty was spending money and pulling strings in a vain effort to block passage of Roosevelt's Public Utility Holding Act. The February 15, 1937, issue of *Time* reported that Doherty spent $200,000 to lobby against public regulation of utilities. Politically, F.D.R. and Doherty were poles apart.

Byoir, too, was then getting unfavorable publicity. His initial service for the Cuban government of Dictator Machado had brought him sharp criticism. Another tourist account, this one with the German government, was exposed and criticized in 1934 by a House of Representatives Committee investigating Nazi propaganda in the United States. According to testimony given to the Committee, on October 1, 1933, eight months after Adolf Hitler had come to power, Byoir's firm signed an 18-month contract with the German Tourist Information Office to promote travel to Germany for a fee of $108,000. Testimony revealed that the old-time German propagandist, George Sylvester Viereck, then busily engaged in trying to sell Hitler to the American people, had been the go-between and, in return, had been put on Byoir's payroll at $1,750 a month.[41] These charges would be reiterated against Byoir in 1940 by Congressman Wright Patman, then engaged in a political fight with a Byoir client, the A. & P. Tea Co. In 1940 Byoir demanded a hearing and received a clean bill of health on the charge that he had done anything more than provide tourist publicity for the German nation. So Byoir, too, needed the prestige that public association with F.D.R. brought in the turbulent New Deal years.[42]

It would appear that Doherty and Byoir got the deep satisfaction that comes from promoting a worthwhile cause and much favorable personal publicity for their efforts, but nothing more from a canny Franklin D. Roosevelt. In his final appearance as executive director of the Birthday Balls Byoir told the 1937 nationwide radio audience and the celebrants, "You are the painters of rainbows in lives clouded by pain and sickness and lost hope." The real painter of the brilliant hues in those rainbows of hope had been Carl Byoir. Thus Colonels Doherty and Byoir made their exit from the polio crusade!

The March of Dimes—1938

Keenly aware of the fading appeal of the Birthday Ball celebrations, Basil O'Connor and Keith Morgan moved ahead with their plans to establish a permanent, independent polio fund-raising organization of a nonpartisan character. On September 22, 1937, President Roosevelt announced, from his Hyde Park home, the establishment of the National Foundation for Infantile Paralysis to coordinate the three-pronged attack on polio: to promote research into its causes and cure; to care for patients struck by the disease; and to find a cure for the aftereffects of the paralysis. F.D.R.'s press statement read in part: "the general purpose of the new Foundation will be to lead, direct, and unify the fight on every phase of this sickness. It will make every effort to ensure that every responsible research agency in this country is adequately financed to carry on investigations into the cause of infantile paralysis and the methods by which it may be prevented." It was made plain also that the Foundation would place much stress on a broad-gauged educational campaign "prepared under expert medical supervision." Roosevelt announced that his long-time partner Basil O'Connor would head the new Foundation and that it would continue the Birthday Balls.[43] The *New York Times* endorsed the Foundation as "a constructive answer . . . finely and humanely conceived . . . touches every root and fiber. . . . What [Roosevelt] proposes is a fairly large experiment in socialized medicine." This was before the American Medical Association had made socialized medicine an epithet!

On November 7 Roosevelt directed that "because sufficient time has not elapsed for organization of the National Foundation for Infantile Paralysis . . . that the 1938 Birthday Balls celebration be planned and carried out by the treasurer of the Warm Springs Foundation, Keith Morgan." Morgan, deeply involved in organizing and promoting the previous parties, was well-equipped for this assignment. With Roosevelt's approval, he quickly announced that all funds received in 1938 would be given to the new National Foundation, and none would go to Warm Springs Foundation, and that the name of the committee would be Committee for the Celebration of the President's Birthday for Fighting Infantile Paralysis. This was the beginning of the shift away from honoring Roosevelt to "fighting infantile paralysis" in campaign appeals. As members of his executive committee to plan the celebration, Morgan selected W. Averell Harriman, George E. Allen, Edsel Ford, S. Clay Williams, Marshall Field, and Walter J. Cummings.

Headquarters were established at 50 East 42nd Street, New York City, under the direction of Colonel William H. Rankin, the publisher of the official programs for the previous fund-raising balls. On November 15 Morgan announced the appointment of George Allen as executive director of the 1938 campaign. Allen, presidential crony, in turn appointed Tom Wrigley as director of publicity and Robert Berger as director of radio. In the revised March of Dimes organization separate departments were created for Public Relations, Radio, Motion Pictures, and Fund Raising. This would indicate that O'Connor and his aides thought of public relations as synonymous with publicity in those years. All of these departments contributed to the success of the March of Dimes.

Wrigley, a native of Elmira, N.Y., was a veteran newspaper man. He had started as a cub reporter on the Elmira *Gazette* in 1909 and by 1920 had worked up to the post of managing editor. From 1920 to 1922 he worked for Hearst's International News Service, in 1923 returned to Elmira to serve as managing editor of the Elmira *Star-Gazette*, and then returned to the Hearst organization. From 1923 to 1925 Wrigley worked for Hearst as city editor of the Boston *Advertiser* and the Boston *Sunday American* and for the next four years, 1925–1929, in Universal News Bureau in Washington, D.C., then until 1933 in the New York office of Universal News, the old Hearst morning news wire. With the onset of the depression Wrigley was cut loose by Universal and, like many another unemployed newsman, he went into publicity work. At International News Service, Wrigley had worked with the talented Dorothy Ducas and he hired her to direct the women's activities. Miss Ducas would ultimately play a key role in the public relations work of the Foundation. When she reported to Wrigley for work in October, 1937, Miss Ducas began an association with the polio crusade that would last until June 1, 1960, when she resigned from the new National Foundation. In those years Dorothy Ducas would write fund-raising and public relations history. From 1937 through 1942 she worked only during the four-month campaign period—October through January.

This trio of publicists—Wrigley, Berger, and Ducas—set to work with the enthusiasm of beginners and the flair of professionals to produce a public relations campaign that was, in Carter's words, "without precedent as a promotional raid on the mind, heart, and pocketbook of the United States." It set a pattern for getting dimes and dollars from millions of people that would later be copied and envied by every disease-battling national agency. The talents and skills of advertising men and women, public relations practitioners, organization leaders, and leaders from every trade and profession were activated in planning and promoting this first campaign under the aegis of the new Foundation. Wrigley and Miss Ducas quickly shifted the main appeal from one of paying tribute to the nation's President to one of unashamed exploitation of the pathetic appeals of crippled children. With them the noble purpose of the cause justified the means of emotional appeals.

It was in this campaign that the now famous March of Dimes was conceived. Morgan, O'Connor, Wrigley, and others had been acutely aware of the need to broaden the appeal and create new channels of giving. Stimulated by the success of the birthday telegrams, the idea of asking the people to send birthday gifts to the President at the White House had come up in previous years, had been discussed and then dropped because of fear of adverse public reaction. It was the beloved radio comedian Eddie Cantor who introduced the March of Dimes idea. There is no dispute about this among Foundation old-timers. Cantor, who gave much to philanthropic fund raising, died on October 10, 1964.

As in the past, a Hollywood committee had been appointed to obtain and channel the support of radio and motion-picture stars for the 1938 Birthday Ball celebration. Cantor, a loyal volunteer in the previous public appeals, suggested at a committee meeting in Hollywood in late October, "We could ask the people to send their dimes directly to the President at the White House." Then he quickly added a phrase that was to perform money-raising miracles in the years to come: "We could call it the March of Dimes." Cantor is reported to have said later that the idea was suggested by the "March of Time," then a popular feature in motion-picture theaters and on radio. The idea was brought back to New York for O'Connor's approval. Some of his aides vetoed the idea on the ground that this strengthened, not loosened the appeal tie to F.D.R. O'Connor decided to take it up with F.D.R. He telephoned the White House and talked to Grace Tully, a secretary. "Check it with the President and see if he'll stand for it," O'Connor told Miss Tully. She brought back F.D.R.'s terse reply, "Go ahead." [44]

With this green light, Wrigley and his staff went to work to spread the idea to the radio personalities of the day, with the strong assistance of the popular Cantor. Cantor, Jack Benny, Bing Crosby, Rudy Vallée, Deanna Durbin, Lawrence Tibbett, Jascha Heifetz, Joe Penner, Kate Smith, Edgar Bergen, and the Lone Ranger all went on the air in late January with repeated appeals for dimes to be mailed to the White House. George Allen had casually reassured the White House staff, "You may get a trickle of dimes."

Two days after the first appeals had gone out over the nation's airways an irritated, concerned Marvin McIntyre, White House press secretary, called Keith Morgan and said, "We're in trouble. You fellows have ruined the President. All we've got is $17.50. The reporters are asking us how much we've got. We're telling them we haven't had time to count." Morgan summoned Wrigley and the latter suggested switching the mail to local addresses or to local postmasters. Called back, McIntyre vetoed this idea, reporting that "the damage is done. The President has got his Dutch up and insists he'll see it through." Once more the President proved more perceptive about public reactions than his public relations advisers. The next morning about ten o'clock McIntyre called Morgan to report gleefully that the mail truck had just arrived at the White House with 23 bags of mail. McIntyre told Morgan: "Everybody's taking a holiday. The mailroom is swamped. There are mail trucks and bags all over the place. Nobody can find the official mail." [45]

In the final week of the 1938 fund-raising effort the dimes poured into the White House—30,000 the first day, 50,000 the second day, 150,000 the third day. The final total of letters was put, months later, at 230,000. Dimes came loose in envelopes, taped or gummed to cardboard, jammed in cans. They came with warm personal letters to the President. Tom Wrigley recalled later, "The President was tickled pink." Desks and offices were stacked high with this flood of money-laden mail. The White House staff did little but open envelopes, sort mail, and count dimes for several days. All told, a total of 2,680,000 dimes ($268,000) were received in this first historic March of Dimes. "For weeks before this showmanly climax the atmosphere was saturated with polio information. Publicity and hundreds of thousands of dollars in donated advertising appeared in hundreds of publications. Physicians were persuaded to talk polio on the radio and in the press, and were sometimes easier to deal with than they had been in previous years, because . . . the new foundation possessed medical credentials that the old birthday-ball group had lacked." [46]

Tom Wrigley and Dorothy Ducas knew how to get publicity. Miss Ducas used Mrs. Roosevelt, Mrs. Cordell Hull, Mrs. Charles Evans Hughes, and other prestigious leaders to rally the nation's women. Wrigley persuaded Walt Disney to make a special Mickey Mouse cartoon for the nation's theaters. Warner Bros. produced and released two short subject films. Transit companies provided free car-card advertising. Match companies printed promotional matchbooks. Newspapers, prodded by a special Publishers' Council, provided miles of publicity clippings. Even children were brought into the act with buttons proclaiming, "I'm glad I'm well." Wrigley and Ducas exploited the emotional appeal of the crippled child as it had never been exploited before. When the sound of the new staff's publicity drums had rolled away and the tired dancers had found their way home from more Birthday Balls, a total of $1,823,045.46 had been raised in the first campaign for the National Foundation for Infantile Paralysis. Of this sum, 42 per cent went into promotional expenses—a fact that brought public controversy and contention about the Foundation's fund-raising costs which continues to this day. However expensive, however controversial, fund-raising history had been made in these five years with the introduction of modern high-pressure public relations. From the patterns fashioned by Byoir and improved upon by Tom Wrigley and Dorothy Ducas would flow the money that would ultimately drive the scourge of polio from the land, and these patterns would be duplicated in other fields of health and welfare.

Typical of the criticism of the Foundation's campaign methods and costs was this poke at O'Connor:

> Polio is no longer a great menace to children and adults—but in fact, it never was in this nation. In a big year there were thirty or thirty-five thousand cases. Yet because of the symbol of the child in braces, and because of astute public relations, this disease was built up as though it were cancer (250,000 deaths per year), heart disease (900,000 deaths per year), and mental illness (filling better than 50 per cent of the hospital beds in the nation)—all in one. The National Foundation for Infantile Paralysis did a very fine job indeed with patient-care, the establishment and expansion of rehabilitation facilities and services, and education. But it took the NFIP twenty years before Dr. Salk's vaccine was announced as safe and effective for widespread use. During those twenty years, the NFIP spent but one dollar out of every fourteen—7 per cent of what it collected—on research. Could scientists have used more than that? Certainly. . . . But the NFIP built itself up into a powerful organization—the most successful fund-raising organization of its type yet known—by doing a job on patient care and minimizing research.[47]

O'Connor would like to have kept all of the more than a million dollars net, raised in 1938, for the new National Foundation but was thwarted by the precedent that had been set in the previous Birthday Ball campaigns. Half remained in the community, to be used in caring for polio patients; half went to the Foundation and from there, after a healthy bite for administrative costs, the funds found their way to the nation's medical researchers. With the magic of the March of Dimes discovered and the appeal of themes to fight polio strengthened, it was clear that there would be enough money to care for the patients and to support medical research. This division of funds actually worked out very well. Money to support local services generated the motivation and enthusiasm of local committees to raise money each year. The other half of the sums raised was sufficient to build a strong national organization that was "able to advance all aspects of its program at top speed."

The Foundation officially began operations in Basil O'Connor's law office in January, 1938, with O'Connor as president. The board of trustees included George E. Allen, William Clayton, Marshall Field, Edsel Ford, James V. Forrestal, Jr., Averell Harriman, Robert E. Mc-Math, Carroll B. Merriam, Jeremiah Milbank, Edward R. Stettinius, Jr., Thomas J. Watson, Robert W. Woodruff, and Clarence M. Woolley. "Accepting the new responsibility, O'Connor faced the fact that the most sweeping pledge in the world's history of public health programs had been made—that, in addition to the financing of a full research program, each victim of the disease who could not pay for treatment would have the finest total care provided for him. No private group or government had ever dared make such a promise." [48] To keep this promise would take skilled public relations.

From 1938 through the 1952 March of Dimes-Birthday Ball campaign, the new Foundation and the Committee for the Celebration of the President's Birthday were kept as separate entities, the first to spend the money and the second to raise it. In those early years O'Connor and Morgan did not see the need for a full-time public relations program despite the educational commitment that had been made when the Foundation was set up.

For the campaign years of 1939, 1940, 1941, and 1942, each October 1 Tom Wrigley and Dorothy Ducas reported for the four-month assignment of conducting the intensive drive to raid the hearts and pocketbooks of the American people. The fund-raising department, under the late Warren Coss, sought out potential donors in their homes, in their offices, in their taverns, in their bowling alleys, in their movie theaters, in their clubs, in the street, and at the basketball games. No one escaped the appeal. Increasingly the emphasis was shifted to the March of Dimes and dimes were collected in canisters and in door-to-door solicitations, not by mail to the White House. In Dorothy Ducas' opinion, "The March of Dimes caught on big and it was a much cheaper way to raise money. The Birthday Balls and similar functions took so much for overhead. Surely the March of Dimes is the most successful example yet of mass philanthropy." [49]

After the 1942 March of Dimes campaign, Miss Ducas became chief of the magazine bureau of the Office of War Information and Wrigley carried the brunt of the 1943 campaign after which he, too, left the Foundation. His place was taken by George La Porte, who served as a full-time director of public relations until he quit to take a similar post with the Greater New York Chapter of the Foundation.

In March, 1944, Miss Ducas (in private life Mrs. James B. Herzog) came back to the Foundation to pick up the crusade banner she would wave for the next sixteen years. O'Connor brought her back as a part-time consultant "to do what you think ought to be done." One of her first projects was to overhaul the Foundation's annual report, making it a readable narrative, not a dry compilation of statistics and finances. She set about to get more magazine articles published, suggesting some, writing some herself. There was a discernible shift in emphasis from the intensive short-term fund-raising publicity to a longer-range goal of winning support for research and care programs.

Increasingly, after Roosevelt's death in April, 1945, O'Connor felt the need for a Washington representative to maintain liaison with Congress and with officials in the executive branch of government. With the all-powerful, always helpful F.D.R. gone, O'Connor no longer had easy access to the White House and through it to the government. In 1946 Tom Wrigley was recalled to active duty as "Washington consultant," a post he still held in 1960. Wrigley was by now, in 1946, sixty-four years old. After the 1949 campaign La Porte, for reasons not readily apparent, was shifted to the Greater New York Chapter and O'Connor asked Miss Ducas to take on the position full time. She demurred, hesitating to give up the freedom her consultant arrangement provided. In June, 1949, she consented to take it on an "acting" basis until O'Connor found someone to fill the post permanently. In January, 1950, she confronted O'Connor and asked when he was going to get a replacement for her. "I haven't been looking for one. You're doing all right," he replied in his characteristic way. She took the job on a permanent basis and thus began what she terms "ten exciting years of the Foundation's history."

In June, 1959, Miss Ducas became a consultant again for a year and then retired for part-time work in other fields so that she could spend more time with her family. She said she felt the new program required new leaders in public relations as well as in the medical field, with perhaps new techniques appropriate to the new diversified program. Her inclination to make way for new leadership was given impetus when she had some differences with O'Connor on public relations matters. Under Dorothy Ducas' deft hand the Foundation's public relations program had broadened and matured.

The first thing this capable publicist did was to institute a program of publicity the year around. Until that time the Foundation, and before that Byoir's Birthday Ball celebrations, had done a terrific four-month job of intensive promotion to raise money and get attendance at fund-raising events. But once this had been done the publicity was put aside until time for another money-getting celebration. "We instituted a great diversity of activities so that if we didn't reach people one way we would another. Those we didn't interest by staging fashion shows we would reach by having benefit bowling tournaments. Each year the Foundation added a new event to its array of fund-raising devices. This served the dual function of providing a fresh news peg and of reaching even more people. Our goal, always, was to appeal to many for little gifts and in this way raise a lot of money," Dorothy Ducas recalls.[50]

She found that the year-round publicity was quite effective because it showed, among other things, that "we weren't always just asking for money or for money-raising publicity. We tried deliberately to operate as a news office, putting our chips on factual stuff. As a consequence we became the polio information bureau for the whole country." By the same token the National Foundation became the headquarters and spearhead for the nationwide battle against this infrequent but deadly crippler. The fund raising gathered momentum as it went. Leading the way, always, was O'Connor, who in Dorothy Ducas' words, "had a perfect genius for getting things done." Before they were through they had raised $551.8 million in the years from 1938 through 1958 and almost everyone in America knew of the March of Dimes. In a nationwide opinion survey in February, 1954, the American Institute of Public Opinion found that 83 per cent of the people could identify the March of Dimes—a remarkably deep penetration of the public mind.

Not all the lucrative fund-raising ideas originated with O'Connor and his aides. The most successful device of all, the Mothers' March on Polio, originated in Wausau, Wis., in the 1950 drive. This was the idea of having residents of a city leave their porch lights on for a period of one hour, say from 7 to 8 P.M., as a signal to a volunteer collector to stop for a contribution. The million-dollar idea was born of necessity, the practical answer to the problem every fund-raising committee faces—not enough canvassers to do the job. It was conceived by Neal Rothman, Wausau newspaper editor, and John Van Gnechten. In 1950 Van Gnechten was county chairman and Rothman city chairman for the March of Dimes in Marathon County. They made plans for a door-to-door canvass in Wausau, using newsboys and members of the American Legion as volunteers. They found they did not have enough manpower to cover the city so they had the idea of asking people to turn on their porch lights "as a signal they were willing to give and thus save the time of our volunteers." [51] Not only did the burning porch light save the volunteer's time; it made the task more inviting because the timid collector was not worried about angry rebuffs. And, no doubt, the neighbor whose front light was not burning felt the heat of social pressure from the lighted porches in the block. A student of the polio crusade volunteers writes:

> The campaign activity which has the broadest appeal for March of Dimes Volunteers as a participant activity and which is widely regarded as the single most effective technique for obtaining mass support is the Mothers' March on Polio. . . .
> The Mothers' March is both a highly-organized activity and one which provides many opportunities for local improvisation. Organization-wise it borrows much from military strategy. The woman in charge of each ward is a Colonel, and her assistants are Block Captains and Lieutenants; the event itself is a *march* against a common enemy. The headquarters office features a large map of the city, divided into areas of responsibility; in cities the size of Philadelphia, for example, 65,000 Marching Mothers are needed for complete coverage. And the quasi-military character of the event is highlighted by the fact that timing is an important feature: the goal is to visit every house in the county during one hour. . . . "Turn on Your Porch Light! Fight Polio Tonight!" is the theme of the advance publicity.[52]

The national headquarters staff was quick to see the great potential of this volunteer-originated idea and the next year it was used across the nation. The features were standardized by Miss Ducas and her staff, later utilized everywhere, and it was eventually copied by other health fund-raising campaigns, particularly the drive for muscular dystrophy. But, as Sills pointed out, "the methods of heralding the event, and of obtaining public cooperation, are infinitely diversified. The use of bells, sirens, whistles, and searchlights to announce the start of the Mothers' March is suggested by National Headquarters, but there is a wide variety of local refinements." [53]

But it takes more than publicity and spotlights stabbing the night sky to raise the millions of dollars that have been given to the National Foundation, first for polio and then for battling arthritis and birth defects. It takes volunteers' time, ringing doorbells to ask for money. In the peak years before the discovery of the Salk vaccine the Foundation had the loyal, enthusiastic help of more than two million volunteer workers. Sills found in his study that most workers were initially recruited into the Foundation as March of Dimes volunteers, and for those who do not participate in patient care activities fund raising is the major rationale for their membership in the Foundation. "The key word which summarizes the satisfactions provided by the patient care program is 'service'; the parallel term to describe the rewards of fund-raising is 'performance.'"

The appeal and success of the Foundation in getting money and recruiting volunteers goes deeper than the magnetic leadership of a gallant Franklin D. Roosevelt, deeper than the hard-driving leadership of a Basil O'Connor, deeper than the public relations skills of a Carl Byoir, a Tom Wrigley, or a Dorothy Ducas. It goes to the satisfactions millions of people find in this kind of activity in our present-day society. Sills found in his study that the Foundation, even before its change of name and change of goals, had acquired an institutional status transcending its then-current goals. Volunteers perceive the organization as a "social movement" and this provides them "an ideological rationale for their own participation." Sills rightly concludes: "The March of Dimes through its basic strategy of obtaining small gifts from millions of contributors has become not only a fund-raising campaign, but an institutionalized aspect of American life." [54]

Little did Carl Byoir, Henry Doherty, and Keith Morgan foresee what would come of their sessions around a crackling pine log fire in Warm Springs, Ga., that November of 1933. The casual beginnings of the President's Birthday Balls have had a profound effect on the character of the National Foundation and on American philanthropy. The Foundation's almost total dependence on getting money from millions of people in small sums traces back to the decisions to solicit gifts from the people of Georgia for a new building at Warm Springs and to raise funds nationally by staging the President's Birthday Balls.

Sills holds that "the characteristically middle-class composition of the Foundation's Volunteer membership may be traced in large part to the decision to ask postmasters, Democrats, and persons of civic prominence generally to organize these Birthday Balls." Surely the patient care program was a direct outgrowth of the decision, starting with the 1935 President's Birthday Ball, to leave half the money in the local communities so as to provide incentive for local effort.

In the strong words of a British physician, "Here was the apotheosis of organized philanthropy, of 'planned giving,'" which will "stand forever as a monument to what ruthless and energetic fund raising can do, for good or evil, if allowed to run riot." [55] Writing out of his medical knowledge and the perspective permitted by time and distance, Dr. John Rowan Wilson sees the March of Dimes as typically American, and rightly so. "When the American nation decided that poliomyelitis could be conquered, they went about it in what can be regarded as a characteristic way—with great urgency and energy, wastefully, expensively, and with the maximum of publicity, some desirable and some thoroughly obnoxious." [56] But as Dr. Wilson readily admits, "Success justifies a great deal." The numbing fear of polio has been forever lifted from the hearts of anxious parents.

NOTES

1. Robert Hamlin, *Voluntary Health and Welfare Agencies in the United States* (New York: Schoolmasters' Press, 1961), p. 66.

2. For this little-known story, see Lela Stiles, *The Man Behind Roosevelt* (Cleveland: World, 1954), and Alfred B. Rollins, Jr., *Roosevelt and Howe* (Alfred A. Knopf, 1962).

3. Turnley Walker, *Roosevelt and the Warm Springs Story* (New York: Wyn, 1953), pp. 15–16.

4. Quoted in Carter, *The Gentle Legions*, p. 106.

5. *Ibid.*, p. 101.

6. *Ibid.*, p. 103.

7. Frances Perkins, *The Roosevelt I Knew* (New York: 1946), p. 36.

8. Victor Cohn, "Start of Fund Raising for Polio Fight," Minneapolis *Tribune*, April 25, 1955.

9. Perkins, *op. cit.*, p. 35.

10. The Federal Trade Commission, during the 1920's, issued several cease and desist orders on products similar to those peddled by Byoir. For example, Stipulation No. 101 of the FTC for March 31, 1926, ordered that a firm stop falsely advertising certain bath salts as having the property of reducing obesity. See: *Federal Trade Commission Decisions*, Vol. 10, Nov. 28, 1925–Nov. 4, 1926, pp. 544–545. See also *ibid.*, Stipulation No. 136, p. 578: A firm selling a colorless liquid said to restore gray hair to its original color was ordered to cease and desist in the claim that "It not only restores the former shade to the hair; it banishes dandruff and stops falling of the hair." Such were the ethics of making money in the 1920's.

11. This summary of Byoir's pre-1933 career is based on his obituary in the Feb. 4, 1957, *New York Times*, p. 19; Spencer Klaw, "Carl Byoir: Opinion Engineering in the Big Time," *Reporter*, June 10, 1952, pp. 30–33; biography of Carl Byoir written by one of his aides on file in Byoir firm, and interviews with his early associates—Gerry Swinehart, Carl Dickey, and George Hammond.

12. George Creel, *Rebel at Large*, pp. 121–122.

13. Alfred M. Lee, *The Daily Newspaper in America*, p. 422.

14. *Newsweek*, Vol. 1 (May 6, 1933), pp. 23–24; *Time*, Vol. 29 (Feb. 15, 1937), pp. 76–77.

15. This account is based primarily on that given by Turnley Walker in *Roosevelt and the Warm Springs Story*, pp. 219–222.

16. Interview with Carl C. Dickey, who was at that time an associate in the Byoir firm, March 18, 1959.

17. Ickes, *The Secret Diary of Harold L. Ickes:* The First Thousand Days (New York: Simon & Schuster, 1953), pp. 565–566.

18. John T. Flynn, *The Roosevelt Myth* (New York: Devin-Adair, 1948), p. 271.

19. Frank Freidel, *Franklin D. Roosevelt:* The Ordeal (Boston: Little, Brown, 1954), p. 249.

20. Eleanor Roosevelt, *This I Remember* (New York: Harper, 1949), p. 45 and Appendix II.

21. Walker, *op. cit.*, p. 196.

22. Based on recollection of Carl C. Dickey, who says Byoir repeated this remark to him. Dickey reported this remark in an interview with the author, March 18, 1959. Later, upon reading this chapter, he said he couldn't recall Byoir's having said it.

23. Cohn, *op. cit.*

24. Carter, *op. cit.*

25. *The President's Birthday Magazine*, January, 1937, p. 42, published by the 1937 Birthday Ball Committee.

26. *New York Times*, Jan. 31, 1934, p. 2.

27. *Ibid.*, May 10, 1934, p. 20.

28. *Ibid.*, May 10, 1934, p. 4.

29. This account based on Turnley Walker's, p. 230.

30. *New York Times*, Nov. 20, 1935, p. 3.

31. Audited Report by Haskins & Sells, dated July 22, 1935. In writer's possession.

32. Allen, *Presidents Who Have Known Me* (New York: Simon & Schuster, 1950), pp. 76–77.

33. Eleanor Roosevelt, *op. cit.*, pp. 154–155.

34. *New York Times*, Jan. 19, 1936, p. 35, for text.

35. Eleanor Roosevelt, *op. cit.*, p. 155.

36. This story is interestingly, fairly told in Rollins, *Roosevelt and Howe*.

37. *New York Times*, Feb. 12, 1936, p. 2.

38. *The President's Birthday Magazine*, Jan. 30, 1937, p. 3.

39. Carter, *op. cit.*, pp. 108–109.

40. "Doherty: Drops High Power Sale of Cities Service Stock," *Newsweek*, Vol. 2 (Aug. 5, 1933), p. 22.

41. See Hearings, House of Representatives, *Investigation of Nazi and Other Propaganda*, 73rd Congress, 1934.

42. It is the recollection of Byoir's aides that the firm never charged

nor received a fee for promoting the President's Birthday Balls. The first two years the work was carried as part of the Doherty account and all campaign costs charged to the hotel-utility tycoon. However, in subsequent years the out-of-pocket expenses were paid out of the funds raised. Byoir's records on this account were discarded years ago.

43. *New York Times*, Sept. 23, 1937, p. 3.

44. Based on O'Connor's recollections.

45. Cohn, copyright article, *op. cit.*

46. Carter, *op. cit.*, pp. 111–112.

47. Hank Bloomgarden, *Before We Sleep* (New York: Putnam, 1958), pp. 107–109.

48. Walker, *op. cit.*, p. 256.

49. Interview, March 9, 1960.

50. Interview with Miss Ducas, March 9, 1960.

51. Statement of Neal Rothman, April 25, 1962. The American Legion-sponsored porch-light canvass was staged on Jan. 22, 1950. The term, "Mothers' March on Polio," was used in a porch-light drive on Jan. 31, 1951, arranged by the Altrusa Club of Wausau, Wisc. National Foundation records show there was a Mothers' March in Phoenix, Ariz., in 1950. The "first" here again is in dispute.

52. David L. Sills, *The Volunteers* (Glencoe, Ill.: Free Press, 1957), pp. 158–159.

53. *Ibid.*, p. 159.

54. *Ibid.*, p. 271.

55. John Rowan Wilson, *Margin of Safety* (New York: Doubleday & Co., 1963), p. 59.

56. *Ibid.*, p. 5.

10

Fund Raising in World War II

Federated Fund Raising Brings in $900 Million

The dark clouds of the depression had barely begun to recede in the United States when the darker, more ominous clouds of World War II, rolling in from Hitler's Germany and Hirohito's Japan, began to cast their shadows across American lives. By the time war broke in Europe, United States fund raisers had largely perfected the art of raising money from the public in sums both large and small. This time, when America was engulfed by war, her fund raisers were ready with experience, patterns of procedure, and plans of organization that would prove equal to the task of raising the astronomical sums required to build a war machine, and to finance war-related social welfare services on a global scale.

The fund-raising lessons of World War I, the twenty years' experience with federated fund raising, and the dramatic lessons taught in the depression, were to be reflected in the money raising of World War II. This time there was less lost motion in getting to the task of unifying appeals and building organizations to provide money for the religious, recreational, and welfare needs of a nation in uniform and in total war production. The promotional patterns of World War I would be repeated, albeit with more style, more skill, more finesse—and bigger totals. For this second war the fund-raising professionals had the new and powerful medium of radio to use in their exhortations.

Long before the Japanese struck on December 7, 1941, Americans were being bombarded with war-born appeals to provide relief to the wounded and the hungry abroad. Everywhere Americans turned—in school hallways, in college corridors, in banks and stores—they were being greeted with posters which read: "Bundles for Britain," "Help British War Victims," "China First to Fight," and other slogans. In making these appeals, fund raisers and welfare leaders were unknowingly gearing up for the tremendous task that would confront them in World War II. Many women had been "knittin' for Britain" for two years before the "day of infamy" at Pearl Harbor.

Illustrative of these pre-Pearl Harbor campaigns to raise money to help the victims of war abroad was that staged in 1938 for Chiang Kai-shek's Republic of China. The Chinese government retained Carl Byoir & Associates to plan and promote raising money in the United States for the Chinese people. By organizing Bowl of Rice dinners in scores of American cities, Byoir, in a single night, netted approximately $175,000 for China. The account proved an unhappy one from Byoir's standpoint though for the hard-pressed Chinese government ceased paying its monthly fee. Byoir's firm had financed, all told, a dozen fund-raising events for China and the firm had a deficit of $104,000 on this account. Until Chiang was forced to flee from the mainland to Formosa the persistent Byoir firm sent a bill for that amount every month, which was obviously ignored.[1] The John Price Jones firm directed the United China Relief Campaign of 1941–1942 and was more fortunate than Byoir. Jones's firm was paid $25,482 for its assistance with this drive, in which the claims for credit were many. *Time* publisher Henry Luce, son of a China missionary, had his own representative on the job at all times, often to the annoyance and not infrequently to the obstruction of the Jones staff.

It will be recalled that the various agencies that responded to the task of giving aid and comfort to U.S. soldiers and sailors in World War I became hotly competitive in their drives for funds and in their desire for public acclaim. Much bickering and wasteful overlapping of effort resulted. Consequently, late in 1918, Secretary of War Newton D. Baker, acting with President Wilson's approval, coerced the YMCA, YWCA, National Catholic War Council, War Camp Community Service, American Library Association, Jewish Welfare Board, and Salvation Army to unite in the United War Fund campaign.

With enactment of the military draft and expansion of defense industries late in 1940, large numbers of young men were being concentrated in military camps and industrial cities, where they found more boredom and sinful temptations than opportunities for

wholesome recreation. Experienced World War I social and welfare agencies could foresee the demands to be made of them. As a
result, the YMCA, the YWCA, the National Catholic Community
Service, the Salvation Army, and the Jewish Welfare Board voluntarily joined forces in the National United Welfare Committee in
November, 1940.

This time these agencies moved to unify and coordinate their
efforts before government compulsion was exercised. The Committee offered itself to President Roosevelt with a plan to promote a
joint fund-raising campaign to finance activities in communities
affected by wartime dislocations.[2] But nothing came of this proposal. There were many to deplore the development of services
"on religious lines of demarcation" and to assert "it indicates failure to profit from twenty-five years of experience in community
organization."[3] Meantime, the strains on the health, welfare, and
recreational resources imposed by a nation rearming for a war that
was moving inexorably to its shores grew in number and in stress.
It became apparent that the United Welfare Committee was too
loose a federation to cope with the task that was becoming larger
with each passing day.

On Tuesday, February 4, 1941, representatives of Protestant,
Catholic, and Jewish groups agreed on forming the United Service
Organizations for National Defense, Inc. Thus the famed USO of
World War II was born. Walter Hoving, a New York City department store executive and Salvation Army volunteer, chairman of
the United Welfare Committee, guided the many series of conferences that culminated in the USO. The United Welfare Committee
was disbanded. Hoving's first word to the public on organization of
the USO was that "we plan a public appeal for funds throughout
the nation in March or April." The USO was organized by the
YMCA, YWCA, National Catholic Community Service, Salvation
Army, Jewish Welfare Board—all represented in the earlier committee—plus the National Travelers Aid Association.

The promised nationwide appeal was launched on April 6, 1941,
when Hoving announced a campaign for $10,765,000 to begin on
June 3. Slogans such as "Don't forget our own soldiers and sailors"
and "The USO is behind the soldiers and sailors of the USA" provided the themes used in urging people to give. Reflecting lessons
taught by the depression, when the nation's welfare needs far out-
stripped the resources of private philanthropy, there was much com-

plaining that providing recreational facilities for soldiers and sailors
was a governmental, not a philanthropic function. Hoving took note
of these complaints. "People may say, 'why doesn't the government provide the money for these programs?' but we want the
public to provide the funds so the soldiers and sailors can feel the
citizens are behind them." At the time this drive was launched there
were already 1.4 million men in uniform.[4] The *New York Times*
confidently asserted that "The present appeal for our new citizen
army will assuredly bring a warm response."

Providing the recreational facilities and morale-building welfare
services for U.S. airmen, soldiers, sailors, and Marines became a joint
government-people's effort. This was a pragmatic, common-sense
and humane answer to a need that neither could effectively meet
alone. President Roosevelt took the initiative early in 1941 to get
Congress to appropriate $150 million for recreational facilities—to
become known as USO Huts—near military bases and large war
manufacturing centers. When the USO launched its first fund drive
in mid-1941, 339 such facilities were in existence. F.D.R. thought
the government should provide the buildings and facilities but that
private agencies, financed by public giving, should operate them.

Thus the President was quick to endorse the USO's appeal for
funds. On April 8, 1941, F.D.R. told America: "This duty of maintaining morale on the home front is one in which every American
shares. The Federal Government . . . stands squarely behind the
USO. The USO should and will have our united support, in financial contributions and in personal efforts." *Survey Midmonthly*
commented: "The tacit approval given to the USO represents the
first step in the complicated and difficult business of formulating a
comprehensive program of community welfare services uniting
public and private endeavor to meet the challenges and the strains
imposed by the defense upheaval."[5] To guide the cooperative
effort in this phase of first the defense, then war program, F.D.R.
directed Paul McNutt to serve "as coordinator of all health, medical, welfare, nutrition, recreation and other related fields of activity affecting the national defense." McNutt soon recruited Charles P.
Taft, son of the former President and experienced lay leader in
community chest work, to assist him in aiding and guiding the new
USO. This time government and philanthropy were partners in
looking after the welfare of the nation's fighting men and their
families.

Leaders of the newly organized USO were quick to turn to the John Price Jones firm. The Jones records show that the firm was retained as counsel for the 1941 and 1942 national USO campaigns and also by the New York City USO Committee those same two years. The goal for the 1941 USO campaign was $10,765,000 and $14,827,419 was actually raised, reflecting the rising war fervor of the American people. This campaign cost was $58,634 plus the Jones fee of something near $50,000. Jones, Harold J. Seymour, H. M. Weeks, Wolcott Street, Pelle Aavatsmark, and Humphrey Redfield staffed the first USO drive. Erwin Tuthill, later to become president of the reorganized John Price Jones Corp., was assigned to the national USO as part of its administrative staff. He was lent to USO on a half-fee basis, Jones's records show. The second national campaign of 1942 had a $32 million goal and records show a "net probable income" of $31,675,547 as of January 20, 1943. The campaign costs, excluding the Jones fee, jumped sharply in comparison with the 1941 drive, reaching $887,045.[6]

In the New York City portion of the national drive the 1941 goal was $3.5 million but only $2,300,788 was raised. Campaign expenses totaled $178,293, of which $19,060 was the Jones fee. Four Jones men were assigned to the New York City campaign. The firm of Tamblyn & Brown also worked on this drive, and cost records show a fee for that firm of $3,600. In the second New York City campaign for the USO, from February to August, 1942, $4,450,000 was sought and $4,263,739 was obtained at a campaign cost of $306,555. The Jones fee on this drive was $54,749. Twelve men were assigned full or part time to raising this money.[7]

Like most of the nationwide appeals for funds, the USO drives brought the Jones firm acclaim, criticism, wild rumors of costs—and profits. In a confidential memorandum written for Jones by David M. Church, the staff was told that a rumor was circulating to the effect that "the John Price Jones Corporation got a million dollars for running the USO campaign."[8] Theodore S. Ruggles, now a vice-president of the firm, thinks these rumors arose from the charge made by the Hearst press about the Emergency United Relief campaign during the depression. These charges had proved groundless, when the Hearst organization—acting on Chairman Harvey Gibson's challenge—sent auditors to check the Jones books. But the rumors persisted.

One of the leaders for the USO campaign was Mrs. Winthrop W.

Aldrich, socially prominent wife of the banker. She served as chairman of Metropolitan New York's Women's Division. On June 23, 1941, Mrs. Aldrich forwarded a biting letter from one of her vice-chairmen, Mrs. Brock Pemberton, wife of the theatrical producer. In her forwarding note, Mrs. Aldrich wrote: "Dear Mr. Jones: The enclosed letter from one of my vice-chairmen will show you that the inefficiency of this office is no mere dream of mine. Sincerely, Harriet Aldrich." The letter from Mrs. Pemberton was written on USO stationery and undated. It read:

> Dear Mrs. Aldrich
>
> I have always been so successful in any drive for the theater which I have headed for various causes—especially the Theater Wing—that I naturally would far rather resign from the USO than have my name connected with a failure which I am sure will be the case in this attempt of Jane's [Jane Watson] and mine to raise money from the theater. I have been doing my best to get out letters etc. and have received no help whatever from this organization—the only work I have accomplished was at home with Mr. Pemberton's secretary . . . wish I could remain to the end but it seems hopeless. Better luck next time.[9]
>
> > Sincerely
> > Margaret Pemberton

It was nearly a year after America's entry into World War I, in April, 1917, before the first war chest developed. In sharp contrast, the first World War II model came within weeks after Pearl Harbor. By September, 1942, there were nearly three hundred war chests in as many communities. The demands for federated fund raising came quicker and stronger this time. As early as September, 1941, Tom K. Smith, chairman of the Community Chests' 1941 Mobilization for Human Needs, was writing: "Born of the First World War, grown up to fight in this one, the Community Chests and the Councils of Social Agencies of the United States are two good signs and signals that this country will see it through."[10] By December, 1941, the patterns of America's public philanthropy had been largely set. From then on, there was more repetition than innovation in getting people to give.

The by-now strong community chest movement had been the offspring of the war chests organized during World War I to bring order and efficiency out of a confused duplication of appeals. Thus it was natural that the basic idea of federating the multiplying wartime appeals into a national war fund appeal would come early in World War II. By June, 1942, Americans were being bombarded by campaigns for British War Relief, for United Service Organizations (the USO), for relief of the war victims in China, Greece, France, Holland, Norway, and other enemy-occupied lands.

On the very eve of Pearl Harbor, Newbold Morris, president of the City Council of New York City, had pleaded for a consolidation of the many appeals for funds. "The persons with means should not receive thirty or forty appeals every year." Morris said, hopefully, that he looked forward to the day when independent drives for charitable institutions would be eliminated to abolish the duplication of time and effort.[11] More than a year earlier the noted social leader Mrs. August Belmont had urged a central planning agency to coordinate the multiplying fund drives stimulated by the consequences of war.[12]

In the words of Winthrop W. Aldrich, who was to become president of the National War Fund, "it was time we achieved some order and system along with our high endeavor." As he recalls, "Community leaders everywhere found themselves with too little time for too many causes, too little information about too many projects, and no notion whatever regarding the relative urgency of one cause as against another, or of the proper relationship between the conflicting total amounts our people were being asked to give." [13] In the more colorful language of the veteran fund raiser Harold J. Seymour, "by the middle of 1942 the situation was just about as well in hand as a greased pig at midnight."

The multiplicity of appeals for aid abroad can be seen in the following figures: After Hitler's barbaric invasion of Poland in September, 1941, the United States government issued an order requiring all appeals for aid to foreign countries to be registered with the U.S. State Department. This regulation was instituted more so that the government could keep a close eye on all matters involving nations at war than to protect American givers from unjustified or fraudulent fund appeals. Before this federal process of registering fund-raising drives for foreign countries was completed, by the war's end, a total of 596 agencies for foreign relief had been registered, and by their own records, had collected a total of $597,621,-366. Consequently, in June, 1942, community chest leaders and war appeal fund raisers met in Cincinnati to bring order to this muddled confusion. Given the experience of World War I and later, the answer appeared obvious—federate the appeals into one fund, one campaign. In an influential speech at Cincinnati, Aldrich proposed a limited form of federation which he tentatively titled "Allied Relief Fund."

Out of the Cincinnati conference came agreement to request President Roosevelt to bring order out of the fund-raising chaos of early months. On July 25, 1942, President Roosevelt complied by signing Executive Order 9205, which took registration and control of agencies raising money for foreign relief out of the State Department and lodged the authority in "The President's War Relief Control Board." The Board was empowered to supervise and regulate money-raising agencies, a power the State Department had not had. Members of the Board appointed by the President were: Joseph E. Davies, former ambassador to Russia, chairman; Charles P. Taft, lawyer, USO official, and noted church and civic leader from Cincinnati; and Frederick P. Keppel, former president of the Carnegie Corp. Keppel died on September 8, 1943, and was succeeded by Charles Warren, historian and former Assistant Attorney General of the United States.

Shortly after the annual conference in Cincinnati, the Community Chests and Councils appointed two national committees to deal with problems that could only be handled on a national basis—setting budgets for the nationwide war appeals and establishing community quotas. Gerard Swope was persuaded to take the chairmanship of the budget committee. From that committee's deliberations came this allocation of America's gift dollars for war appeals:

First National Budget of War Relief Appeals [14]

British War Relief Society	$7,000,000
United China Relief	7,000,000
Queen Wilhelmina Fund	500,000
Greek War Relief six months	6,000,000
Polish American Council	2,000,000
Russian War Relief	5,500,000
American Social Hygiene Assn. for work in "defense communities"	330,000
War Prisoners Aid, YMCA	1,479,000
National Board of YWCA overseas	350,000
United Service Organizations	32,000,000
Unallocated reserves	13,500,000
Total	$75,659,000

Meantime Allen T. Burns and Ralph Blanchard of the Community Chests and Councils organization were urging community chests to become war chests and promoting creation of a war chest in communities where there were no community chests. Efforts were initiated to arrive at quotas for the national war-related drives wishing to be included in the community chest campaign for the fall of 1942. Competition, confusion, and conflict in fund-raising circles was mounting.

In the recollection of Harold J. Seymour:

> Here, then . . . were all the grass-roots elements for creating a national chest for war-related appeals: local demand, official demand in Washington, efforts toward clarity by the national body representing local chests, dissatisfaction among many of the agencies, and incidentally, increasing pressure from the Treasury and the Office of War Information to keep the decks clear during longer periods of the year for war-bond drives and other promotional efforts essential to the military conduct of the war.
>
> The general scramble simply had to stop.[15]

Late in the autumn, Davies, on behalf of the War Relief Control Board, asked five men to set up an organization to end the confusion in fund appeals and to channel gift dollars to causes of merit and need. Chosen for this difficult, delicate task were Winthrop W. Aldrich, then president of the British War Relief Society; Gerard Swope, president of General Electric and long-time leader in the community chests and the Red Cross; Henry M. Wriston, president of Brown University, who had taken the lead in organizing a state-wide war chest for Rhode Island; Ralph Hayes, executive director of the New York Community Chest and vice-president of the Coca-Cola Co.; and Chester I. Barnard, president of the New Jersey Bell Telephone Co., and on leave to serve as full-time president of the USO. These five added a sixth man to their committee, Prescott S. Bush, banker, later to serve as a U.S. senator from Connecticut. Bush had been chairman of the recently completed 1942 national campaign that had raised $32 million for the USO and it was to get the benefit of his recent national fund-raising experience that the committee added him as a member.

These six men first met around a conference table in a window-less, pine-paneled conference room on the fourth floor of New

York's Chase National Bank on December 15, 1942. Out of this conference on "what to do about the war fund raising muddle?" came the National War Fund, Inc., "a philanthropic federation with three simple aims; first, to determine the nature and the extent of the war-related needs; second, to see that everybody has a chance to contribute to the funds required; and third, to channel the sums raised for its member agencies wherever American help is currently most needed—enough and on time." [16] Guiding these men in their quest for answers to these old, but still troublesome problems was the veteran fund raiser we first met in the Jones-directed Harvard Drive of 1919. A Harvard man, "Si" Seymour had joined Jones in his new firm and new field of fund raising, contributing much to the success of both. His great achievement in managing the work of the National War Fund was born of the expertise, experience, and drive that comes from dedication to a good cause. Seymour has recorded the history of the National War Fund in his book, *Design for Giving*.

These six men, aided by Seymour's counsel, set down four basic policies: the fund would represent no single interest but would do its best to represent both the organizations seeking money and the Americans giving the money; full and unreserved acceptance of the principle of federation; organization based on the principle of maximum decentralization; the fullest exercise of simplicity and economy in operation. In Seymour's view, "the Fund was designed, and was operated, as a voluntary nation-wide project in the area of public relations." Seymour was soon joined by Allen T. Burns who resigned as executive director of the Community Chests and Councils federation to devote full time to his job as executive secretary of the National Budget Committee for War Appeals. Ralph Blanchard succeeded Burns as executive head of Community Chests. These three veteran fund raisers worked in close cooperation to meet the greatly enlarged welfare needs of wartime.

The National War Fund was, in Swope's words, simply "an extension of the community chest or united campaign idea to seventeen national war appeals which have become its member agencies" with membership limited to agencies established to meet needs growing out of the war. The basic purposes to be served by the Fund were: provision of welfare and recreational services to the U.S. armed forces, their auxiliaries, and the merchant marine; to provide relief to occupied countries; to give assistance to unoccupied areas and aid to refugees.

Given the two decades of federated fund raising and fund allocation, it was predictable that a multiplicity of national appeals would quickly force a federation of the drives. Even before the National War Fund was organized four states had set up statewide war chests, with Alabama, Rhode Island, Arizona, and Nebraska leading the way. Here was the war chest idea carried to a wider level, from which it was possible to reach down to the small towns and rural counties that had no chests. By 1943 all forty-eight states had organized statewide war chests. No potential giver to war appeals was to be overlooked, no matter how remote his abode on a rural route.

In promotion of the National War Fund's first nationwide drive—from October 1 to November 20, 1943—the sponsors set forth these purposes for the War Fund:

1. Give impetus to the united appeals of established foreign relief and war service agencies certified by the President's War Relief Control Board.
2. Stimulate the development in communities of united campaigns to raise the necessary funds for these national organizations and for local community health and welfare needs.
3. Administer the sums received for the national foreign relief and war service agencies, applying them wherever help is most urgently needed.
4. Spread the opportunity to everyone to contribute money to the war-connected services.
5. Eliminate duplicating war appeals and needless waste of manpower in raising separate funds.
6. Reduce substantially the cost of separate appeals.
7. Bring unity of purpose and effort into wartime philanthropy.[17]

To handle the delicate and difficult task of budgeting and determining quotas for each agency, Gerard Swope was chosen as chairman of the War Fund Budget Committee. Swope had been chairman of the Community Chests and Councils budget committee in 1942 and was known for his sense of fairness. He soon drafted Allen T. Burns to handle the administration of this task. To assist them in their budgeting task, Swope and Burns called in the National Information Bureau's staff to serve as advisers. The first job was to determine a goal for the 1943 drive, "knowing full well, in advance of budget hearings, that the need for relief was virtually unlimited, and that the USO alone would probably require at least $60,000,000.

"There were two sets of known factors; first, how much each agency had raised by its own efforts in 1942, and second, what proportion of any national goal was ordinarily taken by a number of local communities." [18] Out of these studies and hearings came a campaign budget of $125 million which Swope assured the American people "has been carefully arrived at in the light of rock bottom needs."

Actually, as Seymour points out, there could not be a truly national goal because money is always raised locally. Budget, he thought, was a better term for the over-all national figure. The War Fund established the policy of extending the national quota system of fund raising only to the state level, giving each state a percentage of the $125 million to raise as its quota. This was necessary because fund raisers need quotas and goals to use in exhorting their troops. The War Fund did not solicit gifts nationally, but concentrated on promoting giving at the local level. Seymour and his associates in the National War Fund sought to guide the state and community war chest campaigns and to back them up with national publicity. He says, "we suggested method, but never sought to impose it."

The biggest headache for Seymour and his staff in dealing with the local funds came with the so-called "95 Per Cent Clause." This clause in the agreement the War Fund signed with local war fund campaigns provided that if local chest campaigns reached 95 per cent of their goals, the campaign proceeds would be shared proportionately between the local agencies and the Fund; but that if failure exceeded 5 per cent, the Fund would take the brunt of the loss. This clause was no problem in the 1943 and 1944 drives when booming war prosperity put every campaign appeal over the top, but in the 1945 drive, which came after V-J Day, campaign failures of 10 per cent frequently cost the Fund as much as 30 per cent of local quotas. Seymour thinks, in retrospect, that share and share alike should have been the guiding principle. Another problem was that posed by "buck a month clubs" and similar efforts, stemming from the successful patterns of small gifts in the March of Dimes nationwide fund raising. The National War Fund discouraged the March of Dimes approach and insisted that local campaigners emphasize the "principle of proportionate giving." Everyone was to be solicited but each person was to be persuaded to give according to his financial ability.

The National War Fund was essentially an agency for approving appeals for money to meet wartime needs, a coordinator of effort in raising these funds. "With little or no real authority, and with virtually all its operations dependent on good will, the National War Fund in all its aspects was essentially a public relations operation. Its entire framework of policy . . . might well be characterized as public relations policy." [19] The War Fund restricted its own publicity operations to the affairs of the Fund itself and left the promotional work of fund raising to each agency participating in these federated appeals.

As one example, the suspicion, hostility, or just plain disinterest of labor union leaders and members has long represented a difficult public relations problem for community chests. The community chest movement, it will be recalled, was born in the board rooms of the Cleveland, Ohio, Chamber of Commerce and the movement was nurtured and guided by businessmen. Workers had long resented employer pressures on them to give and the fact that credit for their gifts more often went to the company than to its employees. The exigencies and emotions of World War II brought organized labor and the chest movement together when the Community Chests and Councils, Inc., the American Federation of Labor, and the Congress of Industrial Organizations signed a three-way agreement.

In Allen Burns's opinion, "of all the new elements brought into the Chest leadership by the emergence of the War Chest, the most outstanding is labor." Through this national agreement the way was paved for full-fledged cooperation between labor unions and war chests. But the by-now public relations-minded union leaders insisted on credit for their cooperation and their gifts. As Burns wrote, "National pledges by great corporations have often made the headlines. Labor now also insists upon separate recognition of its gifts. It knows the public relations values which may be useful by-products of this kind of war service. Giving the unions proper credit for their gifts will be a familiar form of cooperation, well understood by the Community Chests." [20]

Guided by such able men as Seymour, Burns, and Blanchard and counseled by such wise men as Aldrich and Swope, the legions of federated fund raisers fanning across the nation with emotional war appeals achieved a record in public philanthropy that is likely to stand for a long time. The joint harvest of the National War Fund agencies and the local war chest agencies for the war period was $744,033,636. This astronomical total does not include some $150 million in the value of materials collected in gifts-in-kind campaigns conducted by the agencies and financed by the Fund, such as Bundles for Britain. When it was finally liquidated, the National War Fund had raised and paid out some $320 million to give aid and comfort to the fighting men and women, their families, and to America's allies and the victims of war abroad. It was a fund-raising feat of great magnitude, dwarfing all comparable efforts that had gone before it, as can be seen in Tables 14 and 15.

TABLE 14. NATIONAL WAR FUND, INC. SUMMARY SCHEDULE OF DISBURSEMENTS FROM INCEPTION AND ESTIMATE OF CASH REQUIREMENTS TO COMPLETE AUTHORIZED PROGRAM AS OF MARCH 15, 1947

	Total NWF payments to March 15, 1947 (including "quota-credits")	Estimated additional require- ments *	Total *
Belgian War Relief Society	$ 2,207,299.63	$ 12,000.00	$ 2,219,299.63
British War Relief Society	5,944,033.18		5,944,033.18
Bundles for Britain	108,775.19		108,775.19
Catholic Welfare Conference, National	10,893,507.42	70,159.00	10,963,666.42
China, United Service to	32,379,196.19	154,944.67	32,534,140.86
Czechoslovakia, American Relief for	2,099,725.68	154,981.30	2,254,706.98
Denmark Relief, America	254,457.28		254,457.28
European Children, U.S. Com- mittee for the Care of	296,751.58	76,953.62	373,705.20
Field Service, American	680,191.97		680,191.97
France, American Aid	6,643,021.18	75,132.77	6,718,153.95
Greek War Relief Association	7,909,478.38	262,703.58	8,172,181.96
Holland, American Relief for	3,630,234.60	7,464.43	3,637,699.03
Italy, American Relief for	5,664,402.60	27,906.90	5,692,309.50
Lithuanian Relief Fund, United	808,370.88	4,500.00	812,870.88
Luxembourg, Friends of	295,410.47	5,096.60	300,507.07

TABLE 14 (*Continued*)

	Total NWF payments to March 15, 1947 (including "quota-credits")	Estimated additional require-ments *	Total *
Near East Foundation	802,101.34	12,000.00	814,101.34
Norway, American Relief for	2,527,637.95		2,527,637.95
Philippine War Relief	1,462,186.93	122,507.69	1,584,694.62
Poland, American Relief for	6,648,382.81	232,000.00	6,880,382.81
Prisoners Aid Committee, YMCA, War	9,597,044.29	152,118.13	9,749,162.42
Prisoners Aid, Inc., War	12,794.65		12,794.65
Refugee Relief Trustees	4,921,425.69	59,203.42	4,980,629.11
Russian War Relief	16,028,952.67		16,028,952.67
Seamen's Service, United	12,632,845.14	122,632.51	12,755,477.65
Social Hygiene Association, American	933,529.43	15,000.00	948,529.43
World Emergency & War Victims Fund, YWCA	1,655,244.30	6,728.81	1,661,973.11
World Student Service Fund	240,163.04		240,163.04
Yugoslav Relief Fund, United	3,051,682.65	106,635.08	3,158,317.73
Total Agencies (Exclusive of USO)	140,328,847.12	1,680,668.51	142,009,515.63
USO (United Service Organizations)	175,175,959.24	400,000.00	175,575,959.24
Total Agencies	315,504,806.36	2,080,668.51	317,585,474.87
Headquarters and Campaign Expense	2,142,867.07		2,142,867.07
Expense of Labor Campaign Committees	1,145,737.10		1,145,737.10
Liquidation Expense and Contingencies	381,908.49	146,212.51	528,121.00
Total	$319,175,319.02	$2,226,881.02	$321,402,200.04

* Subject to adjustments for commitments, refunds, income, etc., as disclosed in Auditors' reports—and for over- or underexpenditures of agencies now in liquidation.

Budget Office—National War Fund, Inc.—March 17, 1947.

TABLE 15. CONSOLIDATED STATEMENT OF STATE QUOTAS AND CONTRIBUTIONS
RECEIVED FOR CAMPAIGN YEARS—1943–1944–1945 AS OF MARCH 15, 1947

State	Combined quotas 1943–1946	Total net amount applied	Percentage
Alabama	$ 3,187,500.00	$ 3,138,750.00	98.47
Arizona	888,000.00	866,456.00	97.57
Arkansas	1,988,250.00	1,783,519.19	89.70
California	25,453,750.00	24,439,118.35	96.01
Colorado	2,697,250.00	2,743,034.18	101.70
Connecticut	7,850,000.00	6,425,544.65	81.85
Delaware	1,230,000.00	1,277,400.26	103.85
District of Columbia	3,357,325.00	3,008,200.00	89.60
Florida	3,774,500.00	2,201,773.69	58.33
Georgia	4,525,500.00	3,786,551.27	83.67
Idaho	1,083,000.00	1,085,165.35	100.20
Illinois	26,332,750.00	23,438,986.51	89.01
Indiana	8,564,665.00	7,281,665.02	85.02
Iowa	6,198,500.00	6,198,500.00	100.00
Kansas	3,537,000.00	3,236,252.03	91.50
Kentucky	4,063,250.00	3,817,315.55	93.95
Louisiana	3,739,750.00	3,433,471.46	91.81
Maine	1,964,250.00	1,646,772.19	83.84
Maryland	5,452,826.00	4,941,114.14	90.62
Massachusetts	13,600,000.00	11,737,478.06	86.30
Michigan	16,428,967.00	15,573,845.26	94.80
Minnesota *	6,874,160.00	6,843,249.11	99.55
Mississippi	2,144,000.00	1,865,638.52	87.02
Missouri	9,576,750.00	8,891,934.81	92.85
Montana	1,203,750.00	946,824.33	78.66
Nebraska	2,710,338.00	2,658,359.74	98.08
Nevada	388,000.00	426,340.21	109.88
New Hampshire	1,281,250.00	1,337,320.21	104.38
New Jersey	12,519,409.00	9,062,747.09	72.39
New Mexico	680,000.00	612,657.31	90.10
New York	61,064,079.00	50,596,242.03	82.86
North Carolina	5,313,750.00	4,907,564.59	92.36
North Dakota	1,030,000.00	1,032,592.79	100.25
Ohio	21,745,700.00	19,367,561.55	89.06
Oklahoma	3,636,796.00	3,254,525.70	89.49

TABLE 15 (*Continued*)

State	Combined quotas 1943–1946	Total net amount applied	Percentage
Oregon	3,194,250.00	2,928,070.39	91.67
Pennsylvania	29,085,743.00	26,037,742.62	89.52
Rhode Island	2,350,745.00	2,126,019.00	90.44
South Carolina	2,112,750.00	1,827,151.20	86.48
South Dakota	1,063,843.00	958,684.63	90.12
Tennessee	4,522,416.00	4,522,416.00	100.00
Texas	13,184,700.00	11,931,301.71	90.49
Utah	1,131,500.00	1,096,539.72	96.91
Vermont	807,750.00	734,826.98	90.97
Virginia	5,188,851.00	4,960,782.01	95.60
Washington	5,106,000.00	4,761,195.57	93.25
West Virginia	2,851,500.00	2,456,248.99	86.14
Wisconsin	8,090,700.00	7,295,304.21	90.17
Wyoming	495,750.00	428,216.70	86.38
	$355,271,513.00	$315,928,970.88	88.93
Non-Quota and Miscellaneous Contributions		5,644,097.49	
Total Campaign Receipts		$321,573,068.37	

* Minnesota paid their 1943 and 1944 assigned quotas in full and paid $107,088.87 in excess of their accepted quota for 1945.

The Red Cross Is Prepared

World War I had found the American National Red Cross in a weak, disorganized state. As already recorded, the ARC had not by then mastered the twin arts of public relations and fund raising. When World War II came to the United States, the Red Cross was far better equipped for the somewhat different role that would be assigned it. The organization's accumulated wartime and disaster relief experience, its large membership, strong treasury, and its art of raising money could be, and were, quickly mustered. The degree of popular support that could be commanded by the ARC had been clearly and repeatedly shown in its many previous fund drives for disaster and foreign relief in the 1930's, save one. The exception had been the abortive China relief campaign in 1938 to raise $1 million which netted less than half that amount. All other drives had raised substantially more than the announced goal.

This time, when the war storms broke, the American Red Cross had officers seasoned in meeting disasters and in raising the money to finance its work. Before the war began the Red Cross had obtained agreement that it would be the only nonmilitary agency permitted directly to serve U.S. armed forces overseas. It will be recalled that during World War I the Red Cross was but one of several agencies in the field and, hence, the competition for funds and acclaim among the Red Cross, Salvation Army, YMCA, and religious agencies became quite bitter. In World War II there was no such competition.

Due to recent advances in military medical services, the Red Cross no longer would be required to maintain base hospitals, recruit ambulance sections, and provide medical supplies, now delegated to the armed services. By December, 1941, the Red Cross already had in operation a basic program to provide welfare service to U.S. armed forces. And it had in readiness a plan for raising funds to expand these services should war come. On the very night of December 7, 1941, when every minute of President Roosevelt's time was precious, the Commander in Chief saw Norman Davis, president of the Red Cross. F.D.R. authorized full speed ahead on fund raising. The President launched the public appeal for $50 million on December 12, with a presidential proclamation and a plea to the people to give generously.

This goal of $50 million was only half that asked in the first appeal of World War I. Members of the Red Cross staff thought the goal much too low but "both Davis and members of the campaign committee were convinced that a larger goal would be inadvisable." [21] James K. McClintock, vice-chairman in charge of finances, was sure that this sum would carry the ARC through the first year of the war. "We should make up our minds that it would be impossible again for the Red Cross to raise $400,000,000 in a two-year period as was done in 1917–1918," he told the finance committee. On another occasion McClintock asserted that "we should throw out the window any ideas the Red Cross can raise three hundred to four hundred million dollars, that we should go out for fifty million dollars and be smart enough to make it do for our program!" [22] Obviously Davis and McClintock lacked the boldness and daring to think in terms of raising big sums of money through public giving. How wrong Davis and McClintock were is shown in the spectacular sum of $666,510,000 that was raised by the Red Cross during four years of World War II.

After Congress had declared war against Japan and Germany on December 8, the previously agreed upon fund-raising drive was initiated by telegrams to all Red Cross chapters. The nation was given this breakdown of the requested $50 million: [23]

Services to armed forces (care, welfare, morale of
  troops, men in hospitals, family problems) $25,000,000
Disaster and Emergency Civilian Relief 10,000,000
Civilian Defense Services 5,000,000
Service and Assistance Through Red Cross Chapters ... 4,000,000
Other Official Services (an "insurance fund" against
  some surprise development) 6,000,000

The Red Cross's experienced team of publicists and field workers immediately began the appeal. The people were told by radio, by press, by periodical, and by poster: "You cannot give too generously to the Red Cross and no gift is too small to be of use."

The intensive promotional campaign was directed by G. Stewart Brown and his seasoned staff in ARC headquarters. Brown had succeeded Douglas Griesemer as director of public relations for the ARC in 1939. He came to the job from the United Press bureau in Rome, where he had been bureau chief. A graduate of the University of Arizona, Brown had worked for the Arizona *Republic,* the Tucson *Daily Star,* the Los Angeles *Times,* and the Paris *Herald Tribune* before joining UP in 1929. When Brown came back from Europe to take the ARC post he knew what to expect and had set to work to assemble a public relations staff capable of handling the Red Cross wartime assignments.

The prewar expanding activities of the Red Cross had brought growth in the ARC's publicity program and staff. During 1941, for example, Brown and his staff were required to develop promotional campaigns for Services to the Armed Forces, Nursing Enrollment, Home Nursing, and the new Red Cross Blood Program.

Publicizing and promoting the Red Cross war relief activities prior to America's entry into World War II had also given impetus to strengthening the Red Cross public relations staff and ironing out procedures that would serve well in an intensive war campaign. Indicative of the prewar output is this report by Brown to the Red Cross chairman: "Almost 12,500 newspaper editorials, cartoons, and pictures mentioning the war relief activities of the American Red Cross and printed in newspapers throughout the country from May 10 to August 16, 1940, have been received from the clipping bureaus. Since these agencies do not guarantee better than 40 per cent coverage of the nation's press, it is safe to say that the actual total of these clippings is more than 31,000. During the same period we have received approximately 2,000 clippings having to do with other Red Cross activities." [24]

Berens says: "Although there was a rapid expansion of the public relations function in the Red Cross during World War II, it was not accompanied by the unabated enthusiasm and awe of the World War I period. It had come to be accepted as a matter-of-fact part of the organization's operations; practitioners and the public had become more sophisticated." [25] Public relations, like fund raising, had greatly matured in the intervening twenty years. Fortunately the Red Cross had not heeded Ivy Lee's advice, at the end of World War I, when he mistakenly predicted that "clearly such a thing as a publicity program will no longer continue to exist" and urged "the steady demobilization of the Publicity Department."

From a public relations standpoint, the Blood Donor Program, started on January 9, 1941, proved a great asset, both during and after the war. Berens points out: "It did much to fill the traditional Red Cross role of medical assistance to the wounded, which was largely lost to the military service during the period between the wars." The Blood Donor Program provided an excellent opportunity for participation in a Red Cross activity under emotional circumstances. Newspapers, magazines, and radio stations gave the fullest cooperation. Even the comic strips helped out when Milton Caniff dramatized the value of plasma in "Terry and the Pirates." Overseas broadcasts provided the public with direct evidence of how the wounded themselves felt toward blood donations.[26] Between February, 1941, and the end of World War II the Red Cross raised and spent nearly $16 million providing more than 13 million pints of blood. The Blood Donor Program also generated some bitter criticism, most of it without justification. The most vicious attack came over the handling of Negro blood, with the ARC caught in the vise of the unreasoning ignorance of many persons in the South. On balance, the program brought wide acclaim.

The Red Cross feat in raising $666,5 10,000 and reaching a peak membership of 36,645,000 members by 1945 was not accomplished without many difficulties and strenuous effort on the part of millions of volunteer workers. Although the Red Cross had cleared its World War I competitors out of the field of wartime fund raising, it still had to compete with the appeals for the USO, for War Bond drives, and the expanded demands of community chests and other fund drives across the nation. Although the Red Cross had been designated before the war as the only agency to provide morale services to our fighting men overseas, conflicts inevitably developed with the USO. Eventually, in 1943, the spheres of service were worked out by army regulations. The Red Cross would provide its traditional camp services in the United States, would furnish all relief for the sick and wounded in army hospitals, and would operate Home Service in conjunction with the Red Cross chapters. The USO would provide, in cooperation with Army Special Services, on-post entertainment and recreation, maintain clubs, hostels, information centers, and railroad station lounges for men on leave. The USO was also authorized to present camp shows at foreign posts under the auspices of Special Services.[27]

Difficulties with the community chests flared anew over the issue of one fund drive in a community versus many such drives. The Red Cross Central Committee, with the approval of President Roosevelt, restated its policy forbidding any Red Cross chapter to participate in a joint fund-raising campaign. This policy ultimately was to crumble under public pressure in the postwar era.

The biggest public relations and fund-raising headache for the Red Cross during these wartime campaigns was the continuing suspicion and criticism of organized labor. Labor, long critical of the Red Cross and of community chests because of the dominant role played in these agencies by businessmen and the social elite, had grown powerful in the New Deal years and now demanded recognition. A feud had erupted between organized labor and the Red Cross in the thirties when the Red Cross repeatedly refused to give aid to strikers and their families. Early in the war both the AFL and the CIO, then separate organizations, threatened to stage their own fund-raising drives to provide services to the men and women in military service. This threat was averted when the Red Cross was able to reach agreement with both labor groups in 1942 that assured labor support for the Red Cross through the cooperation of special AFL and CIO fund-raising committees. Subsequently many steps were taken to enlist greater labor cooperation, and this continued into the postwar era by giving organized labor leaders more prominent roles in these agencies.

Reflecting its awareness of the growth of popular philanthropy since World War I, the Red Cross this time made its appeals to a broader base of public support than had Ward and his associates. Red Cross now moved to strengthen its relationships with all groups, not merely organized labor. Much stress was placed on the theme "Partnership of the People." Red Cross public relations and fund-raising officials developed systematic channels of communication with farmers, Negroes, women's clubs, church members, and other organized groups.

Nonetheless, the business community, now broadened to include labor, continued to be the focus of most effort. "Business and industrial leaders and leaders of labor have united in building a strong Red Cross which recognizes 'no border, no creed, no birth' in its work of preventing and relieving human suffering. It is this spirit which makes possible the success of our chapters in the solicitation of men and women at their places of work. Through the Commerce, Industry, and Labor Division the individual will be reached under conditions which permit the widest dissemination of factual material and provide the best method of giving everyone an opportunity to contribute." [28] Every effort was made to appeal to prospective givers in all walks of life and to eradicate long-standing identification of the Red Cross with the rich and the social elite.

In sharp contrast with World War I, when there was little cooperation between Ivy Lee's public relations department in the Red Cross and George Creel's Committee on Public Information, in World War II the Red Cross publicists worked in close cooperation with the Office of War Information headed by Elmer Davis. For instance, G. Stewart Brown told the chairman of the Red Cross that in the 1944 Red Cross war fund appeal, "The full publicity resources of the Office of War Information were brought into play, and the active cooperation of that office, along with the unusual assistance of radio networks and local stations, were high points in the over-all publicity program." [29]

It will be recalled that Creel and Lee had clashed in the dispute growing out of the Colorado Fuel & Iron strike prior to their entering the nation's service in World War I.[30] Creel had written critically of Lee's role in that strike with the consequence that neither one had any inclination to work with the other. In World War I the advertising division of Creel's CPI organization did arrange for public service advertising supporting the Red Cross appeal for money. No such blocks to cooperation existed between Elmer Davis and Red Cross officials. It is doubtful if any appeal for funds has achieved the support of publicity equal to that achieved by the Red Cross and its allies in loading the nation's news channels with fervent heart-moving Red Cross appeals during the Second World War.

Demonstrating the Red Cross's mature experience in money raising and its supporting public relations techniques, these twin tasks were tied closely together for the all-out war effort. The actual campaigns for funds were directed by the National Fund Raising Committee which was headed by G. Stewart Brown, vice-chairman of the Red Cross for public relations. In the Office of Public Relations under Brown there was a Fund Raising Department. This department, headed by Robert A. Shepard, was primarily a planning and preparations office. The campaigns were directed by Brown's Fund Raising Committee working through the area offices and field staffs. Each area had a fund-raising staff to plan the campaign and to distribute campaign supplies to the chapters. In accordance with the practice initiated by Brown in 1940, the public relations personnel from the areas were periodically called to a national conference for coordinated planning.[31]

The nation was saturated with the Red Cross story, as the drive of March, 1943, illustrates. In that month alone orders for 69,000 newspaper mats were placed. A total of 40 feature articles, picture stories, and editorials appeared in national magazines. Red Cross themes were shown on the covers of 10 periodicals. The March 27 issue of *Collier's* carried a feature story by Walter Davenport. *Look*, the picture magazine, had a feature picture story on blood plasma in its April 6 issue available at newsstands in late March. The March 13 issue of the *Saturday Evening Post* cover featured a girl in a Red Cross Military and Naval Welfare Service uniform, and the March 8 issue of *Time* presented a feature story on the Red Cross in its U.S. at War section.

In that same month Movietone, News of the Day, Paramount, Pathé, and Universal newsreels brought Red Cross pleas to the eyes and hearts of millions of moviegoers. One hundred and eighteen regional network-sponsored programs carrying Red Cross spot announcements were broadcast. There were also 55,800 local broadcasts resulting from Red Cross-produced publicity. Twenty-four half-hour Red Cross programs appeared on the radio networks.

The Red Cross public relations department sent out 1,529 news and feature pictures to newspapers, syndicates, periodicals, and employee publications. The foreign-language section distributed news releases in 26 different languages to 980 publications. Twenty-five special releases were made to the largest Negro newspapers and also to the Associated Negro Press. Many metropolitan newspapers featured Red Cross war service stories in their total support of the 1943 fund drive. It would have been a rare hermit indeed who escaped this bombardment of pleas to give to the men and women in uniform through the Red Cross.[32]

In that one month of the 1943 drive both William Green, president of the AFL, and Philip Murray, president of the CIO, made recorded pleas for the War Fund. Two pamphlets, *Organized Labor's Part in the American Red Cross* and *Railroad Labor's Part in the American Red Cross* were published and distributed through union channels. One important means of channeling the Red Cross plea to special groups was its Speakers' Bureau in the Office of Public Relations. This bureau obtained speakers for clubs, schools, Red Cross and other civic gatherings. It prepared speeches and planned the itineraries of speakers as well as providing guidance to the chapter and area speakers' bureaus. In the 1943 drive speeches were made by 24 "public figures," 259 Red Cross field directors, and 31 top army and navy officers.

Motion-picture stars appeared in 28 cities on behalf of the Red Cross fund drive and there were 25 events in which stage stars participated. In addition, fifty-four speakers were provided for various conventions held in March. To reach the farmer—a source of money generally overlooked by the urban-oriented Red Cross prior to World War II—the publicity staff sent out three different feature stories to 3,200 weekly papers through the Rural Press Section of the OWI. A special story was prepared for the *Ohio Farmer*.

This deluge of publicity echoed and re-echoed the pleas of Commander in Chief Franklin D. Roosevelt to give to the Red Cross: "Wherever our fighting men are—all over the world—the American Red Cross is at their side, extending always the arm of helpfulness and comfort." [33] In view of these ringing endorsements by the nation's leaders in war and the avalanche of publicity, it is little wonder that the 1943 War Fund drive brought in $147.5 million—$22.5 million over the announced 1943 goal of $125 million.

But the most intensive drive was yet to come. As the Red Cross accumulated new ways of telling its story, plus new insights on appeals to get money, and as the war neared its climax, it was logical that the 1945 drive would be the most intensive and the most lucrative. Publicity for the 1945 War Fund drive began almost as soon as the 1944 drive ended. Radio broadcasts, news stories, magazine articles, and motion pictures were directed toward March 1—the first day of the drive. The drive began with an intensive radio publicity program on February 28—tagged Red Cross Radio Day—when every listener heard a War Fund message an average of five and a half times. On March 20, President Roosevelt broadcast a Red Cross message from the White House, his last public address over the medium he had used with such great effect in his brilliant career.

The motion-picture industry showed a documentary film, *Seeing Them Through*, in 15,000 theaters. Some 80 million moviegoers saw Ingrid Bergman featured in a moving appeal to give to the Red Cross, followed by taking a collection in the theater. These receipts ultimately brought in approximately $7 million in the 1945 drive. The device of using a movie plea to give, followed by a collection in the theater, was a fund-raising gimmick introduced in the 1930's in the March of Dimes drives. Every known tool of the public relations practice was used to enroll and guide 4 million volunteer workers, operating mainly at the chapter level. The Red Cross never lost sight of the basic fact that raising money is done at the local level, by many volunteer workers asking many, many others to give—and to give now. One public relations practitioner, Glenn Griswold, said, "No single campaign ever gave public relations techniques a broader test than the 1945 American Red Cross war fund drive."

Griswold was describing a massive publicity program that produced and disseminated:

3,500,000 booklets for volunteer solicitors
35,000,000 information leaflets for contributors
1,500,000 posters for billboards, stores, postoffices, etc.
84,042 separate advertisements reaching 2 billion readers
2,500,000,000 radio listener impressions
70 magazine features; 30 front covers
234,000,000 movie impressions
Speeches reaching an estimated 1,500,000 persons.

In addition, wide use was made of other publicity devices such as window displays, postage meters, interurban train schedules, posters in Pullman cars, dining-car menus, calendars, and advertising syndicate services. It was estimated that this vast promotional effort cost the Red Cross only 3 cents on the dollar collected in donations. Much of the work and materials were contributed. The full publicity resources of the OWI were utilized and the Red Cross had the valuable contributions of the advertising industry through its War Advertising Council. The Red Cross brought experience, imagination, and polished performance to the art of money raising in this 1945 drive which brought in $231 million in exactly 31 days—some $31 million over the announced goal. The power of a good cause, careful organization, sound planning, intensive publicity, and systematic solicitation of money has never been more effectively demonstrated.[34]

The American Red Cross collection of more than a half billion dollars in World War II will long stand as a high-water mark in a people's philanthropy.

Kate Smith's Radio Bond Drives

In the years after World War I America developed a new and powerful medium of mass communication—radio broadcasting. That radio was a medium especially susceptible to the exploitation of emotional appeals had been amply demonstrated by the time the fury of war fell upon America on December 7, 1941. Just a few years previously most Americans had looked on in amazement as citizens in the New York-New Jersey area panicked as a result of Orson Welles's dramatic show, *The Invasion from Mars*. President Franklin D. Roosevelt, with his famed "Fireside Chats," had been one of the most effective users of this new medium which reached all the people at one time, yet reached each person as an individual.

Wartime fund-raising appeals brought the radio marathon broadcast to stir the emotions and engage the vicarious participation of vast, unseen audiences. The power and reach of this fund-raising device was dramatically demonstrated by Kate Smith, popular singing star and radio personality of the 1930's and 1940's. She could use the radio to raise money, though Al Smith could not. Kate possessed "a symbolic fitness for the task of selling bonds." The political leader, Alfred E. Smith, lacked this though he too possessed a widely mimicked radio voice. Early in 1932 the John Price Jones firm undertook direction of a fund-raising campaign, the Democratic Victory Campaign, designed to raise enough money to pay off the Democrats' deficit before the 1932 presidential campaign. In this drive Governor Smith made a fervent nationwide appeal for funds over the radio but his plea brought in only 46 gifts totaling $308. John W. Davis, the party's 1924 presidential nominee, Governor Albert Ritchie of Maryland, and National Chairman Jouett Shouse had joined in another radio appeal that netted only $37! Certainly there was nothing automatic about raising money over the radio.[35]

Kate Smith had been a top radio star for a decade when America entered the war. An ex-student nurse who never took a vocal lesson, she was a large, bulky woman with a genial personality, a melodious voice, and boundless energy. She weighed 235 pounds in her days of stardom. She left Broadway musicals to take a 15-minute singing show on the Columbia Broadcasting System in 1931 and was placed opposite the National Broadcasting Company's hit show of the period, "Amos 'n' Andy." Despite this handicap she quickly won a wide and adoring following. In 1941 it could be said that Kate Smith had led all radio polls for ten years. Truly "Radio's First Lady," she oozed sincerity and goodness in her radio personality. Many older Americans today fondly recall her theme song, "When the Moon Comes over the Mountain." Others remember that it was she who popularized Irving Berlin's "God Bless America," a song he had written in World War I and then put away in a trunk. Others recall her friendly philosophizing. Though she never married, she was indexed with "a mother image."

Kate Smith plugged not only songs but causes she considered worthwhile. In radio appeals she had raised an estimated $4 million for the American Red Cross in several drives, an estimated $500,000 for the American Legion, and unknown amounts for other charity appeals. Once, when Miss Smith appealed to her listeners to contribute dolls for needy children, her loyal fans swamped the mails with 20,000 dolls in three days. A Broadway columnist once wrote, "No one in public life has more power to inspire donations than Kate Smith." [36]

By 1943, midway in the war, it was estimated that some 23 million Americans listened to her daytime program and 21 million persons tuned in on her weekly nighttime show. She was truly a radio star and a magnetic public personality. In her first radio marathon to sell U.S. War Bonds, Miss Smith obtained pledges by phone and by mail totaling more than $1 million. A second such effort in 1942 brought in more than $2 million. But in September, 1943, she set a high mark for all performers: she obtained pledges from listeners to buy bonds in the amount of $39 million, in just one long day's marathon broadcast. How many bonds were actually bought as a result of the pledges mailed or phoned to Kate there is no way of knowing. *Time* magazine asserted in 1944 that "it was no secret in the radio industry that there had been too much personal publicity for stars, too many unfulfilled bond pledges" in these radio bond sales campaigns.[37] Also, undoubtedly a portion of these sales represented a reallocation of sales—that is, bonds bought now instead of later.

September 21, 1943, was War Bond Day for the Columbia Broadcasting System and for 18 hours—from 8 A.M. until 2 A.M. the following day—Kate Smith came on at repeated intervals to plead with listeners to buy bonds in support of U.S. fighting men across the seas.

> On sixty-five distinct occasions in the course of the day, she begged, cajoled, demanded that her listeners buy war bonds. Within the narrow borders of her brief messages, Miss Smith managed to touch upon a variety of themes enshrined in American culture. She talked of neighbor boys from American towns and villages, now facing danger and death in other lands. And people listened. She told dramatic tales of generosity and sacrifice by soldier and civilian alike. People continued to listen. She invoked themes of love and hate, of large hopes and desperate fears, of honor and shame. . . . This was presented as a personal message, iterated and reiterated in a voice often broken, it seemed, by deep emotion. And people did more than listen.[38]

As nightfall neared, Miss Smith began to announce large totals of bond pledges that were jamming the telephone lines of CBS and its affiliated stations across the nation. CBS was forced to announce "all regular business at this station has been suspended with the entire staff manning the telephones." By the next day CBS said that the pledges totaled more than $39 million worth of U.S. War Bonds. Fortunately we have a careful record of this radio marathon because a group of social psychologists at Columbia University made a scholarly study of this fund-raising effort, a study subtitled "The

Social Psychology of a War Bond Drive." These investigators found that "as the investigation developed it became abundantly clear that the basis of persuasion by Smith included far more than the manifest content of her radio appeals. It was a larger configuration in which the audience's images of Smith, the class structure of our society, the cultural standards of distinct strata of the population, and socially induced expectations, feelings, tensions were all intricately involved in the patterns of response to the bond drive." [39] In Merton's opinion, listeners brought to the Kate Smith broadcast a wealth of wants and experiences their society had fashioned for them; wants, experiences which caused them to respond with emotional fervor and gifts of cash. Depth interviews with a representative sample of the listeners revealed clearly the strong ego involvement experienced by a large portion of Miss Smith's radio audience. Those who made pledges "participated."

At the outset of this radio marathon Kate told her listeners that this was not going to be an ordinary broadcast: "I'm going to appear on CBS programs throughout the day from now until one o'clock tomorrow morning. . . . I've been in radio quite some time, folks, but in all those years I don't think anything even remotely like this has ever been done before." As indicated earlier, this was not the first radio marathon to raise charity funds or to sell bonds but none had been so widely publicized and as spectacularly successful as this one was. "Commentators on other CBS programs wove their comments into the fabric of expectation. There was little possibility of escaping the atmosphere of excited anticipation." [40]

An analysis of the themes used by the singer to sell bonds shows that not once did she urge purchase of bonds as a sound investment. Nor did she use the anti-inflation argument. She put all her chips on the appeal to sacrifice for one's country in its hour of peril, on "the higher sentiments." Over half of her broadcast time was devoted to the theme of sacrifice. "Twenty-six per cent went to stories of the sacrifices of servicemen; almost as much, 20 per cent, to the sacrifices of civilians and 5 per cent to the sacrifice of one civilian in particular, namely, Kate Smith herself. Sixteen per cent of all Smith had to say dwelt upon the theme of *participation*, setting forth the view that the bond campaign was a common enterprise in which all of us could shuffle off our private egoisms and take part in a massive communal effort. . . . Twelve per cent of her time was devoted to the *competition* theme, which urged listeners to help Smith surpass her earlier bond sale records and to help their own community outdo others in purchasing bonds from her." [41]

Other themes used were the *facilitation* theme—the ease with which they could phone in pledges—and the personal appeal of Miss Smith. Merton points out that the use of the telephone not only made the purchase of bonds easier, it afforded a "simulacrum of personal contact." The recurring theme throughout the marathon was essentially "Buy a bond and bring your boy back home" and it was to this theme that persons responded. Of course the Smith radio appeals did not affect all listeners in the same fashion. Some listened continuously with mounting interest, and others, quite unmoved by her appeals, soon turned to other pursuits. Some bought bonds, many did not. Nor, as Merton points out, "is there any assurance that all those who bought bonds were actuated by the same aspects of her broadcasts." Nor did everyone approve and applaud Miss Smith's efforts to sell bonds by selling sacrifice. Merton's staff quoted one listener: "It's a sad commentary that the American people have to be entertained to make them buy something as important as war bonds."

Kate Smith's spectacular radio marathon did more than dramatize a new way of raising money. This broadcast appeal demonstrated anew that the medium of radio provided a means for building strong public figures who could exploit the listeners' emotions in mass persuasion. In this she was simply underlining a fact that Franklin D. Roosevelt had emphatically demonstrated many years before.

Miss Smith's salesmanship should be viewed in the larger context which made this selling effort possible. The elements that blended into this pattern of persuasion extend far beyond the gross emotional symbols she utilized in the 18-hour broadcast. In this context were blended the emotional fervor of a people at war and the long-accumulating public image of Kate as a sincere, selfless patriot. Merton concluded: "It was this imagery, also, that permitted the bond pledge to become simultaneously an expression of their fealty to Smith and to their country." [42] In this way war bonds were sold and USO funds raised. Since then millions of dollars in funds for health and charity drives have been raised over the airwaves of radio and television with similar techniques.

The Cancer Society Giant Awakens

As should now be clear, it takes more than a good cause to raise the millions of dollars needed by America's popular philanthropy. It takes a cause with public appeal that is fully exploited by shrewd public relations which, in turn, paves the way for systematic solicitation of funds. Public participation in an organization is another requisite for widespread giving. All this is amply illustrated in the story of the American Cancer Society, today one of the fund-raising giants; since 1959 it has been the biggest money raiser in the health field. As already noted, the Cancer Society was long a slumbering giant after its founding in 1913. Some thirty years later, in 1944, the American Society for the Control of Cancer had only 986 dues-paying members, about half as many as it had in its early years. The ACS headquarters was receiving, on the average, about three phone calls a day from persons seeking information about cancer. The Society had been tightly controlled by physicians through these years and was without a strong public relations program or lay participation.

Yet the toll of cancer was steadily mounting; it had become the second major cause of death in the United States. There was a desperate need for cancer research but little could be done because there was no money to pay for it. When the Society was taken over in 1944 by an imaginative lay leadership, led by a smart, spunky Mrs. Mary Lasker, which knew and used the skills of public relations, the Society boomed, in volunteers, in funds raised, and in research support. In 1943 the American Society for the Control of Cancer raised some $350,000 in its annual fund drives; in 1961 the American Cancer Society raised $36,942,955—or more than a hundred times the sum raised before it turned to intensive promotion and high-pressure fund raising. By 1959 the ACS had become the largest voluntary health agency in the country in point of public support.

Leaders of the Cancer Society had long realized the need for effective public education but until the advent of the Albert Laskers they had done little about it. In February, 1923, the Society created the post of managing director and selected Dr. George A. Soper, the "epidemic fighter," largely responsible for the location and detention of "Typhoid Mary," to fill it, at a salary of $10,000 a year. Dr. Soper saw the Society's functions as "epidemiological and educational," adding that "it is not enough that a person know what to do, he must be induced to do it. The Society must make skillful use of the principles of practical psychology." One of Dr. Soper's first contributions was a "statement of principles and policies": [43]

1. The development of the information-gathering function of the Society.
2. The insistence upon accuracy of statement and the use of fear as a motive force.
3. The necessity of obtaining an endowment fund to meet the minimum running expenses of the Society.
4. The importance of encouraging the establishment of cancer clinics and cancer institutes.

The Cancer Society's lack of resources and skill in carrying out the educational function is shown in the stark fact that though Dr. George N. Papanicolaou's vaginal-smear technique of detecting cervical cancer in its early, manageable stages was discovered in 1926, it did not get widespread acceptance until "sold" to the public by the revitalized public relations program dating from the mid-1940's. This amply illustrates the value to society of constructive public relations programs. In 1929 Dr. Clarence Cook Little succeeded Dr. Soper as managing director and served until forced out in the 1945 reorganization of the Society. Dr. Little recognized the need for a nationwide integrated program of lay education and in 1930 the Society started plans for a major educational effort. These plans, like so many other projects of this period, were crimped by the onset of the depression.

The first effort to build lay support to fight cancer came from outside the physician-controlled Society for the Control of Cancer. In November, 1933, the General Federation of Women's Clubs decided to launch a cancer education program in their various field units. Out of this plan came, in 1936, the Women's Field Army, a separate educational group distinct from the General Federation of Women's Clubs. The Women's Field Army was largely the result of the concern and efforts of Mrs. Grace N. Reynolds, federation president, and Mrs. Marjorie B. Illig, chairman of its committee on public health. Dr. Little said their efforts "were absolutely invaluable in bringing about the turn of events." [44] In 1938 the first volunteer enlistment drive was conducted and the "mobilization of American women to vanquish this disease was begun." This was the first large recruitment of volunteers in the conquest of cancer that would ultimately build a volunteer army of more than two million cancer crusaders.

Although the close relationship of the Women's Field Army and the American Cancer Society presented many problems, the results established the Society as a national organization and provided a base of volunteer workers upon which it could later build. Mrs. Illig served as commander until 1943. Her place was taken by Mrs. Harold V. Milligan as national commander of the Women's Field Army, and she served until this office was discontinued by the Society in 1951. But, as Mefford Runyon recalls, "even with these developments the Society, in the early forties, was still small and its program incomplete because the disease was not being attacked in a fundamental way which would ultimately develop a cure or means of prevention." It was clear that before the disease could be attacked "in a fundamental way" there would have to be an effective program to obtain the money needed for such an attack. Such a program to build nationwide support for the crusade against cancer had its inception on a windy afternoon late in November, 1943.

Albert Lasker, the father of modern advertising, and Mrs. Mary Woodard Reinhardt were married June 21, 1940, some fifteen months after they first met. This was Lasker's third marriage, her second. This marriage proved to be an ideal mating of two dynamic, yet diverse personalities. Their brief but happy life together was to have widespread impact on the worlds of medicine, art, and public affairs. The marriage ended all too soon with Lasker's death on May 30, 1952, as the result, ironically, of cancer.

Mrs. Lasker was born Mary Woodard in Watertown, Wis., of Puritan Yankee and North Irish stock. She was educated in Milwaukee-Downer Seminary, the University of Wisconsin, and Radcliffe where she received her degree in 1923 *cum laude*. She then went to England to do postgraduate work at Oxford and study art in Europe. Her major was art history. Upon her return to the United States, Miss Woodard took a job in the Reinhardt Galleries and married Paul Reinhardt in 1926. They were divorced in 1934 and Mary went into the dress pattern business on her own. She was earning $25,000 a year when she met Albert Lasker at a party; a fateful meeting for them, and for the American Society for the Control of Cancer.[45]

Mrs. Mary Lasker had been shocked into action by the death of her

cook from cancer and the maddening fact that medical science could
offer so little help in stemming the ravages of this disease. A dynamic woman with capacity for unsparing devotion to a cause, she
decided to do something. Thus in November, 1943, she called on
Dr. Little at the Society's offices at 350 Madison Avenue. When Dr.
Little told her that the Society had no funds for research, she was
amazed and angered. Mrs. Lasker left the Society's office that
November afternoon a dedicated worker in the cancer movement.
She immediately confronted her talented husband with the demand that "we do something." Mr. Lasker shared his wife's dismay
and concern about the deplorable lack of cancer research but insisted
that his health and the press of business affairs would not permit
him to tackle the job of public education that was urgently needed.
But surely it was wishful thinking on Lasker's part, as subsequent
events would prove, to think that he could remain aloof from this
challenging new interest of the wife he loved so dearly.

Lasker told his wife that his able associate in the Lord & Thomas
advertising agency and now the head of the successor agency, Emerson Foote, might be willing to take on such a task. The previous
year Lasker had dissolved his pioneering advertising agency, which
had done more than $750 million worth of business over seventy
years, and turned the accounts over to the agency started by three
of his top executives, Emerson Foote, Fairfax Cone, and Don Belding.
The new Foote, Cone, Belding firm opened for business on January 1, 1943, and Lasker turned his energies to building support for
the Planned Parenthood Federation, another public service that was
sparked by his new wife.

Foote was ready to help. Both his parents had been victims of
cancer, with the result that he was excited by the possibility of
launching a public crusade to raise research funds. His acceptance
of Mrs. Lasker's challenge brought the promotional skills of an experienced advertising executive to the Cancer Society, a move that
was to prove significant.

Mrs. Lasker was quick to bring Foote and Dr. Little together. They
spent hours discussing ways and means of enlarging the cancer
control movement and building a mass base of support for its work.
In their initial conferences Foote assured Dr. Little that an annual
fund-raising campaign "that was intelligently handled and comprehensive in scope would receive at least five million dollars." [46] Dr.
Little relayed Foote's recommendations to his board, saying, "The

Managing Director believes that the time for the development of a broad and creative statesmanship in the field of cancer control has come, that it is the duty of our Society wholeheartedly and immediately to take the leadership in this effort. The next few years should see the beginning of a new era of public support of cancer control." [47] This was the beginning of the reorganization of the Society and the reorientation of its program which culminated in 1945.

Lay leadership, increased public relations, and intensive fund raising were soon to bring profound changes in the management and impact of this volunteer health agency. The Society had stood in urgent need of the talents of the modern promoter and efficient businessman, talents the Laskers and Emerson Foote would supply in full measure. The Laskers had been appalled to learn that of the $350,000 raised in the 1943 fund drive not one cent had gone to research. They felt equally strongly about the need for an intensive program of public education. Mrs. Lasker immediately gave Dr. Little $5,000 to pay for a pamphlet on the existing state of research in this field. Foote was equally dismayed by the antiquated business methods of the Society. He found the "best fund-raising promotion ideas were impractical because the society had little talent for implementation. Foote complained to the Laskers that the 1944 fund drive would bring in far less than it should for these reasons." [48]

A bare hint of what the infusion of these new talents would mean to the battle against cancer was given in the March, 1944, fund-raising drive. Despite the very limited central office staff and extremely meager publicity efforts, the Society's 1944 drive brought in $820,000, the most successful fund raising in the Society's 31-year history. Acting on Foote's recommendation, the Society dropped "for Control of Cancer" from its name and became the American Cancer Society. Also at his suggestion, the Women's Field Army was renamed the Field Army "to suggest that both sexes had a place in fund raising and community service." Pleas for money for research comprised the basic appeal for the 1944 drive. Nonetheless, the Laskers thought this $820,000 a pitifully inadequate sum against the needs for cancer research and education and, characteristically, decided to take action.

"It had been obvious to both the Laskers and to Foote that the 1944 campaign had failed to be more successful because it lacked full-time experienced leadership." [49] The Laskers told ACS officials

that they would help finance and guide the 1945 campaign on condition that one-fourth of all new funds would go to research and
that the rest would go to public dissemination of knowledge about
cancer. The proposal was accepted and the Laskers went to work.
Lasker often said, "To raise money you have to have it." He was a
great exponent of "seed money." "First, they supplied $80,000 from
various sources, some of it contributed by Albert himself, to help
pay for the campaign." Next they agreed to pay half the salary of
a campaign director for 1945 if the Society would hire Leo Casey,
who had established a good reputation as a fund raiser and political
publicist. This, too, the Society agreed to do.

Leo Casey brought to the task wide experience gained in political
fund raising and publicity work, as well as the asset of numerous
contacts among wealthy influential people and mass media executives. He had served the moderate wing of the Republican party in
several campaigns. Casey had directed the publicity in Thomas E.
Dewey's campaigns for district attorney in Manhattan, and for
governor of New York in 1938. In 1940 he handled Wendell Willkie's
pre-convention publicity, and after Willkie became the GOP nom-
inee for President, Casey was made director of publicity for the
Republican National Committee. He again worked for Willkie in
the latter's short-lived campaign for the GOP nomination in 1944.
Once Willkie's hopes had died in the Wisconsin primary in the
spring of 1944, Casey was looking for a job. Casey also had gained
widespread recognition for his work as publicity director for the
1939 New York World's Fair. Shaughnessy describes him as a "public
relations man of wide experience and great charm."

Casey plunged into his task with vigor and enthusiasm. His first
coup was to get Eric Johnston, president of the United States
Chamber of Commerce, to serve as chairman for the 1945 campaign.
One of the first stumbling blocks Casey encountered in his publicity
planning for the 1945 fund appeal was the taboo against the men-
tion of cancer over the radio. These were still times in which cancer carried a stigma in the minds of its victims and their families,
times in which newspapers feared to report cancer as a cause of
death in obituaries. Casey astutely enlisted Albert Lasker and Emerson Foote to bring pressure on the radio networks to rescind this
ban. Network officials listened with respect to this request from
two men who had made radio a multibillion-dollar advertising medium. "A number of radio stars, like Bob Hope and Fibber and

Molly McGee, lent their assistance freely, and at last the ban on mentioning cancer on the air was broken." [50]

As Casey and Foote mapped plans for a massive nationwide publicity campaign along the lines set by the March of Dimes drive, they felt the pinch of lack of funds. Once again Mary Lasker came to the rescue. One day in August, 1944, she and Emerson Foote were having lunch in New York City to discuss the forthcoming 1945 Cancer Society fund drive. Mrs. Lasker noticed at a nearby table an old friend, Lois Mattox Miller, then an outstanding medical reporter and an editor of the *Reader's Digest*. Mrs. Lasker recalls:

> I told her the sad facts about the inadequate funds for cancer research and for treatment and care and education of doctors, that the Society was raising no funds for research whatever—but still one out of eight would die of the disease, and one out of five over thirty-five would die of it. She was very moved by our enthusiasm and wrote, with the help of Emerson Foote, an excellent short piece which took about a third of a page in the *Digest* and she got DeWitt Wallace to allow her to add a line asking for contributions to be sent to the Society. [51]

The *Digest*, then as now the nation's most widely read magazine, quickly demonstrated its pulling power. The first article by Mrs. Miller appeared in the October, 1944, issue and contributions started rolling in. This article and two other short ones she wrote in the spring of 1945 brought the Society more than $120,000 in direct contributions. "The opening of envelopes and the counting of the money from this source alone was a great bother to the then very inadequately staffed Society." [52] But now the Society had money to finance the expense of posters, pamphlets, mailers, etc., for the 1945 fund drive.

Just when everything appeared to be moving smoothly toward the announced goal Leo Casey resigned. Shaughnessy says that Casey, "though brilliant and imaginative, had evidently found his talents uncongenial to the massive amount of detail which campaign planning had involved." Campaign hopes looked dark as preparation for the drive was abruptly halted. Once more the untiring, determined Mary Lasker came to the rescue. She called John Price Jones and persuaded him to take over the campaign, though the time for preparation was perilously short. Mrs. Lasker agreed to pay Jones's fee, again with the stipulation that 25 per cent of all money raised be allocated to research. The executive committee agreed, Jones's firm took charge, and the campaign went forward. (The Laskers had earlier given $55,000 to the Society to start its research program.) Erwin D. Tuthill was the Jones executive assigned to direct the 1945 fund appeal.

Prodded by Emerson Foote, who now had the support of the fund drive chairman Eric Johnston, the Society agreed to the creation of a planning board and an executive council to provide a policy committee to guide the campaign. More important, prominent lay leaders could bring prestige, influential contacts, and organizational expertise to this national appeal for funds for a Society that was still not widely known. Enlisted on the executive council were James Adams, head of Standard Brands; Elmer Bobst, president of a pharmaceutical company; Thomas Braniff, airline owner; Lewis Douglas, former director of the U.S. Budget Bureau and now head of Mutual Life Insurance Company; and Foote and Lasker. "Along with Adams and Bobst, Lasker proved to be one of the 'strong men' of the reorganization movement. He traveled widely, using his influence, persuading his friends on behalf of the Society, and shattering almost singlehandedly the unseen barrier that forbade the use of the word 'cancer' over the air waves. He was a tremendous storehouse of ideas and optimism." [53]

The 1945 drive, the first to be fully planned, organized, and promoted, was a resounding triumph. Some $4,292,000 was raised in gifts large and small, mostly small. About half this sum was collected by the newly expanded Field Army which found the public aware of the cancer crusade and ready to give. There is some difference on the exact amount raised: John Price Jones records show the total as $4,022,000, ACS records it as $4,292,000. In any event it was far more money than the ACS officers, long accustomed to hand-to-mouth contributions, believed possible to get in gifts. They reckoned without the modern publicist and fund raiser.

Foote and the Laskers were quick to insist that $925,000 be earmarked for research as had been stipulated and to insist further that the Society's board of directors be expanded to include lay leadership. "Flabbergasted at what had happened in the fund drive," most of the Society's board members were ready to accede to the Foote-Lasker demands. But a few, in John Gunther's words, "fought it like tigers." In the end the board was made half-medical, half-lay, as the Laskers wished. Gunther quotes an unnamed physician as saying: "The American Cancer Society and all its beneficent work is no more than the shadow of one man, Albert Lasker." [54] In the reorganization Dr. Clarence Cook Little was swept out of the Society. In Carter's words, "He had wanted a fresh breeze, but had been given a cyclone."

There are two pointed ironies in this story. Both involve the controversy over the link between cigarette smoking and lung cancer. It is ironic that the Cancer Society's modern benefactor was the same Albert Lasker who promoted social acceptance of smoking by women. In the early 1920's Albert Lasker had the American Tobacco Co. as one of his advertising accounts. Industrialist Paul Hoffman, then a Lasker client, suggested to Lasker that he could double the cigarette market by making it fashionable for women to smoke. He and George Washington Hill, the president of American Tobacco Co., set out to do just this. Their advertising campaign was supplemented by the public relations efforts of Edward L. Bernays and the Ivy Lee firm, both of whom were retained by Hill. Lasker's work on behalf of Lucky Strike cigarettes is one of the classics of advertising history.

Cigarettes, heavily consumed by men, women, and teen-agers, have been found to be a possible source of the disease that Lasker helped fight in his last years, before he himself died of abdominal cancer.

The other irony involves Dr. Clarence Cook Little, biologist, former university president, and always stormy petrel. Before becoming managing director of the American Society for the Control of Cancer in 1929, Dr. Little had served as president of the University of Maine and the University of Michigan. In his service to the Cancer Society from 1929 to 1945 he did much to build the foundation and promote the change which made the Society today's fund-raising champion in the volunteer health field. In 1954 Dr. Little came out of retirement to become the scientific director of the Tobacco Industry Research Committee. Creation of this committee and financing the research it directs was the tobacco industry's answer to the growing evidence, albeit still circumstantial, of cigarette smoking as a cause of lung cancer. In the early 1960's the American Cancer Society, which he did so much to build, and the tobacco industry, which he currently serves, frequently engaged in bitter and vitriolic exchanges as to whether smoking was a cause of the rapidly increasing deaths from lung cancer. Perhaps at times

Dr. Little may wistfully wish he had left the slumbering giant asleep!

The reorganized Society moved steadily ahead. The 1946 drive, again directed by the John Price Jones firm, brought in $10.3 million—more than twice the amount raised the year before. Jones's firm also directed the 1947 campaign, which raised $12,075,000. The American Cancer Society was on its way to adulthood and the power to start winning the battle against this dread disease.

When the Society started its research program in July, 1945, not more than $1.5 million was being spent annually in the entire United States for cancer research and half of that amount was for the work of the National Cancer Institute of Bethesda, Md. Within two years after the reorganization of the Cancer Society the amount of money spent for research increased threefold. And this was only the beginning. Perhaps the Society's greatest contribution was to build the public opinion that led Congress greatly to expand the government's research program, which today completely overshadows the comparatively little the Society, despite its fund-raising successes, can provide. In building the fires of public demand under Congress, it was Albert Lasker who again played the key role.

Lasker told his fellow ACS board members that, because the danger of cancer involves the welfare of all the people, the federal government was obligated to finance a research program equal to the danger. "This meant long, careful and persistent education of those who control the government's purse strings. Mr. Lasker and Mr. Adams took the initial lead in arranging for expert testimony to be given before appropriations committees. . . . Mr. Lasker early realized that this problem of informing Congressmen on these health subjects was a difficult and continuing one. . . . He urged the Society to provide a full-time representative in Washington whose responsibility it would be to bring to the attention of Congressional leaders, at all appropriate times, the cancer challenge." [55]

The great difference that can be made by organized public pressure, backed by intensive public relations, is seen in the fact that in the 1946 fiscal year Congress appropriated $1,772,000 for cancer research in 1947, while the much-abused Eightieth Congress, the following year, appropriated $14 million to the National Cancer Institute. By 1952 Congress was appropriating more than $20 million annually in the research battle against cancer. In line with Lasker's recommendation, Colonel Luke Quinn, a public relations consultant and lobbyist specializing in the field of medicine, was retained as of January 1, 1952, for this purpose. Mefford Runyon is quite right in suggesting that "in the long run this initiation and sponsorship of the cancer research program . . . and the persuading of the Congress of the part which the government must necessarily play in the total fight on cancer will prove to be the most important contribution made by the American Cancer Society in the war on this disease."

Although the government's multimillion-dollar research program today dwarfs the some $9 million the Cancer Society spends in research, the Society's educational program continues as a useful contribution in the campaign to conquer cancer. One of the arguments used to resist federation in a single annual health fund drive is that the separate drive is needed to focus public attention on each particular disease, and with some validity. The Society's campaign publicity has had, as one of its by-products, the propagation of cancer facts.

Dr. Frank E. Adair, long-time president of the Society, wrote in the Society's 1947 annual report: "The Campaign which the Society conducts annually to raise money is in itself the greatest contribution that can be made to cancer education. The campaigns . . . have done more to awaken and educate possible cancer victims than could have been done through any other means. In virtually every city and hamlet of the nation, citizens have been aroused to work for this cause." The brunt of this educational task is shared by the large staff and by the two million volunteer workers. Much progress had been made in making citizens aware of the nature of cancer and its early detection; much remains to be done, and this is probably the most valid argument for continued support of the Cancer Society.

NOTES

1. Letter to Hubert Kelly of *American Magazine* from Ralph Wallace, member of Byoir's staff, dated March 6, 1941. Copy in files of Byoir firm.

2. Gertrude Springer, "For Soldiers Off Duty," *Survey Midmonthly*, Vol. 77 (March, 1941), p. 75.

3. *Ibid.*

4. *New York Times*, April 7, 1941, p. 12.

5. Springer, *op. cit.*

6. Letter from T. S. Ruggles, John Price Jones Co., July 19, 1962.

7. *Ibid.*

8. Memorandum, JPJ: Church, "Adverse Word of Mouth Publicity as It Affects the John Price Jones Corporation," dated Oct. 24, 1941. In John Price Jones Papers.

9. "Complaints about the John Price Jones Corp." In John Price Jones Papers, Vol. 331.

10. Tom K. Smith, "Giving We Unite," *Survey Midmonthly*, Vol. 77 (September, 1941), p. 251.

11. *New York Times*, Dec. 6, 1941, p. 13.

12. *Ibid.*, Nov. 19, 1940, p. 25.

13. In Foreword to Harold J. Seymour's *Design for Giving* (New York: Harper, 1947), p. viii.

14. Burns, "Rise of the War Chests 300 Strong Since Pearl Harbor," *Survey Midmonthly*, Vol. 78 (September, 1942), p. 229.

15. Seymour, *op. cit.*, pp. 4–5.

16. *Ibid.*, pp. 6–7.

17. "The National War Fund," *Survey Midmonthly*, Vol. 79 (September, 1943), p. 229.

18. Seymour, *op. cit.*, p. 17.

19. *Ibid.*, p. 20.

20. Burns, *op. cit.*

21. Foster R. Dulles, *The American Red Cross*, p. 361.

22. *Ibid.*

23. "Why the Red Cross Wants $50,000,000," editorial in *Collier's*, Vol. 109 (Feb. 28, 1942), p. 62.

24. Memo Brown to the Chairman, Aug. 26, 1940, "Subj: Editorial Comment." ARC Archives.

25. Ralph Berens, "The History of Public Relations in the American National Red Cross" (unpublished thesis, University of Wisconsin, 1961), p. 230.

26. Dulles, *op. cit.*, p. 417.

27. *Ibid.*, pp. 368 ff.

28. *Red Cross War Fund Campaign Plan Book*, 1943, ARC, p. 22.

29. Memo, "Subj: Report on Publicity for the 1944 War Fund," dated May 2, 1944, Brown to the Chairman. ARC Archives.

30. Creel, *Rebel at Large*, p. 131.

31. Memorandum, Brown to the Chairman, "Organization and Responsibilities of the Office of Public Relations," July 25, 1944. ARC Archives.

32. These data from Public Information Service report, March, 1943, Mimeo No. 719000, ARC Archives.

33. St. Louis *Post-Dispatch*, March 1, 1943, Sec. B, p. 3.

34. For accounts of the 1945 drive see: Red Cross *Annual Report*, June 30, 1945, pp. 143 ff.; Glenn Griswold (ed.), "Best Public Relations Case Studies of 1945," *Public Relations News*, 1946; Memorandum, Brown to the Chairman, "Report of Publicity for the 1944 War Fund," May 2, 1944, ARC Archives.

35. Humphrey E. Redfield's campaign report in Staff Papers, John Price Jones Papers, BF 9.

36. Hildegarde Dolson, "Kate Behind the Mike," condensed from *Movie-Radio Guide, Reader's Digest*, Vol. 40 (January, 1942), p. 35.

37. "Kate's Appeal," *Time*, Vol. 44 (July 3, 1944), p. 50.

38. Robert K. Merton, *Mass Persuasion* (Harper, 1946), p. 2.

39. *Ibid.*, p. 9.

40. *Ibid.*, p. 23.

41. *Ibid.*, pp. 50–51.

42. *Ibid.*, p. 177.

43. Talk by Mefford Runyon, Managing Director, "The American Cancer Society—a Profile," Oct. 29, 1959.

44. *Ibid.*

45. For fuller account of the Laskers' courtship, marriage, and public services see John Gunther, *Taken at the Flood, the Story of Albert D. Lasker.*

46. Donald F. Shaughnessy, "A History of the American Cancer Society" (unpublished Ph.D. thesis Columbia University), p. 205.

47. Annual Report American Society for the Control of Cancer, 1945, p. 7.

48. Carter, *The Gentle Legions*, p. 156.

49. Shaughnessy, *op. cit.*, p. 208.

50. John Gunther, *Taken at the Flood* (New York: Harper, 1960), p. 322.

51. In interview with Donald F. Shaughnessy, July 26, 1955. See his thesis, p. 209.

52. *Ibid.*, p. 210.

53. *Ibid.*, p. 211.

54. Gunther, *op. cit.*, p. 324.

55. Mefford Runyon, *op. cit.*

11

The Cheats in Fund Raising

The Charity Charlatans

Cruel exploitation of man's urge to help his less fortunate fellow man is an ancient evil. It remains an evil in American philanthropy for which no fully effective safeguard has as yet been found. In the early centuries of philanthropy the charity frauds were perpetrated mostly by the itinerant beggars, making false claims in their tearful appeal for alms, or of local fund appeals of questionable merit. These were of no great public consequence. But with the advent of America's twentieth-century surefire methods of fund raising and multibillion-dollar philanthropy, dishonest and wasteful fund raising has become a serious social problem. We use "fraudulent" in this chapter rather more in a moral than in the strictly legal sense. Few of the charity bandits actually run afoul of the law.

The charlatan usually stays within the bounds of the loosely written laws covering fund-raising appeals and charitable agencies. There can be no legal limit set, for instance, on how much is spent on fund raising and on an extravagant administrative overhead. As the Tompkins Committee observed: "The sparsity of data on the activities of organized charity tends to make this field a playground for the unscrupulous." When the Tompkins Committee undertook its investigation in 1953, the postal authorities estimated that there were 1,100 charitable organizations operating in New York City alone. Such a figure illustrates the task of the prober who would make a detailed audit of charitable giving. It also dramatizes the problem of the giver, who must sort out the honest, meritorious appeal from the dubious or dishonest one. Not only does dishonest or wasteful fund raising divert needed dollars from the many real

441

needs of our society, but these practices put all fund appeals under a cloud of suspicion.

F. Emerson Andrews of the Russell Sage Foundation testified in 1953 that of the estimated $750 million collected for charitable purposes in the state of New York in 1950, "about 3% or between $20,-000,000 and $25,000,000 goes into outright charity rackets." These figures were substantiated by other experts in the field testifying before the Tompkins Committee. Other leaders of philanthropy and fund raising put the estimate at 2 per cent. The veteran fund raiser David Church thinks that with the advent of state regulatory laws the percentage is less than 2 per cent. All agree that $1 given to a fraudulent operator is $1 too many. As a nationwide television audience was told in 1962 in a dramatic documentary, *The Charity Bandits:* "The appeals of the worthwhile groups are echoed by others which are honest but incompetent, and imitated by outright frauds. In the resulting confusion, the individual contributor finds it all but impossible to know where to spend his charity dollar." [1]

The growth in the extent and number of fund-raising frauds was first brought to national attention by the hearings of New York State Senator Bernard Tompkins' Joint Legislative Committee on Charitable and Philanthropic Agencies and Organizations in 1953 and 1954. New York State has pioneered among the states in an effort to legislate and prosecute the charity charlatans out of this lucrative field for chicanery. In 1949 the New York State Attorney General Nathaniel L. Goldstein, instructed an assistant, Jerry Glucksman, to step up his investigation of fraudulent practices by cemetery associations and other groups using the membership corporation as a vehicle for shady business. Glucksman recalls: "Peering under the blanket, it was found that charitable solicitation took three forms predominantly: money was solicited either personally, by telephone or by mail. As soon as word got out that this investigation had been started information and complaints started to flow in." [2]

One of the first schemes uncovered by Glucksman was that of fraudulent operators using paid solicitors to collect money in front of Broadway's many theaters. Persons standing in line or on entering a theater would be pressured to drop coins for "the needy" in coin containers held out by the solicitor. In his probing Glucksman discovered that "quick talking promoters went to various religious and charitable organizations with a proposition that they would send solicitors into the street, thus taking the pressure from the membership of these organizations. The solicitors would be paid for their services out of the income dropped into the containers. The promoters would take an override and would bear all of the expenses of obtaining the containers, printing the legends, etc. and the net would be turned over to the charitable or religious organization." [3] The net turned out to be less than 30 per cent of the amount collected as "over seventy per cent of the take went to the promoters and their helpers."

Another charity "racket" soon uncovered by Glucksman's probe is one known as the "boiler room" operation. A slick promoter opens an office and equips it with a battery of telephones. He employs smooth-talking solicitors and a "pitch" is made in the name of charity to known contributors to charitable causes. The "pitchmen" are paid commissions ranging from 25 to 40 per cent. The promoter takes from 5 to 25 per cent to cover his expenses and his profits. As Glucksman says, "What person can resist an appeal to send home a disabled serviceman for the Christmas holidays . . . or to send a child from an underprivileged area away to a summer camp?" As this New York State official points out, "This is not to say all of these appeals are wrong, shady or improper; but what a lovely place to grab a few unmarked dollar bills. The expenses are high; as the expenses go up the result to charity is a deprivation of a few more dollars. Sometimes less than four cents out of every dollar goes into the charity use." [4] One of these boiler-room operators chuckled as he recounted to the committee how on one occasion he impersonated a priest and another time a police representative, in soliciting money over the phone. He admitted that he had been convicted and fined $250 in 1951 for soliciting funds without a license for the Bronx Chapter of the Disabled American Veterans. The witness said he sometimes got as much as 60 per cent of the collections in his "fund drives."

Such discoveries as these led, in turn, to the creation of the Tompkins Committee by the New York State Legislature, March 31, 1953. This Committee concluded nearly a year later that "The public is being mulcted of millions of dollars each year" and that "These vast sums are being diverted away from worthy and necessary philanthropies." [5] The Committee asserted in its final report, *"The generosity of our citizens has been consistently and flagrantly abused by a small minority of frauds operating as 'charities' which have mulcted*

New Yorkers out of an annual amount probably in excess of $25,000,000. In addition, an even vaster sum of dollars contributed by the public is cut down to pennies before reaching intended beneficiaries by excessive fund raising and administrative costs of inefficient charities." [6]

At the conclusion of its hearings and deliberations the New York legislative committee classified charities as follows: Group A—the well-intentioned, well-administered; Group B—the well-intentioned, poorly administered; Group C—the outright frauds of commercial enterprises. "The Committee accepted the expert estimates that Group C *represents approximately 3 per cent of the field*, but it was impossible to approximate the distribution of the remaining 97 per cent into Groups A and B." [7] The Committee's hearings pointed up five areas where "there is a considerable breach of the public trust by the unscrupulous who operate in this field." These were:

1. *Misrepresentations.* Some agencies were found continually to misrepresent their true program. Though they appealed for funds to alleviate human distress, this was never their intent. Some organizations promised to do things their charters did not permit them to do.
2. *Fradulent Sponsorships.* Unauthorized use of the names of public-spirited citizens as sponsors to lend a dignity and reputable sanction to an appeal for funds. Often names were used without the consent or knowledge of the individuals. Unauthorized use of sponsors' names is a favorite technique of the "boiler room" operator.
3. *Inadequate Records.* Because they are not required to give any financial or progress accounts to the general public, some marginal agencies keep what the Committee described as "sloppy records." This practice permitted diversion of funds by unscrupulous fund raisers or administrators.
4. *Fronts.* Some so-called charities are nothing but fronts for commercial enterprises or for the personal aggrandizement of those in control.
5. *High Costs.* Because the light of public scrutiny has not been cast on their administrative practices, numerous agencies incur fund raising and administrative costs which are excessively high.[8]

The extent to which the generous but gullible citizen can be tricked by high-powered promoters exploiting charitable appeals was illustrated in the extreme by the Tompkins Committee's exposure of the National Kids' Day Foundation, Inc., which collected $3,978,000 in five years—June, 1948, to June 30, 1953—and spent this sum in fund-raising, promotion, and administrative services. Not one dollar ever went to the direct aid of a needy child. If a donor had closely scrutinized the glib appeals he would have discovered that the Foundation's function was merely to promote the *idea* of aiding needy children.

Of the $3,978,000 given to the National Kids' Day Foundation, Inc., $3,252,000, or 82 per cent, went to unscrupulous fund raisers; $302,000, or 7.5 per cent, to the promotion of National Kids' Day; $95,000, or 2.5 per cent, to administrative expenses. This left $329,-000, or 8 per cent, to be used in future promotional efforts; in other words, capital for next year's fleecing operation.[9] Until March, 1953, just prior to the Tompkins Committee hearings, the Foundation's promotion was handled by the J. Walter Thompson advertising agency. The unpaid chairman lamely insisted that it cost $100,000 to raise $18,000 in a nationwide fund-raising campaign when an organization did not have volunteers to solicit money for it.

In one year two Chicago promotion firms raised $1,040,000 in the Foundation's name by mailing out unordered merchandise, and turned over $15,000 to the Foundation. These firms were Gayton Associates, Inc., and Wesco, Inc., retained in an arrangement worked out with Abraham L. Koolish.

Gayton's "pattern of activity was to mail fountain pens or name stickers imprinted with the names of recipients to a mailing list which it supplied. About 2,000,000 such pens were sent out, Gayton receiving 56½ cents plus postage of 6½ cents for each mailing. In addition, Wesco, Inc. had a cost-plus contract to open mail received by the Foundation, for which it received approximately $154,000. Receiving a fixed amount for each mailing, Gayton was therefore also in a position to earn large sums of money regardless of the charity's income. . . . The only possible limitation from the point of view of such a fund raiser is that he must be certain that the golden goose receives at least a subsistence diet."[10] In short, for every dollar the donor gave the Kids' Day Foundation, 82 cents went to the cost of soliciting it, mainly to the Gayton and Wesco firm owners. In order to give $1 to the Foundation the donor would have had to have given $5.56 to further its vaguely phrased objectives.

The National Kids' Day Foundation also was found to be using prestigious sponsors' names without authority. The most notable name exploited was that of the popular actor and singer Bing Crosby. In the contract between the Foundation and the charity operator Gayton it was agreed that the Foundation would supply a Bing Crosby memorandum for use in solicitation. The promoters produced an appealing flier with a picture of Bing in front of a microphone that read: "Here's a grand way to help kids who aren't getting the breaks they should. Whatever you can give will be wisely invested to bring happiness and health to youngsters needing special care and attention. So please don't delay. Send what you can—*Today!* Bing Crosby." In an affidavit to the Committee, Crosby denied that he had given the sponsor permission in any way whatsoever to use his name in connection with this activity.[11] The Foundation's main activity was to promote National Kids' Day each September in cooperation with local Kiwanis Clubs across the country and enable Kiwanis Clubs to use this as a vehicle for well-meant projects for underprivileged children. This part of the activitiy was not impugned in the Committee's exposé. These shocking revelations led to the Foundation's demise early in 1954.

The Committee's hearings exposed several other fleecings of the gullible givers. Another example was that of the Guide Dog Foundation, an organization dedicated to the training of guide dogs and their masters, a most laudable purpose. The Committee's chief accountant testified, after examining this Foundation's books:

> For the year 1952, there was a total of $153,000 raised. Of that amount $92,000, or 60 per cent was the cost of fund-raising. The administrative expenses were nine per cent, or $13,000.
>
> The moneys spent on dog training and other welfare was 14 per cent, or $22,000. And there was $6,000, or four per cent, retained by the promoter for future costs of fund-raising to defray him against any losses which he might sustain in the future. And there was also $20,000, or 13 per cent, available for subsequent periods.[12]

Thus, out of every dollar given by the donor that year, only about 14 cents was actually expended for the training of dogs and blind students. Again the big profit went to the charity operator. "The Guide Dog Foundation for the Blind, Inc., employed Donard, Inc. (owned by Willard Kauth, his son and daughter) as its fund-raiser. Donard prepared and managed the Foundation's direct mail solicitation, turning over all letter-shop and mailing work to another corporation, Noddra, Inc., also controlled by Kauth and his family. Kauth, either in his individual or corporate capacity, raised funds for a number of charities including The Boys Brotherhood Republic of New York, School Settlement, Inc., Girls Town, Inc., Boys Athletic League, and Girls Vacation Fund. . . . That charitable work can pay quite well, especially when one can control the expense aspects, is clear from the testimony of Mr. Kauth, that his expected income for 1953, from these organizations, would reach $75,000." [13]

Ralph Lee Smith, formerly on the staff of the Better Business Bureau, records the next chapter in the Kauth story:

> In 1954 Guide Dog Foundation for the Blind discontinued use of the Kauth organizations. Willard's son Donald promptly swung into action, creating a new organization, Guiding Eyes for the Blind, Inc. of which he became salaried director. He started mass fund-raising mailings, using the family-owned Noddra, Inc., for part of the work. . . . Donard, Inc., became inactive in 1957 though it was not disbanded. . . . Donald Kauth continues as director of Guiding Eyes for the Blind. Willard Kauth's salary as director of Boys Athletic League has gone up to $26,000 a year. His wife serves as executive director and treasurer of Girls Vacation Fund, receiving no salary. However, she thoughtfully retains her husband as general manager, at a salary of $16,000 per year. Fund-raising costs for 1960 for Boys Athletic League ran 41 per cent; for Girls Vacation Fund, 42.3 per cent.[14]

Another flagrant fleecing of the public exposed in these hearings was that perpetrated by the National Cancer Hospital of America, described by the Committee as "never more than a parcel of Detroit real estate with a posted notice of a building to be erected." This was a mail-order operation originating in Michigan but directed from New York City. Contributions received in this campaign totaled approximately $630,000 and the cost of raising this sum was $435,000, or 69 per cent. This left $190,000 for charitable use. Of this sum 12 per cent, $76,000, went to buy the lot in Detroit, $5,000 to settle a lawsuit, leaving only $114,000 out of a contributed total of $630,000.

This sum was raised by the mailing out of dollar bills, not merchandise. The scheme was a simple one: mail out a crisp new dollar bill to a prospective contributor and ask him to return the dollar with a matching donation. "Starting with 2,000 crisp new bills put up by the fund-raiser, donations pyramided the operation to a point where 740,859 dollar bills had been sent, with total contributions amounting to $630,427.50." [15] In the course of this dollar bill mailing 164,725 dollar bills mailed out were lost, presumably kept by the not so gullible prospects. Therefore about 26 cents out of every dollar sent in by a contributor was in effect a gift to those keeping the dollar bills they received. The operator of this scheme used the DeHaan, Inc., firm as the fund raiser. DeHaan collected $146,936.95, or about 24 per cent, in mailing fees alone.

The state of New York brought legal action to halt this fund-raising fraud which was taking dollars desperately needed in the crusade against cancer. The state produced the hospital's appeal letter and brochure which indicated that over 70 per cent of its patients were non-paying. When questioned as to how over 70 per cent of the patients in a nonexistent hospital could be non-paying, the defendant replied that she meant a present small hospital in Michigan, which had a different name and consisted of two small brownstone buildings. This hospital could not show it had received any benefits from the more than $600,000 given by the public. The Attorney General of New York was successful in getting an injunction to halt this fraudulent appeal. The judge held that "The fact is that the National Cancer Hospital does not and never has operated a hospital and does not and never has treated a single patient" and "The representations made by the defendants in the letter and pamphlet stating the purpose for which the funds are solicited are false because they do not disclose the whole truth." [16] The Attorney General obtained control of the $68,000 that remained after the operators had taken their cut but the perpetrators of this scheme went unpunished. Law-enforcement officials told the Committee that to convict a charity charlatan of larceny by false pretenses is a "back-breaking" job.

The nation's sense of gratitude to those who have fought its wars has long been a source of easy money for fund raisers. The prime example of this has been the Disabled American Veterans which has its headquarters in Cincinnati, Ohio. The Tompkins Committee uncovered the fact that of the millions of dollars being given the DAV to help needy and disabled veterans only a few cents out of each dollar were used to assist the veteran. The DAV raised its money by mailing unordered merchandise—fountain pens and license plate Ident-O-Tags to car owners—and by the promotion of puzzle contests. The certified financial statements prepared for the DAV and its fund-raising arm, the DAV Service Foundation, showed that in three years, 1950 to 1953, the DAV had collected a total of $21,480,000 from the merchandise and the puzzle contests. The bulk of this sum went to the promoters, not to veterans: [17]

> The cost of fund-raising, which also includes the manufacture of the Ident-O-Tag was $14,529,000, or was 68 per cent of the total funds collected through these various campaigns. In addition thereto, the administrative expenses of the organization amounted to $2,401,000, or 11 per cent. There were certain welfare disbursements totaling $4,837,-000 or 18 per cent . . . and there was also left over and available to subsequent periods a total of $713,000, or 3 per cent of the total amount collected. The net proceeds after fund-raising and administrative expenses for the fiscal year ending June 30, 1949, and the net proceeds after deducting fund-raising and administrative costs were:
>
> | | |
> |---|---|
> | 1949 | 47% |
> | 1950 | 39% |
> | 1951 | 26% |
> | 1952 | 8½% |
> | 1953 | 9% |

In the light of this damning evidence, Senator Tompkins asked Miles H. Draper, president of the DAV Service Foundation, "Do you think that where the impression is given that the contributors' dollar is doing a worthwhile service that it is right for an organization to spend 90 or 91 cents on every dollar for fund-raising costs . . . and only 9 or 10 cents for the purpose of the charity?" Draper replied: "I agree with you, that is too small a percentage of return, net return. I agree with you on that." [18]

The fact was that the DAV, organized in 1920 for a laudable purpose, had come under the corroding influence of Abraham L. Koolish, the man who made the killing in the National Kids' Day Foundation scandal. Koolish became a multimillionaire through his shady fund-raising enterprises until, in 1963, he was convicted of fraud for his part in looting the Sister Kenny Foundation. Koolish testified in 1952 that his net worth was $4,382,348. As Smith notes, "The story of Koolish and his associates is the story of the new-style fund-raising promoters who have taken advantage of the huckstering atmosphere of modern charity to make a personal fortune." [19]

Koolish, seventy-three years old when finally convicted in 1963, started out peddling punchboards in the depression. In 1930 the Federal Trade Commission issued a complaint against K. & S. Sales Co., a punchboard firm, charging it with misleading advertising and with conducting lotteries. Koolish was a partner in this firm. In February, 1937, the FTC issued an amended complaint against K. & S. and in January, 1938, it handed down a cease and desist order. Koolish's firm refused to heed the order and in 1939 K. & S. was fined $4,500 for violation of the FTC order. Koolish then switched to a new firm, Universal Industries, Inc., to promote a so-called "sales stimulator plan" with tableware. The FTC soon caught up with his new enterprise, issued a complaint in 1939, and a cease and desist order in 1941.

Koolish's next venture to make the easy dollar was to establish the Ident-O-Tag Co. to manufacture the now familiar miniature auto license plates for car owners' key rings. For this fund raising, Koolish used his firm, Gayton Associates. He made a deal with the DAV whereby the veterans' organization would receive a small percentage of the money raised from the mass mailings of Ident-O-Tags in exchange for the DAV's sponsorship. The project proved lucrative at the outset—that is, lucrative for Koolish.

Gayton Associates "utilized this shrapnel sales approach for the greater part of its [DAV] support, sending out Ident-O-Tags. Later the D.A.V. purchased the Ident-O-Tag operation from Gayton for $1,300,000 and in addition kept Gayton's president, Abraham L. Koolish, on the D.A.V. payroll at $12,000 per annum for a period of five years. Ident-O-Tag is a non-patentable novelty and thus a rather tenuous asset for a welfare organization." [20] Yet DAV paid more than a million dollars for this non-patentable novelty! Little wonder the Tompkins Committee labeled the DAV fund-raising costs as "grossly excessive."

No part of the over $21 million raised in the 1950–1953 period was given in direct money to any veterans. President Draper admitted, "Nationally our organization does not give individual aid to veterans, except in counselling them or advising them in regard to their claim." Yet the DAV continues to collect millions of dollars from the public on the promise of providing aid to America's disabled veterans. The DAV was discovered using the names of prominent men without permission, including the then President of the United States, Dwight D. Eisenhower. "In connection with their ballpoint pen solicitation, they sent out a piece of literature bearing photographs of and statements of President Eisenhower, General Carl Gray, the Administrator of Veterans Affairs, and General Omar Bradley, seemingly endorsing the fund-raising drive. The record shows that all three vehemently repudiated the use of their names as completely unauthorized." [21]

Another case of major-league overhead and minor-league aid exposed by the Tompkins Committee was that involving the Kings County (N.Y.) Council of the Marine Corps League. The contributor was told by the professional solicitor that his donation would go to the hospitalized and disabled. How the money actually was used could not be determined by the Committee because the Council later destroyed its records. A chart prepared by the Committee's auditors shows that this organization's cost of fund raising was approximately 85 per cent during the period April 1, 1952, to March 31, 1953. When other expenses were added, the sad result is that only 6 cents out of the contributor's dollar went for the intended purpose. [22]

The Marine Corps League quickly revoked the Kings County Council's charter but this illustrates the difficulty of national organizations in effectively policing the fund-raising honesty and efficiency of its local units. As the national commander of the American Legion testified before a Congressional committee in 1958: "As we see it, much of the trouble stems from fund raising at the local level, usually by free lancers and drifters. Obviously, it would be impossible for the American Legion to attempt to police the activities of its 17,004 posts. This is a matter of great concern to the national organization." [23]

The Tompkins Committee hearings brought these expensive and questionable fund-raising practices into the national spotlight, setting off public debate and passage of regulatory legislation in New York and other states. In 1954 the *Saturday Evening Post*, in an article entitled, "Who Gets Your Charity Dollars?" told the nation that some $120 million in philanthropic gifts was going to absolute frauds. Jerome Ellison wrote of the Tompkins hearings: "Revelation piled on shocking revelation" that to the giving public "were gratuitous slaps in trusting faces." [24] The Milwaukee *Journal* called the hearings "an eye opener on the extent to which they [the people] are unwittingly supporting private greed far more than human need in falling for some high pressure 'charity' drives." [25] The hearings set in motion debate and action, which currently continue, on the elimination of the wasteful and fraudulent fund raiser from America's popular philanthropy.

Fund Raising for Veterans

An exhaustive, detailed picture of the wasteful and dubious ways of raising funds in the name of the American war veteran was provided in the hearings before the Committee on Veterans' Affairs of the House of Representatives in the 85th Congress. Representative Olin E. Teague of Texas, veteran chairman of this Committee, presided at these hearings which ran intermittently from February 11 to March 20, 1958. The hearings had been authorized in a resolution passed by the House on February 7, 1957, to determine:

(1) the extent to which appeals for charitable contributions are made to the American people, or segments thereof, in the name of American veterans by appealing to the desire of the American people to assist such veterans . . . ;

(2) whether an undue proportion of such charitable contributions is used to meet the expenses of conducting such appeals and for other administrative expenses rather than providing services for or benefits to veterans;

(3) whether any of such appeals are fraudulent in nature;

(4) whether additional supervision of the fund-raising activities conducted . . . in the name of veterans are [sic] necessary or desirable; and

(5) the existence of any other abuses connected with charitable appeals made in the name of veterans.[26]

Plentiful examples of waste, abuses, and highly questionable practices in fund raising were found by the Committee. As the story of the many veterans' organizations using a multiplicity of methods, most of them wasteful, to get money from the public unfolds, one is forced to wonder if all this extra-government effort is justified. As committee member Representative William H. Ayers observed: "I have a very deep feeling that we are scattering ourselves too thin, relating to this problem of aiding the veterans. There are too many organizations. . . . And if it is necessary to have all of these veterans organizations in order to give the benefits to the veteran that he is entitled to, to go through all these campaigns, all of this outside help, all of these appeals to get money into the organization, I think . . . somebody in the Veterans' Administration is doing a bad job." [27]

Perhaps the greatest fraud perpetrated against the public in the guise of aiding veterans was that effected by an organization calling itself the National Association of Veterans' Employment Councils and "dedicated to the proposition that many handicapped veterans are deserving of and in need of special attention which they are not getting elsewhere." NAVEC, organized July 29, 1955, in the District of Columbia, was very lucrative for a few shrewd operators. From September 1, 1955, to June 30, 1957, NAVEC obtained contributions totaling $2,121,104.31 but when the fund-raising costs were written off there remained only $206,701.11, or 9.7 per cent, as net proceeds. And for all this money taken from a well-intentioned but gullible public, NAVEC's only record of accomplishment was its questionable claim that it had helped 450 handicapped veterans get jobs. The Committee could verify only 126 placements. The big profiteer in NAVEC was Harold A. Keats, a Washington public relations man.

This Association's main purpose, in the opinion of Melvin J. Maas, Marine Corps general and chairman of the President's Committee on the Employment of the Physically Handicapped, was "to raise funds, and it was capitalizing on the great publicity that the President's Committee had generated in connection with . . . jobs for handicapped men and women." [28] Exploiting such publicity with the double appeal of the war veteran and of the handicapped person was largely the creation of Harold A. Keats, F. William Hart, and John Mark. There were no dues-paying members to provide a check on their manipulations. Keats had been "immersed in veterans' problems since 1946" as a former national commander of AMVETS and as a member of the American Battle Monument Commission. He got the idea for NAVEC when the Handicapped War Veterans National Organization failed to survive in the wake of the exposure of the California Handicapped War Veterans which ran afoul of the law. Keats testified: "We decided that a good idea should not be abandoned whatever the origin of the idea may have been. There no longer was a handicapped war veterans national organization. We adopted the basic idea. We enlarged and improved upon it." [29]

NAVEC's antecedent organization, the Department of California Handicapped War Veterans, had disbanded in 1955 when its organizers were indicted for postal frauds in the U.S. District Court for Northern Illinois, Eastern Division. (The indictments were dismissed October 20, 1960, on motion of the government.) Abraham L. Koolish and his son, David F., operated NAVEC through Empire Associates, a subsidiary of Bankers Life & Casualty Co. of Chicago. Empire Associates was principally engaged in mailing unordered merchandise, accompanied by literature, soliciting purchases in the name of one charity or another, and also operated the LeMarge Mailing Service. Empire Associates had a contract with Leo Slaton, head of a California firm that mailed out unordered merchandise in the name of charity, the Dudley Sales Co. This firm retained William E. Mealer as an agent, again illustrating how manipulators work together. John E. Chambers was the executive secretary of the California organization.[30]

NAVEC raised more than $2 million by mailing out cheap ballpoint pens that cost 15 cents to persons whose names had found their way to commercial mailing lists maintained and sold by mailing list brokers. The prospect's name was stamped in "24-karat gold" on the pen which, Keats asserted, "the public has overwhelmingly agreed is of more than a dollar value." NAVEC mailed the pens with a heart-tugging letter describing the plight of the unemployed handicapped war veteran, a stamped return envelope so the donor could mail back his donation, an order blank in case the recipient wished to order more pens, and a "guarantee slip." If the recipient did not respond to the first mailing, he received a follow-up postal card telling him to send the donation or return the pen. Keats told the Committee that the mailing lists were obtained from five different brokers at a cost ranging from $15 to $25 per thousand names.

NAVEC's approach to the prospect was that the handicapped did not want charity. "Our whole program of finding jobs for handicapped veterans centers around the theme that they don't want charity. They want only a chance to earn their own way. . . . That is why we are not asking for charity." Keats told the Teague Committee, "NAVEC employs exactly the same techniques of fundraising used by other veterans, rather by veteran organizations." He asserted further, "Our association raises its own funds. Unlike some others, it has no contract with any outside professional fund raisers." [31] It should be noted that no reputable fund raiser would be involved in such an operation.

Keats used the NAVEC income to pay himself a salary of $17,-401.41 over a two-year period, and several thousand dollars more for travel expenses and for the office rent for the Keats, Allen, & Keats public relations firm in Washington. Keats also collected what appeared to be a "kickback," a common kind of compensation in this dubious kind of fund raising. The Teague Committee's records show that the Merit Pen Corporation paid Harold A. Keats $7,600 for the purchase of a cavity injection mold that it never used. NAVEC bought approximately $315,631.40 worth of merchandise from the Merit Pen Corp., from September 1, 1955, through June 30, 1957.[32] Yet Keats and his associates would assert with a straight face: "Some of you may have seen newspaper reports about how the bulk of gifts to charities go toward fund-raising expenses. This may be true of some fund-raising drives, but it certainly IS NOT TRUE OF NAVEC's program and that of some others which send merchandise on approval." [33] The way the public was fooled can be seen in the NAVEC financial summary prepared by the Teague Committee staff, in Table 16.[34]

Much of the fund raising carried on in behalf of veterans is wasteful. AMVETS is a case in point here. The American Veterans of World War II (AMVETS), which Keats had served as an officer and as public relations consultant, is chartered by Congress and dates from the end of World War II. Its fund-raising operations were also brought under the scrutiny of the Teague Committee and found, at the least, to be wasteful. The AMVETS told the Committee it relied on direct mail appeals and the mailing of unordered merchandise to finance its service programs for veterans. But when all the fund raising was paid for only a sixth or so of the income was left for such service work, as AMVETS' business manager testified:

"The direct-appeal campaigns conducted by AMVETS are of the same variety utilized by many organizations. The format is composed of an appeal letter, a minimum-cost attention catcher, in the nature of a sheet of seals and a reply envelope. The literature, as in all cases, is written by AMVETS. . . . The various products and services required to complete the mailing are obtained from commercial sources on a competitive basis." [35]

Illustrating the high cost of this method of fund raising, AMVETS

TABLE 16. [NAVEC] INCOME AND EXPENSE STATEMENT FOR THE PERIOD
SEPTEMBER 1, 1955, THROUGH JUNE 30, 1957

(The figures used are from statements furnished by NAVEC, except as noted)

Amount of contributions received $2,121,104.31

EXPENSES

Material and pen costs:
Material and pen costs	$992,769.83	
Donation solicitation material	117,154.07	
		$1,109,923.90

Mailing costs:
Mailing costs	348,835.88	
Postage	237,807.91	
		586,643.79

Processing of receipts costs:
Wages—mail handling	123,774.56	
Payroll taxes	5,558.13	
Supplies	4,683.24	
Fees paid Brinks	2,036.41	
Truck rental	1,136.80	
Rent	5,237.86	
Pen room set up	2,573.17	
Bank charges	5,748.27	
		150,748.44

Administrative expenses:
Salaries *	33,822.66	
Payroll taxes *	1,831.38	
Office supplies †	6,123.39	
Telephone †	4,233.79	
Rent ‡	5,334.16	
Professional fees	13,693.89	
Insurance	1,892.35	
Personal property tax	74.78	
Interest expense	80.67	
		67,087.07

Total fund-raising expenses (including
inventory, $42,743.95) 1,914,403.20

Net Proceeds from Fund Raising (9.7 Per Cent) 206,701.11

TABLE 16 (*Continued*)

Program expenses:

Salaries *	$ 38,069.11	
Payroll taxes *	1,831.39	
Office supplies †	3,061.69	
Telephone †	2,116.89	
Rent ‡	2,300.00	
Organization expense	130.87	
Program and field organization §	100,539.64	
	148,049.59	148,049.59
Excess of revenues over expenditures		58,651.52

* Salaries for administrative expenses is all national staff and employees' salaries except the persons assigned for program work. Mr. Keats' salary is divided, one-half for administrative and one-half for program expense. The estimate on salaries would give the program expense their portion or a little more. Payroll taxes were divided in half—small amount.

† Office supplies and telephone expenses were estimated two-thirds for fund raising and one-third for program work.

‡ Rent was estimated on the space used by program employees.

§ NAVEC lists program and field organization expenses as $100,539.64. This is a questionable figure. Listed below are some of the questionable items that go to make up this figure.

Car rentals (rentals mainly in Florida)	$ 954.09
Travel agencies vouchers (mainly trips to Florida)	1,652.63
Airline vouchers (trips to Chicago, New York, and Florida)	4,612.74
Hotel bills	3,896.34
Restaurants	2,101.25
Arthur Lasker (lawyer, expenses)	4,038.59
Thos. B. Sawyer (director, expenses)	4,963.54
Wm. F. Hart (director, expenses)	7.45
John Mark (director, expenses)	4,956.90
Geo. Harris (director, expenses)	3,128.28
H. A. Keats (executive director, expenses)	3,484.93
	$33,850.74
Reimbursements to fieldworkers for expenses	$22,571.89
Fieldworkers' salaries	$12,233.95

The national staff does not itself make placements and all placements are made either by volunteer or part-time and full-time placement directors in the field. It is interesting to note that out of $2,121,104.31 gross contributions, or net proceeds from fund raising of $206,701.11, the sum total of $22,571.89 was given these field volunteer and paid workers for expenses in placing veterans in jobs. In addition, these field workers received in salaries and wages, $12,233.95.

reported that it had staged five mail campaigns in 1956 that grossed $1,969,629.58 but netted only $307,778.15 for AMVETS after the costs of mailing and merchandise had been paid.[36] In every case examined by the Tompkins Committee, "organizations which attempt to raise funds by sending out unordered merchandise, without exception, receive the smallest proportion of net proceeds from the gross contributions sent to them." The high costs of direct-mail fund raising, using either seals or merchandise, can be see in Table 17.[37]

This method of raising funds is also costly for the U.S. taxpayer who foots part of the bill through losses to the Post Office Department. Queried by a Congressional committee, the Office of the Chief Postal Inspector wrote Congressman John Blatnik of Minnesota as follows:

> Dear Congressman Blatnik: Replying to your request for an estimate of the annual loss of postal revenue from unordered merchandise and from mailings by charitable institutions, I have to advise that this particular information is not available. . . .
>
> The estimated loss on all third-class mail for fiscal 1957 was $269,-800,000. It is obvious that losses in the categories mentioned by you were substantial.
>
> Mailings of third-class matter at special rates by organizations or associations not organized for profit . . . amounted to approximately 1,300 million pieces for which $13,500,000 postage was paid. It cost the Department approximately $37,000,000 to handle these mailings, with a resultant loss of $24,100,000. . . .
>
> D. H. Stephens, Chief Inspector.[38]

In 1956 the AMVETS made a direct appeal for funds by mailing out AMVET seals at a cost of 6 cents apiece and then subsequently mailing out unordered wallet identification cards, neckties, greeting cards, and garden seeds in four separate mailings. The last-named was a test project, originated in cooperation with the W. Atlee Burpee Seed Co., and resulted in a loss. Boxes of unordered Christmas cards is a common fund-raising gimmick used by veteran and other fund-seeking organizations. The Military Order of the Purple Heart (MOPH) used this method, which nets the greeting card maker a lot and the organization a little. In 1952 the MOPH entered into a contract with the Lipschutz Co. of Philadelphia, Pa., which provided that the firm would be paid all expenses of the mailing

TABLE 17. AMVETS' FUND-RAISING, 1952–1956

	Fiscal year ended Sept. 30				
	1952	1953	1954	1955	1956
Gross income	$1,499,454.32	$2,353,283.04	$1,702,469.74	$1,722,019.80	$1,631,949.42
Less, costs:					
Direct*	1,224,193.79	1,838,410.34	1,376,919.79	1,405,780.52	1,267,060.05
Indirect†	118,399.06	93,129.18	95,383.14	103,236.29	94,621.99
Subtotal	1,342,592.85	1,931,539.52	1,472,302.93	1,509,016.81	1,361,682.04
Net funds available for AMVETS programs	156,861.47	421,743.52	230,166.81	213,002.99	270,267.38
Actual expenditures for AMVETS programs	181,101.20	222,291.67	223,852.95	238,346.81	245,605.97

* Direct costs include all costs incurred up to the time of receipt of the funds by AMVETS.
† Indirect costs are those processing and administrative expenses incurred after receipt of the funds.

and the profits would be divided on a 50-50 basis. In 1955 the total Christmas card sale was $109,000 and after Lipschutz had deducted $79,000 for its costs the firm and the Order divided $30,000 profit. This same firm also entered into the same deal with the Jewish War Veterans and with the Pennsylvania Department of the American Legion. The Veterans of Foreign Wars also had a contract with Lipschutz and in 1956–1957 its receipts totaled $414,000 of which the VFW got only $62,000. One year the Pennsylvania Legion had a gross card sale of $194,000 but the Legion netted only $15,000.

This led Congressman Paul Fino, a member of the House Veterans Committee, to charge that the Lipschutz firm was "an organization of chiselers." He continued: "This is an organization that maintains only one office and they are doing your [MOPH's] work and the Jewish War Veterans' work and other organizations' work, all with the same purposes, and charging the same expenses and so on, and they come up with these lists of expenditures . . . they are using your organization and the good name of your organization to make money." [39]

The Teague Committee continued what the Tompkins Committee had begun, in exploring the fund-raising operations of the Disabled American Veterans organization. Paul E. Frederick, Jr., national commander of the DAV, attempted to justify its high fund-raising costs on the basis of the difficult public relations imposed by the public's impression that the federal government provides for disabled veterans (as indeed it does) and by the fact that the National Information Bureau will not accredit a fund-raising campaign by a veterans' organization. These problems "make our returns much lower than for most other charitable causes." [40] He also tried to argue that the costs of employing 500 disabled veterans in DAV's national headquarters should be excluded in computing fund-raising costs because these jobs aided disabled veterans.

Smarting under the devastating disclosures made before the Tompkins Committee, the DAV subsequently embarked on an expensive public relations effort that, in its opinion, resulted in "a rise in income, and a reduction in the ratio of costs of fund raising." This public relations program was launched by a television show, "Hidden Treasure," designed as both a public relations vehicle and as a fund-raising contest: ". . . it was hoped that the contest phase would draw enough contestants to make the venture self-liquidating so we might sponsor additional programs." [41] The DAV put some

$300,000 of funds raised through the Ident-O-Tag program into this TV show. Commander Frederick justified this expenditure by saying, "We feel that what public relations we received from the program in the long run justified this amount." Chairman Teague sharply disputed this use of money raised on the promise of aiding disabled veterans.

Figures brought out in the Teague Committee hearings showed that the DAV had brought its net return on the Ident-O-Tag fund raising operation up to nearly 20 per cent. The DAV's income for 1956 from the mailing of these miniature license plates to auto owners was $4,254,750.38 while expenses totaled $3,444,727.63, leaving a net of $810,022.75, or 19.04 per cent of the gross income. It was brought out in testimony before this Committee that Abraham Koolish was responsible for DAV's getting into the Ident-O-Tag operation. Chairman Teague, probing the lavish expenditures of DAV funds by its national adjutant, Vivian D. Corbly, asked Corbly why he sent an expensive Christmas present to Koolish and got this reply:

> Because of the many nice things he did for the DAV. . . . Mr. A. L. Koolish was responsible for us getting the Idento-Tag [sic] operation. During the early years when he had the operation, he expended thousands upon thousands of dollars for our organization. If you come to headquarters, you will find about 20 paintings that he purchased and presented to the organization.[42]

Thus the trail of Mr. Koolish winds from one dubious fund-raising scheme to another, from peddling punchboards to exploiting the fear of polio.

The Sister Kenny Scandal

The ease with which dishonest men can gain control of a worthwhile cause supported by a none too discerning public and exploit it for selfish ends is clearly illustrated in the scandal that overtook the Sister Elizabeth Kenny Foundation, Inc., in the 1950's. The Sister Kenny Foundation, as it was popularly known, was incorporated in 1943 in the state of Minnesota as a nonprofit corporation. The Foundation was set up in response to the determined drive of Kenny to support her method of treating polio patients and other victims of crippling diseases. It was organized "for the general purpose of combating infantile paralysis by providing hospitalization, research, treatment and training facilities." Thus this Foundation, financed by popular giving, was directly competitive with the F.D.R.-sponsored National Foundation for Infantile Paralysis. The Kenny Foundation raised its funds in nationwide drives and developed institutes in Minneapolis, Detroit, Buffalo, New York City, and Jersey City.

Sister Kenny, an Australian nurse, enlisted early in the battle against polio by developing a helpful therapy for patients. In this work she was supported for a time by grants from the National Foundation for Infantile Paralysis. Then Nurse Kenny turned scientific theoretician with the declaration that poliomyelitis was a disease of the muscles, not of the spinal cord. This led to a rift with the polio foundation and she became a sharp critic of Basil O'Connor and his associates. Before the split, the polio foundation had provided Sister Kenny with more than $2 million in research and treatment grants. Carter describes her as "incredibly temperamental." She participated in organizing the Foundation and served actively as a director until December, 1950, when she became an honorary director. This connection ended in 1952.

According to the Attorney General of Minnesota, who investigated and exposed the manipulations of the Sister Kenny Foundation's executives, "Prior to 1950, the Foundation appears to have been managed in a sound, reasonable, and businesslike manner." This does not say that the millions of dollars given by the public from 1953 to 1950 were all usefully spent on meritorious research or treatment; the Attorney General simply vouches that up to 1950 the money was fully and legally accounted for by the Foundation officers. The extent to which the public can be bilked is amply demonstrated by the stark fact that the Foundation's executive director, from 1946 to 1959, took a total of $773,013.18 out of the Foundation directly or indirectly, honestly and dishonestly. These three-quarters of a million dollars had been donated by the generous, unquestioning public.

The Sister Kenny Foundation received $30,674,000 from public gifts in the period from 1952 through 1959 and of this sum $16,260,000 went not to fight polio but to finance fund-raising, public relations, and administrative overhead—53 per cent of the amount collected. Thus only 47 cents out of each dollar given by a donor went for the purpose he intended, to finance hospitalization, treatment, research, and training facilities.[43] These exorbitant administrative costs were heavily boosted by graft and wasteful fund-raising methods.

The looters of the Sister Kenny Foundation were:

Marvin L. Kline, former mayor of Minneapolis and former executive director of the Foundation. He was convicted April 6, 1961, in a Hennepin County court of grand larceny for illegally raising his Foundation salary from $25,000 to $48,000 a year. He appealed the conviction, but it was upheld.

Fred Fadell, Minneapolis public relations man who handled the Foundation's public relations and fund raising from 1948 to 1960.

Abraham L. Koolish, father, and David F. Koolish, son, of Chicago, operators of Empire Associates, Empire Industries, Inc., Le-Marge Mailing Service Co., Inc., and the New Century Corp.

These men, along with John B. Carnell and Philip G. Rettig, both of Chicago, and former presidents of the Koolishes' New Century Corp., and J. George Zimmerman, Minneapolis, former Foundation auditor, were indicted on January 29, 1962, by a federal grand jury on charges of using the mails to defraud in the U.S. District Court at Minneapolis.

The indictments were announced the following day by Attorney General Robert Kennedy. Kline and Fadell were indicted for taking "kickbacks" amounting to $360,000 from the Koolish-controlled mailing firms. The mail firm executives were accused of diverting to the two Foundation employees some of the money paid to the firms for soliciting contributions. The auditor was accused of falsifying audits of the Foundation's books.[44]

On Wednesday, May 29, 1963, a jury in Federal District Court found five of the defendants guilty of mail fraud and conspiracy. Convicted were: Marvin L. Kline, Abraham L. Koolish, David Koolish, John B. Carnell, and J. George Zimmerman. Earlier Fred Fadell, the publicist, had pleaded guilty during the 12-week trial. Rettig was ill at the time of the trial and his case was severed from the others.[45] On September 13, 1963, Federal Judge Edward J. Devitt meted out these sentences:

Marvin L. Kline: Sentenced to 10 years imprisonment—the sentence to run concurrent with the 10-year term he faced in Stillwater, Minn., prison as a result of the grand larceny conviction in Hennepin County District Court.

Abraham L. Koolish and *David Koolish:* Each sentenced to 10 years in prison and fined $17,000 and assessed court costs estimated at $16,000.

John B. Carnell: Sentenced to five years in prison.

Fred Fadell: Sentenced to a year and a day in prison.

J. George Zimmerman: Sentenced to five years in prison but immediately placed on probation.[46]

Before handing down the sentences, Judge Devitt delivered a scathing denunciation of the plunderers in these words:

> These defendants were properly convicted on strong evidence of the commission of serious crimes. They deserve substantial punishment. The criminal acts of these defendants are reprehensible because they deprived crippled children and adults of needful physical rehabilitation; because they destroyed public confidence and support, almost irreparably, in a meritorious charitable foundation serving a large public need; because, in effect, they stole the dimes and dollars donated with sacrifice by so many warm-hearted benefactors, most of them little people, for their own selfish purposes.

Kline appealed his federal court conviction but dropped his appeal in July, 1964, while serving the ten-year term in Stillwater (Minn.) prison on the state court conviction for illegally boosting his salary as head of the Foundation. Dropping the federal appeal opened the way to serving the two terms concurrently, according to Kline's attorney.

Kline, a professional engineer, had been one of the incorporators of the Foundation in 1943 and served as an unpaid director and officer until 1946 when he was prevailed upon to become the full-time executive director at a salary of $12,500 a year. Kline was president of the Foundation when he left the mayor's office in 1945 and he testified at his first trial that he continued to conduct foundation business from the office of his engineering firm. Early in 1946 he told the board of directors that he could no longer carry this extra burden and they responded by asking him to take the job on a full-time basis.

In 1943—the year the Sister Kenny Foundation was started—Fred Fadell was employed by his brother, Mike Fadell, who operated the Fadell Publicity Bureau. The Fadell firm conducted a fund-raising campaign in Minnesota for the Foundation in 1943.

From 1944 to 1948 the Foundation retained another firm to handle its promotion and fund raising. In 1948 Fred Fadell was hired by the executive committee of the Foundation to furnish publicity services for the Minnesota Area Campaign at a fee of $1,990 per month. No other written agreement was ever entered into between the Foundation and Fadell. In 1950 Fadell's company offices were moved into the Foundation's offices and he became head of its Promotion and Information Service.

Fadell's firm was housed rent-free and he used Foundation personnel on many of his outside accounts. Fadell was paid a total of $140,000 in salary from 1951 through 1959, and another $59,300 in fees, $13,809 in contributions for his pension plan, and another $1,000 for an annuity. His car and travel expenses were provided at the expense of the Foundation. As Fadell steadily increased his take, the Foundation's public relations expenses mounted accordingly, going from $59,856 in 1951 to $261,891 in 1959 when the roof caved in on Fadell's cozy setup. The nine-year total public relations expenses for Fadell and his staff totaled $1,497,603—all paid with the public's dollars.[47]

The Koolishes' mailing firms, first Empire, then New Century, were retained on the basis of letter agreements negotiated between them and Kline acting on behalf of the Foundation. There was no evidence that Kline had sought competitive bids. This relationship began in 1949 when John Carnell, an employee of Empire Industries, persuaded Kline to try a test mail campaign of 100,000 pieces. This test produced $5,994 in contributions at a cost of $5,100, netting the Foundation exactly $844! In 1950, 3,173,000 pieces were mailed at a cost of $173,000 and produced $103,000 in excess of the mailing cost. The relationship with Empire continued until 1955, when it went out of business.

Thereafter the Sister Kenny Foundation mail campaigns were conducted by the New Century Corp. whose principal officers were former employees of Empire. New Century Corp. "has no substantial physical plant. . . . The actual work of the mail campaign has been conducted by LeMarge Mailing Service Co., which is managed by David Koolish. LeMarge also handled the letter-shop services for the mail campaign conducted by Empire for the Foundation. Although there appears to have been some effort to hide the identity of the true owners of the New Century and LeMarge, there is substantial evidence that they are both controlled by the Koolish family." [48]

The Koolish-controlled mailing firms, from 1952 through 1959, conducted two mail campaigns a year. The spring campaign was a mail appeal to persons on the list of previous or regular contributors to the Sister Kenny Foundation. The autumn, or "Cold Shot," campaign consisted of mailings to a much larger list of names rented from Empire Industries. An analysis of the results of these direct-mail campaigns, from 1952 through 1959, is summarized in Table 18: [49]

TABLE 18

	Spring	Fall	Total
Contributions received from public	$9,110,617	$10,341,354	$19,451,971
Cost of Mailing	3,120,116	7,845,162	10,965,278
Total	$5,990,501	$ 2,496,192	$ 8,486,693
Processing Expense	219,327	313,099	532,426
Net Proceeds to Foundation	$5,771,174	$ 2,183,093	$ 7,954,267
Per Cent of Net Proceeds to contributions received	63.3%	21.1%	40.9%
Number of Pieces Mailed	30,282,421	107,829,309	138,111,730

The waste in these campaigns is clearly evident in the figures for the 1956 autumn campaign which brought in $1,542,339 in contributions at a total cost of $1,485,630 for mailing and $33,270 for processing the contributions. This left a net return to the Foundation of $23,738, or 1.5 per cent of the money contributed. These figures do not reflect the costs of administration and promotion charged off to the national headquarters in Minneapolis. And these were high, too!

Attorney General Mondale's thorough probe of the Foundation's finances and testimony at Kline's first trial made it abundantly clear that Kline, Fadell, and the Koolishes were sharing the spoils on a fairly equal basis. "A month by month analysis of the payments from Empire and New Century to Mr. Fadell and from Mr. Fadell to Mr. Kline indicates an equal division of the Empire-New Century payments until 1957 although there is some minor variance." [50] The tabulation of Kline's take, for example, shows he received $113,-750.00 in "consultant fees" from Fadell's public relations firm. These payments from Fadell to Kline extended from 1952 to 1957 "on a fee basis which ranged between fifteen thousand and twenty-three thousand dollars annually." The fees to Kline stopped after the latter learned the Bureau of Internal Revenue was probing his tax returns.

In turn, Empire Industries, and later the New Century Corp., paid substantial fees to Fadell for promoting the Sister Kenny fund appeals. These Koolish-controlled mailing firms paid to Fred Fadell the sum of $344,300 between 1951 and 1959. Fadell, in a letter to the board of directors dated April 13, 1960, claimed that he received these fees from Empire-New Century for promoting and publicizing the Kenny Foundation on a national scale, "thus protecting New Century against loss on its guarantee that the foundation would at least break even on the national mail campaign." This was the very same thing for which he was being paid a handsome salary and expenses from the Foundation! Fadell also took "consulting fees" from other firms doing business with the Foundation.

Carnell, as president of the New Century Corp., got "gravy," too. He was paid $15,225 by the Foundation between 1956 and 1959 for services as a consultant. Beginning on May 1, 1957, he was paid $400 per month until March 8, 1960, shortly after the commencement of the Attorney General's investigation of the Foundation. "Mr. Kline stated that Mr. Carnell was paid this amount for advice and help in connection with fund campaigns in New York and California, and was, in general, evasive and equivocal as to specific advice and help rendered." [51] The records show also that Fadell paid Carnell the sum of $600 in each of the years 1958 and 1959.

The extent of this grafting can be seen in the 1951 mail campaign for public gifts. "In 1951, Empire Industries mailed about 16,000,-000 pieces for the Foundation, producing about $1,272,000 in contributions. After payment of $1,022,000 in direct mailing costs, of which $48,000 was the cost of processing incoming contributions, the Foundation netted about $250,000 or 20% of the mail contributions." [52] Kline and Fadell, of course, knew that these padded fund-raising costs would not stand public scrutiny. Arthur Anderson & Co., a certified public accounting firm, was engaged to prepare the Foundation's financial statement as of December 31, 1951. "The national direct mail campaign for that year produced roughly $1,-

240,000 in contributions; direct mail costs were $975,000 resulting in net proceeds before processing incoming mail of about $265,000. Mr. Kline insisted that the financial statements reflect only the net proceeds from the mail campaign of $265,000 without disclosing the direct mail costs. Arthur Anderson & Co. refused to certify the financial statements unless the direct mail costs were disclosed therein, and withdrew from the engagement." [53]

The Koolish enterprises also profited greatly from rentals of the Sister Kenny mailing list to other fund-raising organizations. By 1960 this list included some 3.5 million names, mostly of persons who had given to the Foundation, and thus was of great commercial value. "From July 11, 1956, to December 31, 1959, New Century acknowledged the rental of 15,094,174 Kenny Foundation names for which it was stated they charged rates ranging from $17.00 to $25.00 per thousand for a gross rental of $298,106.60. Of this amount the foundation was credited with $118,180.63 applied against the cost of maintenance of its list by New Century. Foundation records reveal authorization for rental of only about 10 per cent of the number of names acknowledged by LeMarge and New Century to have been rented." [54]

Publication of Attorney General Mondale's report exposing the wholesale diversion of the moneys given by the public to the Sister Kenny Foundation led to its reorganization as the Sister Kenny Institute late in 1960. The emphasis of the new board and new leadership is regional. In September, 1960, the new president of the Institute, Dr. Frank H. Krusen, promised the public "We're going to live in a goldfish bowl from now on. We will have a monthly financial report. There'll be no question about the constant check on every expenditure of the organization." The reorganization brought a distinguished authority on physical medicine to the presidency and added twelve new directors to a holdover nucleus of three. The Minneapolis *Star* voiced the hope that "The new management will not soon forget that those who serve on the boards of charitable organizations have a heavy responsibility to know what is going on and to keep a vigilant watch on both policies and staff." The *Star* added, "This lesson was bitterly learned through the old foundation's failures." [55]

The "old foundation's failures" effectively underline many of the dangers and problems in America's multibillion-dollar people's philanthropy. First of all, the story demonstrates the public's willingness to respond in large numbers to the many skillfully phrased calls to fight disease and human affliction without really knowing much about the merit of the appeal. There was sharp difference among medical leaders over the merit of Sister Kenny's scientific theories, yet the public generously responded to her emotional pleas for help. Bloomgarden's observations are pertinent here:

> Most of the voluntary agencies active in medical research and related fields were created and developed by people whose intentions were good and whose only purpose was to attack some specific disease with which they were involved or concerned. But their involvement, concern and purposes were usually framed by what they felt emotionally, and not by what they had discovered objectively . . . an appeal for funds must be made and a campaign of proselytism for additional members and additional contributions is undertaken. However, if this drive or campaign is to have any success, it requires a professional touch. . . . At this point the trouble begins.[56]

How prophetic he was in this instance.

When questioned by Attorney General Mondale's staff, directors of the Sister Kenny Foundation had only the vaguest understanding of Fadell's arrangement with the Foundation and none of them knew Kline had been drawing a salary of $48,000 since July, 1957. Directors who did question Kline's actions were dropped from the board or quit in disgust. These directors were replaced by close friends of Kline who would not question what he was doing. Thus, in time, he was able to get a board that gave him a free rein for his exploitation. Consequently, in the absence of a close watch by a responsible board and in the absence of effective state regulation, millions of charity dollars were easily diverted to the pockets of unscrupulous men.

The Federal Association for Epilepsy

Another Congressional hearing, held in 1958, laid bare still another example of wasteful fund raising where most of the money went to the fund raisers. These hearings were held in July by a subcommittee of the House Committee on Government Operations to inquire into the relationship of several federal agencies to philanthropy. Representative John A. Blatnik of Minnesota presided.

He explained the Committee's purpose this way: "Our immediate aim is to examine into current solicitation and expenditure practice and to determine whether the departments in our jurisdiction, and charged with responsibility toward philanthropy, are performing their duties efficiently and honestly." [57] Most of the testimony focused on the sad story of the Federal Association for Epilepsy—a health agency organized by well-intentioned persons who were taken in by smooth if not wholly ethical fund raisers. Harold A. Keats, public relations man and organizer of the National Association of Veterans' Employment Councils (NAVEC), reappears in this story.

The moving spirit in organizing this Association to aid epileptic children was Mrs. Nellie M. Broyhill, mother of a congressman, Representative Joel T. Broyhill of Virginia. The Association was founded on April 12, 1954, under a Virginia charter "with national powers . . . to enroll children from all states in the Union and to be able to solicit funds from any and all States when necessary." Mrs. Broyhill, a religious woman, told the Committee, "I would never have entered this field without His laying His hand on me." "The first year we floundered. . . . Then began the frantic months of financial strain. . . . The child we wanted to help was in an untouched field: uncontrolled epileptic children with multiple associated afflictions brought on by brain and nerve damage." [58]

Mrs. Broyhill told the Committee of the Association's first three years, as it cast about in futile efforts to raise money to equip a treatment center and provide a staff to care for epileptic children: ". . . we launched a fund-raising program, using the trial and error plan, testing, testing, testing. I held a charity ball in my home similar to two previous cancer drives I had held, and two telethons. We derived about $2,500 from this. I held ladies' luncheons, dinner meetings of men's service clubs, and induced people to hold teas, card parties and other things to raise money. This helped us to carry the load but we had to launch a big-scale fund-raising program if we were ever to build a national organization able to support a hospital-school institution of any size on a modern scientific basis.

"With this in mind the directors agreed to investigate the possibility of public education and fund-raising through a large scale direct mail campaign. . . . We felt that we could kill 2 birds with 1 stone by sending out millions of leaflets and brochures to educate and inform the general public on this little known malady." [59] And this quest led to Harold A. Keats whom the officers "convinced . . . after much urging, that he should do this job."

This move came when Mrs. Broyhill and her associates admittedly "were frantic for funds." She even made a futile appeal to Basil O'Connor and the National Foundation. She told the committee:

". . . when it came out in the papers that the Salk vaccine had been discovered and that polio had been licked—I went to New York City. I had my son's office call and make an appointment with Mr. O'Connor, the president. . . . When I got there he was not available. . . . I talked with his assistant.

" 'Will you people here in New York, the National Foundation for Infantile Paralysis, take the $20 million that you have laying in the banks . . . and help us get this institution started in the Greater Washington area?'

"The answer was, 'No, we cannot. . . .'

"So there was nothing left for us. We have tried everything." [60]

She explained that they turned to Keats only after national fund-raising organizations she did not name told her that there would have to be an intensive program of public education preceding a fund-raising drive. "The national fund-raising people made a lot of suggestions to us, but they still left it open to us to work out the education first and pave the way."

Mrs. Broyhill could not remember exactly when Keats was first hired by the Association. A contract dated January 22, 1957, between Keats, Allen & Keats, Public Relations, and the Federal Association for Epilepsy, Inc., authorized Keats to direct a mail campaign for funds "similar to the previous mailing of household seals" and to be paid 15 per cent of the gross cost of the mailing for this work. This contract with Keats was abruptly terminated on June 25, 1958—on the eve of the Blatnik Committee's hearings—when Mrs. Broyhill wrote Keats: "On June 11, 1958, the board of directors of the Federal Association for Epilepsy, Inc. met and decided to terminate all of their current contracts with you forthwith. The reasons have been generally discussed with you in May of this year." [61]

In the meantime Keats set to work to demonstrate anew that a direct-mail campaign to a prime list of contributors can bring in dollars for an unknown cause. In his 1957 direct-mail fund-raising campaign Keats raised a total of $465,204.99 in gifts at a cost of

$280,230.42, or 60 per cent of the money given by the public. Another $16,132.44 went to the Association's administrative overhead, leaving a total $71,759.88, or 14.8 per cent, for operation of the rehabilitation center at Leesburg, Va., where only nine children were cared for in 1957.[62] As of May 31, 1958, the FAE had eleven children at Leesburg. The FAE's 1957 audit was the first audit made of its finances.

In short, as Representative Blatnik told the press, the Association had raised almost a half million dollars, yet had cared for only nine epileptic children. Mrs. Broyhill and her associates quickly branded

TABLE 19. RECONCILIATION OF AUDITOR'S AND COMMITTEE STAFF ALLOCATION OF EXPENSES, FEDERAL ASSOCIATION FOR EPILEPSY, INC.

Statement of operations for the year ended Dec. 31, 1957

	Per 1957 Credit Report	Adjustments		Adjusted Balances
		Debit	Credit	
Operating receipts:				
Contributions:				
Mail solicitations	$442,328.84			$442,328.84
Telerama	22,876.15			22,876.15
Total Contributions	$465,204.99			$465,204.99
Hospital fees	16,865.70			16,865.70
List rentals	637.50			637.50
Total Receipts	$482,708.19			$482,708.19
Operating expenses:				
Campaign expenses:				
Mail solicitations	$162,524.51			
Telerama	11,008.39			
Total Campaign Expenses	$173,532.90	$71,168.05 *		$280,230.42
		35,529.47		
		310.96 †		
Natl. Children's Rehab. Center.	$ 71,448.92		$71,168.05 *	
Printing and Publications	71,168.05		35,529.47	
Public Information-Education..	35,529.47		310.96 †	
Administrative	16,443.40			
Total Operating Expenses ...	$368,122.74			$368,122.74
Net increase to general fund ..	$114,585.45			$114,585.45

* To transfer back attempted separation of fund-raising costs.
† To transfer NCRC expenses as shown per ledger, Dec. 31, 1956.

Blatnik's charge "less than half the truth." In any event, Keats and his associates had been well cared for. Keats had received $25,642.32 for his services in 1957 and had been paid $8,000 for work in 1958 before he was summarily dropped.[63] The exorbitant cost of the FAE's 1957 Keats-directed fund drive, which relied mainly on the mailing out of unordered merchandise (household labels), is seen in Table 19 prepared by the Congressional Committee staff:[64]

In carrying out the mail appeal Keats once more turned to the Koolishes for mailing service. FAE's records show that the Koolish subsidiary, New Century, was paid $64,067.64 for mailing out 3,132,-892 pieces of mail at a net cost of $20.45 per thousand, much higher than the going price. In the same period, Capital Mailers, a Washington firm, was providing the same service at $13.70 per thousand pieces. What arrangement there was, if any, between Keats and the Koolishes was not brought out in these proceedings.

Reviewing the findings of his Committee which heard the New York State legislative committee's findings from Senator Tompkins, reviewing the NAVEC testimony taken by the House Committee on Veterans' Affairs, and the exposures of the exorbitant fund-raising costs spent by the FAE, Congressman Blatnik concluded: "In most of these instances the privileges which the Government grants to encourage philanthropy were shown to have been abused and the public trust breached."

NOTES

1. Script, "The Charity Bandits," produced for the Armstrong Cork Co., and provided by the National Information Bureau.
2. Text of speech provided author July, 1962, by Gluksman, then assistant attorney general of the State of New York, in charge of the Charity Frauds Bureau.
3. *Ibid.*
4. *Ibid.*
5. Tompkins Committee Report, p. 37.
6. *Ibid.*, p. 16. Italics the Committee's.
7. *Ibid.*, p. 16. Italics the Committee's.
8. *Ibid.*, pp. 17–18. Paraphrased.
9. *Ibid.*, see Fig. 7.
10. *Ibid.*, pp. 24–25.
11. *Ibid.*, p. 31.
12. *Ibid.*, p. 19.
13. *Ibid.*, p. 24.
14. *The Bargain Hucksters* (New York: Crowell, 1962), p. 121.
15. Tompkins Committee Report, p. 26.
16. Quoted in *ibid.*, pp. 27–28.
17. *Ibid.*, p. 20.
18. *Ibid.*, p. 21.
19. Smith, *op. cit.*, p. 128.
20. *Ibid.*, p. 25.
21. *Ibid.*, p. 29.
22. *Ibid.*, pp. 19–20.
23. "Fund Raising By or In Behalf of Veterans," Hearings Before the Committee on Veterans' Affairs, House of Representatives, 85th Congress, Second Session (Government Printing Office, Washington, D.C., 1958), p. 2641. Hereafter these hearings will be referred to as Teague Committee Hearings.
24. *Saturday Evening Post*, Vol. 226 (June 26, 1954), p. 27.
25. Editorial on p. 2, Part V, Dec. 20, 1953.
26. Teague Committee Hearings, p. 2625.
27. *Ibid.*, p. 2777.
28. *Ibid.*, p. 3060.
29. *Ibid.*, p. 2875.

30. The indictments brought by the U.S. District Court grand jury named the Department of California, Handicapped War Veterans, a California corporation, Handicapped War Veterans, National Organization, a District of Columbia corporation, Bankers Life & Casualty Co. (including Empire Associates and LeMarge Mailing Service), Dudley Sales Co., Marlowe Pen Co., John E. Chambers, Abraham L. Koolish, David F. Koolish, William E. Mealer, and Leo Richard Slaton. These indictments were dismissed by order of the Honorable Edwin A. Robson on Oct. 20, 1960, pursuant to Rule 48 (a) of the Federal Rules of Criminal Procedure. See Teague Committee Hearings, pp. 2797–2874, for details of this fund-raising scheme.

31. *Ibid.*, p. 2871.

32. *Ibid.*, pp. 3306–3307.

33. Quoted from NAVEC newsletter dated Feb. 23, 1956, Vol. 1, No. 3, and found on p. 3292 of the Teague Committee Hearings.

34. *Ibid.*, pp. 3313–3315.

35. *Ibid.*, p. 2692.

36. *Ibid.*, pp. 2705–2707.

37. *Ibid.*, p. 2704.

38. "Federal Agencies and Philanthropies," Hearings Before a Subcommittee of the Committee on Government Operations, House of Representatives, 85th Congress, Second Session, p. 35. Hereafter these proceedings will be referred to as Blatnik Committee Hearings.

39. *Ibid.*, p. 3387.

40. *Ibid.*, p. 3387.

41. *Ibid.*, p. 3390.

42. *Ibid.*, p. 3466.

43. Report of Investigation of the Sister Elizabeth Kenny Foundation submitted to the Foundation's board, June 27, 1960, by Walter F. Mondale, Attorney General of Minnesota, p. 3. Hereafter this will be cited as the Mondale Report.

44. Associated Press dispatch from Washington, D.C., Jan. 30, 1962, as printed in Milwaukee *Journal* of that date.

45. Minneapolis *Morning Tribune*, May 31, 1963, p. 10.

46. Minneapolis *Star*, Sept. 13, 1963, p. 1.

47. See Exhibit D of Mondale Report for detailed breakdown.

48. Mondale Report, pp. 4–7. Also see Teague Committee Hearings, p. 2844.

49. Mondale Report, p. 4.

50. *Ibid.*, p. 9.

51. *Ibid.*, p. 7.

52. *Ibid.*, p. 4.

53. *Ibid.*, p. 24.

54. *Ibid.,* pp. 11–12.
55. Editorial, Sept. 13, 1960.
56. Bloomgarden, *Before We Sleep,* pp. 93–95.
57. Blatnik Committee Hearings, p. 2.
58. *Ibid.,* p. 40.
59. *Ibid.,* pp. 40–41.
60. *Ibid.,* pp. 130–131.
61. *Ibid.,* p. 138.
62. *Ibid.,* p. 54.
63. *Ibid.,* pp. 111–112.
64. *Ibid.,* p. 55.

12

The Postwar Years:
"Fabulous Dimensions"

Public Giving Climbs Ever Higher

The American historian Arthur M. Schlesinger, Sr., observed in 1953: "This philanthropic streak in the national character, an index of the pervasive spirit of neighborliness, appeared early and has in our own day reached fabulous dimensions. It is another of the distinguishing marks of the American way." [1]

The total amount of American annual giving reached more than $10 billion in 1963, a $725 million increase over the 1961 total and more than eight times the $1.25 billion donated to charitable causes in 1940. Roughly half of this annual outpouring goes to churches and related religious institutions. Nearly all religious contributions come from individual givers and most of them are given in response to the annual church or parish campaign.

The American Association of Fund Raising Counsel reports: "Over the eleven year period from 1950 through 1960 Americans increased their investment in the nation's philanthropically supported institutions at a faster pace than either personal income or the gross national product advanced. Private support of our religious, educational, health, and social welfare organizations increased 100 per cent in this period, while personal income rose 78 per cent, and the gross national product 77 per cent." [2]

These figures indicate that Americans were becoming more generous, the fund raisers more skillful, or perhaps the multiplication of appeals being directed at the American giver brought results. Voluntary agencies, benefiting from America's charitable impulse and the skills of the fund raiser, had rapidly increased in number. It is

estimated that there are more than 100,000 voluntary health and welfare agencies soliciting contributions from the American public. Add
to this staggering total another 100,000 fraternal, civic, veterans', and
related organizations that sponsor some health and welfare activities.
National and regional voluntary agencies in the health and welfare
field grew from 15 in 1940 to some 100 in 1960. United funds and
community chests spurted from 549 in the 1940's to more than
2,000 by 1960; money given these two organizations is passed on to
some 26,000 local, regional, and national member agencies. The more
than 300,000 churches, 3,346 hospitals, and the some 2,040 institutions
of higher education add to the intensive pressure on the American
donor to contribute money and to ask his neighbor to do so. There
is small chance of escaping the relentless pressure applied by the
fund raiser for the church, the community, the college, and countless
other causes. Almost daily United States citizens are confronted by
demands to give—at the front door, in the mailbox, in newspapers,
on television screens, and at places of work, worship, and play.

Little wonder that experts in this field predict that by 1970 Americans will be giving some $15,000,000,000 a year to religious, health,
welfare, and educational agencies. The Hamlin Committee which
studied gifts to health and welfare agencies predicted that by 1970
public giving will "approach $13 billion, more than ten times the
1940 total." [3] The American Association of Fund-Raising Counsel
estimates that by 1975 philanthropy in the United States may have
assets approaching $100 billion. Thomas Karter, program analyst in
the Social Security Administration, Department of Health, Education, and Welfare, has made these projections of philanthropic giving for the next decade: [4]

	1965	*1970*
Total (millions)	$10,410	$13,070
Individuals	9,810	12,320
Living Donors	9,000	11,300
Bequests	810	1,020
Corporations	600	750

Surely the ceiling on public giving is not in sight. Yet as each
new crest of public giving has been reached in the swelling tides
of American philanthropy there have been those who thought
"surely the people can't and won't be able to give more than this."

In the grim depression years a prominent American educator direfully predicted that "there would be no more large gifts to education in the future." He explained, "Great fortunes . . . which made former large gifts possible . . . have been dissipated." Later, in the New Deal years, it was gloomily predicted that the high taxes imposed by the Roosevelt Administration would injure, if not kill, philanthropy outright. One irate industrialist placed full-page advertisements in the newspapers to assert "destructive taxes will eventually cripple college, church, and charity," a dire prediction echoed over the years by those fearful of Big Government's mounting budgets and deficits. On the contrary, however, higher taxes, with their charitable deduction provisions, have induced philanthropic giving. Indeed ours might well be termed a "tax deductible" philanthropy.

Figures compiled by Marts & Lundy show that the percentage of personal income given by Americans to philanthropy has risen from 1.22 per cent in 1929 to 1.61 per cent in 1960, an increase of nearly 30 per cent. The individual donor remains the major source of philanthropy in the United States despite the growth of foundations and the rise of corporation giving. These persons are the same 60 million or more taxpayers who take the standard deduction or claim philanthropic deductions on their income tax returns.

Internal Revenue Service records for 1958 show that 96 per cent of those filing returns, or a total of 19,960,353 persons, claimed a record total of $5.7 billion for contributions, and some 38 million individuals took a standard deduction for their contributions.[5] In 1960 about 96 returns of every 100 made to the U.S. Internal Revenue Service made a deduction for charitable contributions. The total deduction in 1960 returns for contributions was $6,750,326,000 reported on 23,106,000 returns.[6] In 1961 the University of Michigan Survey Research Center, in a nationwide survey of a representative sample of adult citizens, showed that 62 per cent of these adults reported making some kind of charitable contribution. This survey indicated that, though the ways of voluntarism have been changing, contributions in the United States to church, charities, and colleges are still substantial. Such data validate our term "people's philanthropy" to characterize American fund raising and American fund giving.

Fifty-five Years and Eighty Millions Later

The evolution of the art of American fund raising can be dramatically demonstrated in three representative fund drives carried out by Harvard University—those of 1904–05, of 1919–20, and of 1956–60. Bishop William Lawrence's effort in 1904–05 to raise $2.5 million to increase faculty salaries at Harvard has already been described. As the first organized fund-raising campaign on behalf of a college or university it became, in some ways, the prototype for countless educational fund drives carried on since.

Also recounted earlier is the Harvard Endowment Fund Campaign of 1919–1920 to raise $10 million, directed by John Price Jones, assisted by Robert Duncan, Harold J. Seymour, and Chester E. Tucker, all Harvard men. This drive not only brought Harvard $14.2 million but led to the founding of the Jones firm. Harvard's next fund drive, 1956 through 1960, brought in the staggering sum of $82,775,553.

It will be recalled that when the shrewd and skillful Bishop Lawrence set out to raise the sum of $2.5 million for Harvard he had no professional fund raiser to assist him, no patterns of organization to guide him. This was, as he later stated, before the word "drive" had been invented, when the only "central office" was under the bishop's hat, and when he, as director of the campaign, would insist that there "be no crowding or jamming for subscriptions." The only professional help utilized by the bishop and his fellow committee members was provided by the nation's first public relations firm, George Michaelis, for a "few syndicated articles" for the sum of $500. Even the term "professional" might be questioned as publicity was still in its infancy. But Bishop Lawrence not only raised $2.4 million, he successfully developed the idea of alumni giving and dramatized the need for more public support of the nation's colleges and universities.

In the Harvard campaign of 1919, when Jones, Duncan, Seymour and Tucker joined forces, they not only made fund-raising history; they changed the course of higher education. Using their wartime experiences, their mastery of the art of publicity, and the intensive drive techniques developed for the YMCA by Ward and Pierce, this quartet developed many of the patterns and procedures that are currently used in educational fund raising.

Since the early 1920's there has been little in the way of true innovation in directing fund-raising campaigns, but rather a case of polishing and perfecting the detailed methods developed in World War I and in the formative years of the fund-raising business. In the 1919–1920 Harvard drive, Jones and his aides carefully organized the campaign, thoroughly prepared the statement of the case, and paved the way for systematic solicitation of all possible prospects with a hard-hitting publicity program. With the success in raising what was then a most dramatic sum, $14.2 million, not only was "the big movement of organized giving to American education under way" but fund raising had become a task for the specialist, skilled in organization and public relations.

How perfected the basic procedures and pressure-building techniques of fund raising had become over a span of thirty-five years can be seen in the spectacular success of the Harvard drive staged from 1956 to 1960, which went over its $82.5 million goal by more than a quarter of a million dollars. Granted that the Harvard campaign came in a period when gifts and grants were pouring into the nation's hard-pressed colleges at an unprecedented rate, nonetheless this was a monumental tribute to the power of highly organized, shrewdly promoted fund raising on behalf of a meritorious cause. In the period of this drive, from 1954–1955 to 1958–1959, gifts and grants to higher education increased 94 per cent, according to the Council for Financial Aid to Education. The Harvard College Program drive, announced by President Pusey at a press conference on October 31, 1956, exceeded its goal on January 20, 1960.

Playing key roles in this massive effort were Robert F. Duncan, Carl A. Kersting, Byron W. Shimp, Wolcott D. Street, Donald L. Kersting, and Kendrick Smith. Duncan acted as campaign director for the first six months, then became consultant. After an interval of five months he was succeeded as campaign director by Shimp, long associated with the firm of Tamblyn & Brown, and in 1957–1962 the president of Kersting, Brown & Co. Shimp directed most of the technical aspects of this university campaign, the largest up to that time, from September, 1957, to its successful conclusion.

These men brought all the accumulated knowledge of modern fund raising to the Harvard campaign, much of it learned in association with John Price Jones. Duncan had served as Jones's right-hand man in the 1919 drive. Street joined the Jones firm in 1928, one year after graduating from Harvard. Carl A. Kersting worked for the Jones firm from 1932 to 1935, and again from 1941 to 1943, when he formed his own firm, now Kersting, Brown & Co. This was the firm retained for the Harvard Program campaign, largely through the influence of Duncan, who joined the Kersting firm as president when he left Jones in 1950. For their part in this effective campaign the fund raisers were paid approximately $300,000, a relatively small fee in view of the sum raised.[7] Although Kersting & Brown was the firm operating behind the scenes in this Harvard drive, the methodical, relentless ways of John Price Jones were fully utilized by his former aides. Duncan has written: "I have always felt that the J.P.J. shop of the '30s and early '40s was the best training ground this business has ever seen or ever will see."[8] Jones watched this drive from the quietude of retirement, having sold his firm in 1955.

In sharp contrast to the "few syndicated articles" used by Bishop Lawrence in his 1904–05 drive, these professional fund raisers used an intensive publicity-promotion that ultimately totaled some two million words written for folders, letters, manuals, bulletins, magazines, newsletters, and a book. "If radio and movie scripts, local bulletins, speeches, news releases, special presentations to individual donors, and other campaign miscellany were piled on top, the total wordage would be doubled or tripled."[9] This public relations program was directed by Laurence O. Pratt, '26, under the guidance of a policy committee composed of some of Harvard's most distinguished alumni in communications. Members included the late Arthur W. Page, long-time public relations director of American Telephone and Telegraph Co., *Look* publisher Gardner Cowles and *Time* publisher Roy E. Larsen, TV producer Robert Saudek, William I. Nichols, John C. Robbins, Jr., Edward Streeter, and until his death Henry Salomon, Jr.

A second public relations committee was set up in Cambridge to serve as an operating group focusing the talents of the University on the over-all program. It was Pratt's task to coordinate the work of these two committees in New York and Cambridge and direct the operations of the publicity staff. The two public relations offices were operated throughout the four years of the campaign. The Cambridge office turned out the major printed pieces, while the New York office served the campaign with bulletins, the *Newsletter* and *Progress Report*, and fed the story into the nation's mass media. Wolcott Street prepared the basic presentation of Harvard's case that provided the backbone of the publicity disseminated on a wholesale scale.

All of this was carried forward in compliance with a carefully predetermined Public Relations Plan. The targets of the program's publicity were clearly defined—campaign aids for the program workers, special programs for Advance and Special Gift prospects, the college alumni as a whole, alumni of the Graduate Schools, parents and widows of Harvard men, the faculty, corporations, foundations, and the general public. The prime emphasis was directed at Harvard's alumni in the belief that this was "essentially an alumni show." And this paid off, for nearly 60 per cent of all the men of Harvard College gave to the program. This rate of alumni giving was unprecedented in college fund raising. At the height of the campaign seventy-one persons were employed full time in the Cambridge and New York City offices.

As to naming this a "program," Harold J. Seymour wrote, "Calling it a Program instead of a fund was an act of inspired wisdom . . . for it made the fund-raising process itself a means toward an end, not an end in itself." [10] The idea was President Pusey's and when he voiced it at a meeting at the Harvard Club in mid-July, 1956, those present, including Duncan, enthusiastically endorsed it. Following this campaign, the title "program" was adopted by many other university campaigns, just as, thirty-two years before, the title "development campaign," suggested in the autumn of 1924 by President Ernest DeWitt Burton of the University of Chicago for its 1924–25 campaign, was widely copied. Today many colleges and universities have Departments of Development and a drive is often labeled a "development campaign." The fund-raising campaign was undertaken at President Pusey's direction early in his administration and he worked untiringly in giving it imaginative leadership and vigorous support. Pusey, a college president of the modern era, recognizes that money raising is now a phase of the college president's task that cannot be completely delegated to fund raisers.[11]

Pusey first foreshadowed what was to come in a speech to the Associated Harvard Clubs at Miami, Fla., on April 7, 1956, "the most serious and important speech I have made since coming to Harvard as president." His appointment in 1955, as the successor to James B. Conant, had stimulated a searching appraisal of Harvard's goals and needs, which culminated in the proposed Harvard Program to raise

$82.5 million. This was a fund drive on a scale hitherto thought impossible to organize, even by veteran fund raisers. Again, as in 1919, the dimension and drama of Harvard's fund drive served to focus the nation's attention on the urgent needs of all her colleges and universities. Its success stimulated a number of similarly large campaigns by other universities.

Although the basic campaign methods utilized were those tested in the crucible of fund raising in the earlier days of Ward, Pierce, and Jones, this drive employed, in effective and dramatic ways, many of the newer tools of mass persuasion: public opinion polls, television, motion pictures, closed circuit telephone and television hookups of meetings in different parts of the country. An opinion survey of Harvard's alumni was conducted, well after the drive was under way, and results of this poll guided efforts that culminated in pushing alumni participation in the campaign to some 26,000 givers—a record-shattering figure in any college campaign. Until this survey was analyzed the campaign's leaders had resisted the notion of a direct-mail appeal to alumni. The opinion survey revealed that campaign workers were reluctant to re-solicit alumni who had already given but that many alumni were ready to give again. With these guidelines, a direct-mail campaign was prepared and carried out over a three-month period, bringing in $1,125,454 in 4,807 gifts and pledges.

The campaigners broke another precedent when an hour's time was purchased on a national radio network to celebrate Harvard Day on March 28, 1958, a world-wide event unique in fund-raising annals. "This plan had the advantage of assuring a complete network without holes, gave Harvard greater freedom in planning its own show." [12]

Harvard's campaigners got an unexpected bonus when another network re-broadcast the show without charge, evidence that it had been of high entertainment quality. Around the radio program, major events were held in Cambridge, New York, Washington, and a few other cities, but the main purpose was to reach alumni beyond the reach of campaign events. The aforementioned alumni survey indicated that more than half the Harvard family around the globe had been reached through this program.

Early in the drive, at Kersting & Brown's suggestion, a series of closed circuit telephone lunches were held to help knit the program workers together and infuse them with the "go get 'em" spirit. Another modern touch was the production of a powerful motion picture, *To the Age That Is Waiting,* under the sensitive and skillful direction of Robert Saudek. This film was the central piece in the campaign's "kick-off" dinners and was intensively used in subsequent campaign events and alumni club meetings and was shown over many TV stations. "Even when poorly projected, as it often was, handkerchiefs were generally in evidence when the lights went up." Famed Harvard-trained authors, Van Wyck Brooks, John Dos Passos, and Walter D. Edmonds were recruited to write "old school tie" appeals.

The pressure of these and countless other methods ultimately propelled the fund drive across the goal line with dollars to spare. Quite different from Bishop Lawrence's day, there was plenty of "jamming and crowding." Most fund raisers recoil from the idea that their job is to build pressure on prospects. Among the more candid of the veterans in this field is Harold Seymour. He admits: "There is ground for rejoicing by all students and practitioners of organized fund-raising that the Program made no bones at all about 'pressure.' It is usually called 'high' pressure by those who oppose or dislike big fund-raising campaigns, especially by those innocents who still think that there is substantial nourishment to be found in 'quiet special gifts efforts.' Whatever it is called, there was lots of pressure in this Harvard affair." [13]

This fund raising on a grand scale confirmed and illuminated some of the basic laws of modern fund raising as well as demonstrating modern-day scope. Seymour sums it up:

> The case must be bigger than the institution. . . . No voluntary organization is ever stronger than the quality of its leadership, or ever extends its constituency beyond the degree to which the leadership is representative. . . . Personal contact by laymen, whether for enlistment of workers or the solicitation of gifts, should be established on the same or higher level. . . . Duly proportionate quotas, whether for dollars or units of work, should be established and accepted, by advice and consent, for every part of the campaign structure; for every division, every team, every worker, and every prospective contributor. . . . The best prospects are those who have already contributed. . . . Standards should be set from the inside out. . . . Money flows to promising programs, rather than to needy institutions. [14]

The amazing results of this Harvard Program campaign, coupling Seymour's principles with powerful publicity and systematic solicitation, can be seen in Table 20, taken from the March 19, 1960, issue of the *Harvard Alumni Bulletin*:

Dramatic evidence of the accelerating sums of money raised in organized drives is seen in the more recent campaign of Massachusetts Institute of Technology which brought it nearly $100 million in three years of intensive fund raising. On May 24, 1960, the Institute announced a Second Century Program "for broad advances in education and research to help fulfill its national responsibilities" and set a target of $66 million to be raised to meet this goal. A total of $26 million had been pledged or contributed in advance gifts when the drive was announced. The remaining months of 1960 were used to solicit special gifts, approach large donors, and perfect plans for the broader campaign launched in 1961. Strong appeals backed by saturation publicity were made to 48,000 alumni, to industry, foundations, and to the general public in a campaign directed by John J. Wilson, Boston industrialist. The halfway mark in the Second Century Fund drive was reached in February, 1961, when the Martin Company gave a half million dollars. On May 7, 1963, almost three years after the drive's start, Wilson announced that gifts, grants, and pledges from private sources had reached the undreamed-of total of $98 million—$32 million above the goal. For once, Harvard had been exceeded in money getting!

In these days of a $100 billion federal budget and of multimillion foundation gifts the raising of nearly $100 million through an organized promotional campaign may not seem unusual. The magnitude of Harvard and MIT's fund-raising power is better appreciated when shown against the backdrop of earlier college drives.

Largely because of the depression and World War II, there were few big capital campaigns between the late 1920's and the late 1940's. Smith College raised some $7 million in 1946–1950, and the New York University Bellevue Medical College drive in 1947–1951 produced $22 million.

One must go back thirty-five years, to 1928, when the successful Yale campaign also raised $22 million, to find any effort of comparable size. The University of Chicago was the first to set today's high postwar pace with a goal of $32,799,000 in a campaign launched in June, 1955. This drive produced $31,241,000 by the spring of 1958.

TABLE 20. THE HARVARD PROGRAM DRIVE

Tabulation of Receipts

	Semi-annual basis	Cumulative
July 1, 1956–December 31, 1956	$ 6,573,723	$ 6,573,723
January 1, 1957–June 30, 1957	8,176,069	14,749,792
July 1, 1957–December 31, 1957	14,953,689	29,703,481
January 1, 1958–June 30, 1958	12,764,464	42,467,945
July 1, 1958–December 31, 1958	12,614,373	55,082,318
January 1, 1959–June 30, 1959	12,658,659	67,740,977
July 1, 1959 to the end of the Program (January 20, 1960)	15,034,577	82,775,554

B. EXPECTATIONS AND REALIZATIONS

Table of Gifts

	Anticipated		Actual	
Size of gift	Number of gifts	Amount	Number of gifts	Amount
$10,000,000 and up	1	$10,000,000	None	None
5,000,000–$9,999,999	2	12,000,000	None	None
1,000,000– 4,999,999	7	10,000,000	15	$30,127,169
100,000– 999,999	110	29,000,000	115	27,144,352
50,000– 99,999	100	5,000,000	45	2,867,100
10,000– 49,999	500	9,000,000	537	9,704,376
5,000– 9,999	400	3,000,000	519	3,119,944
1,000– 4,999	1,500	2,000,000	3,408	5,743,472
Less than 1,000	20,000	2,500,000	23,124	3,814,105
Group Gift Donors	—	—	3,933	255,036
Total	22,620	$82,500,000	31,696	$82,775,554

C. WHERE THE MONEY CAME FROM

Sources of Funds

	Anticipated	Actually received
Alumni	$62,000,000	$54,779,179
Bequests	10,000,000	14,481,002
Corporations	2,000,000	1,453,225
Foundations	7,500,000	6,766,469
Friends	1,000,000	5,295,679
Total	$82,500,000	$82,775,554

MIT moved into large-scale fund raising with its 1948–1951 drive which raised $28 million in a campaign begun by Marts & Lundy. Prior to this the Institute had not intensively campaigned for funds but its systematic, high-pressure fund drives have brought in more than $150 million in fifteen years—another indication of the power and potential of today's tightly organized, high-pressure fund raising.

Health Drives Multiply

Persons interested in fighting other diseases were quick to see the lessons of nationwide fund raising as taught by the National Tuberculosis Association, March of Dimes, and, more recently, by the American Cancer Society.

Total contributions for health and medical care in 1958 were $680 million, much of it raised in annual fund drives. This represented 3 per cent of the total public and private expenditures of $22.9 billion spent for medical care in the United States that year. Nearly half of this $680 million, or $325 million, was given in 1958 to about sixty national and regional voluntary agencies with a primary interest in health.

Louis I. Dublin once wrote, "The voluntary health movement has had its fullest flowering in the United States. . . . The voluntary health agencies of the United States have grown since the beginning of the century from a mere handful to over 20,000. They cover the land. . . . Like other expressions of the free initiative of our people, these organizations naturally overlap at some points, duplicating effort." [15] Marion K. Sanders reports that in the spring of 1957 "a spot check of Chatham County, Georgia, the Savannah *Morning Herald* tallied up nineteen organizations passing the hat for the blind; seven for disabled veterans; six for the crippled; four for mental illness; five for cancer; two each for muscular dystrophy, polio, leprosy, brain injury, alcoholism; and one apiece of heart disease, retarded children, cerebral palsy, deafness, tuberculosis, multiple sclerosis, arthritis, myasthenia gravis, nephrosis, facial disfigurement, tropical diseases, diabetes, epilepsy, allergic diseases, hemophilia, and paraplegia." [16] Little wonder that one Stamford, Conn., business leader said wearily, "We are punch drunk trying to keep up with all these appeals."

The rush to reap the dimes and dollars can be seen in the rapid-fire organization of the following agencies which were conducting annual fund drives in 1962:

Name of Agency/Society	Year Founded	Time of Drive	1958 Drive Result
Arthritis and Rheumatism Foundation	1948	Nov. 15–Dec. 15	$ 3,026,400
Damon Runyon Memorial Fund for Cancer Research	1946	Year around	885,000
United Cerebral Palsy Assn.	1948	January	11,248,000
National Cystic Fibrosis Research Foundation	1955	September	276,000
American Heart Association	1948	February	22,962,700
National Kidney Disease Foundation	1950	Dec.–March	698,000
National Association for Mental Health	1950	May	4,482,700
National Multiple Sclerosis Society	1946	May 8–June 19	2,807,000
Muscular Dystrophy Assn. America	1950	November	5,466,200
National Association for Retarded Children	1953	November	2,300,000

These agencies, hotly competitive for the public's heart and purse, also brought rising controversy about their role in man's battle against the ills of disease and of society. One sharp-tongued critic wrote in 1958:

. . . the voluntary agencies have failed down the line to admit to themselves that their own resources would not do to support a proper offensive employing every possible line of attack. This is my first criticism of the voluntary agencies—their selfish refusal to recognize their own limitations. They have always assumed (or found it more profitable so to believe) that conditions were not ripe for anything but the tin-cup approach to disease. . . . By so doing and, through public relations, making it appear that this was the correct and sane avenue of approach, these agencies have rendered a distinct public disservice. . . .

Is it defensible, from any logical or ethical point of view, to persuade the public that the way to attack cancer (250,000 deaths a year), heart disease (900,000 deaths a year), mental illnesses (which fill better than one of every two hospital beds in the nation)—or the other great killers and cripplers—is by direct-mail campaigns, spot announcements on radio and television, telethons, free publicity, and public relations and "promotion" when, in fact only a fraction of the dollars contributed goes into research? [17]

According to Bloomgarden, this is how the American Cancer Society spent the $29,650,000 it collected from the general public in 1957: [18]

   30 per cent to research projects
   30 per cent went to education (18 per cent for public education,
       12 per cent for professional education)
   23 per cent went to service the cancer patients
   8 per cent went to administration
   9 per cent went to fund raising

"Thus, 70 per cent (or more) of the total contributed went into programs other than research." According to his figures, the American Cancer Society was spending some 17 per cent of its income for administration and fund raising. This is expensive philanthropy, to be sure. Yet, would there have been an aroused public opinion to force the federal government to move in a broad-scale attack on cancer without the American Cancer Society's campaigns?

The disquieting fact is that the public's dimes and dollars go to the causes with the ablest leaders, publicists, and fund raisers. In a recent conference on philanthropy sponsored by the National Bureau of Economic Research it was concluded: "The distribution of funds available for the voluntary national health agencies is certainly not proportional to the number of deaths resulting annually from the diseases which are the special targets of the national health agencies. . . . There does seem to be a need for some kind of policy . . . to be used as a basis for judgment about the distribution of these funds among the disease categories, whether they are public funds, such as those of the National Institutes of Health, or the funds of voluntary agencies." [19] Such disparity is inevitable in a system of voluntarism, short of a national united health fund drive that would turn its funds over to a central board for allocation in the manner of the local community chest. In 1958 it could be said, for example, that Americans were contributing more money in behalf of 150,000 victims of muscular dystrophy than for the 9 mil-

lion persons mentally ill. As Marion Sanders wrote with bitterness, "Crusades are built on pity and terror, not statistics." But that
is not the whole of the matter, either.

The disparity is quickly seen in a comparison of infantile paralysis with multiple sclerosis, a less-publicized but just as common and
as deadly a crippler of people. Both causes could and did exploit
emotional appeals. Multiple sclerosis—a harder name to pronounce
than polio—is a disease that attacks the nervous system and leaves
its victims paralyzed for life. MS, as it is often called, strikes
without warning and attacks men and women between the ages of
twenty and forty, especially the younger people. While rarely fatal
in its early stages, it may be progressive and cause long incapacity.
As of 1964 there was no cure in sight. "At present MS research
stands engulfed in that despairing darkness which always precedes
the scientific dawn." [20]

In 1961 it was estimated that there were 500,000 victims of multiple sclerosis and other related demyelinating diseases in the United
States.

A comparison of the number of deaths from MS and from polio
between 1949, when MS became a definitely diagnosable disease,
and 1955, when the Salk vaccine was fully introduced in the United
States, follows: [21]

Year	Multiple Sclerosis	Infantile Paralysis
1949	1,379	2,720
1950	1,278	1,904
1951	1,418	1,551
1952	1,531	3,145
1953	1,431	1,450
1954	1,394	1,368
1955	1,409	1,043

These diseases were, before polio's cure, roughly comparable in
the way they strike, in their role as a crippler, and in their effects.
Yet there is a wide disparity in their public support. In 1954—the
year the Salk vaccine was tested on a nationwide scale amid much
excitement and controversy—the National Foundation for Infantile
Paralysis had an income of more than $42 million, more than $40
million of which came from public contributions. In the same
year the Multiple Sclerosis Society was floundering in its effort to
raise a mere $1.1 million in a national drive guided by the John Price

Jones firm. "At last reports, although only about a quarter of a million had been collected nationally and locally, some thirty-five campaigns are still going and we have a trustworthy forecast of $1,228,-000 . . . that figure depends on some pretty big 'ifs.' " [22] In 1958, long after Basil O'Connor and the National Foundation had proved "for all time the power of a voluntary organization to solve one of the world's major health problems," the National Foundation was raising nearly $35 million to provide research in the areas of arthritis and birth defects, and care for polio sufferers. In the same year the National Multiple Sclerosis Society received $1,136,400 in contributions to carry on its work in a demonstrably greater cause than that now espoused by the O'Connor-led National Foundation. [23]

In 1954 the National Foundation spent more than five times as much money on administration and public relations as the Multiple Sclerosis Society was able to raise. In the very rough accounting the Foundation gives the public on its administrative expenses, it reported spending $3,541,000 on maintenance of state offices, medical department and public relations services, service and assistance to chapters, and another $1,896,000 on general administrative expenses. [24] Given this budget, Basil O'Connor's imaginative though dictatorial leadership, Dorothy Ducas' skill in public relations, and the loyalty of thousands of volunteer workers, it is little wonder that the Foundation could raise more than $60 million in dimes and dollars in its 1954 nationwide campaign.

That same year the Multiple Sclerosis Society was suffering from what Wolcott Street diagnosed as lack of leadership, lack of funds for promotion, and lack of volunteer workers. When Street was called in to direct the MS group's 1954 national campaign he found the organization "paralyzed by the jealousies and rivalries of those who volunteer their services to its chapters; by their frequently lacerated egos, their inter-group animosities . . . and their mistrust of the parent organization." And as fund raisers know, money has to be raised in the precincts. Street observes: "The national organization per se, while important, is to some extent window dressing. Your success depends on your chapters, on their fund-raising ingenuity and know-how, and on your success in servicing them, keeping them on the track, and maintaining momentum." [25]

In sharp contrast to these early troubles in building community volunteer groups in the Multiple Sclerosis Society is the deep and continuing loyalty of the National Foundation volunteer as documented in Sills' *The Volunteers*. Basil O'Connor and his associates wisely provided, "Volunteers with an opportunity to acquire, through making decisions and assuming responsibilities, a vested interest in the organization; a vested interest, however, which does not interfere with programs toward organizational goals. . . . These characteristics of the Foundation have led many Volunteers to perceive the organization as a 'social movement,' and have thus provided Volunteers with an ideological rationale for their own participation." [26]

Today, it is estimated, there are probably 50,000,000 volunteers participating in fund drives. This figure includes 3,000,000 of America's business and professional leaders, at least 18,000,000 church workers, and over 29,000,000 listed volunteers with 35 national philanthropic agencies.

"Mutiny of the Bountiful"

American fund raising in the post-World War II years continued to be, in the words of Donald Young, "the emotional and disorderly field of benevolence." The pent-up demands for buildings for colleges, churches, and other institutions plus the continuing needs of relief and welfare brought on a public reaction headlined by one magazine as a "Mutiny of the Bountiful." Demands for a surcease of the endless solicitations and unremitting pressure to work in drives brought into existence the United Fund, the United Defense Fund in the Korean War, the United College appeal and numerous other nationwide federations.

". . . Americans are being bombarded as never before by appeals from coast to coast. In San Francisco, a young accountant earning $7,500 a year toted up 178 national and local calls for his financial help last year. A well-known New York businessman, whose yearly income exceeds $50,000, estimates that he annually receives close to 500 pleas for aid. In Chicago, a housewife who has to make do on a $60 weekly budget found she had donated to 31 different drives within the past twelve months and recalls at least two dozen additional requests to serve as a volunteer solicitor." [27]

There was still, however, heated controversy over the issue of "one drive or many." One caustic critic described federation as a "strait jacket on brotherly cooperation." On the other hand, Ralph

Blanchard, a long-time community chest leader, insisted that federation "is inevitable because it is right." This commonsense response had led to the pooling of fund raising on a local basis as early as 1887 with the formation of the Associated Charities of Denver, and again in 1900 in Cleveland; to the war chests of World War I and the community chests of the 1920's and 1930's. The outgrowth of these early efforts to eliminate duplication and gaps in the over-all philanthropic picture is illustrated in the following brief sketches of three major national fund-raising movements.

The United Fund

America's community chests, retooled for World War II under the direction of the National War Fund, had made another important contribution to American philanthropy by pushing the nation's voluntary fund-raising potential to a new height. Millions of people had given to chests for the first time. Business and industry had taken leadership in helping to raise and contribute money on a vast scale. Corporate philanthropy was spreading. Organized labor had demonstrated its concern for welfare and shown great fund-raising capacity. As a result, community chests raised nearly one-third more for national war-related causes, one-third more for war relief, and one-third more for local agencies. When hostilities ceased, community chests sought to maintain the wartime levels of giving but were confronted by a wholly new climate of fund raising. Community needs for new hospitals, churches, libraries, and the like brought a flood of capital building fund campaigns. Colleges increased their campaigns. National health drives mushroomed.

In the face of these competing appeals, community chests across the country began to experience campaign failures. This brought some hard research on why chest campaigns had failed to make announced goals. One significant study of this problem was made in Indianapolis, Ind., by Community Surveys, Inc., in response to the persistent question of chest leaders in Indianapolis, "What's wrong with our Chest?" The researchers found that in one year under scrutiny, 1951, Indianapolis should have been able to raise $3.07 per capita in its chest drive but raised only $2.54. Evidence of what the authors term mass, operational, periodic, secular fund raising pointed in these directions:

The greater the degree of corporate dependency, the greater the disappointingness of the general Chest performance per capita.

The greater the degree of leading donor dependency, the greater the disappointingness of the general Chest performance per capita.

The greater the degree of inequity in the standard for and in the actual executive giving, both the lower the level of executive generosity and the greater the disappointingness of the general Chest performance per capita.[28]

Although community chests found it harder to meet campaign quotas in the 1950's, the demands on chest-supported agencies—dramatized by increased numbers of family breakdowns, a rise in juvenile delinquency, racial problems, and a greatly increased demand for more recreational facilities—steadily mounted.

As early as 1945, complaint about the multiplicity of fund-raising drives, increasingly annoying, costly, and confusing to the public, brought talk of a state package for these appeals. There also was a growing belief on the part of many that the chests could survive only by encompassing more and more campaigns, particularly the national health drives which hold such a strong emotional appeal for the typical giver. At least the latter point was asserted by the health agencies that would not come into the united funds. In the 1950's, just as in Cleveland in 1913, the articulate voice of the businessman demanded that something be done.

As the drives multiplied, employers were not only pressed to give large donations on behalf of their firms but were asked to submit to plant solicitations of employees during working hours and to use up a great deal of valuable corporate executive time on "community relations." As one writer pointed out a decade later: "Corporation executives . . . had to decide in dozens of cases whether to permit solicitation on company property, whether to release personnel to assist in money raising and how much money to give in the corporation name. . . . Many big companies . . . started their own in-plant federated campaigns, closing the door to all solicitors and raising the money in a single office and plant campaign." [29] Plant employees who were solicited and had to do much of the soliciting became equally distraught with the excessive appeals to give. Labor generally supported management's position on this issue.

A united fund "position paper" described the united fund's origins this way:

As everyone knows, the organization of United Funds was largely an outgrowth of the annoyance of businessmen and labor leaders, essentially, at the number of campaigns they were called upon to conduct in their plants.

They realized that to sell the [united fund] idea, they would have to have more publicity. They would need more fanfare. It might even be necessary to change the name [from community chest] in order to make the movement more dynamic.[30]

Henry Ford II took the leadership in the united fund movement. He had taken over the presidency of the faltering Ford Motor Co. in 1945 from the tired, rigid hands of his grandfather. Guided by an astute public relations counselor, Earl Newsom, young Ford was looking for ways and means of establishing himself as an industrial statesman. The United Health and Welfare Fund of Michigan was launched on July 15, 1947, at a meeting called by Ford with the full support of the community chests of Michigan and the blessing of the Three Cs national leadership. This was the stated purpose of the meeting:

> To help create a more balanced program of health and welfare services by cooperating with state and national agencies in the establishment of budgets based on need and capacity to meet need; by determining equitable assignments of quotas, assuring Michigan's fair share of the national quota, and assigning equitable quotas to county units; by federating appeals and conducting one campaign for the entire amount. The Fund will also endeavor to provide information for the guidance of local communities on campaigns to be conducted within the state.[31]

Thus once more the businessman played an influential role in this sector of the American people's philanthropy. On this issue Henry Ford II and Walter Reuther, president of the United Automobile Workers' union, saw eye to eye. The first united fund, federating local chest appeals and national health agency causes, was conceived in the July, 1947, meeting called by Ford and participated in by some 175 representatives of labor, industry, finance, and business in Michigan.

It took more than a year for Ford's united fund proposal to become a reality. The first full-scale united fund drive was staged in Detroit in November, 1949, and went over the set goal of $8,550,000 by a comfortable margin; a total of $8,918,349 was raised. Henry Ford II crowed: "It confirms the belief many of us have had that a united campaign, with everybody giving everything they've got to a single hard-hitting campaign is the best way to get good results." This pioneering effort to couple fund-raising campaigns for the health causes with the traditional chest agencies attracted nationwide attention. *Newsweek* noted: "Detroit's spectacular success in bringing all appeals under a single umbrella may be the ideal solution for hundreds of other communities which have been wrestling with the same problem." [32] The *Saturday Evening Post*, in an editorial commending the idea, said, "Michigan has had enough of multiple drives and is the first state to do something about it." [33] What, the *Post* asked, is wrong with federated peacetime giving?

Many of the national health agencies found something wrong with it. The opposition was led by the American Red Cross, by the National Foundation for Infantile Paralysis, and the American Cancer Society. Basil O'Connor has been a determined, unyielding foe of united fund raising. The Red Cross issued a pamphlet condemning "compulsory federated giving." Critics of the united fund plan raised fears of "a national welfare trust." In a privately published book, reputedly inspired and supported by Basil O'Connor during his term as head of the American Red Cross, Robert Keith Leavitt stated that "a national Super Chest would be controlled largely by professionals drawn from the field of local Community Chest work." Leavitt was certain that this "Super Chest authoritarianism would impose arbitrary and capricious restrictions." [34]

The American National Red Cross and the strong national health groups—O'Connor's Polio Foundation, the Tuberculosis Association, the Cancer Society in particular—fought determinedly and often bitterly against the pressure of large business contributors to force their appeals into a united fund at the local and state level. Much of the debate and difference was reminiscent of the resistance of the National Tuberculosis Association to being forced into the community chests in the 1920's. The American National Red Cross ultimately capitulated under the bludgeoning administered by the influential Mrs. Agnes Meyer: "The Red Cross is the perfect symbol of all the shortcomings of voluntary welfare work because it has preserved the aristocratic, aloof, and egotistical psychology of private welfare organizations to an almost pathological degree. . . . In great and small communities it wishes to dictate. If the Red

Cross will not face the dangers of that habitual authoritarianism, real community harmony cannot be achieved." [35] The Red Cross, after O'Connor left it, took a neutral position and left the matter up to its local chapters. By 1958 some 950 Red Cross chapters were participating in united fund drives.

Initially the American Cancer Society opposed the united fund idea and from 1944 on declared itself in favor of a separate and independent campaign by stating that none of its divisions, branches, or units "shall be a part of any War Chest, Community Chest or similar fund-raising organization or device." In 1950 this nonparticipation policy was modified "to enable Units of the Society to participate in such solicitations under certain specified conditions." Realistically this meant that local units of the ACS could join in communities where the pressure to come into the united fund could not be resisted. Seven years later, 1957, the ACS reversed this policy and ordered all units out of united funds by 1960. The American Cancer Society argued: "With the United Fund movement, the three-way partnership between the agencies, the givers, and the Chests disappeared. In its place came a dual partnership between givers—primarily representatives of business and industry. For the first time in American philanthropy, the programs of vital health and welfare services were being evaluated and directed by the givers and not by those most knowledgeable, experienced and concerned—the professional staffs and dedicated volunteer leaders of the agencies." [36]

The advocates of the united fund argue, with equally persuasive logic: "Federation puts its faith on the principle of 'go it together' as opposed to the cult of 'go it alone.' . . . The first small united campaign discovered a simple formula: cooperation minus competition equals more services to people, plus more dollars for services. After nearly half a century of growth and change the formula still works. Today the united way of community planning, budgeting, and fund raising is accepted by the overwhelming majority of contributors, volunteer leaders and health and welfare workers as the most effective way yet devised to meet the health and welfare needs of people through voluntary services." [37] The basic appeal for the united fund which appears again and again in UGF fund-raising literature is that "people want to do their fair share in support of voluntary health, welfare, and recreation agencies" but that "givers want one annual campaign for all eligible agencies when they can go all out both in work and giving."

Another strong argument used by its advocates in pleading the united fund case is its economy as compared with those of the independent fund drives. Precise, accurate fund-raising costs are difficult to find, in either case. In the Los Angeles Community Chest, where all agencies appealing for funds must comply with a uniform accounting system, the fund-raising costs came to 8.5 cents per dollar raised. The health agencies spend from 12 to 30 cents to collect each Los Angeles dollar. Marion Sanders estimated "health agencies spend no less than $26 million a year to collect $170 million." [38] As noted earlier, the use of seals in a direct-mail appeal is a most expensive way of raising funds. Maas asserted, "Over 23 cents of every dollar you shell out for the National Tuberculosis Association Christmas-seal campaign is really eaten up by fund-raising expenses." He also said that "the National Foundation . . . spent twice as much on fund raising as on research, from 1938 to 1958."

The advocates of individual fund appeals counter this low-cost argument by insisting that a fund drive is also an educational campaign and much of its cost is properly chargeable to education. It is certainly true that the united fund appeals to give must be couched in most general terms and cannot communicate specific information about the scores of agencies financed through the common fund. Much of today's giving comes in response to the "check off" at the place of work and in response to the emotional appeals and catchy slogans fashioned by public relations experts. One writer has observed: "Like religion, philanthropic activities have become a matter of faith and belief. The faith is maintained by what is called good 'public relations' or it may be weakened and destroyed by counterpropaganda and adverse publicity. . . . Today the philanthropic contributor both to independent appeals and to joint campaigns is predominately an individual who contributes to symbols and slogans. This condition has been created not by federated fundraising, but by the growth of urban populations and multiplicity of appeals, and the remoteness of the agencies from the bulk of their supporters." [39]

Whatever the pluses and minuses of lumping all health, welfare, and disaster relief appeals into one federated fund drive—and there are valid points on both sides—the united fund idea took hold in this post-World War II era just as the chest idea had caught on after

World War I. In July, 1957, just ten years after Henry Ford II had sponsored the idea in Detroit, the thousandth united fund was born. The American Red Cross was a partner in 936 of them; several of the lesser national health agencies had joined; but the Big Four— the National Foundation, the National Tuberculosis Association, the American Heart Association, and the American Cancer Society— resisted both the united fund idea at the local level and the federated health fund idea on a nationwide basis.

By 1959 the number of united fund campaigns had risen to 1,217 and 1,261 Red Cross chapters were partners in united campaigns. That year more than one-half of the Red Cross's annual intake came from joint drives. Federated campaigns for 1959 raised, in total, a record high of $427,262,622, an increase of almost $13 million over the previous year, and about $235 million more than was raised in 1950.[40] In the over $10 billion total given to philanthropic causes, the united fund sums are relatively small. Nonetheless these funds, and the people who spend them, play an influential role in American philanthropy—and in the nation's local communities.

The modern symbol of united fund raising, and a mighty effective one it is too, is the Red Feather. The Red Feather was adopted nationally as the official symbol of services, contributors, and united fund raising of the community chests in 1946. Duluth, Minn., was the first city to use this identification of chest givers, introducing it in 1928. The jaunty feather is now widely known and chest agencies are frequently referred to as "Red Feather agencies."

The United Defense Fund

In June, 1950, when the Communist forces of North Korea crossed the 38th parallel, the United States once again found herself in military battle with the forces of totalitarianism; only this time the enemy was Communist led, not Nippon and Nazi led. And this time the war was not called a war but was euphemistically termed a "conflict." The conflict lasted more than three years and took 54,246 American lives. In the Korean War the united way of fund raising to provide for the wartime needs of U.S. fighting men and their families was put to work without debate or delay. The National United War Fund had been born late in the days of World War I and brought to perfection in the National War Fund of World War II. With these precedents to guide welfare and government leaders, and the professionals of the community chest organizations ready to supply the manpower, the United Defense Fund, Inc., of the Korean War came swiftly, as a matter of course. The agency reflects the now standardized procedures of American fund raising in the health and welfare field, wartime or peacetime.

In its five years of activity the United Defense Fund raised a total of $45,053,826, at an overhead cost, covering the fund raising, collection, budgeting, supervision, and accounting, of 6.39 per cent, according to Michael T. Kelleher, the president.[41] The funds raised, less the expenses of raising them, were distributed as follows:

American Relief for Korea	$1,458,912
American Social Hygiene Assn.	1,678,207
Natl. Recreation Assn.	409,941
United Community Defense Services	3,716,433
United Seamen's Service	448,518
United Service Organization (USO)	34,157,138

Given the continuing conflict in the Cold War between Russia and the United States, it was wise, and perhaps prophetic, that the United Defense Fund was not disbanded in 1955, only "put in mothballs" with a reserve fund sufficient to enable it "to resume operations—immediately if called upon to do so." The USO and its allied agencies are now a fixed part of America's military establishment.

The United Defense Fund had its inception on August 18, 1950, at a meeting of the Executive Committee of the National Social Welfare Assembly called by Mrs. Henry A. Ingraham, active social leader from Brooklyn, N.Y., who served as a member of the UDF board during its existence. Those attending the August 18 conference represented sixteen community chests, thirty-five voluntary national organizations, and five federal agencies. Those welfare leaders saw that "the American mobilization of manpower and economic resources to meet the Korean invasion called for a concerted appraisal of . . . voluntary services, and fund raising plans." [42]

There was consensus that a nationwide fund-raising drive was necessary because "the United States would probably sustain an enlarged industrial and military program for some years to come." This national emergency fund was established on November 28 and agencies included were the USO, the United Community Defense Services, American Social Hygiene Association, and National Recreation Association. American Relief for Korea was admitted early in 1951 and terminated as a member at the end of 1954. The United Seamen's Service was admitted in the spring of 1952. United Community Defense Services was dropped on December 31, 1955.[43] The USO was the main focus of the fund's operations.

With a half century's experience and experimentation behind her, the United States could quickly organize and quickly staff a wartime fund-raising effort. Two experienced lay leaders from the community chest movement alternated as president. E. A. Roberts, Philadelphia insurance executive and a former president of the community chests, was the first president. He was succeeded by Michael T. Kelleher, Boston broker and former campaign chairman of the Greater Boston Fund. To provide prestige for the fund-raising appeals to the nation, General James H. Doolittle and then General Omar Bradley, both popular World War II heroes, served terms as national campaign chairman. The work of organizing the fund and raising the money fell to the professionals of the Community Chests and Councils. In fact, the United Defense Fund was something of an unofficial subsidiary of the Three Cs. Ralph Blanchard, executive director of the Three Cs, served as volunteer executive director of the United Defense Fund for several months before turning the task over to his assistant, Bent Taylor. Taylor served as the UDF's executive director from its inception until July 1, 1954, when he resumed his Three Cs hat. The public relations and promotional program was directed by Henry Weber, public relations director of the Three Cs. The chest leaders were in full command of the United Defense Fund from start to finish, though the National Welfare Assembly served as the planning arm.

The United Defense Fund, directed by "united way" proponents, expected to raise its money through united community fund drives. It associated itself and its appeal with such community campaigns wherever possible. Most of the money was raised through chest campaigns. Wherever such inclusion could not be achieved, the Fund, in cooperation with local leaders, organized and conducted an independent campaign. At first "the United Defense Fund did not generally approve raising money through benefits, radio programs, street collections, tag days, canisters or other devices which might defeat plans to ask each contributor to give according to his means. Nor did it regard favorably money-raising efforts within national federations of clubs, fraternal orders, labor unions or other groups that cut across community lines and thus reduce the chance for successful campaign efforts locally." [44] In line with this approach, the basic public relations policy did not initially call for a separate institutional identity for the UDF. Instead the emphasis was put on the easily identified USO symbol.

This beginning policy was modified when it proved unsuccessful. In 1952 a Study Committee was set up by UDF's board to re-evaluate and overhaul the United Defense Fund's operations. This committee recommended "a full-scale publicity program of publicity and education in support of efforts to gain inclusion in local and state funds." By the middle of 1952 the UDF's public relations department "was thinking in terms of national publicity and promotion—syndicate, magazines, radio, television and all other national media." In 1954 the UDF employed its own public relations director, Vilas J. Boyle, and he further intensified the effort to promote the United Defense Fund nationally. On the whole, the Fund's promotional efforts were similar to the nation's war efforts, something less than total when compared to the World War II military and fund-raising drives. Yet throughout the Fund's lifetime the chest professionals recognized that "Fund-raising is basically a public relations operation. Be it a single organization or a federation, it is supported in direct ratio to the impact it, itself, makes on the public: (1) skillful interpretation of its program; (2) degree of emotional response it elicits; and (3) breadth and depth of good will it creates for itself." [45] The union of fund raising and public relations was now fully recognized.

The United College Appeal

In the postwar years of 1919 and 1920, Lyman Pierce had promoted the federated private college fund-raising appeal when he led eight Wisconsin colleges in a joint effort to raise a $5 million endowment to be shared proportionately. The goal was missed by a wide margin. Pierce was ahead of his time in this instance. The federation of private colleges for fund-raising purposes developed on a broad scale in the post-World War II period. In 1919 Pierce exhorted Wisconsin citizens: "The life of many a small college is hanging by a tenuous financial thread." It was ever thus, and probably always will be.

The nation's first successful united fund raising for colleges was carried out by its impecunious Negro colleges. The idea originated with Dr. F. D. Patterson, president of Tuskegee Institute, in 1943. Private colleges, always financially pressed, had been especially hard hit by the rising costs and declining enrollments brought on by the war. Dr. Patterson saw the situation as particularly grave for the Negro colleges. He estimated that private Negro colleges were then educating nearly half the Negroes who received college training. He proposed his plan in a signed article in the Pittsburgh *Courier*, a Negro paper, January 30, 1943, under the headline: "SOUTHERN VIEWPOINT: Would It Not Be Wise for Some Negro Schools to Make a Joint Appeal for Funds?" President Patterson proposed that these colleges "pool the small monies which they are spending for campaigns and publicity and that they make a unified appeal to the national conscience." The source of his plan was obvious: "Negro colleges may well take a cue from the general program of organization which seems to involve most charitable efforts today. Various and sundry drives are being unified with a reduction in overhead for publicity and in behalf of a more purposeful and pointed approach to the giving public." [46]

Interest generated by Dr. Patterson's article resulted in a series of meetings of college presidents, foundation directors, and other educational leaders. Out of much correspondence and many conferences came what today is proudly known as "America's First Educational Community Chest." The united fund was organized in the fall of 1943 but not chartered until April, 1944. Twenty-seven colleges and universities banded together for this first public fund appeal: Tuskegee Institute, Hampton Institute, Fisk University, Howard University, Atlanta University, Bennett College, Bethune-Cookman College, Clark College, Dillard University, Gammon Theological Seminary, Knoxville College, Lane College, LeMoyne College, Lincoln University, Livingstone College, Morehouse College, Morris Brown College, Philander Smith College, Samuel Houston College, Shaw University, Spellman College, Texas College, Tillotson College, Tougaloo College, Virginia Union University, Wiley College, and the Atlanta University School of Social Work. From 1944, the year of the first drive, until 1962 inclusive, the United Negro College Fund raised $46,634,501.78 in nineteen annual campaigns, several special capital fund drives, and from legacies. [47]

The 1944 campaign was for funds to meet the current expenses of those institutions and brought $765,563 from 11,276 contributors. The goal had been set at $1.5 million. Leaders of this campaign were Walter Hoving, then serving as chairman of the USO, chairman of the UNCF campaign committee; Winthrop W. Aldrich, national treasurer; John D. Rockefeller, Jr., chairman of the national campaign advisory committee; William E. S. Griswold, Jr.; and Augustine A. Austin, co-chairman of the New York City Committee.

Hoving said the drive was "the first cooperative nationwide effort between whites and Negroes to establish an academic community chest for the benefit of the Negroes." [48] It may be presumed that Mr. Hoving and his associates of the National War Fund campaign were glad to assist in the consolidation of the many appeals for Negro colleges, to lessen the strident clamor for funds characteristic of wartime. Certainly the national fund-raising ideas and resources brought from the USO group to the Negro fund was highly beneficial. At the center of this pioneering fund-raising effort was its originator, the energetic and determined President Patterson, the Fund's first president. The results of the nineteen annual fund-raising appeals promoted by the United Negro College Fund are shown in Table 21.

All private liberal arts colleges encountered tough financial sledding after the end of World War II, as enrollments of G.I.'s soared, and research requirements increased tenfold. An oft-repeated estimate stated that one-half of all such colleges were running "in the red" every year,[49] and this was strongly supported in 1954 by a survey of colleges and universities in which 753 responses indicated that half of all colleges were running on a deficit.[50] For years many educators had been talking hopefully about federal aid as the panacea for financially sick colleges, for "endowments . . . [gave] lower returns, and ferocious personal income taxes cut down the ability of alumni to make special gifts." [51]

In 1948, however, the president of a private liberal arts college in Indiana suggested an alternative plan, and this idea has developed into the Independent College Funds of America, Inc. One key to the success of the idea is that groups of private colleges join in state or regional organizations and approach corporations with a program akin to community chest drives: one annual donation to be distributed proportionately among a number of colleges. The innovator was Frank H. Sparks, at the time president of Wabash Col-

TABLE 21. UNITED NEGRO COLLEGE FUND ANNUAL CAMPAIGNS, 1944–1962

Year	Amounts raised	Cumulative	Contributions *
1944	$ 765,563	$ 765,563	11,276
1945	1,075,848	1,841,411	22,370
1946	930,012	2,771,423	22,133
1947	1,032,571	3,803,994	26,515
1948	1,072,296	4,876,290	30,020
1949	1,159,065	6,035,355	34,647
1950	1,210,141	7,245,496	34,362
1951	1,310,431	8,555,927	37,458
1952	1,374,475	9,930,402	37,054
1953	1,441,221	11,371,623	46,139
1954	1,477,204	12,848,827	43,575
1955	1,631,292	14,480,119	39,918
1956	1,668,317	16,148,436	38,156
1957	1,774,619	17,923,055	42,659
1958	1,843,033	19,766,088	42,132
1959	1,947,827	21,713,915	48,195
1960	2,035,020	23,748,935	48,418
1961	2,195,821	25,944,756	50,575
1962	2,300,003	28,244,759	53,075

* This refers to the *number of receipts* issued by national headquarters. One receipt, in the case of a gift from a group, may well represent fifty or one hundred donors, depending on the size of the group. This column therefore *does not mean number of donors*. This would be much larger.

lege. The prime promoters of the idea have been college fund raisers and corporate executives, mostly public relations personnel. The influential role of the corporation in post-World War II philanthropy is easily discernible in the broad spread of appeals to include industry made by the independent college fund in the 1950's, in contrast to the 1920's when corporations were little involved in philanthropy, and the idea died at its inception.

Sparks epitomizes the American success legend of the self-made man. This ingenious Hoosier was born in Grant County, Indiana, in 1891, to parents of modest circumstances. He went to work as a youth and by 1929 had risen to the presidency of Noblitt-Sparks (now Arvin Industries), an auto accessory firm which that year did a gross business of $64 million. Now a wealthy man, Sparks decided, at the age of thirty-eight, to return to college for the education his lack of money had denied him when he was young. He enrolled in Butler University on a part-time basis, earned his bachelor's degree by 1935, and made up his mind to become a college president. He quit the business world and went to the University of Southern California for graduate work, receiving the master's degree in 1937 and the Ph.D. in 1941 when he was fifty years old. He was appointed president of Wabash College, but within two years after America's entry into World War II, he was appointed head of the Bureau of Manpower Mobilization in Washington. In this wartime agency Sparks developed a passionate distrust of bureaucratic red tape and deep-seated fears of Big Government. After the war he returned to Wabash College and within four years was leading a group of Indiana college presidents who feared federal aid to education would be accompanied by controls.[52]

Shortly after the war's end Sparks set up the College-Industry program at Wabash, by which a selected group of industries offered summer employment and financial assistance to undergraduates who planned to enter business. In 1948, with the College-Industry program working well, Sparks suggested to other presidents of independent Indiana colleges that industry in Indiana could pay as much as $250,000 a year toward current operating expenses for their colleges. Some of the presidents shied away from this idea at first. President Thomas J. Jones of Earlham College said: "If we follow Doctor Sparks' idea, every newspaper in the state will be saying that we sold out to big business." [53] The other presidents at the meeting apparently took little stock in Sparks' idea of a united college fund appeal directed to Indiana's corporations, but Jones soon became a convert.

Sparks called Jones into a meeting with B. F. Hamilton, president of the Hamilton Cosco Manufacturing Co. and then urged Hamilton to give $1,000 to Earlham College. Hamilton is reported to have replied: "If I do, it will be the thousand that I usually give to you [Sparks]." But Sparks proceeded to convince Hamilton that a corporate rather than a personal gift should be given to support nontechnical liberal arts colleges. Sparks persuasively argued that if federal aid were to be made available to help the small colleges out of their financial plight, this would increase the corporation tax bill several fold, "due to bureaucratic red tape." [54] Later Sparks and Jones tackled the giant Standard Oil Co. of Indiana, which agreed to contribute if state associations were organized in thirteen other states where Standard had marketing areas. This was done, and the oil company gave an initial $150,000 in the spring of 1953. Since then the total given by Indiana Standard had grown to $1,325,000 by 1960, given to fourteen of these state groups of private colleges.[55] The growth of Sparks' united fund idea was slow at first, with the other colleges hesitant to join forces in this share and share alike solicitation. In 1949 only the presidents of Hanover and DePauw colleges joined Wabash and Earlham in a plea to Indiana industry to give to them. A total of $63,000 was raised for the current expenses of those four colleges from about a hundred gifts. Four more Indiana colleges joined the movement in 1950, but no more money was raised than in 1949. It seemed possible that the united college fund movement in Indiana might die.

One block in the path of the movement was caused by state laws controlling the activities of corporations. These laws cast doubts on a corporation's right to give corporate funds—the property of the stockholders—to community and college causes unless it could be shown that such donations would be of immediate benefit to the donor. Historically, dating from the fund-raising days of World War I, there had been a shadow of doubt of the legality of corporate gifts to charitable causes.[56] This problem was eased by the 1953 decisions of state courts in New Jersey which upheld the legality of an unrestricted corporate gift to Princeton University.[57]

Beardsley Ruml's incessant campaign to get corporations to give to the limit of their 5 per cent tax deductible provision also greatly aided the growth of these united college funds.[58] Meanwhile, Sparks' initial appeal—stressing the hobgoblin of higher taxes if corporations did not support colleges, while lauding the independent colleges as an important part of the American Way—had growing success.

This success brought imitators in other states. Ohio was quick to follow suit. Although Indiana gets credit for originating the idea, Ohio was the first state to start a united fund appeal on an incorporated, organized basis. The Ohio Foundation of Independent Colleges conducted the first organized corporate solicitation program in that state on November 13, 1951, with nineteen colleges participating. Ten years later the Ohio united fund had twenty-nine colleges participating in the campaign for corporate gifts, sharing the proceeds on a ratio based on enrollment. The Ohio effort has been directed by Harold K. Schellenger, former Ohio State University publicist, who was hired as full-time director in 1951. By

1960 there were forty united college funds operating on a state or regional basis.[59]

The idea had grown to multimillion-dollar dimensions within a decade. In bold contrast to the $63,000 raised in 1949 by President Frank Sparks in his first "college community chest" campaign, in 1959 these state and regional college chests raised $8,782,901 from 8,639 donors. In this decade a total of $40,597,176 had been raised from some 35,394 donors.[60] By 1959 the Council for Financial Aid to Education reported that voluntary support for all colleges and universities was increasing at the rate of $400 million a year.[61]

Another strong appeal to the corporation was the manner in which the united fund approach simplified the corporation's task in deciding which colleges to aid and which ones to turn down, always a delicate matter. By this time all colleges, private and public, were beating on the doors of corporations for a share in the corporate largess. The corporation's dilemma in handling the growing number of pleas from educators was expressed in 1950 by Claude L. Alexander, executive secretary of the Contribution and Membership Committee of the Standard Oil Company of New Jersey. Now retired, he was something of a pioneer, the first corporate executive to be assigned to such a task on a full-time basis. Alexander wrote: "Many Corporations have discovered that it is frequently harder to give money wisely than it is to make it. . . . Some of them have stated that too much time is spent in determining what and to whom contributions should be made, rather than devoting the time to making money." [62]

What he does not state in plain language is the hard fact that corporate giving is done largely for public relations reasons under the tax-deductible provisions of U.S. revenue laws. Given this purpose of corporate giving, one can imagine the fear of offending those who ask but do not receive. The college community chest offers a convenient method to the corporation in this dilemma. Little wonder that corporate public relations officers have been active in organizing and promoting these united college funds. For example, the Wisconsin Association of Independent Colleges had its genesis in the organizing efforts of the public relations counsel of the Wisconsin Manufacturers' Association. Thus we see old problems and old patterns of fund raising and philanthropy garbed in new dress. Only this time the role of the businessman is much more in evidence.

The Corporation Takes a Hand

Nowadays it is commonplace for the business executive to declare, in a speech written for him by his public relations aide: "Corporations are part of the community in which they operate, and owe to the community a duty equal to that of any individual who gains his livelihood there." Not too many years ago this would have been a startling and disputed doctrine, and there are still some corporate executives who hold that the sole purpose of a business is to make and sell goods or services to earn a profit! The sophisticated professional corporate manager says derisively that these men belong to the "old school." Philanthropy is but one area of American life being influenced by the expanding social role of the modern giant corporation.

The legal concepts governing corporate giving have changed until today the corporation can make gifts out of the stockholders' earnings for most general purposes and the stockholder who may prefer to have his earnings go to other philanthropies, or to none at all, is virtually powerless to object.

As of 1962, forty-four states had laws specifically authorizing corporate philanthropy. The federal government, since 1935, has encouraged corporate gifts through its generous deduction provisions in the tax laws. Court decisions have steadily broadened the permissible scope of corporate giving. Likewise, the motives behind corporate giving have moved far from the local businessman's charity to the poor and ill. Most corporate giving today is motivated by the desire to build that loosely defined asset "good will" and thus maintain an environment favorable to the profit-making enterprise.

Many corporations have made control of contributions a top management function, so important has this become. Contributions committees with full-time staffs are used more and more to guide the corporation's donations. Many firms have adopted carefully worked-out policies and procedures to administer the corporate philanthropy.[63] Many have set up their own charitable foundations. The philanthropic foundation was a rarity at the turn of the century; in 1962 there were some 15,000 foundations giving grants in the United States, for the most part either family or general welfare foundations. Today nearly half of all corporations with 1,000 or more employees have operating foundations or trusts to handle their phi-

lanthropies. It is estimated by W. H. Turner, executive director of
the United States Steel Foundation, that company-sponsored foundations approximate 1,500 with assets of "upward of $1 billion." [64]

To summarize, from the inception of the YMCA's Ward-Pierce
whirlwind campaign, and the Cleveland federated one-drive-a-year
idea, the American businessman has played an influential role in the
giving and raising of funds for America's philanthropy. Until World
War I most businessmen gave to local charities, but their business
firms did not. As recounted earlier, corporate giving had its feeble
and uncertain beginnings in the patriotic fervor of World War I.
In the 1920's and early 1930's corporate giving went mainly to community chest and depression causes. Passage of the 1935 Revenue
Act which permitted—at the insistence of community chest leaders
—corporations to give not more than 5 per cent of their earnings
as contributions to philanthropy spurred corporate giving. From
1936 through 1939, depression years, corporate giving proceeded
along the $30 million a year plateau, most of this money going to
community chests. World War II brought years of high income and
high taxes and wartime pressures to give, causing corporate giving
to climb sharply.

In the postwar years, as the corporation's concern for its public
image as a "good citizen" has grown, corporate philanthropy has
skyrocketed accordingly. This is readily seen in Table 22, compiled
by the American Association of Fund-Raising Counsel.[65]

By 1961 American corporations were giving more than a half
billion dollars annually to philanthropic appeals; a sum relatively
small in terms of the more than $10 billion Americans are giving in
response to the fund raiser's exhortations, but large in the eyes of
the recipient, and thus influential in its impact. Today's fund raising
gets much of its volunteer manpower from the public relations-
minded corporations. Today's corporate executive often plays a
strong, if not the dominant, role in united fund and college fund
drives.

Most corporations eschew giving to religious causes because of
the tender and often unreasoning emotions that surround a person's religious views. For example, a survey made of corporate giving practices in Cleveland found that less than 17 per cent of the
corporations would consider requests from churches or other denominational agencies.[66] A survey of corporate officials by the
Opinion Research Corp. in 1948 found that of those interviewed

TABLE 22. THE RECORD OF CORPORATE GIVING AS SHOWN IN
U.S. TAX RETURNS 1948–1961

Year	Net Income Before Deductions for Contributions (000)	Allowable Deductions for Contributions (000)	Contributions Deducted (000)	% of Allowed Contributions Deducted
1945	$21,405,636	$1,070,281	$265,679	1.24
1948	34,664,361	1,733,218	239,337	0.69
1949	28,417,403	1,420,870	222,566	0.78
1950	42,865,670	2,143,283	252,366	0.59
1951	43,888,629	2,194,431	343,039	0.78
1952	38,854,758	1,942,737	398,579	1.03
1953	39,979,204	1,998,960	494,517	1.24
1954	36,642,199	1,832,109	313,764	0.86
1955	47,949,316	2,397,465	414,759	0.87
1956	46,884,912	2,344,245	417,996	0.89
1957	45,073,370	2,253,666	418,917	0.92
1958	38,522,689	1,926,134	395,362	1.02
1959	47,630,018	2,381,500	481,541	1.01
1960	43,505,174	2,175,258	482,151	1.1
1961	45,893,900	2,294,695	511,872	1.11

a majority "turn thumbs down on company contributions to religious causes because 'Religion is a personal matter and better left
to individuals not companies.'" [67] The national health drives with
emotional "heart appeal" get little corporate support. For causes
that cannot fashion a moving "heart" appeal, the corporate giver is
virtually essential in today's fund raising.

In 1950 the Russell Sage Foundation conducted a survey to determine the pattern of corporate giving, to confirm the distribution
of the corporate gift dollar. The survey covered 326 corporations.[68]
The response indicated that a typical company in 1950 was allocating
44 cents of its philanthropic dollar to welfare agencies, with 36
cents going to the local united fund or community chest. Another
26 cents, with a few extra mills, went to health agencies, including
hospitals, national foundations, and the like. Some 16½ cents went
to education, and of this amount 6 cents was earmarked to support
research. Religious agencies received 4 cents and institutions to promote "understanding of our free enterprise economy" received 5

cents. The other 4 cents went to unspecified causes. The rising demands of colleges upon corporations for support, discussed earlier, had effected a change in the allocation of the corporate gift dollar. According to a study made in 1959 by John H. Watson III, for the National Industrial Conference Board, some 45 per cent of all corporate giving was going to health and welfare causes, 39 per cent to education, and the remaining 16 per cent scattered to civic, cultural, and "free enterprise" causes.

As already indicated in Chapter Eight, the legal right of corporations to give to philanthropic causes was long clouded in doubt. Historically, both in Great Britain and in the United States, the test of direct benefit applied to the legality of corporate contributions to charitable causes. This was the test the courts applied in the Old Mission Portland Cement case. The courts' interpretation of what constitutes direct benefits has steadily broadened through the years. Nagging legal doubts apparently were cleared away in the A. P. Smith case. In what well may have been a deliberate act to invoke a court test of the corporation's right to give, the A. P. Smith Co.— a New Jersey manufacturer of machinery and equipment for water and gas industries—made a gift of $1,500 to Princeton University as a contribution toward the University's general maintenance. The gift was voted by the board on July 24, 1951. The right of the corporation to make this gift was quickly challenged in the New Jersey courts by stockholders.

The corporation then sought a declaratory judgment in the Chancery Division of the Superior Court of New Jersey asking that its action be upheld. The issue, as defined by the court, was "whether a New Jersey corporation, organized in 1896 to engage in industry for the purposes of profit, may lawfully in 1951 donate from its funds for the general maintenance of an educational institution like Princeton University." The Smith firm relied for justification on two New Jersey laws, one passed in 1930 that permitted corporations to participate in the creation and maintenance of community funds "or of charitable, philanthropic, or benevolent instrumentalities conducive to the public welfare" and one enacted in 1950 which expanded that statute to embrace "educational or scientific purposes."

The court upheld the act of the Smith company and thus "recognized that corporation philanthropy had become one of the indispensable means of guarding the external conditions of growth." Richard T. Eells, an authority on corporate philanthropy, says the court's decision "emphatically rejects the notion that immediate and direct benefit to the share owners alone can be the measuring rod of corporate powers. . . . The justification for corporation philanthropy, in short, is not what it achieves for the community alone, but rather what it does to protect the wider corporate environment that sustains the share owners' profitable investment." [69] In October, 1953, the Supreme Court of the United States declined to hear an appeal because of lack of a substantial federal issue. Thus the Smith case stands as a legal landmark in philanthropy.

In its 1953 decision the New Jersey Supreme Court opened the door wide: "Modern conditions require that corporations acknowledge and discharge social as well as private responsibilities as members of the communities within which they operate. . . . Indeed, the matter may be viewed strictly in terms of actual survival of the corporation in a free enterprise system." [70]

This was a great day for fund raisers. In 1952 Alex J. Peet told his colleagues at John Price Jones that a "growing part of our business is making corporate appeals. . . . We expect 40 per cent [of campaign goal] today on many campaigns if they are to succeed." Peet reported that in a campaign for Harding College in Searcy, Ark., 90 per cent of the funds came from corporations. [71] Peet's example of Harding College is an atypical one but it does reveal some of the motivations and dangers of tax-deductible corporate giving. Harding, generously supported by corporations, serves as a propaganda machine for the ultraconservative causes. In a study of the nation's "far right," two reputable newsmen concluded:

> Harding's National Education Program is and has been for many years one of the most aggressive organizations for ultraconservatism in the nation. Every year, a hundred thousand newspaper columns, newsletters, speech reprints, tapes, pamphlets, leaflets, flannelboard presentations, and anti-Communist study guides pour out of Harding's offices for use by newspapers, radio and television stations, businesses, schools, civic groups, and itinerant anti-Communist seminars. The Program consists of unending warnings of periods to the free-enterprise system to be found in communism, socialism, liberalism. [72]

Harding, a small struggling college in the foothills of the Ozarks until George Benson became its president, had an endowment of

$6 million by the early sixties—almost all of it given by industrial donors. General Motors' long-time president, Alfred P. Sloan, gave Harding $300,000 in 1949 to help it launch its motion-picture service, a major component in the Harding propaganda machine. In 1954 the National Education Program was made a separate corporate entity to clear the way for Harding's accreditation. Janson and Eisman believe that "The admiration of businessmen for the Harding program is based in large measure on economic self-interest." Certainly Harding is a prolific producer of "free enterprise" propaganda. Alan F. Westin, associate professor of public law and government at Columbia University, estimates that the business community contributed nearly $10 million to the Radical Right in 1961.[73]

As of 1962 there was little question about the power of the corporation to support philanthropy under the permissive statutes enacted by forty-four states. These favorable court decisions coincided with the big postwar boom in corporation public relations programs.

Most corporations defend their philanthropy on the broad, general grounds of good corporate citizenship. Realistically translated, this means corporate philanthropy is part and parcel of intensified efforts to build a favorable "corporate image." A secondary motive with some, the primary motive with a few, is the frantic fear of "creeping socialism" that gripped American business leaders in the postwar years. This fear became most pronounced after President Harry Truman's election in 1948 when he upset the Republicans' "sure winner," Thomas E. Dewey. The years 1945–1964 witnessed much heated talk on the part of businessmen about the virtues of "free enterprise," much concern for the "corporate image," and the consequent stepping up of corporation public relations and philanthropic programs. Corporation giving to all causes in 1963, including grants of company-sponsored foundations, is estimated to have totaled $536 million.

The basic "good citizenship" theme was sounded early in the 1950's by one of the evangels of corporate giving, Frank W. Abrams, then head of the Standard Oil Co. of New Jersey: "The public today expects corporations to be good and constructive citizens. The people who own and manage corporations wish to meet and fulfill this public expectation. Increasing numbers of business managers, I believe, feel that corporations should not take substantial benefits from their membership in the economic community while avoiding the normally accepted obligations of citizenship in the social community." [74] Most corporations today support fund-raising campaigns with both money and manpower. A 1958 survey by the Chicago chapter of the Public Relations Society concluded that "an increasing recognition among companies that the choice is not *whether* to contribute, but rather *how* to contribute." The public, apparently, overwhelmingly approves this corporate course. The Opinion Research Corporation found in its 1948 public opinion study: "Community leaders as well as the general public overwhelmingly expect companies to support charitable causes. The ORC intensively examined the views of a national cross-section of teachers, clergymen, lawyers, and editors and found that 78 per cent of these influentials said companies should contribute to charitable causes, only 7 per cent said no. Eighty per cent of the general public said companies should give money to charitable causes." [75]

The public relations motivation behind corporate giving can be heard in the formal and informal talk of businessmen, and seen in the literature of public relations and in opinion surveys. For example, officials of corporations participating in the 1948 ORC study, when asked what criteria they employed to evaluate charitable requests, responded that "the public's reaction weighs heavily in their minds, as does how the charity's efforts directly or indirectly affect the company's well-being." The main criteria in the minds of most of those interviewed was "What will be the public reaction if we give or do not give?" Corporate giving is often administered in the firm's public relations department and the public relations director, at the least, has a large voice in determining the distribution of the corporate gifts.

A 1961 conference on philanthropy concluded: "Although the earlier trend of placing corporate giving under the public relations department is undergoing some change, the fact that the directors and top management of corporations have public relations in mind in making corporate gifts will not be changed in the near future." Many corporate executives undoubtedly agree with F. Emerson Andrews that "the favorable public opinion created by knowledge of the gift may be the most important benefit" to the corporation. Unlike the almsgivers of old, "corporations seldom hide their philanthropic light under a bushel, and it is no accident that their contributions committees usually include the director of public relations."

Yet, oddly enough, few corporations make this an item in their annual reports to stockholders.

Writing in 1954, one corporate public relations official described corporate giving as "a very sensitive tool" of public relations. He summed up his company's position thus: ". . . it believes that donations represent an important implement of public relations and to hold successfully that role, payments must be fairly established. From the standpoint of the stockholder, there must be sound reasons for making donations, either to engender good will or sustain public respect for the Company." [76] Eells seriously questions this broad-purpose giving of corporate gifts to promote the corporation's public image or similarly vague purposes. "Corporate giving will run into trouble . . . if it is used to discharge the undefined 'social responsibilities' of the businessman. Least of all can a policy of corporate support be based on narrow expediency, for the purposes of publicity or an easy way to appease all claimants." [77]

The "free enterprise" motivation is freely voiced by the corporate official and frequently exploited by the fund raiser from the private college or university. Irving S. Olds, former chairman of U.S. Steel and another evangel of corporate giving in that period, once said: "Capitalism and free enterprise owe their survival to our private independent colleges. Just as private industry has given us material weapons with which to repel the armies of foreign aggressors, so we have looked to our privately endowed education for the intellectual weapons to resist invasion by totalitarian ideologies."

The private colleges propound this same theme to get the corporations to give. A fund-raising brochure distributed by Gustavus Adolphus College in this period, read in part: "The private colleges of America are the bulwark of our free economy. If they are allowed to disintegrate for the lack of public support, government will have to assume the responsibility of educating all our youth. Therein lies grave danger of our way of life." A brochure used by the Associated Colleges of Illinois in the mid-1950's, held out the threat of higher taxes if state schools had to take care of a larger proportion of the students in Illinois, and then added: "Yes! Statistical investigations of the collegiate origins of leading American men . . . have repeatedly proved that the small liberal arts colleges of this country are its most productive source of leaders and thinkers, upon whom rests responsibility for the progress and safety of

America." [78] This latter assertion cannot be supported by evidence.

The president of Ripon College, Dr. Frederick O. Pinkham, unabashedly asserted in a Ripon fund-raising appeal: "There is one distinguishing mark of the small liberal arts college—independence. The typical small college stands as one of the few institutions left in America which is not under the direct control of labor unionism or the federal government or other centralized authority. . . . The small independent colleges stand virtually alone as bulwarks of independence in its true meaning. They operate under the direction of self-perpetuating boards of trustees and remain free of taxation and tax support." This statement is often mocked by the small college president going, hat in hand, to the corporate giver who sometimes attaches strings to his gift, either stated or subtly implied.

What of the stockholder who has had the choice of where he gives his philanthropic dollars taken away from him to some extent? A survey made in 513 Chicago corporations found that the general attitude of stockholders on this matter was passive. "They feel that if they don't like what the management does, they can sell out." [79]

Many of the corporate profit dollars that are deducted as philanthropic gifts on the tax returns go to the proliferating number of foundations set up to promote and preserve what their sponsors are fond of calling "the American way of life." This stretches the definition of philanthropy to its outermost limits. These organizations to indoctrinate American citizens in the glories of free enterprise were rampant in the 1950's, the era of McCarthyism and the Cold War. Typical are the American Library of Information, the Committee for Constitutional Government, the Foundation for Economic Education, and the Four Freedoms Foundation. The Cleveland survey of corporate giving reported:

> A large number of national organizations have appeared in recent years, advocating, publicizing and otherwise fostering the principles of American democracy, sound economic methods, free enterprise, and individual initiative, as opposed to Communism and other subversive influences. The "American Way" agencies, as a class, have secured encouragement and support from business and industrial sources. Many corporations state they contribute to one or more, but various questions are raised regarding the growing multiplicity of such agencies, the degree of their effectiveness, and the problem of how to select worthy organizations for corporate gifts. [80]

About half the corporations responding to the Cleveland survey said their firms considered "American Way" appeals but some expressed strong doubts about this philanthropy, to use the word loosely. Typical, perhaps, is the company which said: "Our corporation has made such gifts, but is skeptical as to validity of some programs, even when sponsorship is impressive." [81]

But it is to the community chest and the college that most corporate tax-deductible gift dollars go today. About a third of corporate giving is to the community chest-united fund type of philanthropy. The typical united fund campaign is organized about corporate leadership and about two-thirds of the money comes from the corporations and their employees. Many corporate employees give through a payroll deduction plan which in the eyes of many employees amounts to a compulsory tax. Corporate gifts to federated community campaigns in 1959 totaled $152 million, an increase of 96 per cent over the $77,559,000 donated in the 1950 campaigns, according to the United Community Funds and Councils of America. In 1959 the corporate giving represented 35.7 per cent of chest collections. For the corporations these funds represented 29.2 per cent of all giving that year.[82]

However, the main interest of the corporate giver—as manifested by the flow of corporate gift dollars and the activity of the corporate public relations officer—seems to be shifting to higher education. Corporate executives repeatedly and vehemently voice the desire to maintain a pluralistic society in their exhortations to follow corporate leaders to join in support of higher education. The corporation has a strong self-interest in providing a flow of well-trained, highly educated employees to meet its operating needs.

Consequently, industry's contribution to American higher education rose dramatically in the 1950–1960 decade. In 1962, according to the Council for Financial Aid to Education, business concerns gave some $200 million to higher education for specific operating and capital purposes. Major private universities received more than a third of this amount. Publicly supported state universities received 25 per cent, mostly in research grants. Voluntary support increased each year in this decade and the proportion given to public universities increased as well. In 1956–57 business concerns gave slightly more than half of the 1960–61 total—$77 million—to higher education. Private universities received 42.75 per cent of this sum, public universities slightly over 13 per cent. F. Emerson Andrews,

in 1959, said: "Industry is aiding higher education at the rate of
$130–140 million annually. This area of corporate support runs as
high as two-thirds of the company's contribution budget. Just a decade ago the average was about 10% and many budgets failed to include this item at all." [83] In this growing support of the colleges
the corporation is exerting an ever stronger influence on education
as well as on philanthropy.

The bulk of corporate giving to higher education goes to the private college. This is in accord with the corporate philanthropy rationale that it must support the nation's "free and voluntary" institutions against the encroachment of Big Government. Yet, under
growing pressure from America's state universities, many corporations now give to tax-supported colleges and universities. As of
1962 most corporations still did not. To meet the heavy demands
on state universities for research and public service, as well as instruction of the nation's exploding population, these institutions have
joined the fund-raising army—capital fund drives, alumni funds,
development offices, and all the other philanthropic paraphernalia.
In the late 1950's the Association of State Universities and Land
Grant Colleges and the Association of State Universities joined
forces to finance an organized public relations campaign to persuade
corporations to support state as well as private universities, a campaign that is meeting with success.

This, too, poses a public relations headache for the corporate giver.
A state university fund raiser writes a corporation: "I want to register a strong protest concerning the implications of a program for
the benefit of higher education which does not include young men
and women attending state-supported institutions generally. To be
sure, the basic operating expenses of our University are paid by
student fees, supplemented by legislative appropriations of tax funds.
There are, however, many areas of need at all state-supported institutions which cannot, for legal and practical reasons, be met in this
manner." A corporate official responds: "Our position is that corporations are contributing to public institutions through the tax
route in a significant way. Even though many private institutions
receive some support from public sources, by definition, they do
not receive nearly so much as public institutions. To me, it seems
to follow that this differential in support must be made up in part
by means of voluntary contributions."

Many corporations beg the question altogether, others vacillate.

Some have clearly defined philosophies and policies for corporate giving; many do not. In 1962 it was the consensus of those most knowledgeable that much corporate giving was for rather vague reasons and too seldom guided by clear-cut policies. Eells asserts: "Corporate giving, in general, is tied to tax expediency, and the tax laws are the command of the sovereign." He adds, "The charitable 'tax bargain' is entirely legitimate. But it is hard to see how a rational policy of corporate giving can let itself be dominated by tax benefits." [84] The trend is toward definite policies administered by full-time executives, based upon the company's responsibility to the community where its employees live, and to assist those organizations that benefit the corporation directly or indirectly. Even so, public relations motives and public relations officials continue to play the dominant role in corporate giving and in providing manpower for fund-raising campaigns. Here, too, we see the strong influence of public relations on a people's philanthropy.

NOTES

1. Arthur M. Schlesinger, "The True American Way of Life," St. Louis *Post-Dispatch*, Part Two, Dec. 13, 1953, p. 3.
2. *Giving USA, 1962*, p. 7.
3. *Voluntary Health and Welfare Agencies in the United States*, p. 9.
4. *Giving USA, 1962*, p. 10.
5. *Ibid.*, p. 8.
6. *Statistics of Income . . . 1960, Individual Income Tax Returns for 1960*, p. 11.
7. Interview with Robert Duncan, March 28, 1960.
8. Memo to former Jones associates dated Sept. 30, 1959.
9. Laurence O. Pratt, "You Talked Yourselves into It," *Harvard Alumni Bulletin*, March 19, 1960, p. 450.
10. Harold J. Seymour, "Big, Important, and Urgent," *Harvard Alumni Bulletin*, March 19, 1960, p. 475.
11. See President Emeritus Henry Wriston's *Academic Procession*, pp. 164–168.
12. Pratt, *op. cit.*, p. 452.
13. Seymour, *op. cit.*, p. 478.
14. *Ibid.*, p. 477.
15. In Gunn and Platt, *Voluntary Health Agencies*, p. 3.
16. Sanders, "Mutiny of the Bountiful," *Harper's*, Vol. 217 (December, 1958), p. 23.
17. Bloomgarden, *Before We Sleep*, pp. 98–99.
18. *Ibid.*, p. 100.
19. Frank G. Dickinson (ed.), *Philanthropy and Public Policy* (New York: NBEC, 1961), p. 96.
20. Robert Grant, Jr., "I've Got the Most Mysterious Disease," *Saturday Evening Post*, Vol. 226 (May 22, 1954), pp. 26–74.
21. *Facts on the Major Killing and Crippling Diseases in the United States*.
22. Wolcott D. Street, Memo for Staff Conference, June 17, 1954, "Building a National Campaign on Shaky Foundations," in *1954 John Price Jones Staff Conference Proceedings*, in the Jones firm's library.
23. *Voluntary Health and Welfare Agencies in the United States*, pp. 86–87.

24. *Annual Report 1954*, National Foundation for Infantile Paralysis, p. 42.

25. Wolcott Street, *op. cit.*

26. Sills, *The Volunteers*, pp. 270–71.

27. Peter Maas, "Where Does Your Charity Dollar Go?," *Look*, Vol. 24 (March 15, 1960), pp. 40 and 42.

28. Seeley, *et al.*, *Community Chest: A Case Study in Philanthropy* (Toronto: University of Toronto Press, 1957), p. 405.

29. Donald S. Connery, "Business and Charity; The Pittsburgh Skirmish," *Fortune*, Vol. LV (April, 1957), p. 144.

30. Position Paper presented by E. V. Graef, Executive Director, Pittsburgh Health and Research Services Foundation, dated Jan. 29, 1959.

31. "Chronological History of Fund Raising," in files of United Community Funds and Councils of America, Inc.

32. *Newsweek*, Vol. 34 (Nov. 21, 1949), pp. 25–26.

33. *Saturday Evening Post*, Vol. 222 (Oct. 1, 1949), p. 10.

34. Leavitt, *Common Sense About Fund Raising*, published by the author in 1949. O'Connor headed the Red Cross as well as the National Foundation from 1944 to 1949. A high Red Cross official confided to the author that Leavitt was recruited by O'Connor to write this attack on the emerging united fund idea.

35. Mrs. Eugene Meyer, "Judgment Day for the Private Welfare Agency," *Public Opinion Quarterly*, Vol. 9 (1945), pp. 338–345.

36. American Cancer Society, "United Funds and the American Cancer Society," a Confidential Background Report, Dec. 4, 1959. Multilithed and copyrighted by the ACS.

37. United Community Funds and Councils, *Go It Together*, April, 1958.

38. Sanders, *op. cit.*, p. 31.

39. H. L. Lurie, "Private Philanthropy and Federated Fund-Raising," *Social Service Review*, Vol. 29 (March, 1955), pp. 68–69.

40. United Community Funds and Councils of America, Inc., *Trends in Giving 1959* (July, 1959), p. 4.

41. Letter of April 16, 1957, to President Eisenhower submitting final UDF report.

42. *History United Defense Fund, Inc., November 1950–December 1955*, published by the fund in multilithed form, p. 1.

43. *Ibid.*, p. 7.

44. *Ibid.*, p. 18.

45. *Ibid.*, p. 21.

46. Pittsburgh *Courier*, Jan. 30, 1943, p. 7. For brief account of Fund's origins, see Guzman, *Negro Yearbook*, 1952, p. 249.

47. Figures on file, United Negro College Fund, Inc., headquarters 22 East 54th Street, New York City.

48. *New York Times*, May 4, 1944, p. 36.

49. "Liberal Arts Colleges Need Support if They Are to Avoid Federalization," editorial in *Saturday Evening Post*, Vol. 225 (Nov. 1, 1952), p. 12.

50. Council for Financial Aid to Education, Inc., "Institutional Needs for Higher Education and Corporation Practices in Aid," a pamphlet (New York, second printing, 1957), p. 6.

51. *Saturday Evening Post*, loc. cit.

52. This account of Sparks' life is based on the article by Joe Alex Morris, "Small Colleges Fight for Their Lives," *Saturday Evening Post*, Vol. 226 (May 15, 1954), p. 104.

53. *Ibid.*

54. *Ibid.*, p. 107.

55. Based on account, "Colleges Kick Off Drive for Business Donations," *New York Times*, Oct. 9, 1960, Sec. II, p. 1.

56. See Edward F. Potthoff, "Meeting Higher Costs for Higher Education," *College Public Relations Quarterly*, Vol. 5 (January, 1954), p. 17.

57. *A. P. Smith Manufacturing Co. v. Barlow et al.*, 98 *Atlantic Reporter*, 2d 581 (1953).

58. Morris, *op. cit.*, p. 108. Ruml's *The Five Per Cent*, co-authored with Theodore Geiger, published by the National Planning Association, 1951, had wide influence in college fund-raising and corporate management circles.

59. Letter Feb. 10, 1960, from Mr. Schellenger.

60. Treasurer's Report, *Highlights 1959 Solicitations*, Independent College Funds of America, Inc.

61. Council for Financial Aid to Education, Inc., *Where's the Money Coming From?*, a pamphlet, February, 1959, p. 2.

62. "Problems and Practices of Corporate Giving," *Public Relations Journal*, Vol. 6 (December, 1950), p. 5.

63. National Industrial Conference Board, *Company Contributions III. Policies and Procedures*, Studies in Business Policy, No. 89, NICB, 1958.

64. *Giving USA*, 1962, p. 45. Also see: National Industrial Conference Board Report, *Company-Sponsored Foundations*, Studies in Business Policy, No. 73, the NICB, 1955.

65. Data for years 1945–1959 compiled from tables in *Giving, USA*, 1955, 1959, and 1962 eds. Figures for 1960 and 1961 taken from *Statistics of Income . . . 1960–61, Corporation Income Tax Returns*. U.S. Treasury Department, Internal Revenue Service, 1963.

66. *Corporate Giving in Greater Cleveland*, A Survey by the Harvard Business School Club of Cleveland, Inc., December, 1953, p. 18.

67. Opinion Research Corp., *The Public Opinion Index for Industry*, "Meeting the Problem of Charitable Contributions."

68. Andrews, *Corporation Giving*, p. 71.

69. Eells, *Corporation Giving in a Free Society* (New York: Harper, 1956), pp. 25 and 29.

70. *A. P. Smith Manufacturing Co.* v. *Barlow et al.*, 98 *Atlantic Reporter*, 2d 581 (1953).

71. Alex J. Peet, "Corporate Giving," paper for Jones Staff Conference, June 20, 1952. In John Price Jones Papers.

72. Donald Janson and Bernard Eisman, *The Far Right* (New York: McGraw-Hill, 1963), p. 92.

73. Quoted in *ibid.*, p. 100.

74. In "Corporations and Education," *The Lamp*, Vol. 35 (March, 1953), p. 8.

75. Opinion Research Corp., *op. cit.*

76. W. J. Held, "Corporate Giving Sensitive Tool of PR," *Public Relations Journal*, Vol. 10 (November, 1954), p. 9.

77. Richard T. Eells, "The Need for a Positive Corporate Philanthropic Policy," in *The Changing Role of American Corporate Philanthropy*, p. 16.

78. Associated Colleges of Illinois Brochure, circa 1955, Box 16, Hanover Bank Philanthropy Collection in State Historical Society of Wisconsin.

79. Unpublished report, "Key Findings and Basic Statistics—The Study of the Chicago Company Contribution Policies and Practices," directed by Dr. Leo J. Shapiro for the Chicago Chapter, Public Relations Society of America. The data from the Chicago PRSA Study was used by Frank M. Andrews in his *A Study of Company Sponsored Foundations*, published by the Russell Sage Foundation in 1960.

80. *Corporate Giving in Greater Cleveland*, p. 18.

81. *Ibid.*

82. United Community Funds and Councils of America, Inc. "Corporate Support of United Community Campaigns," Bulletin No. 209, 1960.

83. *Management Record*, Vol. 21 (May, 1959), p. 3.

84. Eells, "The Need for a Positive Corporate Philanthropic Policy," *op. cit.*, p. 14.

Epilogue

America's "philanthropic streak"—as Arthur Schlesinger, Sr., terms it—grows in large measure out of this nation's heritage of frontier democracy, its national plenty, and its emphasis on equality as expressed in compassion for the underdog. The concern of every man to be his brother's keeper is a basic trait and "Through the ages, this response to suffering and need has been counted one of the highest attributes of human uniqueness." These and related factors merged in the United States to provide a fertile soil for the seeds of philanthropy.

The American fund raisers, amateur and professional alike, till this soil with the skill and efficiency of American business and the persuasive methods developed by the public relations and advertising professions. The fund raiser has brought American givers from the tin cup to the telethon in little more than a half century. He has both fostered and exploited America's willingness to support an ever-expanding philanthropy out of her abundance, and her highly perfected, uniquely American methods of fund raising have induced her citizens to give more and more money to more and more charitable causes—more than the people of any other nation. The ceiling on American giving is not yet in sight.

What motivates these millions of donors? Not many will share John Steinbeck's cynical view of American giving but most will admit that there is a grain of truth in what he says:

Perhaps the most overrated virtue in our list of shoddy virtues is that of giving. Giving builds up the ego of the giver, makes him superior and higher and larger than the receiver. Nearly always, giving is a selfish pleasure, and in many cases is a downright destructive and evil thing. One has only to remember some of the wolfish financiers who spend two-thirds of their lives clawing fortunes out the guts of society and the latter third pushing it back. It is not enough to suppose that their philanthropy is a kind of frightened restitution, or

526

that their natures change when they have enough. Such a nature never has enough and natures do not change that readily. I think that the impulse is the same in both cases. For giving can bring the same sense of superiority as getting does, and philanthropy may be another kind of spiritual avarice.[1]

In a more balanced view, Merle Curti suggests: "Perhaps in the magnitude of giving, and certainly in the patterns of philanthropy that have found expression here, American experience in philanthropy has both expressed American character and at the same time has helped to shape it."[2] The professional public relations and fund-raising experts are characteristic of our pragmatic society and at the same time help shape America's philanthropy by determining, to a large degree, the causes citizens support and the amounts they give. Certainly one reason for giving today is the social pressure mobilized by the skilled fund raiser.

Systematic solicitation of the general public, not just the rich, for money to support a proliferating number of charity, health, and welfare agencies began in the early 1900's. Such agencies, in growing numbers, were made necessary by the problems posed by swiftly accelerating industrialization and urbanization and were supported by America's increasing wealth. As the nation's expanding cities were crowded by immigrants from Europe and emigrants from the farms, a host of new and complex health and social problems arose. In Norton's view, "there came into the consciousness of American life a new emphasis upon social problems, accompanied by the rise of many social service organizations." As a new problem became apparent it was characteristically American to organize a body of volunteers to solve it. More than three-quarters of a century earlier, the perceptive Frenchman de Tocqueville had observed:

> In no country in the world has the principle of association been more successfully used, or applied to a greater multitude of objects, than in America. Besides the permanent associations, which are established by law . . . a vast number of others are formed and maintained by the agency of private individuals. The citizen of the United States is taught from infancy to rely upon his own exertions.[3]

Responding to a swiftly changing environment and the basic instincts of human nature, American philanthropy has gone through "rapid and radical change" in the twentieth century until, in the words of Seeley and his colleagues, "it is barely recognizable as the offspring of yesterday."

The American trait, seen long ago by de Tocqueville, is amply illustrated in the YMCA movement, which had its roots in England but had its fullest flowering in the United States. To meet the capital and operating needs of the Y, Charles Sumner Ward and Lyman Pierce developed the short-term fund drive that today is a fixed feature of Americans' civic lives. Arnaud Marts estimates that "the creation of the intensive campaign by Messrs. Ward and Pierce has brought into the treasuries and into the service of our educational, religious, character-building, health, and philanthropic agencies over 75 billions of dollars—*more* than the funds these agencies would have received if they had continued to use the fund-raising methods of the nineteenth century." [4] Even though Marts's figure may be inflated, the Ward-Pierce plan was a significant development. In raising ever-higher sums through the short-term, high-pressure campaign, Ward, Pierce, and their imitators utilized the developing power of the mass circulation newspaper, also a twentieth-century development.

As the number of fund-seeking organizations grew and as campaign pressures became more intense, demands for greater efficiency, greater economy, and less confusion mounted. This led, inevitably, to federated fund raising, still a central and controversial problem in American philanthropy. This idea, too, was born in England but found its successful application in the United States, after a few initial failures. The appealing notion of one federated fund was first effectively developed by the Jews of America, a people with a long and proud history of philanthropy. One of them, Martin Marks, brought the plan to the nation's community life. He was greatly aided and encouraged in his pioneering efforts by Cleveland's businessmen who were growing restive under the multiplying pressures to give. Businessmen have been, and still are, the driving force behind the nation's community chests and united funds. There are dangers in this fact, particularly in these days of national chain stores and branch factories. Business leaders too often concentrate their attention on the monetary side of the community, such as the united fund or hospital drive, to the neglect of its social problems.

By the eve of the United States entry into World War I, Bishop

William Lawrence had demonstrated that careful organization, intensive publicity, and systematic solicitation were the keys to raising money. The war itself was the catalyst that set off the nation's first great explosion of public giving. Nonmilitary needs, born of war, were met by welding together the YMCA campaign methods, the organizational efficiency and limitless optimism of Big Business, and the emerging public relations expertise exemplified by Ivy Lee. Community war chests and the nation's first united fund drive gave impetus to the federated principle of fund raising by demonstrating its efficacy. The war years strengthened the greatest fund raiser of modern times—the American National Red Cross, which served as an example to others.

The 1920's saw the principles of mass fund raising and the potentials of public giving extended and refined. The newly learned techniques of public promotion and fund raising were quickly put to work to meet the neglected capital needs of colleges, churches, hospitals, and libraries, as well as the new needs of a burgeoning number of social welfare agencies. The term and concept of philanthropy was replacing the narrower one of charity. This period of "permanent prosperity" saw the formation of professional fund-raising firms and a rapid increase in the number of public relations practitioners. In turn, organized fund raising for colleges, hospitals, and welfare agencies stimulated the growth of public relations departments in nonprofit agencies. Radio, the new medium reaching millions of people, was soon fully utilized by these fund raisers and publicists. This was the Age of Publicity.

The depression diverted public giving to relief and charity needs and demonstrated that private charity could not cope with problems born of widespread economic distress. Government entered the social welfare field in a large, positive, and permanent way. The 1930's saw a halt in large-scale capital fund drives. In their stead came the nationwide dimes-and-dollars drive that would, ultimately, reap millions for those skilled in this technique. The March of Dimes—prototype of today's many national health drives—brought increased emphasis on public relations, and a people's philanthropy. In these years of urgent relief, welfare, and health needs, the skills and methods of fund raisers were polished and perfected. Government gave great impetus to philanthropy when pressures generated by the depression led to the 5 per cent deduction provision in the tax laws. This would, in time, bring large-scale corporate philanthropy.

The perfected ways of raising money were soon put to use in World War II to raise moneys needed for the USO, for the Red Cross, and for other agencies meeting the war-born needs of society. This time the nationwide federated drive was more quickly accepted and utilized. This, in turn, gave new impetus to the united fund movement in the postwar years. The multiplication of the national health drives, adopting the patterns of the National Foundation for Infantile Paralysis, increased the pressure on the public to give, resulting in demands from businessmen, labor leaders, and plain citizens, for the united fund. As corporate gifts to philanthropic causes increased and the problem of giving became more difficult, corporate officials, especially public relations directors, encouraged such developments as the United Givers at the community level, the United College Fund at the state level, and the United Negro College Fund at the national level.

The emergence of the corporation as a powerful force in American philanthropy is perhaps the most significant development in the post-World War II years. Seeley, Junker, and Jones assert that the corporation is replacing the individual as the most important source of philanthropic gifts. This means, in their view:

> "Planned" routines of giving—payroll deduction and the year-round campaign—succeed impulse giving; and the beneficiary becomes ever more remote in space and vividness from the donor. The religious mandate to "charity" becomes the civic duty to "bear your fair share," and the problem for the private conscience—"Let not thy right hand know . . ."—becomes a matter of published performance. . . . The collection plate or the beggar's extended hand . . . is succeeded by a virtual private tax with social penalties.[5]

Out of this evolution has come a multibillion-dollar philanthropy, supported in considerable part by the small gifts of millions of givers as well as by the rich and the business corporation. This people's philanthropy has been made possible by the power of the mass media, now including television, shrewdly utilized by the public relations practitioner and the professional fund raiser in tapping a relatively affluent society. America's philanthropy is typically American—born of the cooperative and generous spirit bred on the frontier, required by the problems of large-scale industrialization and urbanization, made possible by the enormous accumulation of capital wealth, and energized by the high-pressure, publicity techniques. This generous giving, in response to group pressures intensified by mass media promotion, is not without its problems.

Leadership and promotion often makes the difference in whether a philanthropic cause is supported or not. It is a lamentable fact of American philanthropy today that there is no direct correlation between the public need and the amount of money given. The difference these skills make is readily seen in the story of the American Cancer Society, in periods that may be best divided as Before Mary Lasker and After Mary Lasker. In the former period the ACS limped along as a small society of doctors and had little public impact or support. Once it had been infused with Mary Lasker's dynamic drive and the public relations talents of Albert Lasker and Emerson Foote it became a fund-raising giant.

Another illustration is seen in the fortunes of the National Foundation for Infantile Paralysis and the National Multiple Sclerosis Society. In comparing the efforts of these two national organizations to raise funds to combat diseases comparable in incidence, in crippling effects, in death toll, and in dramatic publicity possibilities, we clearly see that there is more to raising money than simply having a good case. It is as much, or more, a matter of Basil O'Connors, Carl Byoirs, Albert and Mary Laskers, Emerson Footes, John Price Joneses, and Dorothy Ducases employing their superior talents in a cause. The National Health Council pointed this out in its 1945 study: "Time and effort spent on a particular problem, say mental health, is not determined by need but by effectiveness of its fund-raising techniques."

Many people are disturbed by the waste and duplicated efforts that go into some of the nationwide campaigns for dimes and dollars, a criticism aimed almost exclusively at the multiple health drives. John Rowan Wilson sees waste and publicity as common factors in all large American enterprises, including our fund drives. He observed:

> Since the project is being carried out for the common man's benefit, and with his money, then, so the reasoning goes, he has a right to know about it. In fact, when any complex technical issues are concerned, he never does know about it, since he lacks the background to assess the significance of whatever facts the public relations officers and journalists decide to give him, but he has been so long flattered

by the illusion of being kept in the picture that he would be outraged if this fiction were not maintained. In this claim to receive oversimplified, fundamentally valueless, and frequently misleading digests of information, he is supported by the most powerful lobby in the United States—the specialists in communication; journalists, television newscasters, public relations men.[6]

Another disturbing factor in today's philanthropy is that once successful fund-raising agencies are developed they tend to perpetuate themselves long after the problem they were created to solve has been alleviated. A case in point is the National Foundation for Infantile Paralysis which changed its name in 1958 to the National Foundation, and switched its objectives to research on birth defects and finding a cure for arthritis. Created to combat polio, the Foundation did not disband once polio had been conquered by the Salk and Sabin vaccines. Instead, it has kept its organization intact and switched the fund-raising engine onto a new track.

At the time the National Foundation was renamed, the Arthritis and Rheumatism Foundation, formed by a merger ten years earlier, was already raising funds to finance research on the causes and cure of those diseases. Because birth defects are not a widespread medical problem, the uncharitable observer might conclude that this objective was included so that the National Foundation's publicists could continue to exploit the appeal of the pathetically crippled child. Nothing will pull the nation's heartstrings and pursestrings more than a brave and beautiful little girl, painfully crippled, being wheeled into the office of the President at the White House.

The National Foundation, in October, 1964, yielded the field of arthritis to the reorganized Arthritis Foundation. This foundation, formerly the Arthritis and Rheumatism Foundation, took over the support of arthritic treatment and research when the National Foundation agreed, henceforth, to concentrate its efforts on combating birth defects.

These criticisms do not apply with equal validity to the capital fund drives for colleges, hospitals, etc. and to community chest or united fund campaigns. Most of these are carried out efficiently and economically. There can be no dispensing with the publicity that Wilson so vehemently criticizes. Yet there is no magic in professional organization and public relations that automatically assures success of every campaign. Many a meritorious appeal for funds fails, however skilled the promoters may be. Nonetheless, it is a hard fact of American philanthropy that no appeal, however worthy, can succeed today without these professional promoters. That the public's philanthropic dollars do not always go to the deserving is an inescapable price of free-enterprise fund raising by voluntary agencies. Many of these enterprises could be conducted more efficiently and with fairer taxation of the whole population if they were carried out by units of government. Even so, volunteerism, with all its waste and duplication of effort, has many priceless values in the American scheme of things which should not be lost.

The root problem was pointed out by the Hamlin Committee:

> The public, in the absence of objective methods to evaluate voluntary agencies, gives too little consideration to the quality of agency services and to the priority of community health and welfare needs. High-pressure publicity methods, the emotional appeal of an agency's program, and the particular timing of fund-raising campaigns have too great an influence on public contributions and involvement in voluntary agency activities. Though emotional satisfaction is and should remain an important basis for the public's decisions about voluntary agencies it needs to be tempered by objective judgment.[7]

It is the hard, lamentable fact that the citizen still, after some fifty years of public fund raising, does not have adequate and accurate information so that he may objectively evaluate the countless appeals he gets in the clamor of today's fund raising. The problem is more acute today than it was in 1912 when Allen wrote, "Nowhere have givers adequate means of learning what is most needed in their communities."

In the wake of World War I, the National Information Bureau was organized "as an information service to protect charitable contributors and to conserve charitable resources." The Bureau is the first to admit that it has not fully succeeded in this laudable aim, though its efforts have been of great help. The NIB is powerless when a national foundation refuses to submit to its auditing procedures. The Better Business Bureau also has been of help on this problem.

Yet in 1961, forty-two years after the NIB was organized, the Hamlin Committee concluded: "If the public is to make wise decisions about voluntary agencies, it must have more objective information about agency purposes, program content, administration, physical facilities, board structure and function, personnel, financing and budgeting, and relations with other agencies in the community." The staff of the NIB is justifiably proud of its performance over the years. On the other hand, it is frank enough to admit that in 1960 it was unable to prevent contributions of something like $75 million going to agencies not deserving of such gifts.

A lesser but not uncommon problem is that posed by the fakers and charity bandits who prey on the uninformed citizen's generous instincts. As pointed out earlier, these parasites on philanthropy can mulct millions from the public without violating the law. It seems clear that federal legislation, requiring annual registration and uniform, public accounting for all nationwide fund-raising agencies, is the only effective solution to this problem. Some state and municipal laws already exist in this area.

As of June, 1964, twenty-six states and the District of Columbia had laws for the control of the solicitation of charitable gifts. Many cities, notably Los Angeles, have similar ordinances. Some of these laws have been of value but they have not provided an effective solution for the problem. Many of these statutes suffer from vague provisions, too many exemptions (for instance, veterans' organizations), and inadequate enforcement. For example, the state of Wisconsin enacted such a law in 1961 in the wake of the Sister Kenny scandal in nearby Minnesota. It has not proved effective. The Milwaukee *Journal*, in a thoughtful editorial, observed:

. . . the law gives the illusion of protection but there is no substance. . . .

To begin with, it is full of holes. Veteran and religious organizations are exempt. So are organizations operating within only one county. No attempt is made to police organizations that solicit by mail from outside the state. The secretary of state's office gives reports a "cursory" examination before filing them away. It can do no more. It has no money for auditing and no manpower for field inspections. It has no way of knowing how many organizations ignore the law and how many file falsified records.[8]

We are not optimistic enough to believe that federal regulation would provide a wholly effective answer. The mass media—particularly the newspapers, radio and television stations—bear a large share of the responsibility for waste, misdirection of gifts, and frauds in today's philanthropy. These media do too much promoting and too little reporting in the field of philanthropy. With the best of intentions, they provide the heart-tugging publicity that sets the climate of giving but with no critical discrimination as to the merits of various appeals. Most newspapers, radio and TV stations whole-heartedly assist the health drives, community chest campaigns, and other drives for public funds, but media executives and editors seldom apply their tough, discriminating news standards to the countless stories, pictures, and programs provided by the money seekers. It takes a brave editor to bring into public question the merit of an appeal to eliminate birth defects or to provide Seeing Eye dogs for the blind. Fortunately a few newspapers and several magazines have, from time to time, exposed the wasters and the charlatans among the fund seekers.

All too often citizens of good will are entrapped by the charity bandits and quite unintentionally serve as fronts for the unscrupulous. Congressman John Blatnik, at the conclusion of his committee's hearings, succinctly summarized this oft-repeated story:

> Officers in an organization, unfamiliar with the techniques and problems of soliciting funds from the public, may receive an offer from such a fund raiser, promising them substantial returns. This offer may entice them to make a contract with him which is not in the best interests of their organization. Some organizations are perfectly satisfied with such an arrangement, since their share still exceeds the results they were able to obtain by themselves, but the lion's share of the proceeds goes to the professional and commercial firms which do the actual work.
>
> The fund raiser's stock in trade is the mailing list of names and addresses of persons who have shown a willingness to respond to charitable solicitations. If the promoter controls several charities, he can keep his lists up to date and add new names from each new appeal. As we have seen, these lists are a valuable commodity. They are paid for by the charity which foots the bills, but the benefits tend to accrue to the promoters.[9]

Ethical fund raisers, members of the American Association of Fund Raising Counsel, and responsible public relations practitioners object to describing these promoters along the shadowy fringes of fund raising as either fund raisers or public relations men. They want them called promoters or operators or worse. The self-accreditation procedures of both the fund raisers' association and the

Public Relations Society of America have not weeded out the incompetent and the charlatan. These fringe operators are parasites on American philanthropy. The honest charities need both the dollars and the public confidence that tighter federal regulation of popular philanthropy would bring. Agencies taking money from the public must be made to account to the public, fully and honestly, for the manner in which the public's money is spent.

The effective protection the public deserves must come from the news media as well as from federal legislation. A federal law would require all charitable causes seeking public gifts to make an annual uniform accounting that would provide a standard yardstick for reviewing groups, by both government and the generous giver. This law would provide for strict enforcement and wide publicity of the annual reports of national fund-seeking groups. Sufficient experience has been accumulated in local and state regulation to guide the drafting of a sound bill to meet this need.

The federated principle of one fund drive, with a central agency collecting and allocating moneys to member agencies, is not the sure, simple answer its proponents claim it to be. These federated funds, as illustrated by community chests, tend to become frozen in a pattern of supporting only the safe, reliable causes they have supported for years on end. New and controversial causes often get a chilly reception from the businessman-dominated united fund or community chest. Support for mental health work and alcoholism are cases in point. Federated fund raising also limits the freedom of the giver to select his philanthropies. There is greater economy and less experimentation in the one-fund plan. There is validity in the finding of the Hamlin Committee that criticized the inauguration of "new and expanded services" by voluntary agencies before the effectiveness of programs already in existence could be determined. But there is also some merit in the intemperate view of Basil O'Connor, who lashed back at the Hamlin report by saying that if the committee report were adopted it would destroy "one of the most cherished privileges of democracy by inflicting on volunteers a government by vigilante."

Seeley, Junker, and Jones and their associates looked at this problem closely in their useful Indianapolis case study. They concluded:

> From the viewpoint of social policy, the problem appears as a problem in freedom and control: whose freedom with respect to what is

it proposed to limit or abrogate for the sake of control over what by whom? The United Fund answer seems to be that some sizeable part of the freedom of all the Big Six to get what they can by their own methods in their own way is to be abrogated—and necessarily, therewith, the freedom of the donor in proportions he "chooses" to a large variety of respectable causes. These limitations upon freedom are ostensibly to be borne for the sake of greater control over "multiplicity of campaigns," over "being bothered," over manpower utilization, over money-raising ("success"), over money-allocation ("budgeting") and gift-load distribution ("standards"). But we have little or no evidence that any of the gains in control that supposedly justify the sacrifice in freedom, actually occur. The evidence on the first three is doubtful; and the evidence for better budgeting or more sensible load-distribution is virtually nil. The classic position in democratic social philosophy has been that the evidence for greater and more valuable control should be overwhelming before a case for the sacrifice of a freedom can be said to be made out.[10]

It is not easy to draw the balance sheet. A federated fund ensures tighter control and fuller accounting of moneys given by the citizen. A federated fund can raise funds more economically than can possibly be done in multiple drives. Yet there is little public education in the generalized slogan "Everybody Gives, Everybody Benefits" and in the reiterated reminders to "Give Your Fair Share." The individual agency, using the fund drive as a news peg, is more likely to get its story through to the public than if submerged in a united fund. Fund raisers influence public opinion by saturating the media with their story and recruit workers in the cause by involving persons in doing something they might not otherwise do. How meaningful is most of the publicity obtained in fund raising is another question. Much of it is emotionalized sloganeering. The multiple drives are inherently wasteful in money and manpower but they allow the giver more freedom and give new causes a better chance. Freedom is usually expensive.

Nor will governmental action automatically provide alternative solutions. Councils, legislatures, and Congress are slow to meet new problems of society until a public demand has been generated by a voluntary group. The federal government, for example, did not adequately support research on the cause and cure of cancer until public opinion was mobilized by the astute Albert Lasker, Emerson Foote, and their association. There must never be a bar to a group of American citizens organizing to meet a problem they deem urgent and in having the freedom to go to the public with their appeal for money and votes. Who will fight the battle against public prejudice for the nation's nearly two million epileptics unless the Epilepsy Foundation fights it? For too many years a great injustice has been done these victims of "falling sickness" in American society. Voluntary action, supported by voluntary giving, is the pragmatic American answer to the host of problems that have arisen in the past and will arise in the future as our society becomes ever more interdependent, ever more complex. Mobilization of public opinion about the problem will bring governmental action in due course, if such be required for the problem's solution.

As our story ends we find that the patterns of America's people's philanthropy seem to be rather permanently set. Modern public relations men, professional fund raisers, and efficiency-minded businessmen have combined their talents to demonstrate the power of raising large sums through small gifts from a broad segment of the population. The carefully organized campaign, with prestigious leaders in front and professional fund raisers behind, that carefully pinpoints prospects, organizes their solicitation, and builds a psychological climate that compels people to give is now a fixture of American philanthropy. There may be debate about the methods, fuss about the costs, arguments over whether there should be many drives or one federated appeal, and questions about the ethics of the hard-sell public relations; but today's high-powered, high-pressure campaign to raise money is here to stay. And it is well that this is so, for Americans could not meet all their urgent welfare, education, health, and recreational needs without the organized fund-raising campaign. The methods of the fund raiser and the public relations practitioner will not go unused so long as there are new causes, new diseases, and social ills—old and new—to move spirited men and women to do something about them in America's pattern of volunteerism. The "how" of fund raising has been widely dramatized and publicized. For what causes and to what ends these skills shall be used is for the public to decide—with its dimes, its dollars, and its votes. To make these decisions wisely it needs more adequate and accurate information than it usually gets from either the fund raiser or the news media. All this is typically "the American Way" of doing things.

NOTES

1. "About Ed Picketts," in *The Log from the Sea of Cortez* (New York: Viking, 1962), pp. lxiv–lxv.

2. "American Philanthropy and the National Character," *American Quarterly*, Vol. 10, p. 437.

3. In the classic work, *Democracy in America*. This quote from p. 95, Mentor Book Ed. edited by Richard D. Heffner.

4. *Financing Philanthropy*, Vol. XXXVI (October, 1963), p. 8.

5. Seeley, Junker, Jones, *et al.*, *Community Chest*, p. 396.

6. Wilson, *Margin of Safety*, p. 5.

7. *Voluntary Health and Welfare Agencies in the United States*, pp. 16–17.

8. Issue of Aug. 28, 1963, p. 18.

9. Blatnik Committee Hearings, p. 34.

10. In *Community Chest*, pp. 431–432.

Bibliography

ALLEN, FREDERICK LEWIS. *The Big Change.* New York: Harper, 1952. 308 pp.

ALLEN, GEORGE H. *Presidents Who Have Known Me.* New York: Simon & Schuster, 1950. 247 pp.

ALLEN, WILLIAM H. *Modern Philanthropy: A Study of Efficient Appealing and Giving.* New York: Dodd, Mead, & Co., 1912. 437 pp.

American Association of Fund Raising Counsel, Inc. *Giving, USA.* New York: The Association. Summary of American giving published annually since 1955 by this association.

American Association for Organizing Charity. *Financial Federations* (The Report of a Special Committee). New York: The Association, 1917. 285 pp.

American National Red Cross. *The Work of the American Red Cross during the War.* Washington, D.C.: American National Red Cross, 1919. 90 pp.

——. *Relief Work in the Drought of 1930–31: Official Report of Operations of the American National Red Cross.* Washington, D.C.: Red Cross, October, 1931. 109 pp.

ANDREWS, F. EMERSON. *Philanthropic Giving.* New York: Russell Sage Foundation, 1950. 318 pp.

——. *Corporation Giving.* New York: Russell Sage Foundation, 1952. 361 pp.

ANDREWS, FRANK M. *A Study of Company Sponsored Foundations.* New York: The Russell Sage Foundation, 1960. 86 pp.

BERENS, ROBERT. "The History of Public Relations in the American Red Cross." Unpublished thesis, University of Wisconsin, 1961. 340 pp.

BERNSTEIN, IRVING. *The Lean Years.* Boston: Houghton Mifflin Co., 1960. 577 pp.

BLOOMGARDEN, HANK. *Before We Sleep.* New York: G. P. Putnam's Sons, 1958. 246 pp.

BOGEN, BORIS D. *Jewish Philanthropy.* New York: Macmillan, 1917. 391 pp.

BRACE, CHARLES LORING. *The Dangerous Classes of New York.* New York: Wynkoop and Hallenbeck, 3rd ed., 1880. 468 pp.

541

BRANDT, LILLIAN. *How Much Shall I Give?* New York: Frontier Press, 1921. 153 pp.

BREMNER, ROBERT H. *American Philanthropy*. Chicago: University of Chicago Press, 1960. 230 pp.

BUCKINGHAM, CLYDE E. *Red Cross Disaster Relief*. Washington, D.C.: Public Affairs Press, 1956. 47 pp.

CAREY, MATHEW. *Miscellaneous Essays*. Philadelphia: Printed for Carey & Hart, Nov. 13, 1830. (Essay, "An Early Effort at Federated Financing" is reprinted in *Social Service Review*, Vol. 29 (1955), pp. 302–305. I quoted from latter source.)

CARTER, RICHARD. *The Gentle Legions*. Garden City, N.Y.: Doubleday, 1961. 335 pp.

CLARKE, JOSEPH I. C. *My Life and Memories*. New York: Dodd, Mead, & Co., 1925. 404 pp.

Council for Financial Aid to Education, Inc. *1960 Corporation Support of Higher Education*. New York: The Council, January, 1962.

CREEL, GEORGE. *How We Advertised America*. New York: Harper, 1920. 467 pp.

———. *Rebel at Large*. New York: Putnam's Sons 1947. 384 pp.

CURTI, MERLE. *American Philanthropy Abroad*. New Brunswick, N.J.: Rutgers University Press, 1963.

Dartnell Corporation. *How 300 Companies Handle Contributions*. Chicago: Dartnell Corp., 1959. A survey. 200 pp.

DICKINSON, FRANK G. *Philanthropy and Public Policy*. Proceedings of a Conference on Philanthropy, June 26–July 7, 1961. New York: National Bureau Economic Research, 1961. 143 pp. Mimeographed.

DULLES, FOSTER RHEA. *The American Red Cross, a History*. New York: Harper, 1950. 554 pp.

EELLS, RICHARD T. *Corporation Giving in a Free Society*. New York: Harper, 1956. 210 pp.

FLYNN, JOHN T. *The Roosevelt Myth*. New York: Devin-Adair Co., 1948. 438 pp.

FOSDICK, RAYMOND B. *The Story of the Rockefeller Foundation*. New York: Harper, 1952. 336 pp.

FREIDEL, FRANK. *Franklin D. Roosevelt:* The Ordeal. Boston: Little, Brown, 1954. 320 pp.

GAEDDERT, G. R. *The American National Red Cross in World War I, Vol. IV, The History of the American National Red Cross*. Washington, D.C.: American National Red Cross, Historical Division, 1950. 456 pp. Mimeographed.

GLENN, JOHN M., LILLIAN BRANDT, and F. EMERSON ANDREWS. *Russell Sage Foundation, 1907–1946*. New York: Russell Sage Foundation, 1947. 2 vols. 746 pp.

GOLDMAN, ERIC F. *Rendezvous with Destiny.* New York: Vintage Books edition, 1959, 4th printing. 372 pp.

GUNN, SELSKAR, and PHILIP S. PLATT. *Voluntary Health Agencies.* New York: Ronald Press, 1945. 364 pp.

GUNTHER, JOHN. *Taken at the Flood: The Story of Albert D. Lasker.* New York: Harper, 1960. 368 pp.

HAMILTON, RAPHAEL N., S.J., *The Story of Marquette University.* Milwaukee: Marquette Press, 1953. 434 pp.

HAMLIN, ROBERT H. (study director). *Voluntary Health and Welfare Agencies in the United States.* New York: Schoolmasters' Press, 1961. 88 pp.

Harvard Business Club of Cleveland, Inc. *Corporate Giving in Greater Cleveland.* The Club, December, 1953. 60 pp.

HEFFNER, RICHARD D. (ed.). *Democracy in America.* New York: New American Library, 1956.

HITCHCOCK, EDWARD. *The Power of Christian Benevolence: Life and Labors of Mary Lyon.* Northampton: Hopkins, Bridgeman, & Co., 1852. 7th ed. 486 pp.

HODGES, LEIGH MITCHELL. *The People against Tuberculosis.* New York: National Tuberculosis Association, 1942. 54 pp.

HOPKINS, C. HOWARD. *History of the Y.M.C.A. in North America.* New York: Association Press, 1951. 818 pp.

HURD, CHARLES W. *The Compact History of the American Red Cross.* New York: Hawthorn, 1959. 308 pp.

ICKES, HAROLD L. *The Secret Diary of Harold L. Ickes:* The First Thousand Days, 1933–1936. New York: Simon & Schuster, 1953. 738 pp.

JACOBS, PHILIP P. *The Tuberculosis Worker.* Baltimore, Md.: Williams & Wilkins Co., 1923. 314 pp.

JANSON, DONALD, and BERNARD EISMAN. *The Far Right.* New York: McGraw-Hill, 1963. 259 pp.

KING, WILLFORD ISBELL. *Trends in Philanthropy.* New York: National Bureau of Economic Research, Inc., 1928. 78 pp.

LAWRENCE, WILLIAM. *Memories of a Happy Life.* Boston: Houghton Mifflin Co., 1926. 452 pp.

LEAVITT, ROBERT KEITH. *Common Sense About Fund Raising.* Published by author, 1949. 75 pp.

LEE, ALFRED McCLUNG. *The Daily Newspaper in America.* New York: Macmillan, 1937. 797 pp.

LINK, ARTHUR S. *American Epoch.* New York: Knopf, 1955. 724 pp.

LYON, PETER. *Success Story: The Life and Times of S. S. McClure.* New York: Scribner's, 1963. 433 pp.

MARTS, ARNAUD C. *Philanthropy's Role in Civilization.* New York: Harper, 1953. 206 pp.

Marts, Arnaud C. *Man's Concern for His Fellow Man.* Geneva, N.Y.: W. F. Humphrey Press, 1961. 64 pp.

MERTON, ROBERT K. *Mass Persuasion: The Social Psychology of a War Bond Drive.* New York: Harper, 1946. 210 pp.

MOCK, JAMES O., and CEDRIC LARSON. *Words That Won the War: The Story of the Committee on Public Information 1917–1919.* Princeton, N.J.: Princeton University Press, 1939. 372 pp.

MORGENTHAU, HENRY. *All in a Life-time.* Garden City, N.Y.: Doubleday, Page & Co., 1922. 454 pp.

MORISON, SAMUEL ELIOT. *The Founding of Harvard College.* Cambridge, Mass.: Harvard University Press, 1935. 472 pp.

MYERS, WILLIAM STARR (ed.). *The State Papers and Other Public Writings of Herbert Hoover,* Vol. 1. New York: Doubleday, Doran & Co., 1934. 622 pp.

National Foundation for Infantile Paralysis. *Annual Reports* for 1952, 1953, 1954, 1955, 1956, and 1957. New York: The Foundation.

National Health Education Committee, Inc. *Facts on the Major Killing and Crippling Diseases in the United States Today.* New York: The Committee, 135 E. 42nd St., 1961.

National Industrial Conference Board, Inc. *Company-Sponsored Foundations.* New York: NICB, Studies in Business Policy, No. 73, 1955. 80 pp.

——. *The Why and How of Corporate Giving.* New York: NICB, 1956. 124 pp. Report of a conference.

——. *Company Contributions, III. Policies and Procedures.* New York: NICB, Studies in Business Policy, No. 89, 1958. 88 pp.

Negro Yearbook, 1952. New York: William H. Wise & Co. Jessie Parkhurst Guzman, ed.

NEVINS, ALLAN. *John D. Rockefeller: The Heroic Age of American Enterprise.* New York: Scribner's Sons, 1940. 2 vols. A one-volume abridgment was published in 1959.

NORTON, WILLIAM J. *The Cooperative Movement in Social Work.* New York: Macmillan, 1927. 373 pp.

Opinion Research Corporation. *Public Opinion Index for Industry: Meeting the Problem of Charitable Contributions.* Princeton, N.J., 1948. Copyright.

PARRINGTON, VERNON L. *Main Currents in American Thought.* Vol. 3, *The Beginnings of Critical Realism in America.* New York: Harcourt, Brace, 1927. 428 pp.

PERKINS, FRANCES. *The Roosevelt I Knew.* New York: Viking Press, 1946. 408 pp.

PIERCE, LYMAN L. *How to Raise Money.* New York: Harper, 1932. 295 pp.

RICHARDS, LAURA E. (ed.). *Letters and Journals of Samuel Gridley Howe.* Vol. 2. Boston: Dana Estes & Co., 1909. 611 pp.

ROLLINS, ALFRED B., JR. *Roosevelt and Howe.* New York: Knopf, 1962. 479 pp.

ROOSEVELT, ELEANOR. *This I Remember.* New York: Harper, 1949. 387 pp.

ROSS, ISHBEL. *Angel of the Battlefield: The Life of Clara Barton.* New York: Harper, 1956. 305 pp.

RUML, BEARDSLEY, and THEODORE GEIGER. *The Five Percent.* Washington, D.C.: National Planning Association, Planning Pamphlet No. 73, rev. ed., August, 1951. 38 pp.

SEARS, JESSE B. *Philanthropy in the History of American Higher Education.* Washington, D.C.: U.S. Government Printing Office, 1922. 112 pp.

SEELEY, JOHN R., BUFORD H. JUNKER, R. WALLACE JONES, JR., *et al. Community Chest: A Case Study in Philanthropy.* Toronto: University of Toronto Press, 1957. 593 pp.

SEELYE, L. CLARK. *The Early History of Smith College, 1871–1910.* Cambridge, Mass.: Houghton Mifflin Co., 1923.

SEYMOUR, HAROLD J. *Design for Giving: The Story of the National War Fund, Inc.,* 1943–1947. New York: Harper, 1947. 182 pp.

SHANNON, DAVID A. (ed.). *The Great Depression.* Englewood Cliffs, N.J.: Prentice-Hall, 1960. 171 pp. A book of readings.

SHAUGHNESSY, DONALD F. "A History of the American Cancer Society," unpublished Ph.D. thesis, Columbia University, 1956. 254 pp.

SHERRILL, HENRY KNOX. *William Lawrence: Later Years of a Happy Life.* Cambridge, Mass.: Harvard University Press, 1943. 179 pp.

SHAPIRO, LEO J. "Report on Key Findings and Basic Statistics—the Study of Chicago Company Contribution Policies and Practices." Chicago: Chicago Chapter, Public Relations Society of America. An unpublished survey.

SHRYOCK, RICHARD H. *National Tuberculosis Association, 1904–1954.* New York: National Tuberculosis Association, 1957. 342 pp.

SILLS, DAVID L. *The Volunteers: Means and Ends in a National Operation.* Glencoe, Ill.: Free Press, 1957. 320 pp.

SMITH, RALPH LEE. *The Bargain Hucksters.* New York: Crowell, 1962. 236 pp.

STEFFENS, C. M., and PAUL P. FARIS. *Adventures in Money Raising.* New York: Macmillan, 1930. 278 pp.

STEINBECK, JOHN. *The Log from the Sea of Cortez.* New York: Viking (Compass Books Ed.), 1962.

STILES, LELA. *The Man Behind Roosevelt.* Cleveland: World Publishing Co., 1954. 311 pp. The biography of Louis McHenry Howe.

United Defense Fund, Inc. *History of the United Defense Fund, Inc.* New York: The Fund, 1957. 36 pp.

U.S. House of Representatives Select Committee on Small Business. *Tax-Exempt Foundations and Charitable Trusts: Their Impact on Our Economy.* Installment One, Dec. 31, 1962; Installment Two, issued Oct. 16, 1963. Washington, D.C.: U.S. Government Printing Office.

U.S. House of Representatives Committee on Veterans' Affairs. *Fund Raising by or in Behalf of Veterans.* Washington, D.C.: U.S. Government Printing Office, 1958.

U.S. House of Representatives Committee on Government Operations. *Federal Agencies and Philanthropies.* Washington, D.C.: U.S. Government Printing Office, 1958.

U.S. Treasury, Internal Revenue Service. *Statistics of Income . . . 1960, Individual Tax Returns, 1960.* Washington, D.C.: U.S. Government Printing Office, 1962. 165 pp.

———. *Statistics of Income . . . Corporation Income Tax Returns* with accounting periods ended July, 1960–June, 1961. Washington, D.C.: U.S. Government Printing Office, 1963.

University of Wisconsin Extension Division. *The Changing Role of American Corporate Philanthropy.* Madison, Wis.: Extension Division, 1962. Proceedings of a conference. Speakers included Merle Curti, Dr. Robert Hamlin, and Richard Eells.

WALKER, TURNLEY. *Roosevelt and the Warm Springs Story.* New York: A. A. Wyn, 1953. 311 pp.

WARD, CHARLES S. *The Intensive Financial Campaign.* New York: Young Men's Christian Association, 1917. In YMCA Library, New York City.

WATSON, FRANK D. *The Charity Organization Movement in the United States.* New York: Macmillan, 1922. 560 pp.

WILLIAMS, PIERCE, and FREDERICK E. CROXTON. *Corporation Contributions to Organized Community Welfare Services.* New York: National Bureau of Economic Research, 1930. 347 pp.

WILSON, JOHN ROWAN. *Margin of Safety.* New York: Doubleday, 1963. 258 pp.

WOODROOFE, KATHLEEN. *From Charity to Social Work in England and the States.* Toronto: University of Toronto Press, 1962. 247 pp.

Index